AF292332

MIDDLE EAST

MIDDLE EAST

CITIES AND SANDS FROM ISTANBUL TO DUBAI

TREVOR NAYLOR

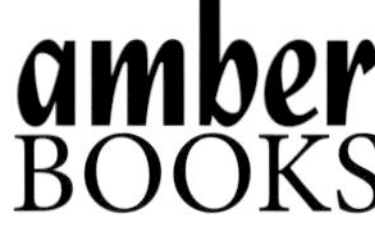

amber
BOOKS

First published in 2026

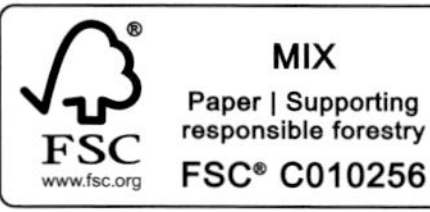

Published by
Amber Books Ltd
United House
London N7 9DP
United Kingdom
www.amberbooks.co.uk
Facebook: amberbooks
YouTube: amberbooksltd
Instagram: amberbooksltd
X(Twitter): @amberbooks

ISBN: 978-1-83886-667-9

Editorial, design and picture research by Amber Books Ltd

Printed in China

Contents

Introduction

T he Middle East is undoubtedly a region of paradox. A place of profound history, burdened by modern strife – but bundling this vast area into such a simple narrative is to miss its deep and complex soul. For centuries, this region was the centre of the known world. Its towns and deserts have served as crossroads of trade, been the crucible of ideas, and contain sites that were the wellsprings of faith for major religions. The very alphabet we use, the numerals with which we count, the principles of mathematics and astronomy that underpin our modern science, all have roots here. Today you can walk through the rose-red city of Petra and feel the echoes of Nabatean merchants or stand in the shadow of a pyramid in Egypt and sense the enduring legacy of the greatest ancient civilization. In the Middle East history is not confined to museums.

But history is only one part of the story. From the breathtaking, almost sci-fi skylines of Dubai and Riyadh to the ambitious green energy projects rising from the desert sands, there is a palpable sense of dynamism and forward momentum. This is a region looking confidently towards the future, investing in technology, art and innovation on an unprecedented scale. There is a youthful energy, a bold, can-do spirit that is infectious. These are countries that are evolving at a staggering pace, with ambitious plans underpinned by a deep past knowledge. It is this beautiful juxtaposition of the ancient and the futuristic that provides the visual chequerboard of this book.

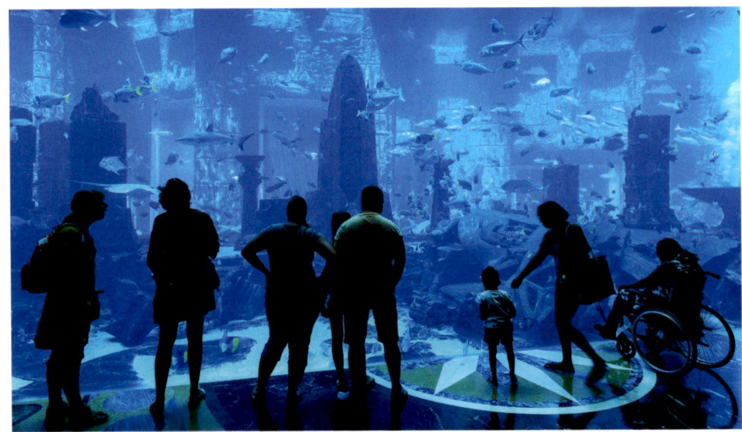

ABOVE:
Atlantis Aquarium at the Palm Hotel, Dubai.

OPPOSITE:
Sand towers in the Lut Desert.

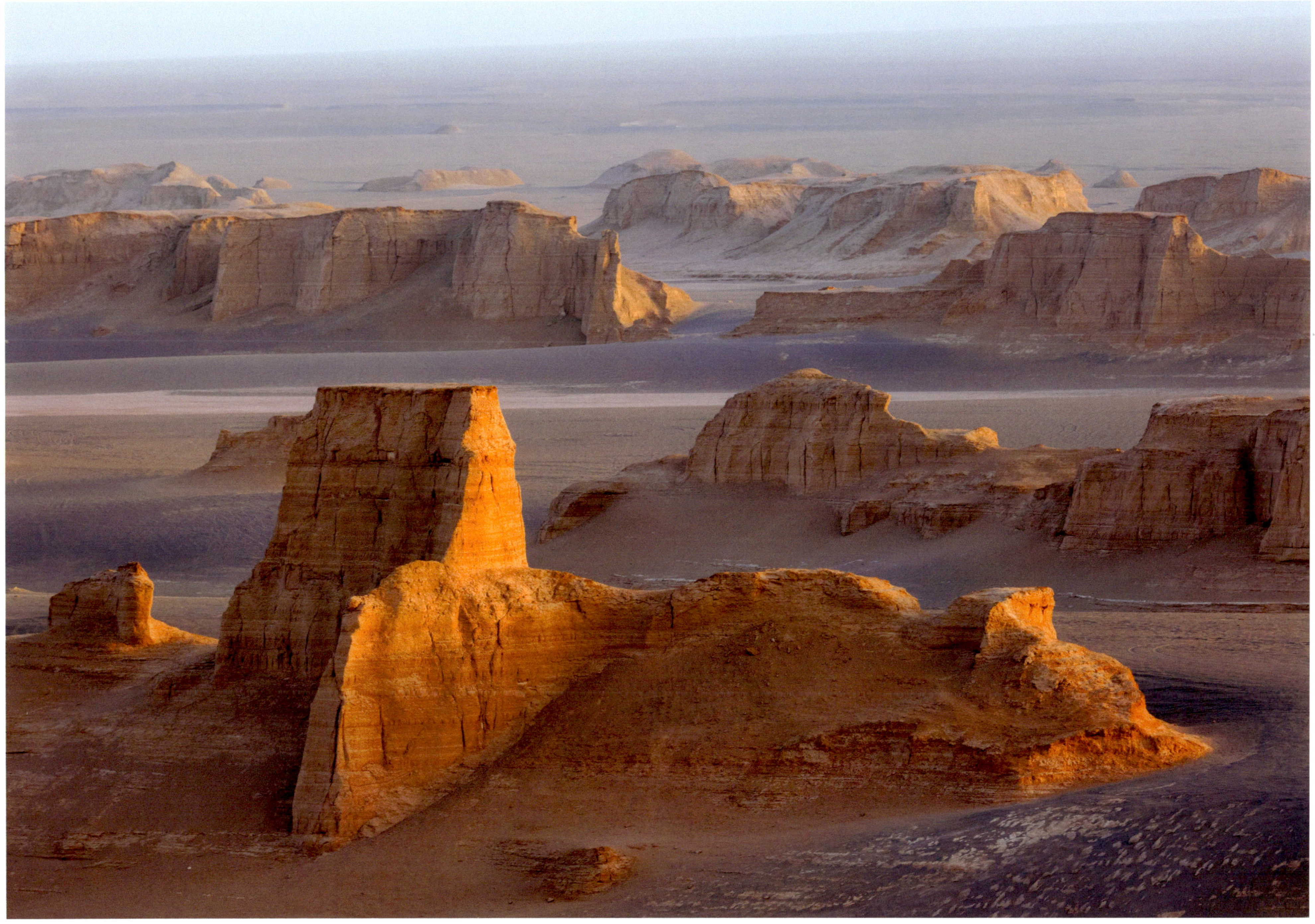

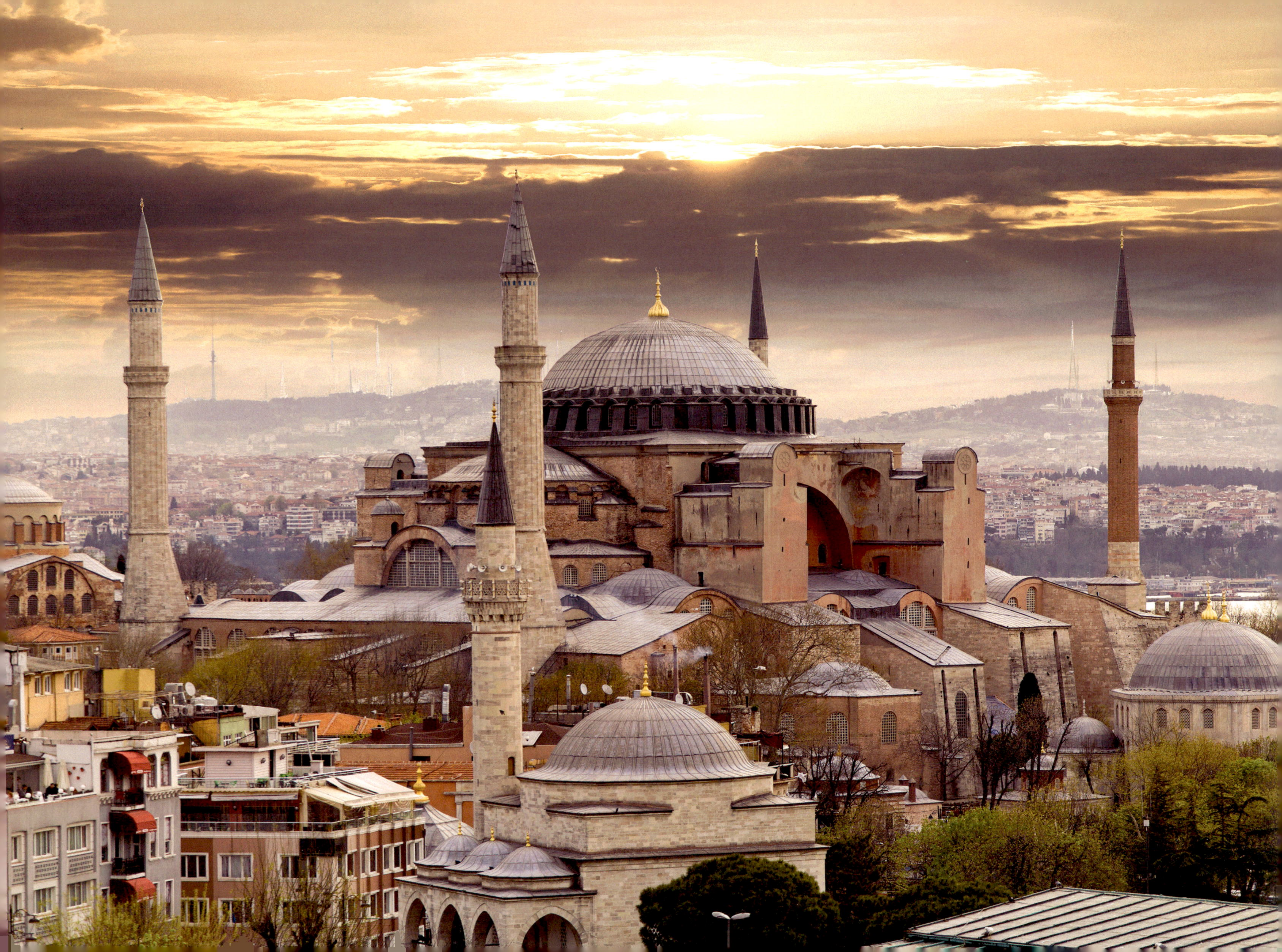

Türkiye

Are you ready to visit a country like no other, a land truly unique in language and attitude? This is where ancient wonders and contemporary style fuse seamlessly. Arriving in Istanbul you stand at the crossroads of Roman, Byzantine, and Ottoman history. On every bustling street the past is woven into the very fabric of daily life. Türkiye – the official name of Turkey since 2022 – has a historic role as a cultural and physical connecting point between East and West, creating a unique buzz that's both fascinating and beautiful. Turkish people are famously independent, and their spirit is warm and contagious, making you feel instantly at home. Engage in conversation and you'll discover the Turkish language, a captivating tongue that ensures you shop extensively in the famous Grand Bazaar. As you tour this land, the food you enjoy provides a culinary journey of its own. Eating is an epicurean delight, from the savoury, slow-cooked, Anatolian kebab to delicious, sweet, and syrupy baklava. Lunch and dinner are both celebrations, for family and friends, of the wealth of fresh food grown across this vast, vibrant country. Türkiye is a thrilling, individual adventure that will captivate your heart and soul.

Hagia Sophia, Istanbul
Originally built as a Christian cathedral by the Byzantine Emperor Justinian I in the sixth century, Hagia Sophia was the world's largest cathedral for nearly a thousand years. After the Ottoman conquest of Constantinople in 1453, it was converted into a mosque, when minarets and other Islamic features were incorporated. In 1934, the secular Turkish Republic transformed the complex into a museum, not just of local history, but also celebrating world culture. It remained a museum for 86 years before becoming a mosque again in 2020.

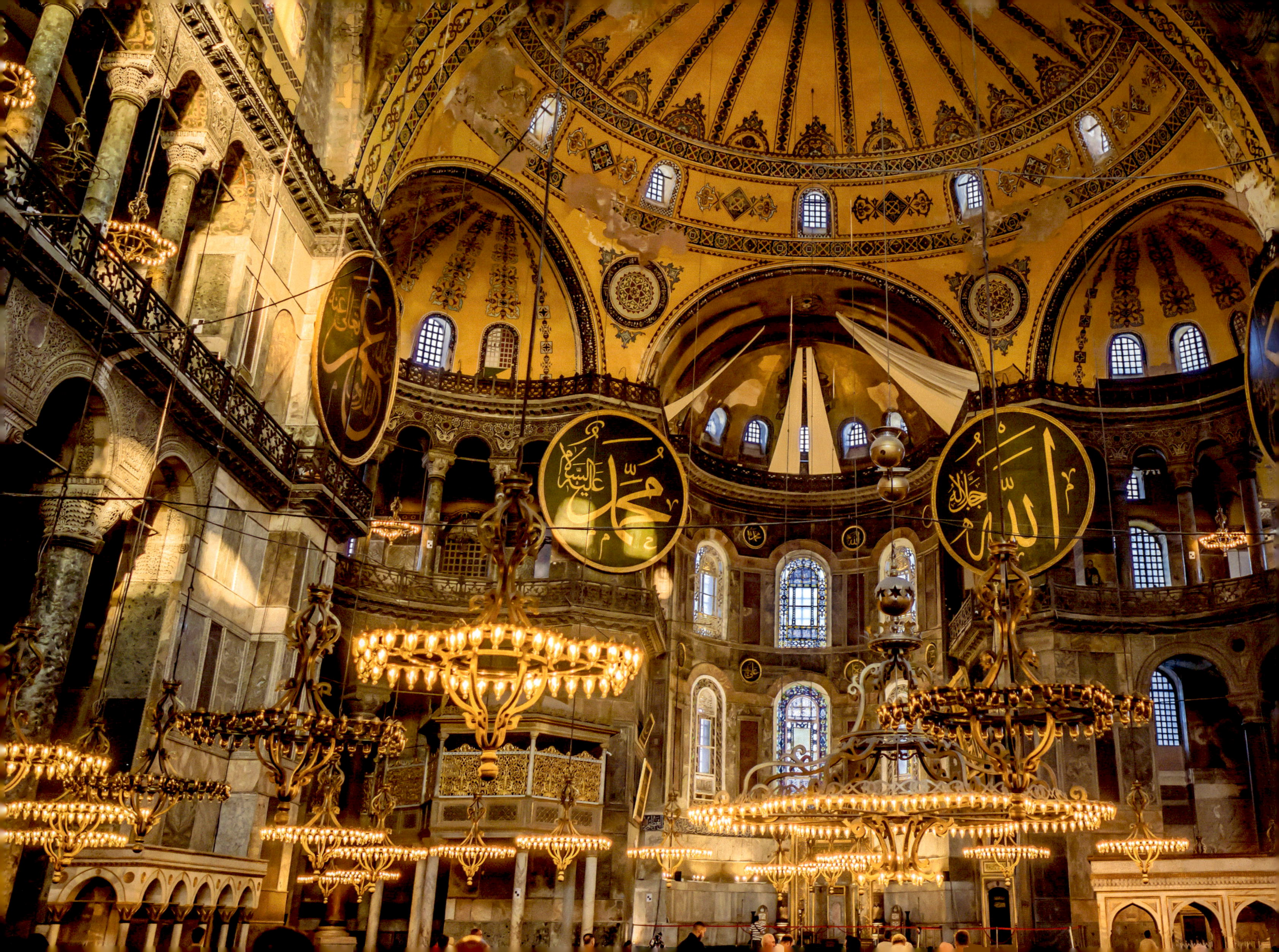

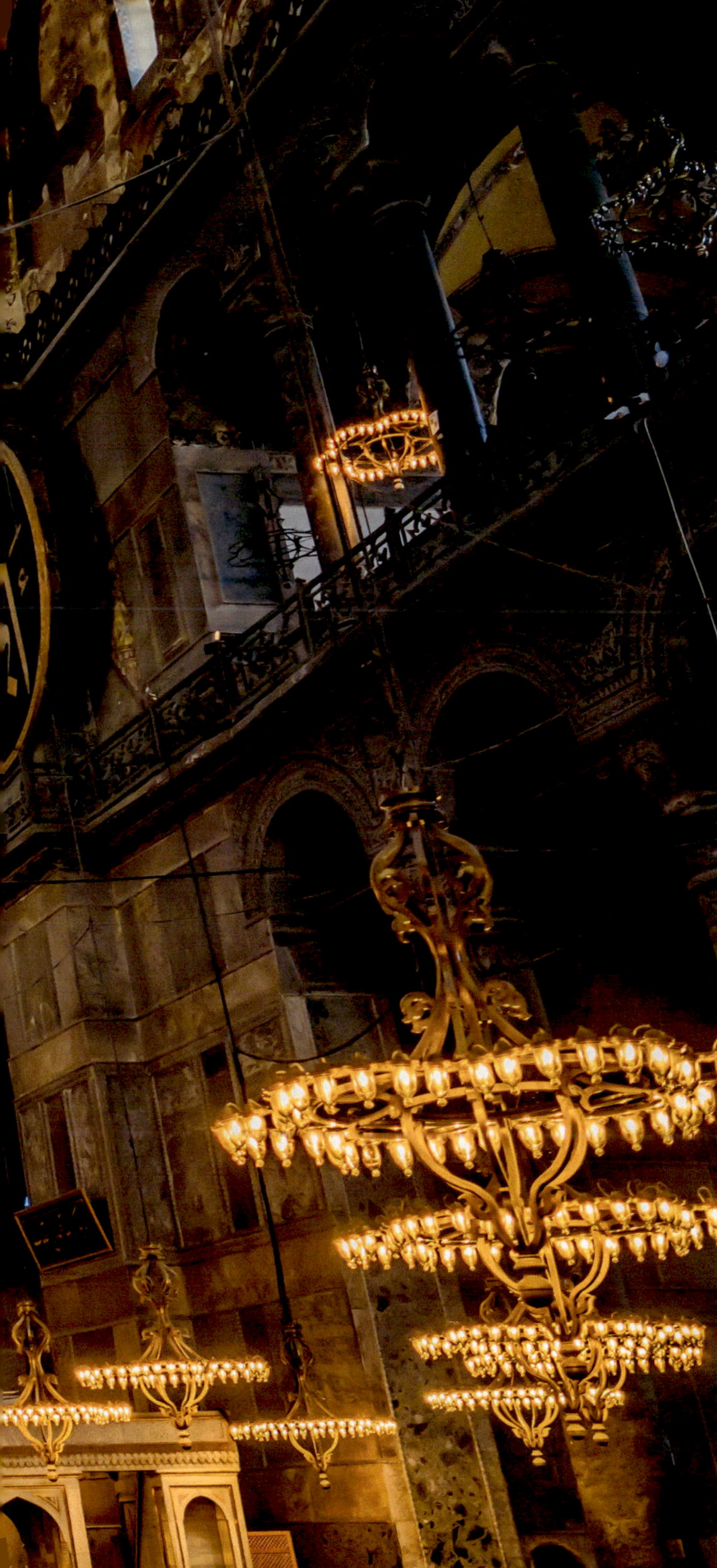

LEFT:

Interior, Hagia Sophia, Istanbul
The interior of Hagia Sophia is a remarkable mixture of styles, revealing the story of its Byzantine and Ottoman past. The massive central dome and walls are decorated with both Christian mosaics and Islamic calligraphic roundels of the largest scale.

RIGHT:

Mosaic of Jesus Christ, Hagia Sophia, Istanbul
This masterpiece of Byzantine art is situated in the south gallery of Hagia Sophia. This image of Christ is part of the building's monumental Deesis mosaic.

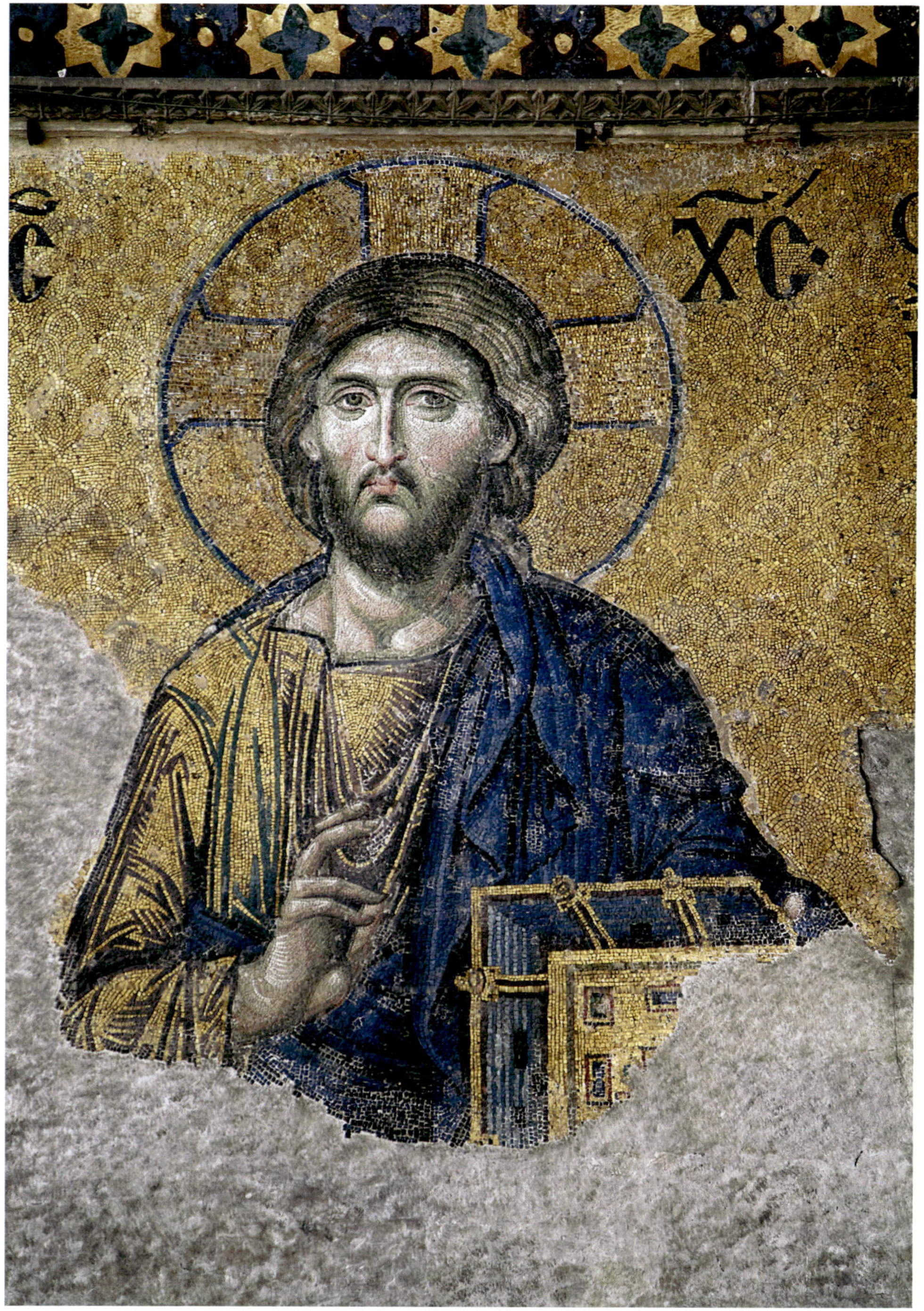

Blue Mosque, Istanbul

The Blue Mosque, officially the Sultan Ahmed Mosque, is an icon of Istanbul's skyline. Commissioned by a teenage Sultan Ahmed I, it was built between 1609 and 1616. It provided proof of this untested Sultan's status and continued to assert the vision of Ottoman power. Its more commonly used name refers to the over 20,000 handmade blue Iznik tiles that adorn its vast, richly decorated interior. The mosque has six minarets and cascading domes, providing graceful balance to its outline while competing with the nearby Hagia Sophia.

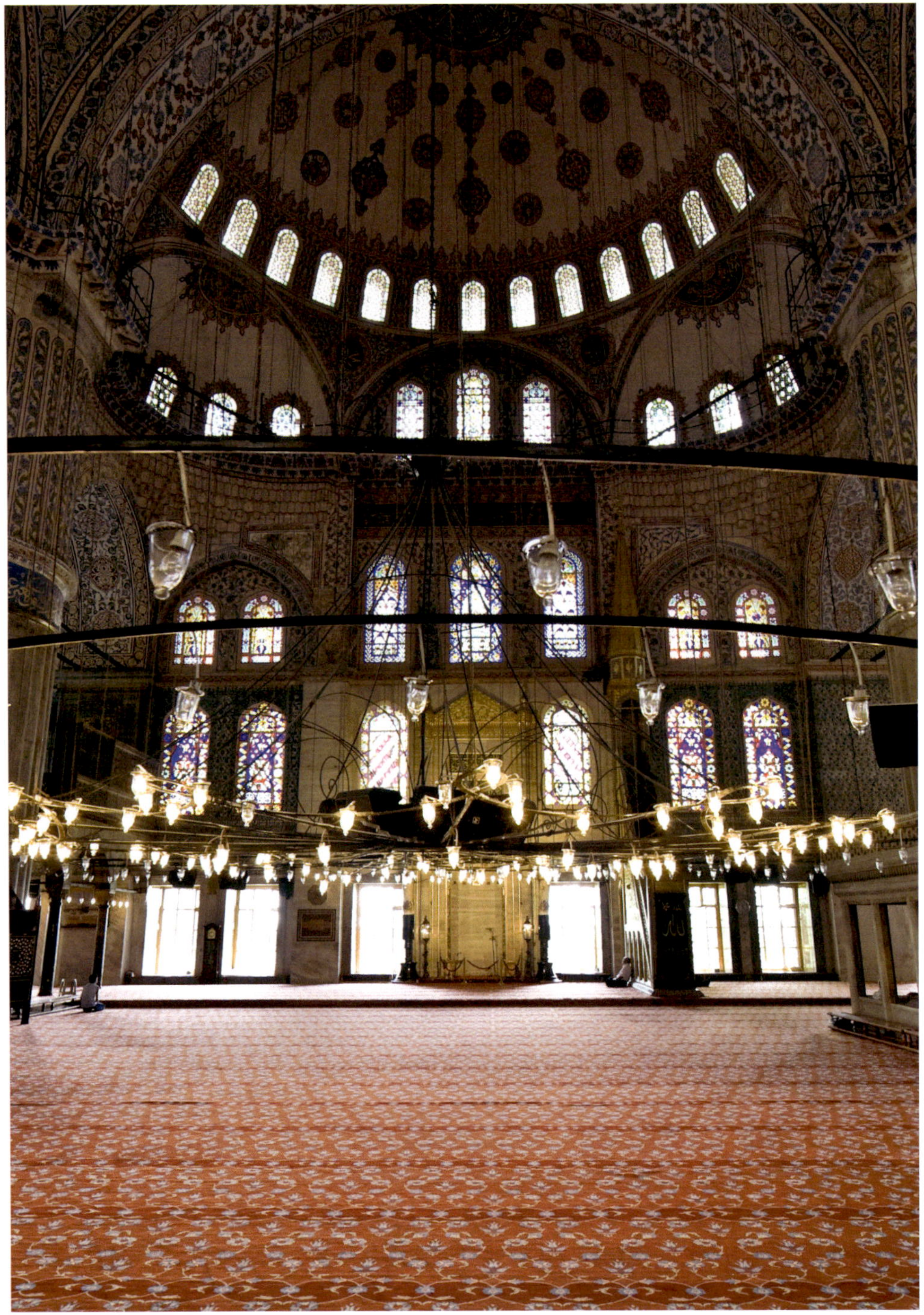

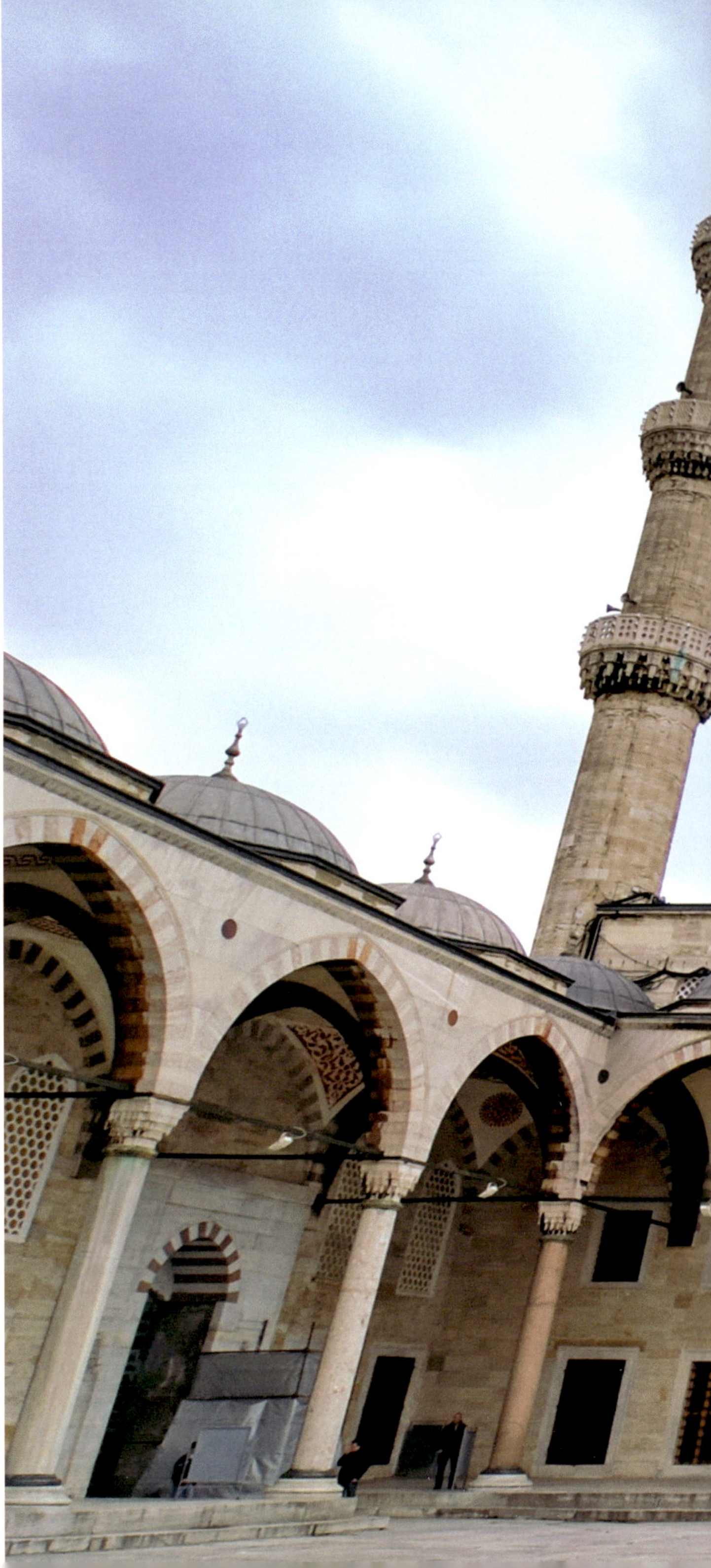

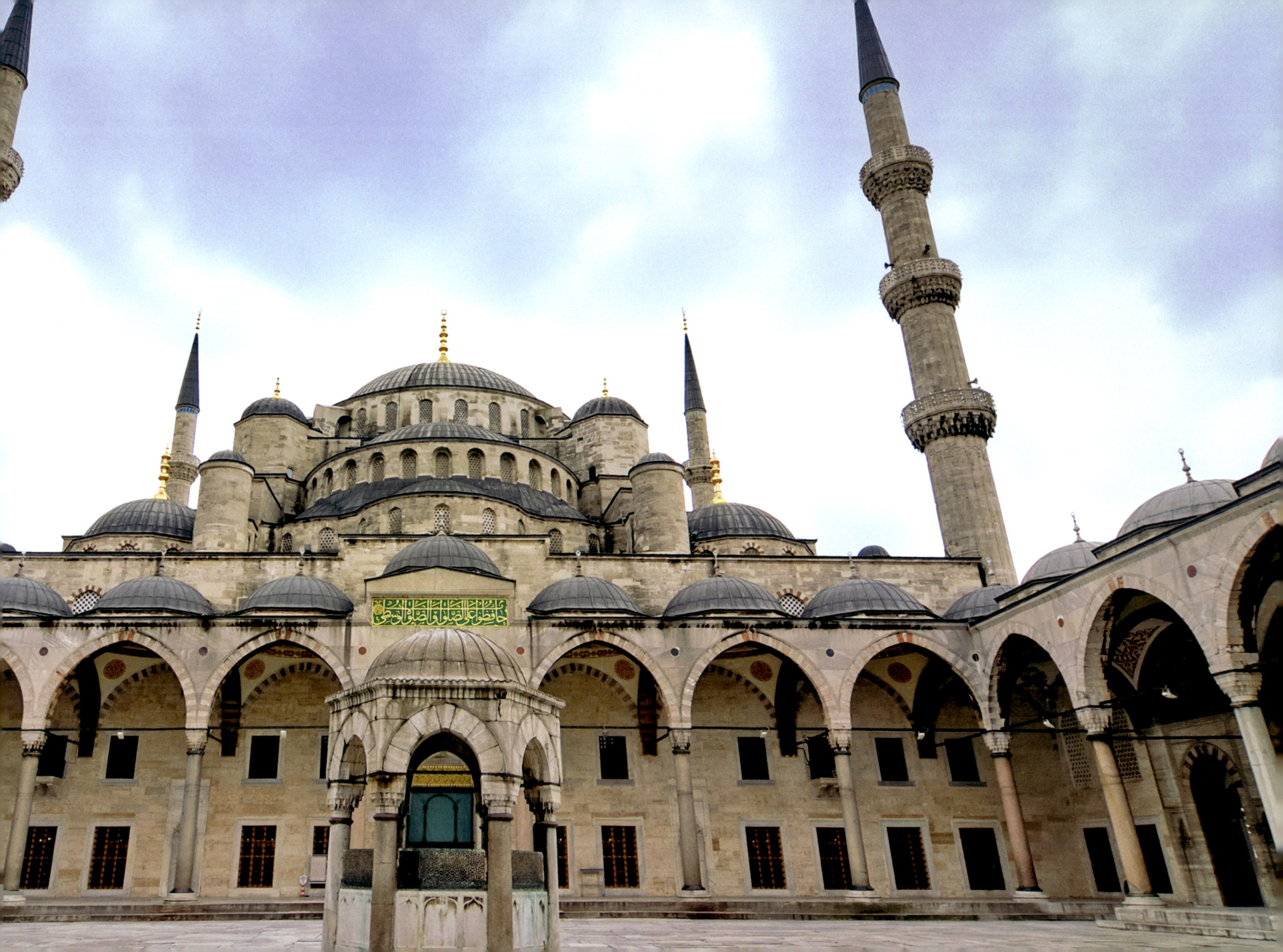

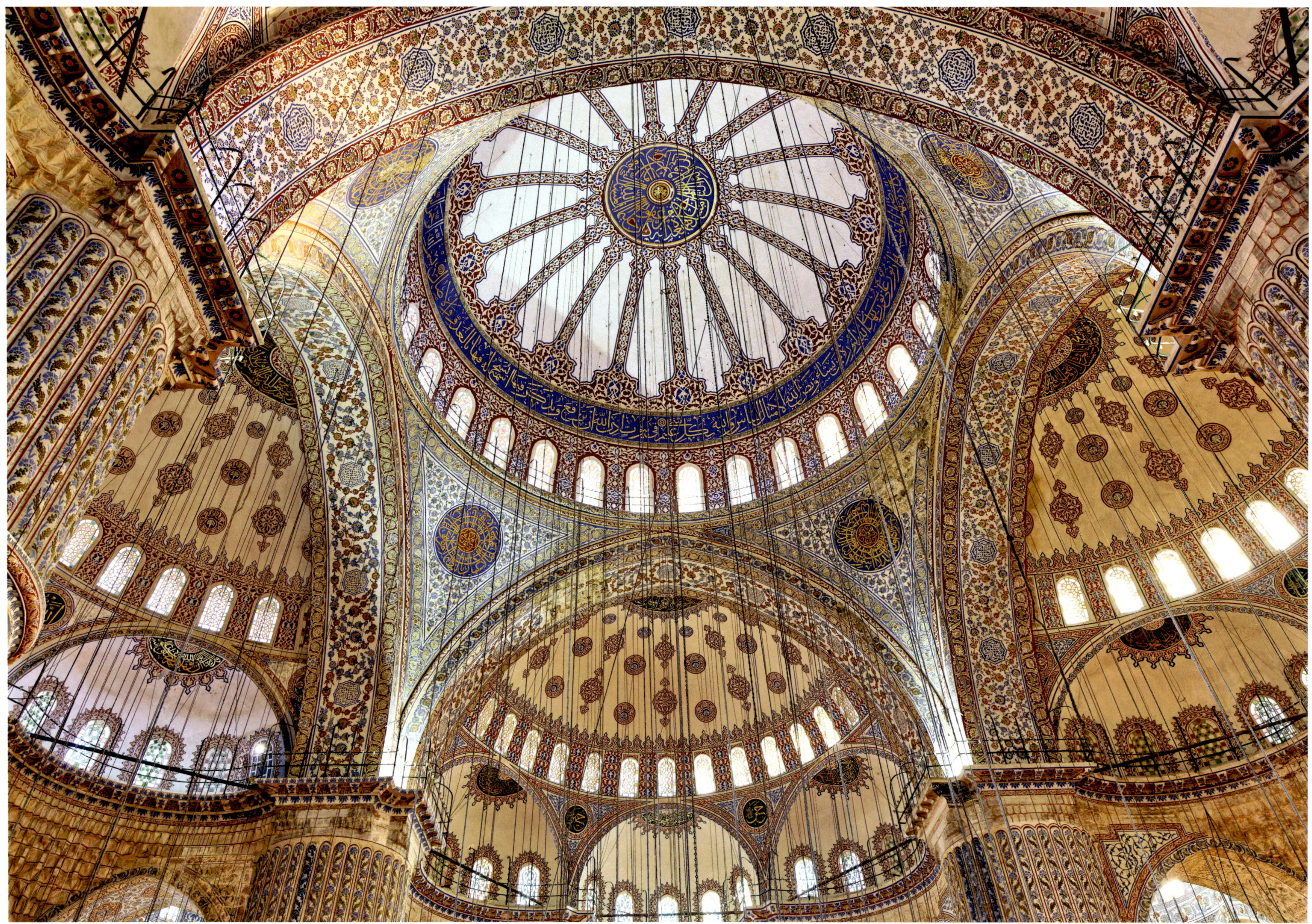

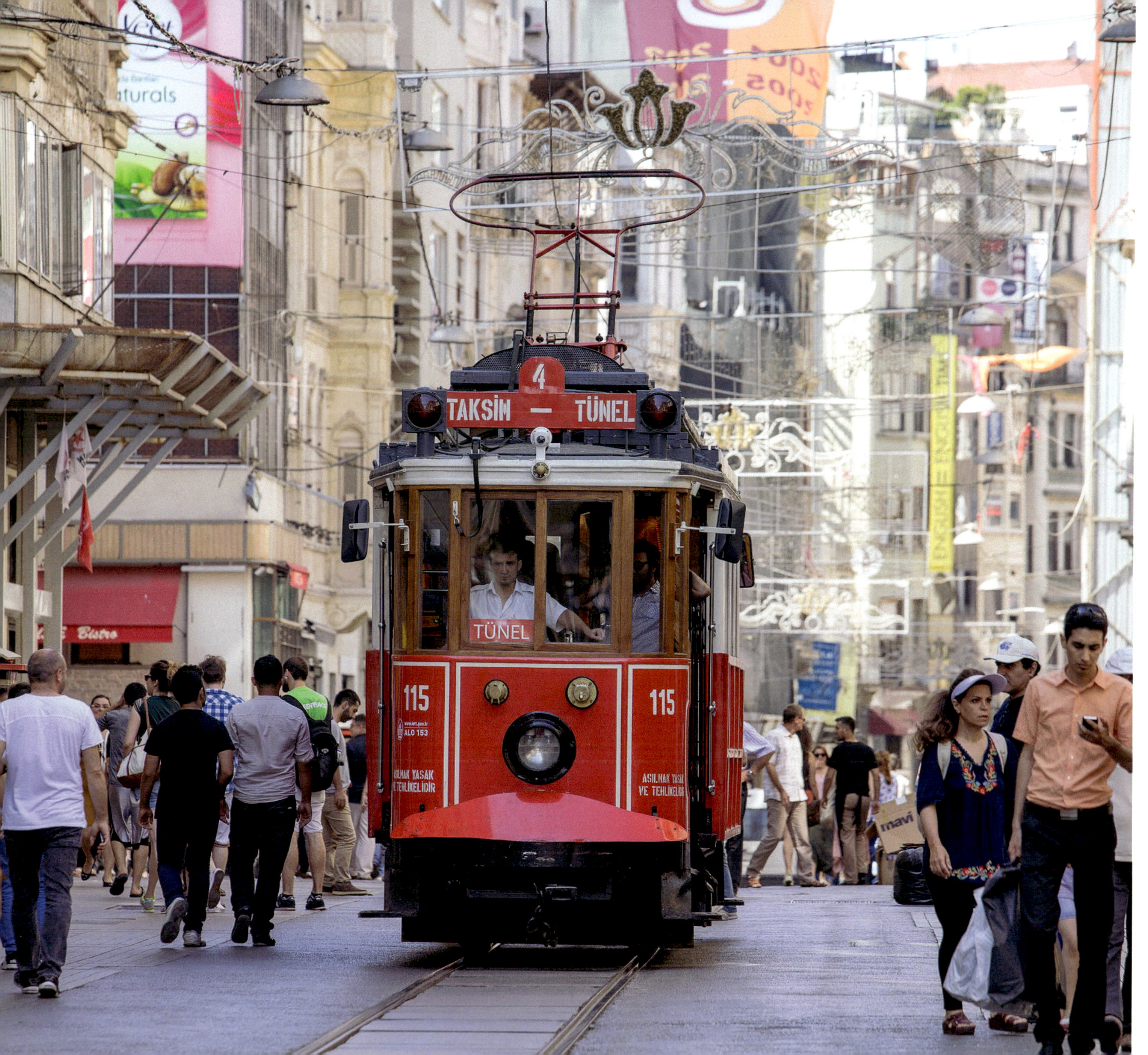

LEFT:

Taksim-Tünel Nostalgia Tram, Istiklal Street, Istanbul

This nostalgic tramway is a bright red icon of the city. It travels, all day long, down the famous pedestrian-only İstiklal Caddesi. Known as the T2 line, it travels between Taksim Square and Tünel, where it connects to a steep, underground railway. This historic and fun tram offers a vintage journey to both locals and tourists alike.

15

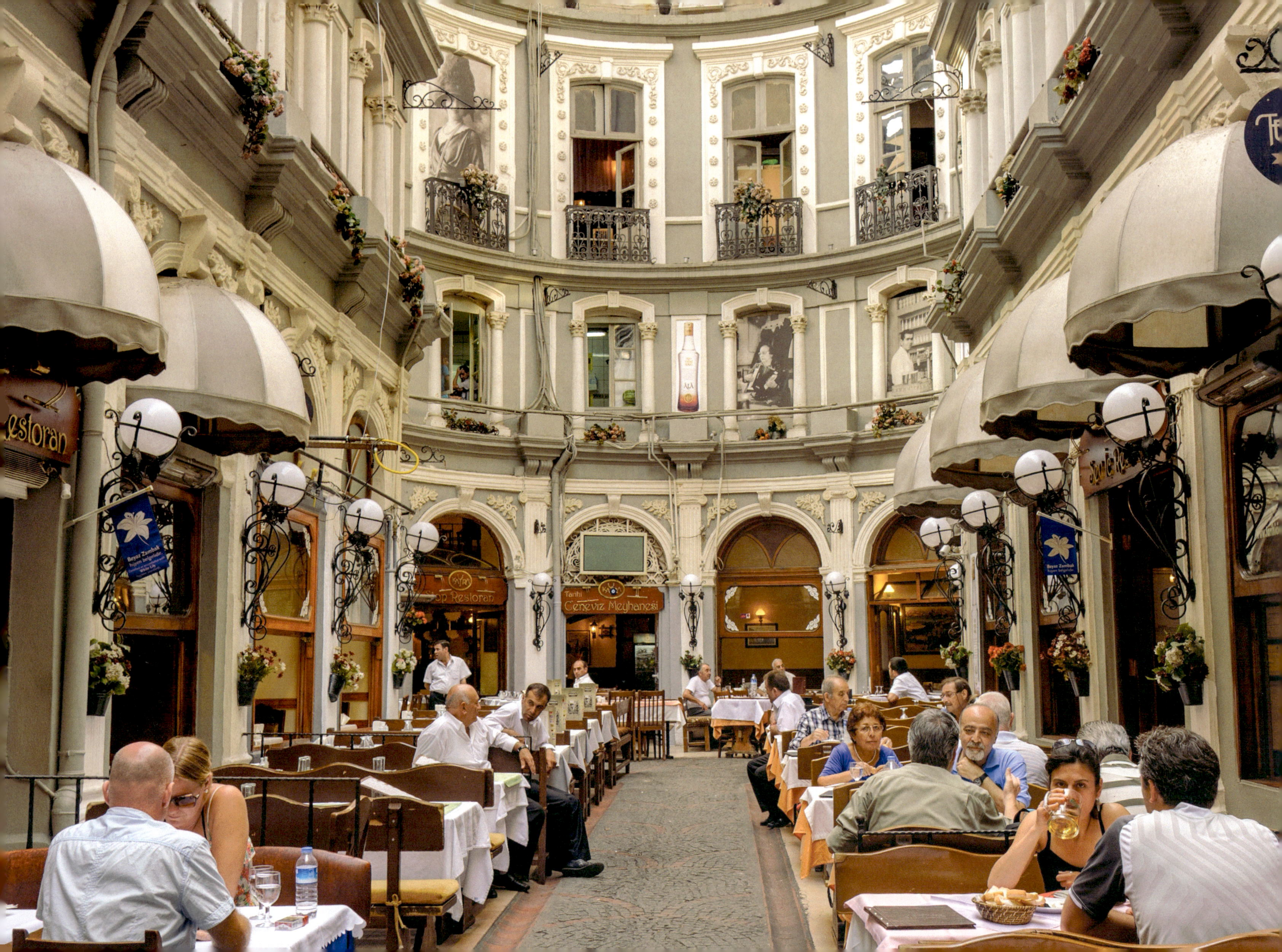

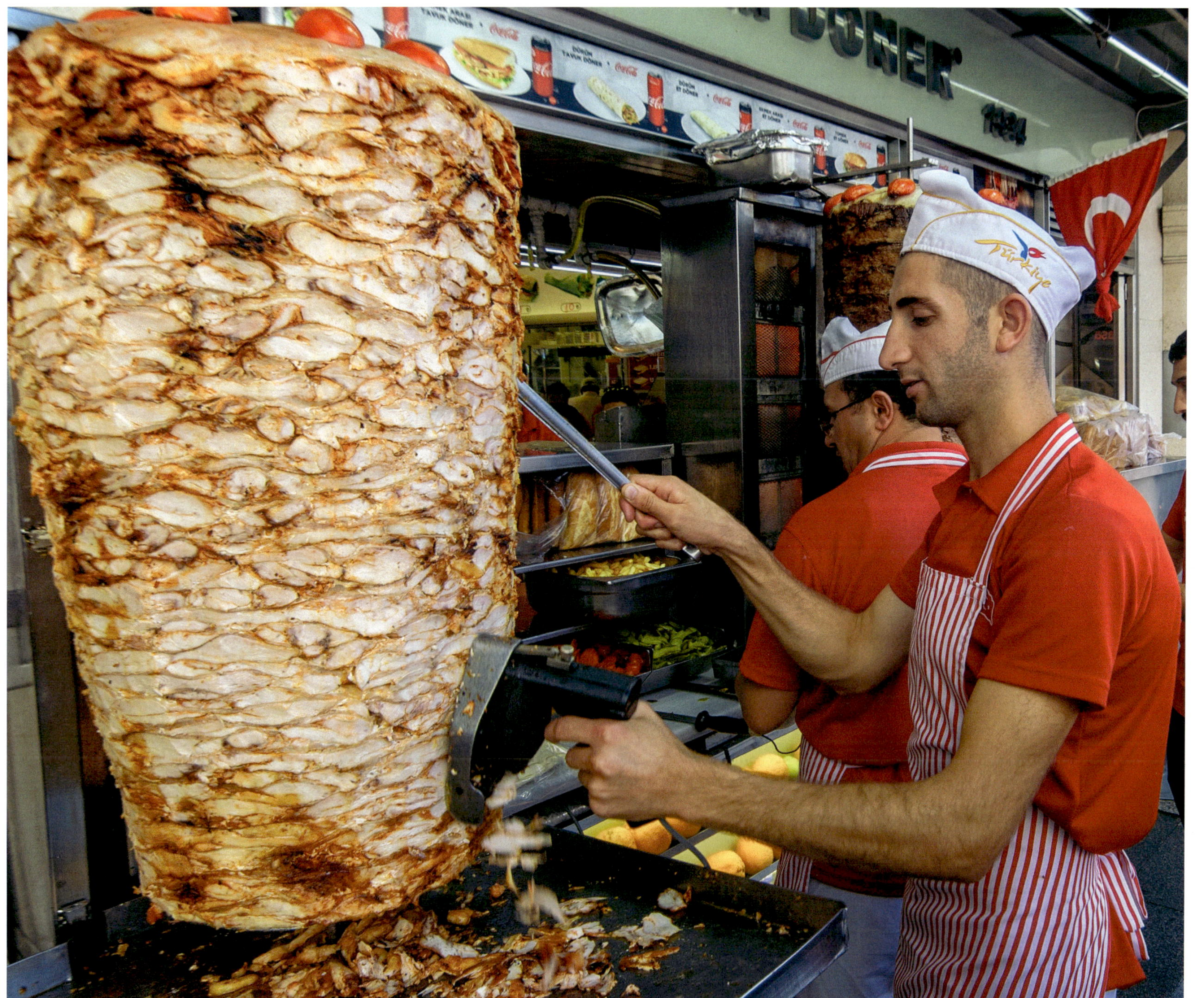

LEFT:

Kebab, Taksim Square, Istanbul

Eating a kebab in Istanbul is a culinary journey rooted in tradition and flavour. While walking you may find the air is often filled with the tantalizing aroma of grilling meat. From the humble döner on a street corner to the many elaborate shish kebab recipes in a fine restaurant, each bite tells a story of spices and tender meat.

OPPOSITE:

Eating out, Istanbul

Restaurants in Istanbul are a special experience. Türkiye's vibrant cuisine, developed during the Ottoman Empire, in a country linking Europe, the Middle East, and Asia, is a unique combination of fresh flavours and spices. For Turkish people, food is a source of immense pride and identity. Their diverse regional cuisines are all shared and enjoyed in Istanbul. Meals are a communal activity, a chance to connect with family and friends, and the city provides thousands of places for visitors to share that experience.

Topkapi Palace, Istanbul
This richly decorated palace was the home and headquarters of the Ottoman sultans from the 15th to the 19th centuries. The buildings reflect a blend of Ottoman, Islamic, and European influences, which grew over centuries. Its glittering interiors are lavishly decorated with Iznik tiles, depicting floral and geometric patterns.

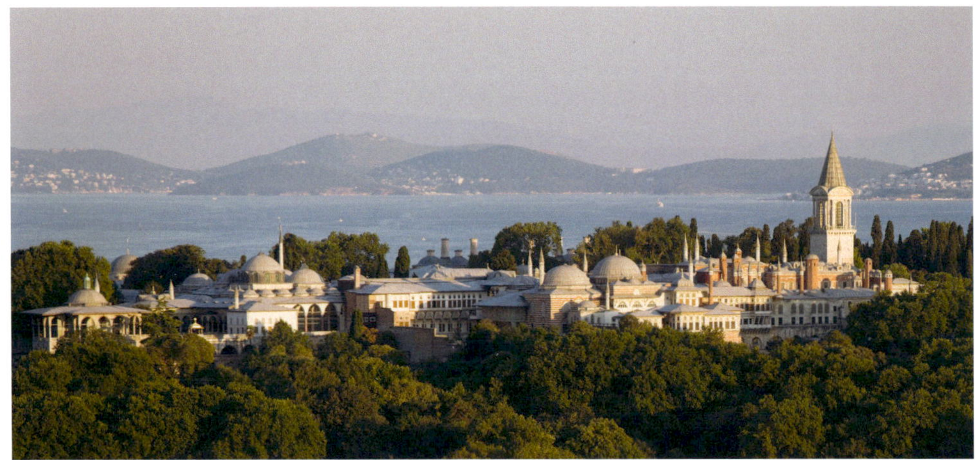

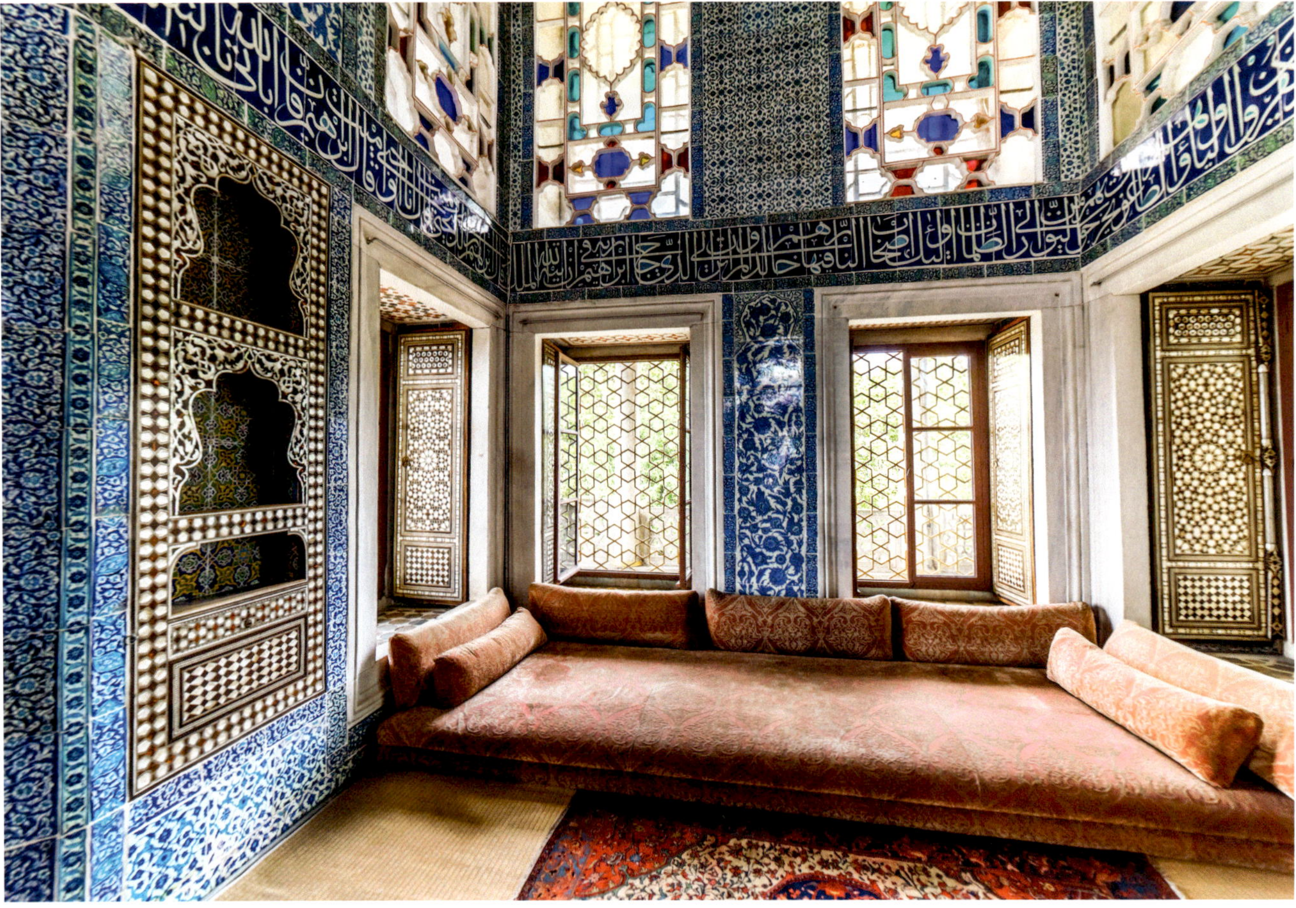

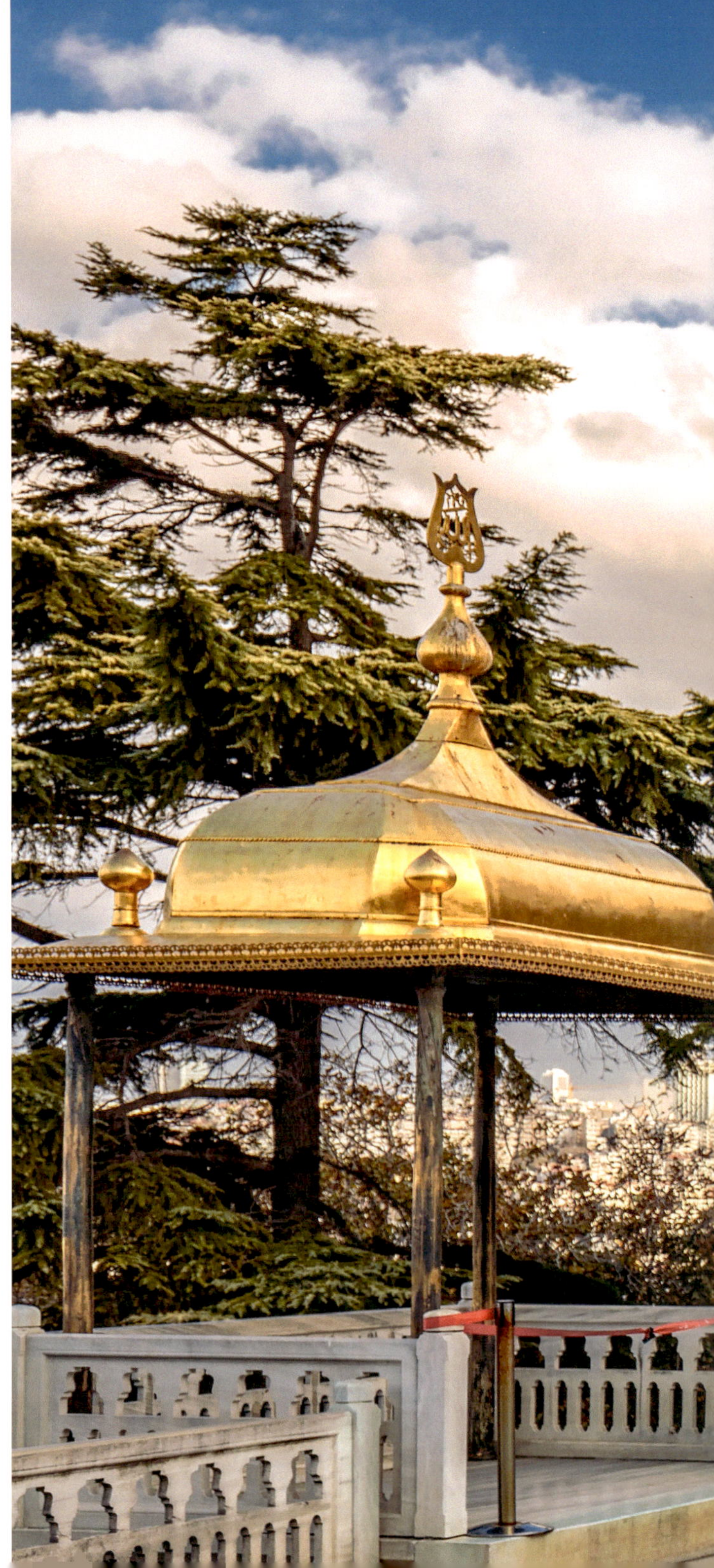

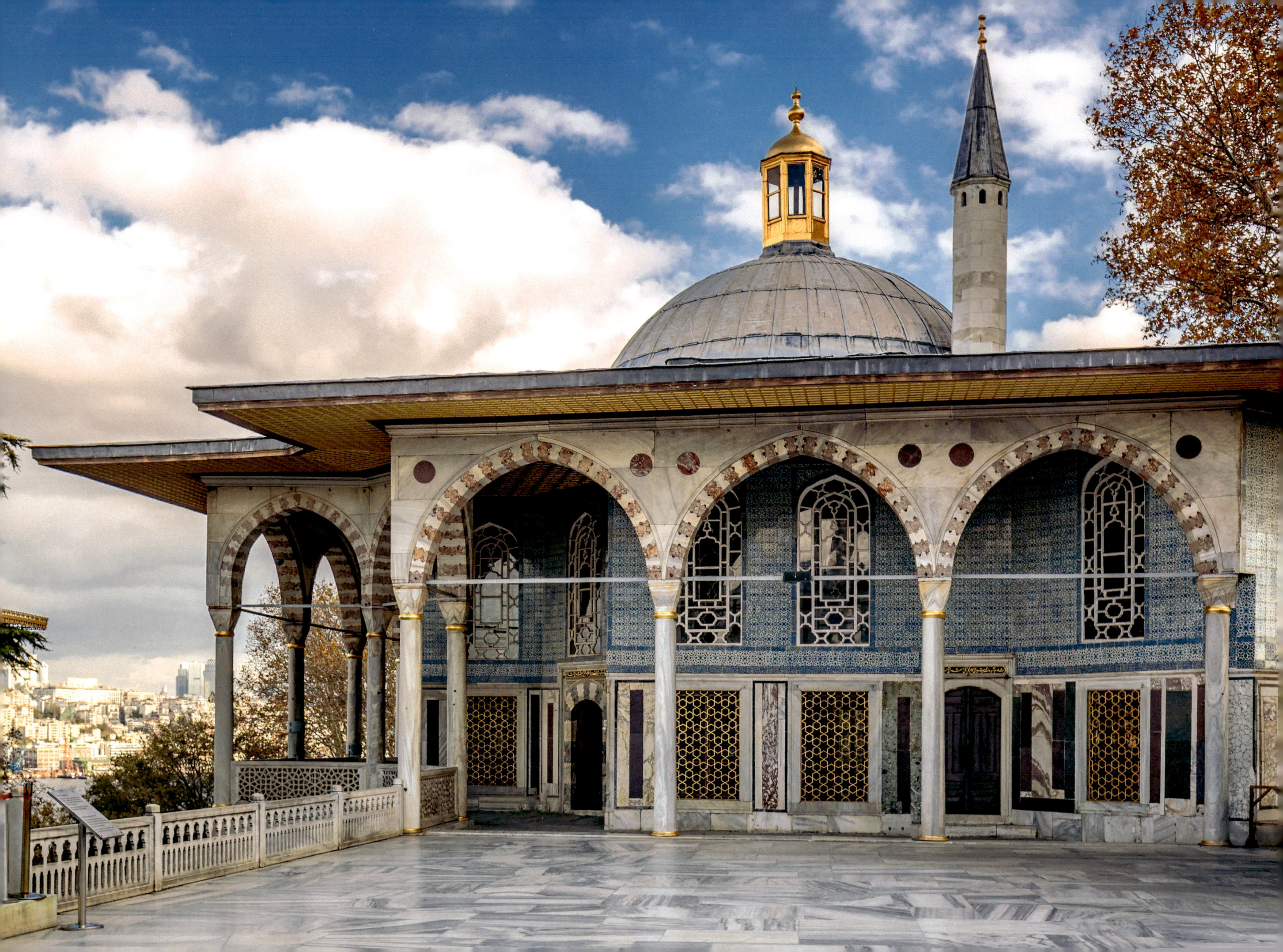

BOTH PHOTOGRAPHS:
Galata Bridge, Istanbul
Spanning the Golden Horn,
Galata Bridge is Istanbul's
vital link between the famed
old city and its more modern,
commercial districts. The
current bridge is the fifth
to occupy the site and was
completed in 1994. The
bridge is now a microcosm of
Turkish life, being a bustling
cultural hub where fishermen
line the top deck, and with
restaurants and cafes on the
lower level offering places
to sit, take coffee, eat fresh
seafood and enjoy stunning
views of the city's skyline and
the Bosphorus.

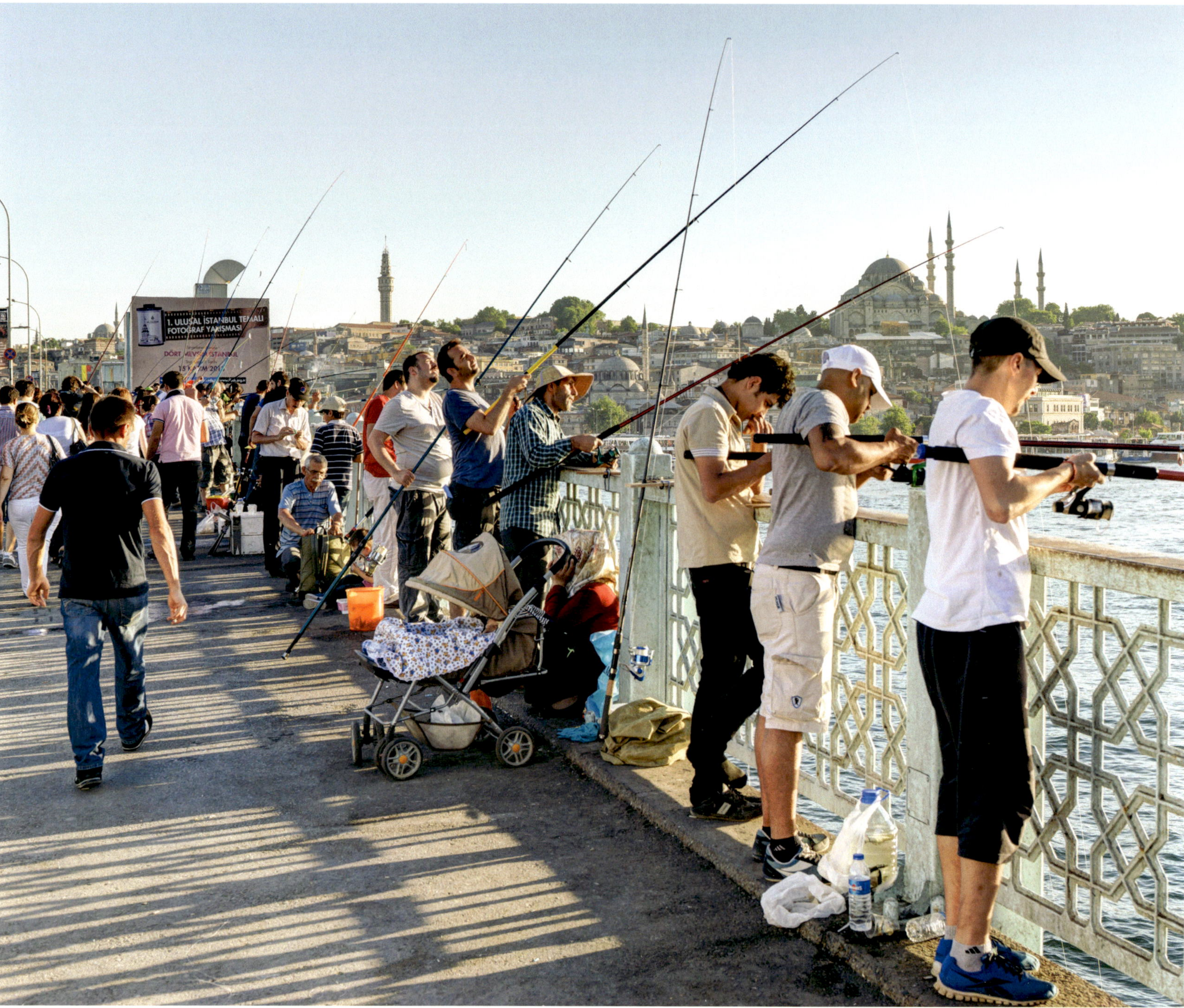

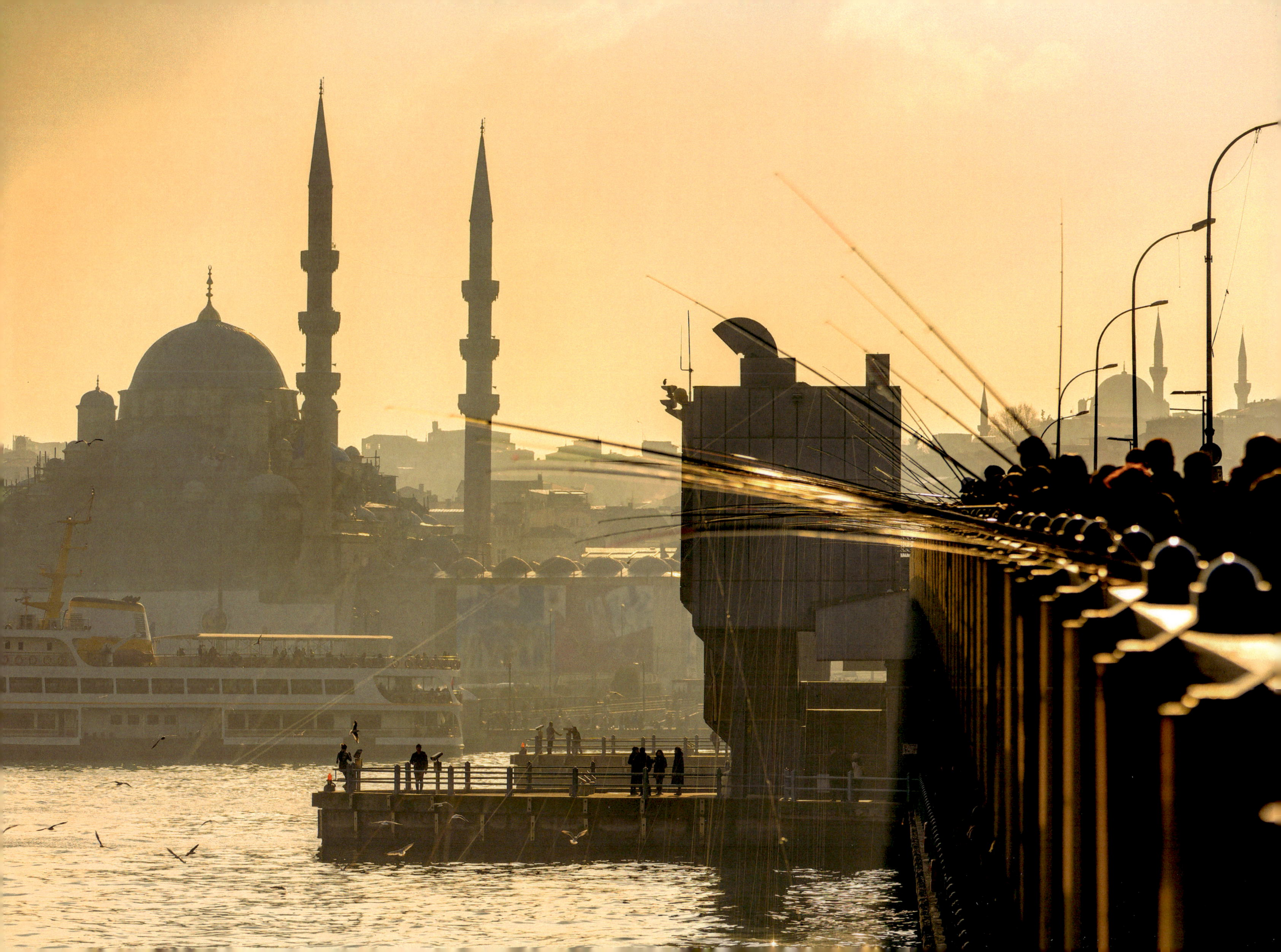

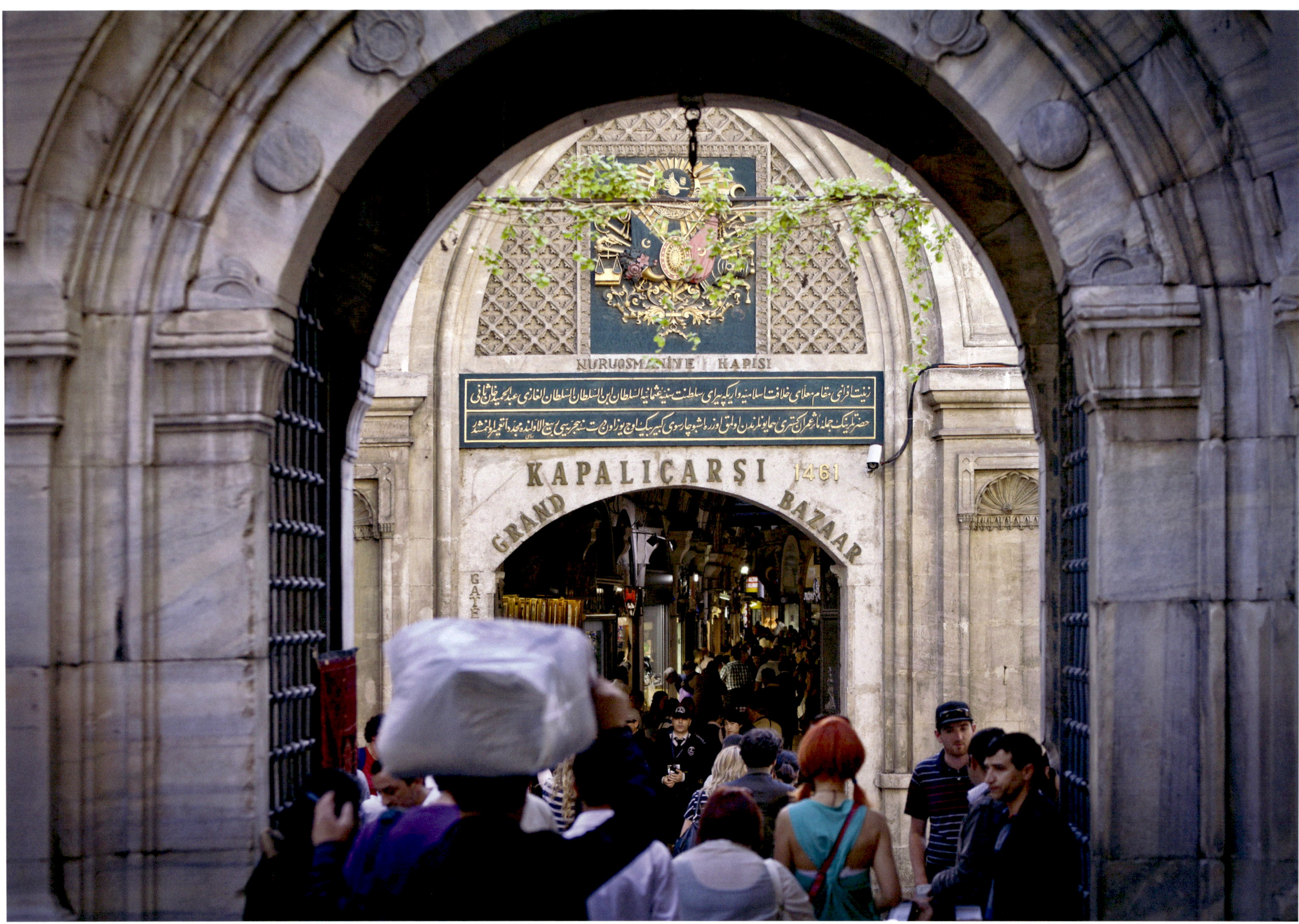
NURUOSMANİYE KAPISI
KAPALIÇARŞI 1461
GRAND BAZAAR GATE

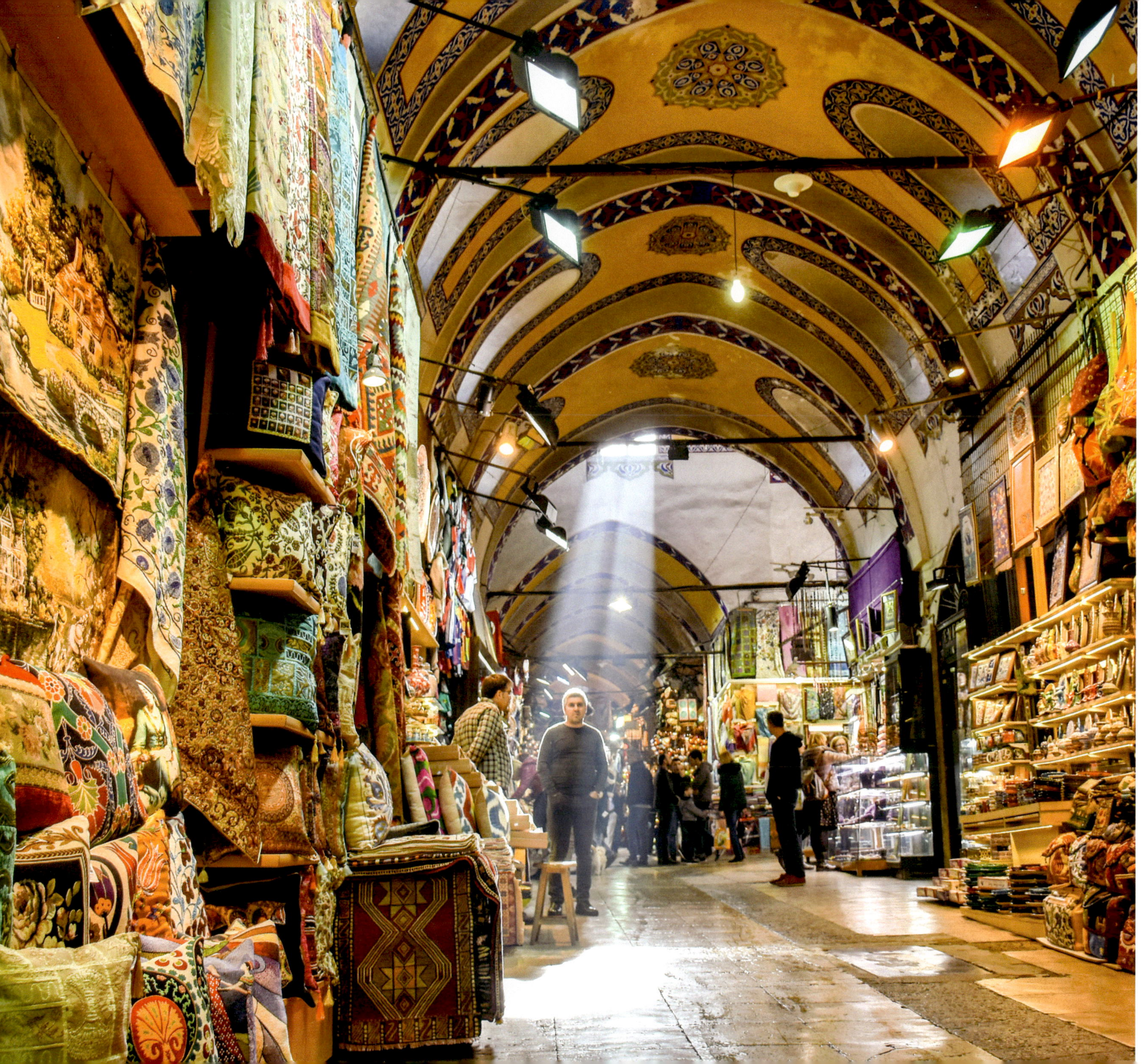

ALL PHOTOGRAPHS:
Grand Bazaar, Istanbul
Known in Turkish as
Kapalıçarşı, this giant
indoor market has been
a cornerstone of Turkish
history. It was established
shortly after the Ottoman
conquest of Constantinople
to stimulate trade. Then, it
was the economic heart of
the empire. Over time it grew
to become a labyrinth of
trade guilds and international
commerce. Till today, it
remains one of the world's
largest and oldest covered
markets, attracting millions
of local shoppers and
tourists. Within its vibrant
atmosphere, customers
can haggle for everything
from handwoven carpets
and intricate jewellery to
spices, ceramics, and Turkish
handicrafts.

Ceramics, Grand Bazaar, Istanbul

Pottery travels to Istanbul from across the country. Key purchases include decorative plates and bowls, often featuring intricate Iznik-style patterns with tulip, carnation, and geometric designs. Many shops also sell tile panels for home decoration.

Perfumed sweets

The famed sweet Turkish delight, or lokum, was first enjoyed by Ottoman sultans. The confectioner Hacı Bekir is known to have brought the modern recipe to market in the 18th century. It became 'Turkish delight' when first brought to the West by travellers. Early flavours included rosewater, lemon, and mint, but modern varieties tease all palates. Pistachio, hazelnut, pomegranate, orange, and more fill shops in the bazaar.

Above the market

The Grand Bazaar spans a vast area of over 30,000 square metres (322,920 sq ft). Located in Istanbul's Fatih district, it lies between the historic Beyazit and Nuruosmaniye mosques. This trading labyrinth encompasses more than 60 streets and thousands of shops.

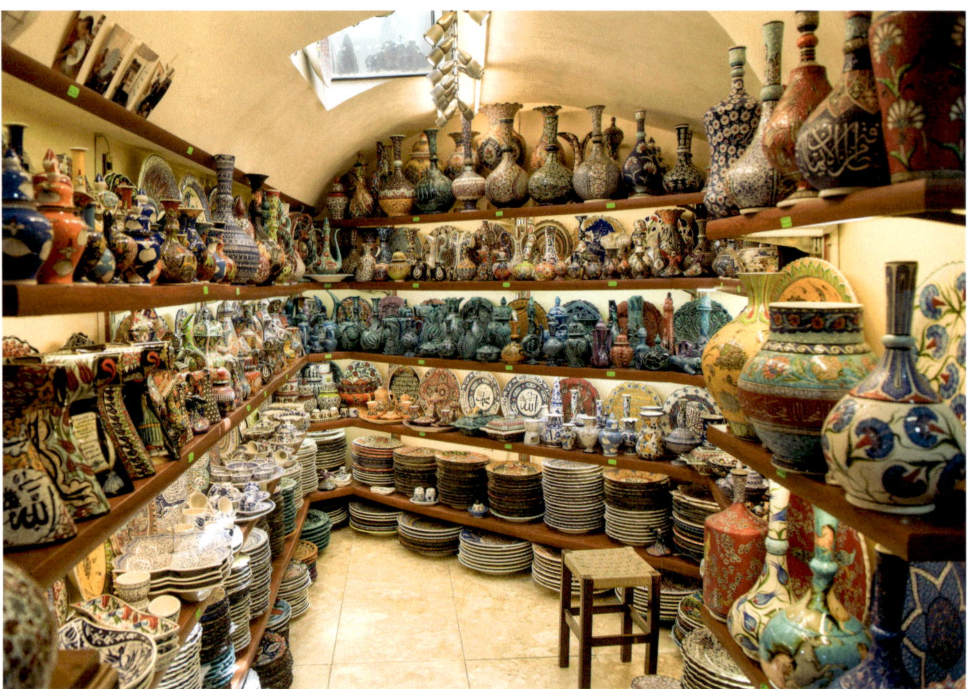

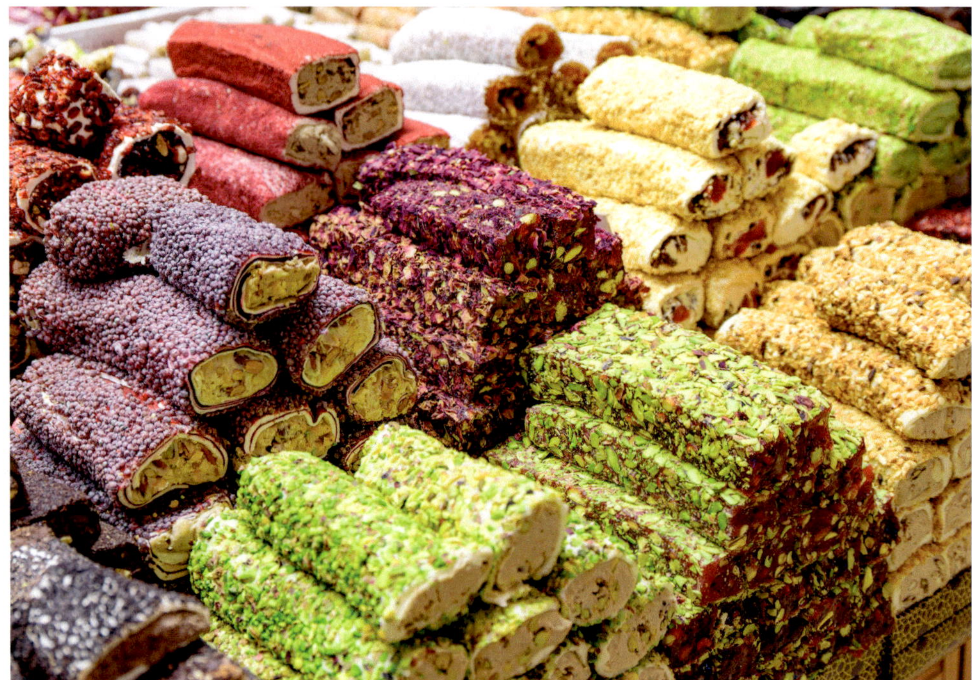

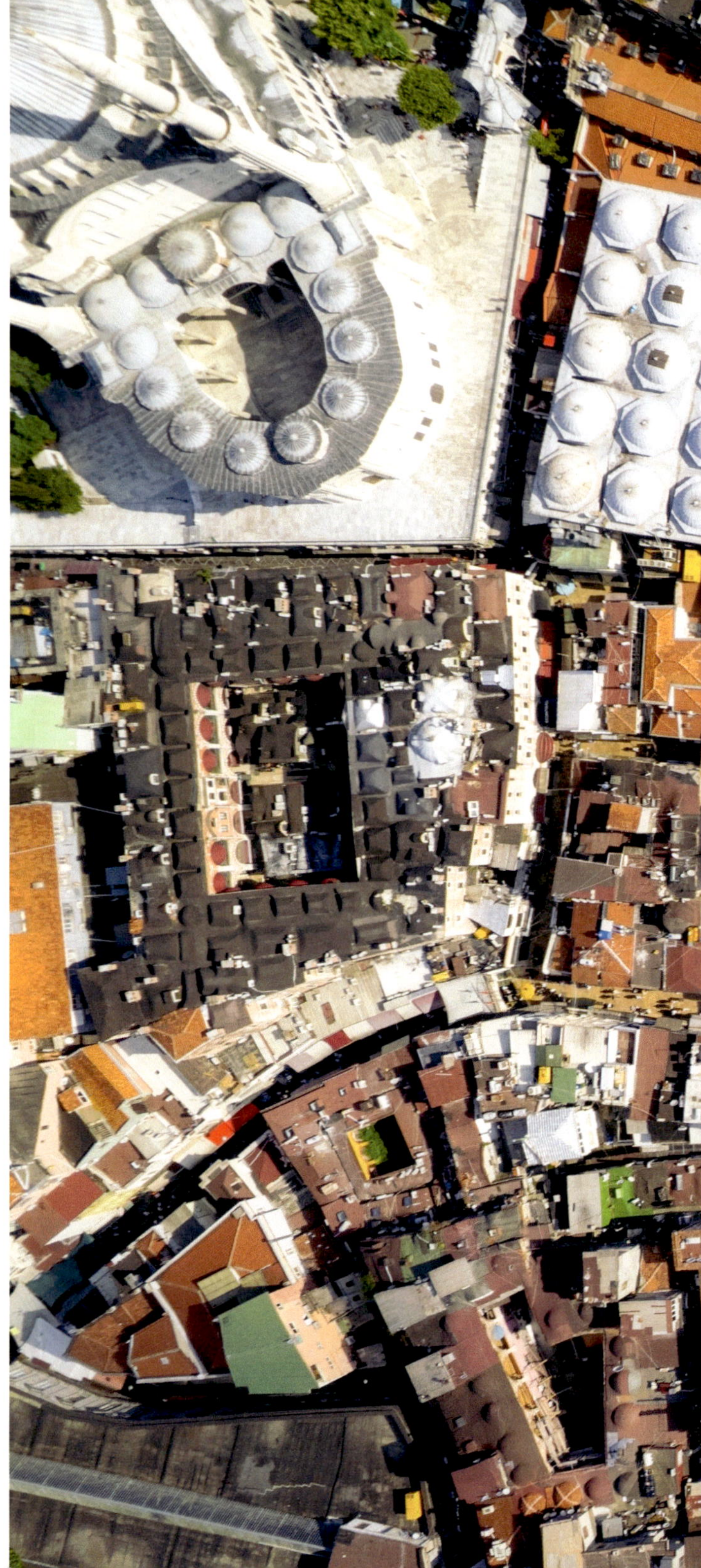

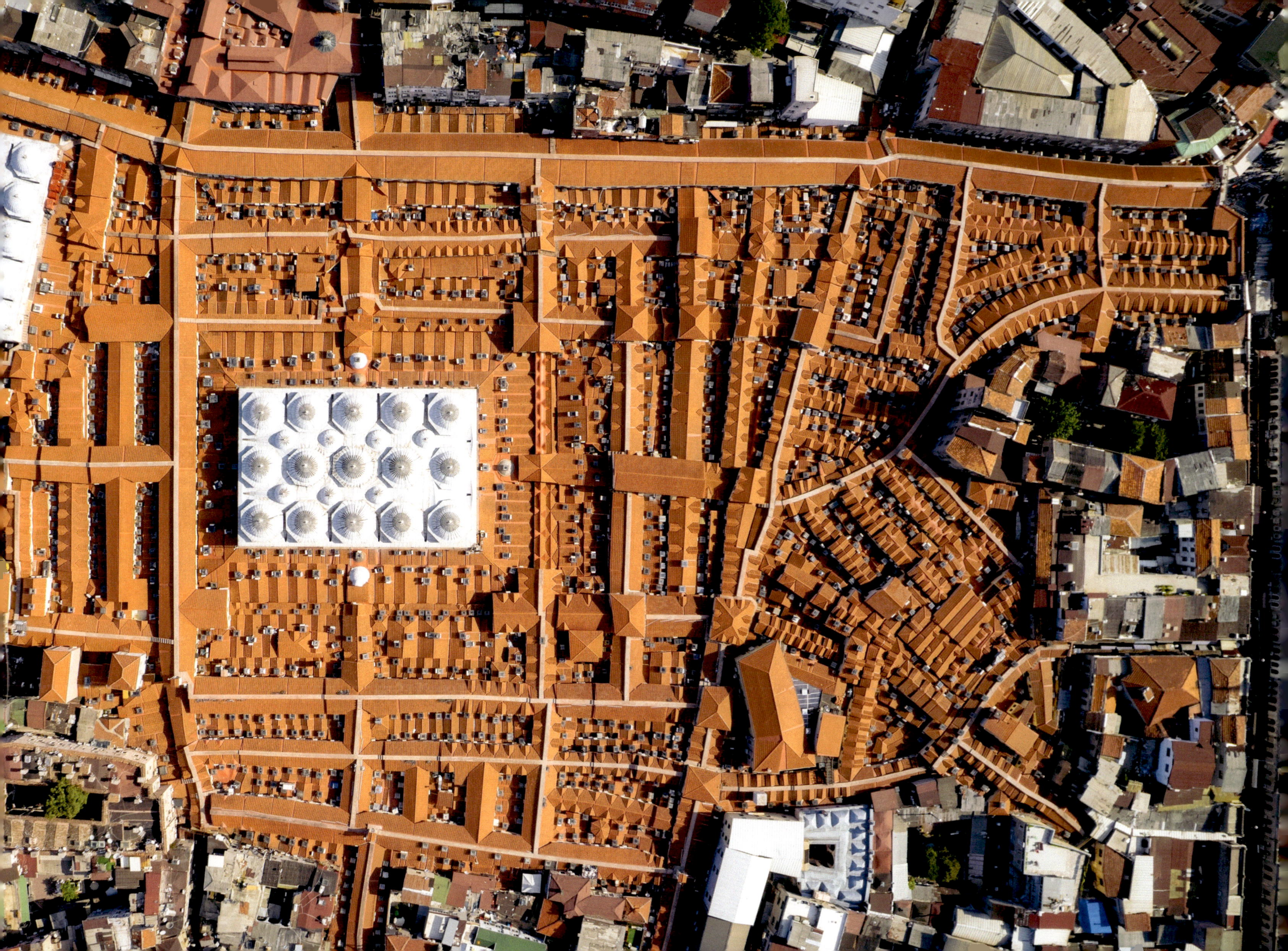

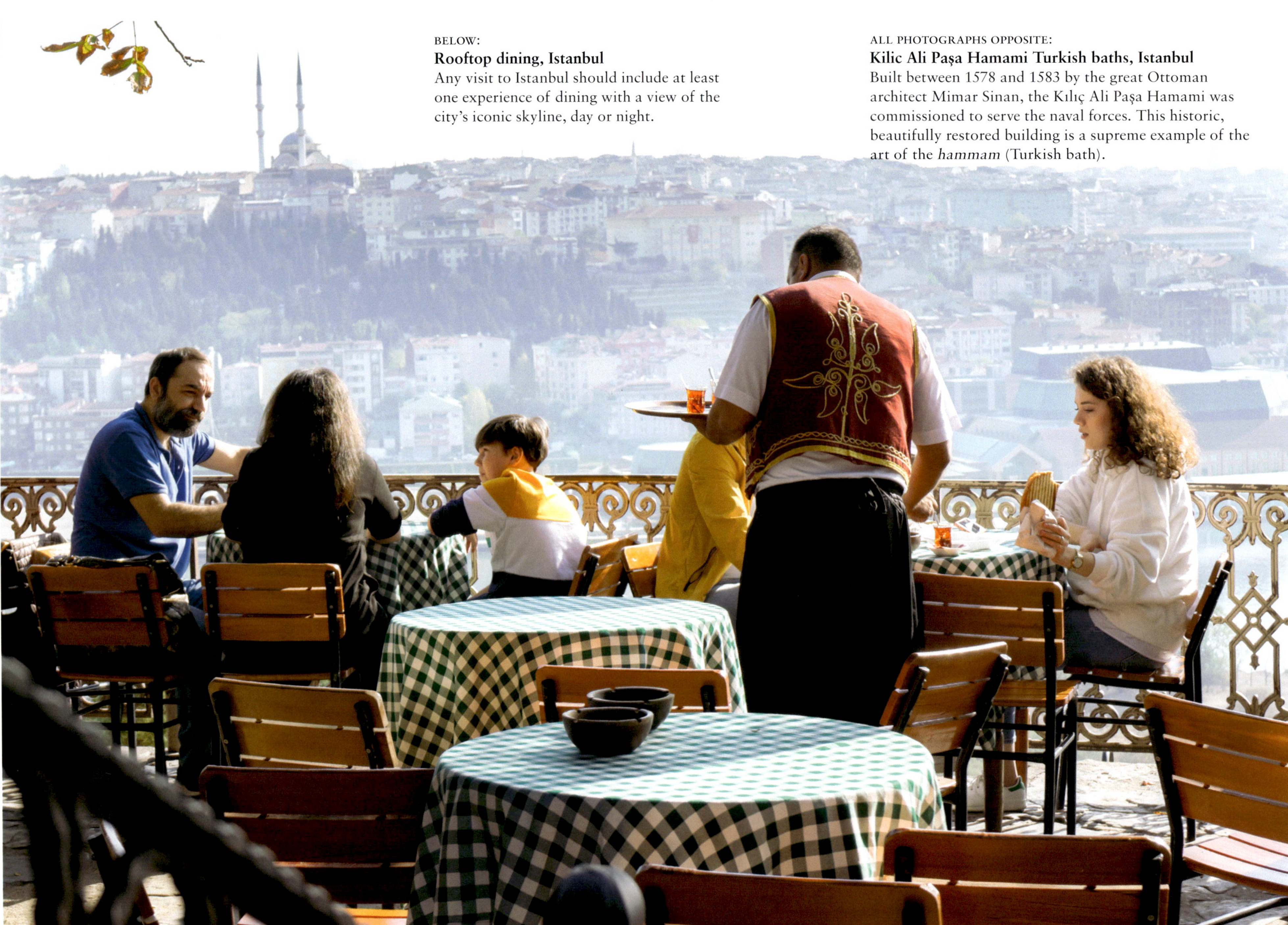

Rooftop dining, Istanbul
Any visit to Istanbul should include at least one experience of dining with a view of the city's iconic skyline, day or night.

Kilic Ali Paşa Hamami Turkish baths, Istanbul
Built between 1578 and 1583 by the great Ottoman architect Mimar Sinan, the Kılıç Ali Paşa Hamami was commissioned to serve the naval forces. This historic, beautifully restored building is a supreme example of the art of the *hammam* (Turkish bath).

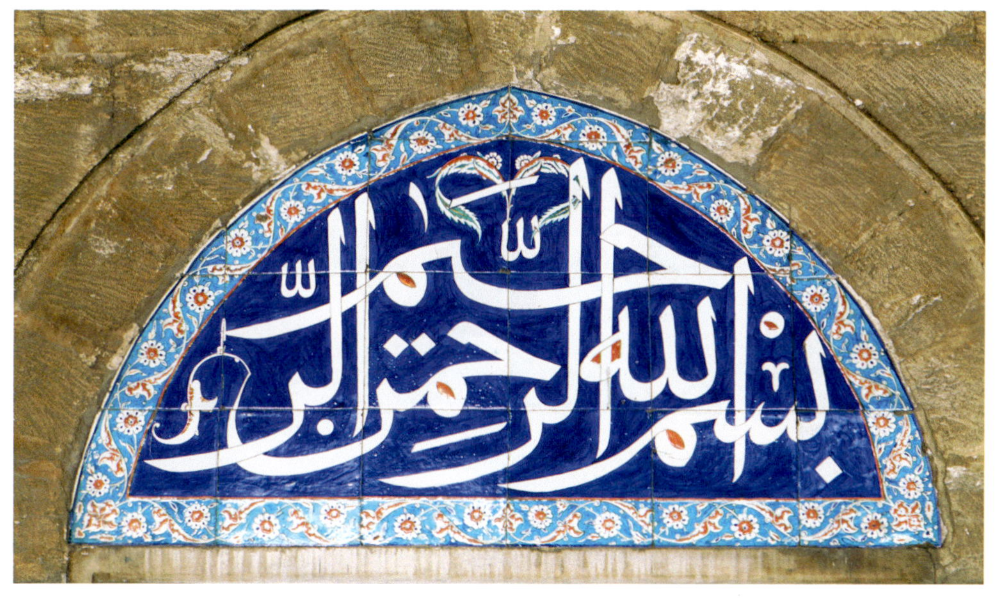

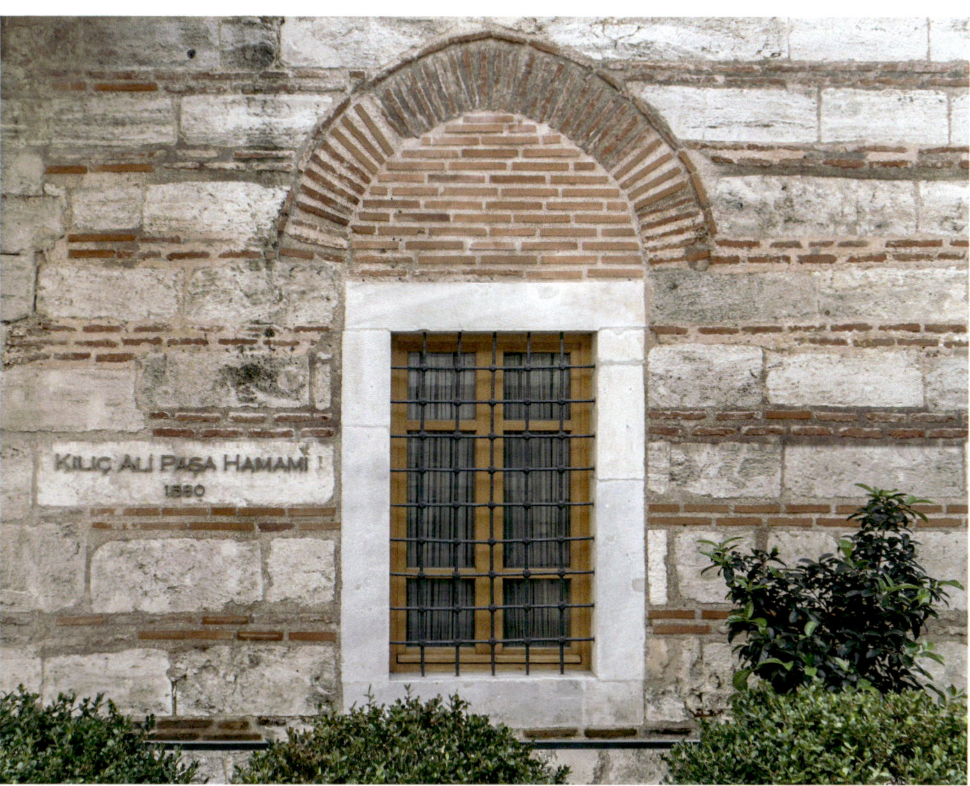

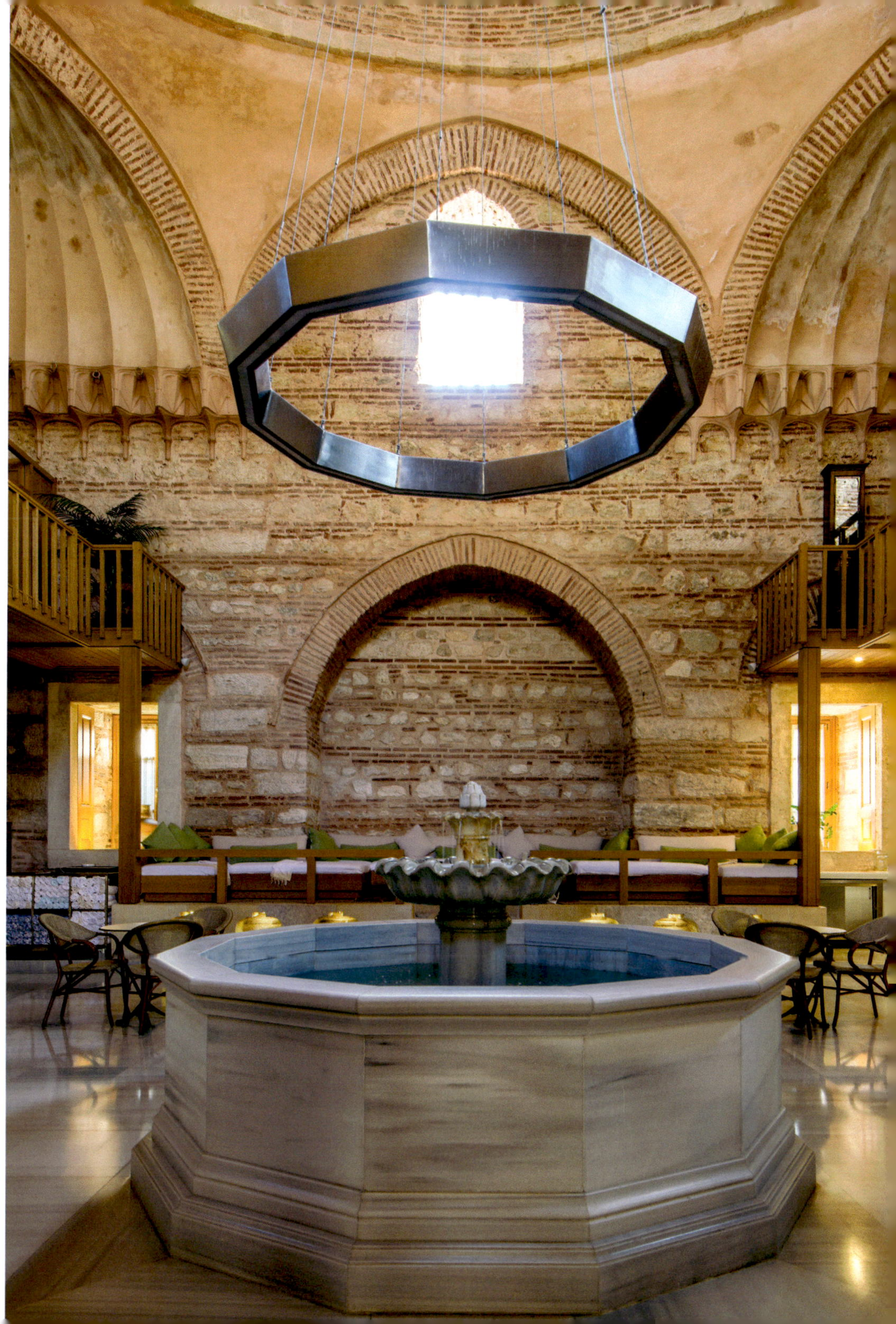

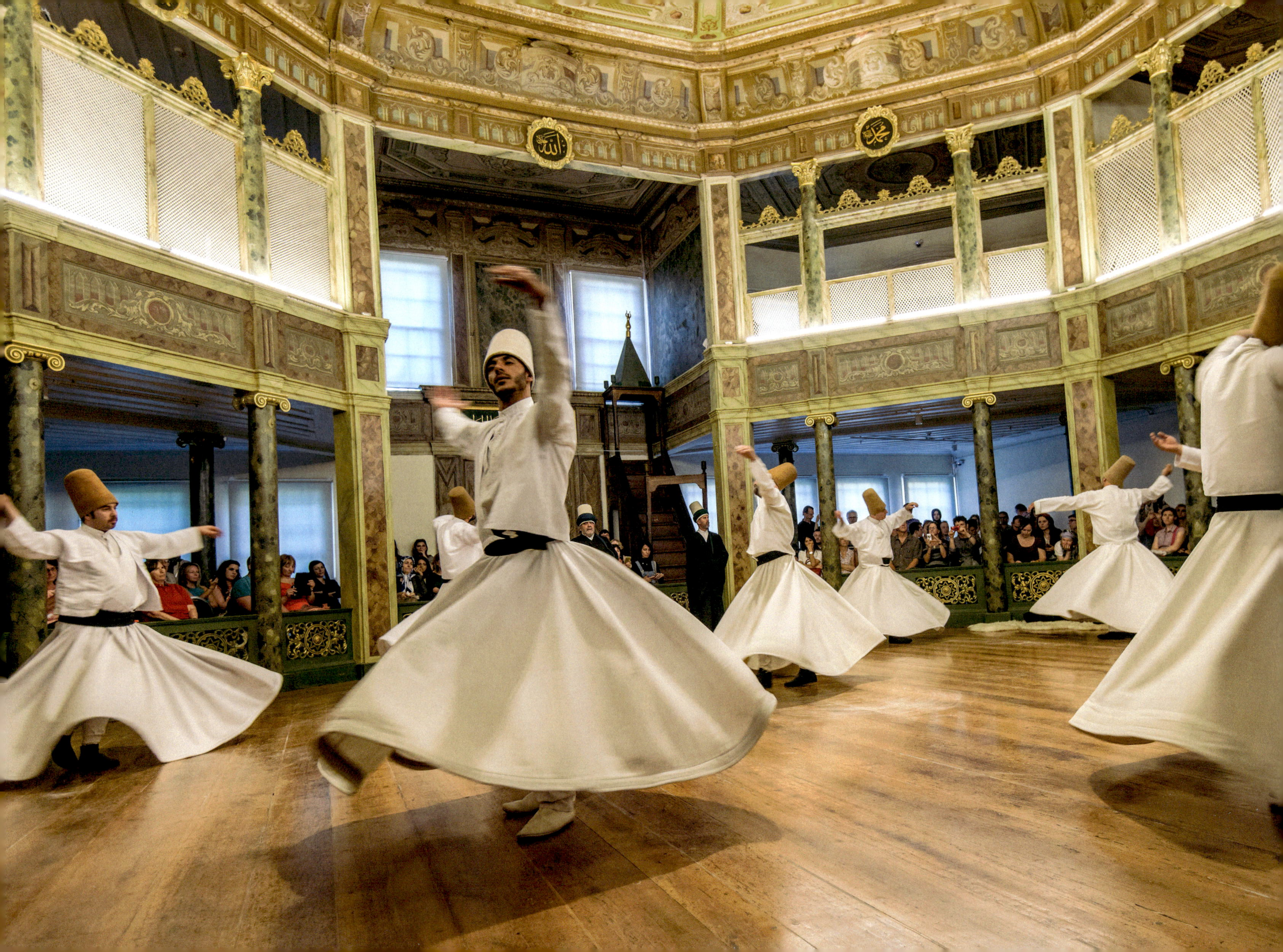

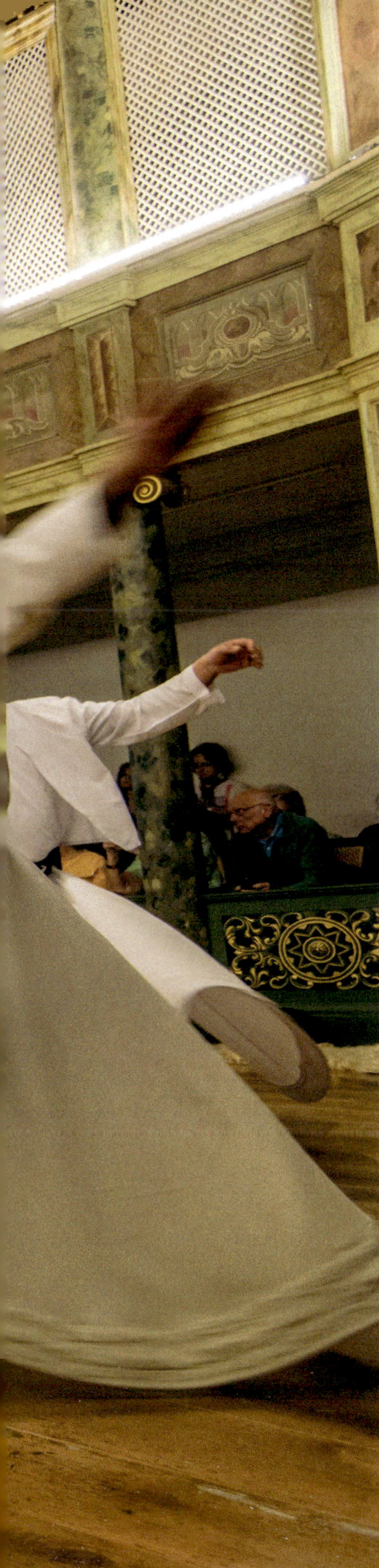

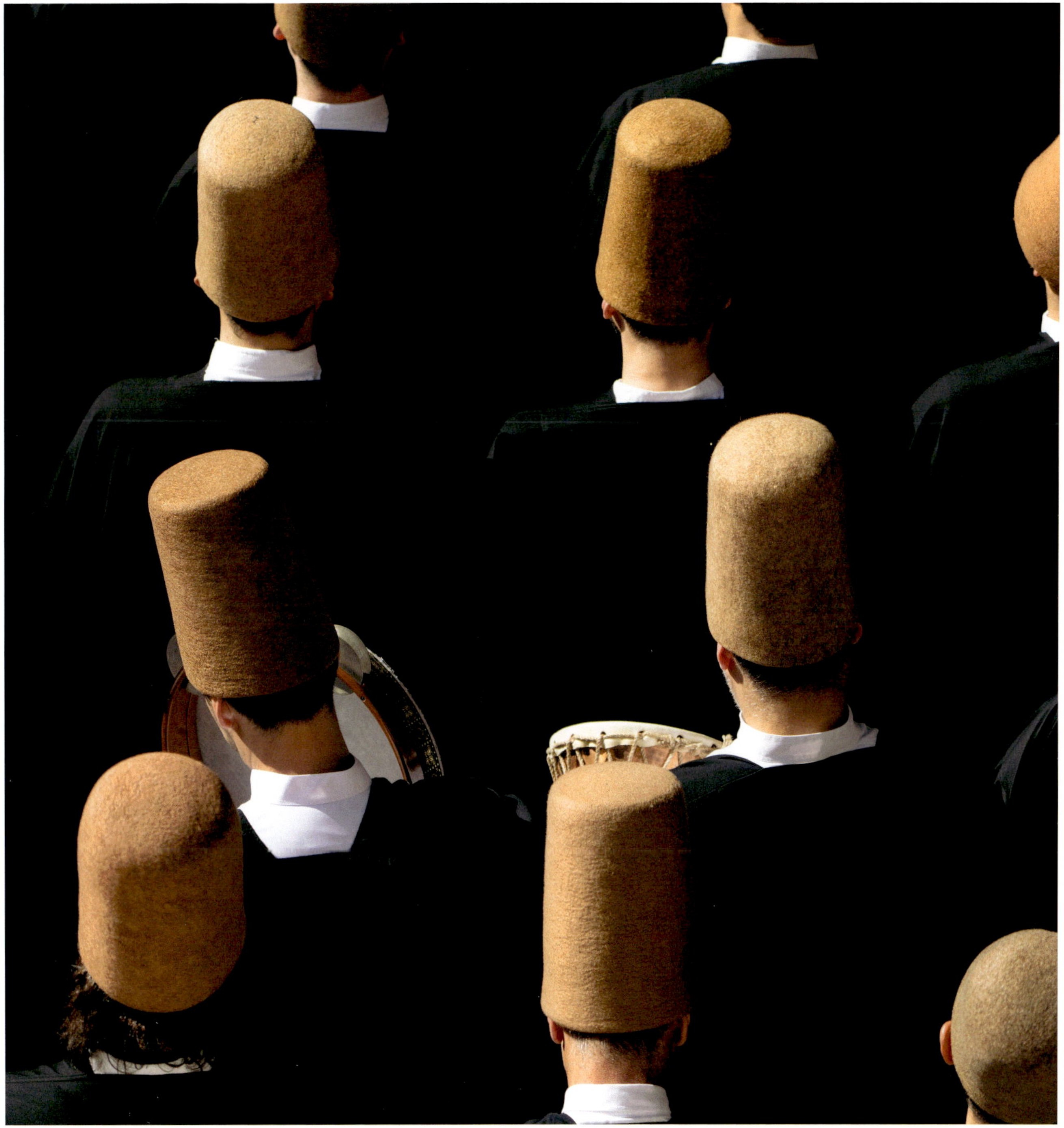

Whirling dervishes, Galata Mevlevi House, Istanbul

The Mevlevi House is a lodge where whirling dervishes perform their famous, sacred dance. It is a form of active meditation and prayer during which dancers abandon their egos to achieve a state of spiritual ecstasy and then reach a communion with God. While spinning, the dervishes, in symbolic clothing, turn gracefully to music.

LEFT:

Sufi dervishes, Eminönü, Fatih, Istanbul

The Mevlevi Order is a mystical branch of Islam founded by followers of the 13th-century poet Rumi. The Sufi dervishes of that order seek a spiritual connection with God through the Sema ceremony, a meditative practice of whirling, as performed at Mevlevi House, Eminönü, and at other locations in the Fatih district of Istanbul.

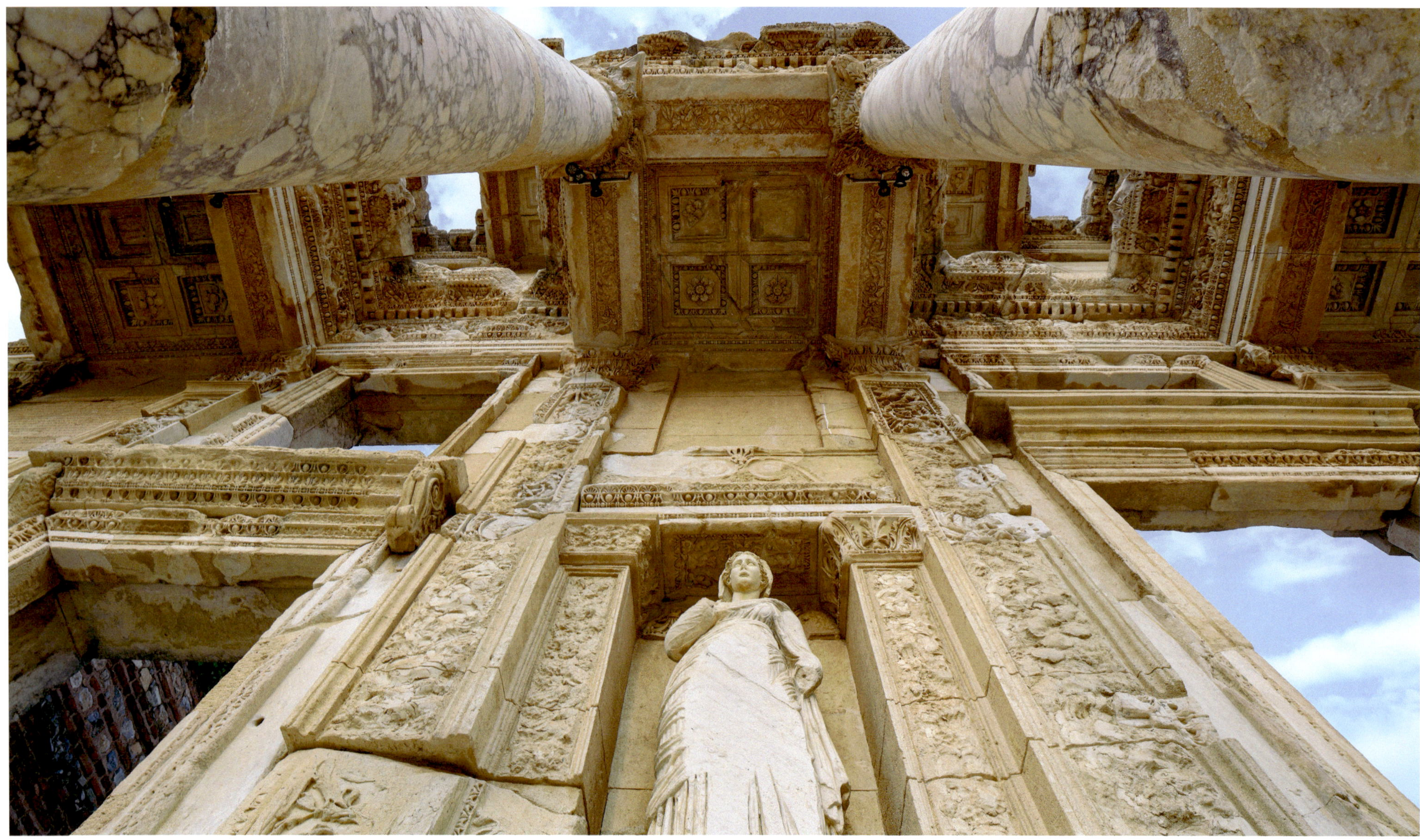

Library of Celsus, Ephesus, Izmir
Located near Izmir, Ephesus was a key commercial and cultural site in the ancient world. The library is a Roman-era building which dates to the 2nd century AD. It once held over 12,000 scrolls and was one of the largest libraries in the ancient world.

Today, its magnificent two-story marble facade has been painstakingly reconstructed, featuring intricate carvings and statues.

Grand Theatre of Ephesus, Izmir
With a seating capacity of up to 25,000 spectators, this impressive site is the largest ancient theatre in Anatolia. Standing on the slope of Mount Pion, the Grand Theatre was a central hub for Roman entertainment, public assemblies, gladiatorial contests, and communal gatherings.

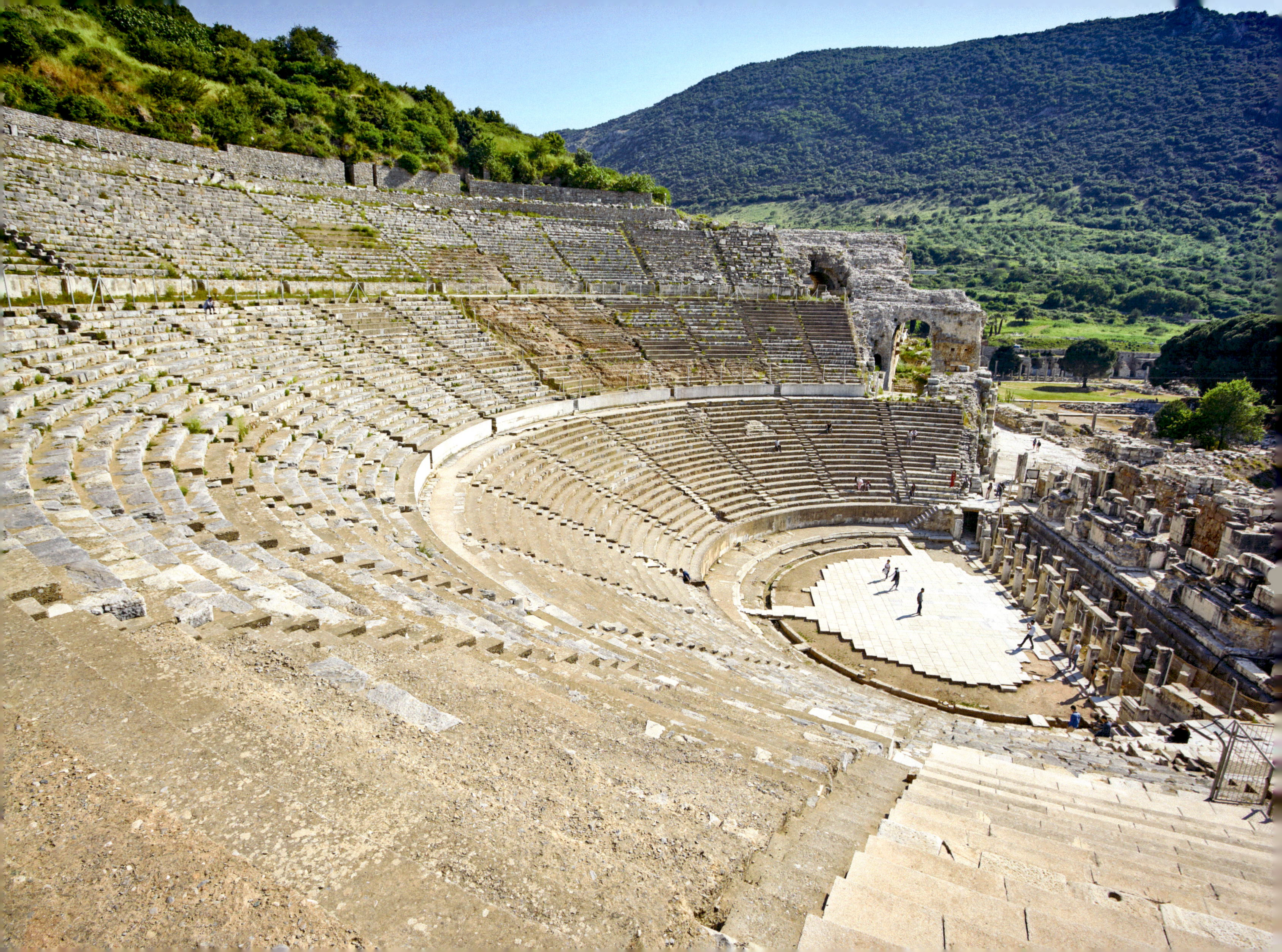

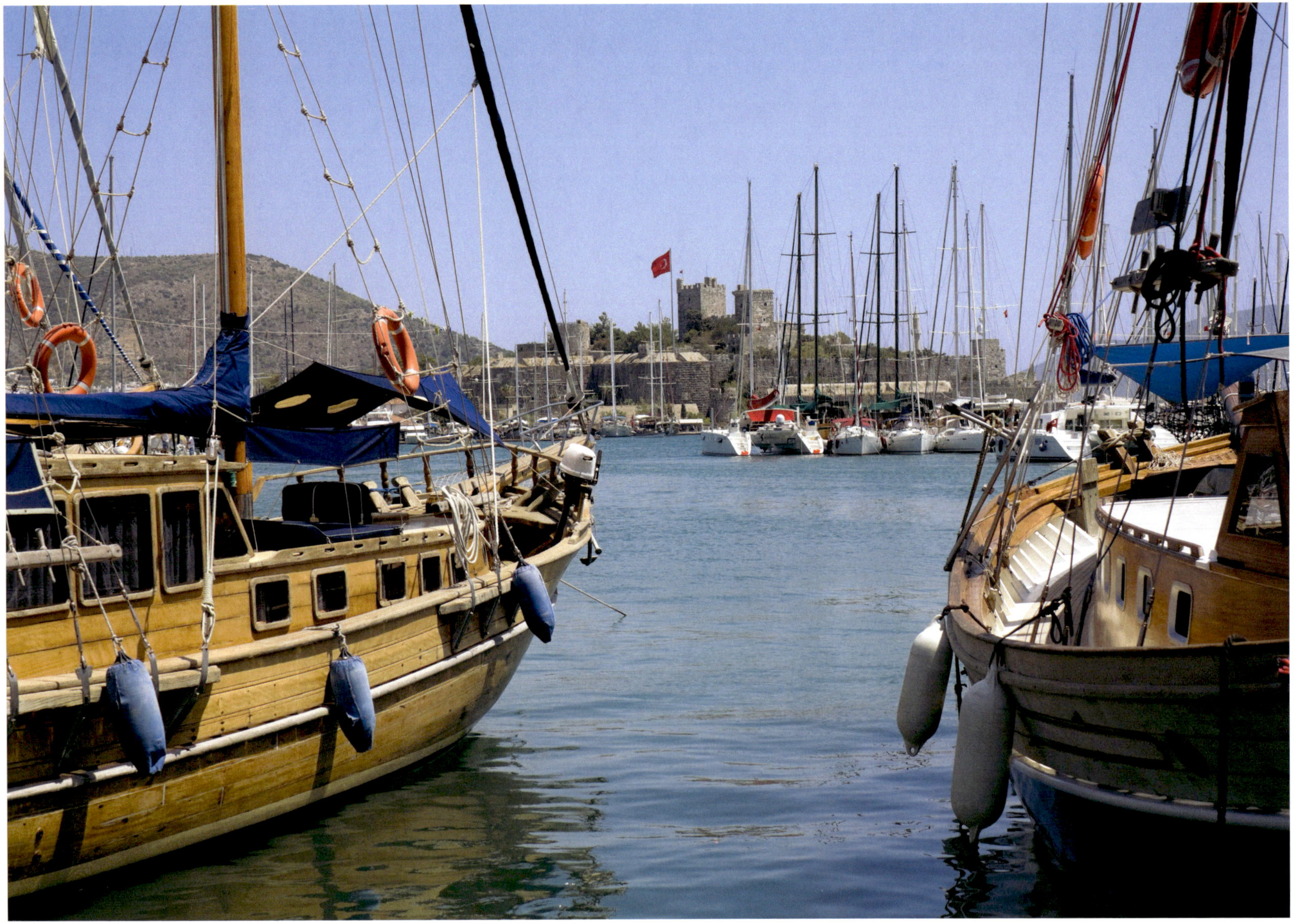

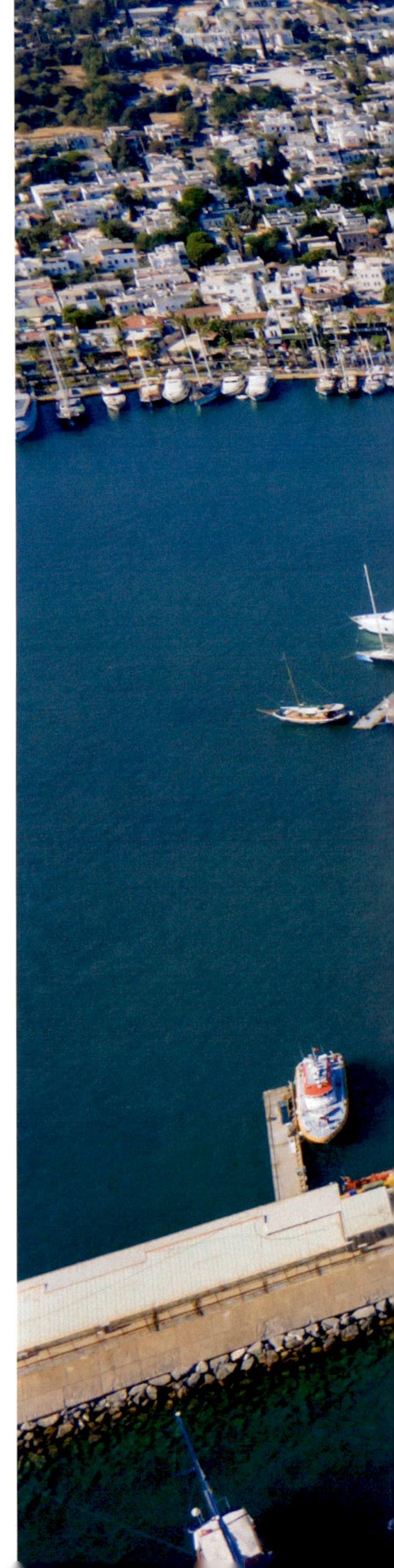

Bodrum Castle

Situated in the southwest, Bodrum is a major Turkish port city, which was known as Halicarnassus in antiquity. Then, it was home to Herodotus and contained the mausoleum we know from the Seven Wonders of the Ancient World. Its castle is the dominating feature of the harbour. This 15th-century fortress was built by the Knights of Saint John between 1402 and 1522. The castle's impressive size and positioning ensured it maintained its role as a formidable city defence while providing a vital stronghold for Christians during dangerous times. Currently it houses the Bodrum Museum of Underwater Archaeology, which exhibits artefacts from ancient shipwrecks.

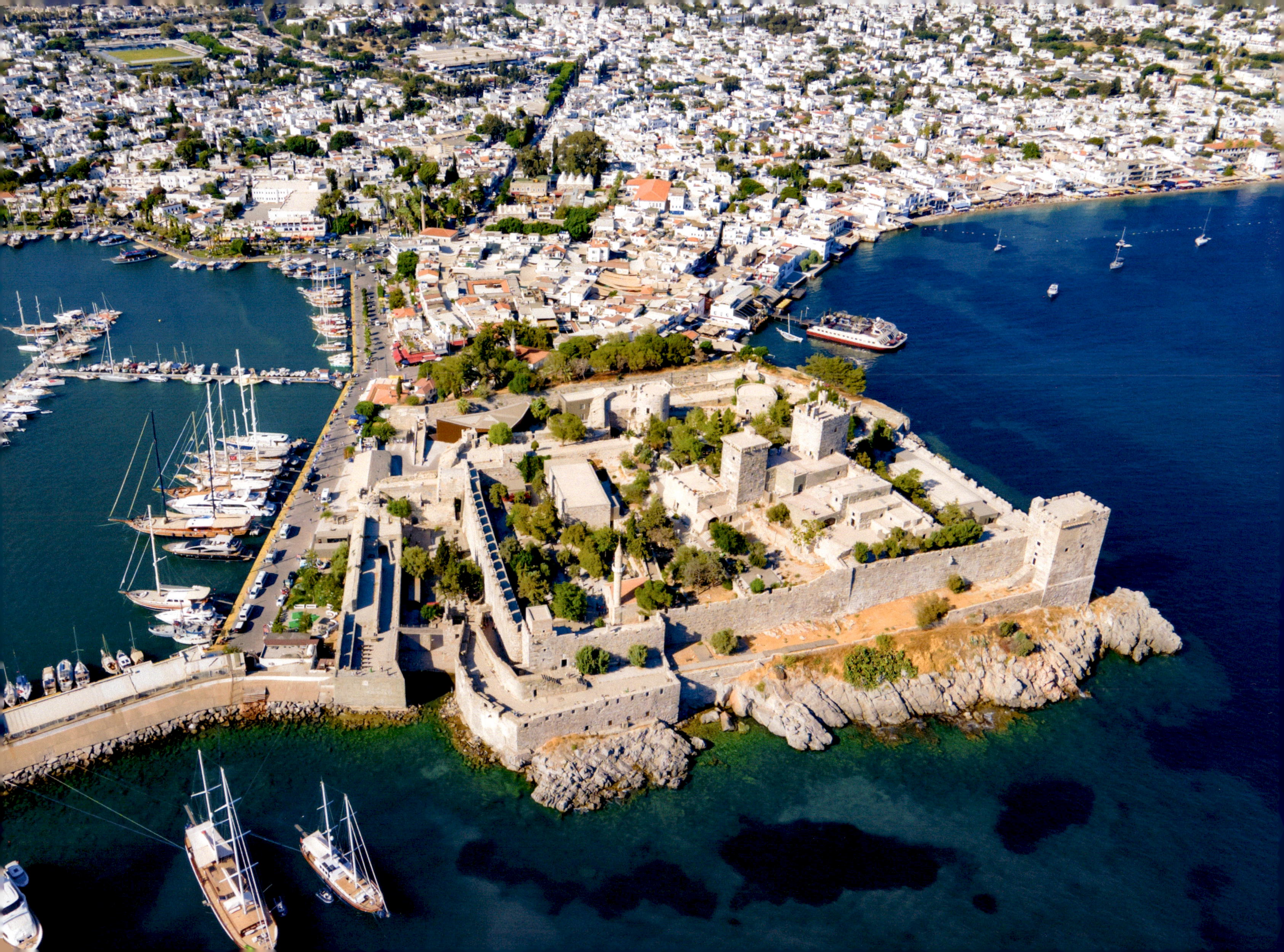

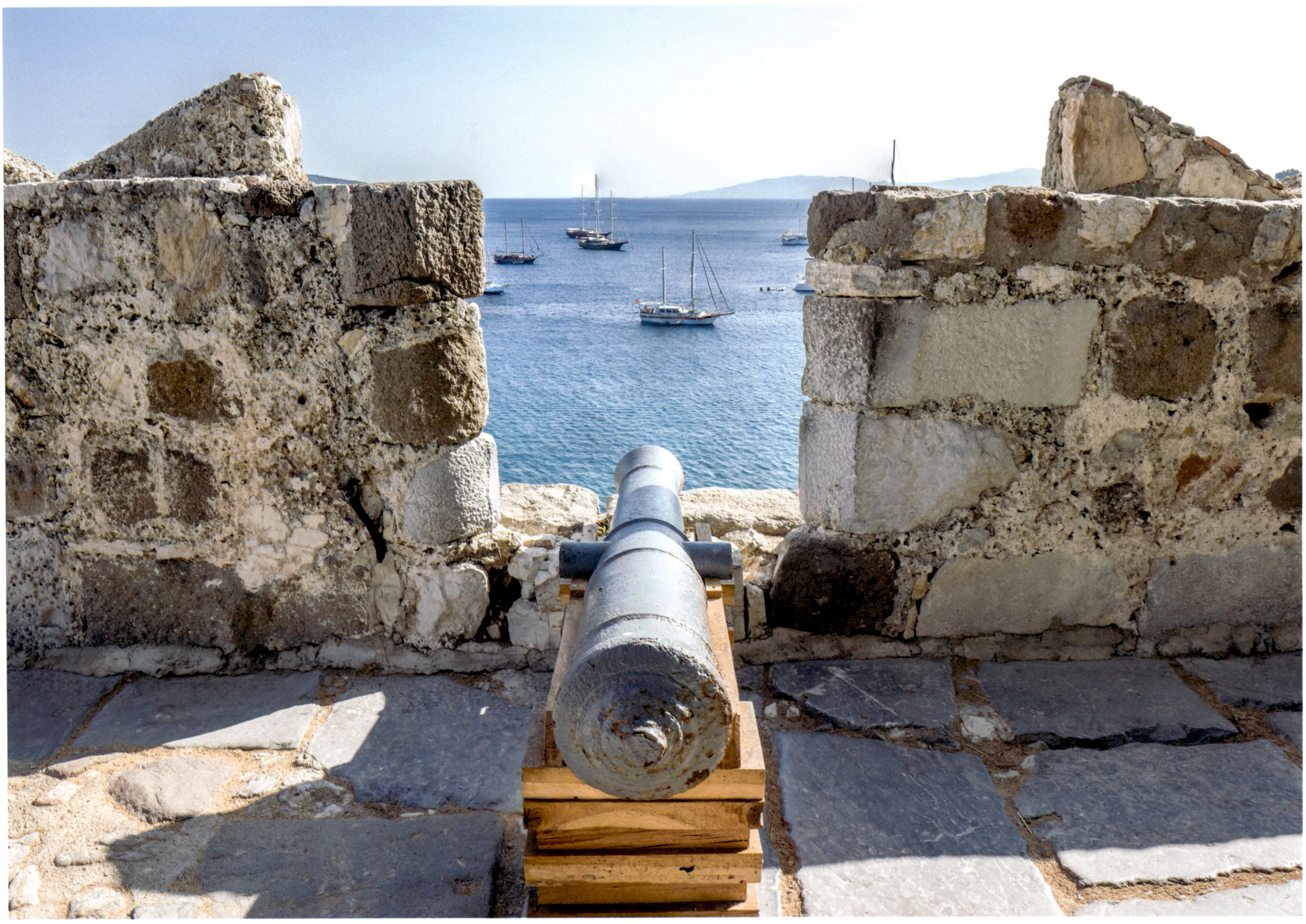

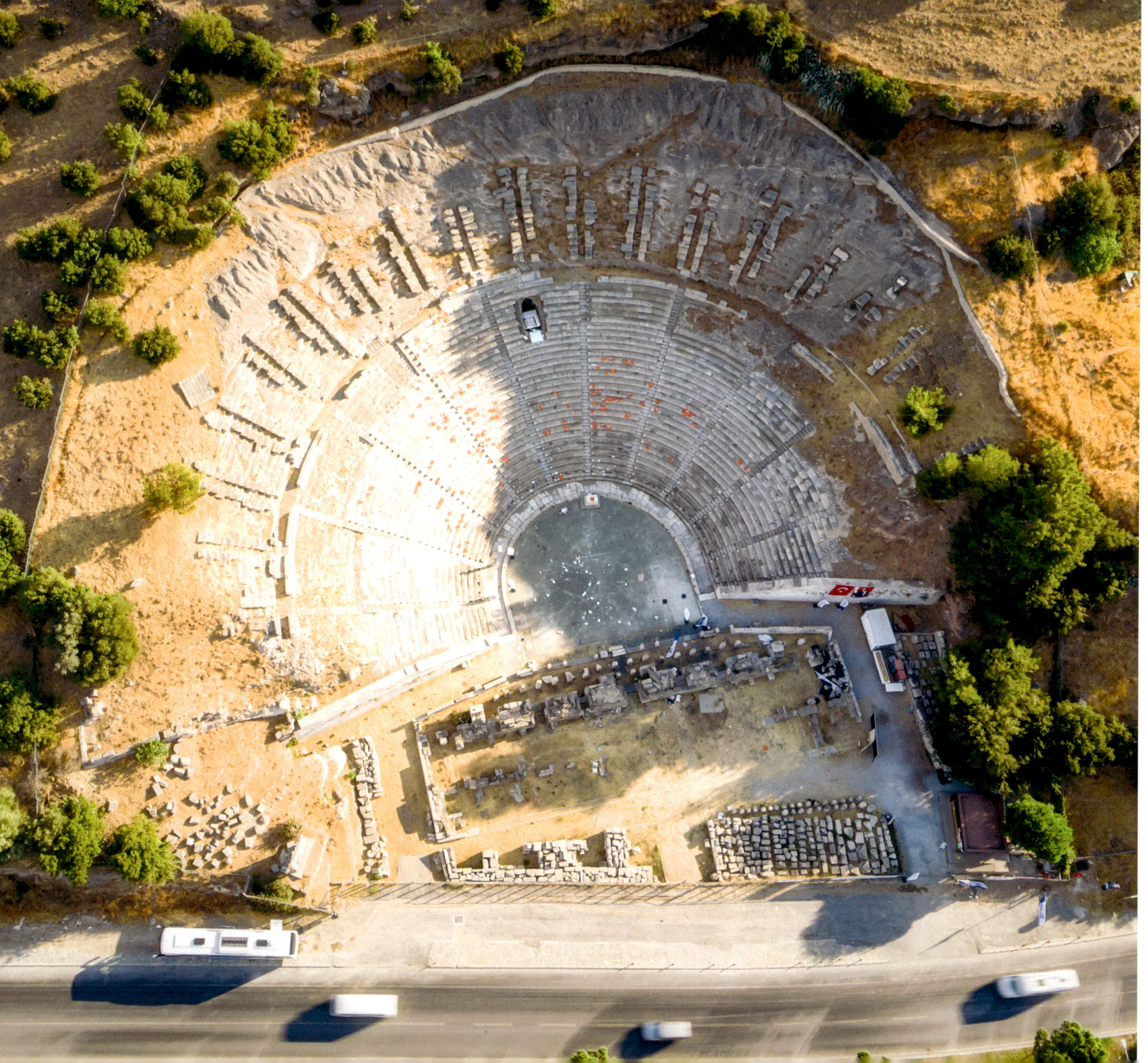

Theatre of Halicarnassus, Bodrum

This impressive ancient amphitheatre was built in the 4th century BC under the rule of Mausolus. He and his wife Artemisia were instrumental in transforming Halicarnassus into a magnificent, and influential, capital. During the Roman period, the theatre was enlarged, seating some 13,000 people. Its stunning hillside location offers the visitor fine views of Bodrum and the coastline for miles around.

**Göreme Historical
National Park, Cappadocia**
Renowned for its unique
landscape of so-called
'fairy chimneys' and rock
formations, sculpted by
millions of years of volcanic
activity and erosion, this
UNESCO World Heritage
site is famed for its ancient
rock-hewn churches and
underground dwellings. These
refuges were carved by early
Christians in search of a
more monastic lifestyle. The
most popular way to enjoy
this vast area is to observe it
from the air. Hot air balloons
rise each morning to look
down on unique geological
landscape and ancient cave
dwellings, giving the visitor
an unforgettable visual
experience.

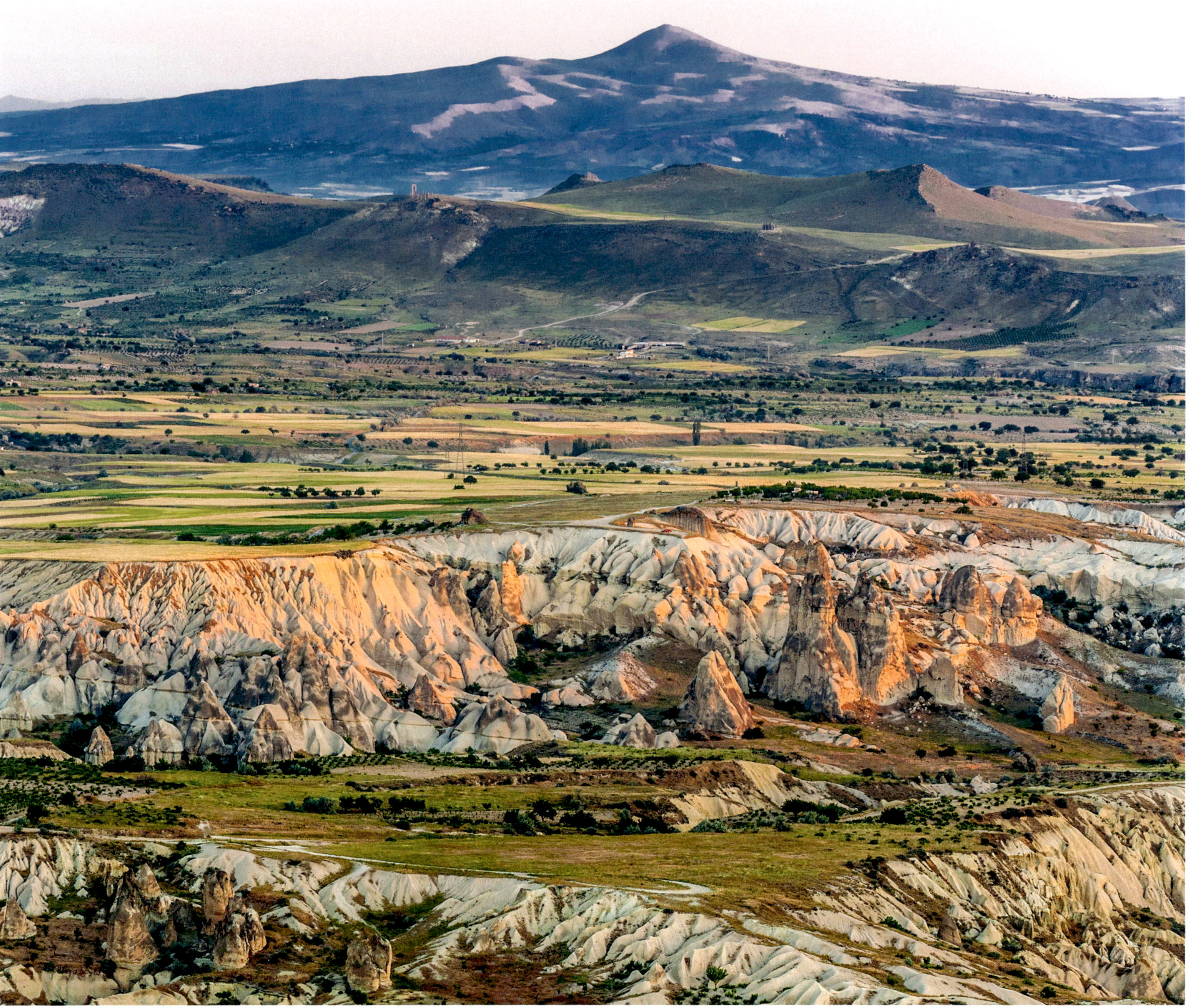

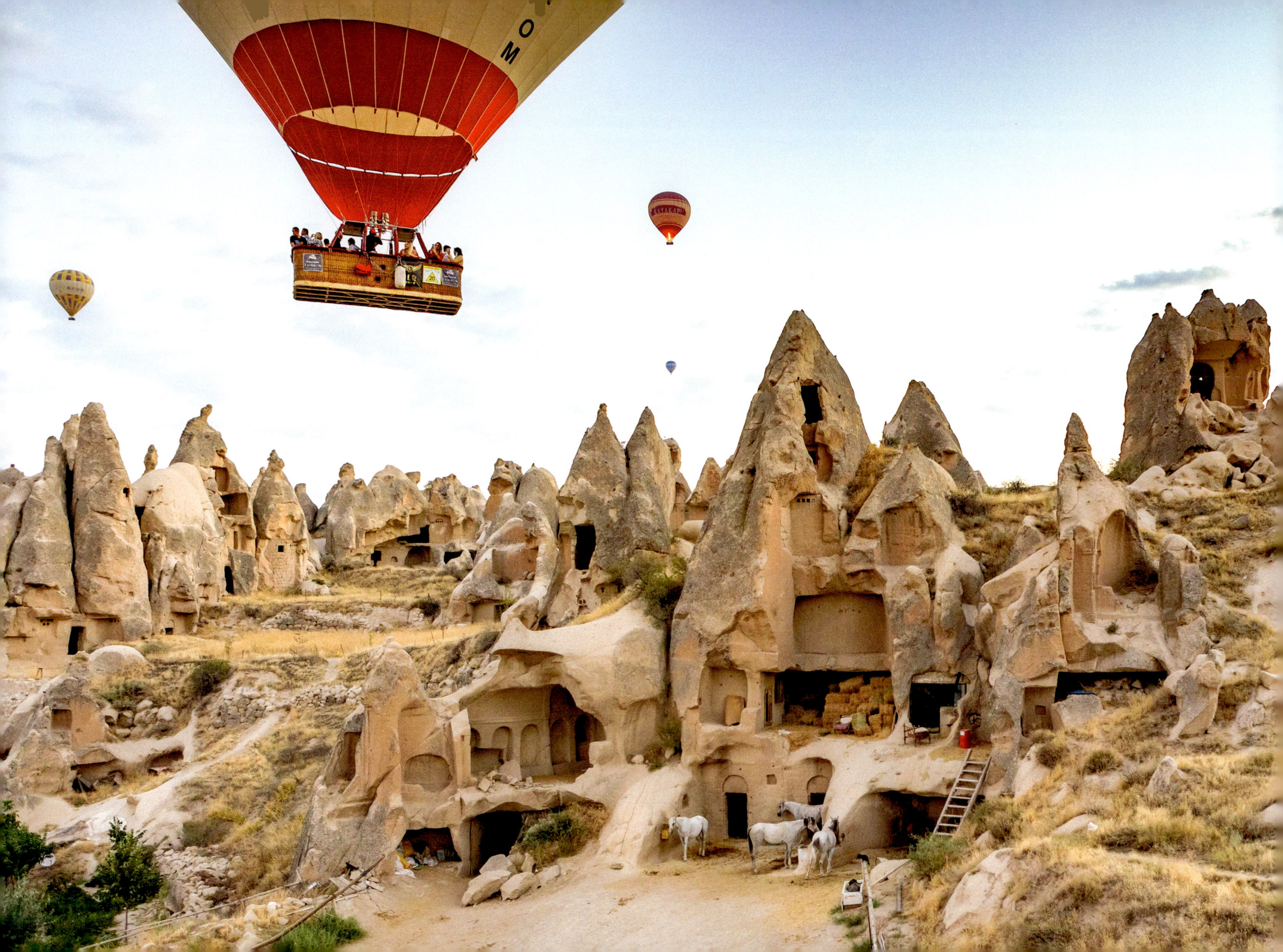

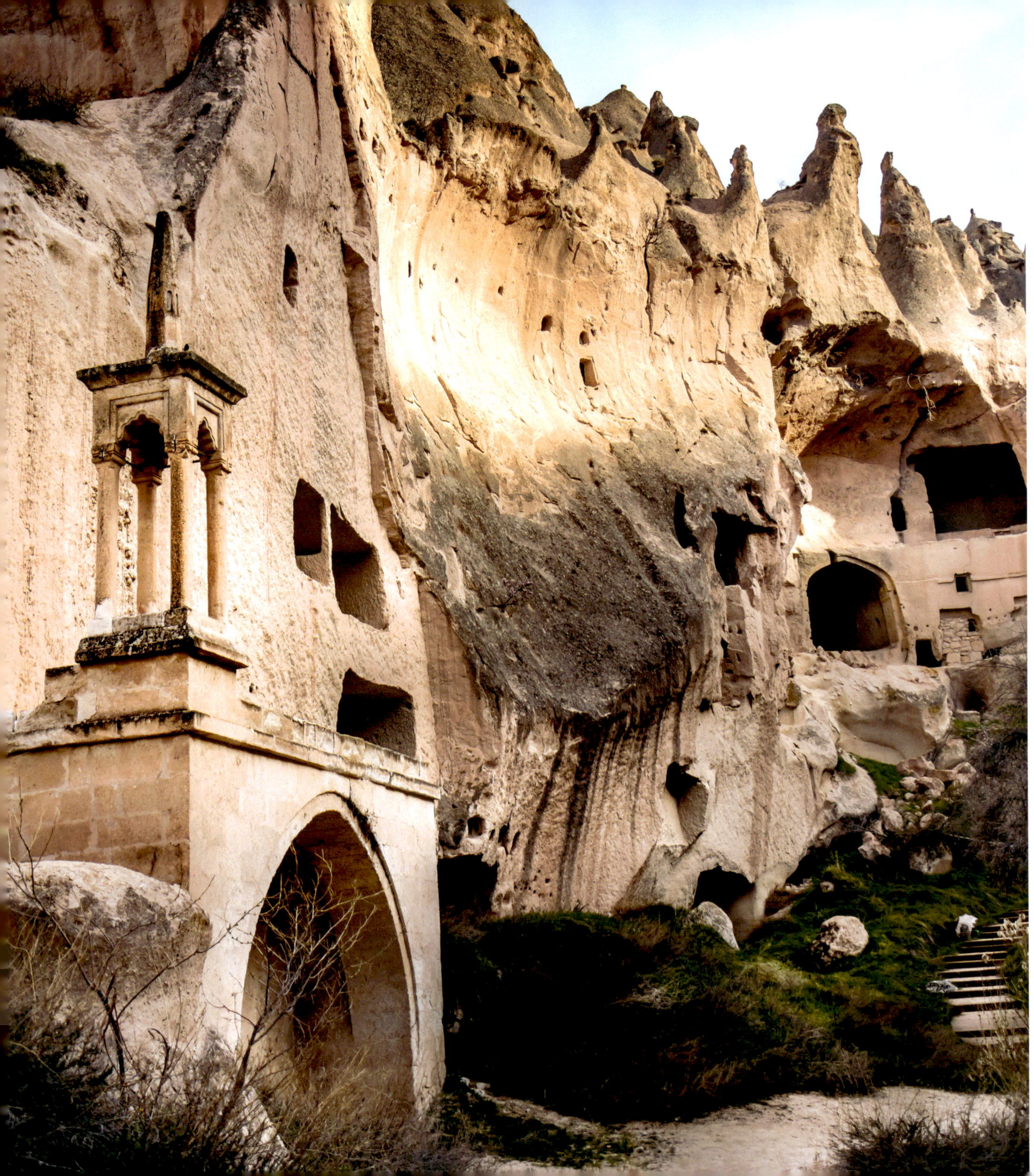

Zelve Open Air Museum, Cappadocia

This former Byzantine monastic retreat and Turkish village tells a special story, for here Christians and Muslims lived side by side for centuries until the 1950s. This open-air experience offers visitors the chance to explore three rugged valleys filled with tunnels, a mosque (left), several churches (pictured right), and many ancient homes where cave dwellers existed. These fascinating spaces are still visible despite the erosion which eventually made life there too dangerous. Zelve is a sprawling museum and those exploring its treasures can enjoy a genuine sense of discovery at every turn.

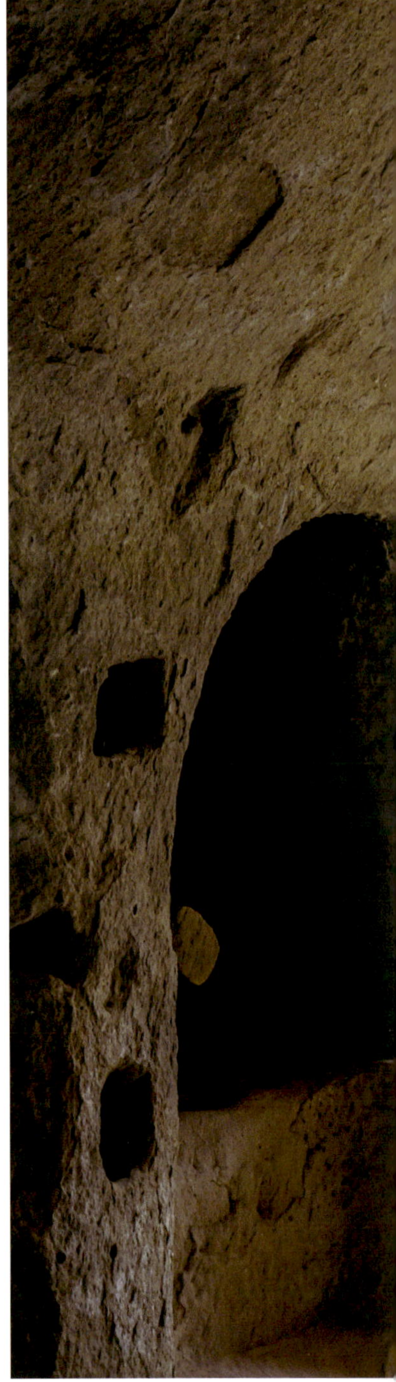

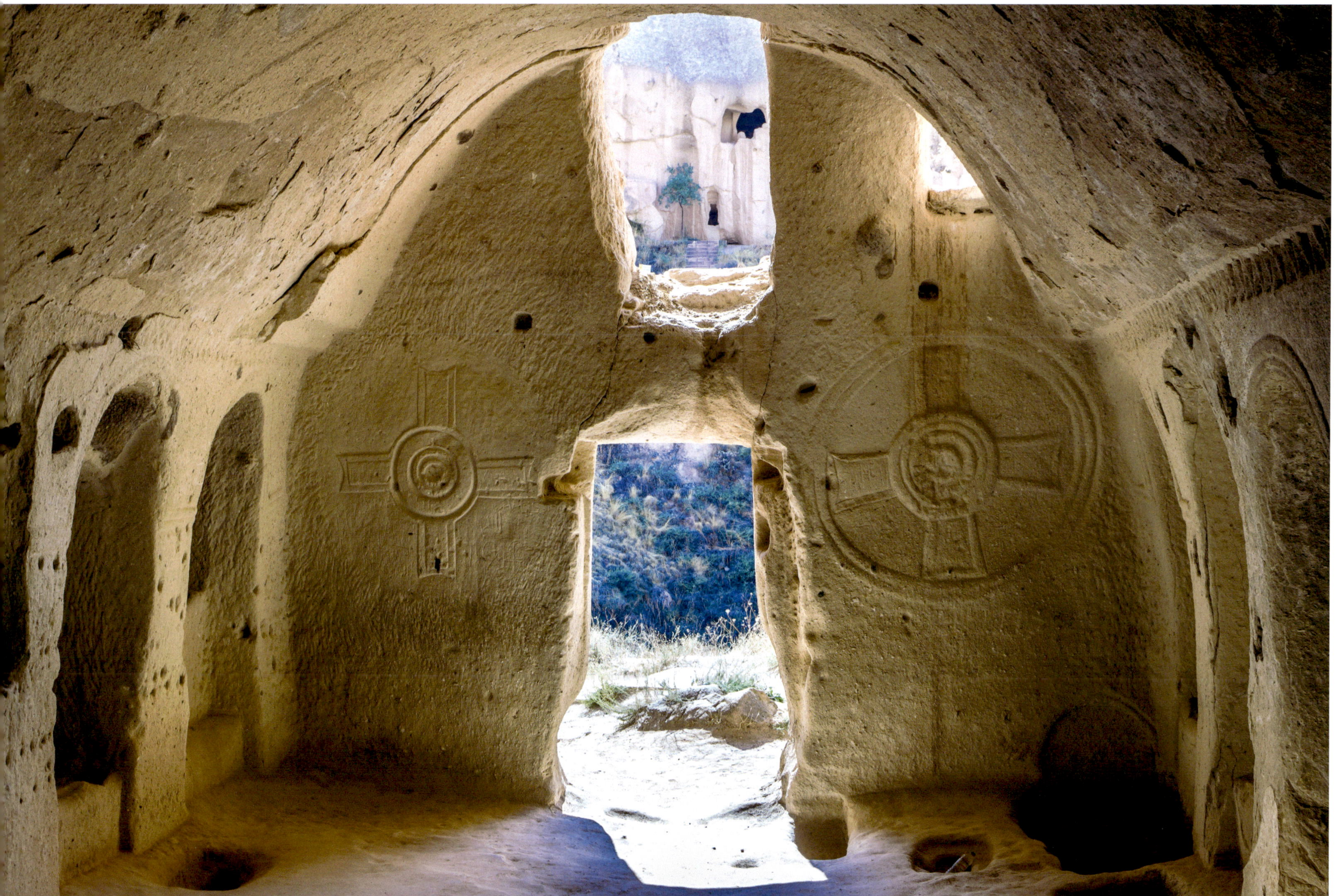

Thermal pools, Pamukkale
The unique beauty, colours, and therapeutic properties of the thermal pools of Pamukkale, a city in western Turkey, have drawn visitors for centuries. This stunning natural wonder in Turkey is a product of the mineral-rich, cascading hot springs, depositing calcium carbonate onto the land and solidifying into brilliant white, salty terraces. This celebrated natural spa was known in Roman times, with Queen Cleopatra of Egypt believed to have been a bather, at least in myth.

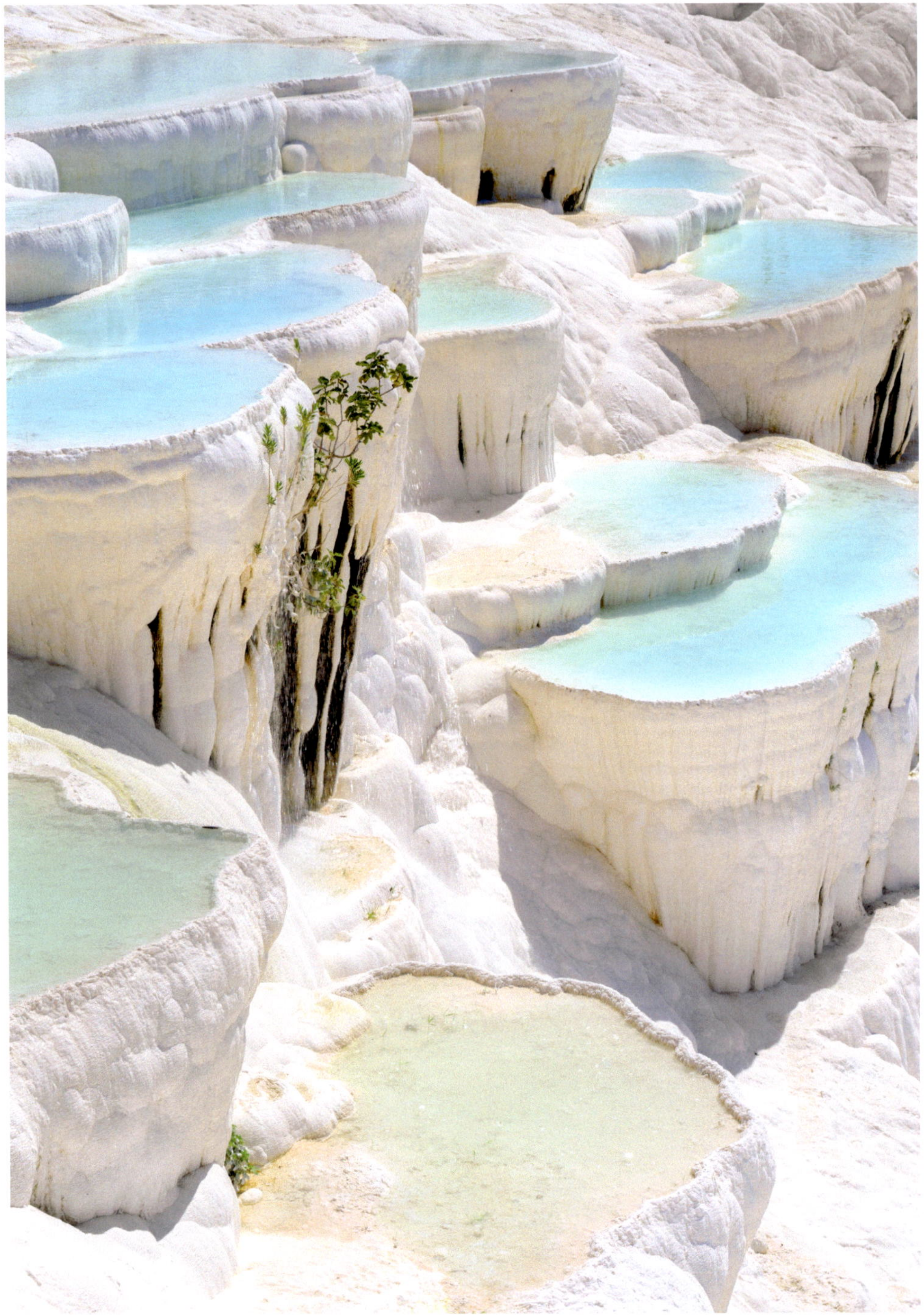

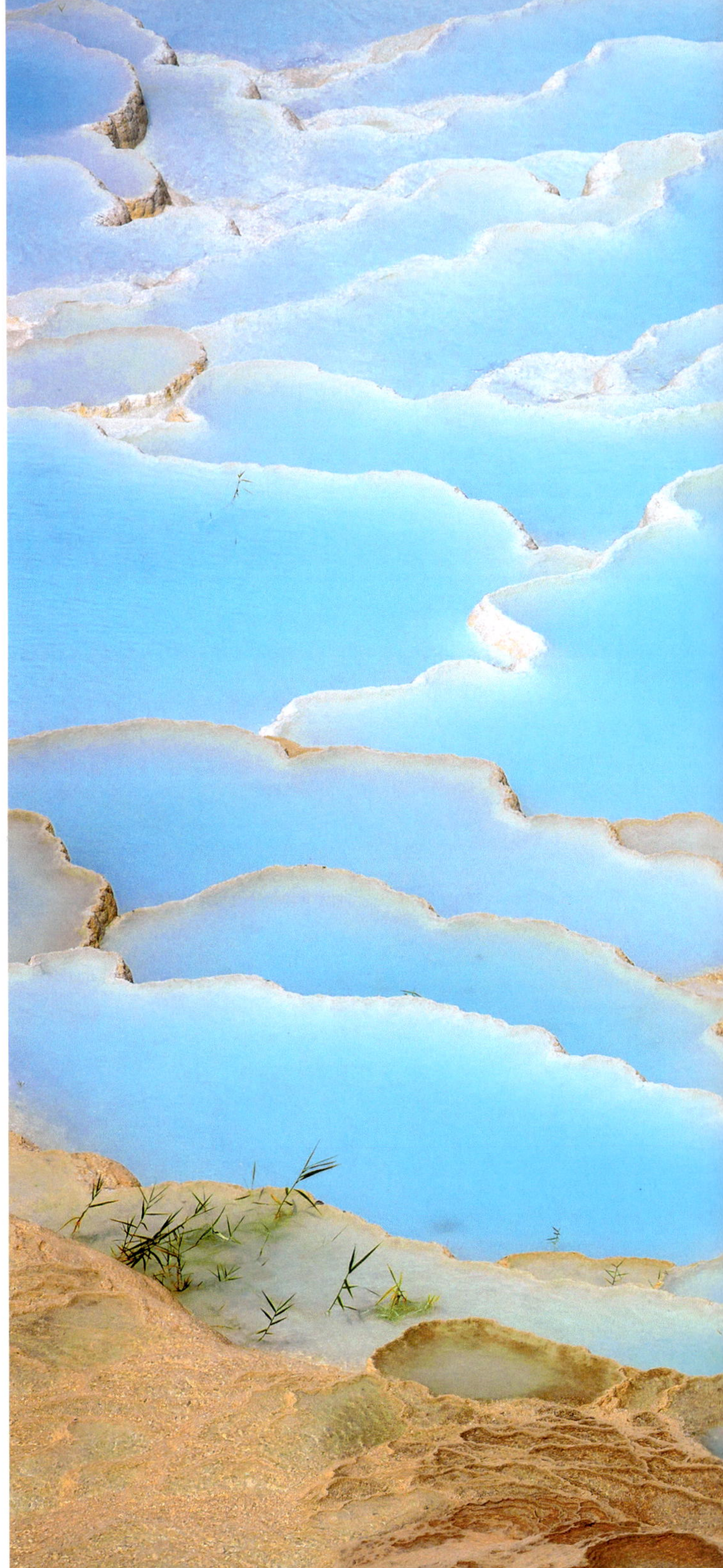

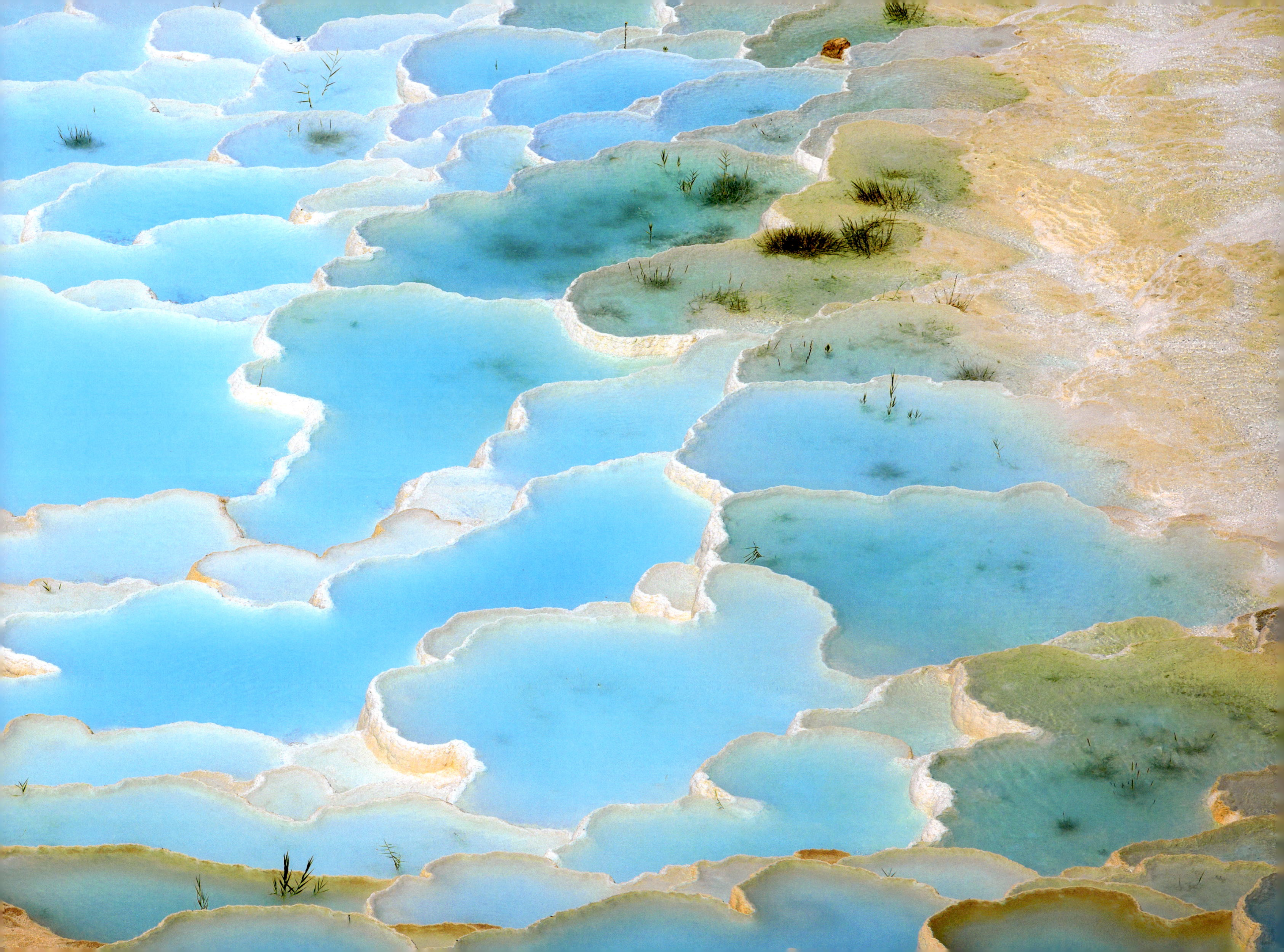

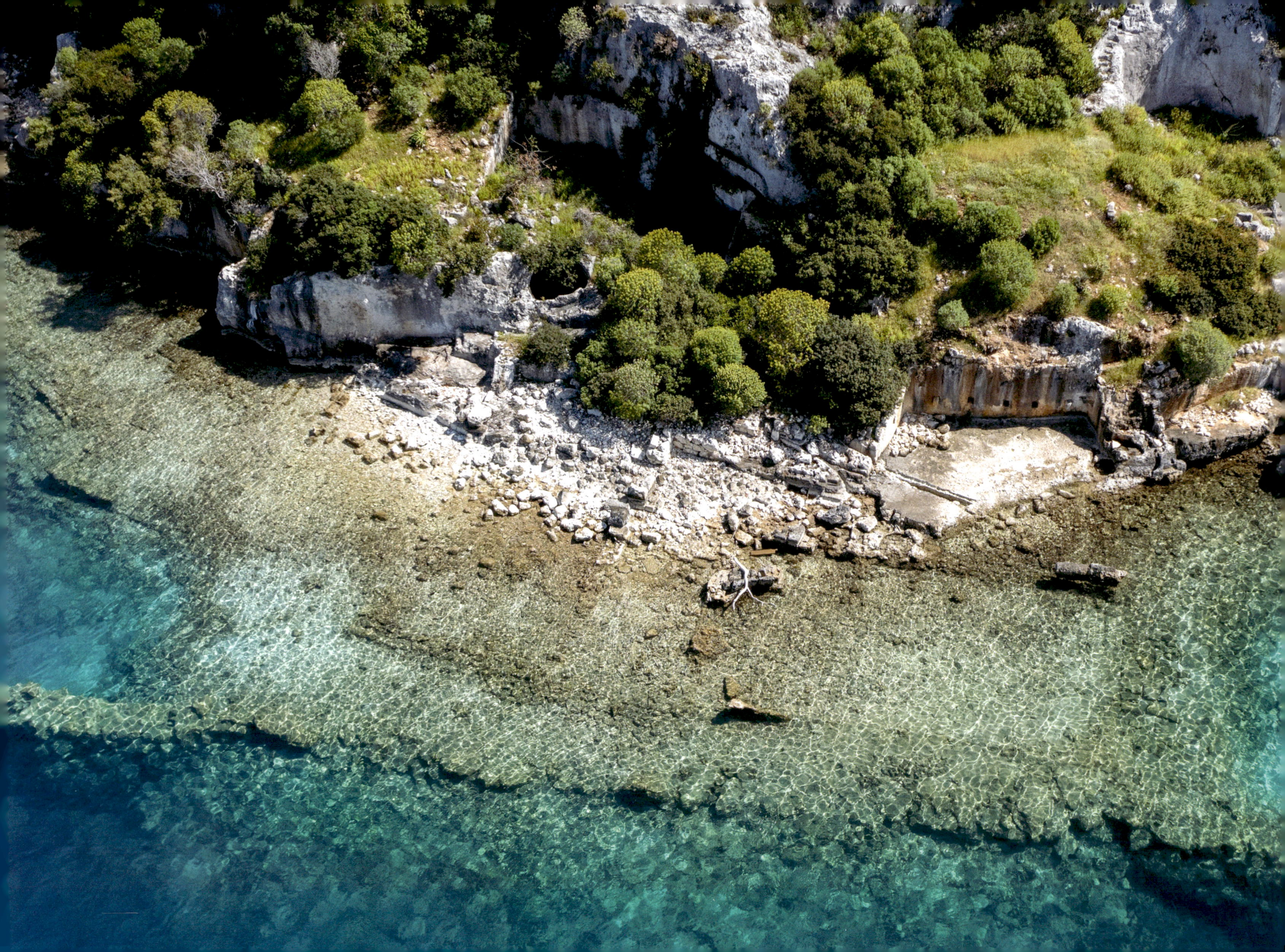

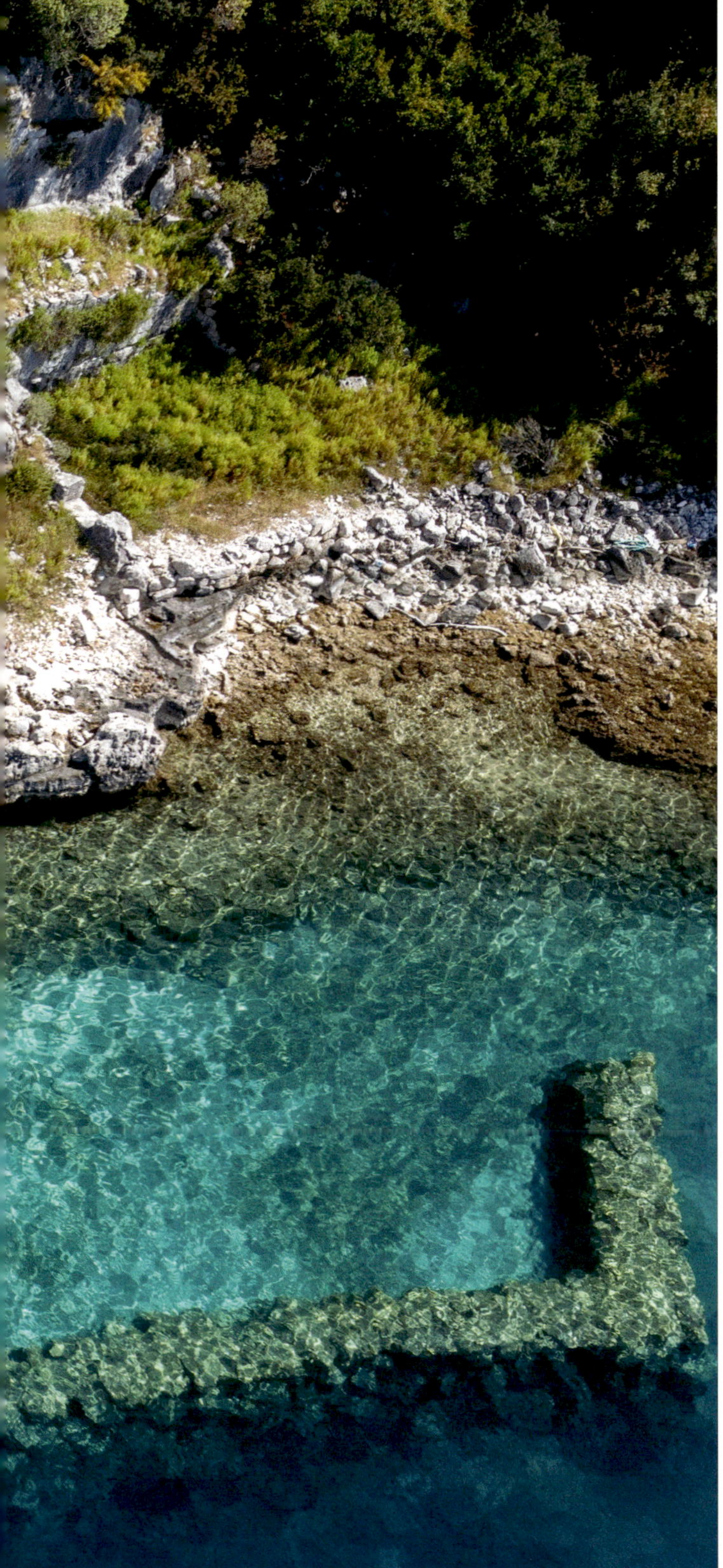

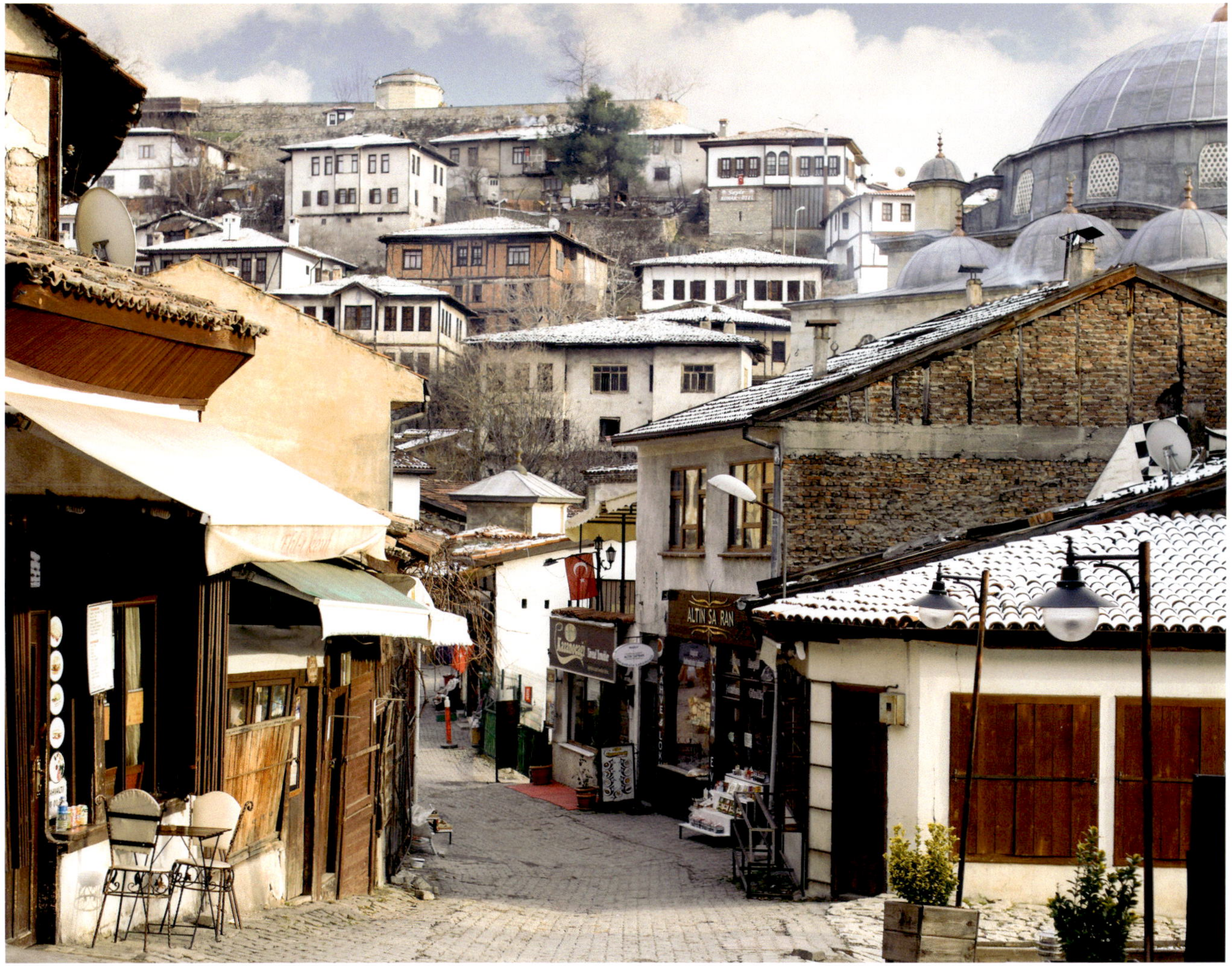

Lycian sunken city, Kekova Island, Antalya

This captivating underwater archaeological site in Antalya marks the ruins of an ancient Lycian settlement. An earthquake in the 2nd century AD caused a thriving coastal city to sink into the Mediterranean. Visitors to the uninhabited island of Kekova now take boat tours over crystal-clear waters and see the remains of ancient streets, staircases, outlines of the city homes, and their foundations.

Safranbolu, Black Sea region

Once a key trading station on the East–West caravan route, the increasing prosperity of Safranbolu in the 17th century led to the construction of magnificent timber-framed, hillside buildings. Now a UNESCO World Heritage site, Safranbolu is renowned for its exceptionally well-preserved Ottoman-era architecture where visitors can immerse themselves in the past. Safranbolu takes its name from its famous saffron production.

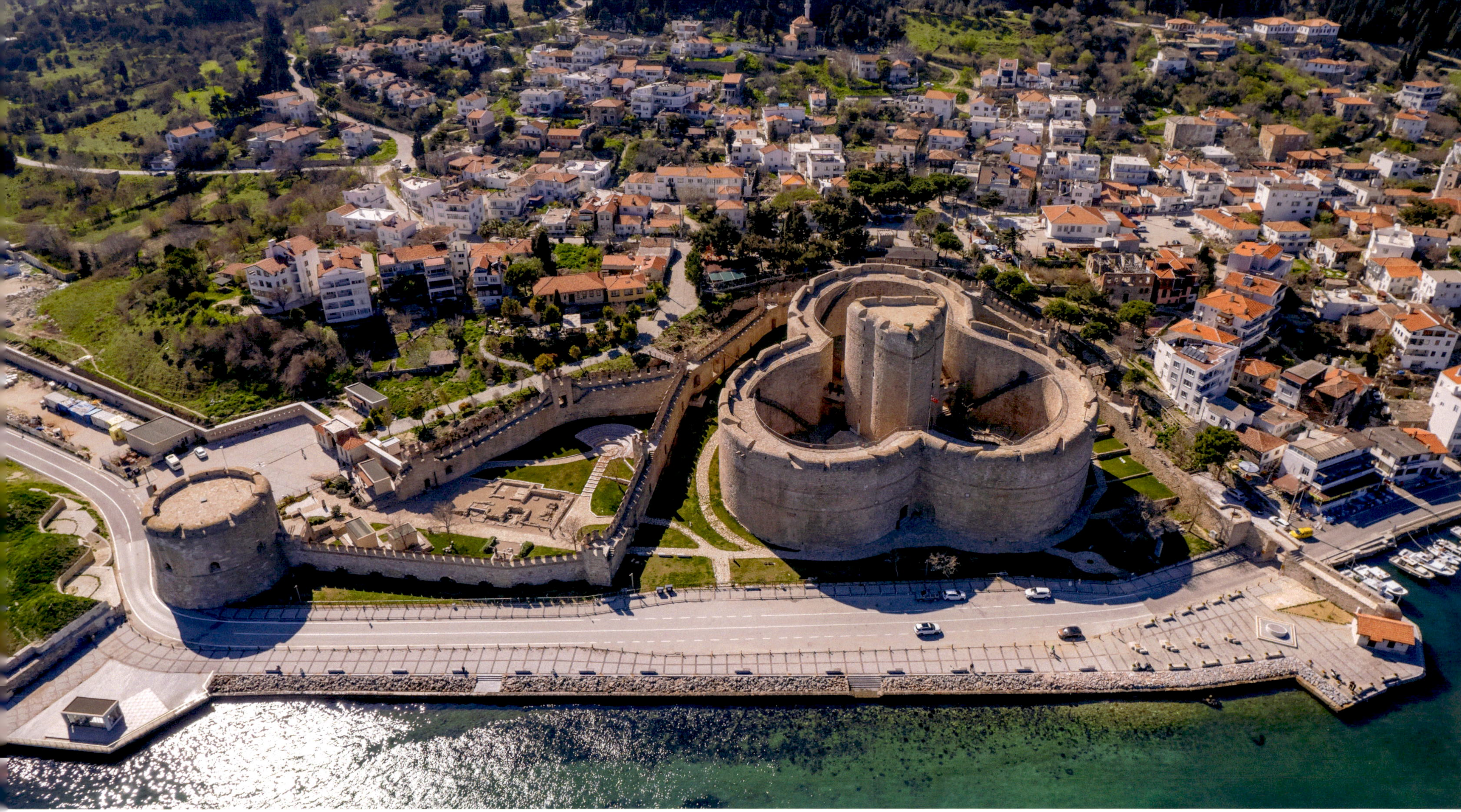

Kilitbahir Castle, Gallipoli National Park
This historic harbour is an entry point to Gallipoli National Park. The harbour area features 15th-century Kilitbahir Castle, now a museum dedicated to Ottoman and naval history. Gallipoli National Park is a significant historical site which includes such World War I sites as ANZAC Cove, multiple war cemeteries and memorials, and the preserved wartime trenches of that time.

Canakkale Martyrs Memorial, Gallipoli
This massive monument is dedicated to the 253,000 Turkish soldiers who died during the Gallipoli campaign of World War I. It was built as a testament to military sacrifice and to mark the Ottoman Empire's victory against Allied forces in 1915 in battle. The very name Gallipoli now represents a defining moment in Turkish history and is a symbol of national resilience and bravery.

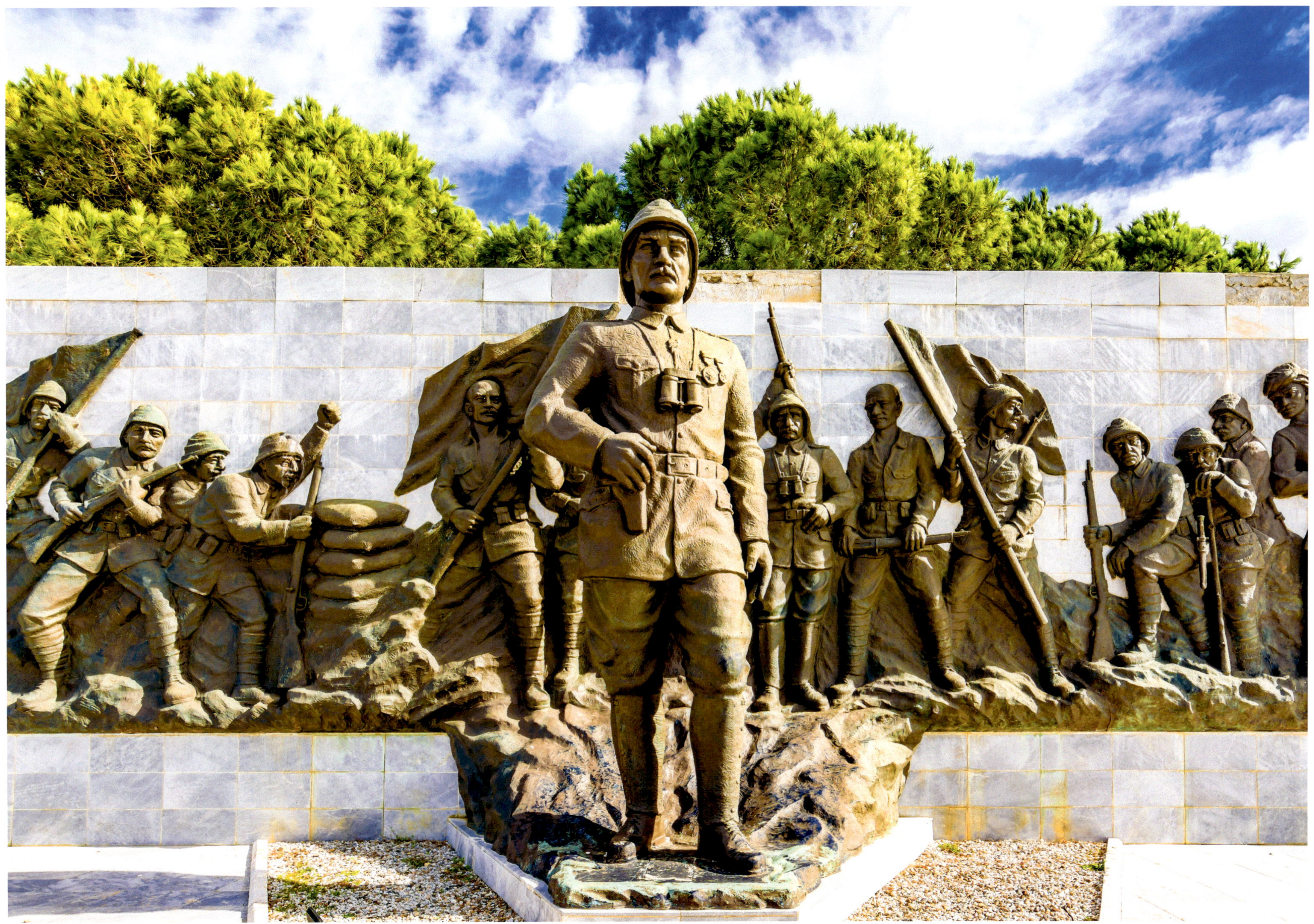

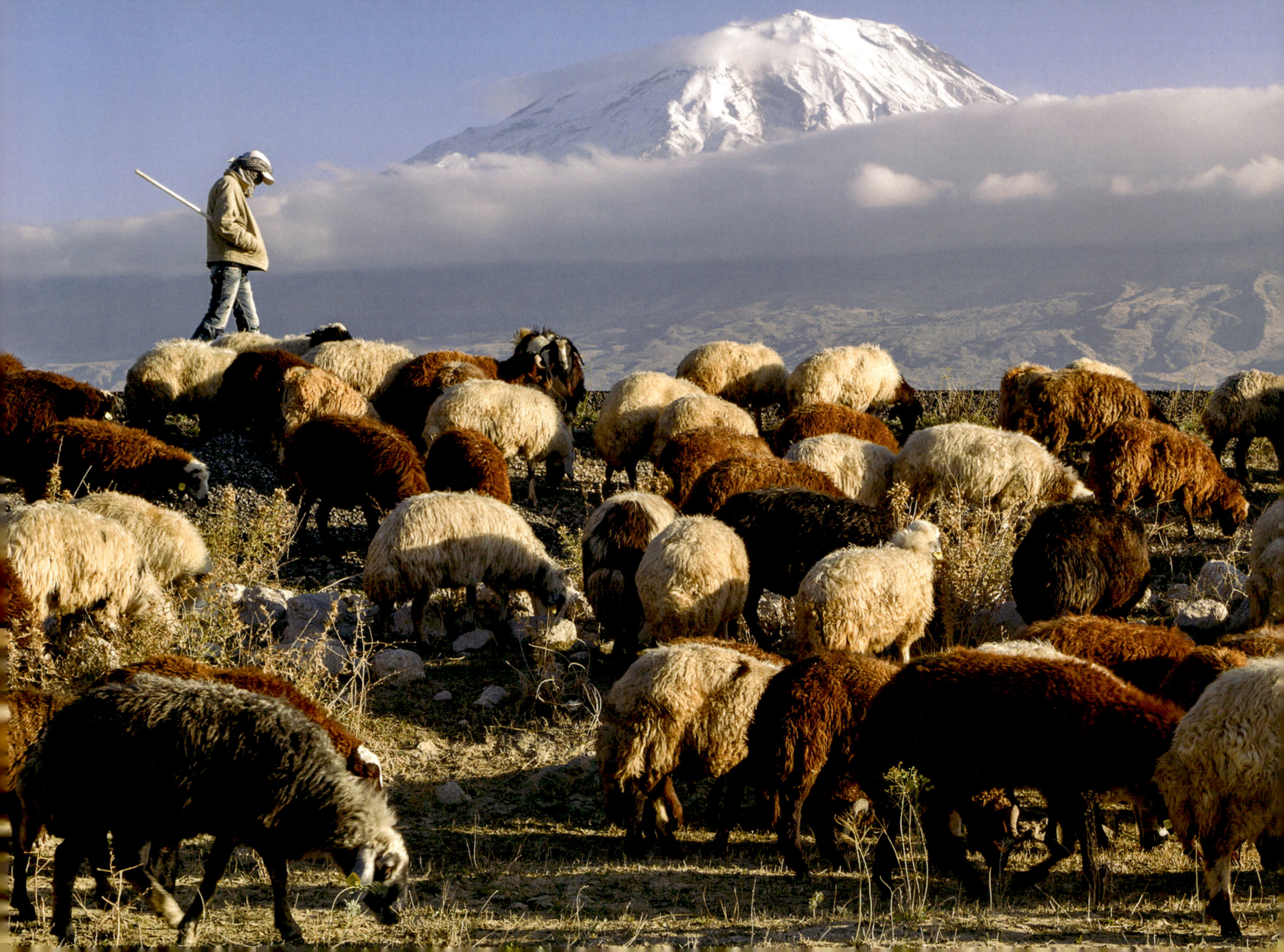

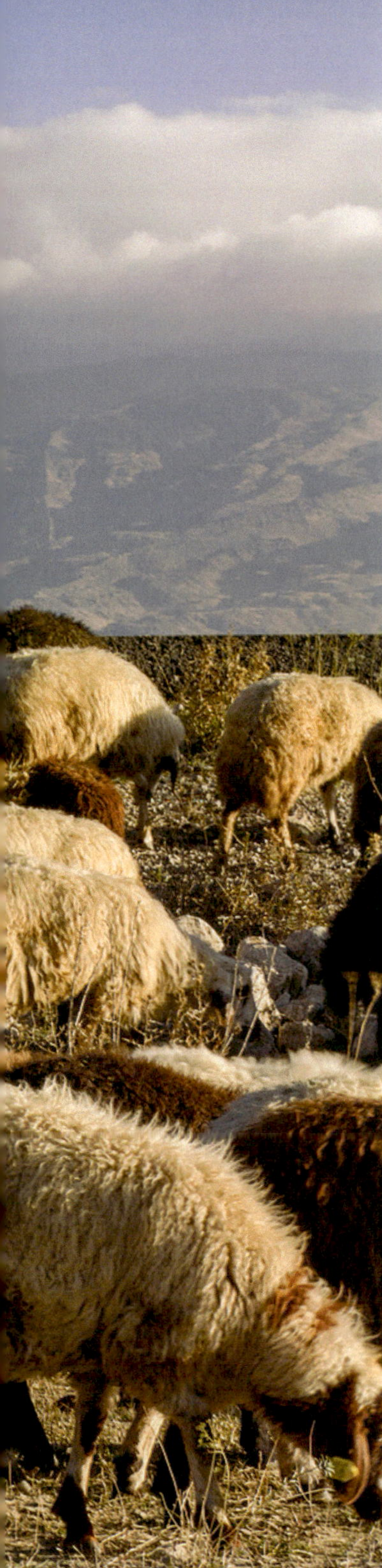

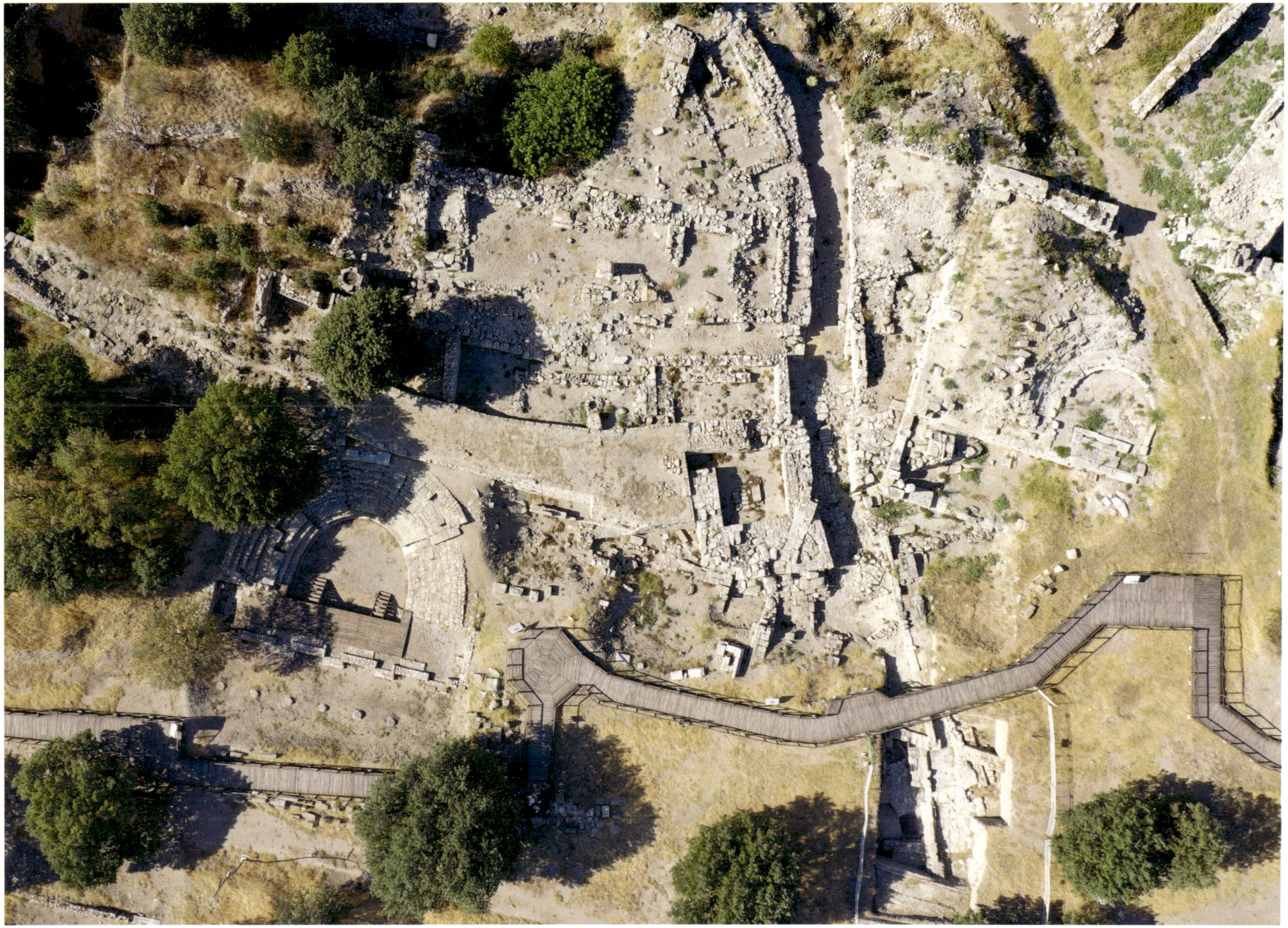

Mount Ararat, Dogubeyazit
Standing at just over 5000 metres (16,400ft), this formidable
mountain is Türkiye's highest peak. Ararat is most famous for
its place in the Bible as the final resting place of Noah's Ark
after the Great Flood. Today it attracts climbers and hikers to
the vast area of the Eastern Anatolia.

Archaeological site of Troy, Aegean coast
This ancient city is most famous as the location for Homer's
epic poem *The Iliad*. However, for over 4000 years Troy played
a key role by controlling vital trade routes between the Aegean
Sea and the Black Sea. Archaeologists have revealed Troy to be
built in ten layers, each representing a distinct period.

Sumela Monastery, Trabzon

This splendid, isolated Greek Orthodox monastery was built directly into a steep cliff face in the Altındere Valley in the 4th century. Seen as a testament to incredible human perseverance and devotion, and situated in a breathtaking location, today it is not only a pilgrimage site but also a major tourist attraction. Its frescoes include Our Lady of the Sign, shown here.

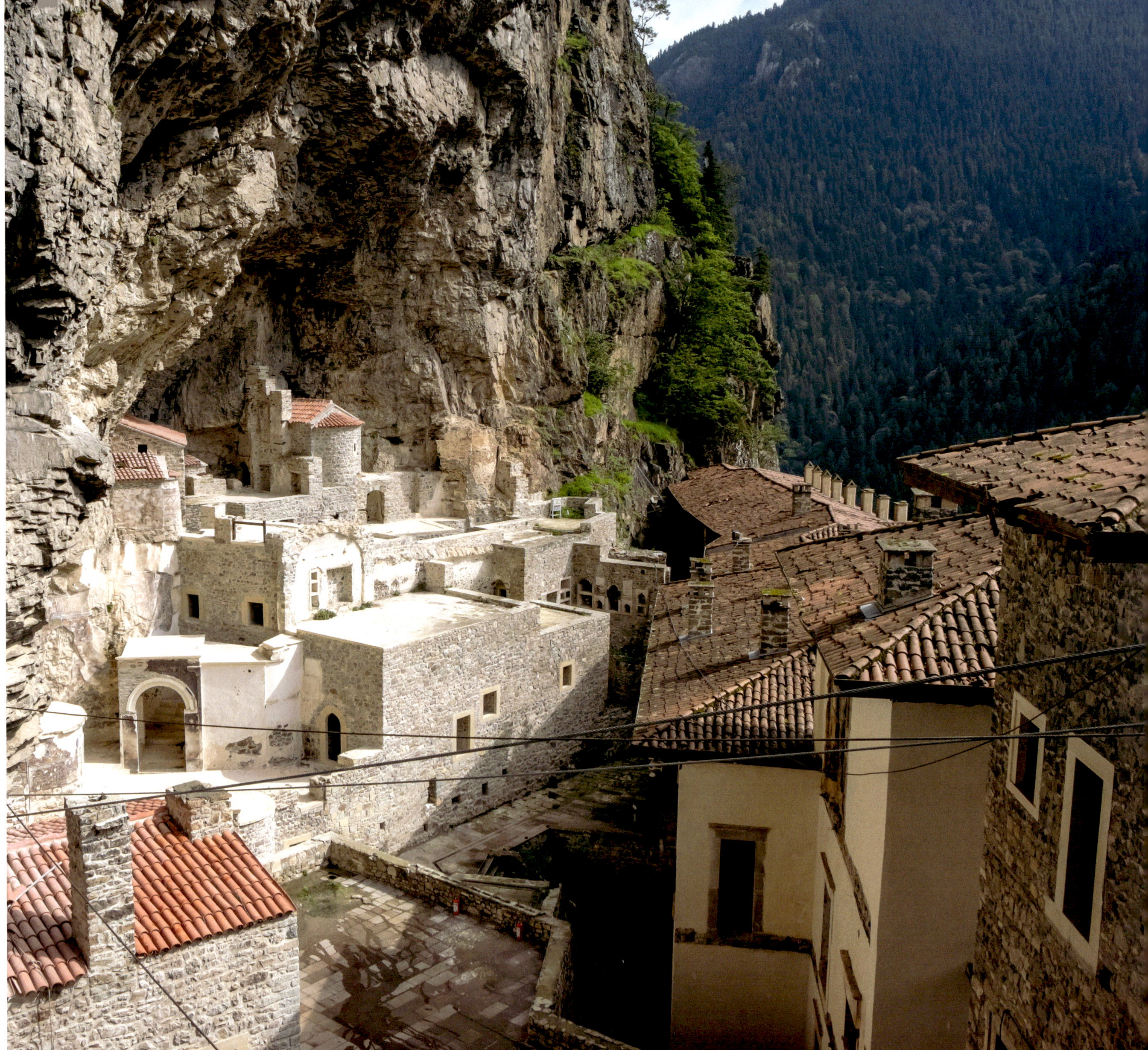

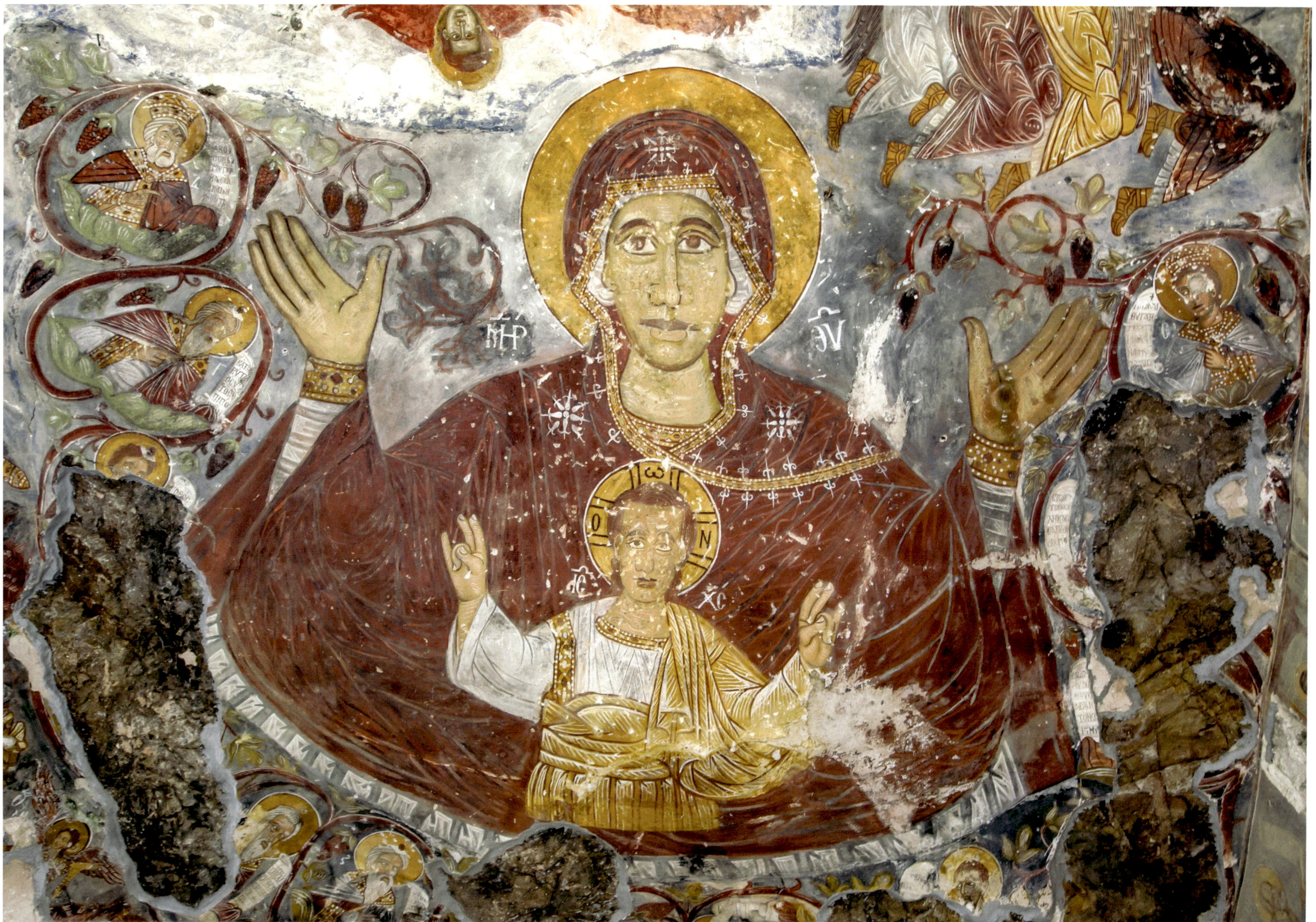

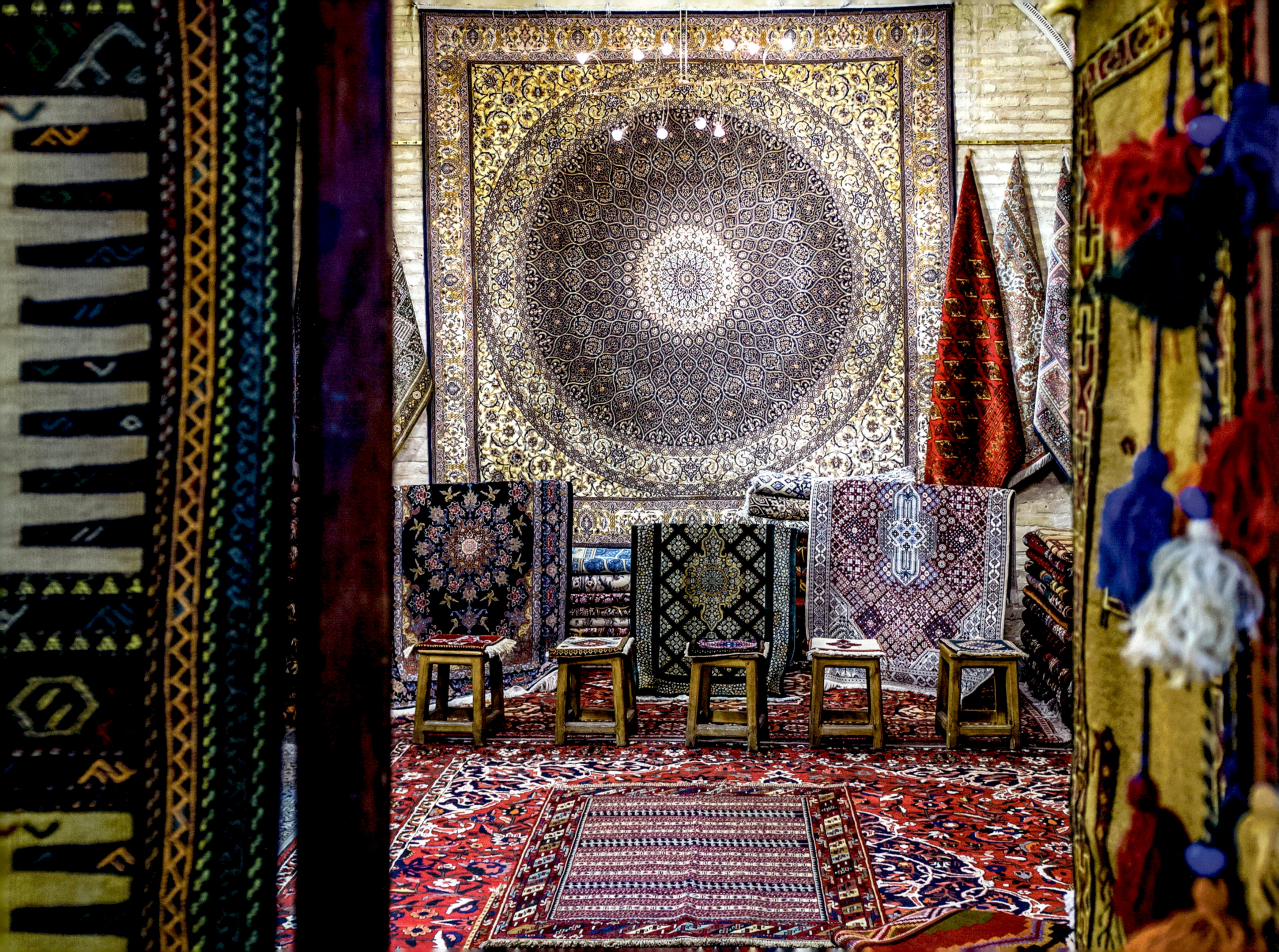

Lands of 1001 Nights

Welcome to a real-life fairytale – this chapter is your guide to the cities and countries of 1001 Nights. Cities such as Baghdad, Isfahan, Cairo, and Damascus live now, long after *The 1001 Nights*, as destinations waiting to be explored. The legendary city of Baghdad is a perfect example. Simply step into the buzzing heart of the city at Al-Mutanabbi Street, Baghdad's iconic book market, and find poets, artists, and students still gathering to share literature and more. While Tehran is the capital, Isfahan is the true Iranian jewel, an oasis of breathtaking Islamic architecture, such as Naghsh-e Jahan Square. This vast space is a masterpiece of design, surrounded by the stunning Imam Mosque, the elegant Sheikh Lotfollah Mosque, and the grand Ali Qapu Palace. Cairo is a city that never sleeps, a thrilling, chaotic, and utterly mesmerizing metropolis. It is also a gateway to ancient Egypt, with the

Pyramids just a few miles beyond the city centre. Here you can literally walk through 7000 years of history. Food is a big part of street life. Try koshary, a comforting mix of rice, lentils, and pasta, topped with a spicy tomato sauce. It's a delicious and filling meal that's a local favourite.

Damascus is one of the world's oldest cities, and its enchanting old town, a UNESCO site, feels frozen in time. The Umayyad Mosque is the spiritual heart of the city, a superb example of Islamic architecture that must be visited. The scent of jasmine, the city's signature flower, seems to be everywhere, a sweet perfume to guide your route as you wander through the labyrinthine alleys of the souqs.

These cities are more than just places on a map. They are vibrant, living museums, and the people, food, and culture are waiting to be discovered.

Carpet shop, Great Bazaar, Isfahan
Across the Middle East carpets and rugs are not just floor coverings; they're a celebrated art form. Arab world carpets, though influenced by nearby cultures, including Persian and Turkish traditions, boast a rich, independent heritage. Using a variety of materials, from the traditional wool and camel hair to luxurious silk, carpet makers create intricate, hand-knotted pieces. Designs often feature stunning geometric patterns, floral arabesques, and even Arabic calligraphy, reflecting Islamic art's emphasis on non-representational imagery.

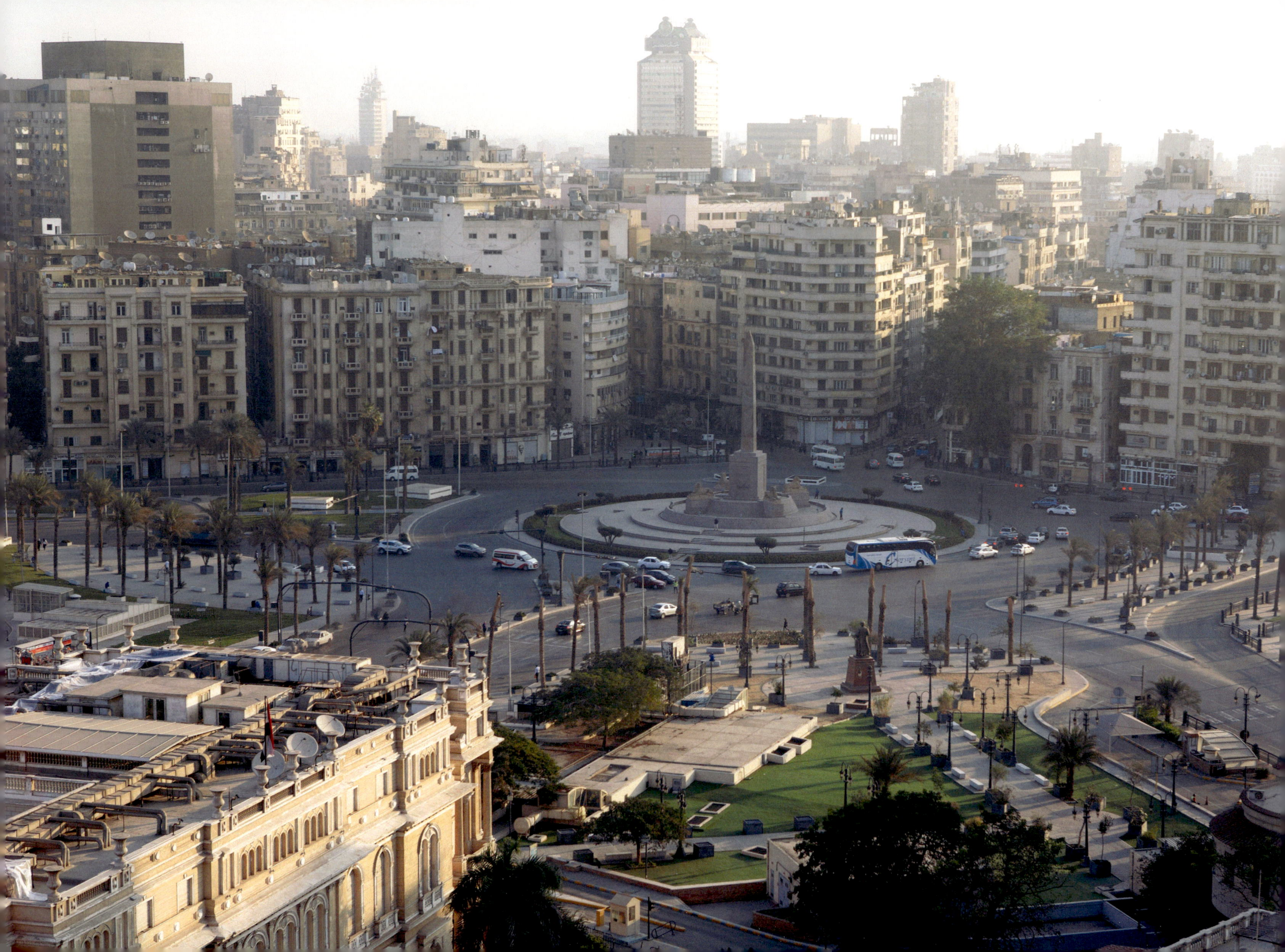

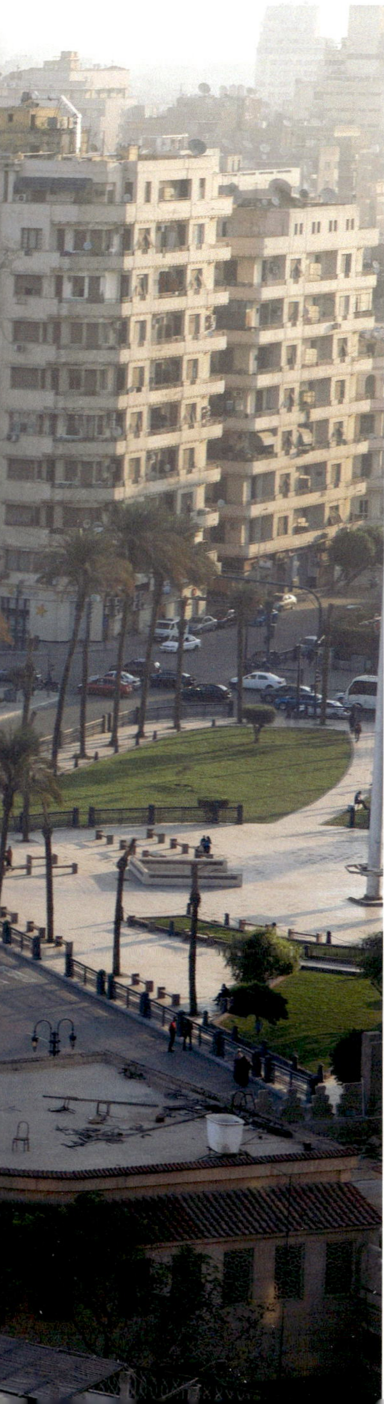

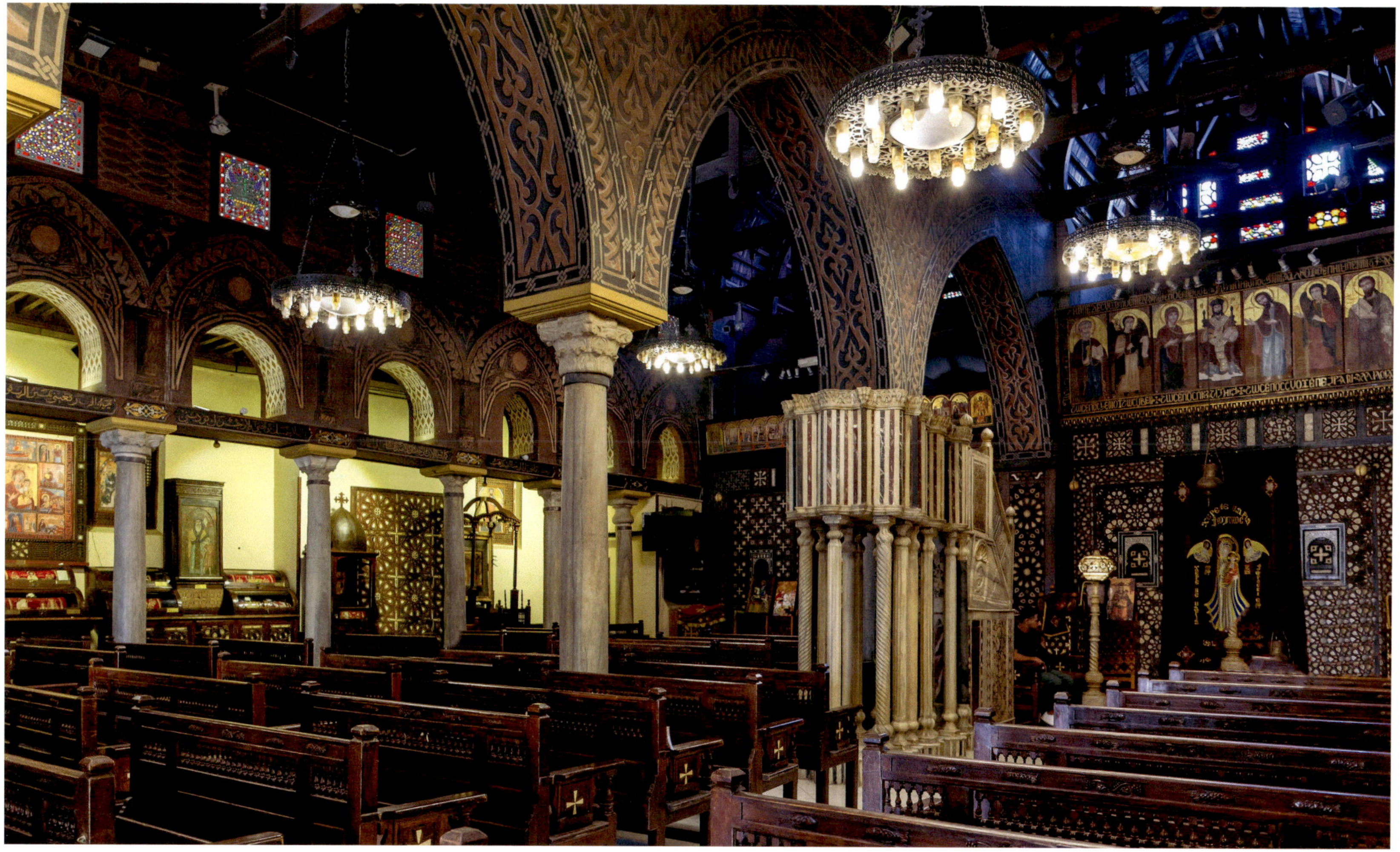

Tahrir Square, Cairo

Tahrir Square is the beating heart of downtown Cairo, a major transport hub and a nexus of significant historical and cultural landmarks, including the Egyptian Museum, home of the Mask of Tutankhamun until recently. Originally designed to be the 'Paris by the Nile', its true importance emerged as a symbol of Egyptian liberation. More recently it has undergone a major renovation along with much of downtown Cairo, bringing back the sense of fin-de-siecle Europe it once enjoyed. The giant governmental building known as the Mogamma is set to become one of the largest hotels in the region, and an obelisk now stands at its centre.

Hanging Church, Old Cairo

Old Cairo is a testament to the city's layered past, a dense and historic area built upon the ruins of a Roman-era fortress known as Babylon. This ancient quarter, also called Coptic Cairo, is a remarkable interfaith complex. The most famous buildings include the Hanging Church, named for its position atop the fortress's gatehouse, and the Church of St Sergius, which tradition holds was built on a crypt where the Holy Family took refuge. Nearby, the Ben Ezra Synagogue, a testament to Egypt's Jewish history, is believed to be where baby Moses was found.

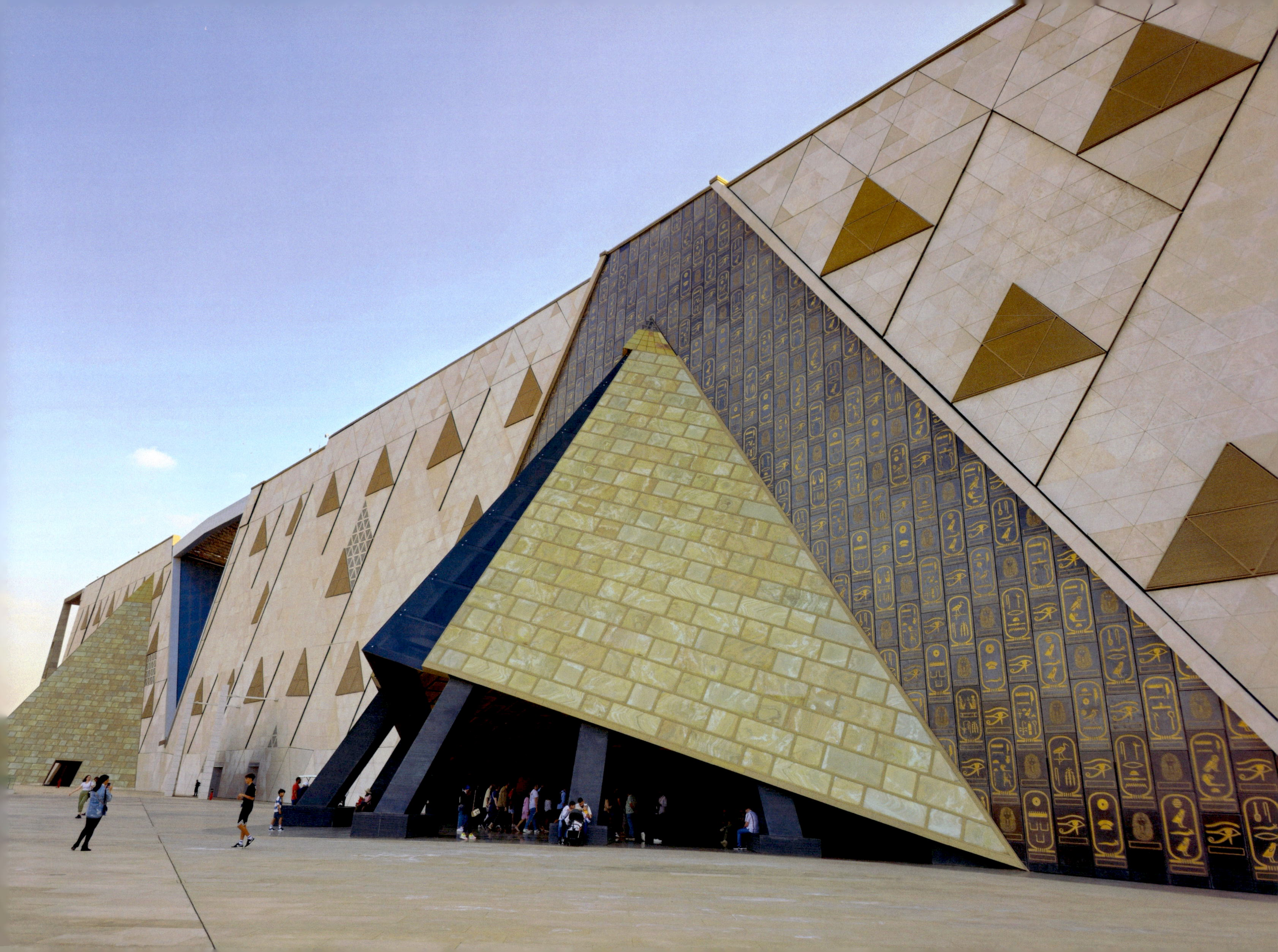

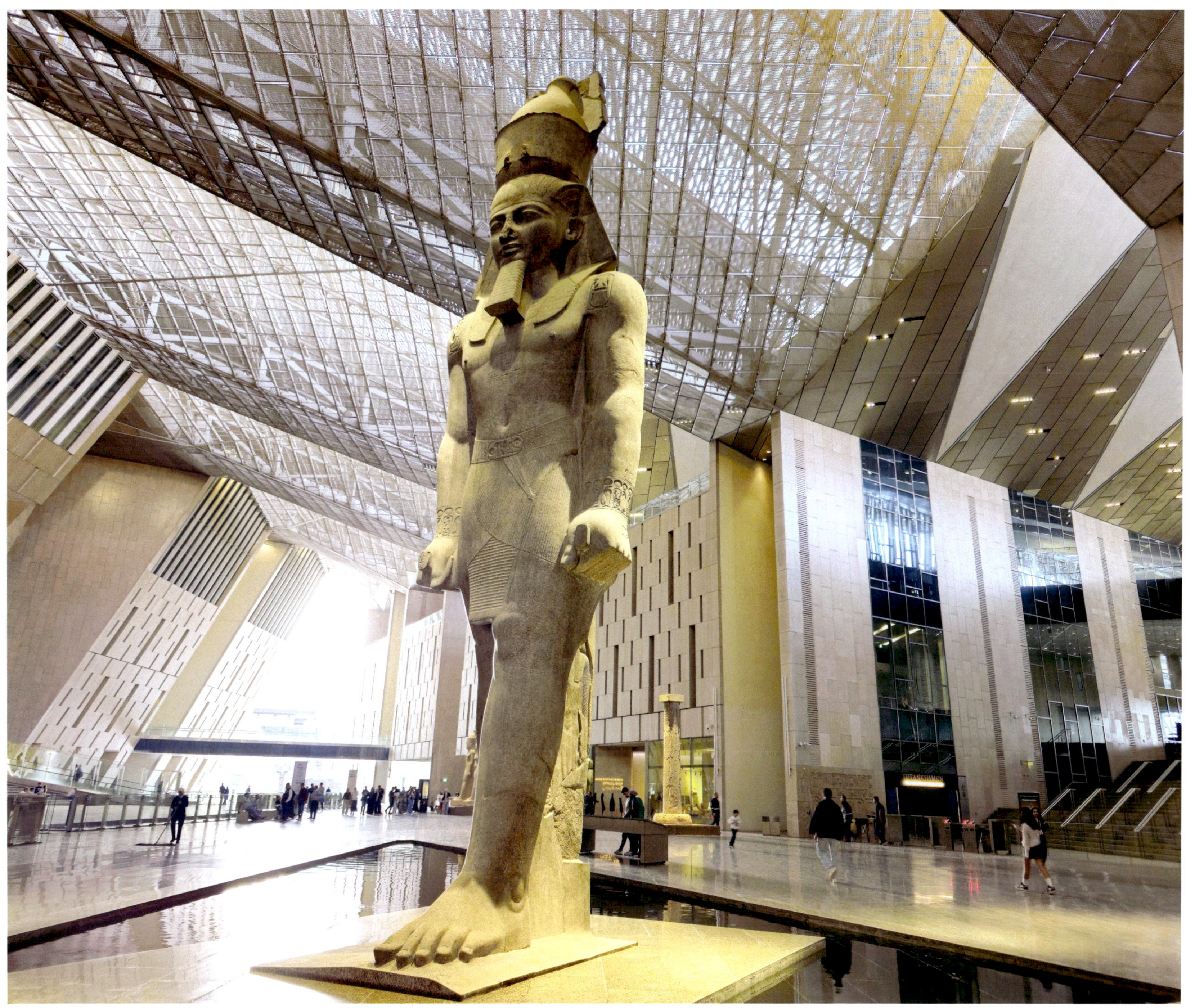

Grand Egyptian Museum (GEM), Giza

Opened in 2025, the GEM is the largest museum in the world dedicated to a single civilization. It houses over 100,000 artefacts, including the complete Tutankhamun collection, displayed together for the first time since the tomb's opening. With main galleries arranged by time period, visitors are taken on a journey from prehistoric times to the Roman era. The museum reclaims Egyptology for Egyptians, and has already fostered a new generation of local archaeologists and curators, inspired by their own past. The museum also features a colossal statue of Ramesses II in its main atrium and a grand staircase lined with impressive statues and relics.

Mosque of Ibn Tulun, Cairo
This vast mosque was built
between 876 and 879 CE
by the Abbasid governor of
Egypt Ahmad ibn Tulun. As
a central element of Islamic
Cairo, Ibn Tulun draws
worshippers from around the
Muslim world. The mosque is
the oldest in the city to have
retained its original form, and
its unique design, influenced
by the Samarran style of Iraq,
is a testament to early Islamic
architecture. Its famous
spiral minaret and extensive
stucco decorations make it
a significant historical and
artistic landmark.

**Mosque of Muhammad Ali,
Cairo**
The 'Alabaster Mosque' was
constructed from 1830 to
1848, after its commissioning
by Muhammad Ali Pasha.
Built to serve as a royal
mosque, it also symbolized
his own power and ambitions
to modernize Egypt as the
country sought independence
from the Ottoman Empire.
The mosque's Ottoman-
inspired design, with its large
central dome and two slender
minarets, marked a move
away from the earlier Mamluk
style. Inside is the tomb of
Muhammad Ali himself,
with the prayer hall lavishly
decorated with alabaster,
intricate carvings, and
elaborate chandeliers.

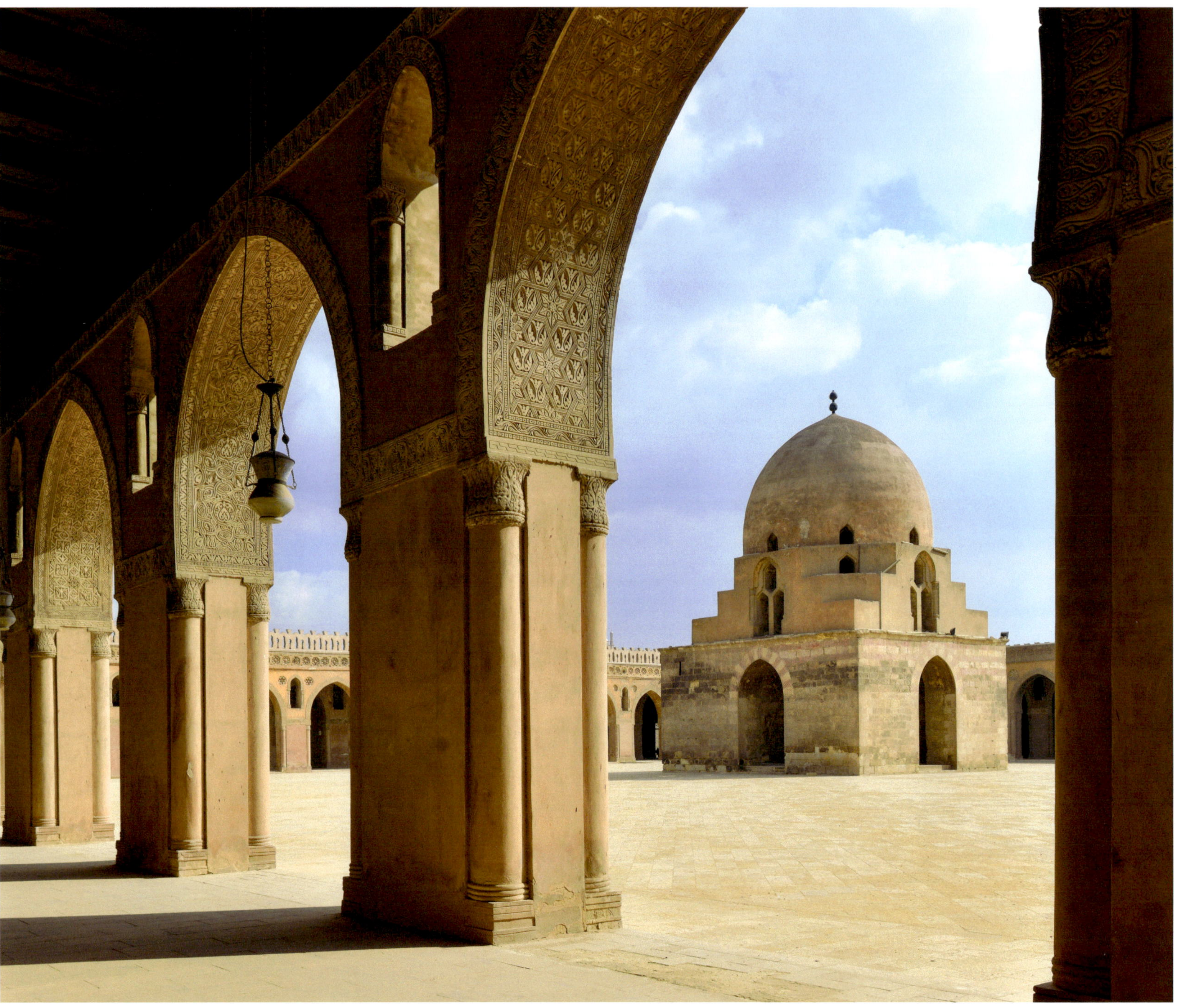

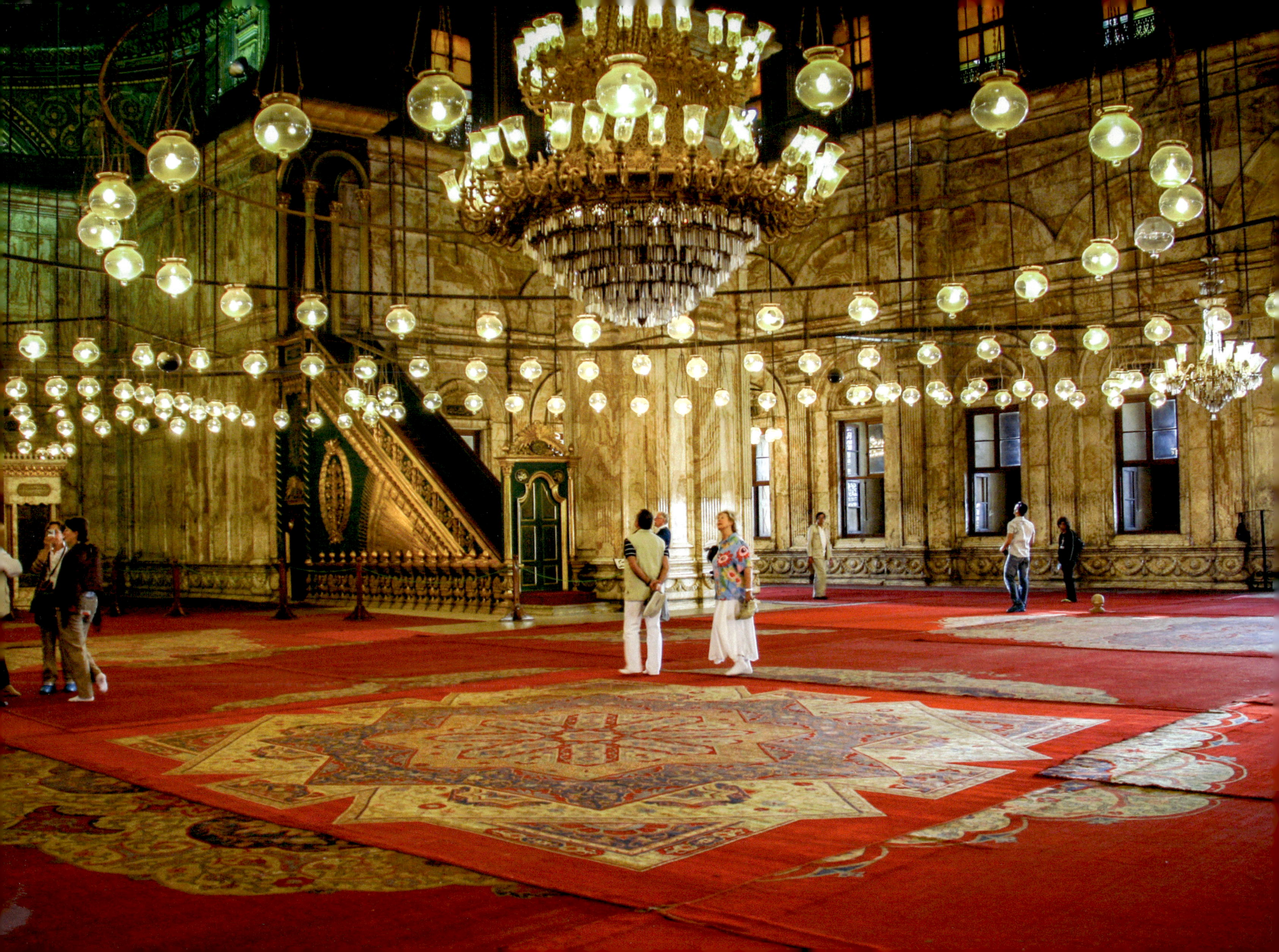

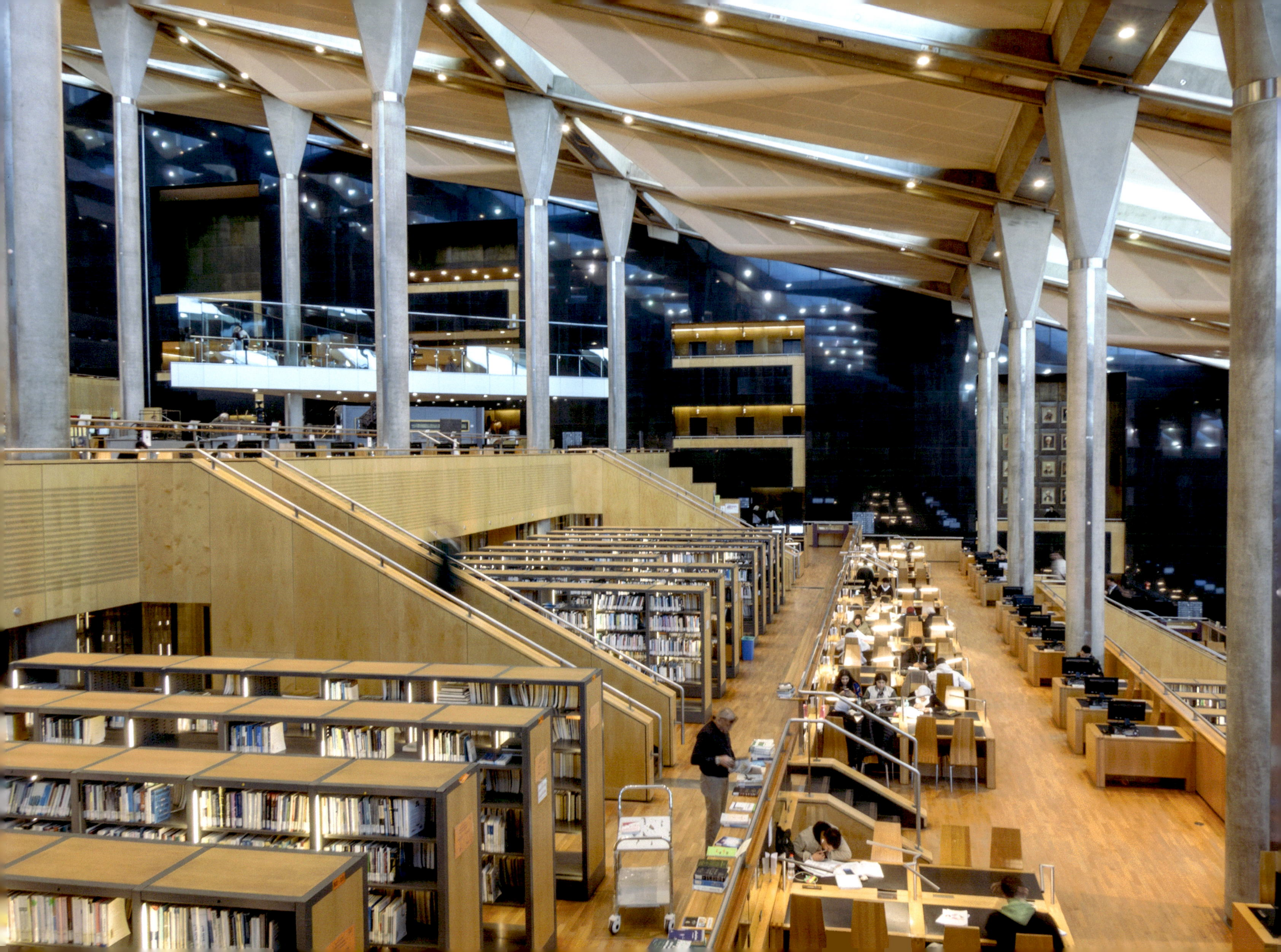

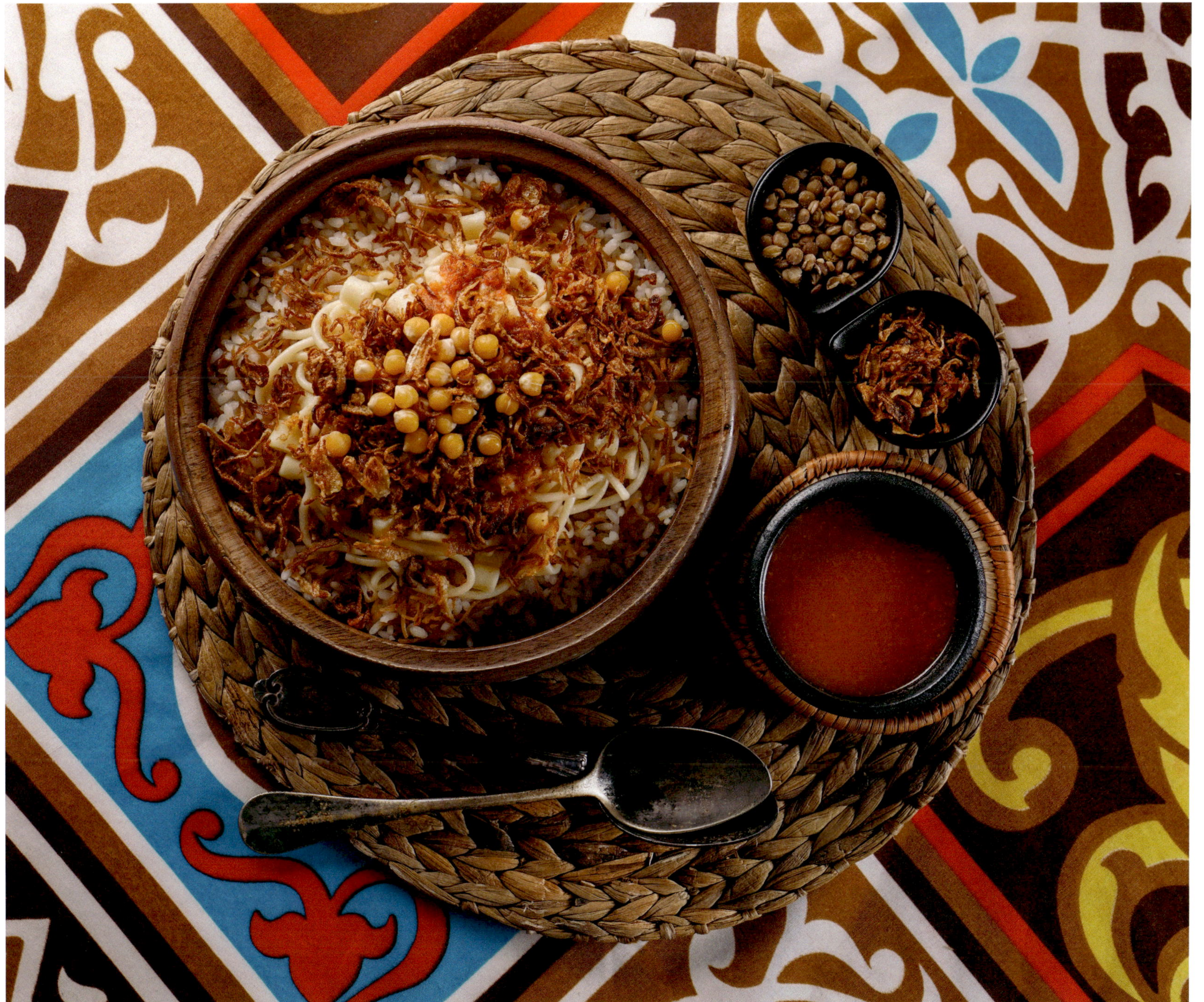

Bibliotheca Alexandrina, Alexandria

The ancient Library of Alexandria was the world's greatest centre of knowledge. Attracting scholars and housing an immense collection of scrolls, it flourished for centuries. The striking building of the new Bibliotheca Alexandrina was completed in 2002 by the Egyptian government and UNESCO. The library now serves as a major cultural and intellectual hub for both Egypt and the world.

Koshary

Koshary, often considered Egypt's national dish, is a quintessential part of life in Cairo. This hearty and affordable comfort food is a layered mix of rice, macaroni, lentils, and chickpeas, topped with a zesty tomato-garlic sauce and crispy fried onions. Koshary is enjoyed by Egyptians from all walks of life, from labourers and students to families dining at home. To eat it is to love it.

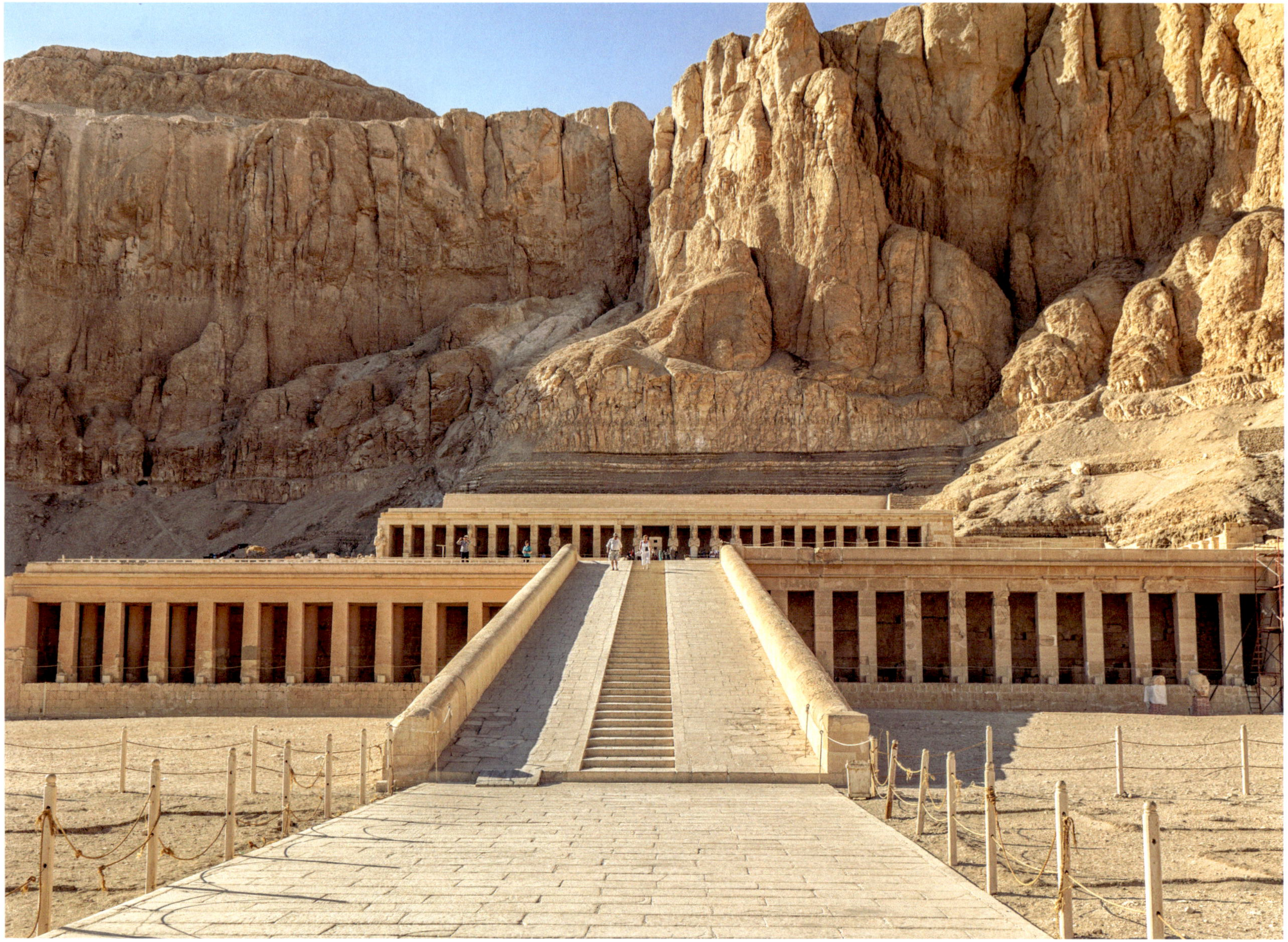

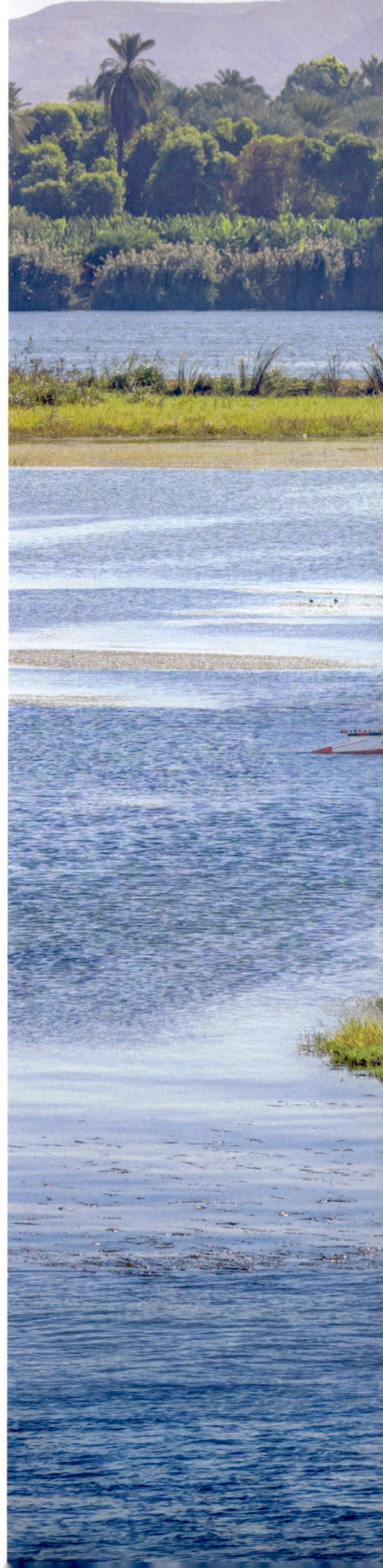

ABOVE:
Temple of Hatshepsut, Luxor
Located on the West Bank of the Nile, this temple is a remarkable testament to the power of one of ancient Egypt's few female pharaohs. Built during the 18th dynasty by her famed architect Senenmut, the temple features stunning reliefs that narrate her divine birth and a famous trading expedition to the land of Punt.

RIGHT:
Feluccas on the Nile, Aswan
Observing these gentle, silent boats weave across the Nile is to truly journey back in time. Feluccas have graced the Nile for thousands of years, providing transport, carrying goods, and delighting Egyptians of all ages on holidays and high days.

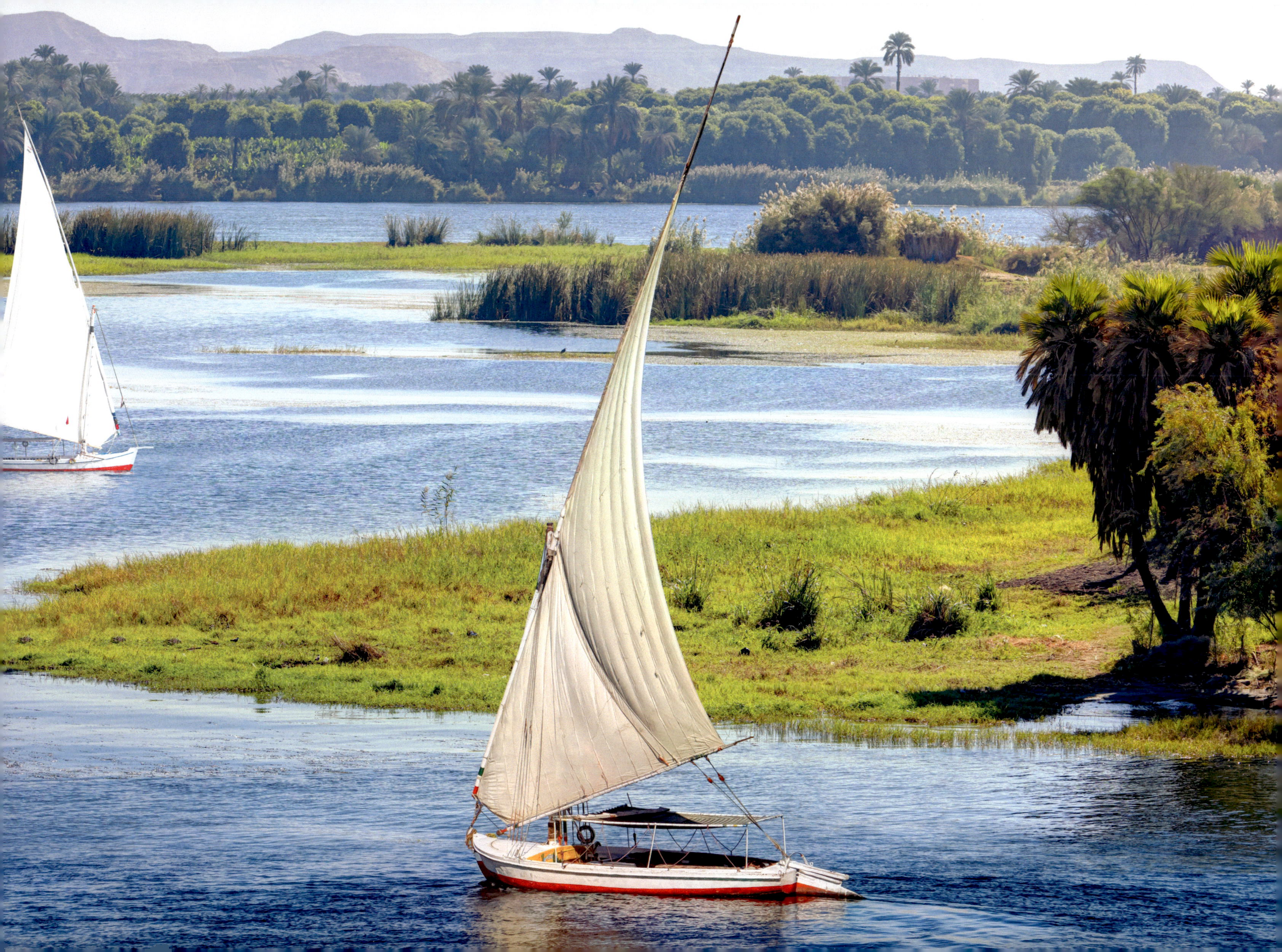

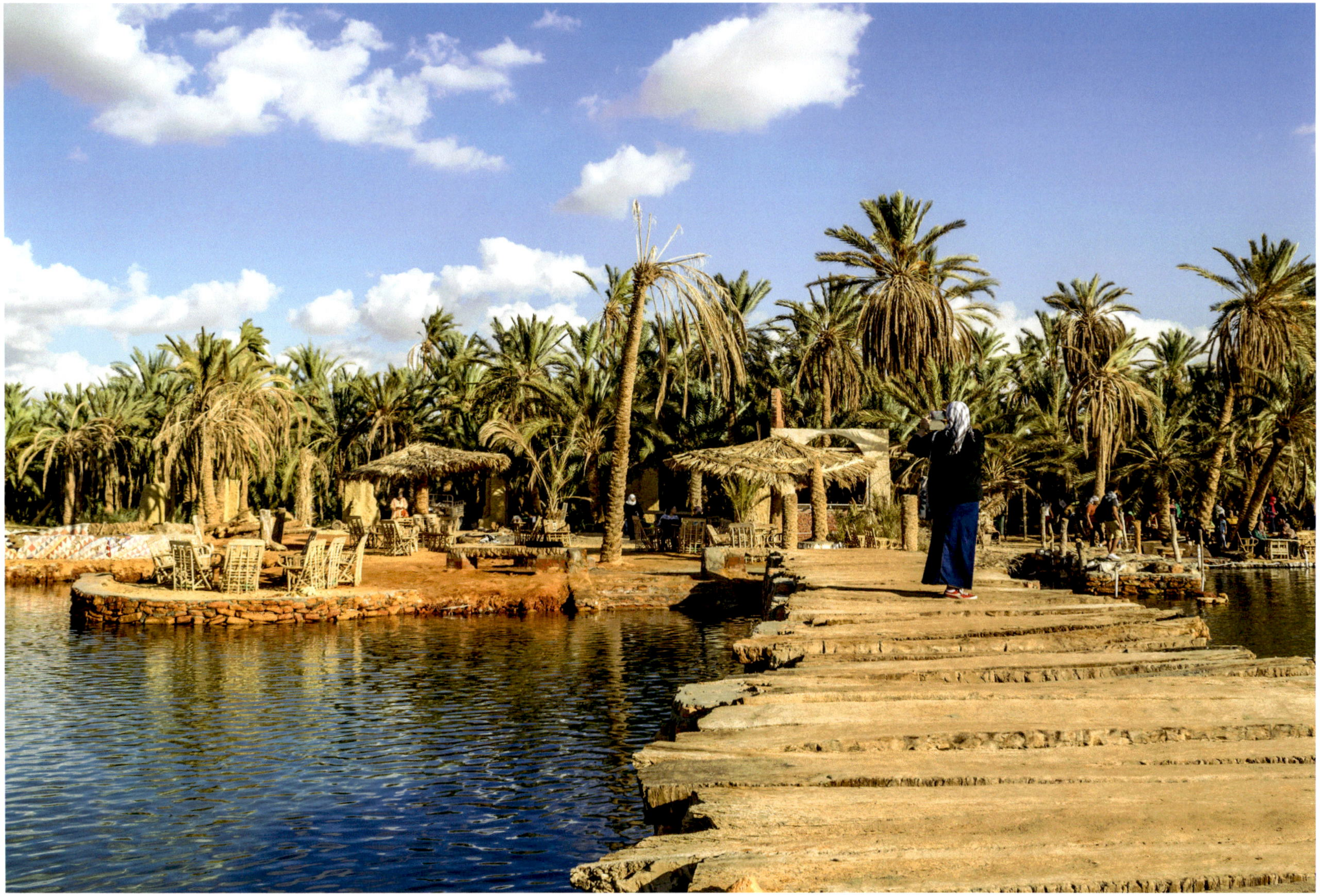

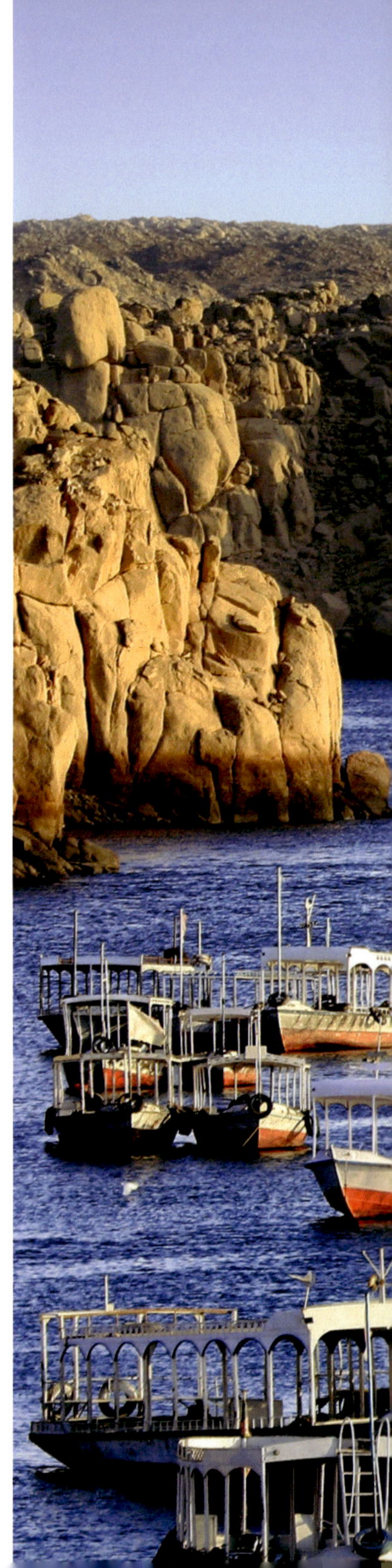

Siwa Oasis, Western Desert

This secluded spot is a significant historical and cultural
sanctuary, far from the city. Visited by Alexander the Great to
consult the famed Oracle of Amun, Siwa continues to draw
people in with its lush palm groves, abundant springs, and
delicious dates and olives. An ancient mud-brick fortress,
known as the Shali, still dominates the town, ensuring a sense
of legend pervades the whole oasis.

Temple of Philae, Aswan

This beautiful island temple is dedicated to the goddess
Isis and stands as a masterpiece of Ptolemaic and Roman
architecture. A longstanding pilgrimage site, Philae was one of
the last places where ancient Egyptian religion was practised.
In the 1960s the temple was endangered by the building of the
Aswan High Dam. Saved by a UNESCO-led appeal, the temple
was dismantled and rebuilt on a nearby island, Agilkia.

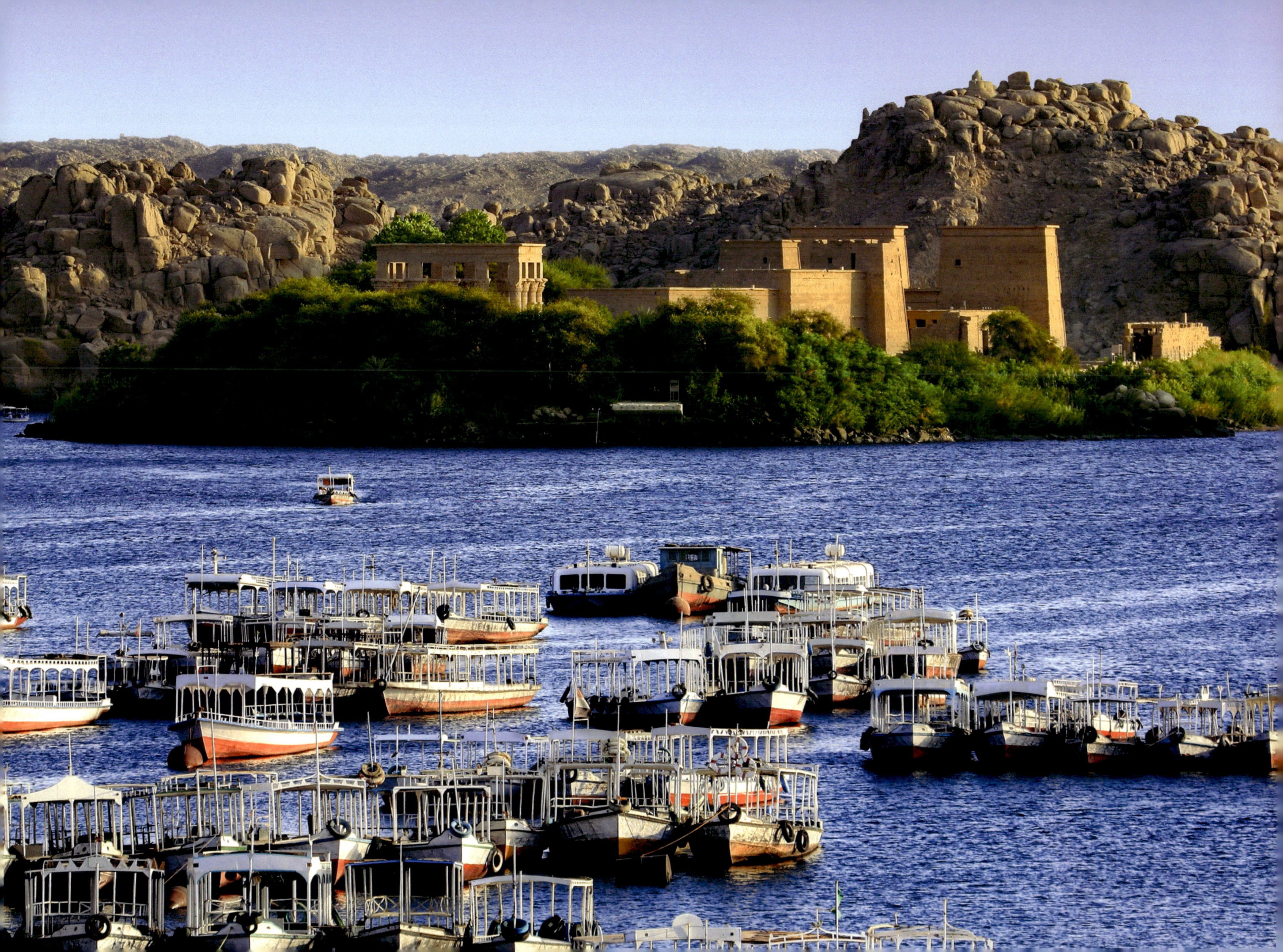

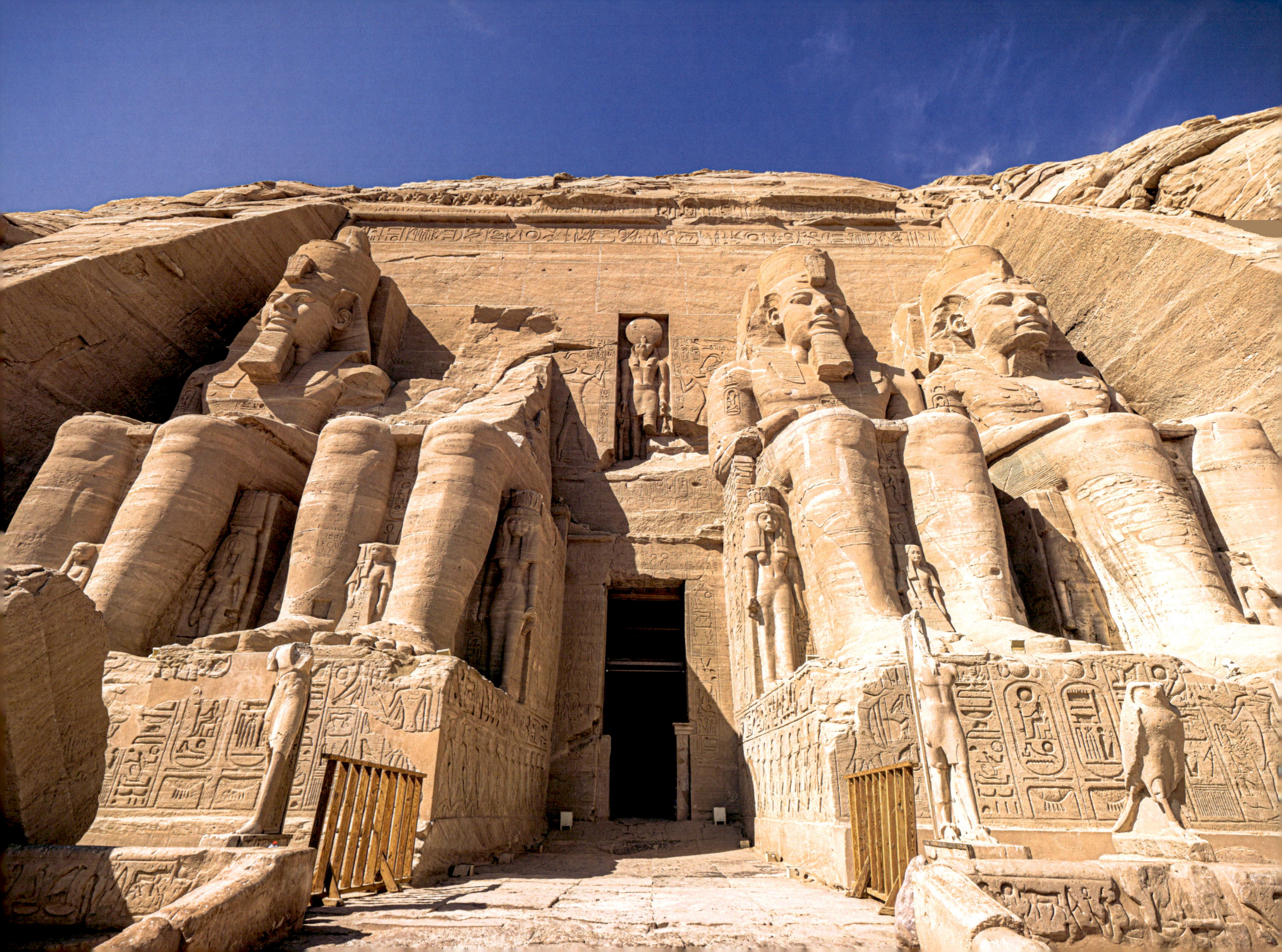

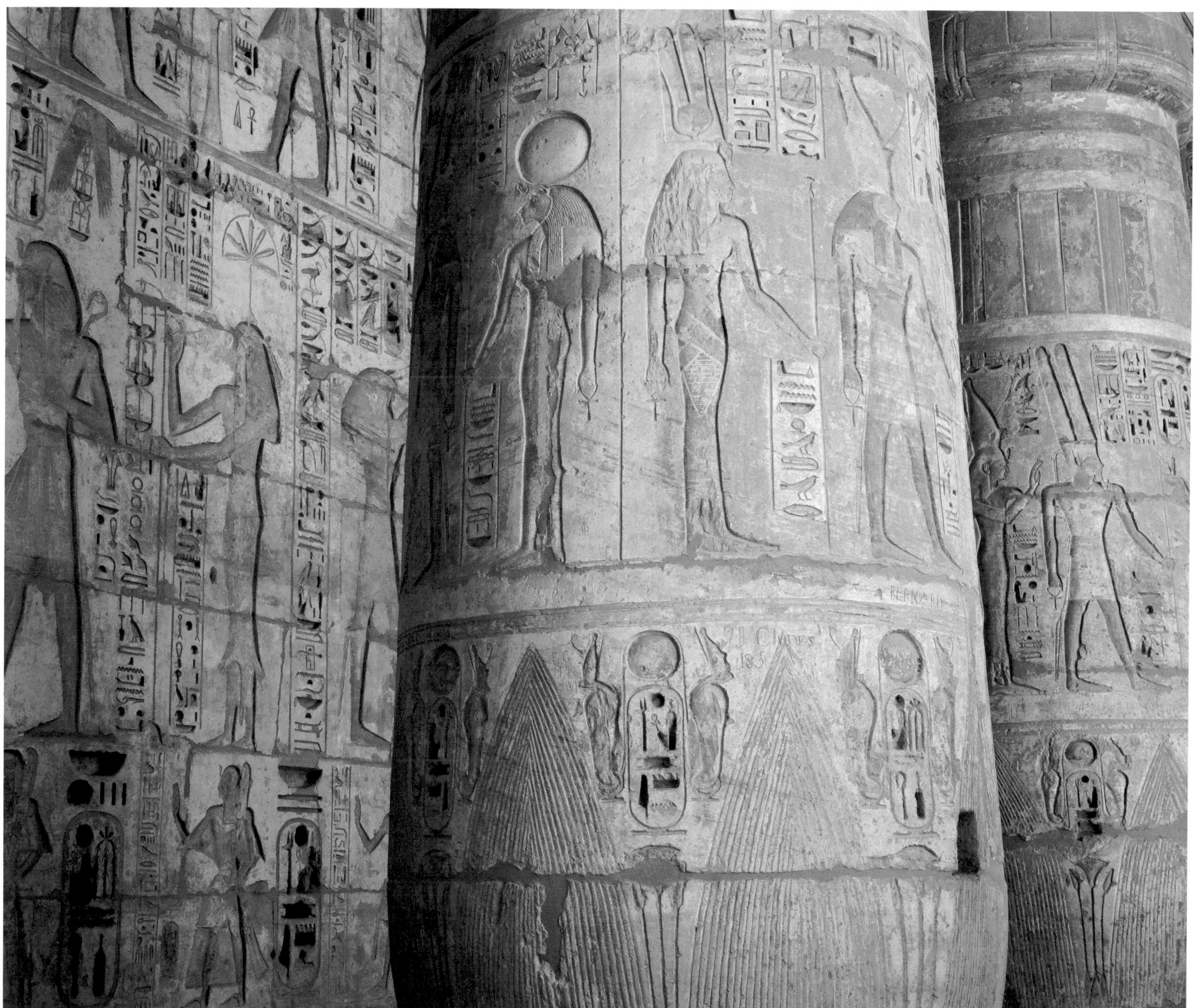

OPPOSITE:

**Abu Simbel,
Aswan governate**
The magnificent and
iconic rock-cut temples
of Abu Simbel were built
by the powerful pharaoh
Ramesses II during the 13th
century BCE. Situated in
ancient Nubia, they were
intended to demonstrate the
might of the Egyptian Empire
to neighbours and enemies
alike. The larger temple is
dedicated to Ramesses II
himself, along with the gods
Amun, Ra-Horakhty, and
Ptah, and its façade features
four colossal statues of the
pharaoh. The smaller temple
is dedicated to his beloved
queen, Nefertari, and the
goddess Hathor.

LEFT:

**Hypostyle Hall, Karnak
Temple, Luxor**
Containing 134 colossal
sandstone columns, some
rising to 24 metres (79ft),
the central hall of Karnak
Temple is awe-inspiring.
The central columns are
taller with open, bell-shaped
papyrus capitals, while the
side columns have closed bud
capitals. The art covering the
hall, primarily by Seti I and
Ramesses II, includes intricate
carvings and reliefs depicting
religious ceremonies, royal
rituals, and military victories,
with some still retaining their
original vibrant paint.

The Old City, Damascus

Damascus is one of the oldest continuously inhabited cities in the world, located at the crossroads of major trade routes. Its past glories are reflected in many stunning monuments, showcasing a blend of Roman, Byzantine, and Islamic architecture. Highlights include the Umayyad Mosque, built on the site of an Assyrian sanctuary, the historic Straight Street (Via Recta), several labyrinthine souqs, and generations-old restaurants, all surrounded by ancient Roman walls and gates.

Old City souq, Damascus

The souqs are truly a journey through time, where the air is thick with the scent of the spice trade and the sound of traditional artisans at work. Here you can enjoy a vibrant, atmospheric mix of history and daily life. Traditional goods like intricate inlaid wooden furniture, handmade textiles, copperware, and aromatic spices and sweets fill the quaint stalls and shops.

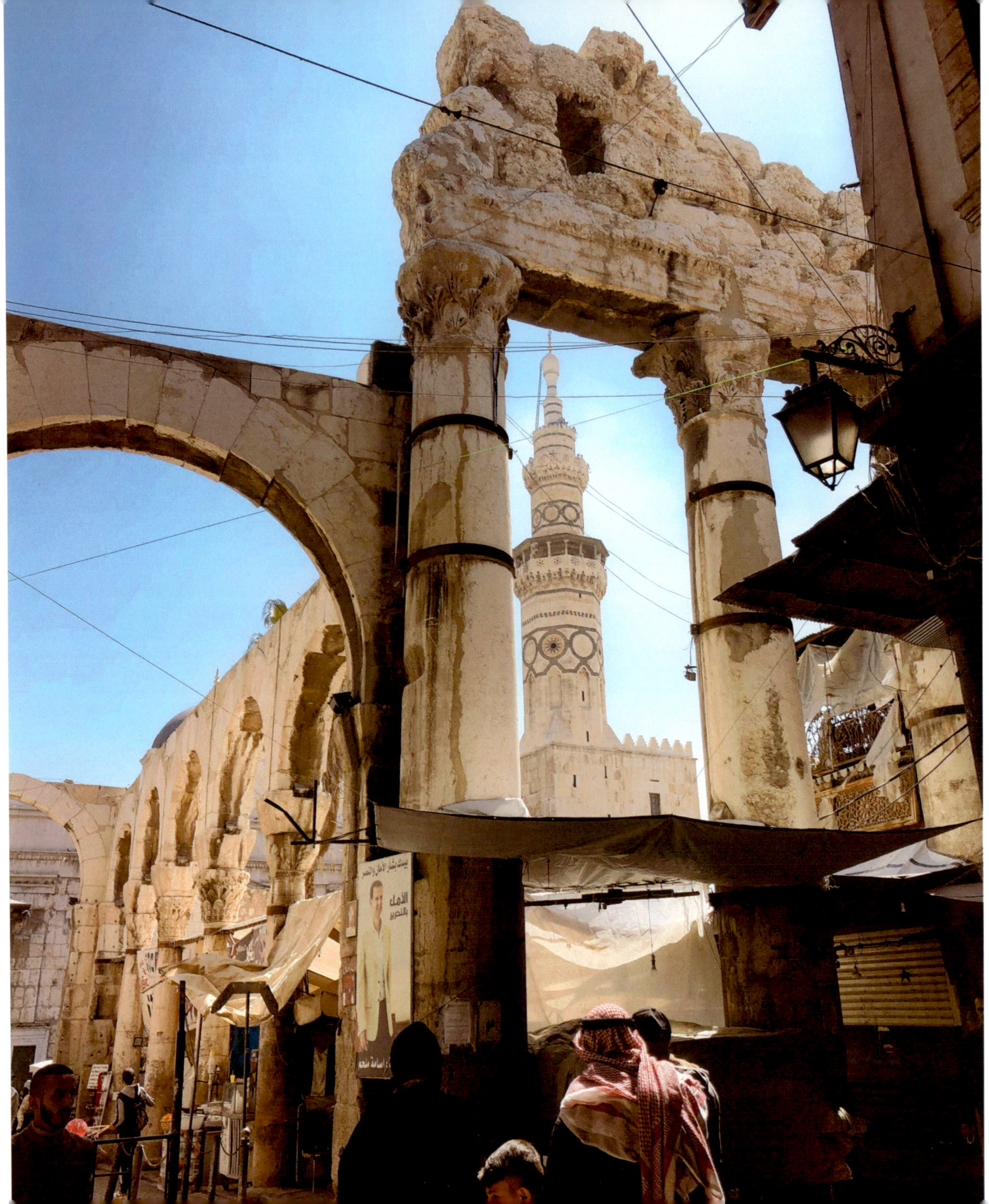

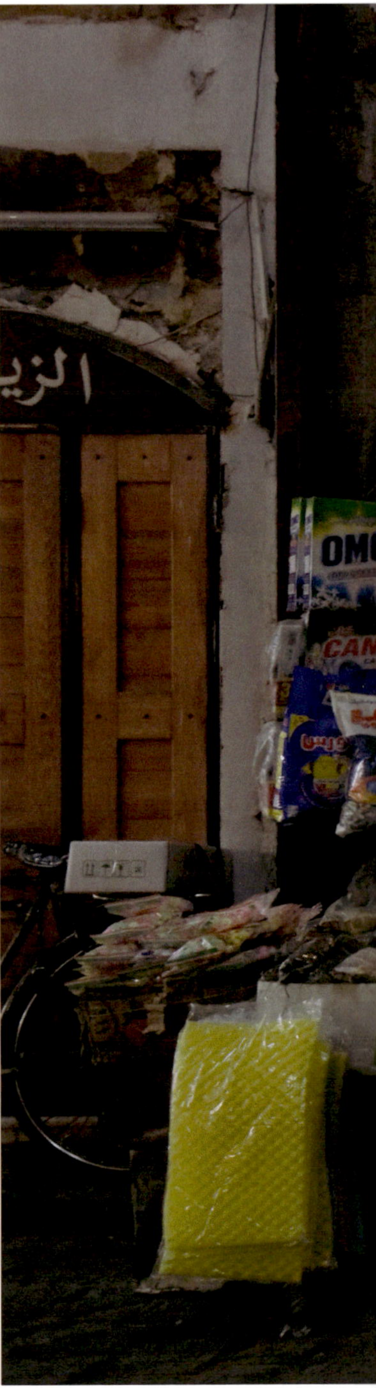

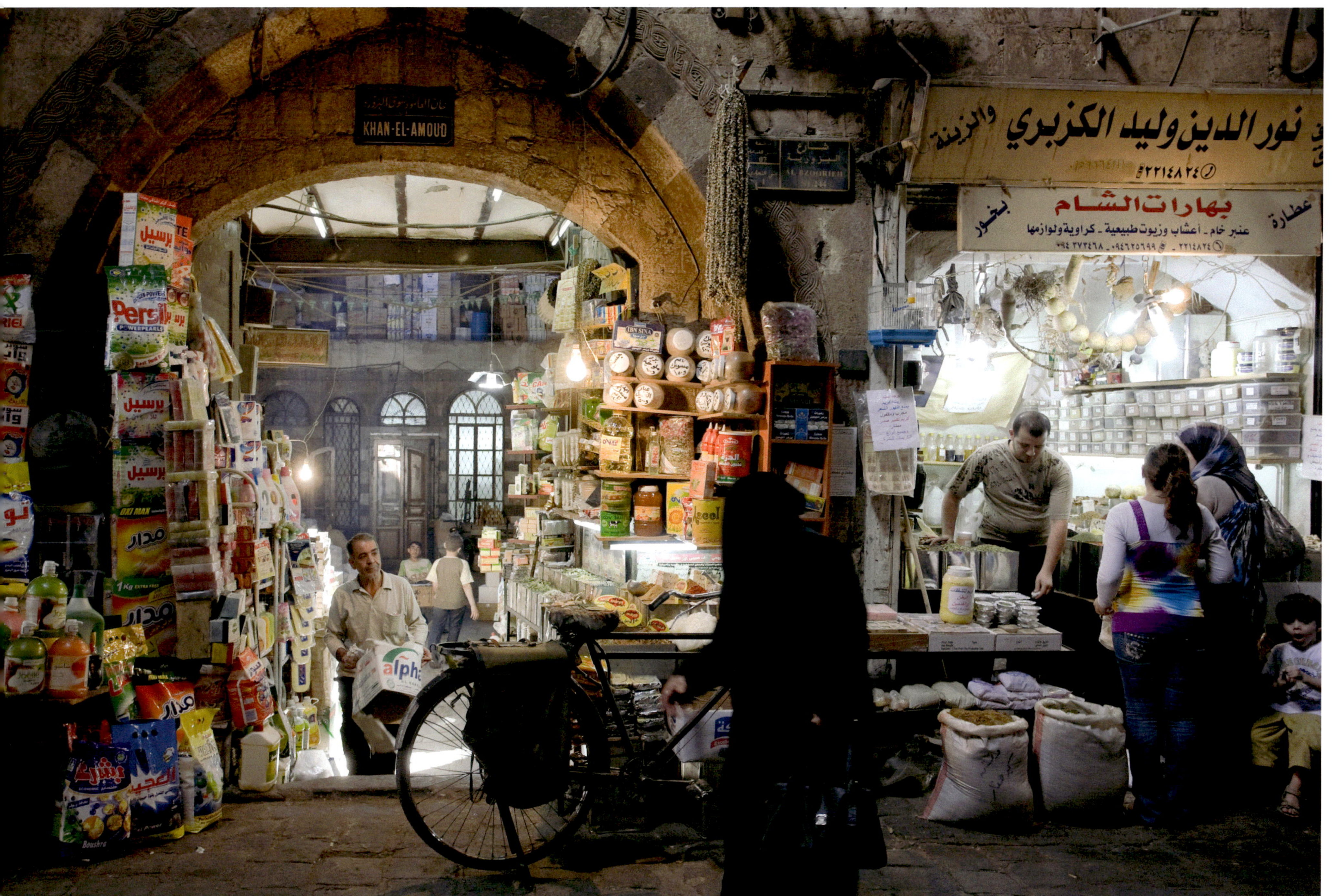
KHAN·EL·AMOUD
نور الدين وليد الكزبري
والزينة
٢٢١٤٨٢٤
بهارات الشام
عطارة
بخور
عنبر خام ـ أعشاب وزيوت طبيعية ـ كراوية ولوازمها
٠٩٤٦٢٥٠٦٩٩ ٠٩٤ ٣٧٣٤٦٨
شارع
البزورية
AL·BZOURIEH
Persil
RIEL
برسيل
OXI MAX
مدار
alpha
Boushra
IBN SINA
Seel

Roman theatre, Bosra
This large theatre was built in the 2nd century CE, providing a majestic venue for many artistic performances. After the Roman era, it became a fortified citadel, employed by the Ayyubid dynasty, which helped preserve its structure. Sadly, it has been a casualty of the Syrian civil war, suffering damage from military activities and shelling, but despite this, it remains one of the world's best-preserved Roman theatres.

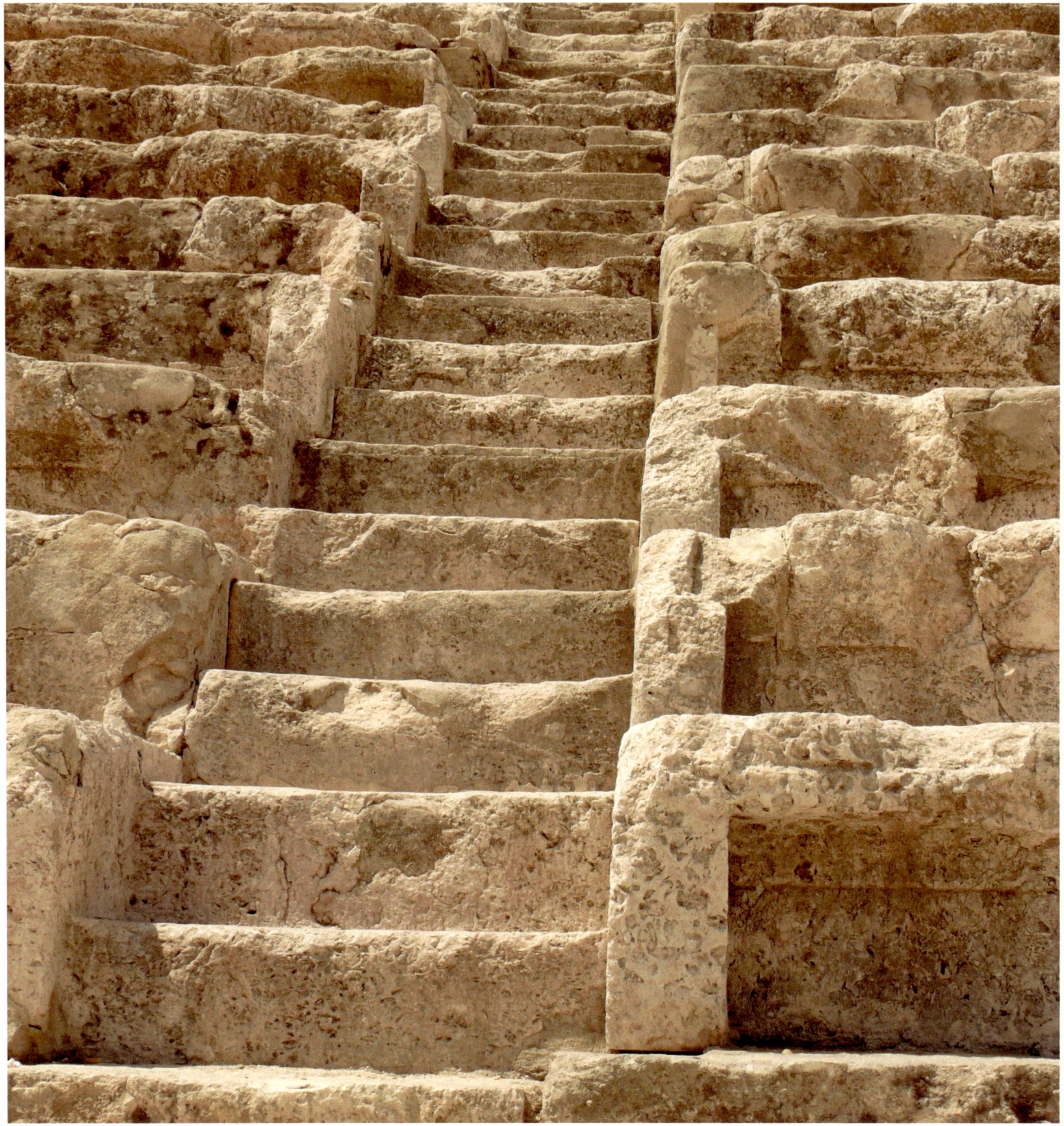

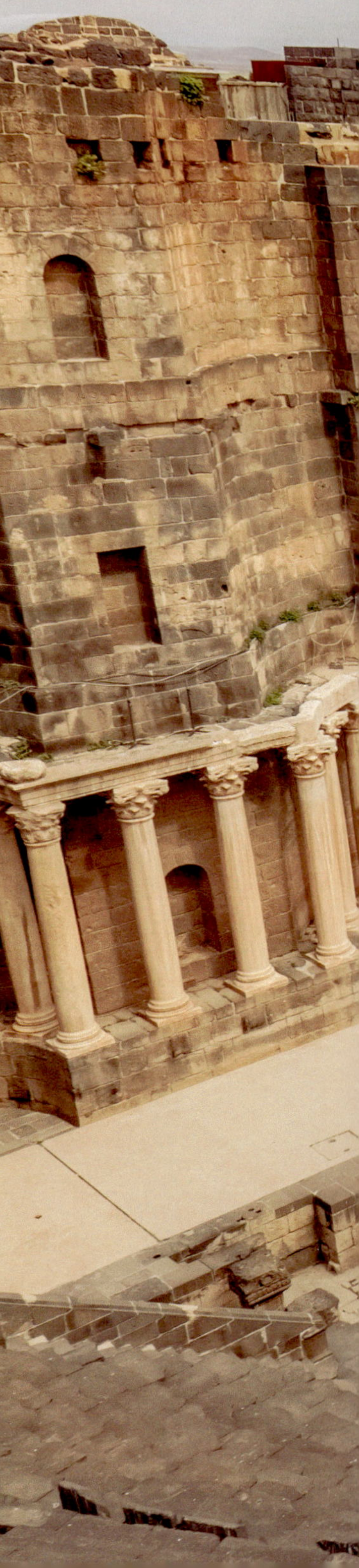

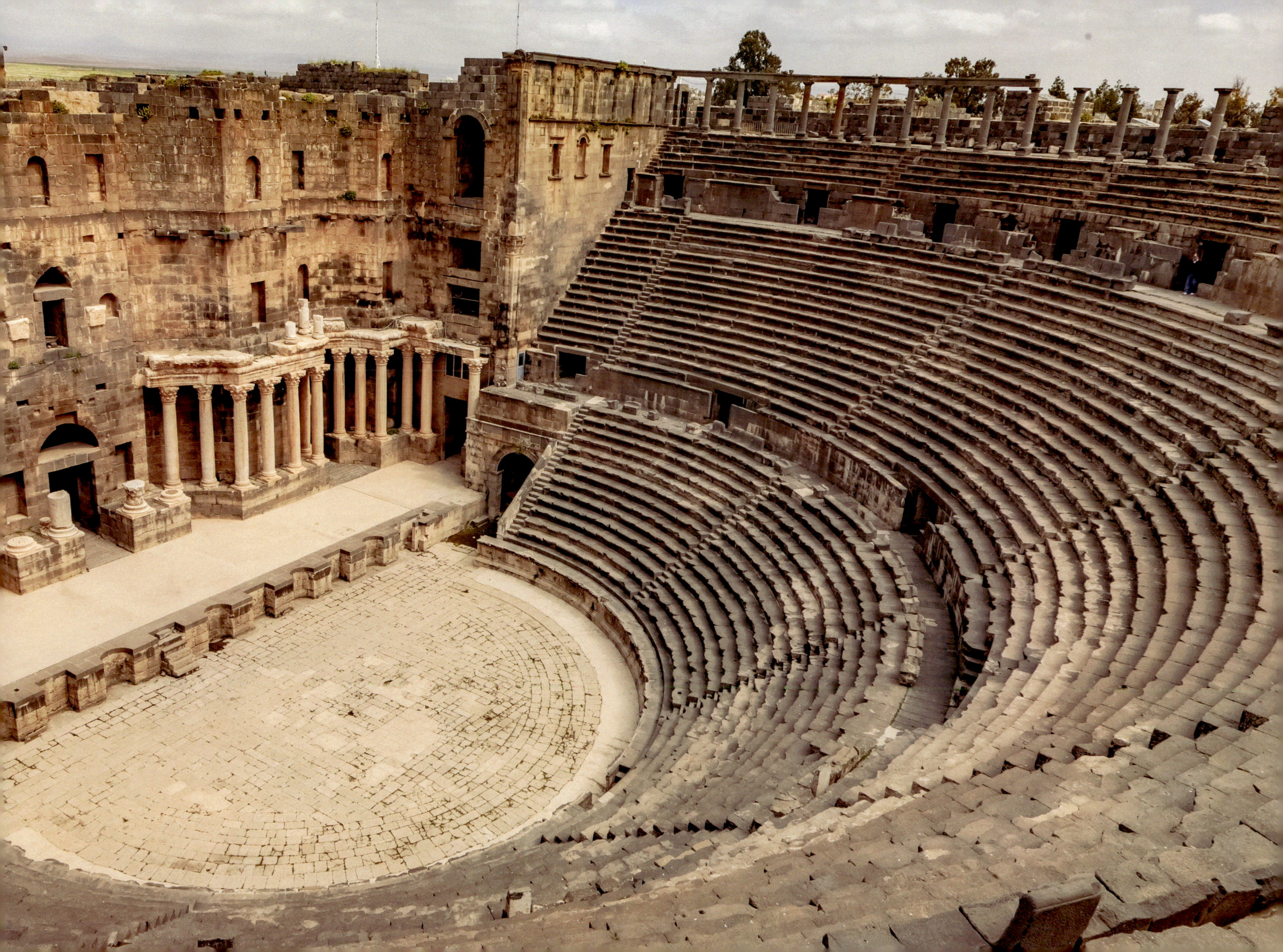

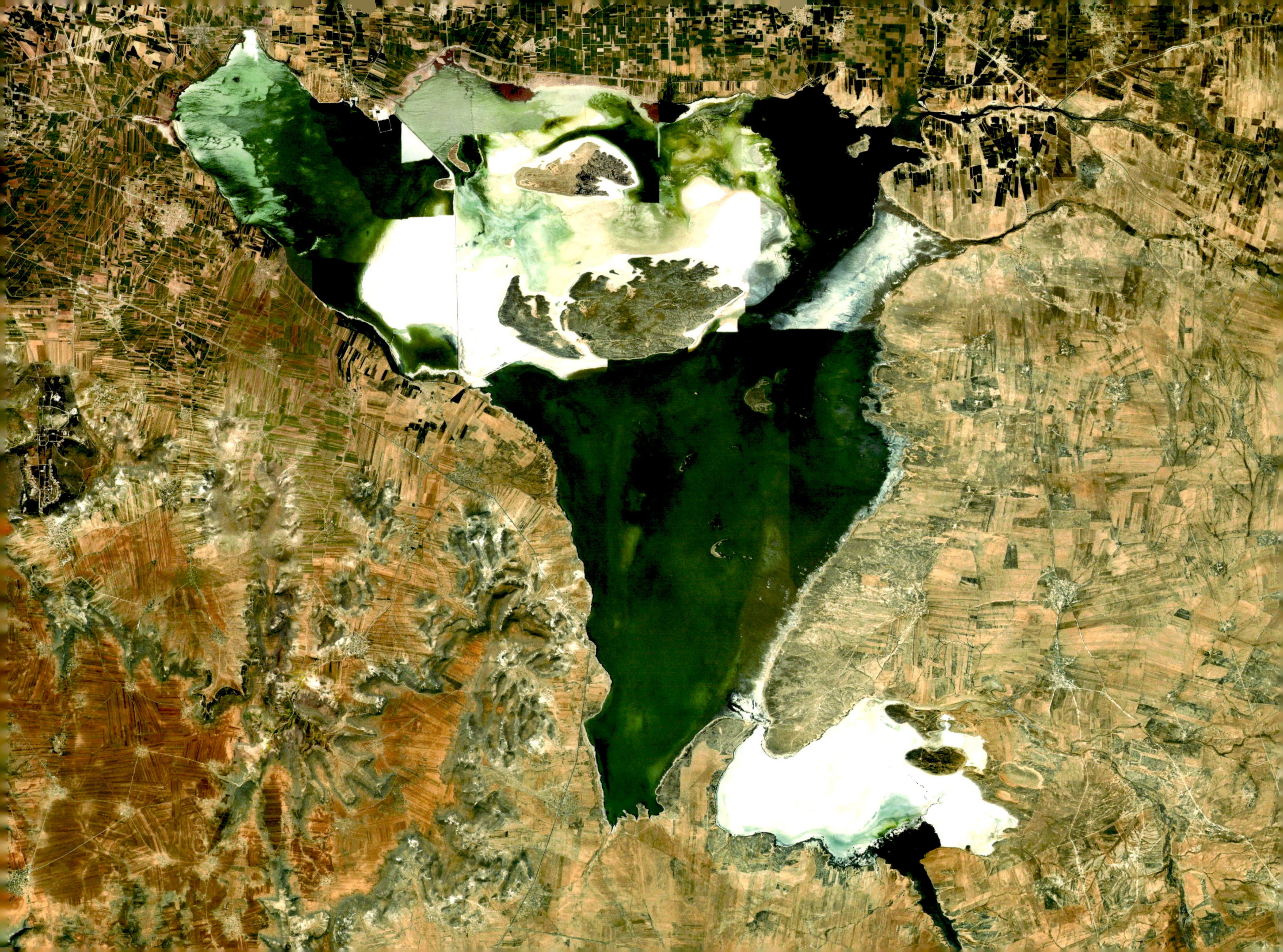

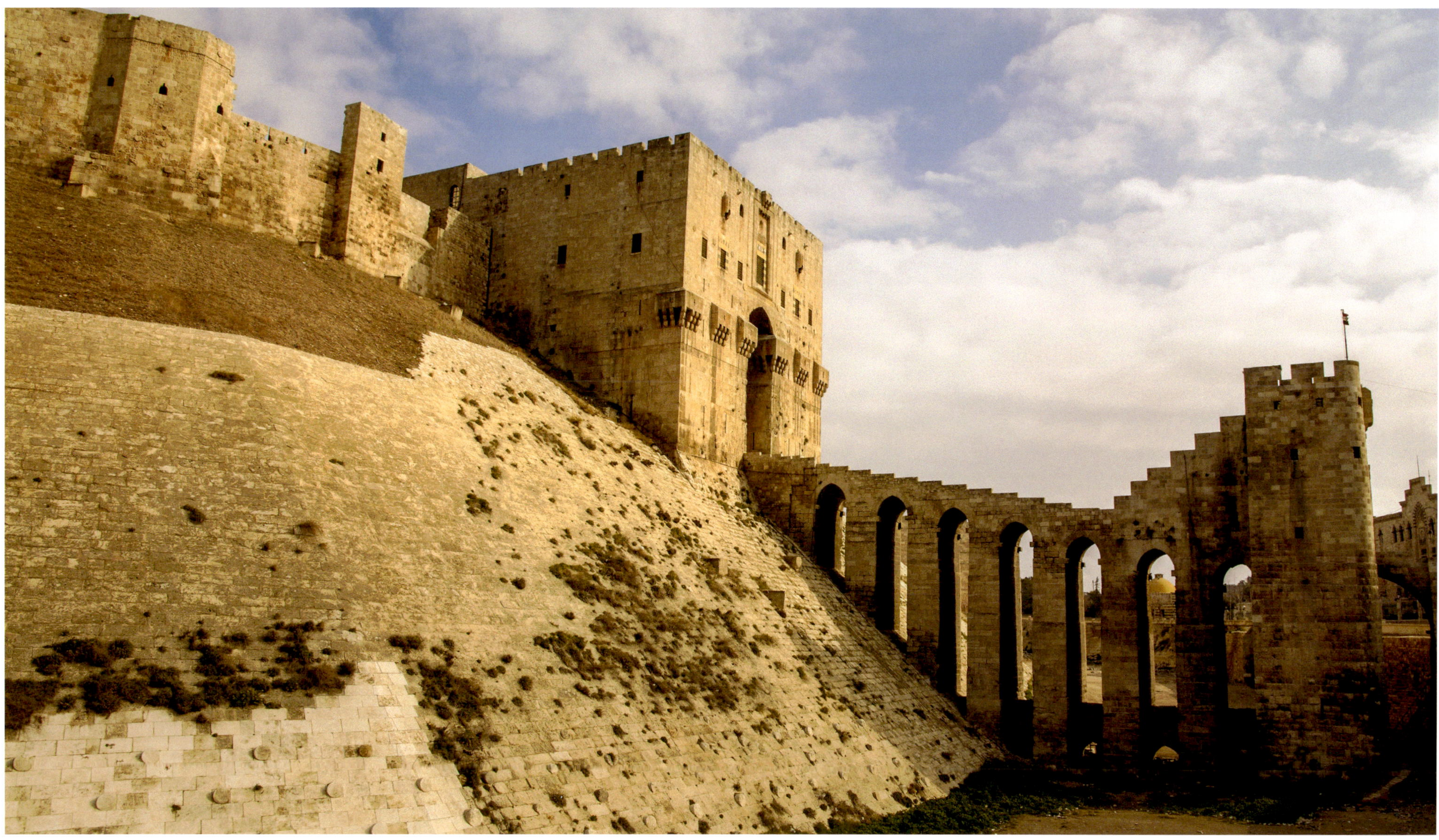

Lake Sabkhat al-Jabbul, Aleppo
This surprising waterhole is the largest natural lake in Syria and is surrounded by extensive salt flats. The lake is also an important ecological site, serving as a critical habitat for migratory birds. It was designated as a wetland of international importance due to its role as a key staging and wintering area for various waterbirds.

The Citadel, Aleppo
This most impressive castle has been a stronghold for various civilizations, including the Hittites, Greeks, Romans, and Mongols, each leaving their mark on its structure. It remains a powerful symbol of Aleppo's resilience. In the 12th century, during the Crusader wars, Sultan al-Zaher Ghazi, the son of Saladin, fortified the Citadel. He dug the massive moat and built the imposing entrance bridge with its series of disorienting pathways, designed to make attackers vulnerable from the defenders above.

Krak des Chevaliers, Tartus, Homs Gap

It was the Knights Hospitaller (Order of Saint John of Jerusalem), a powerful Christian military order, who held and fortified this castle from 1142 to 1271, turning it into an impregnable stronghold. This magnificent Crusader castle is one of the world's best examples of medieval military architecture. The castle was never taken by force, only surrendering to a long siege held by the Mamluk leader Sultan Baybars I in 1271.

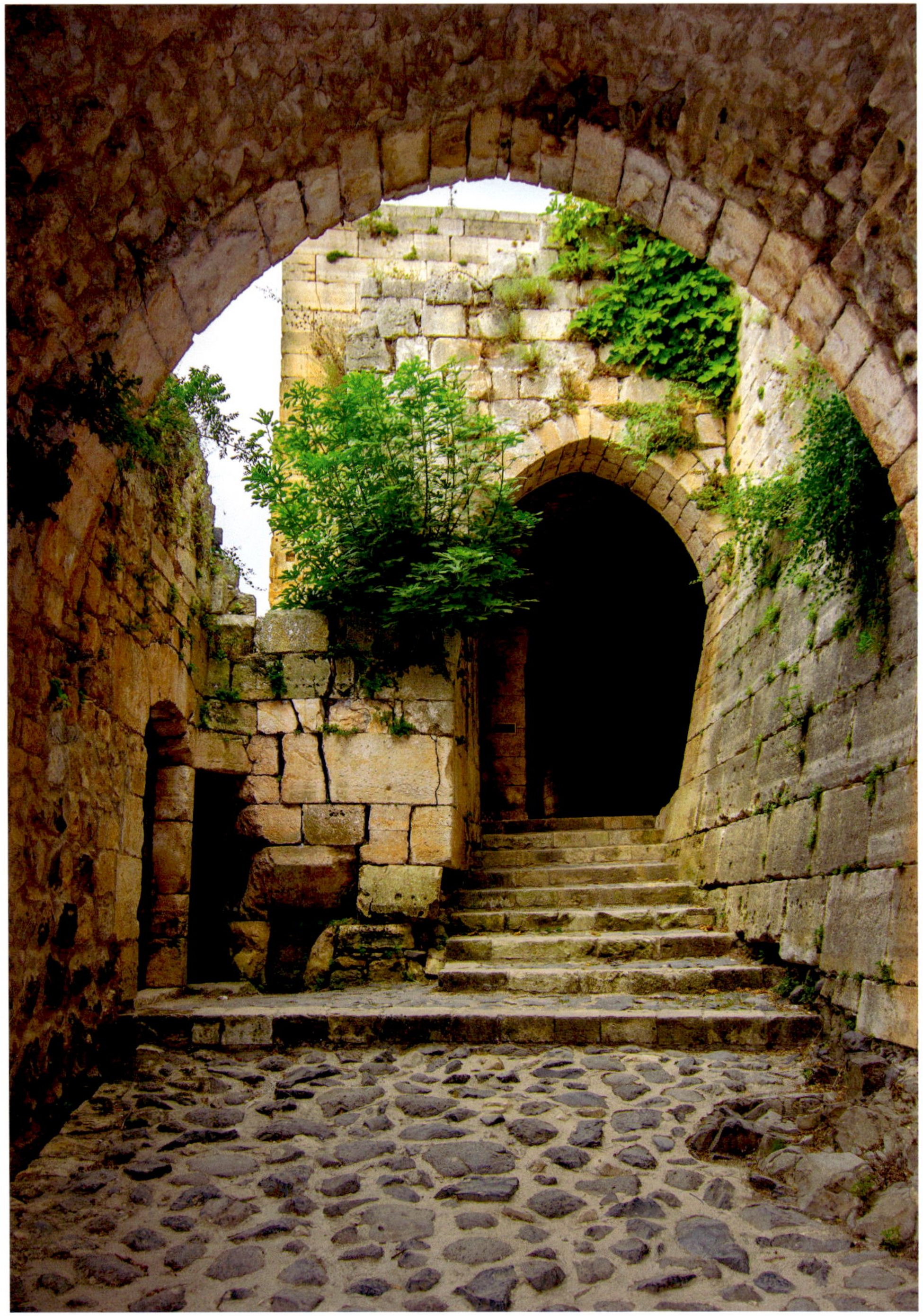

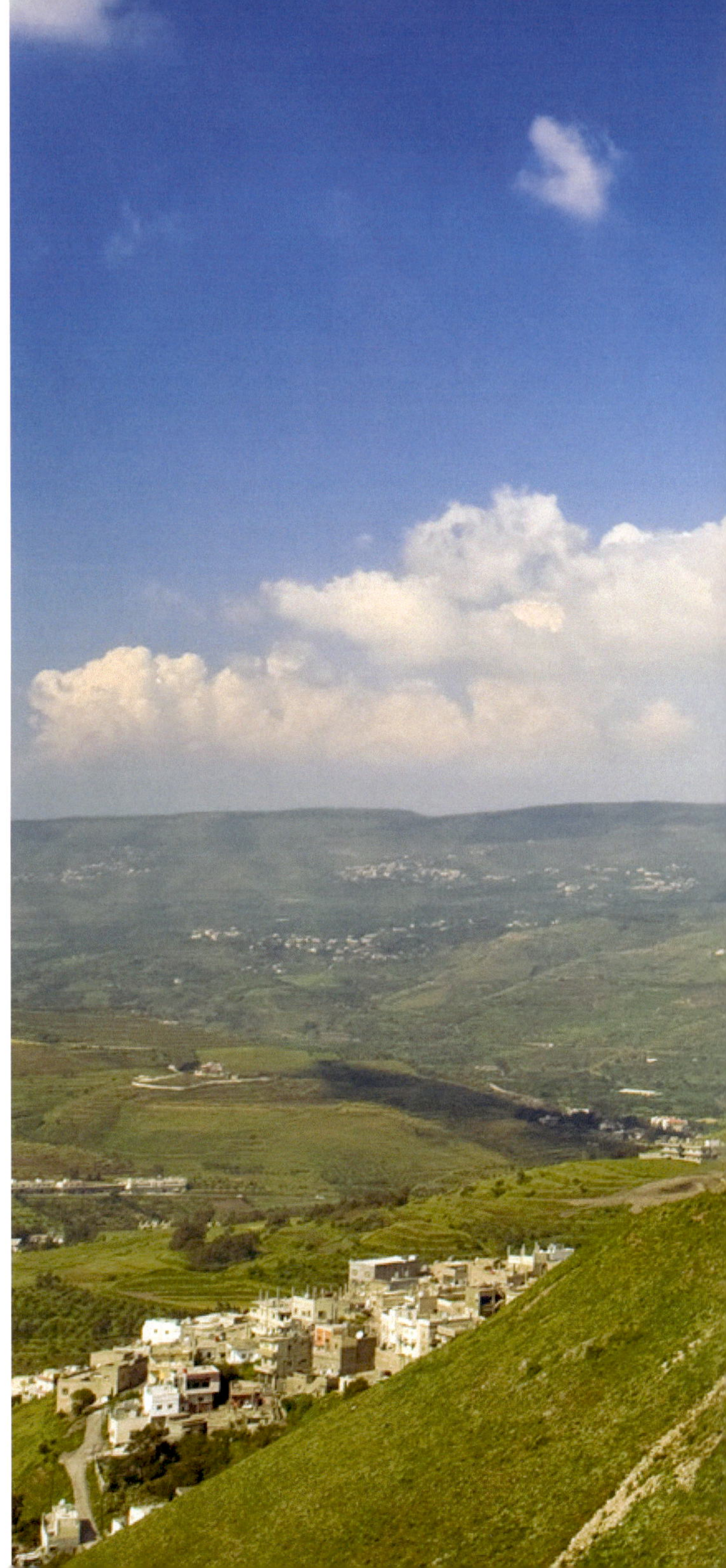

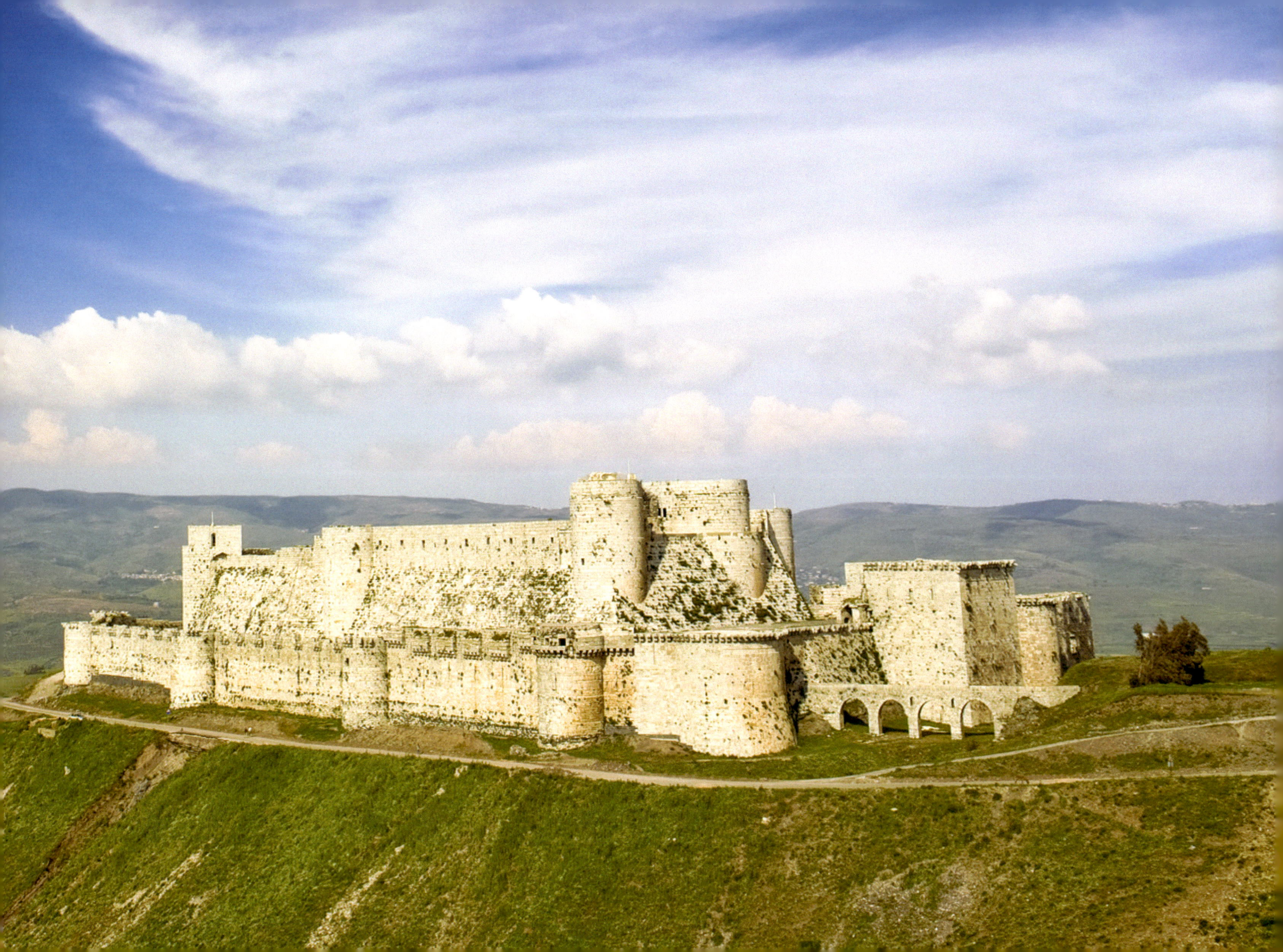

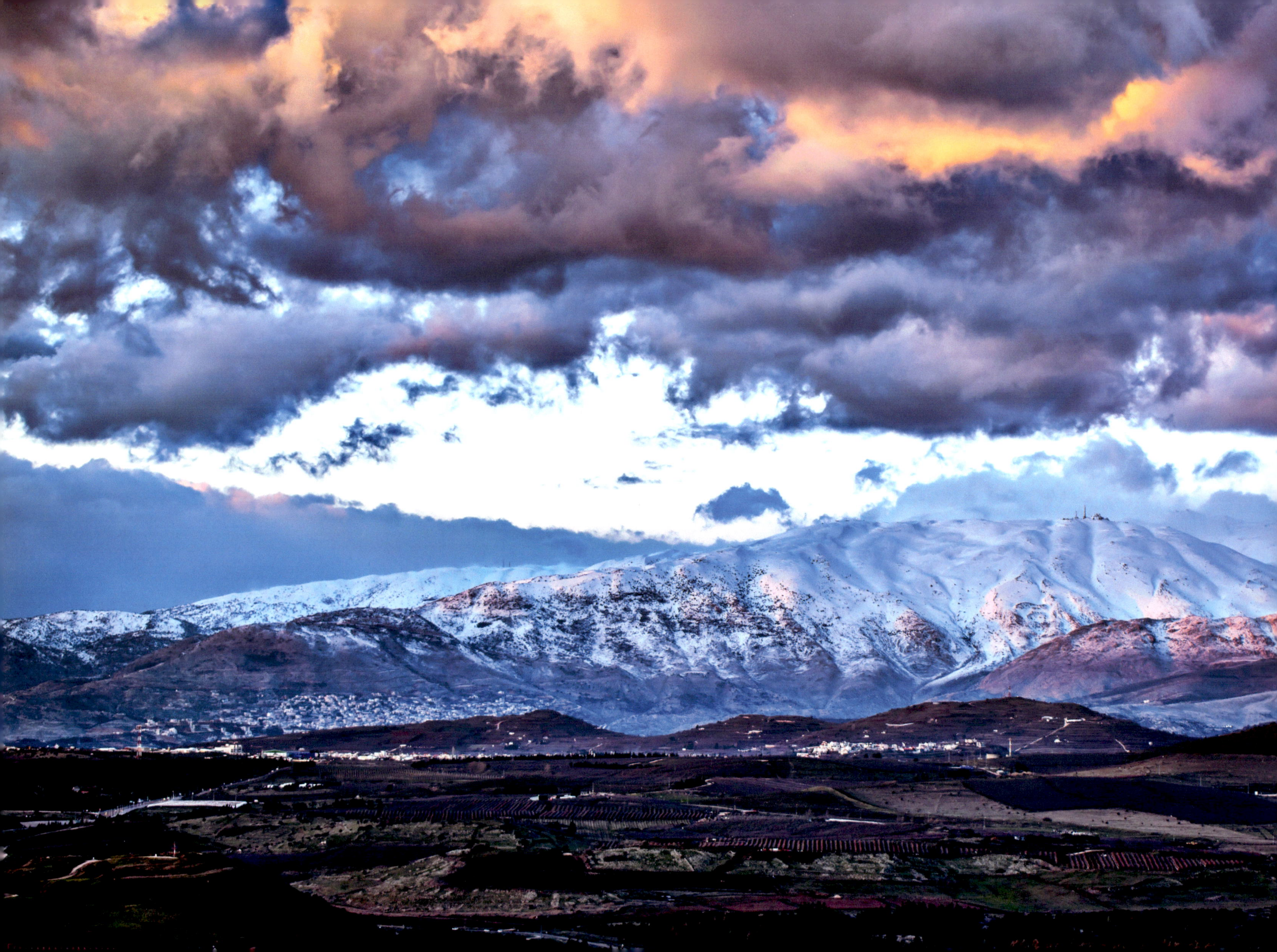

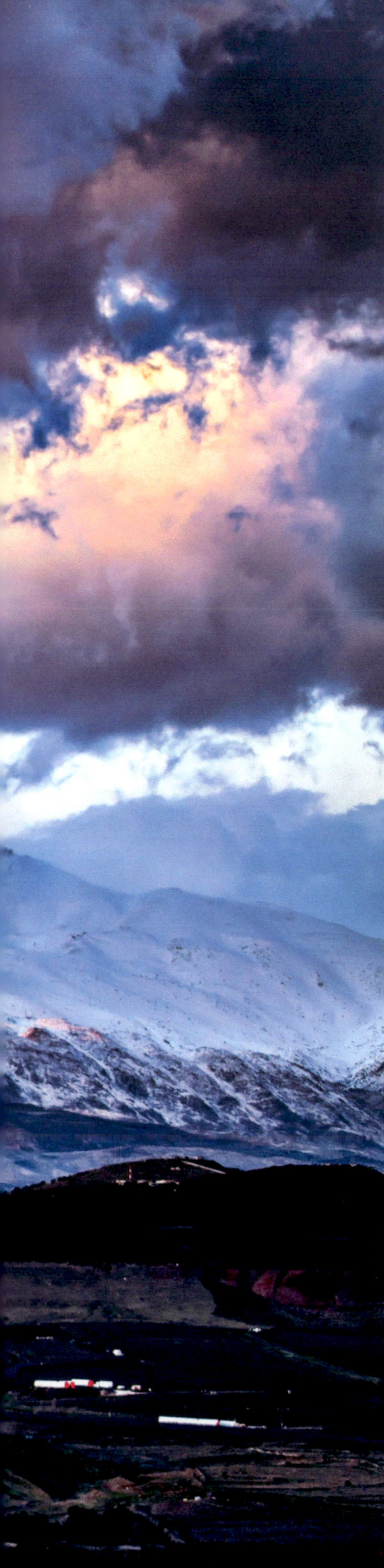

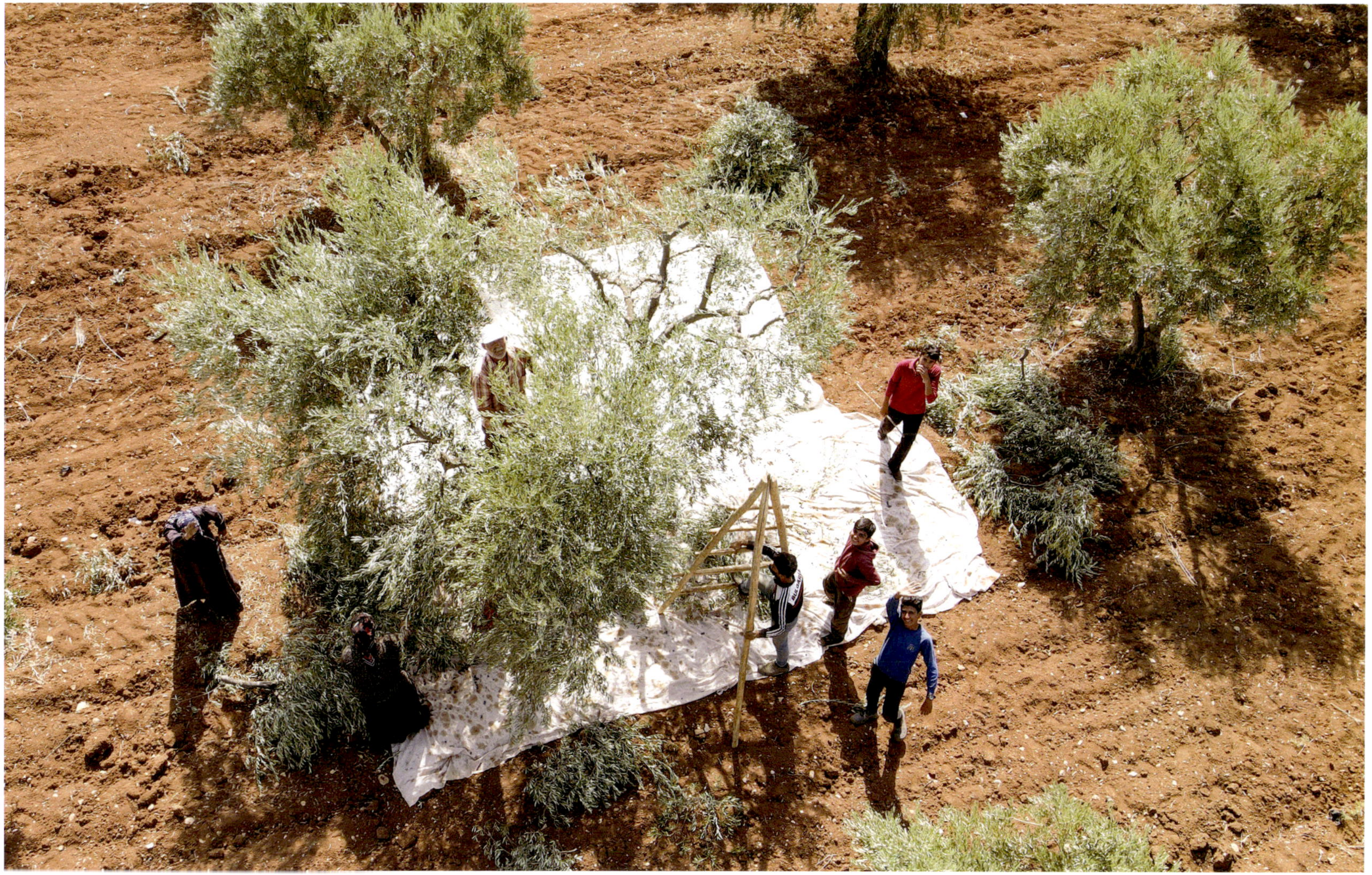

Mount Hermon, Anti-Lebanon Mountains

At 2,814 metres (9,232ft), Mount Hermon is the highest peak in Syria. From its Syrian slopes, Mount Hermon offers breathtaking panoramic views of Lebanon. The mountain is a vital source of water for the entire region, and a welcome natural area for walking, hiking, and skiing.

ABOVE:

Olive groves, Idlib

Syria is believed to be one of the original homes of the olive tree. For millennia, the cultivation of olives has been central to Syrian agriculture and cuisine. The olive tree is a potent symbol to Syrians, representing peace, prosperity, and resilience. Evidence suggests that the cultivation of olives in Syria dates back over 6000 years. The Phoenicians helped spread olive culture from Syria to other Mediterranean shores. A visit to a mountainside Syrian village provides local food, wine, and a table laden with olives.

Great Mosque of the Umayyads, Damascus

This outstanding example of Islamic architecture was built between 705 and 715 CE by Caliph al-Walid I and stands on a sacred site which previously housed an Aramaean temple, a Roman temple dedicated to Jupiter, and a Byzantine church which honoured St John the Baptist. This early mosque's design absorbed elements from these earlier structures into its monumental new look. With a vast prayer hall, spacious courtyard, and three minarets, the Great Mosque established the prototype for subsequent congregational mosques across the Islamic world. Other pivotal features were introduced, ideas that became hallmarks of Islamic architecture, such as the mihrab prayer niche and minarets for the call to prayer.

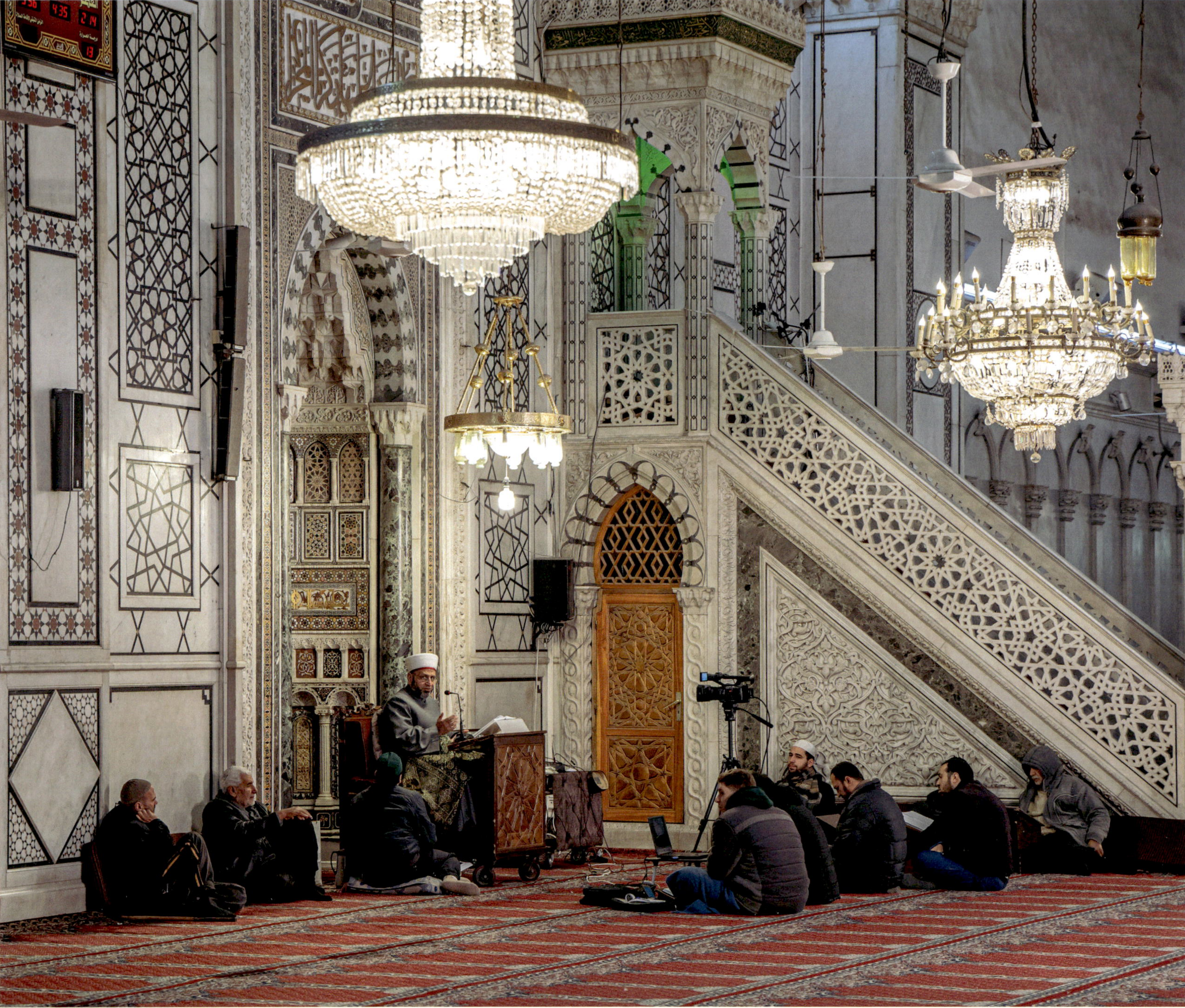

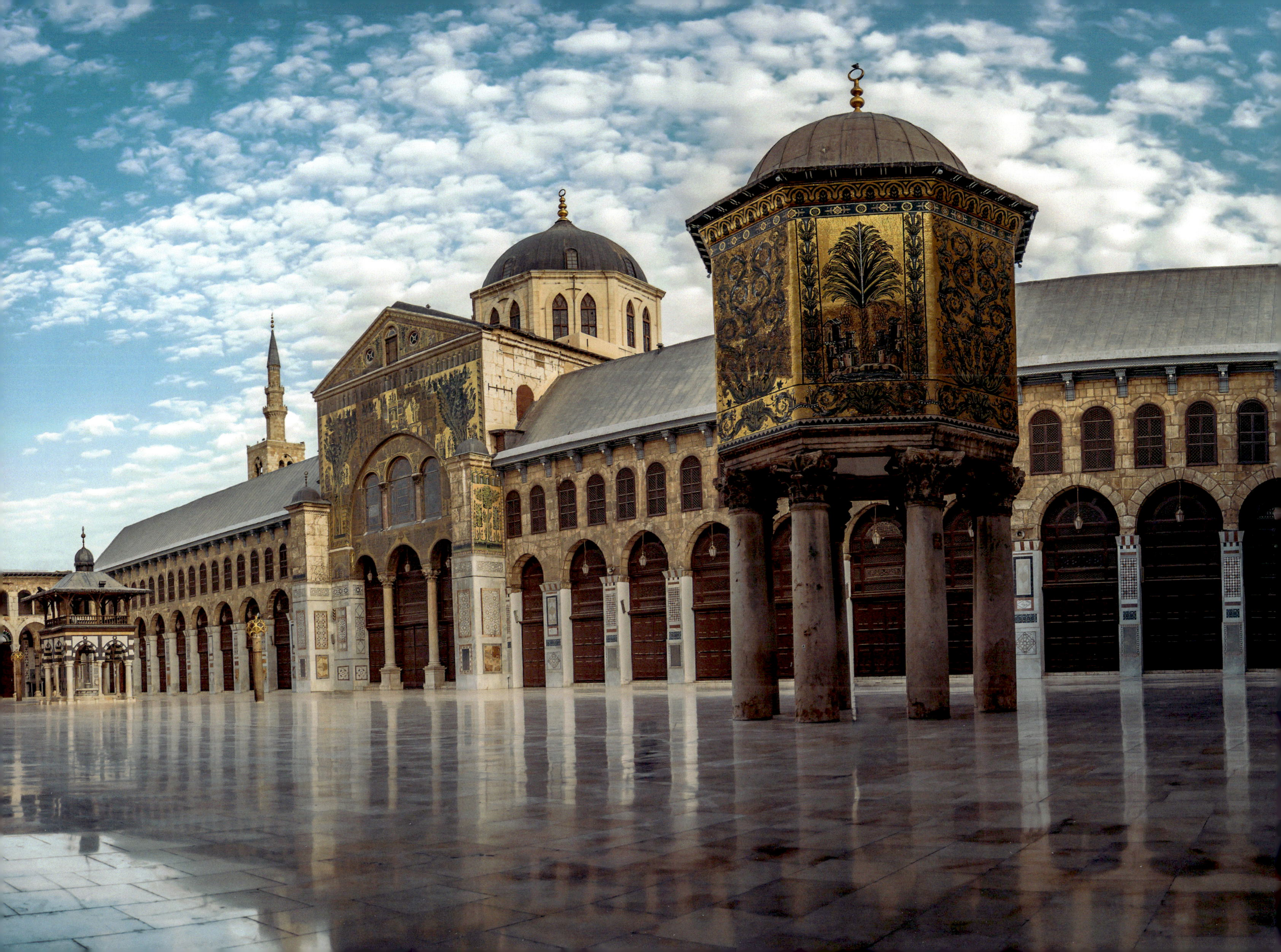

Lake Dukan, Kurdistan
This major tourist area attracts many Iraqis who come to enjoy the natural wonders and cultural history of this beautiful region. The traditional Kurdish villages provide a glimpse of local life and its rich cuisine. Around the lake, people picnic and enjoy hiking and watersports. Many archaeological sites have been excavated, revealing ancient settlements and artefacts from the Stone Age and the Bronze Age Hurrian civilization. The forests by the lake are rich with birdlife, attracting international visitors.

National Museum, Baghdad
Iraq's National Museum is home to a magnificent Lamassu, the famed, colossal Assyrian protective deity. These mythical beings combine the body of a bull or lion, the wings of an eagle, and a human head. The museum's Lamassu, originally from the palace of King Sargon II at Khorsabad, is a vital symbol of ancient Mesopotamian art. They served as guardians, emphasizing the king's power and providing divine protection to kings, palaces, and ancient Bahgdad's city gates.

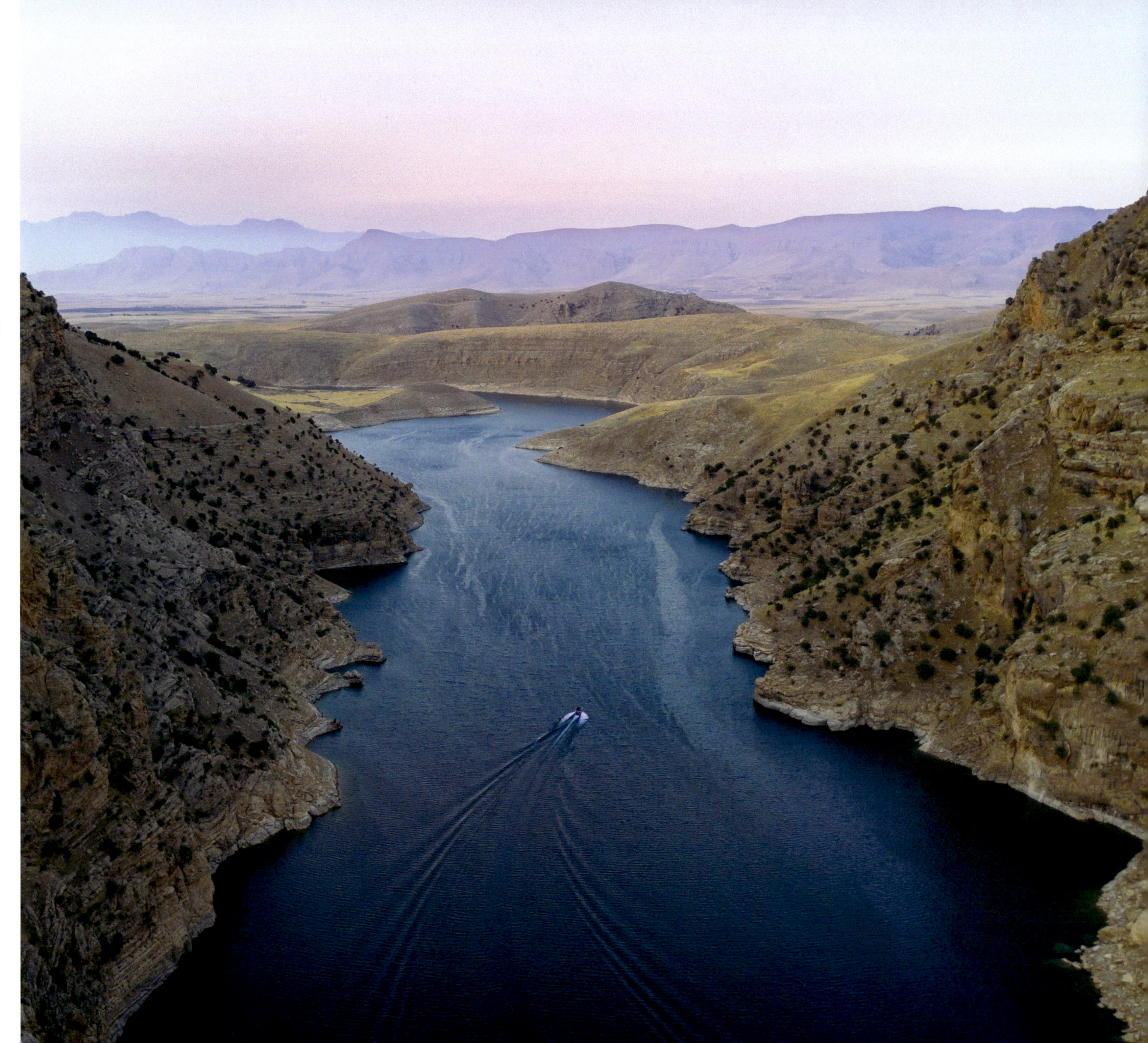

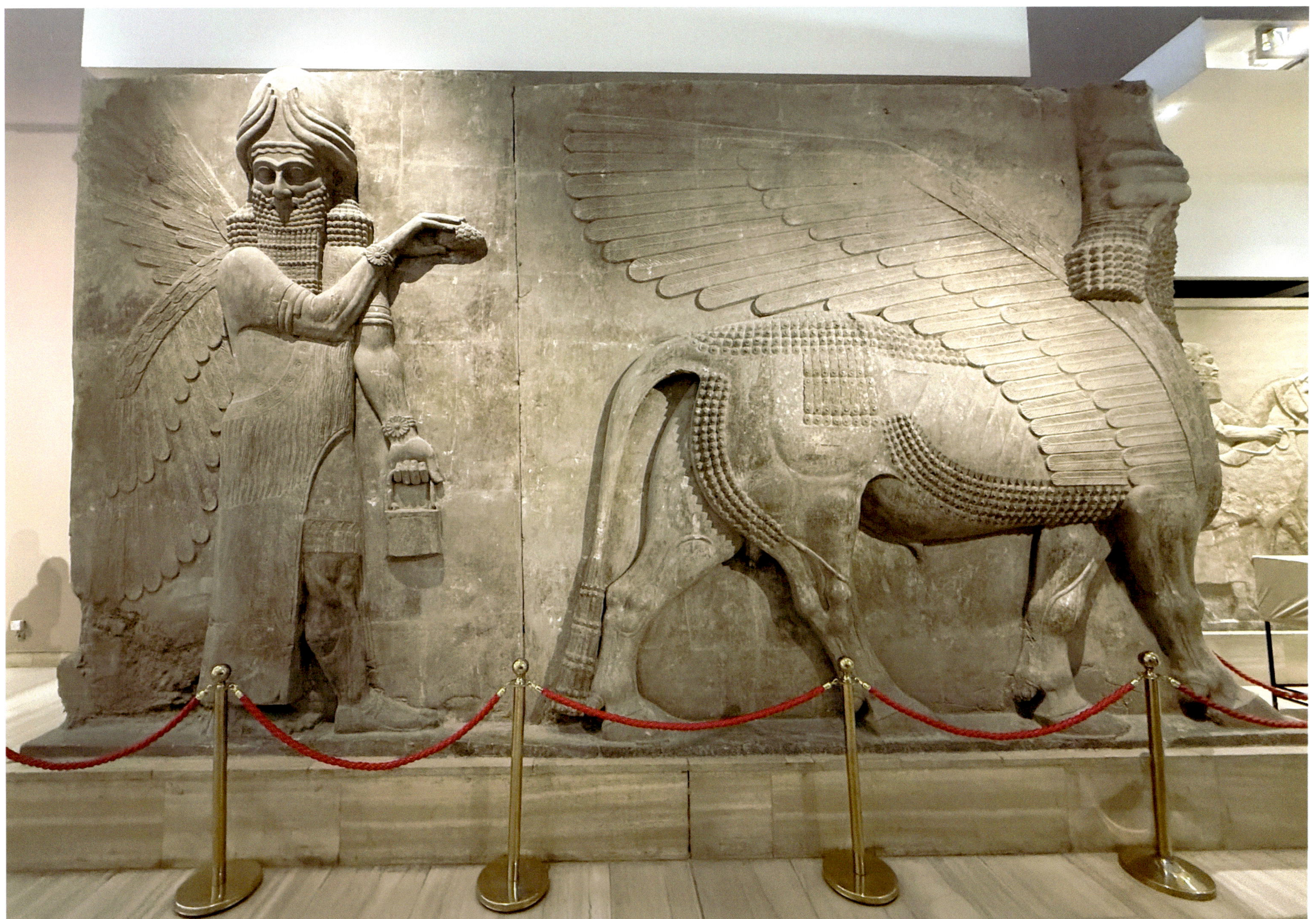

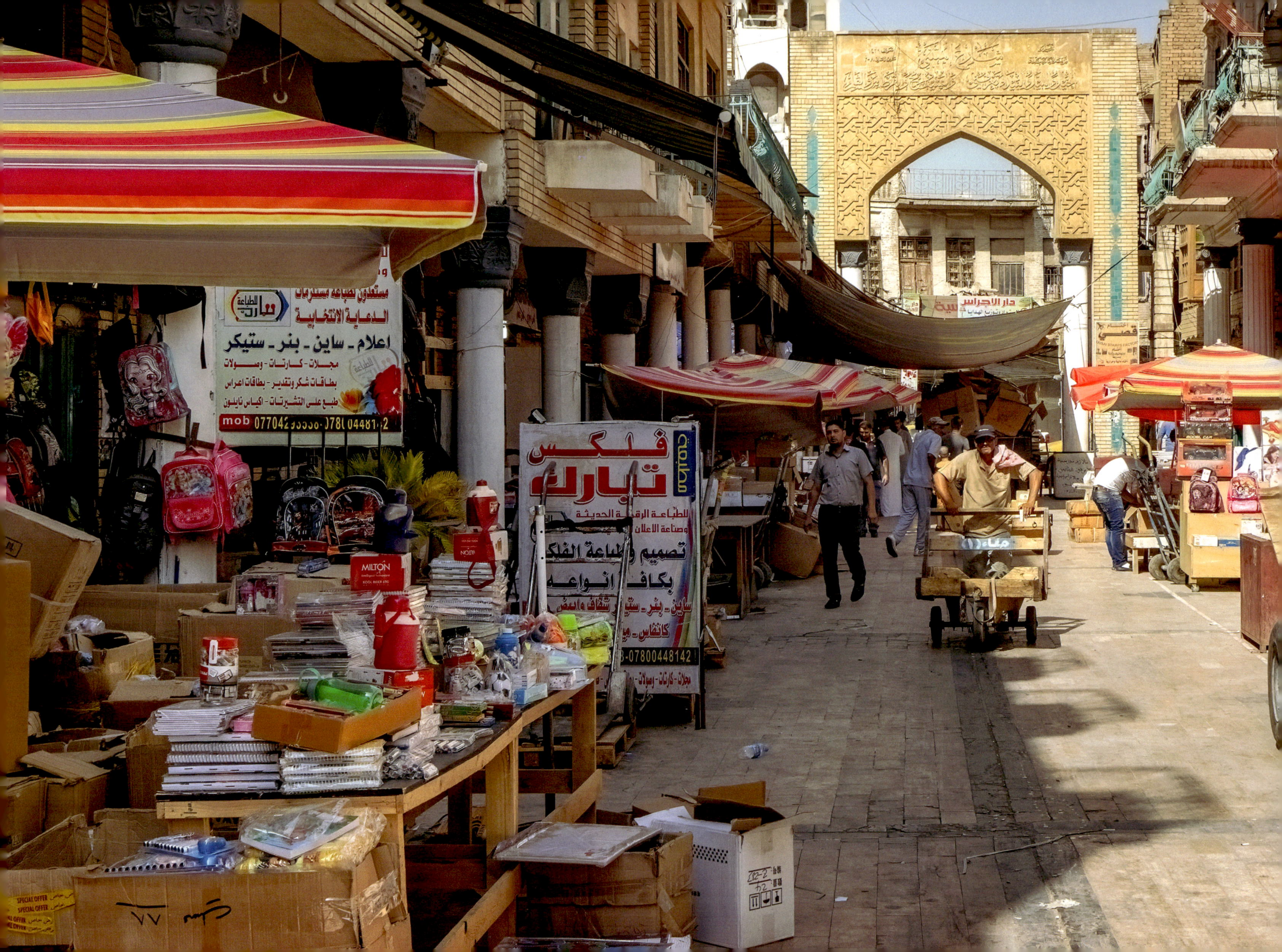
الطباعة
مستعدون لصناعة مستلزمات
الدعاية الانتخابية
اعلام - ساين - بنر - ستيكر
مجلات - كارتات - وصولات
بطاقات شكر وتقدير - بطاقات اعراس
طبع على التشيرتات - اكياس نايلون
mob 07704 0781 0448
فلكس
تبارك
للطباعة الرقمية الحديثة
وصناعة الاعلان
تصميم وطباعة الفلكس
بكافة انواعه
ساين - بنر - ستيكر
كانفاس
07800448142
دار الاجراس
MILTON
SPECIAL OFFER
٧٧

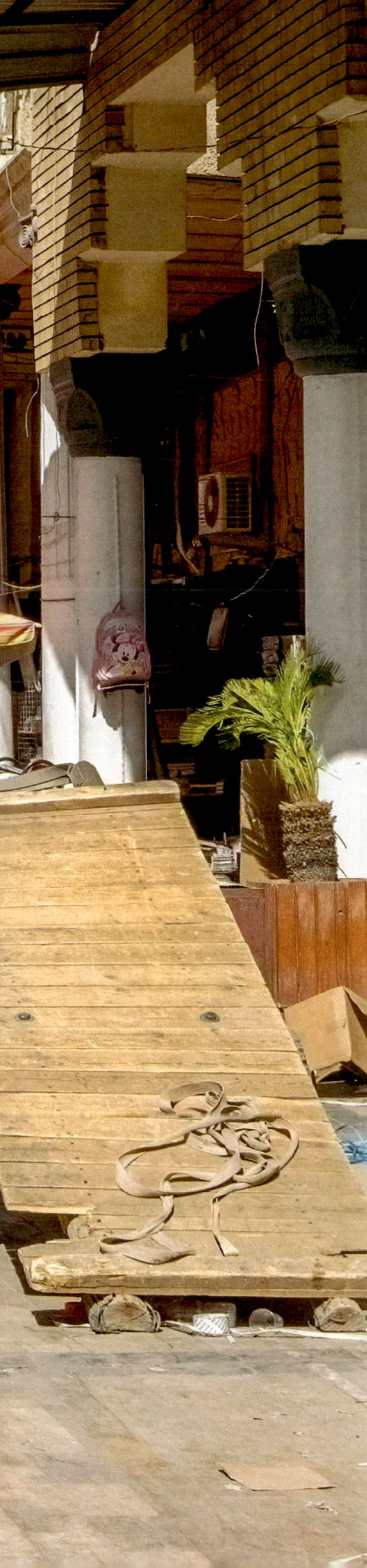

Al-Mutanabbi Street, Baghdad

Famous as the historic heart of Iraq's intellectual and literary community, this thoroughfare is named after a 10th-century poet. For centuries the street has been lined with bookshops and outdoor book stalls, alongside traditional cafes such as Shabandar Cafe. Together they create a cultural hub where writers, artists, and students gather, especially on Fridays. Over centuries of conflict, the street has been damaged but always repaired, ensuring Baghdad's enduring commitment to the written word.

RIGHT:

Rawanduz Canyon, Kurdistan

This breathtaking natural wonder is close to the city of Soran, and is known as Iraq's Grand Canyon. Its dramatic, lush landscape draws visitors to its deep gorges, winding rivers, and stunning panoramic viewpoints. It's a popular destination for nature lovers and adventurers.

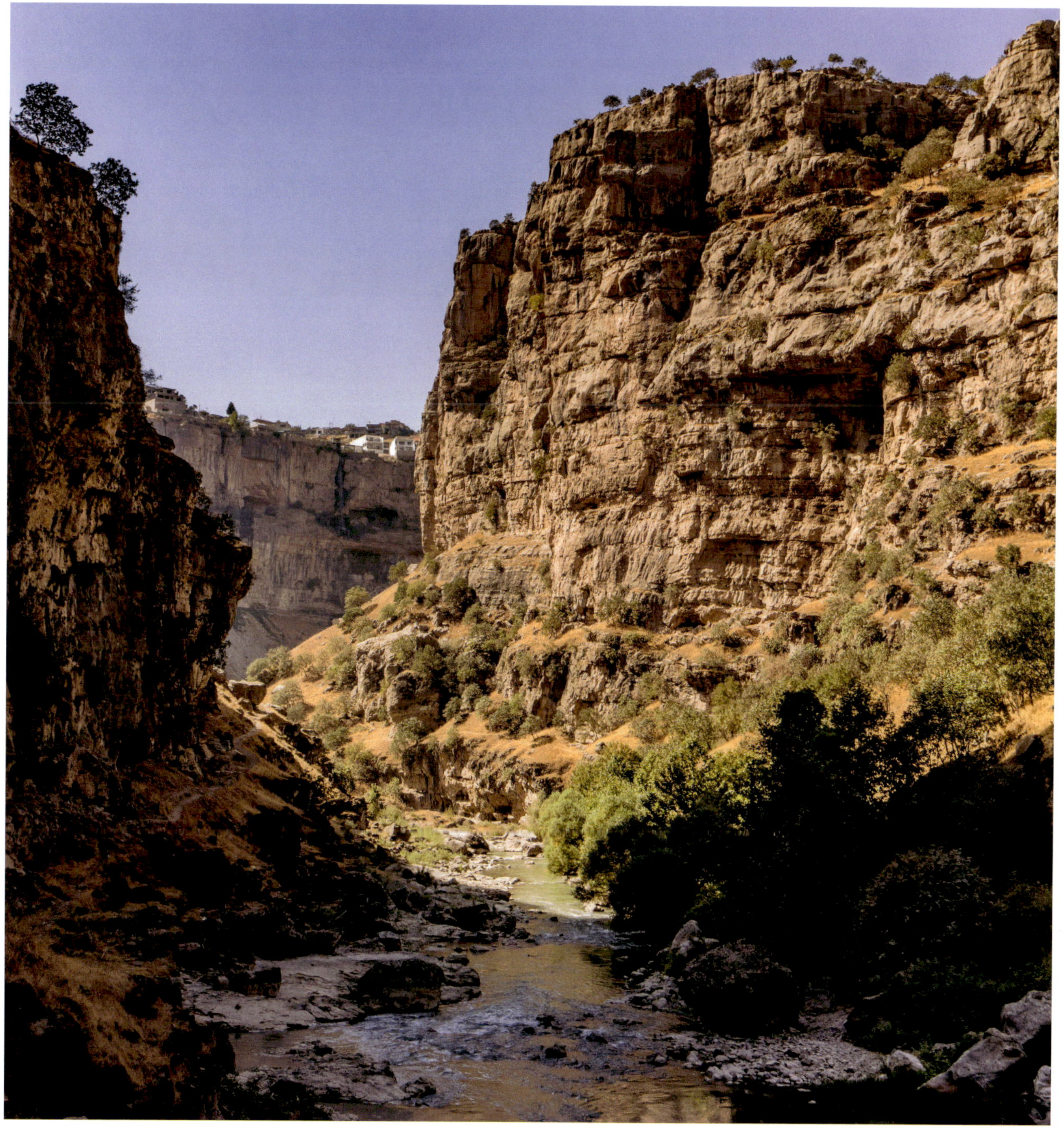

Ishtar Gate, Baghdad
More commonly known
as the 'Blue Gate of
Babylon', this gateway to
the ancient inner city was
built around 575 BCE by
King Nebuchadnezzar II,
making it the eighth and most
important city entrance. The
gate's façade was covered in
a brilliant blue-glazed brick,
a rare material resembling
lapis lazuli, and adorned with
reliefs of bulls and dragons,
symbolizing the famous gods
Adad and Marduk.

Imam Ali Shrine, Najaf
The most important building
in Najaf is the Imam Ali
Shrine. This religious
complex, with its golden
dome and minarets, is a
major Islamic pilgrimage
site and central to the city's
identity. It is understood to
be the burial place of Imam
Ali ibn Abi Talib, cousin and
son-in-law of the Prophet
Muhammad, who became the
first Shia Imam. This shrine is
considered by Shia Muslims
to be one of the holiest
places on Earth, after Mecca,
Medina, and Jerusalem.

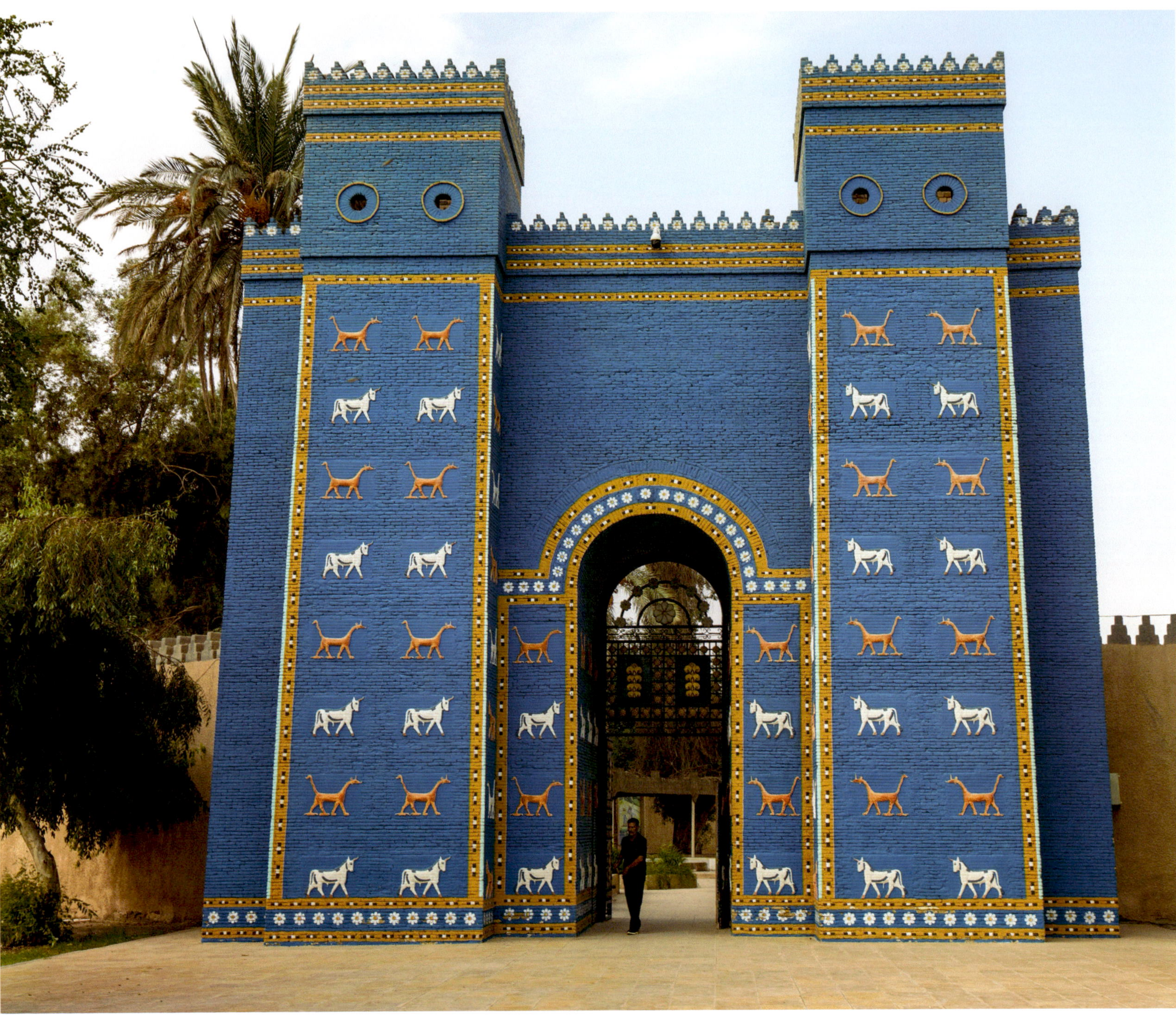

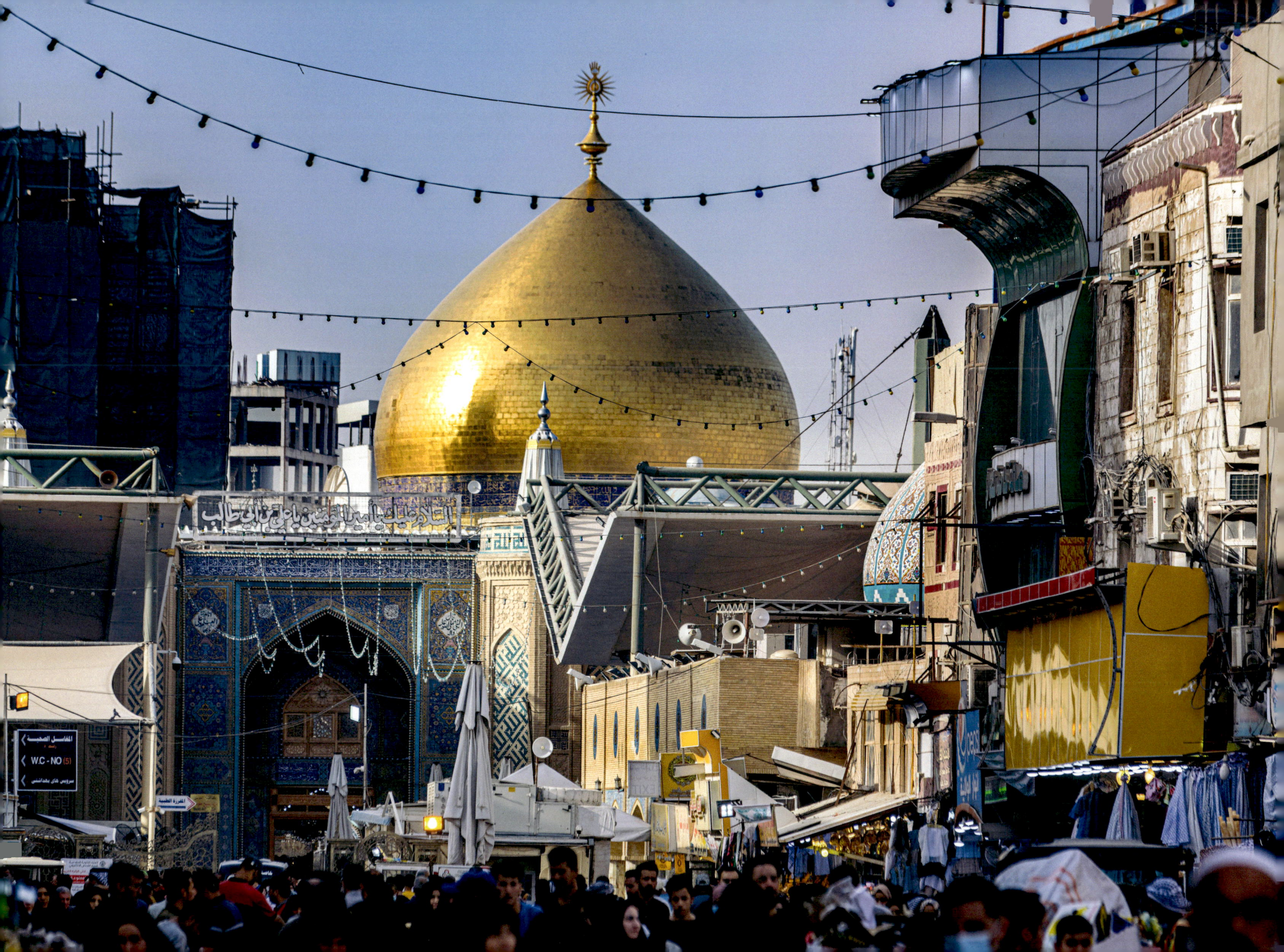

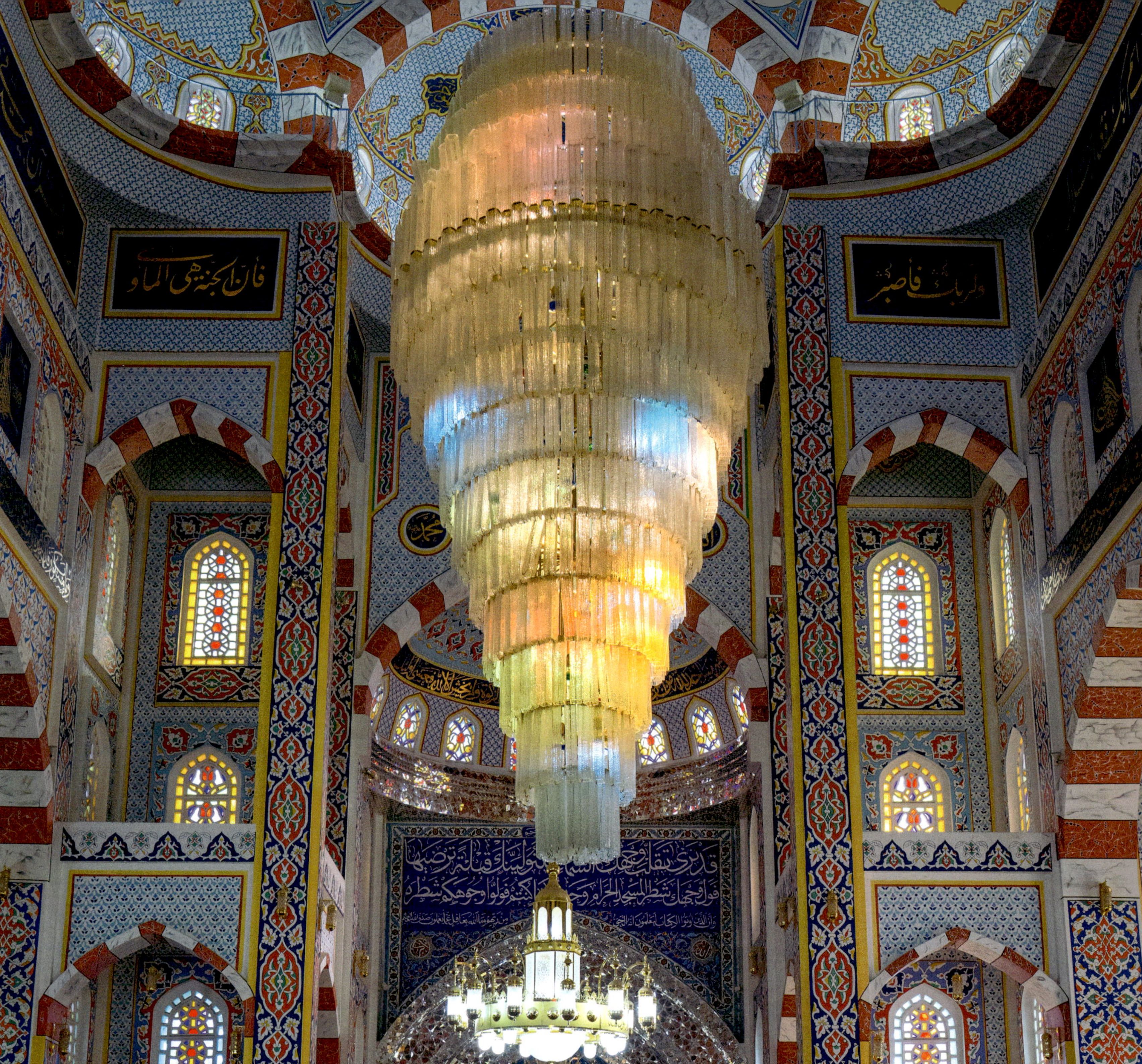

RIGHT:

Jalil Khayat Mosque, Erbil
Erbil's largest mosque was completed in 2007. It blends Ottoman, Abbasid, and Persian styles, representing much of the city's history. Externally it is reminiscent of Cairo's Muhammad Ali Mosque. Its stunning interior has intricate mosaics, calligraphy, and a massive central dome filled with lights.

OPPOSITE LEFT:

Cuneiform tablet, National Museum of Iraq
The museum holds a vast collection of cuneiform tablets including some of the earliest examples of writing in the world. The tablets document everything from administrative records and laws to religious texts and myths, providing unparalleled insights into ancient Sumerian society.

OPPOSITE RIGHT TOP & BOTTOM:

Hatra, Nineveh
This UNESCO World Heritage site was the fortified capital of a small Arab kingdom and a crucial trading hub under the Parthian Empire, famed for its huge double-wall circular defences. Architecturally, it uniquely blends Hellenistic and Roman styles with Eastern decorative features, reflecting its position as a cultural and trading crossroads between the Roman and Parthian Empires.

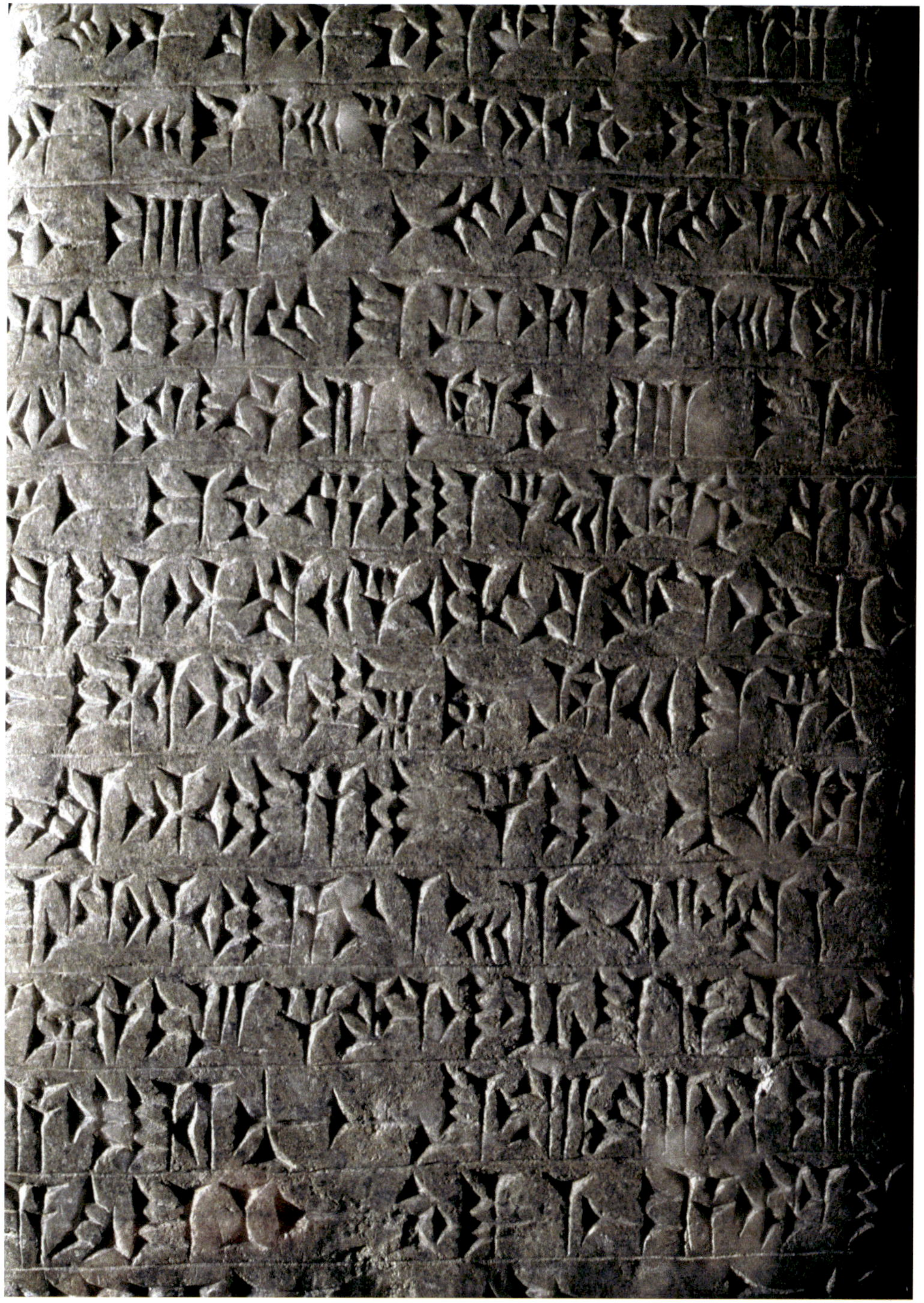

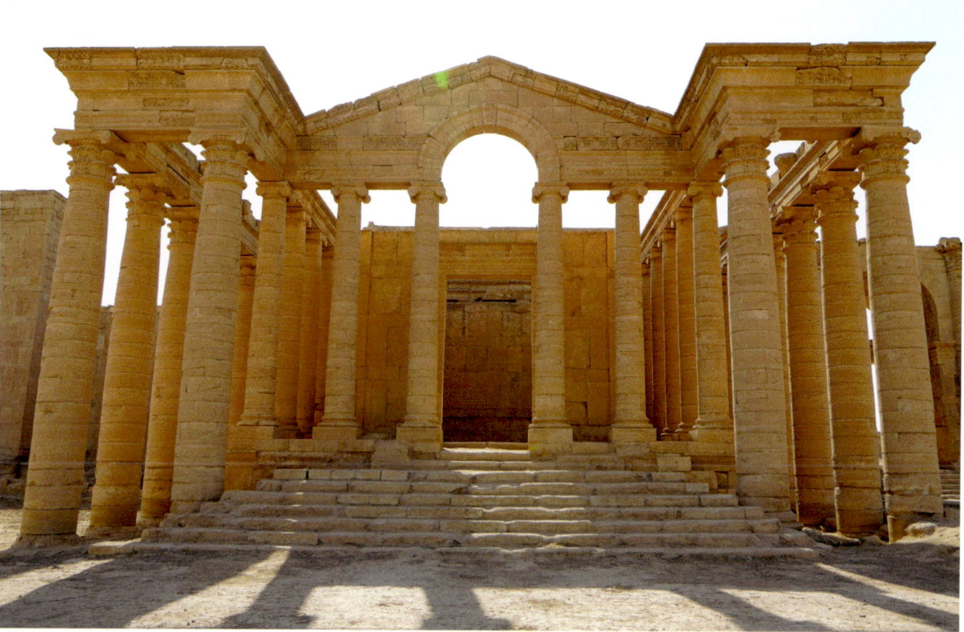

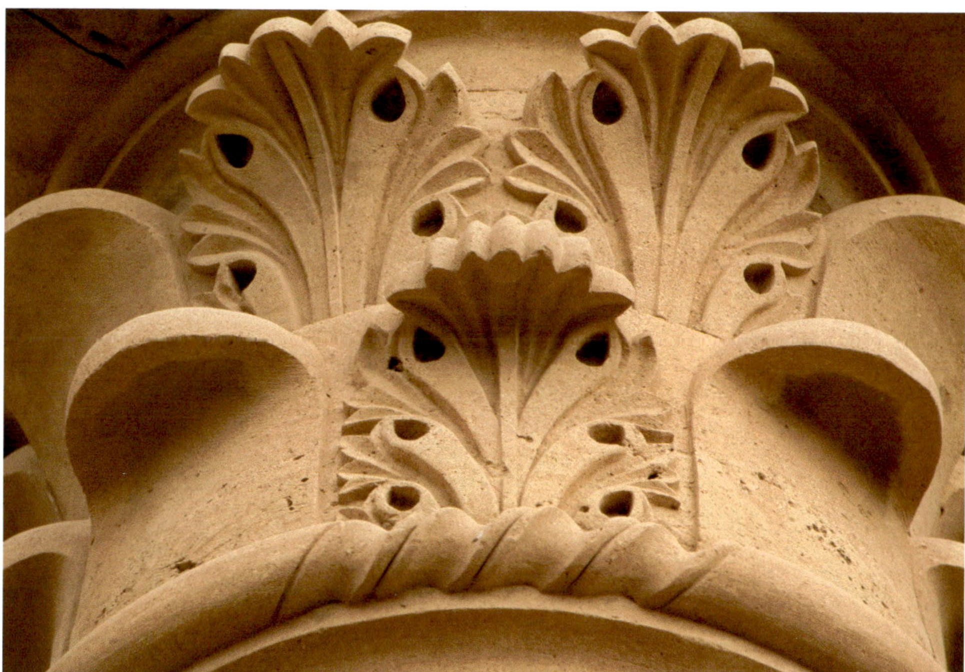

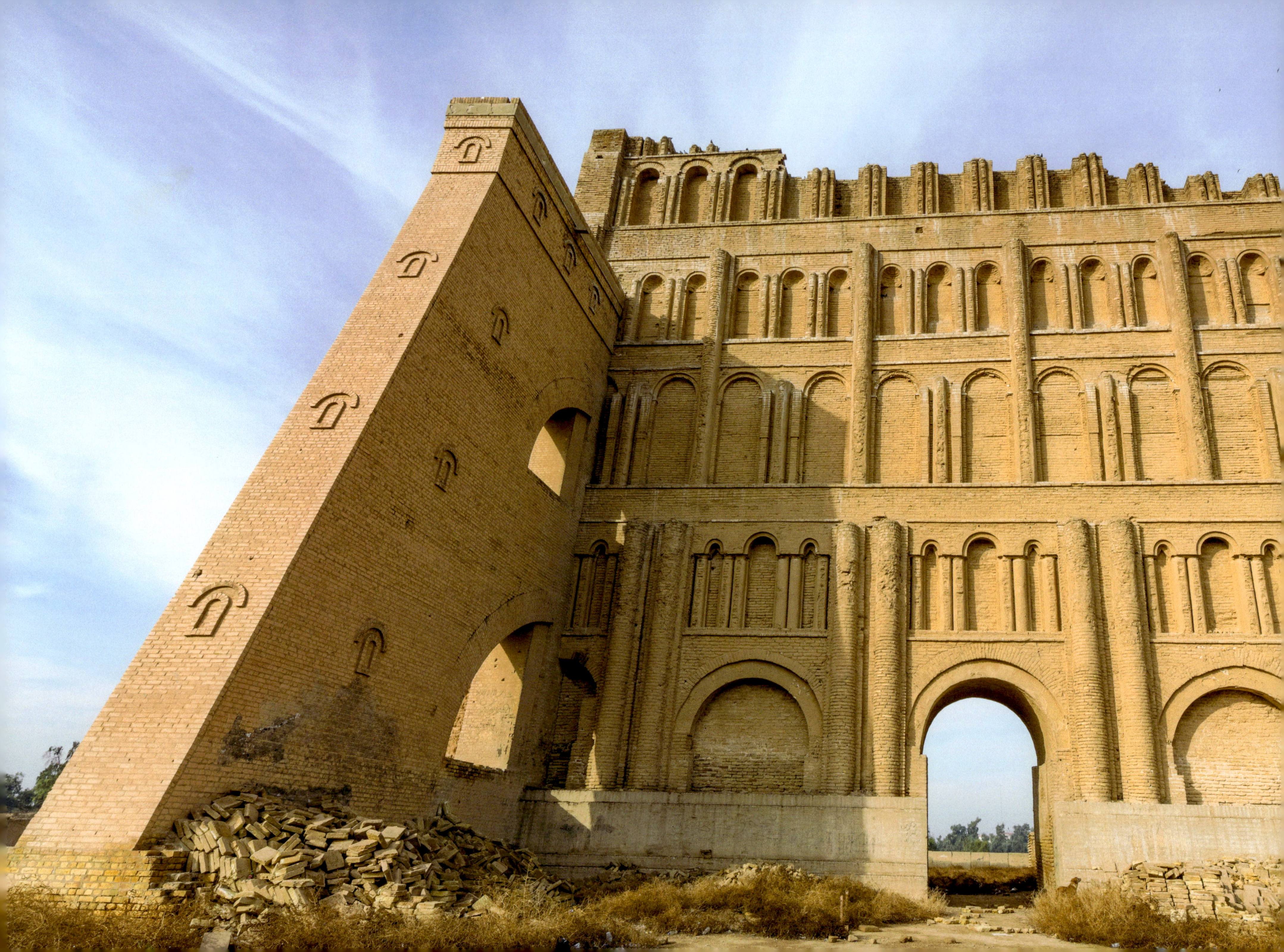

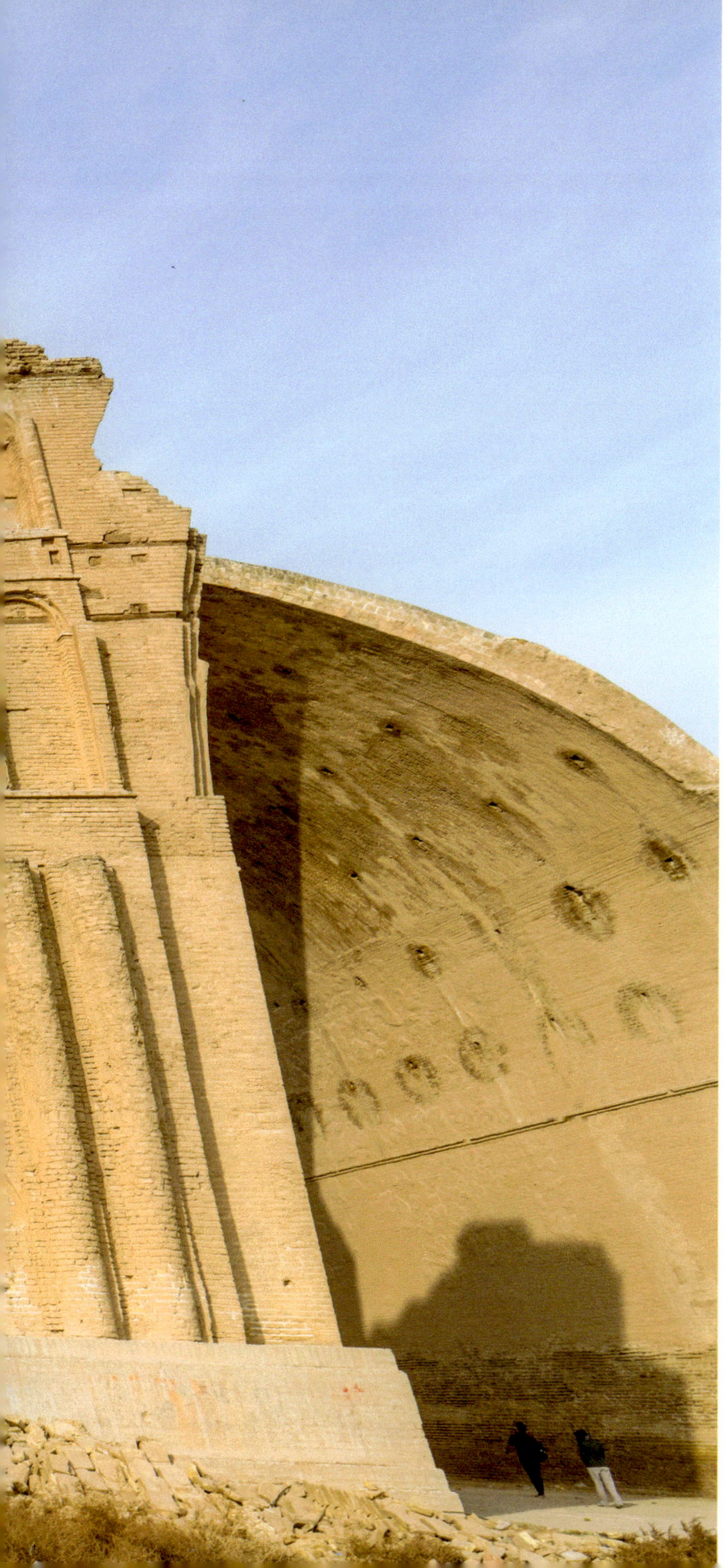

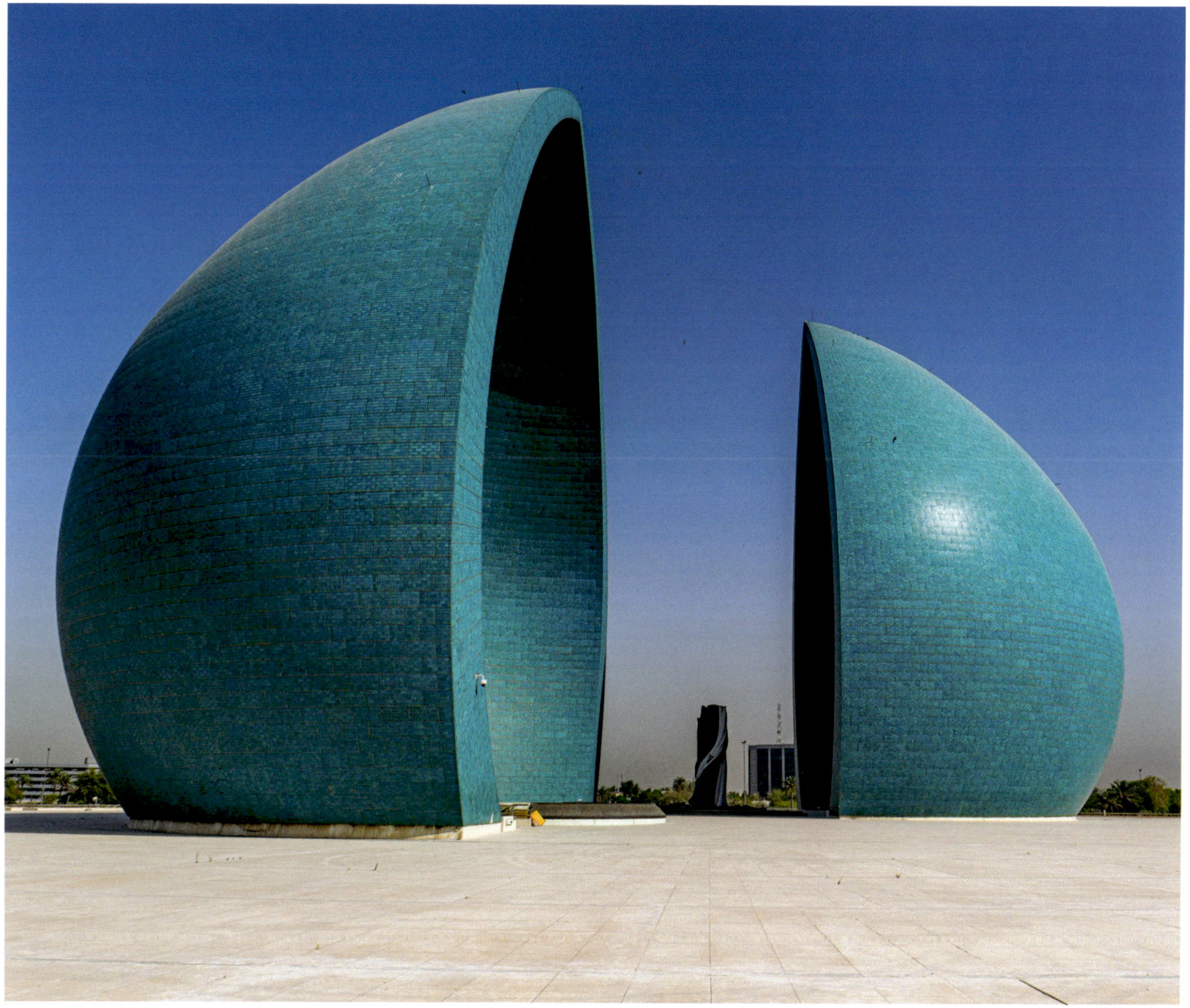

Arch of Ctesiphon, Ctesiphon, Baghdad

For over 800 years, Ctesiphon served as the royal capital of two successive Iranian empires. The city was the political and economic centre of the Parthian and the Sasanian eras, flourishing as a trading hub along the Silk Road. Today, its most famous ruin is the Taq Kasra, a magnificent Sasanian-era arch that is one of the largest single-span brick arches in the world.

Martyr's Memorial, Baghdad

The Al-Shaheed Monument was completed in 1983 and designed by Iraqi sculptor Ismail Fatah al-Turk. Originally, it was built to honour the many Iraqi soldiers who died in the Iran-Iraq War. The iconic design is a huge split turquoise dome, with the two halves offset to reveal an eternal flame and built on a circular platform within an artificial lake. The sculpture now serves as a memorial for all of Iraq's martyrs.

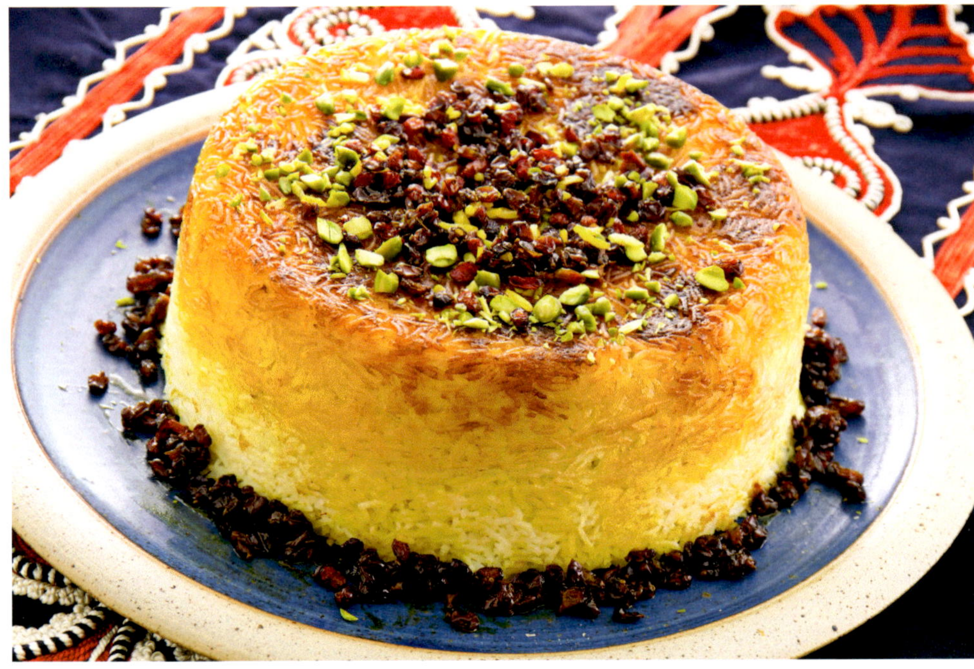

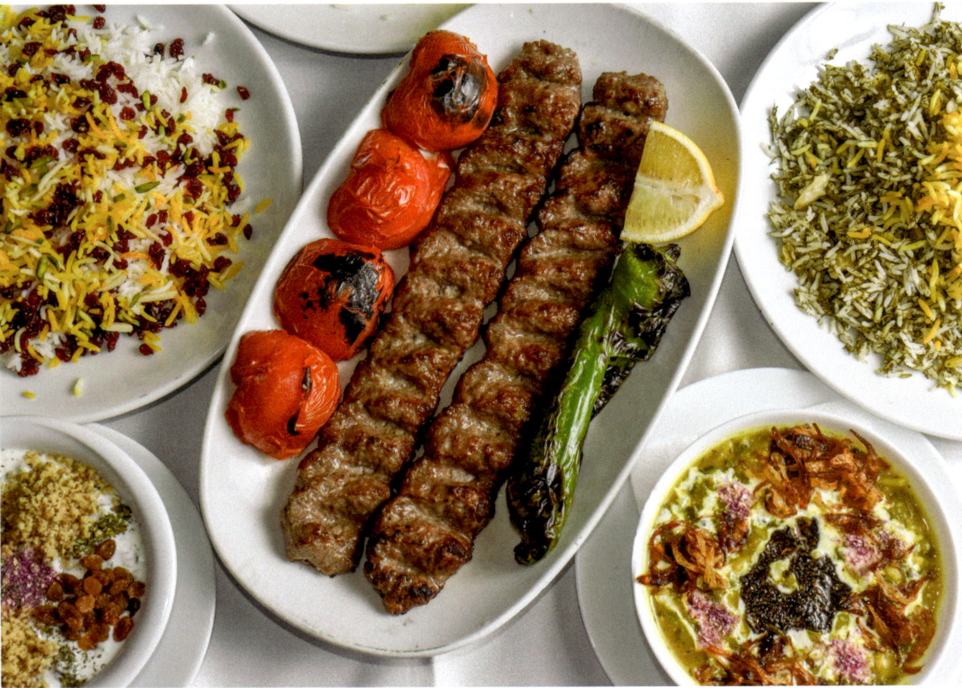

LEFT TOP:

Tah-chin

This Persian rice dish has a name meaning, 'arranged at the bottom'. This refers to a mixture of yogurt, saffron, and egg yolks that forms a crispy, golden crust on the bottom of the pot. The dish is typically layered with chicken or lamb, creating a rich savoury taste.

LEFT BOTTOM:

Persian kebabs

Central to Iranian cuisine, these kebabs are renowned for their tenderness and flavour. Made from ground meat (koobideh) or chunks of lamb, beef, or chicken (joojeh), they are marinated and grilled to tasty perfection, and usually served with saffron rice.

RIGHT:

Tehran traffic

A combination of a large population, a high number of cars, and an insufficient road network leads to severe gridlock, especially during rush hours (mornings and late afternoons). To combat this, the city has implemented a congestion zone where vehicles are charged a fee to enter, and has also developed an extensive metro system and Bus Rapid Transit (BRT) lanes.

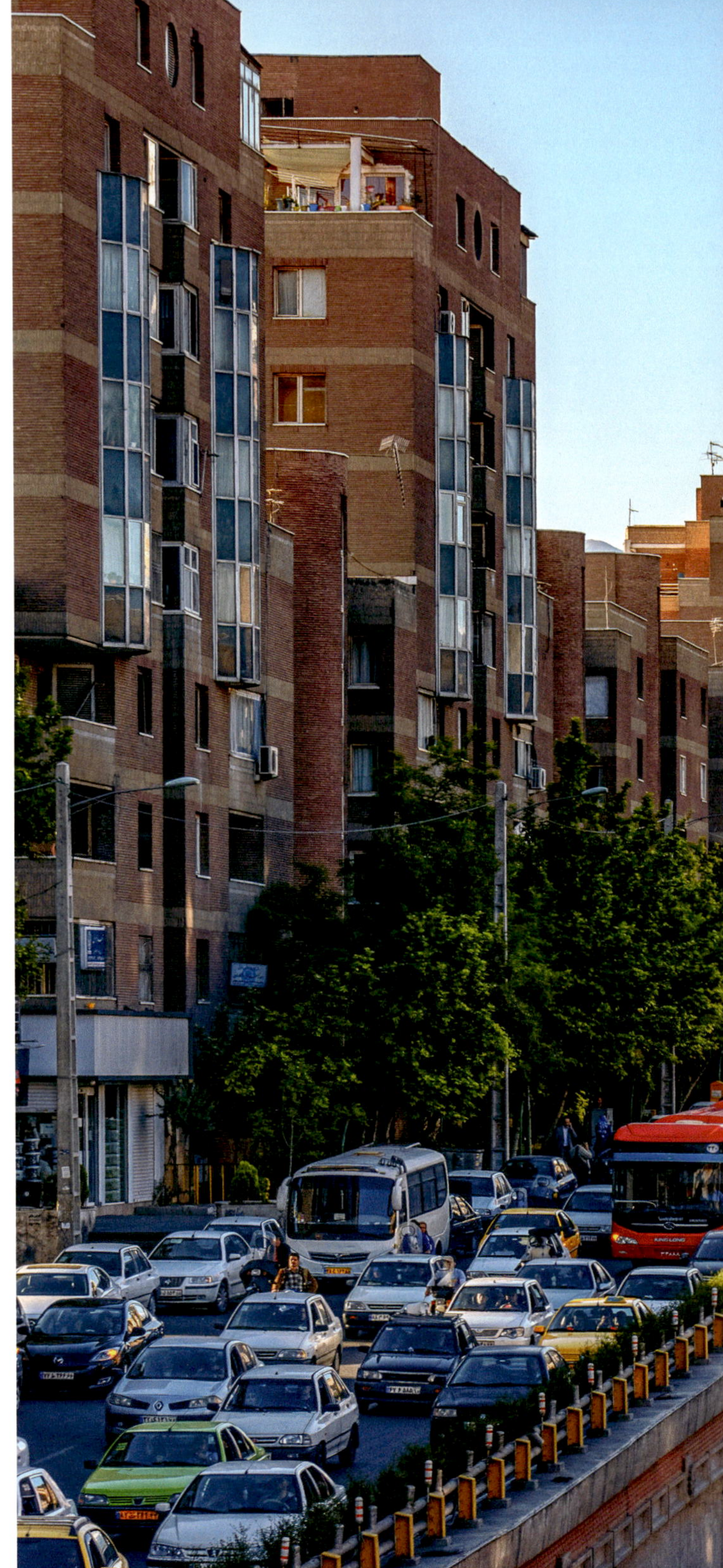

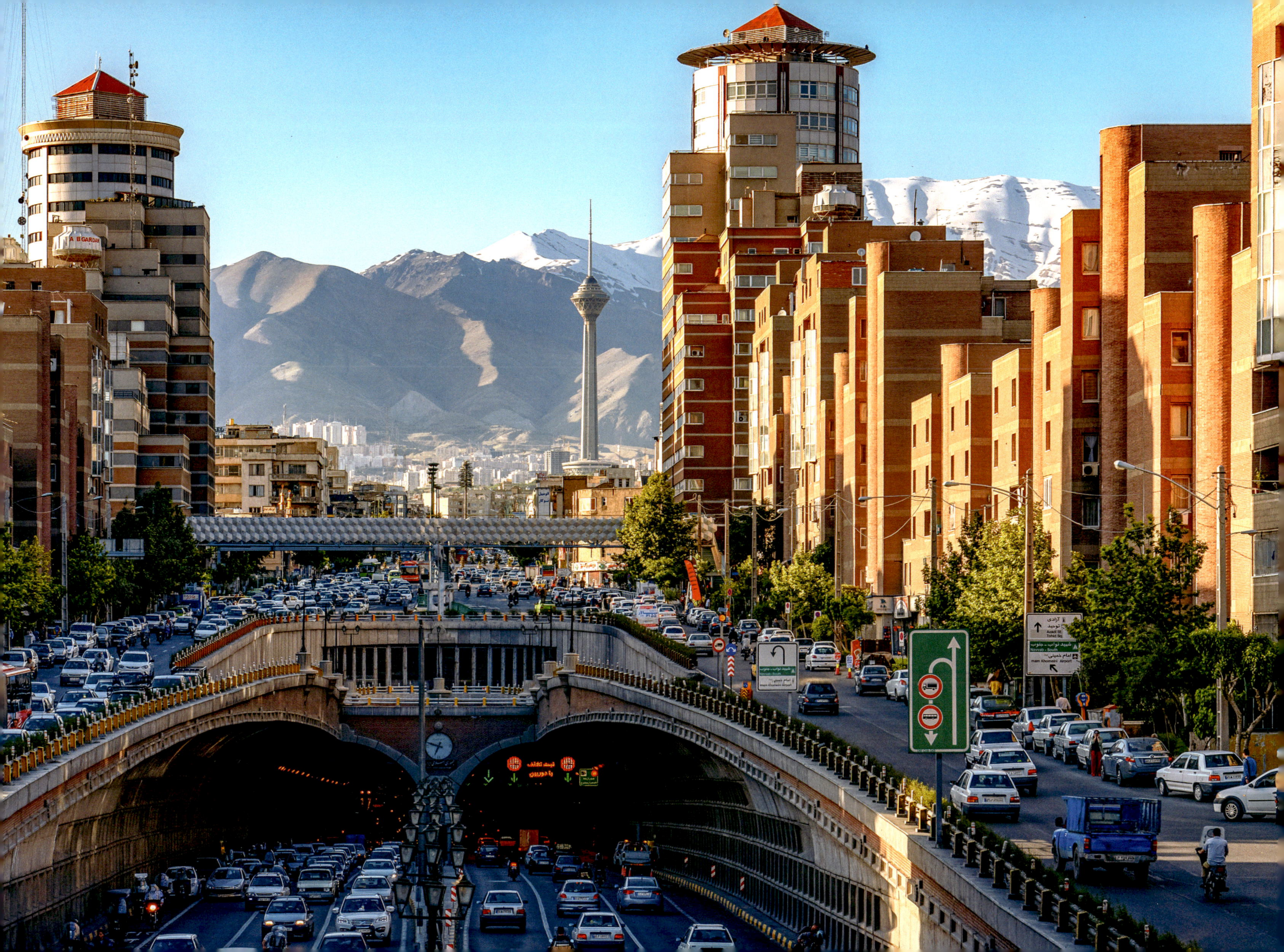

Iranian ingredients
Iranian cuisine is renowned
for its aromatic spices and
the wide array of delicious
dried fruits. Iranian kitchens
and markets are filled with
spices that include saffron,
often called 'red gold' for its
colour and musky fragrance.
Popular too is sumac, with its
tangy citrus flavour, and dried
limes. Popular dried fruits
include dates, figs, apricots,
and zereshk (barberries),
which are used in many
dishes, particularly rice.

Ski resort, Shemshak
Shemshak is known for its
steep runs and awkward
terrain, which tend to attract
more advanced skiers and
snowboarders. Shemshak
is primarily known for its
winter sports, but the area is
also popular in the summer
for hiking and enjoying the
clear mountain air away from
the city.

Alborz Mountains, Tehran
The Alborz rise majestically
north of Tehran and
dominate the city skyline,
especially in winter when they
become a popular destination
for skiing and other winter
sports. These mountains
provide a spectacular escape
from the city, attracting both
locals and international
visitors with their high
altitudes, abundant snowfall,
and well-equipped slopes.

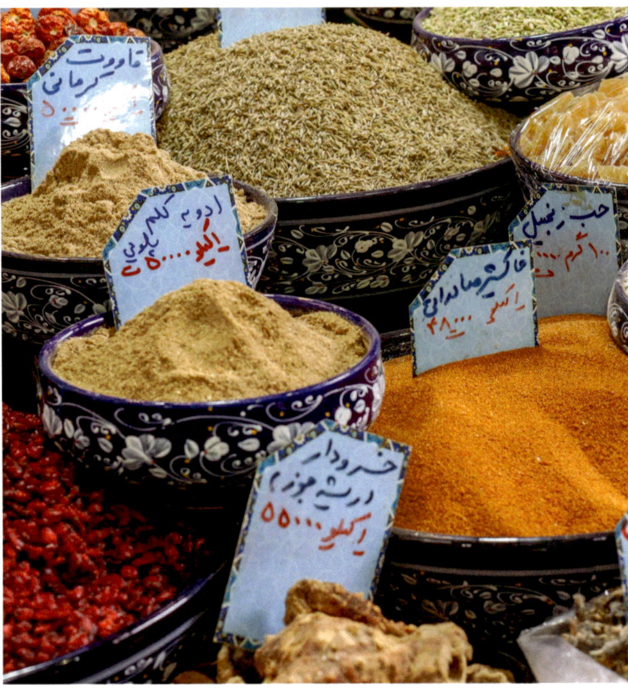

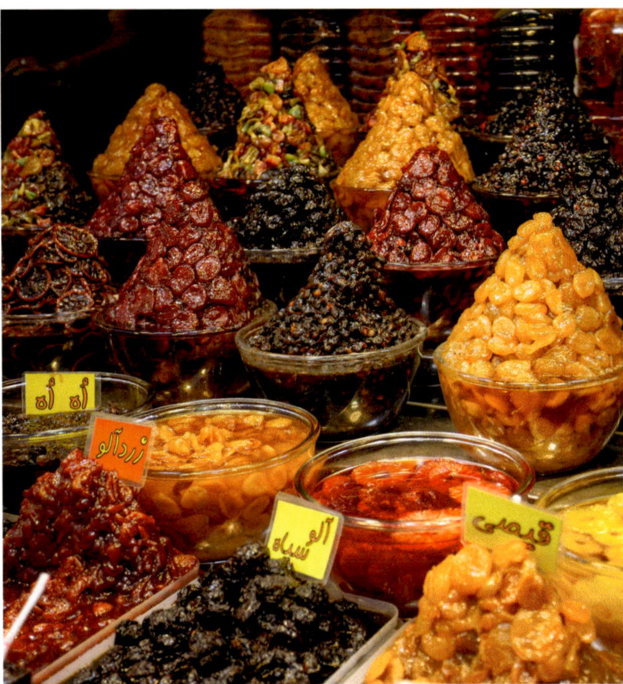

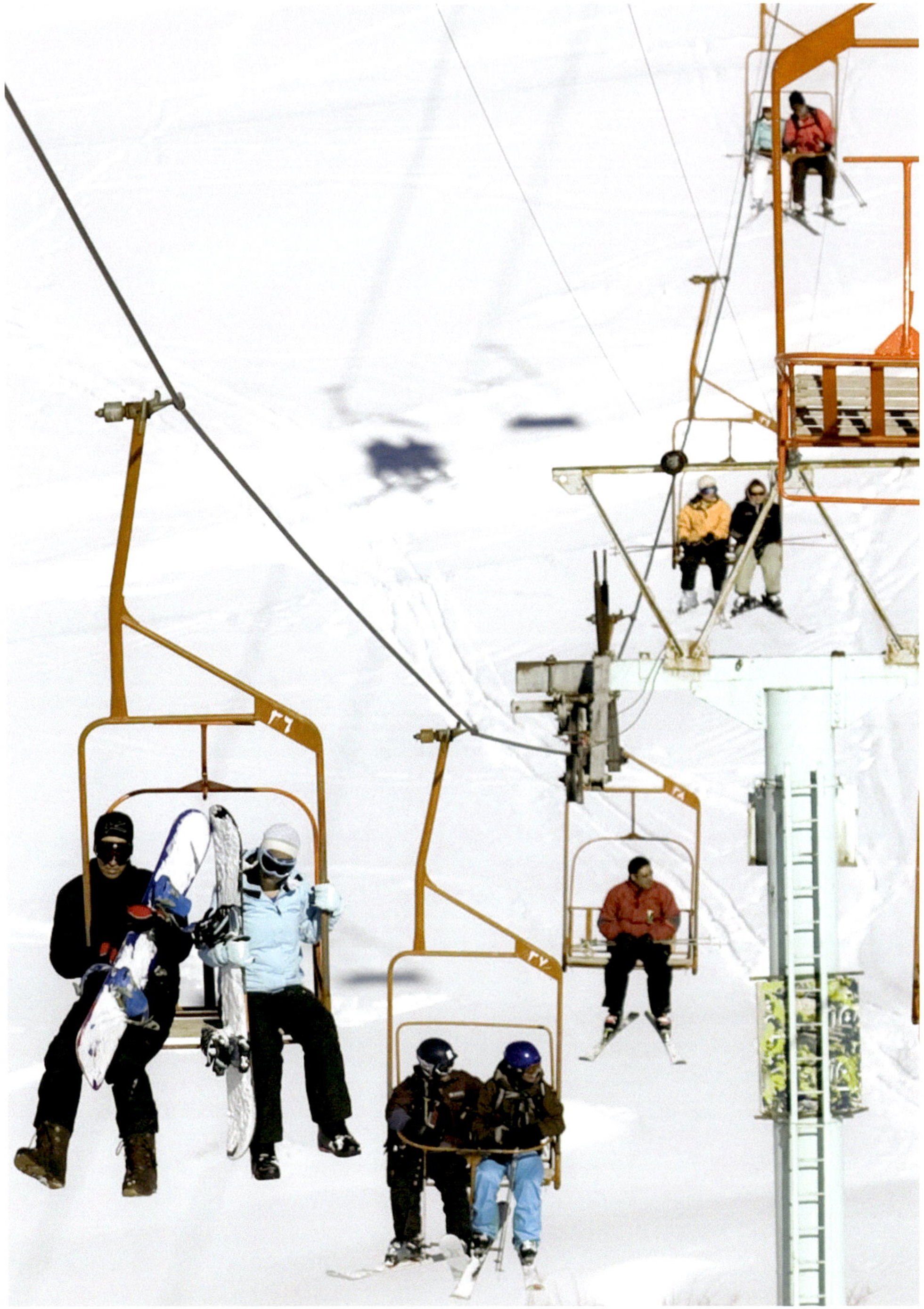

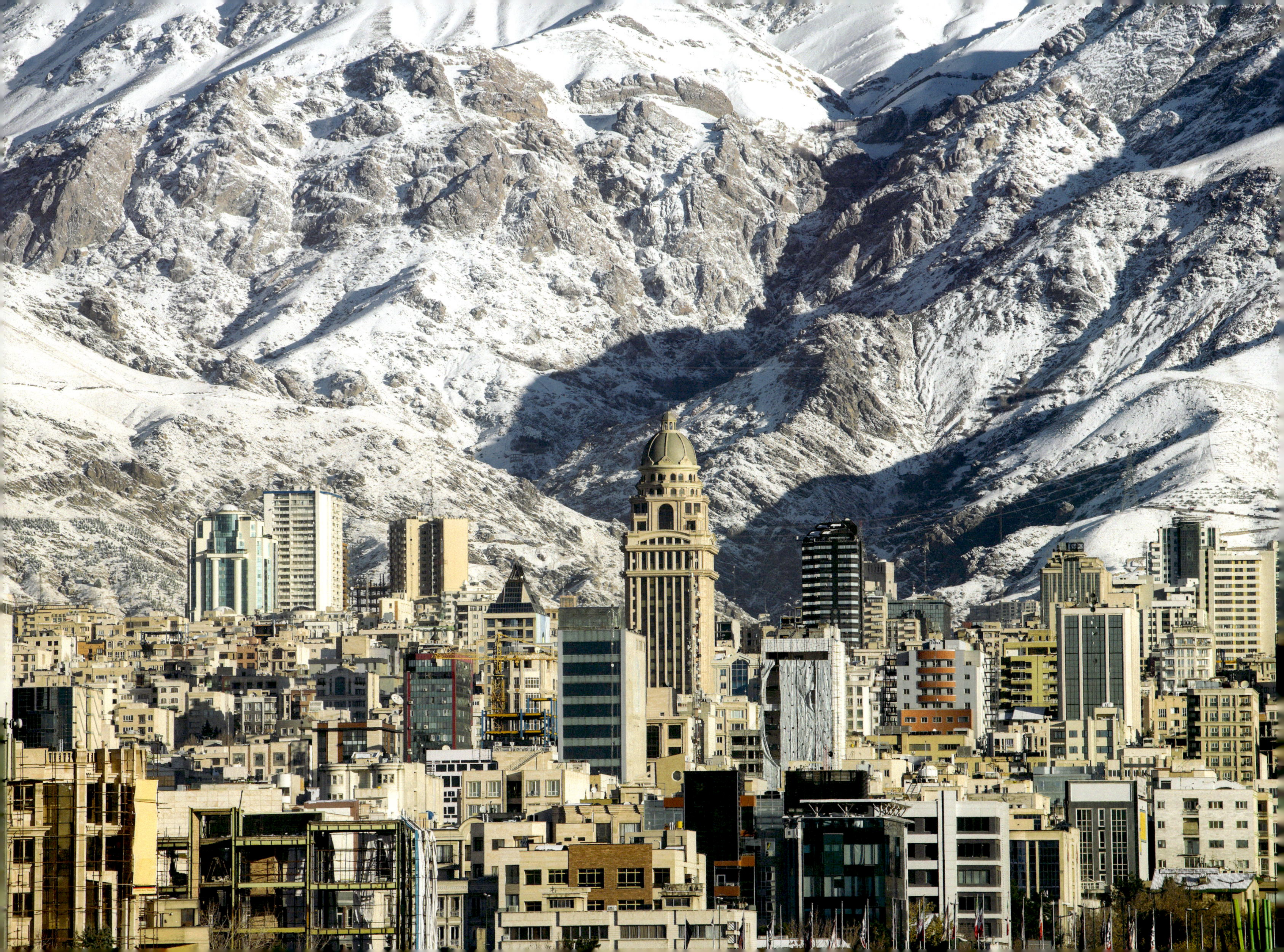

Naqsh-e Jahan Square, Isfahan

This masterpiece of Safavid architecture was built in the early 17th century under Shah Abbas I and designed to be the heart of the new capital. It is bordered by four iconic structures: the Shah (Imam) Mosque, the Sheikh Lotfollah Mosque (a part of its highly decorated ceiling is pictured opposite), the Ali Qapu Palace, and the entrance to the Imperial Bazaar. Imam Square, as it is more usually called, remains the vibrant heart of Isfahan. It is a popular gathering place for Iranians and visitors alike, filled with horse-drawn carriages, fountains and endless traditional cafes. The surrounding buildings are still in use, with a bustling bazaar filled with artisans and merchants, and mosques that are architectural and religious wonders.

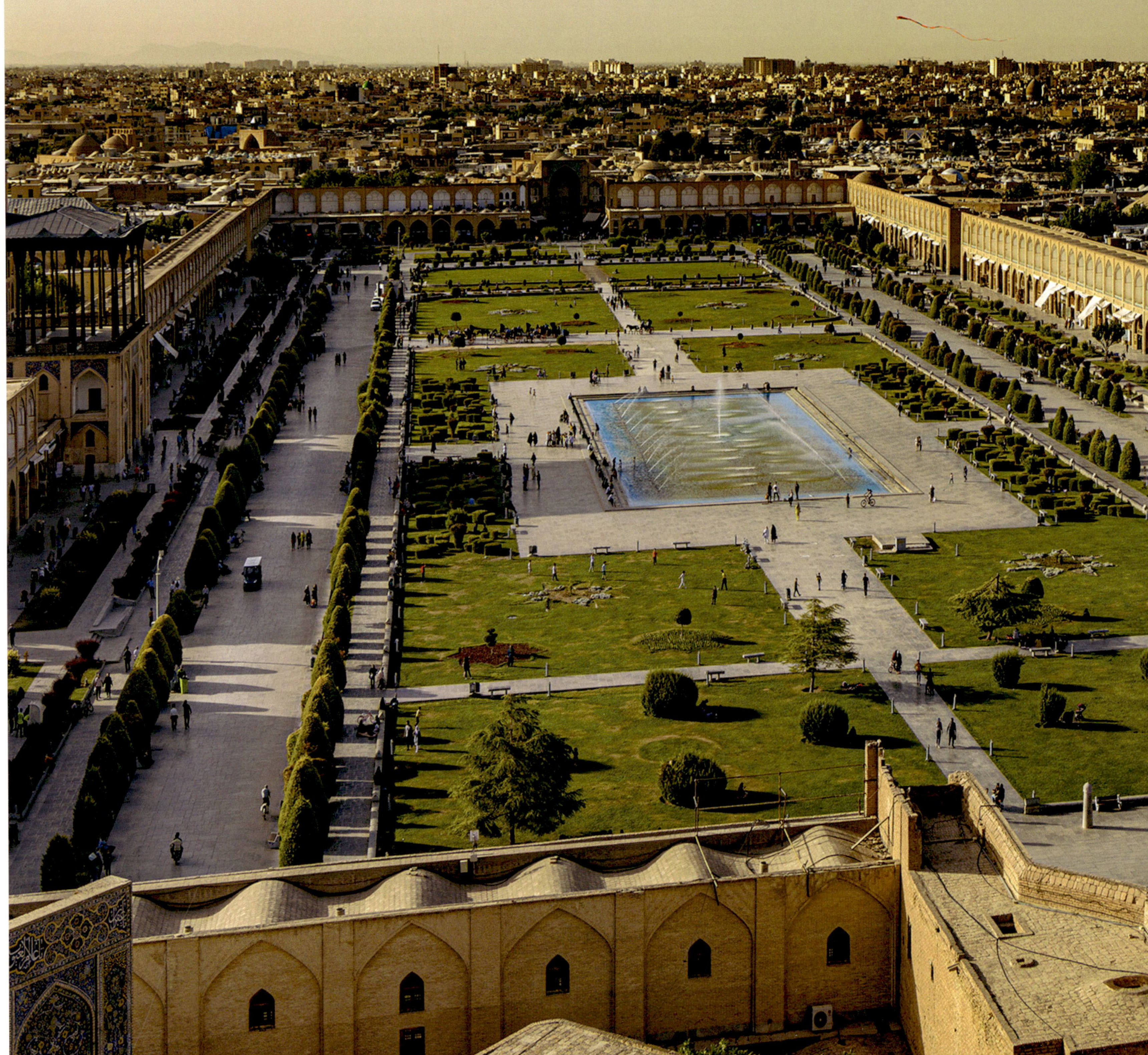

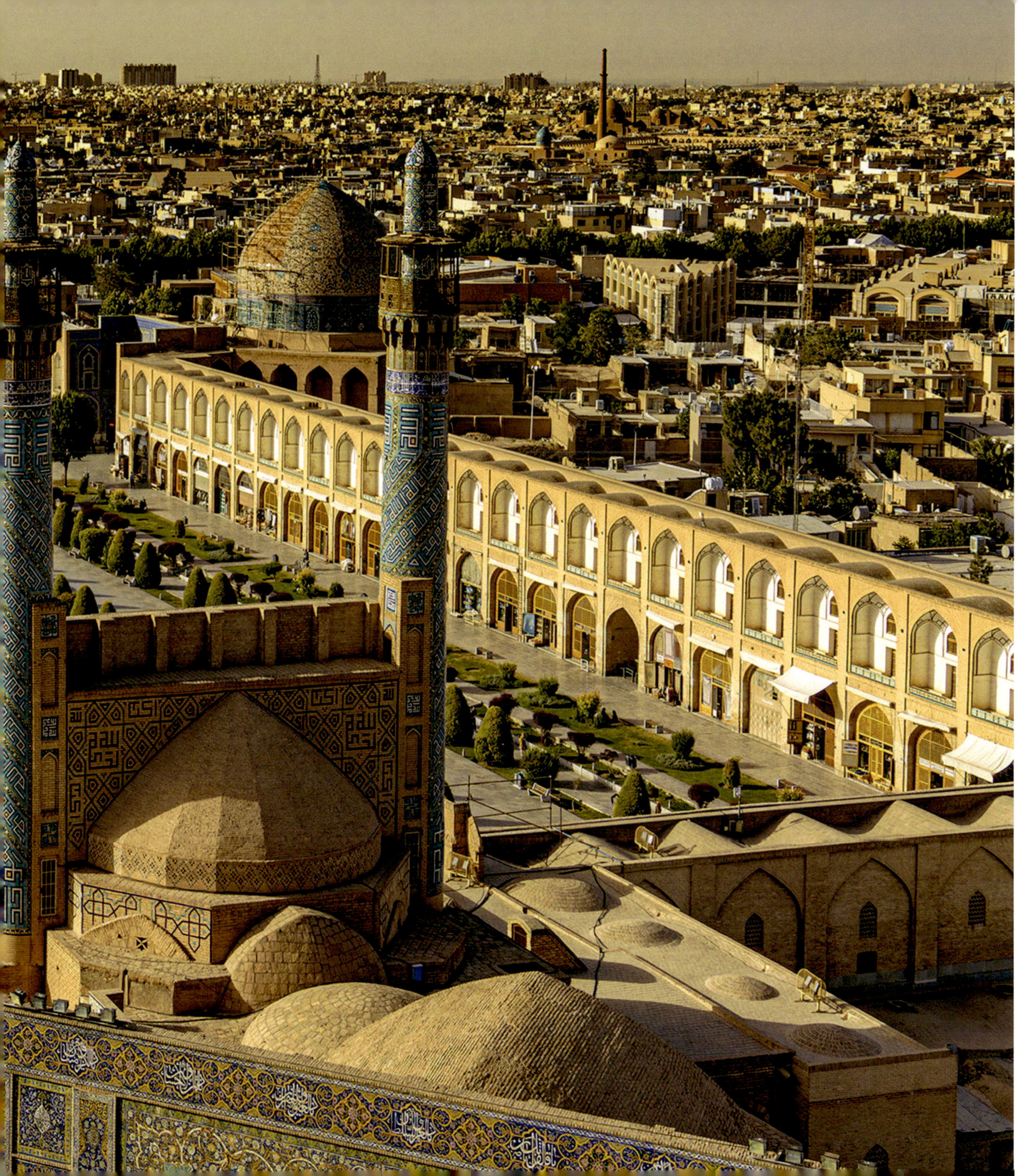

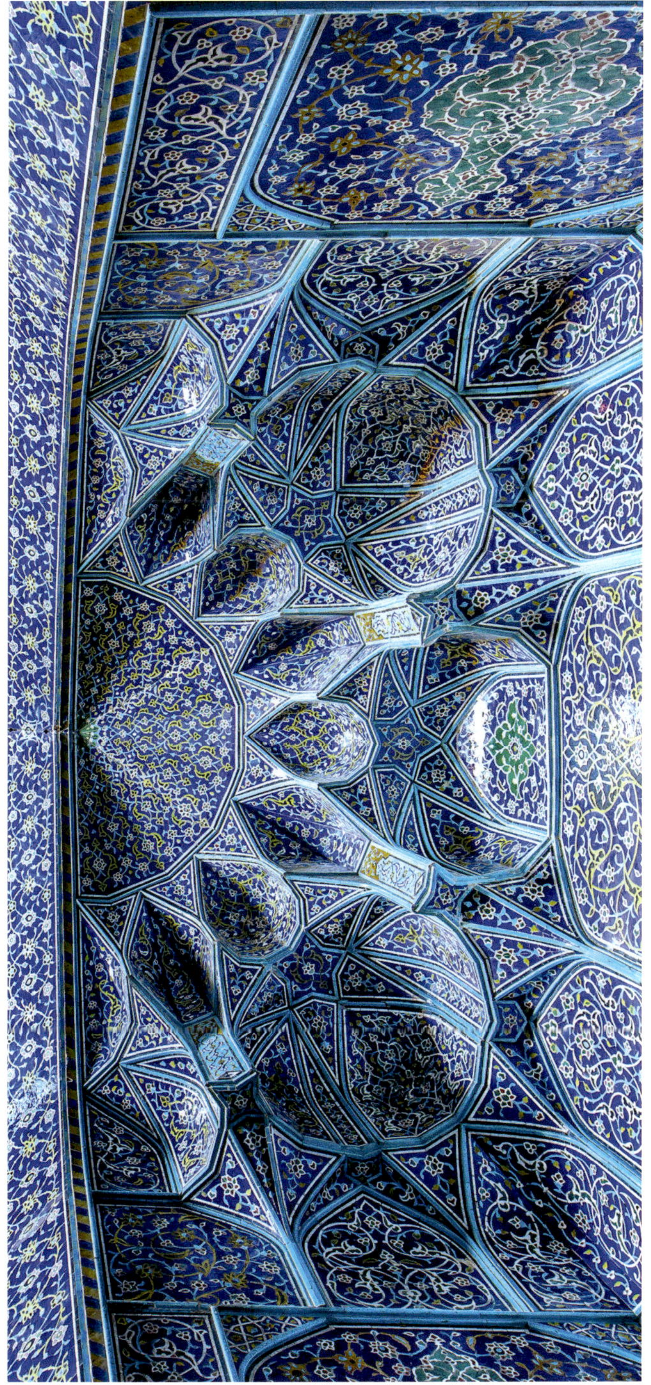

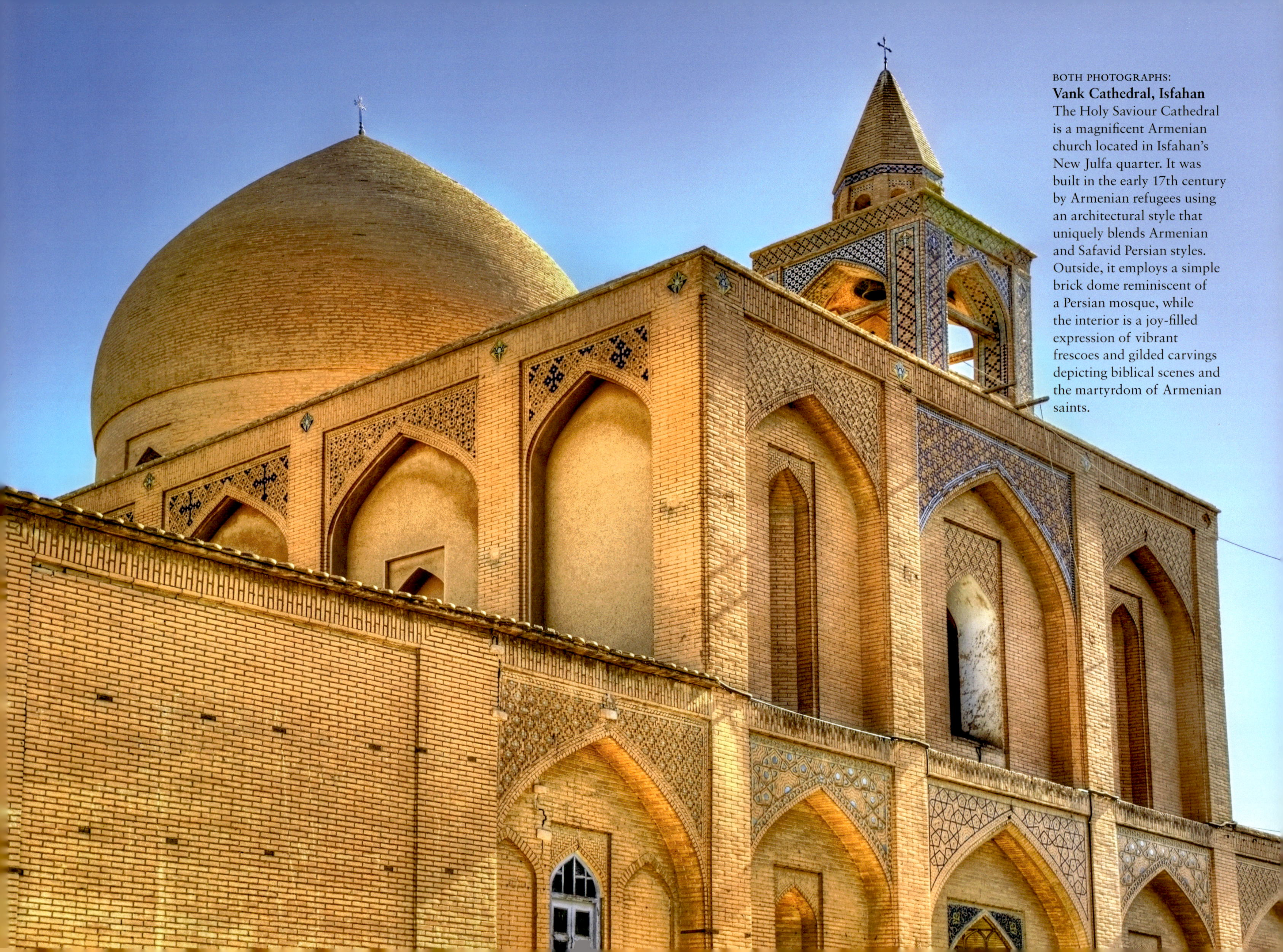

Vank Cathedral, Isfahan
The Holy Saviour Cathedral is a magnificent Armenian church located in Isfahan's New Julfa quarter. It was built in the early 17th century by Armenian refugees using an architectural style that uniquely blends Armenian and Safavid Persian styles. Outside, it employs a simple brick dome reminiscent of a Persian mosque, while the interior is a joy-filled expression of vibrant frescoes and gilded carvings depicting biblical scenes and the martyrdom of Armenian saints.

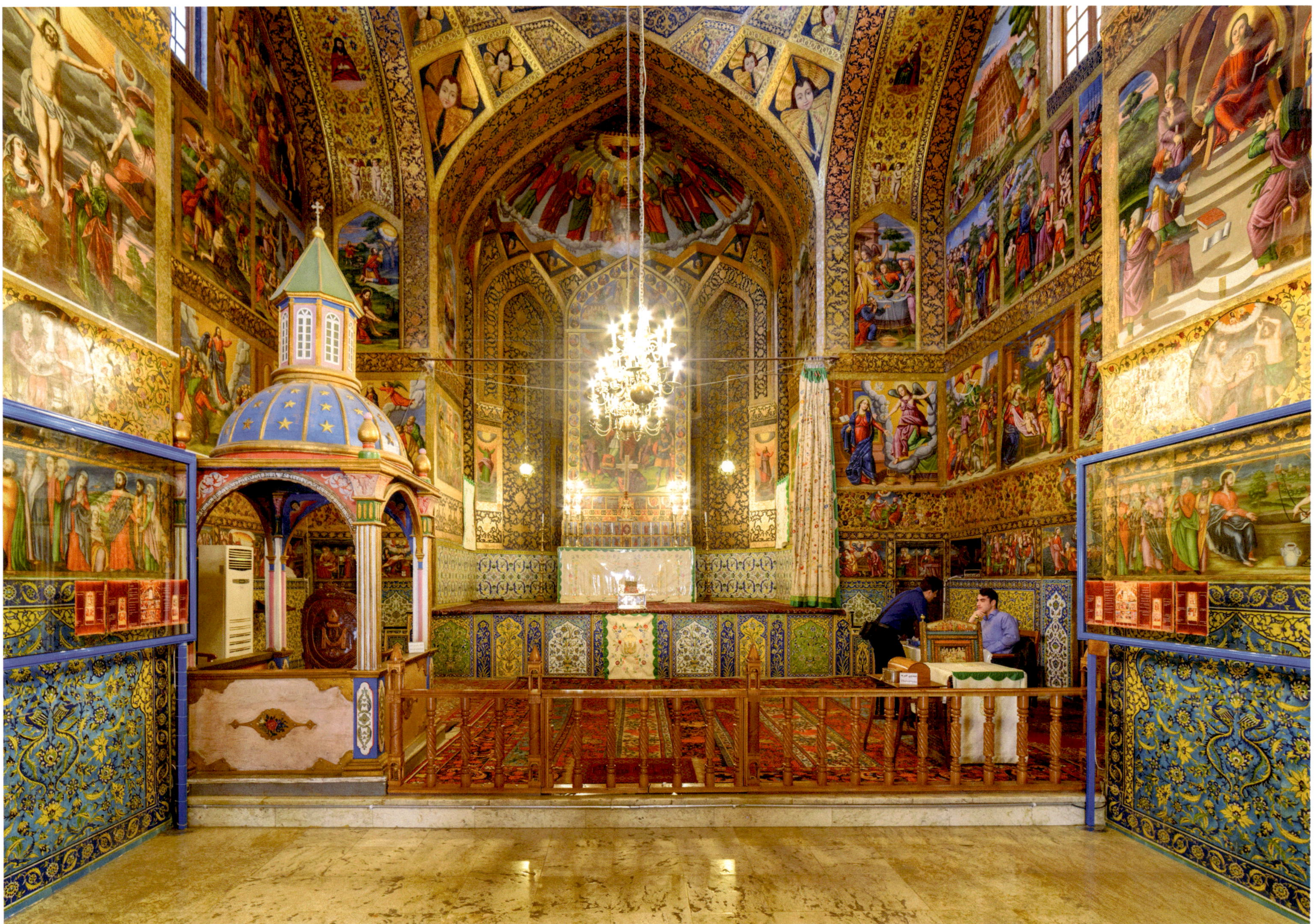

Shah Mosque, Isfahan
The four minarets of
this majestic mosque are
excellent examples of Safavid
architectural mastery. Two
towering minarets flank the
entrance to the mosque, while
two more stand on either
side of the sanctuary's huge
dome. Adorned with intricate
turquoise and blue tilework,
the minarets showcase the
sophisticated craftsmanship
of the 17th century.

Persepolis, Fars Province
Persepolis, meaning 'City of
the Persians', is an ancient
city in Iran that served as
the ceremonial capital of the
Achaemenid Empire. Founded
by Darius I around 518 BCE,
the city was built on a vast
terrace and expanded by
successors such as Xerxes I.

Persepolis was a symbol
of the empire's power and
prosperity, used primarily for
royal receptions and festivals.
However, its glory was short-
lived. In 330 BCE, Alexander
the Great plundered and
burned the city, bringing
an end to its reign. Today,
Persepolis is a UNESCO
World Heritage site that
holds a vital position in Iran's
rich ancient past.

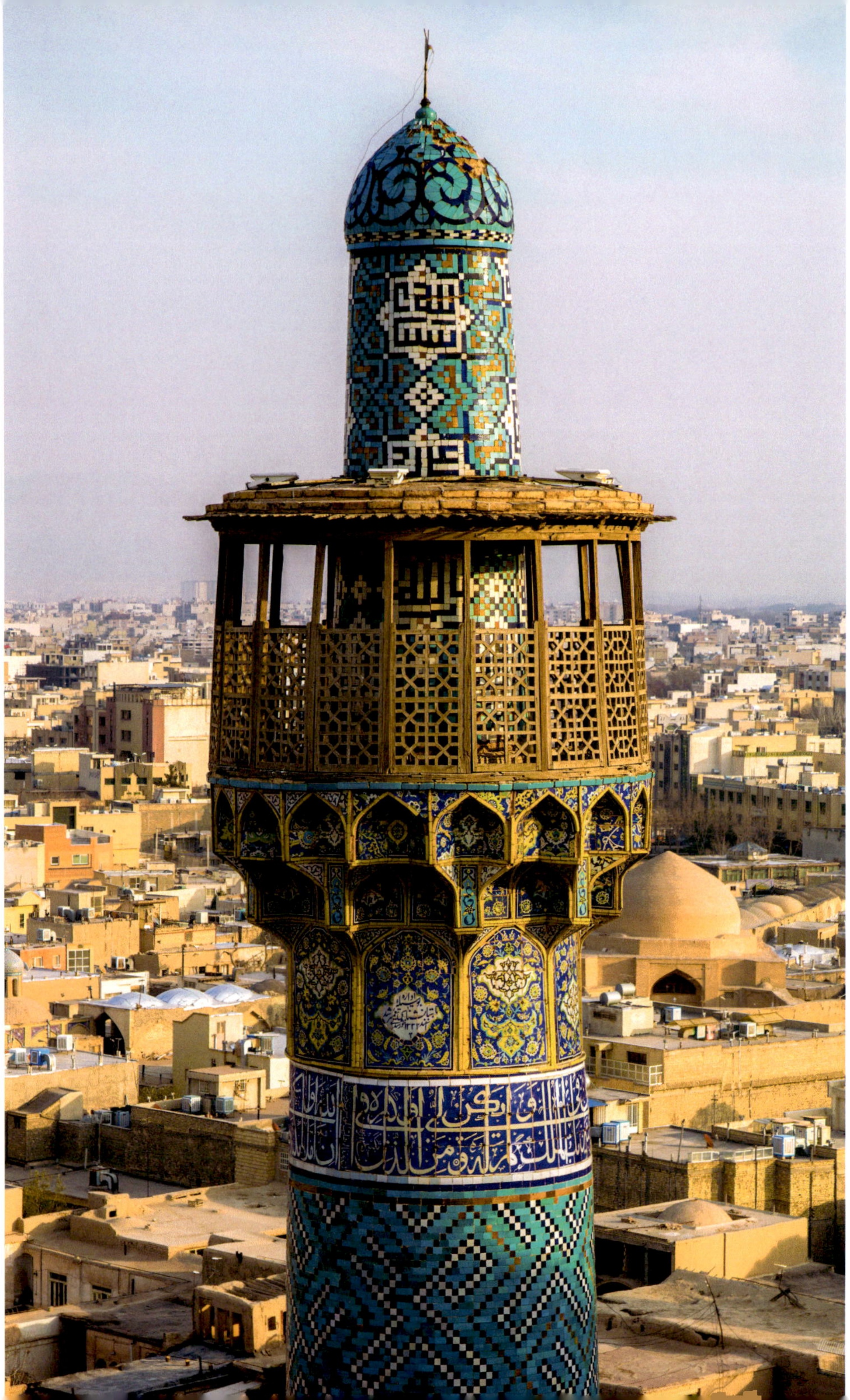

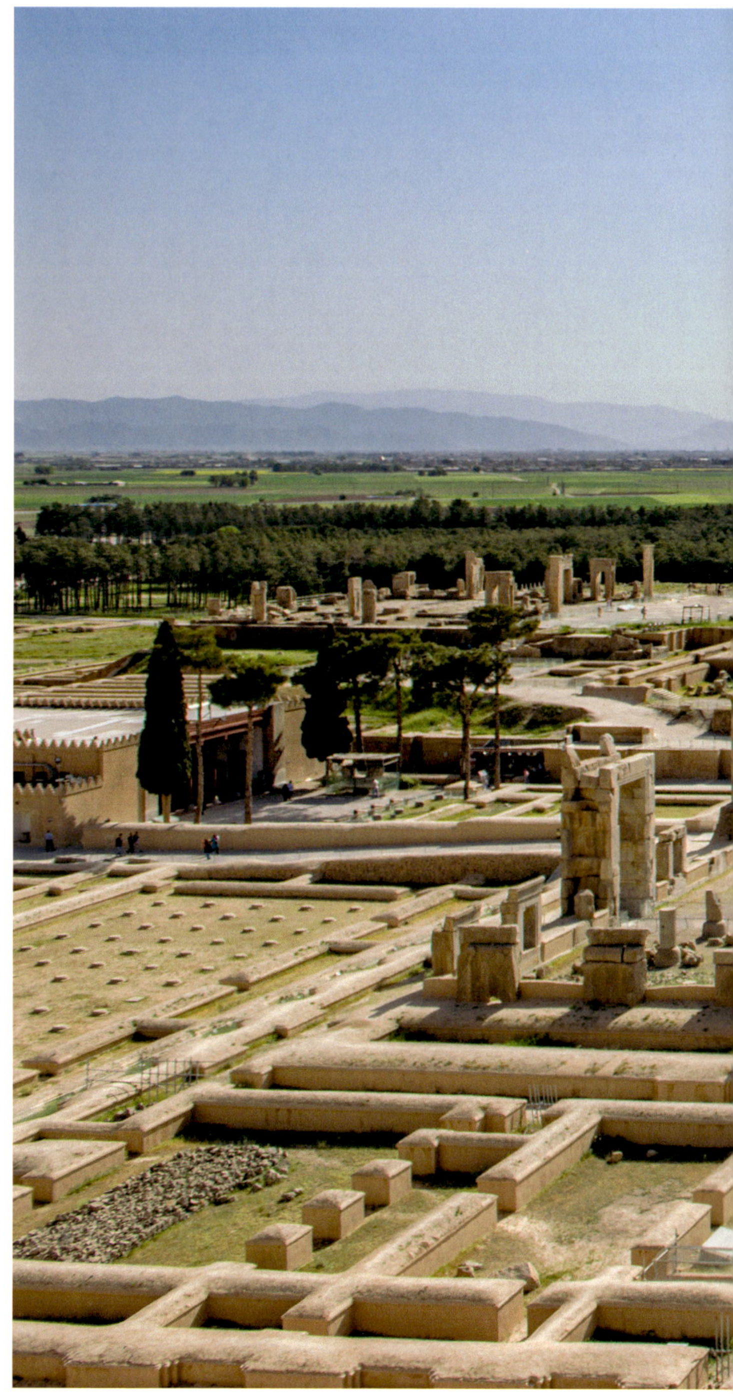

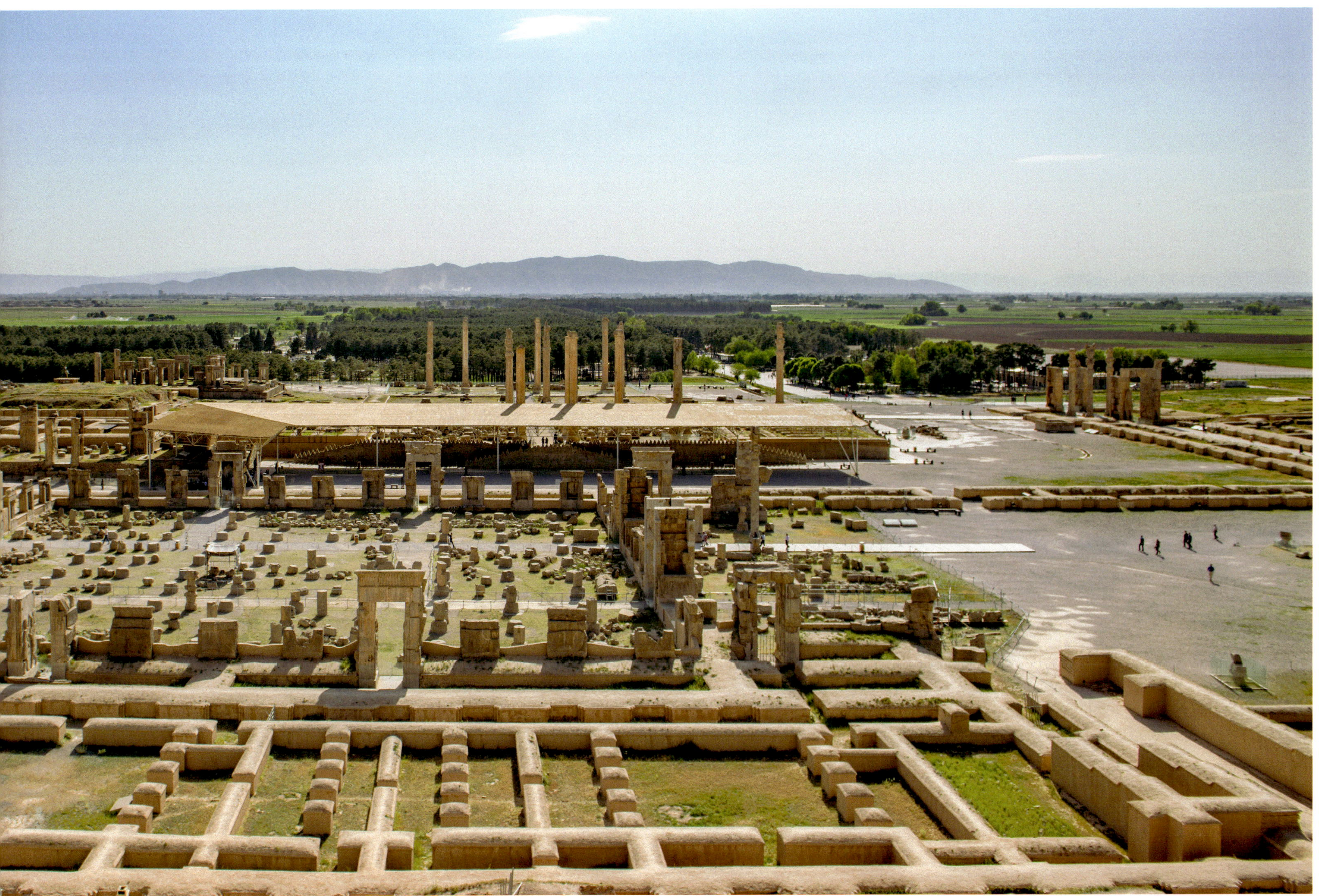

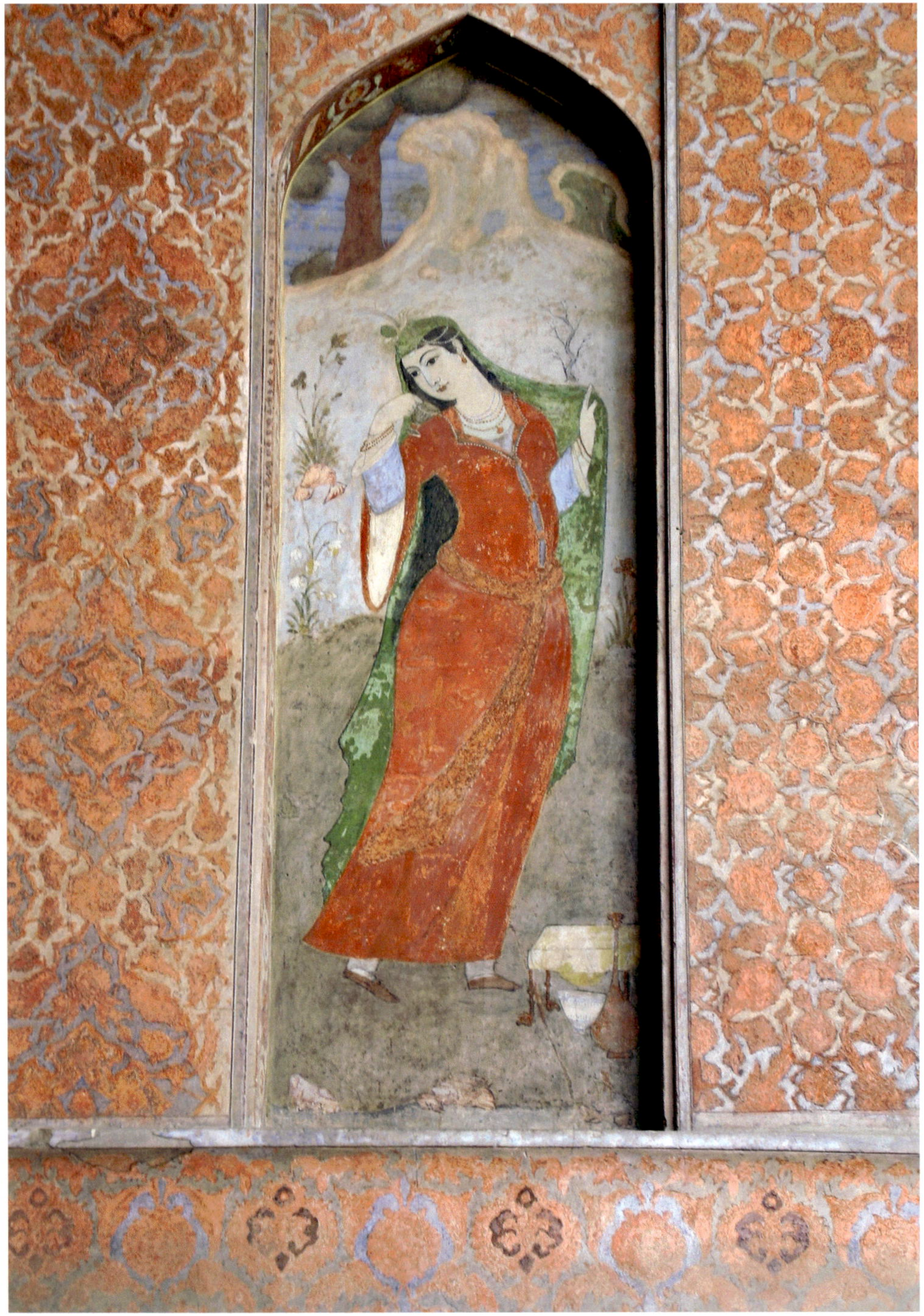

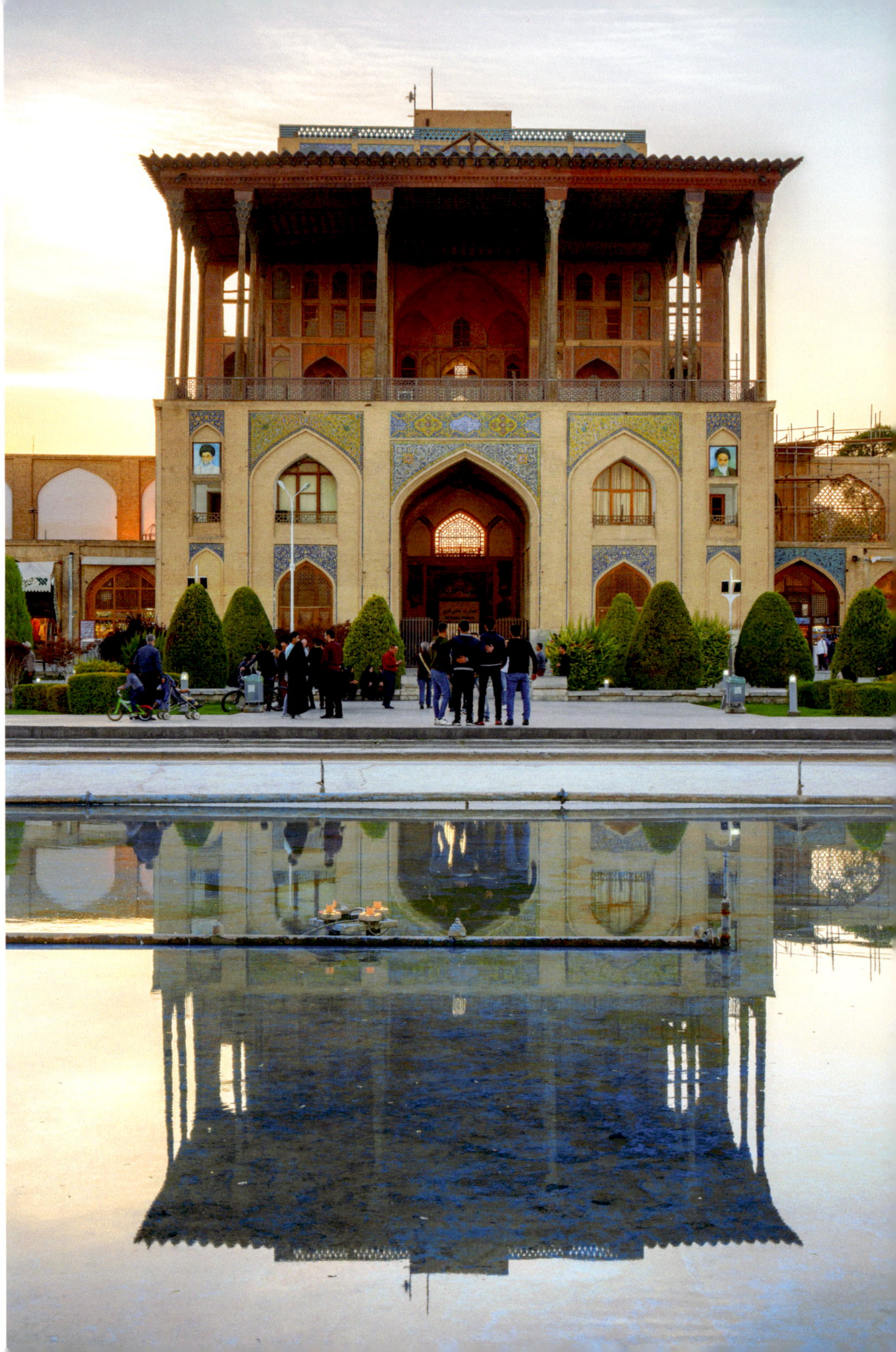

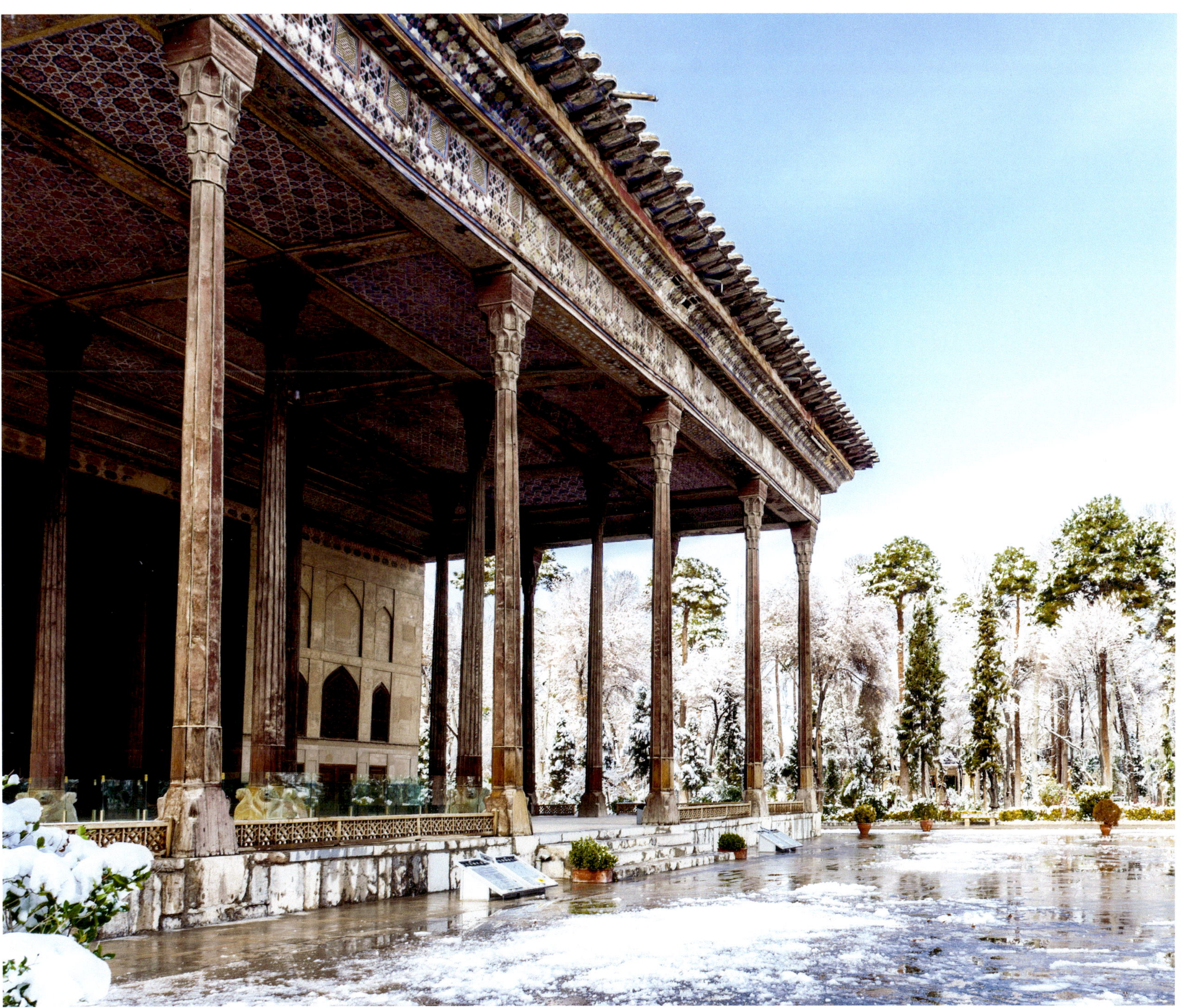

Chehel Sotoun Pavilion, Isfahan

Constructed by Shah Abbas II in the 17th century, the 'Forty Columns' pavilion, set in a stunning Persian garden, was used for royal receptions and entertainment. The name is a clever illusion as the 20 actual columns of the palace are reflected in a long pool, creating the impression of being 40. The Safavid-era palace is renowned for its magnificent frescoes and murals depicting historical events and extravagant courtly life.

OPPOSITE (BOTH PHOTOGRAPHS):

Ali Qapu Palace, Isfahan

This building served as the royal palace and a grand ceremonial gateway to the Safavid court. Built by Shah Abbas I in the early 17th century, this six-storey palace is best known for its magnificent third-floor terrace, giving visitors a panoramic view of Imam Square. Equally notable is the famed 'music room' on the top floor, which was acoustically designed to create an ideal environment for live performances on important occasions.

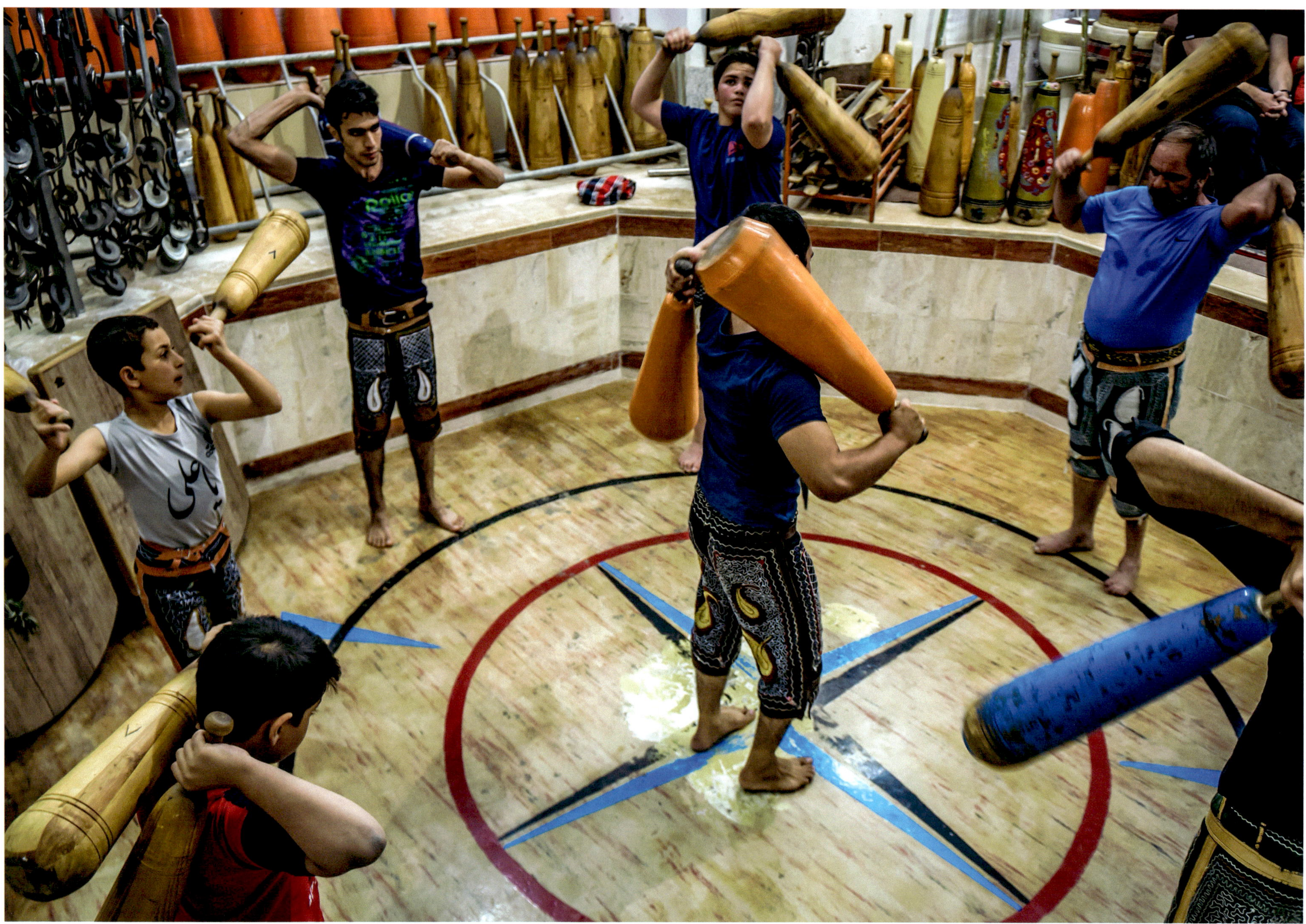

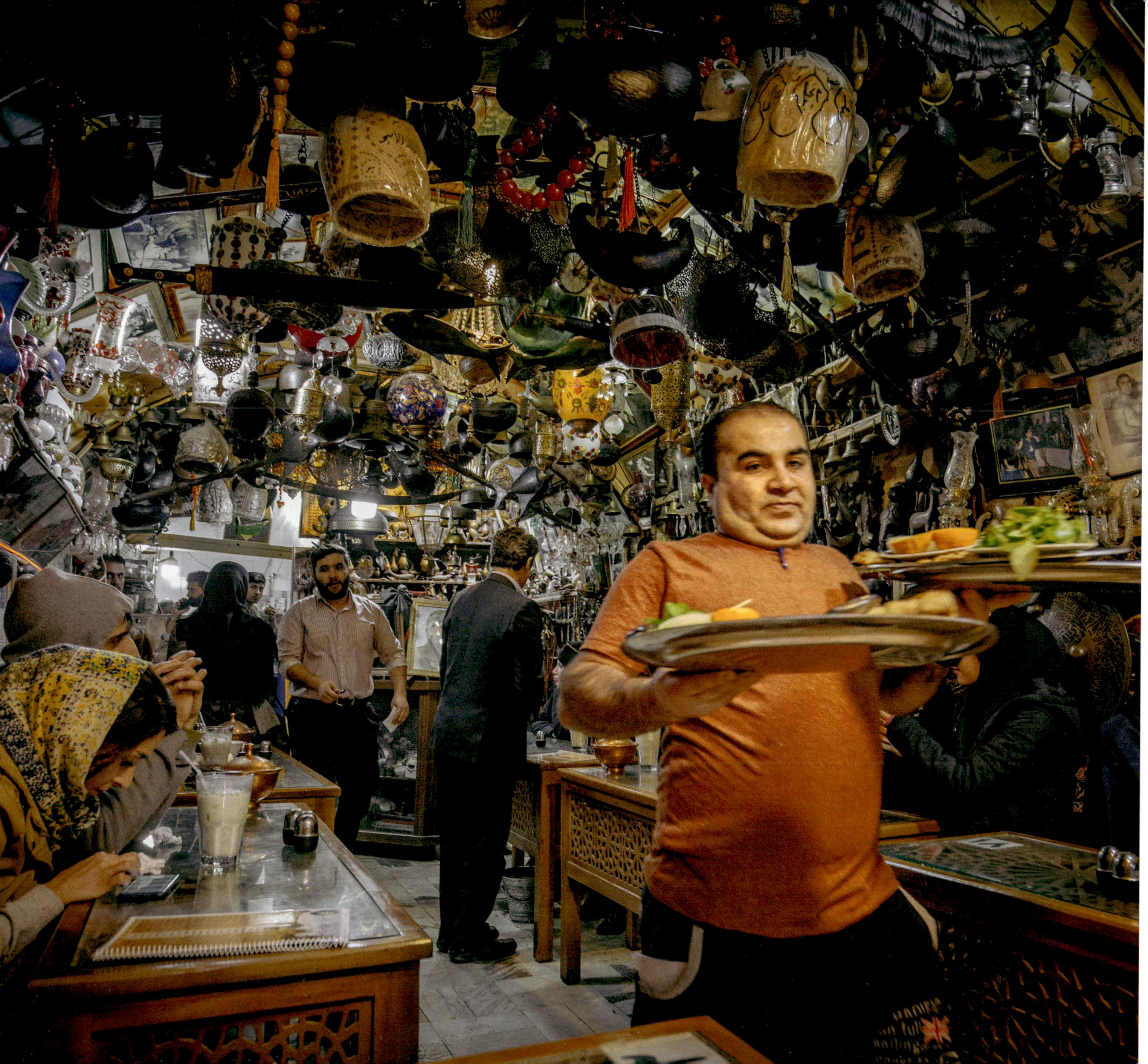

LEFT:

Azadegan Cafe, Isfahan

If you want to absorb both food and atmosphere in Isfahan, then this historic, museum-like teahouse with a quirky, antique-filled decor is ideal. It serves traditional Iranian foods and beverages such as dizi stew, beryan (a meat dish with spices), and doogh and gooshfil, which are sweet drinks and desserts.

OPPOSITE:

Zurkhaneh, Yadz

A Zurkhaneh is a traditional Iranian gymnasium where a form of martial arts and strength training called Varzesh-e Bastani is practised; such places are particularly known in the city of Yadz. The workouts use unique tools like heavy wooden clubs, large iron shields, and a bow-shaped chain. It's a highly spiritual and disciplined practice, often with a musician leading the rhythm, which is said to exercise and strengthen the whole body.

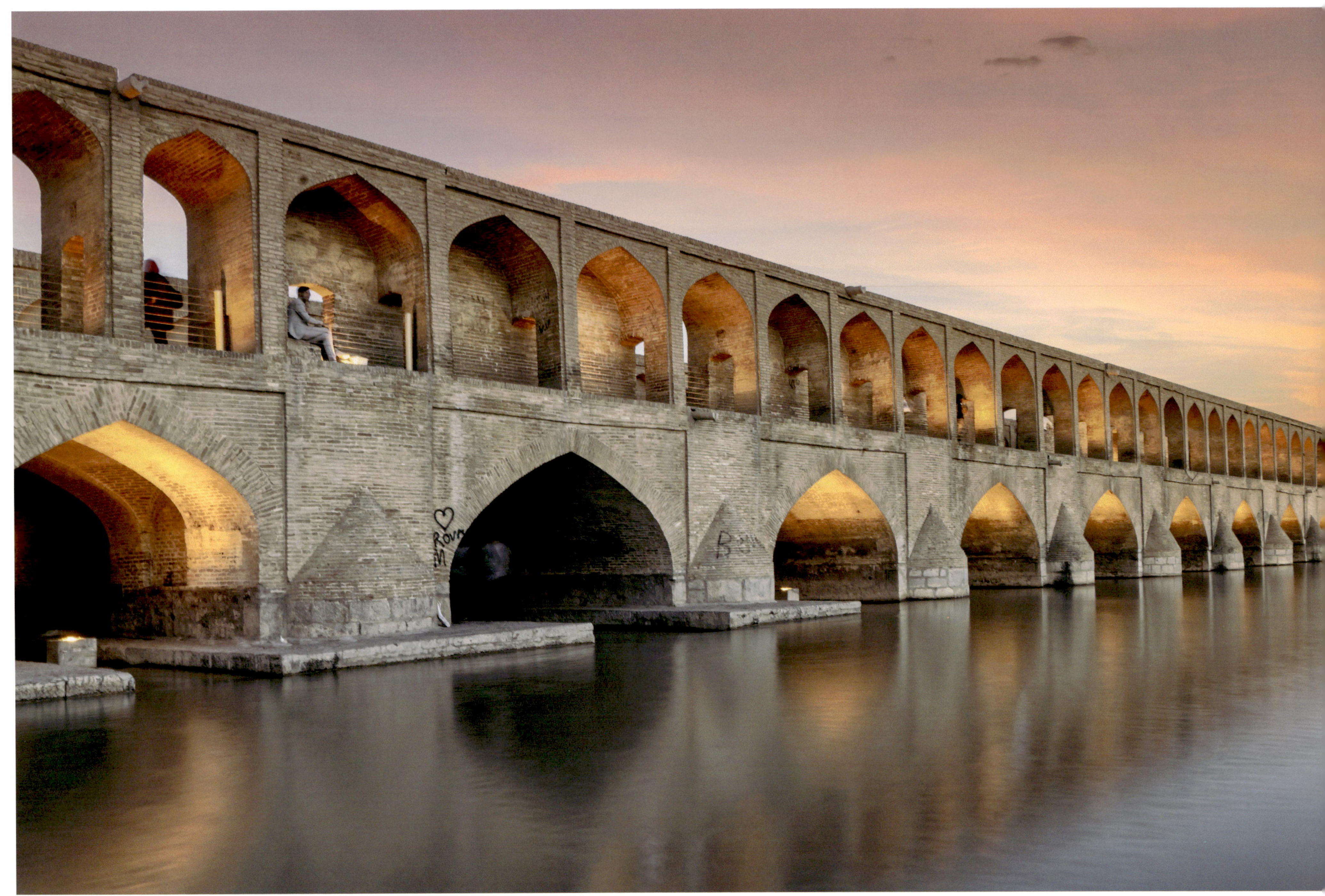

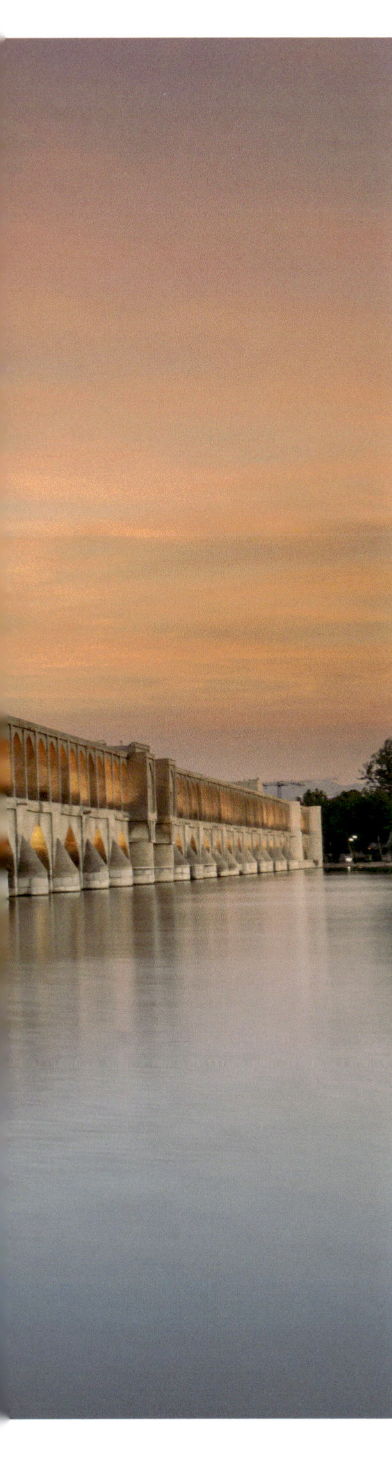

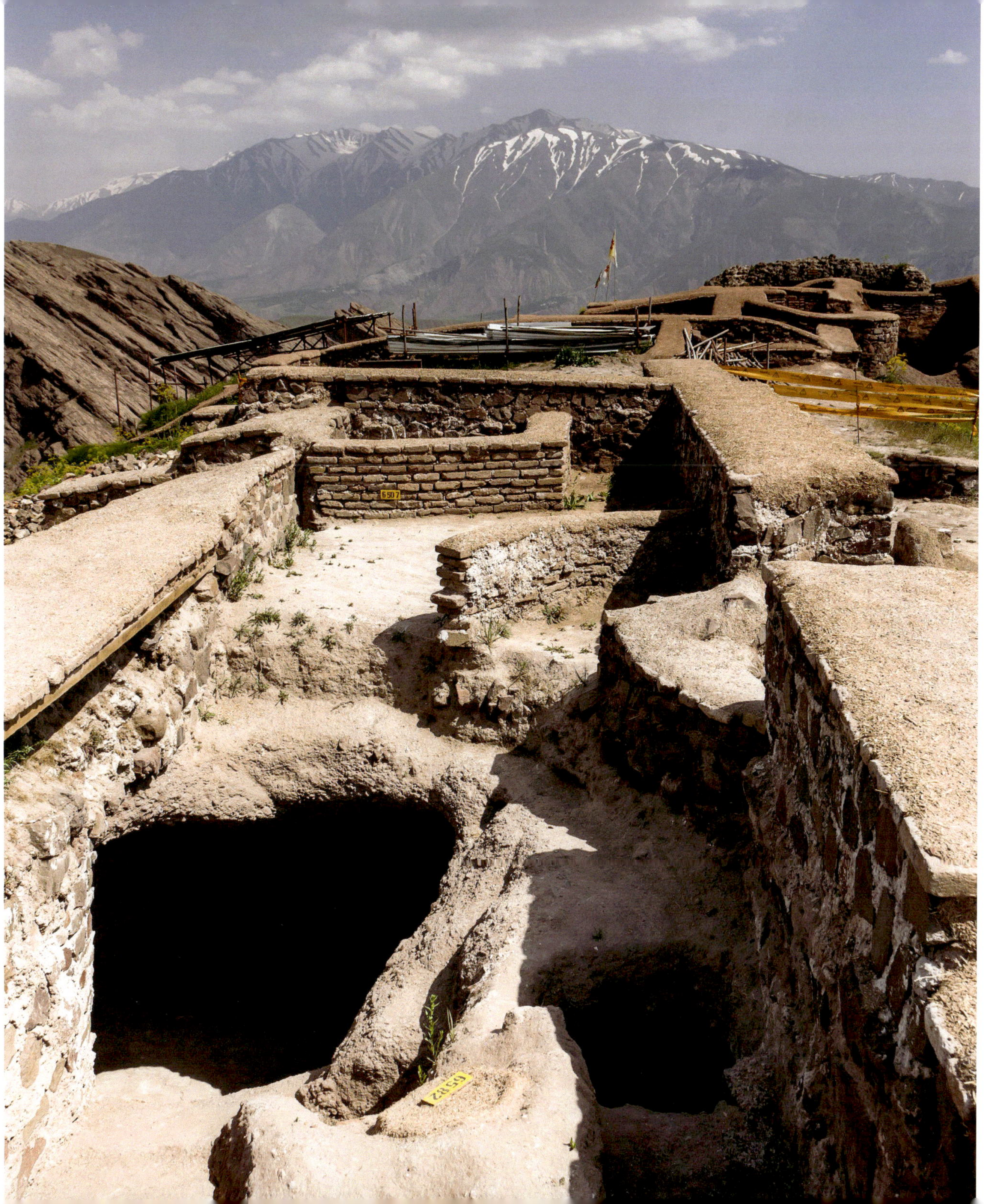

Allahverdi Bridge (Bridge of 33 Arches), Isfahan
This famous landmark of Isfahan was constructed in the early 17th century by Shah Abbas I's commander Allahverdi Khan. The attractive double-deck, arched bridge spans the Zayandeh River and was built to serve as both a bridge and a dam. The bridge originally connected the city centre to the Armenian quarter of New Julfa. It has long been a popular gathering place for coffee drinking, fishing and walking for Iranians of all ages.

LEFT:
Alamut Castle, Alborz Mountains
This historical fortress was the mountain stronghold of the Nizari Isma'ili Sect (known as the Order of Assassins), and the headquarters of its legendary leader Hassan-i Sabbah, who it is said never left the fortress for almost 40 years. The castle was famed for its inaccessibility and housed a massive library created by Hassan-i Sabbah, who was a noted mathematician and philosopher.

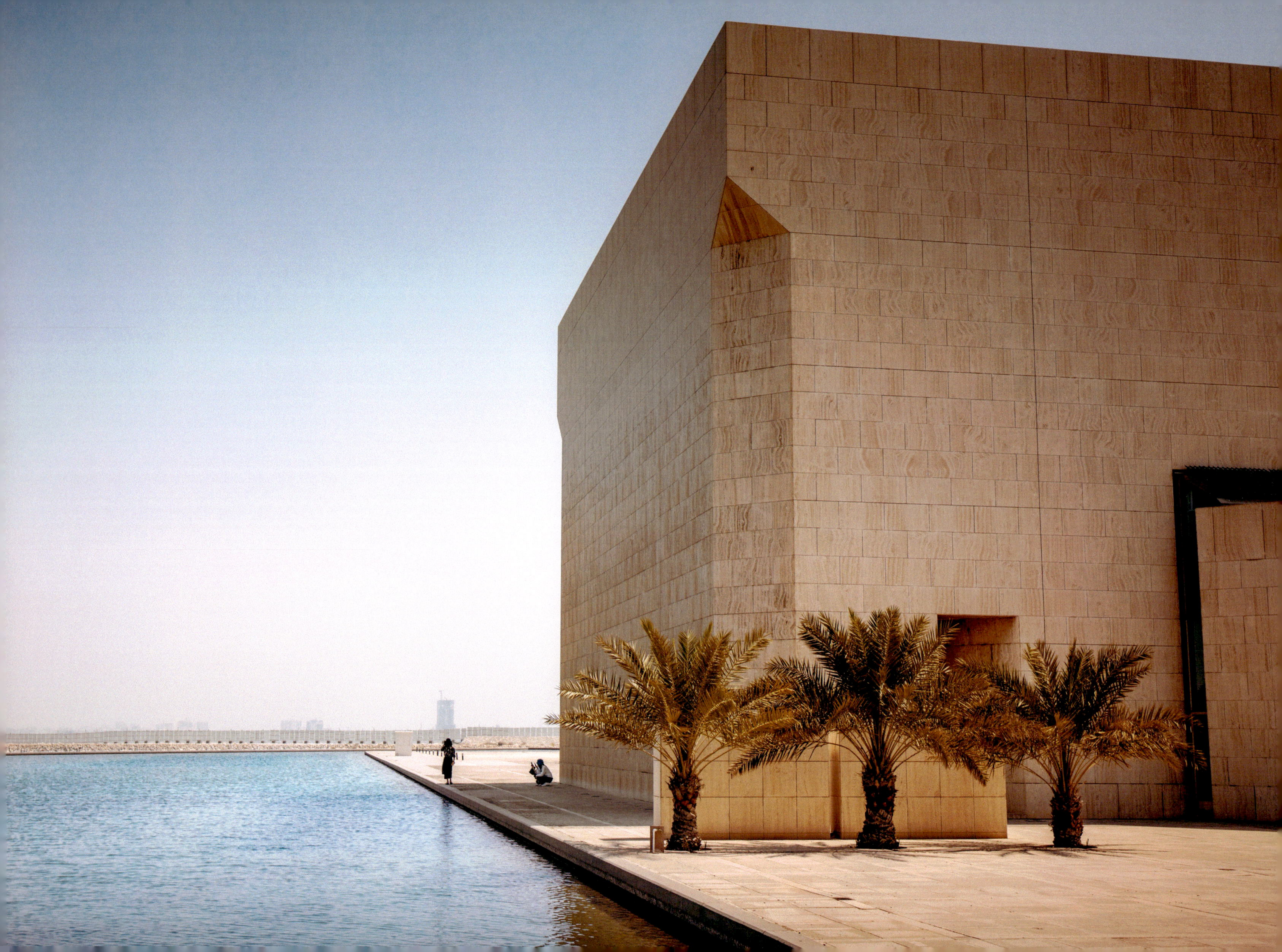

Arabian Gold

The Arabian Peninsula is a land of startling and exciting contrasts. In these countries ancient traditions blend with a fast forward, futuristic ambition. Their histories share similar beginnings in nomadic Bedouin life, before the rise of powerful early peoples such as the Kingdom of Hadhramaut. It was the birth of Islam in 7th century Mecca, however, that provided the basis for today's shared cultural identity. These are the lands of the Arabic language, where generosity and hospitality come first, and where a deep respect for poetry and storytelling provides the literary soul. Food is another source of Arab pride and identity. Rooted in the nomadic traditions of the Bedouin, the cuisine is hearty and tasty, with ingredients from the land such as dates, dried fruit, and meat.

Today, the futuristic skylines of Dubai and Doha, showcasing cutting-edge architecture like the Burj Khalifa and the Museum of the Future, sitting alongside Oman's low-level architecture, wadis and traditional souqs, offer a spectrum of new experiences for the world-weary traveller. Abu Dhabi's cultural offerings, such as the Louvre, have brought fresh impetus to the artistic scene of the Arabian Gulf. Saudi Arabia has fast-paced tourism ambitions, inviting the world to explore UNESCO World Heritage sites like Al-Balad in Jeddah and the tombs of Al-Ula, known as the 'Petra of Saudi Arabia'. The peninsula's natural attractions are also breathtaking. The vast sand dunes of the Empty Quarter, the rugged mountains of Oman and Yemen, and the vibrant marine life of the Red Sea are being carefully preserved as they become open to exploration.

Bahrain National Museum, Manama
This iconic local building, with its white marble facade, is located on an artificial peninsula, creating a striking visual with its reflection in the surrounding water. The powerful modern architectural exterior contains six halls of artefacts and exhibitions explaining 6000 years of history from Bahrain's ancient Dilmun past to the arrival of Islam. Bahrain's customs, traditions, and traditional crafts feature heavily, giving the visitor a taste of why this island country is so distinctly different.

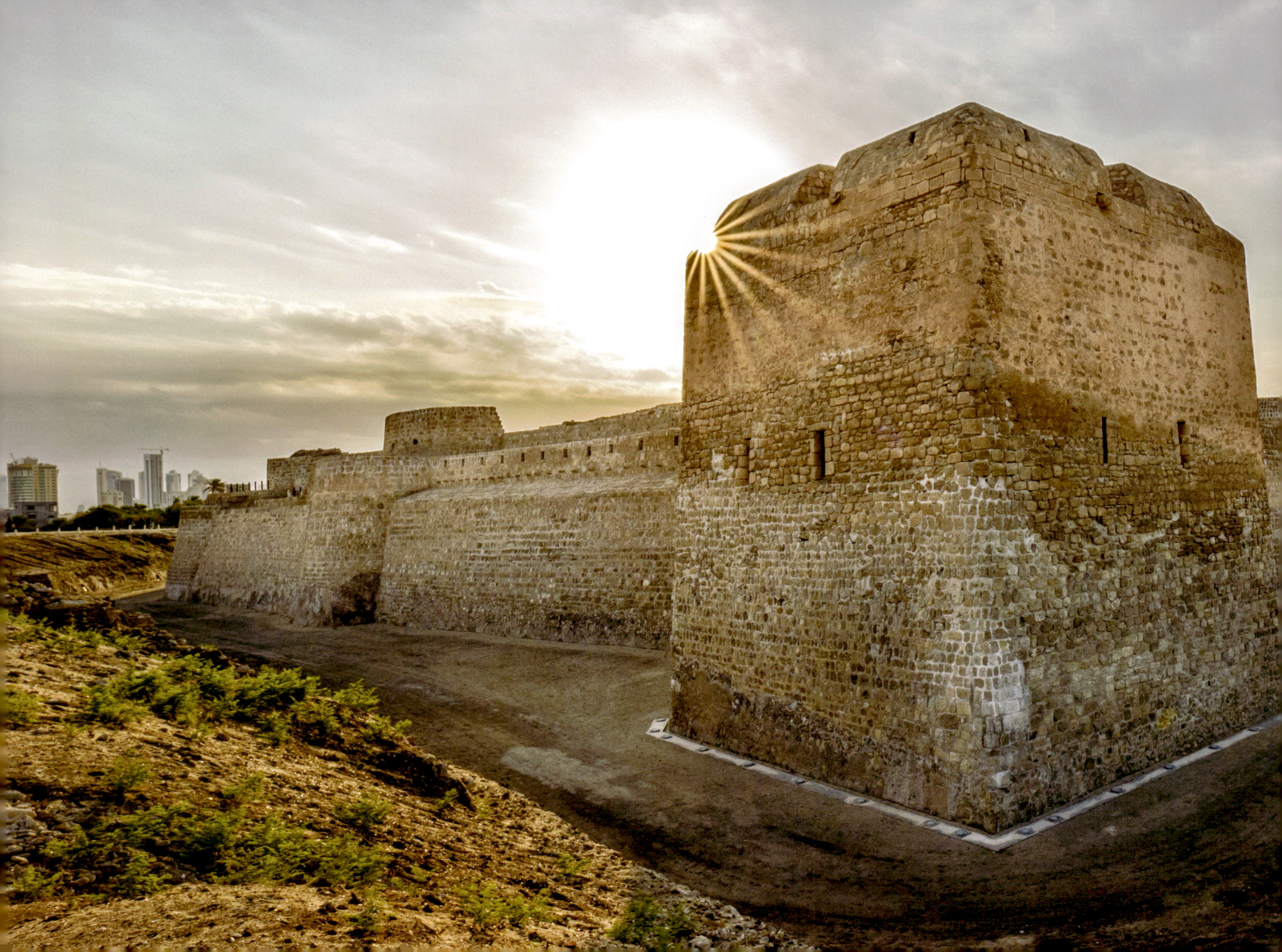

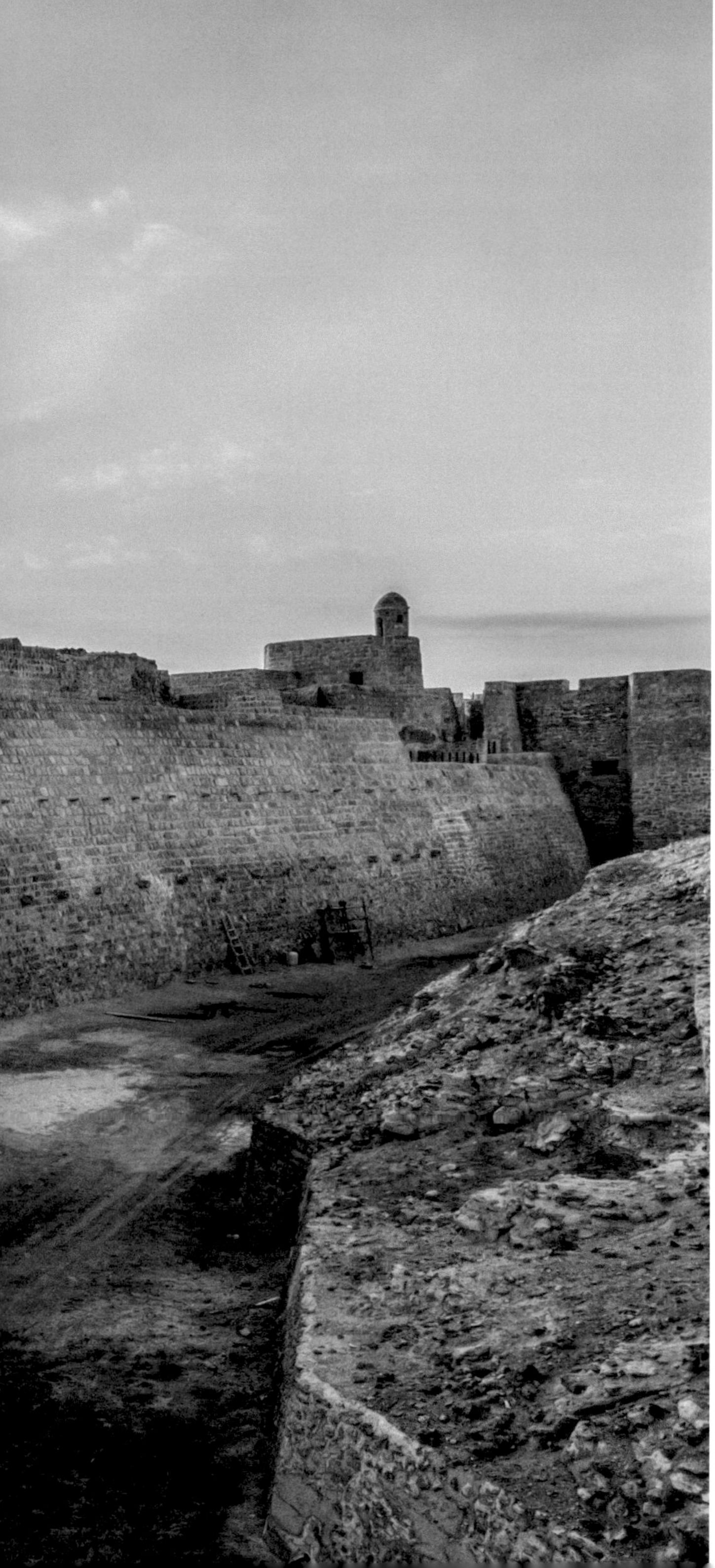

Bahrain Fort
Known locally as Qal'at al-Bahrain, this must-visit attraction is a UNESCO World Heritage site. Built on an artificial mound called a 'tell', it served as the capital of the ancient Dilmun civilization and enjoys a 4500-year history. The current structure, which gave the site its name, is a 16th-century Portuguese fort with a centre that houses artefacts from all eras.

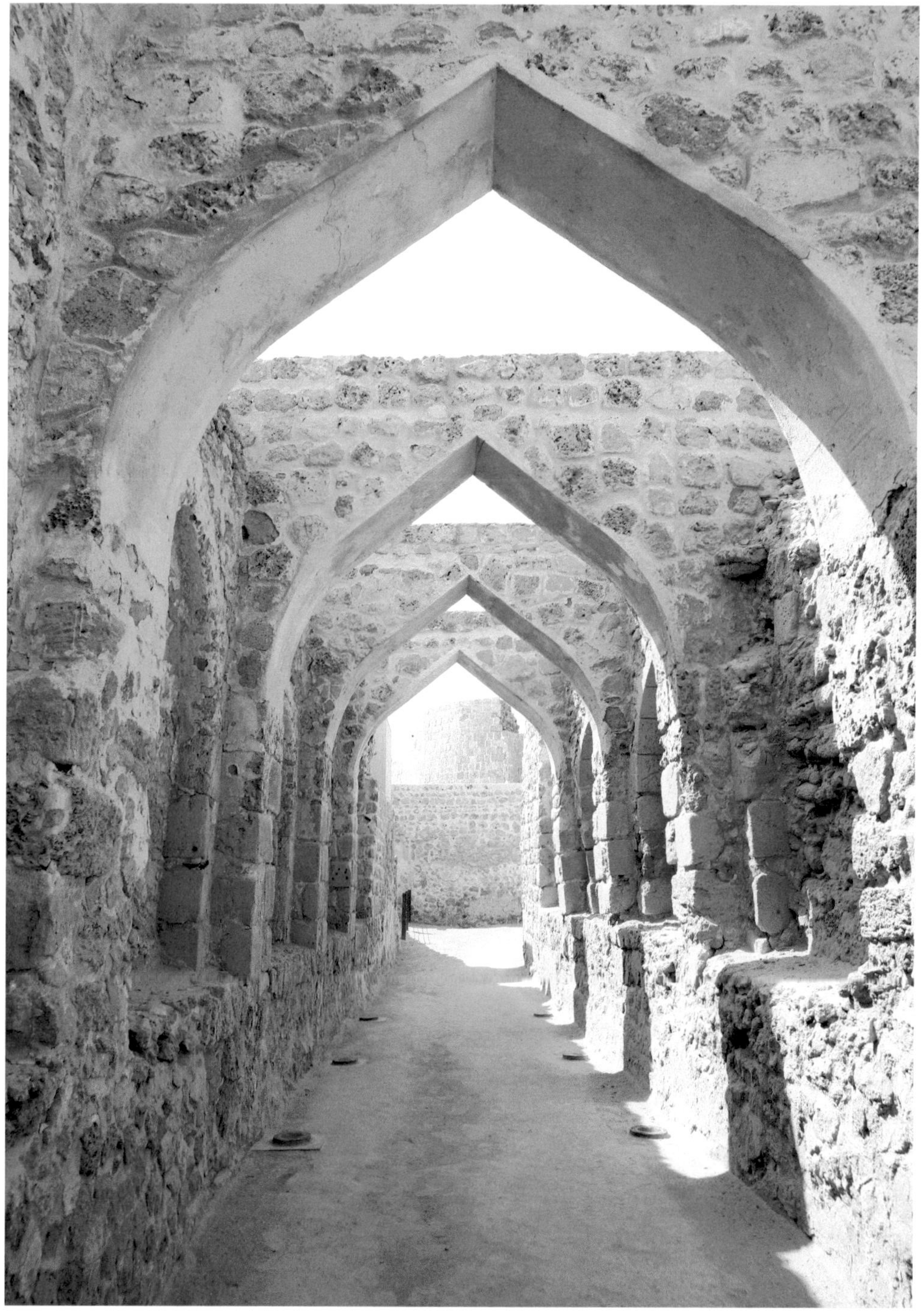

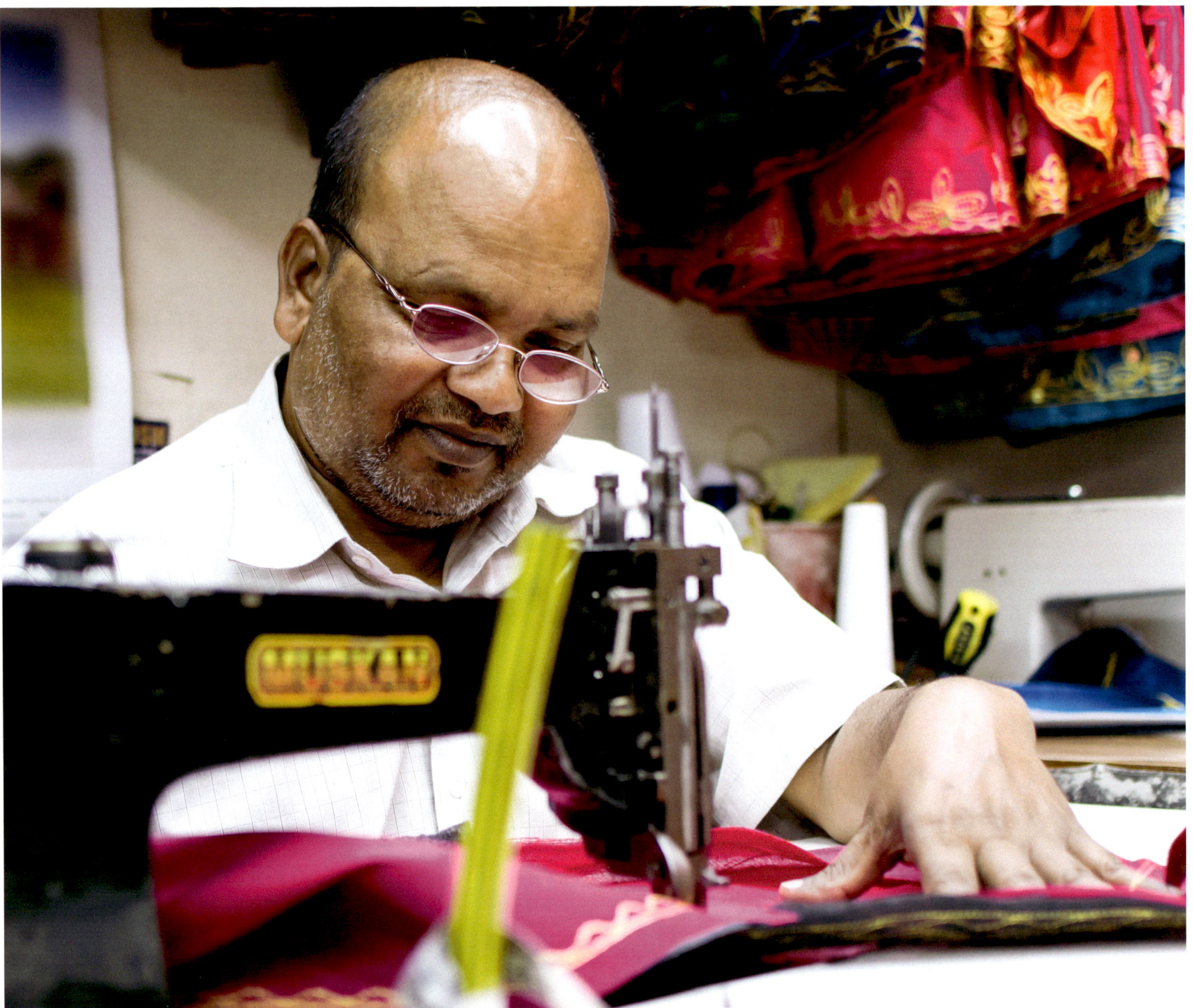

LEFT & OPPOSITE:
The Souq, Manama
Situated by the historic Bab Al Bahrain, this maze of narrow alleyways is filled with shops selling everything from traditional spices, textiles, and handicrafts to modern electronics and jewellery, including the famed local, natural pearls. Traditional crafts for sale include intricate gold and silver, pottery from A'ali village, and basketry made from local palm leaves. Other popular items are aromatic spices, traditional sweets like halwa, and beautiful handicrafts inspired by the islands' rich history.

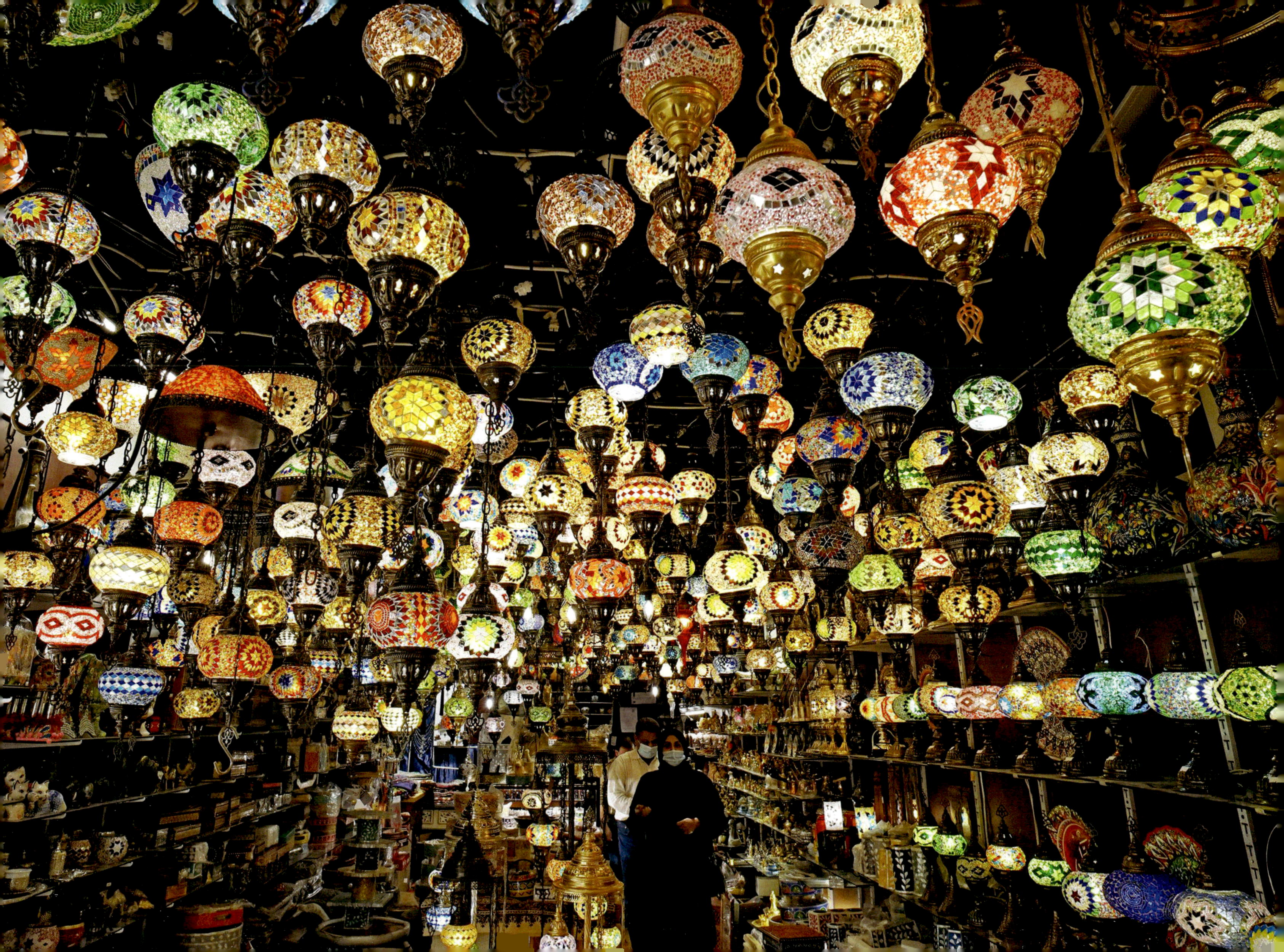

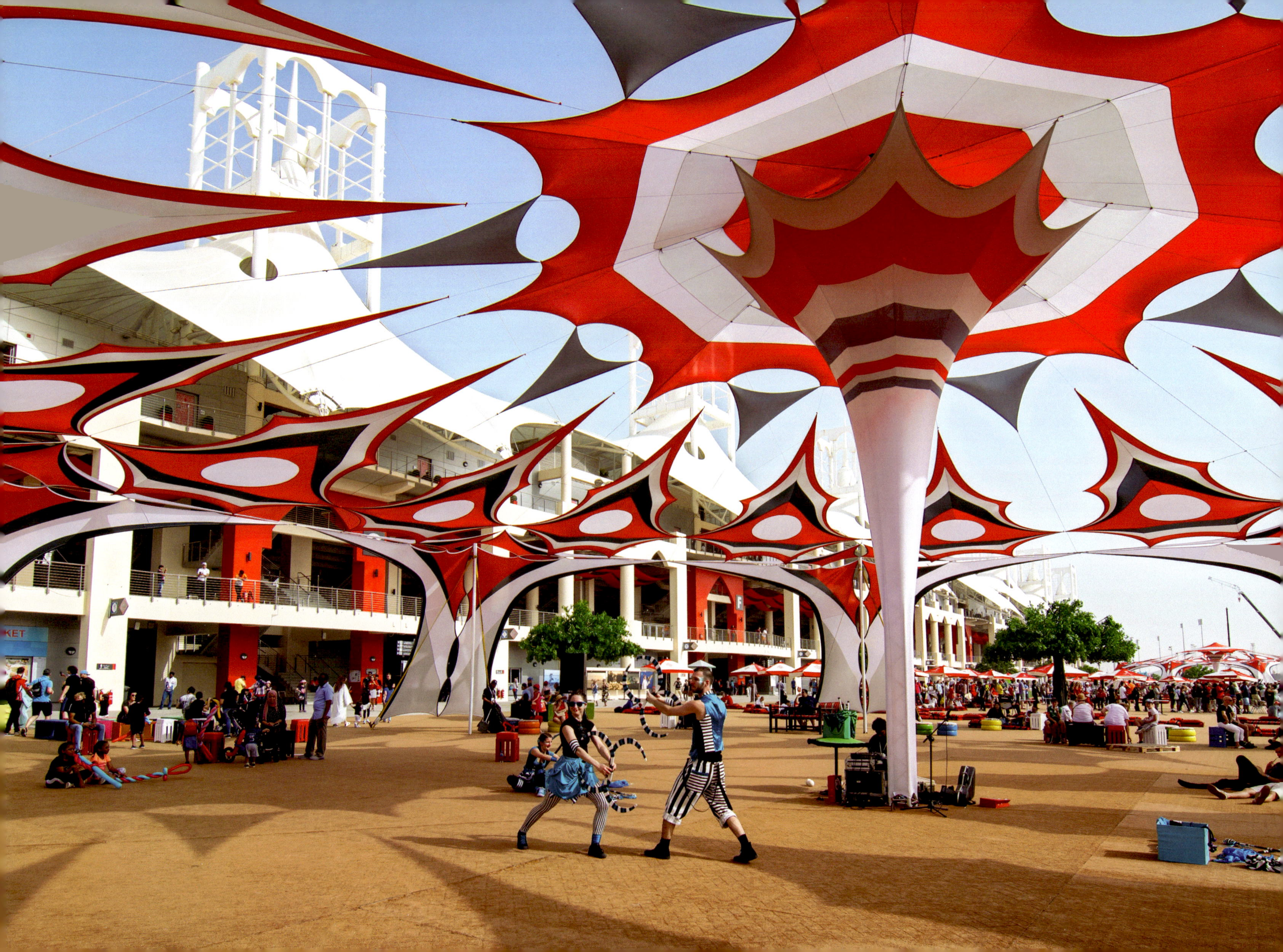

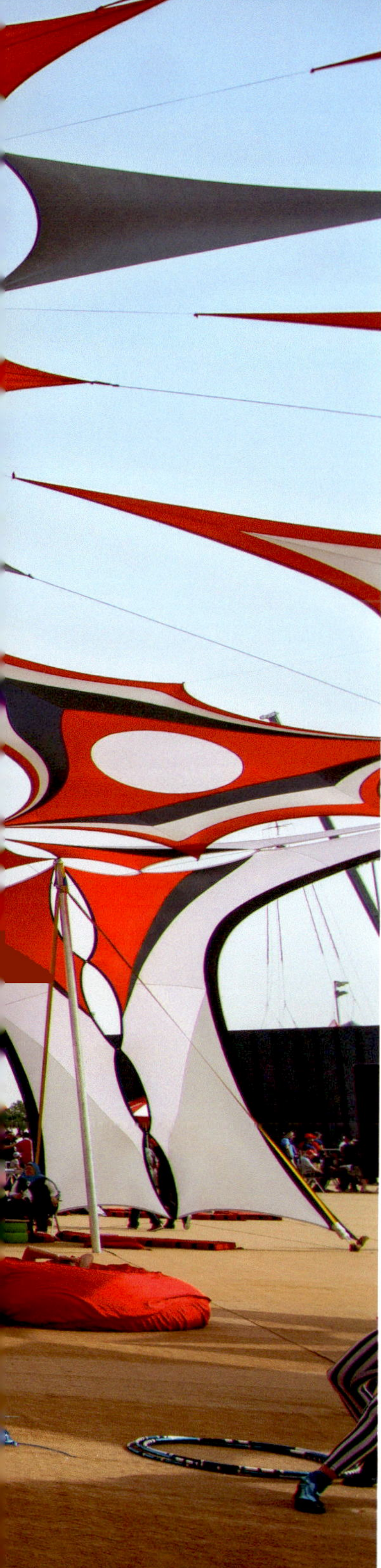

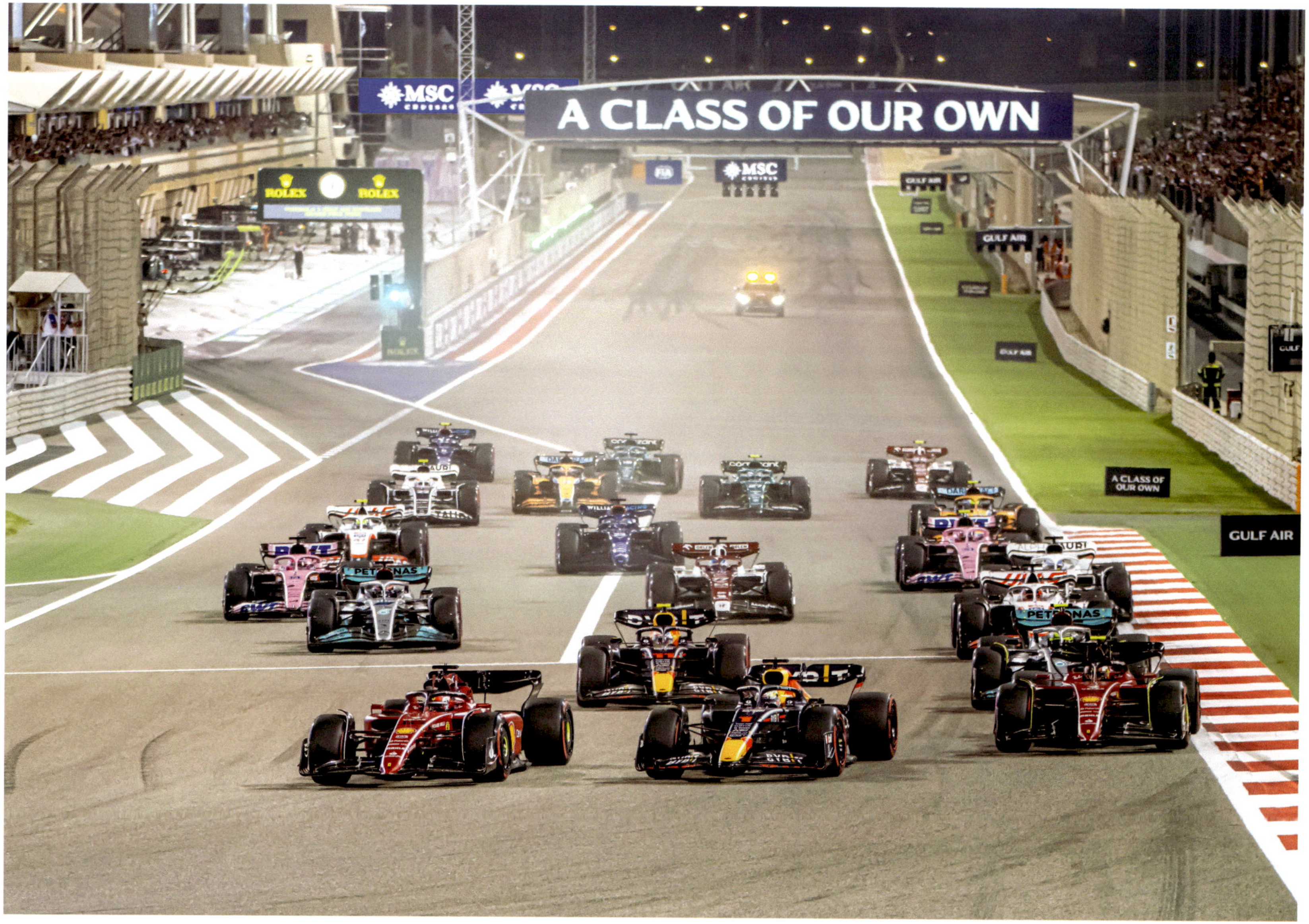

LEFT & ABOVE:

Bahrain International Circuit

Opened in 2004, this modern motorsport venue holds a significant place in the world of F1 racing, for it hosted the first Formula One Grand Prix in the Middle East. It is located in the desert of area of Sakhir. The circuit was designed and completed in a remarkably fast 16-month timeline. The course has several circuits, allowing it to host multiple events. It also enjoys a night-racing capability, ensuring late-night drama in the coolest part of the day.

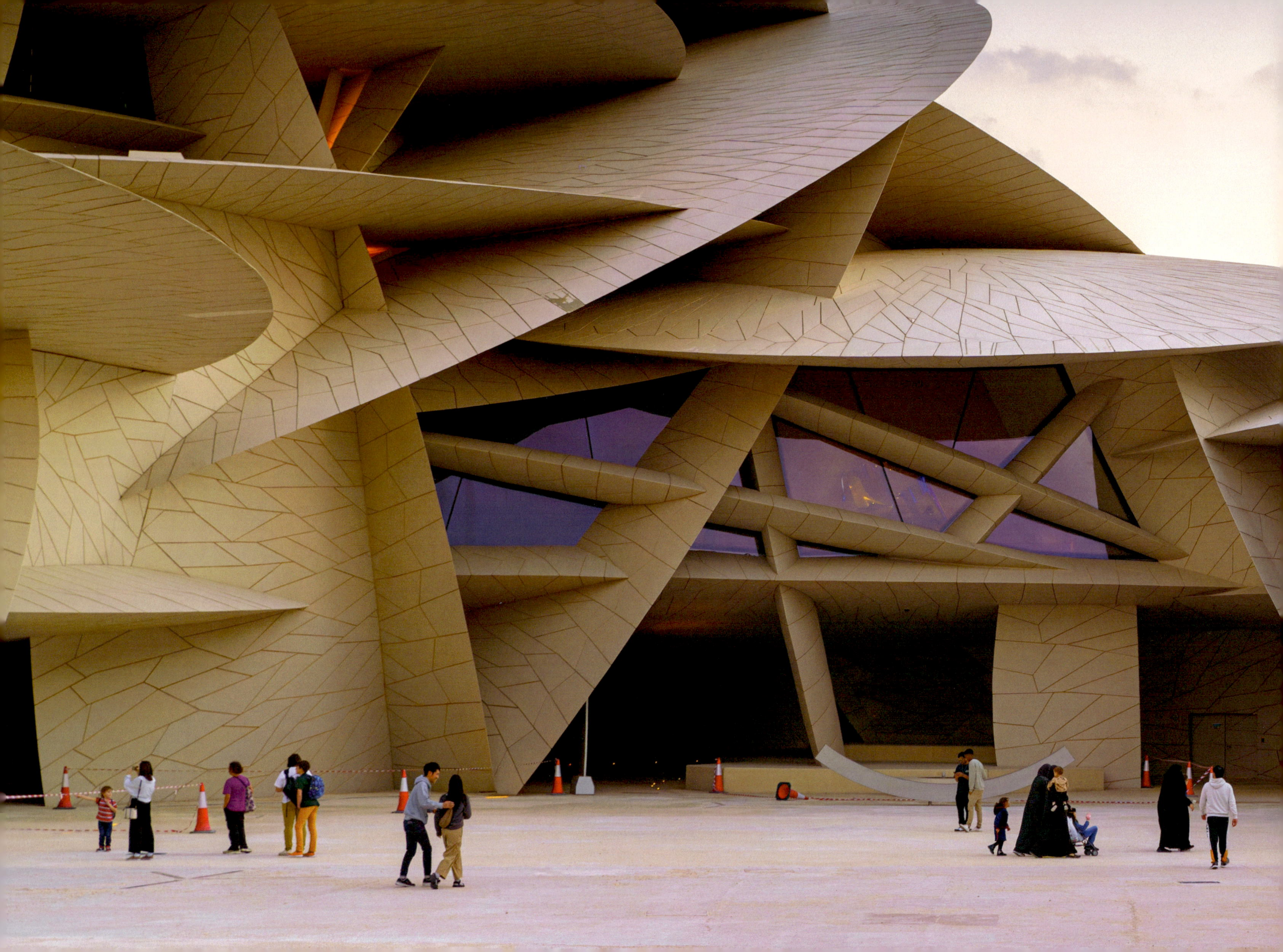

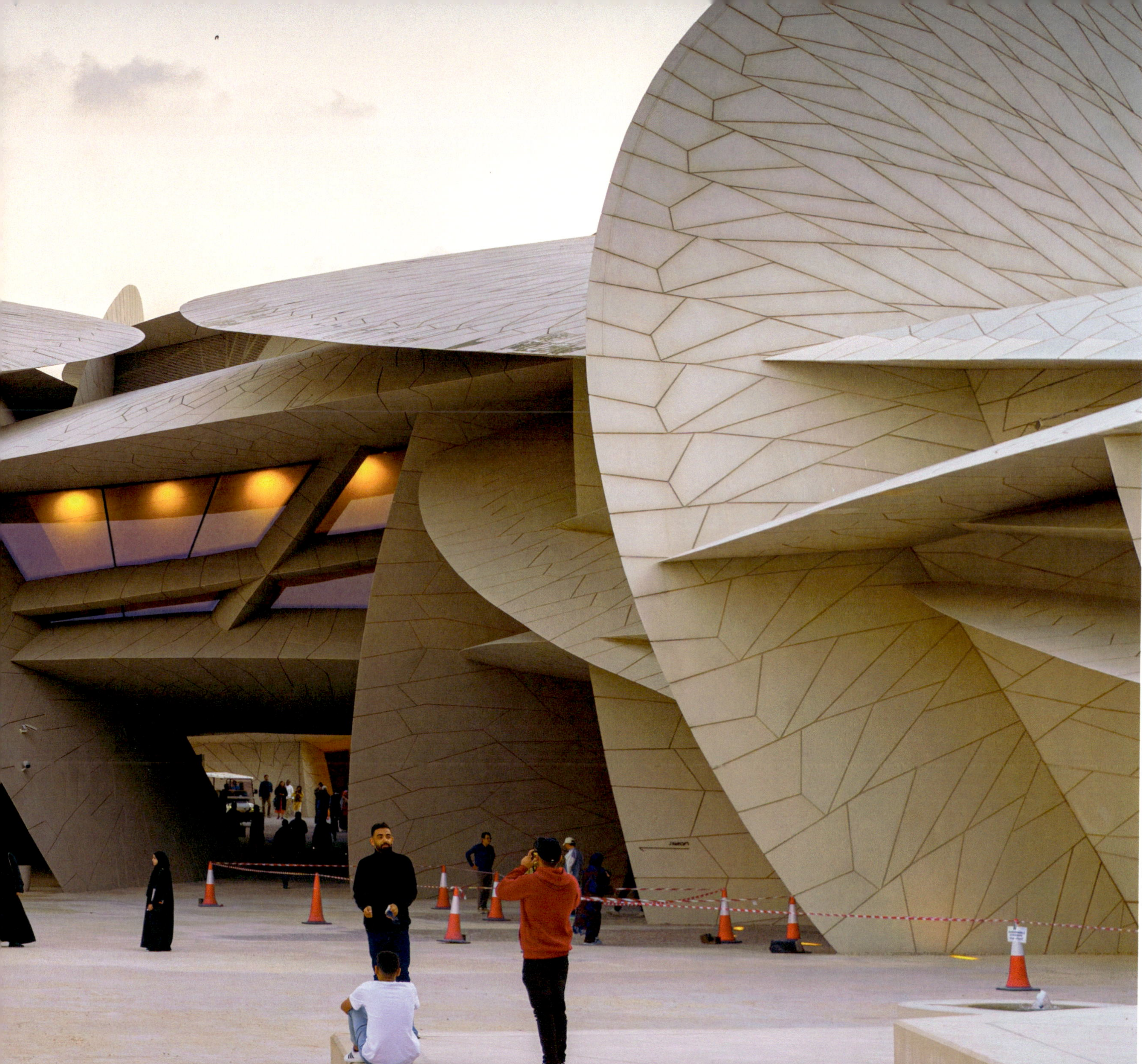

National Museum of Qatar, Doha
This architectural masterpiece was designed by Jean Nouvel. The distinctive shape was inspired by the desert rose and its unique interlocking disc structure houses 11 separate galleries. The museum tells the story of Qatar and its people, from its geological formation to the present day. As well as its curated spaces, the museum incorporates the historic palace of Sheikh Abdullah bin Jassim Al Thani. This vast cultural space was designed to celebrate Qatar's past and inform visitors about its progressive future.

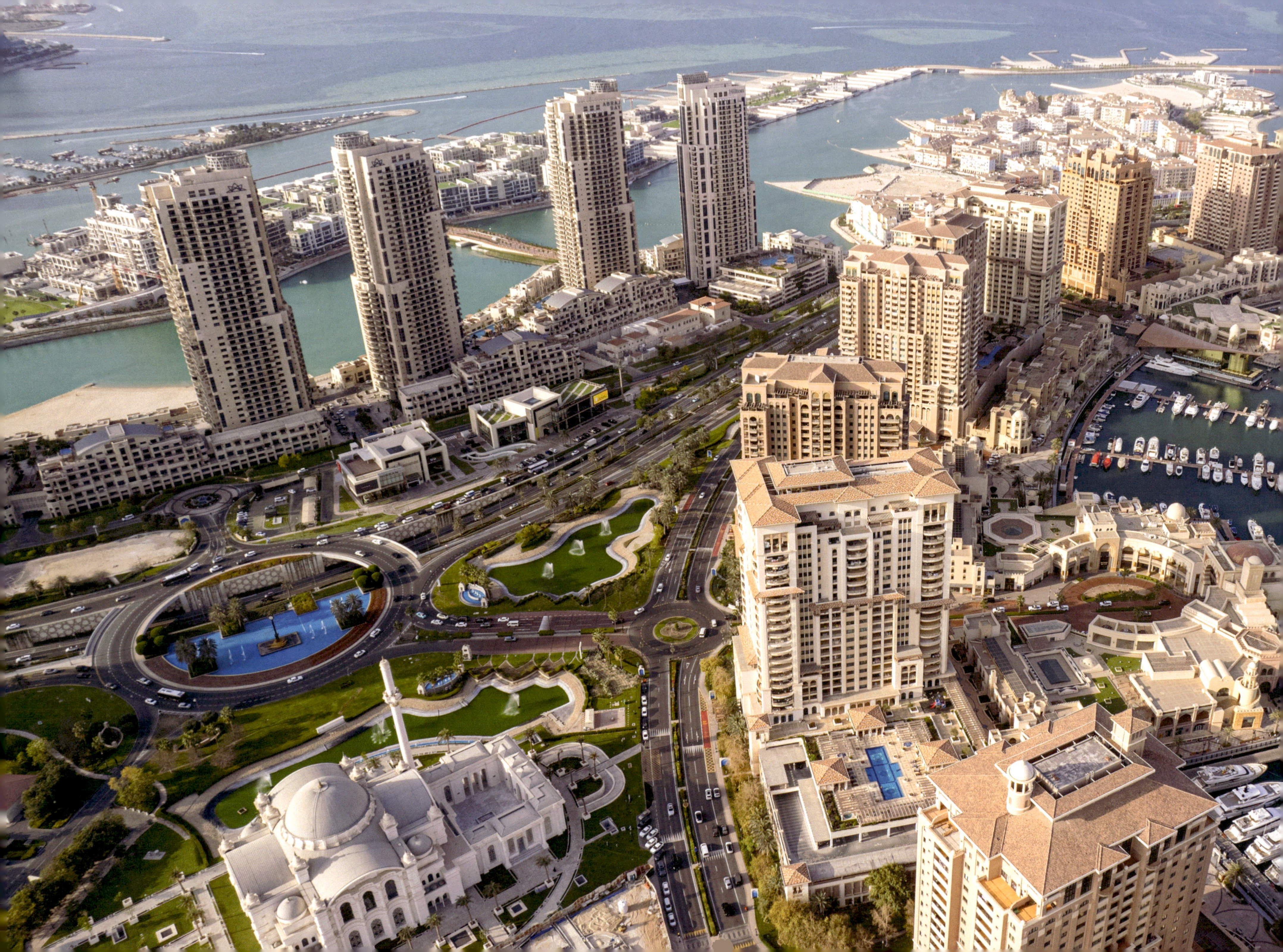

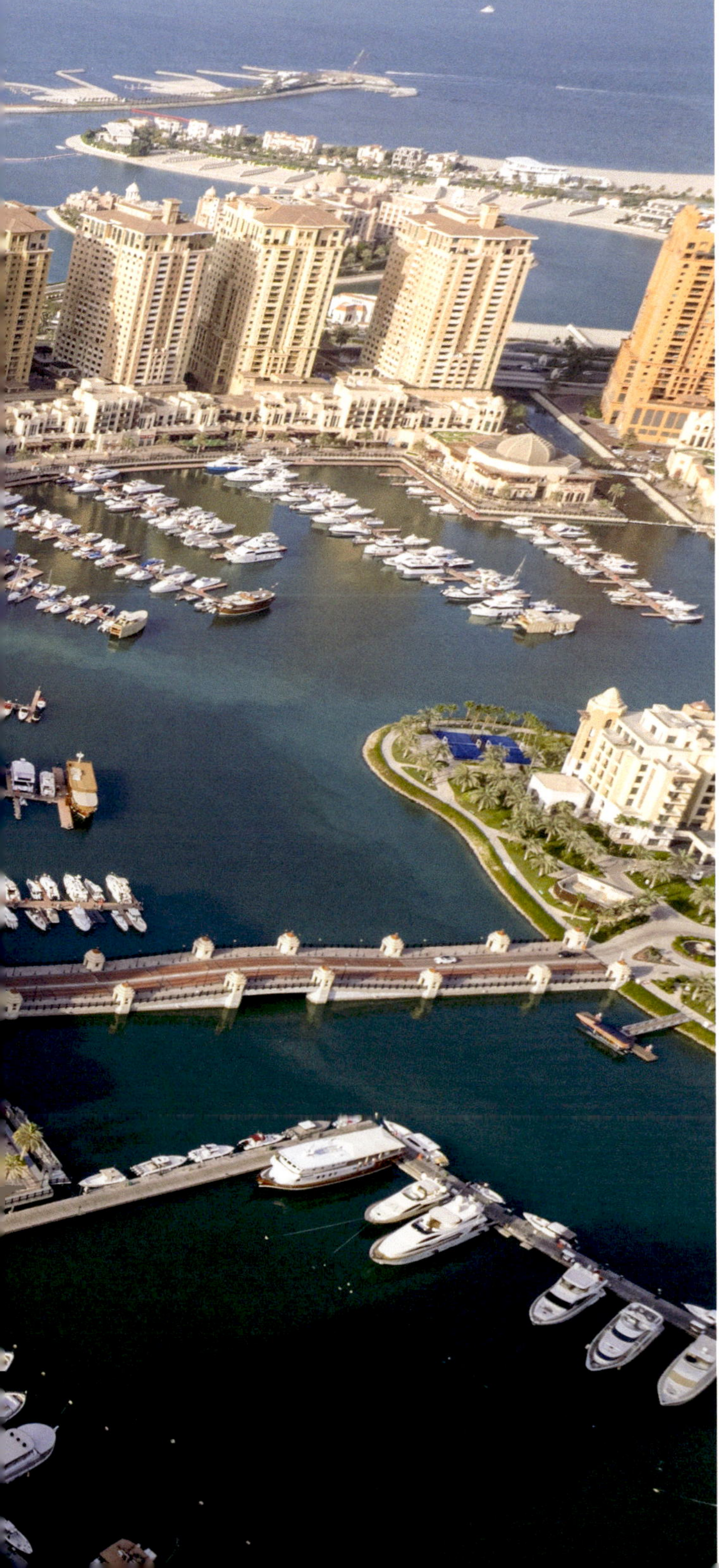

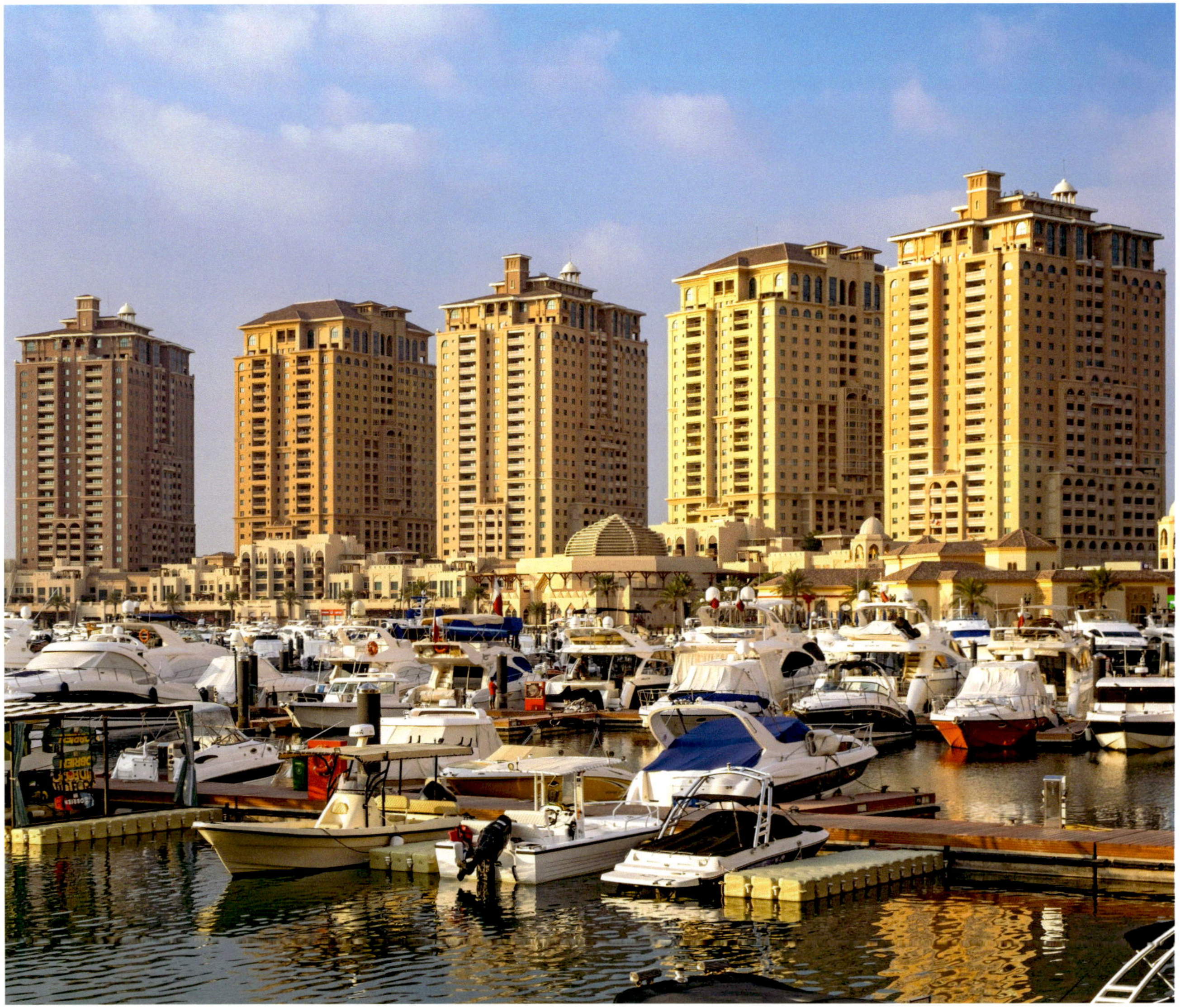

Pearl Island, Doha

This luxurious artificial island pays tribute to Qatar's history as a pearl diving centre. This huge area is known locally as the 'Arabian Riviera'. This is reflected in its Mediterranean-inspired architecture, yacht-lined marinas, and colourful, fashionable waterfront. For those who aspire to a glamorous lifestyle, the island offers high-end residences, luxury boutiques, fine dining, and entertainment. Divided into distinct districts, including the Venice-like Qanat Quarter, it attracts locals and international visitors alike.

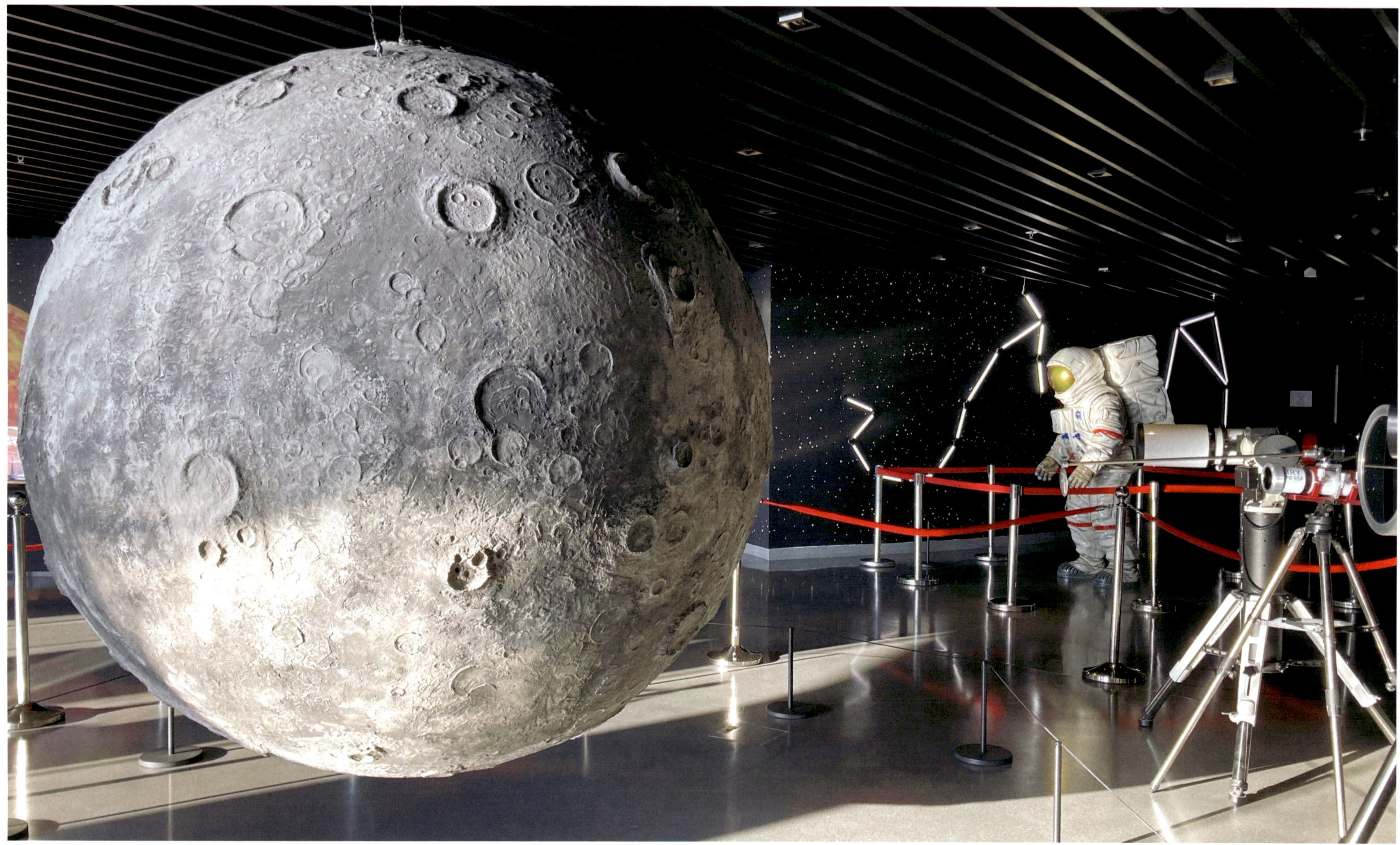

ABOVE:
Al Thuraya Planetarium, Doha
This state-of-the-art scientific facility is named after the
Pleiades star cluster. The planetarium features a museum with
multiple interactive exhibits, including astronaut suits, planet
models, and displays of astronomical history. The planetarium

also offers an immersive experience using a 22-metre
(70-ft) screen and a full-dome digital system. These showcase
educational 2D and 3D films about space and earth sciences.
It's a popular family destination blending entertainment with
scientific discovery.

OPPOSITE:
Doha skyline
The waterfront of Doha is a stunning display of futuristic
architecture. It features illuminated skyscrapers with unique
and unconventional designs, such as the Doha Tower and the
crescent-shaped Katara Towers.

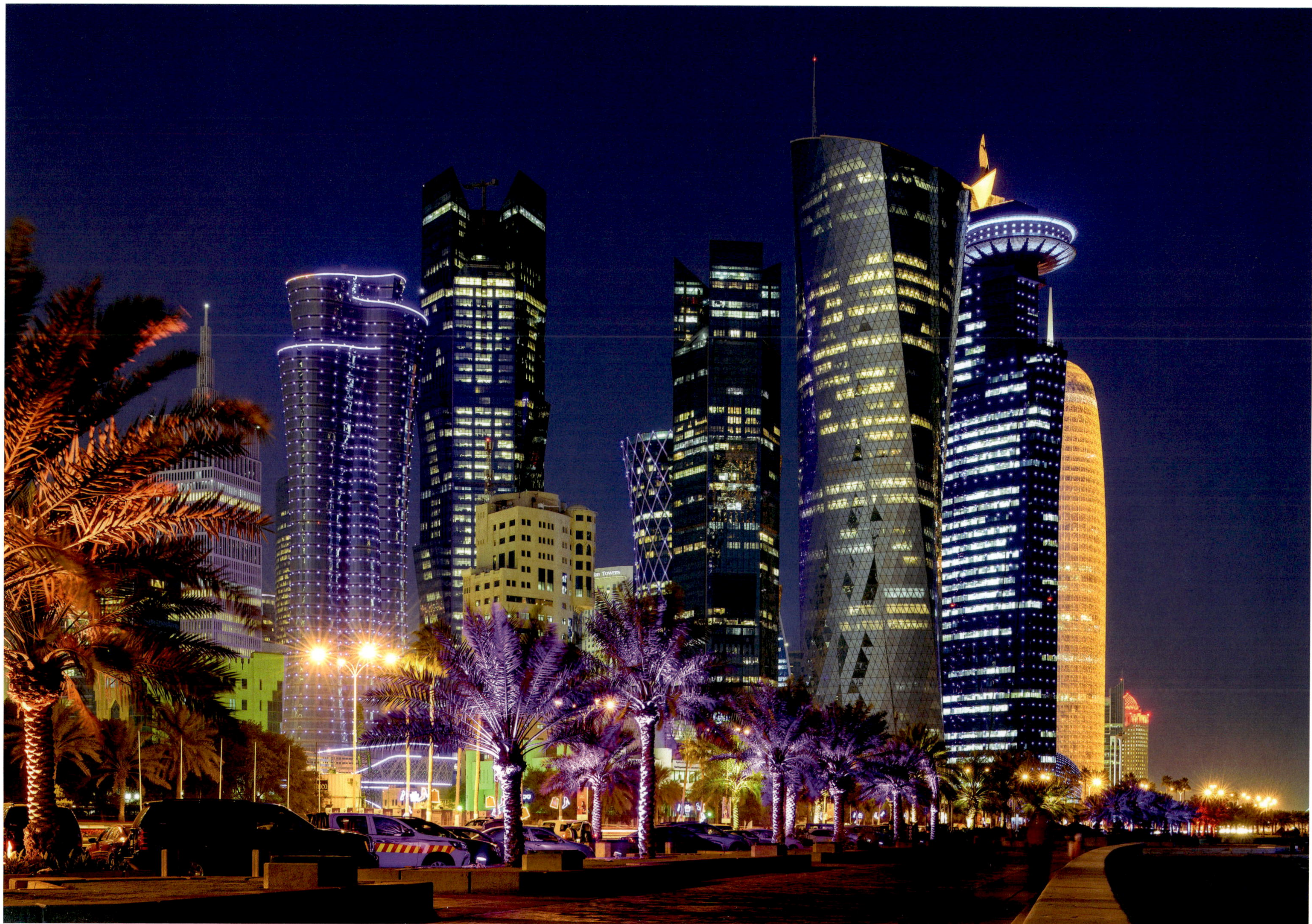

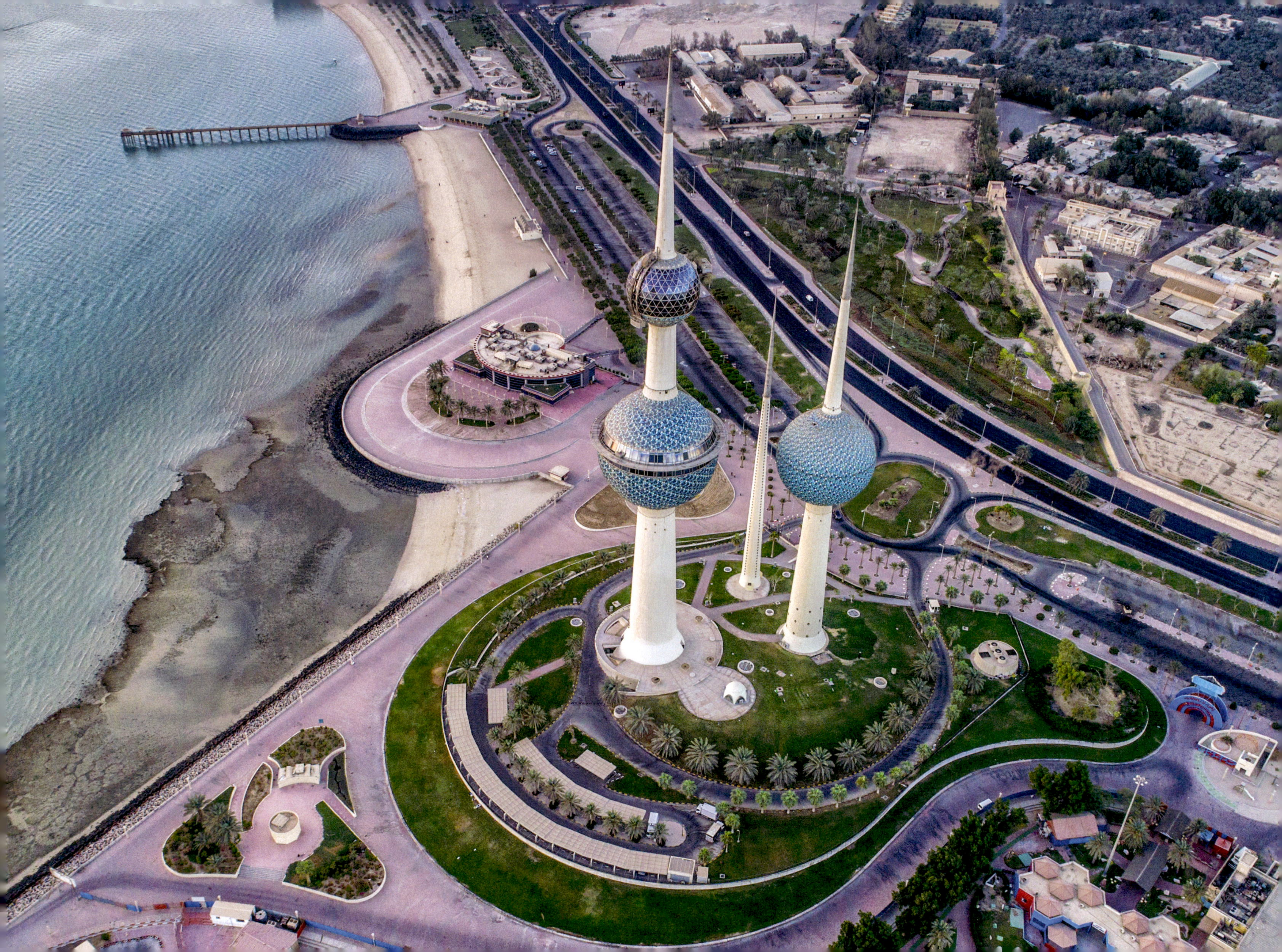

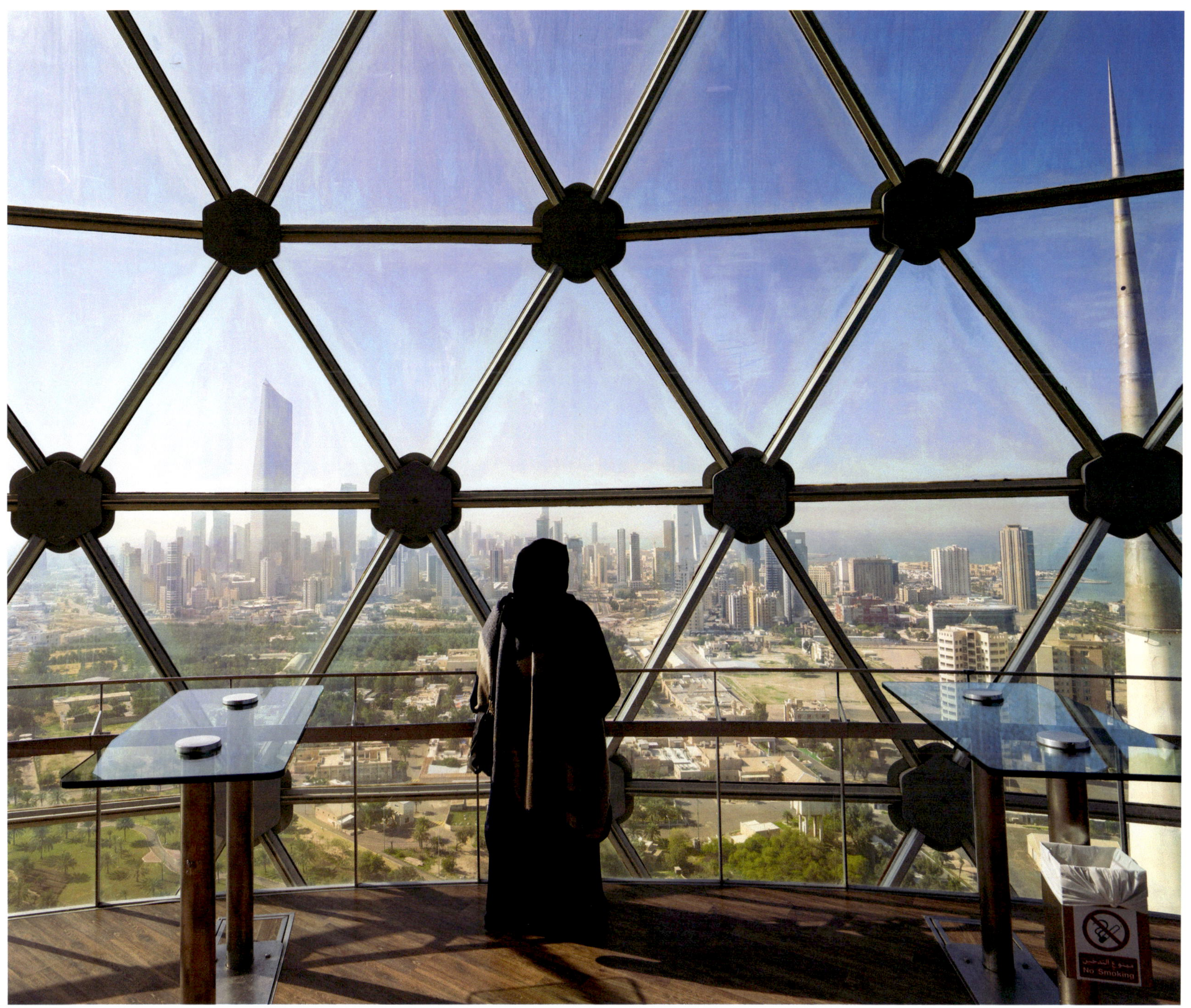

LEFT & OPPOSITE:

Kuwait Towers, Kuwait City
This trio of slender spires are a symbol of modern Kuwait. Inaugurated in 1979, they were originally part of a water supply project, with the spheres on the two taller buildings serving as reservoirs. Designed by Swedish architect Sune Lindström and Danish architect Malene Bjorn, these towers created a modern visual identity for this young country, combined with traditional Islamic motifs. Today, they are a major tourist attraction for visitors and Kuwaitis alike, who come to enjoy fine food and great all-round views of city and sea.

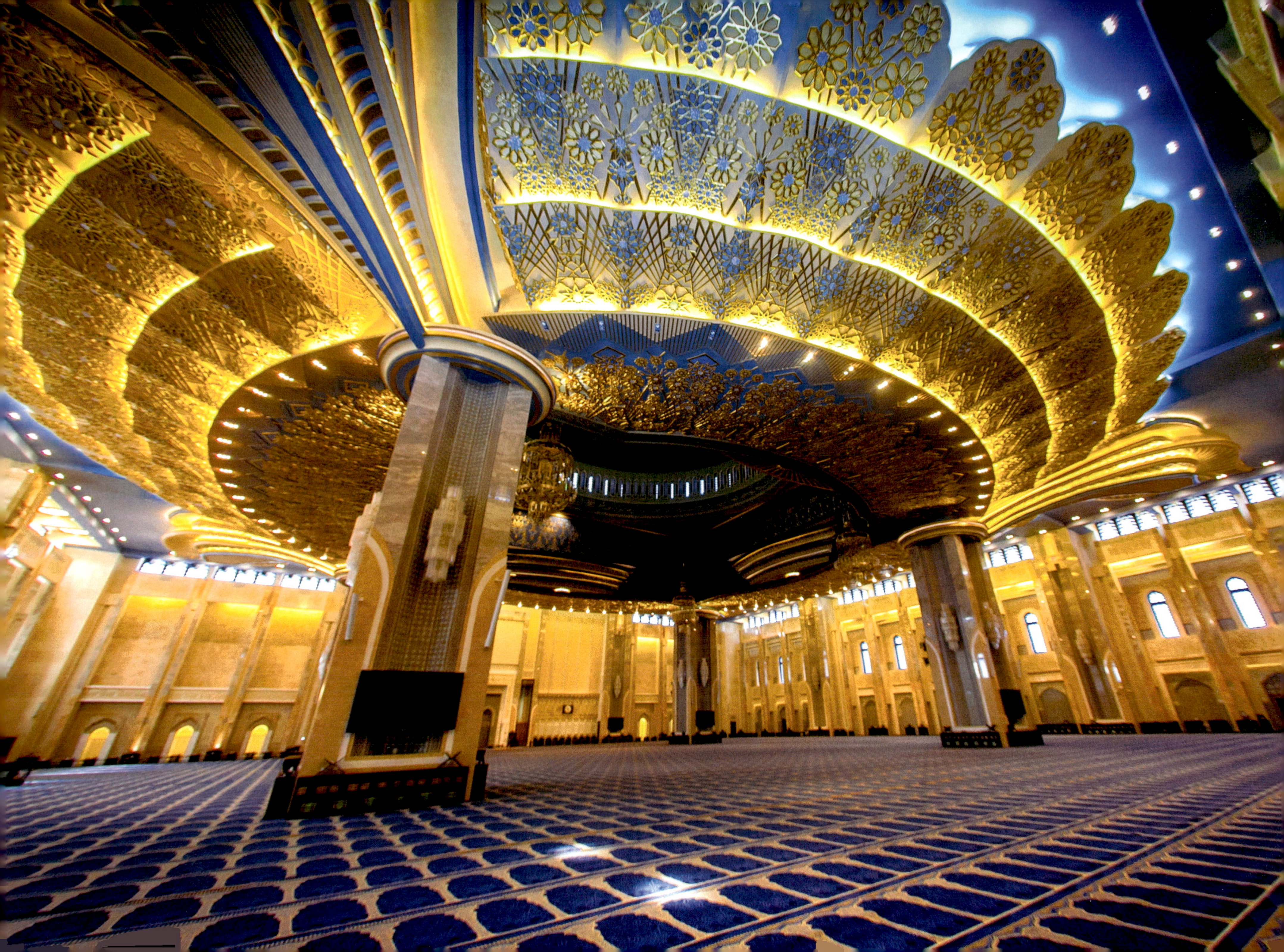

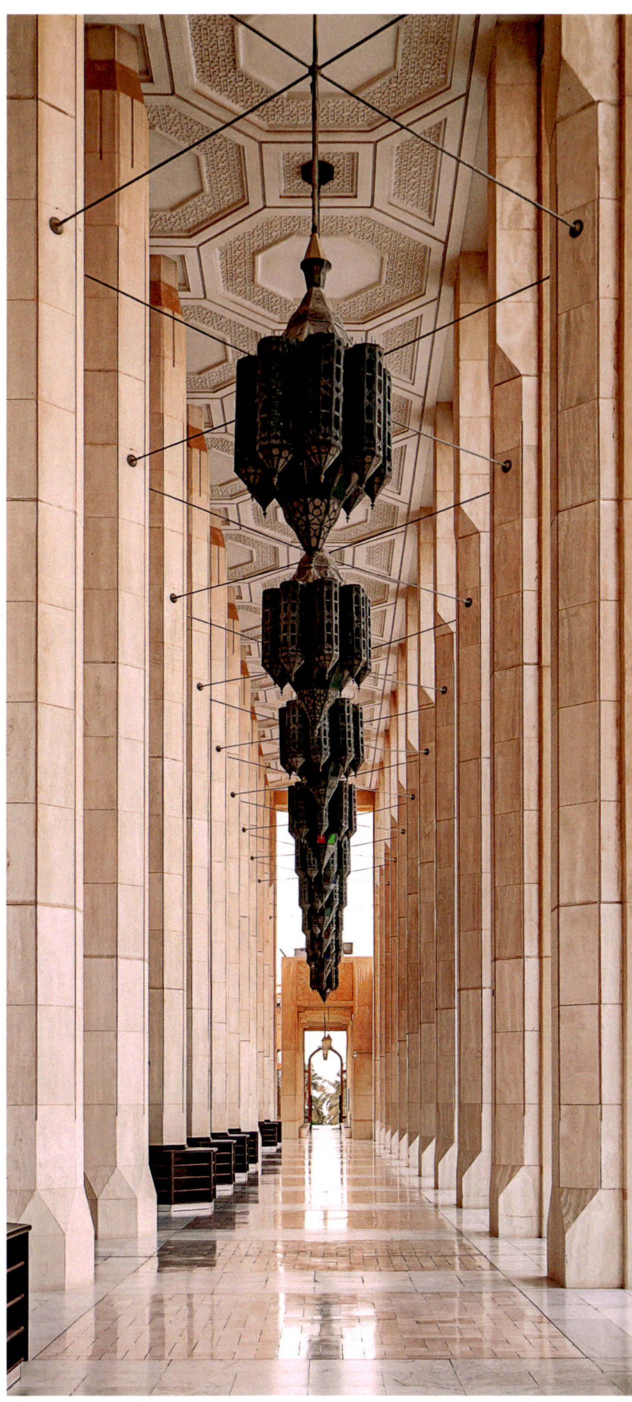

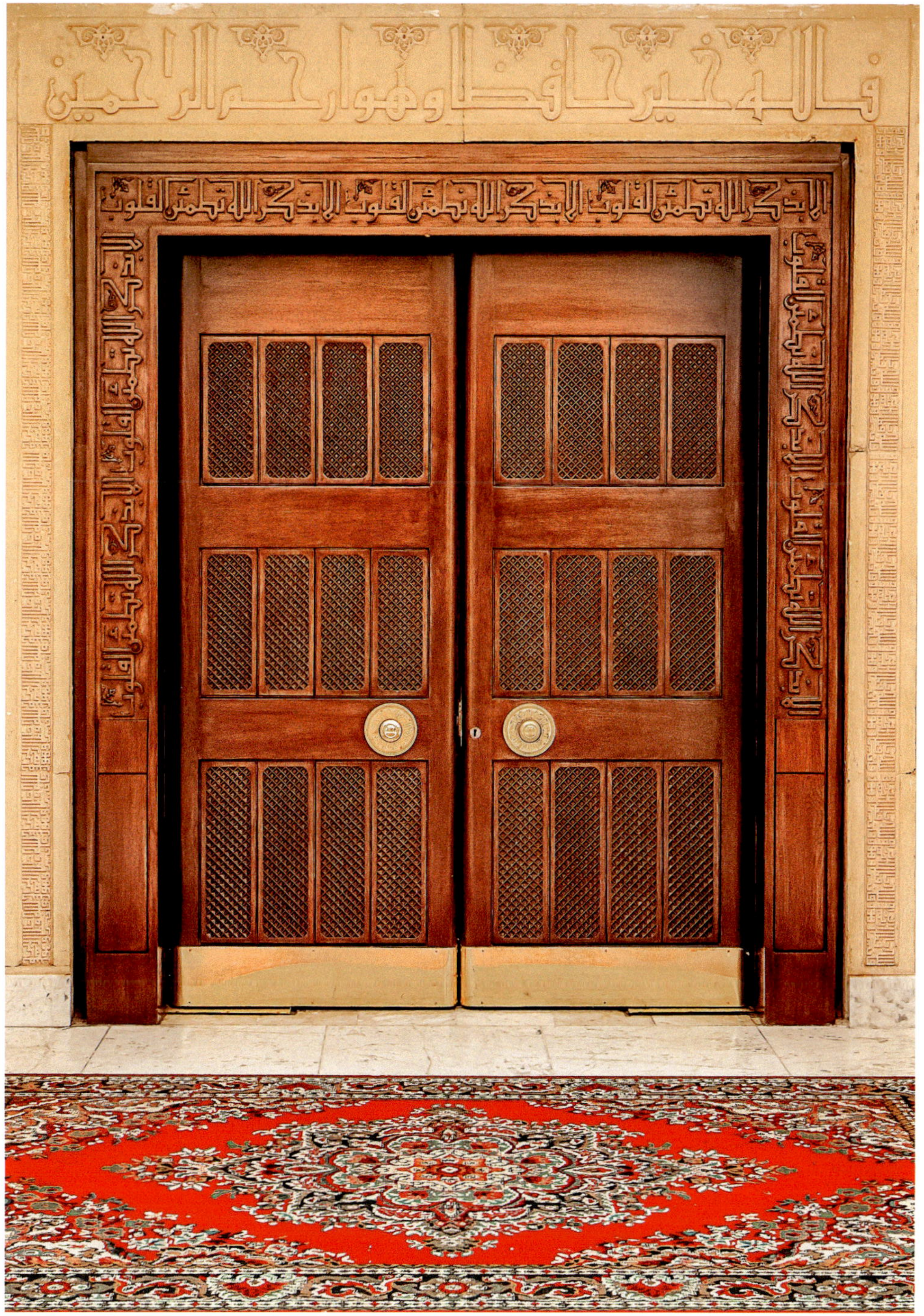

ALL PHOTOGRAPHS:

Grand Mosque of Kuwait, Kuwait City

Commissioned by the late Sheikh Jaber Al-Ahmad Al-Jaber Al-Sabah, construction of this, the country's largest mosque, began in 1979 and was completed in 1986. While the mosque's exterior is understated, with a traditional Andalusian-style minaret, quiet corridors surround the exterior and the doors are in simple, traditional style. Inside lies an astonishing showcase of Islamic art. The huge main prayer hall features a central dome, some 43 metres (140ft) high, that is adorned with the 99 names of Allah in intricate Kufi calligraphy. The mosque is decorated throughout with a mix of traditional geometric patterns, floral motifs, and detailed Arabic calligraphy by artist Hamid Haddad. Materials used include Italian marble, mosaics from Morocco, and specially designed stained glass from France.

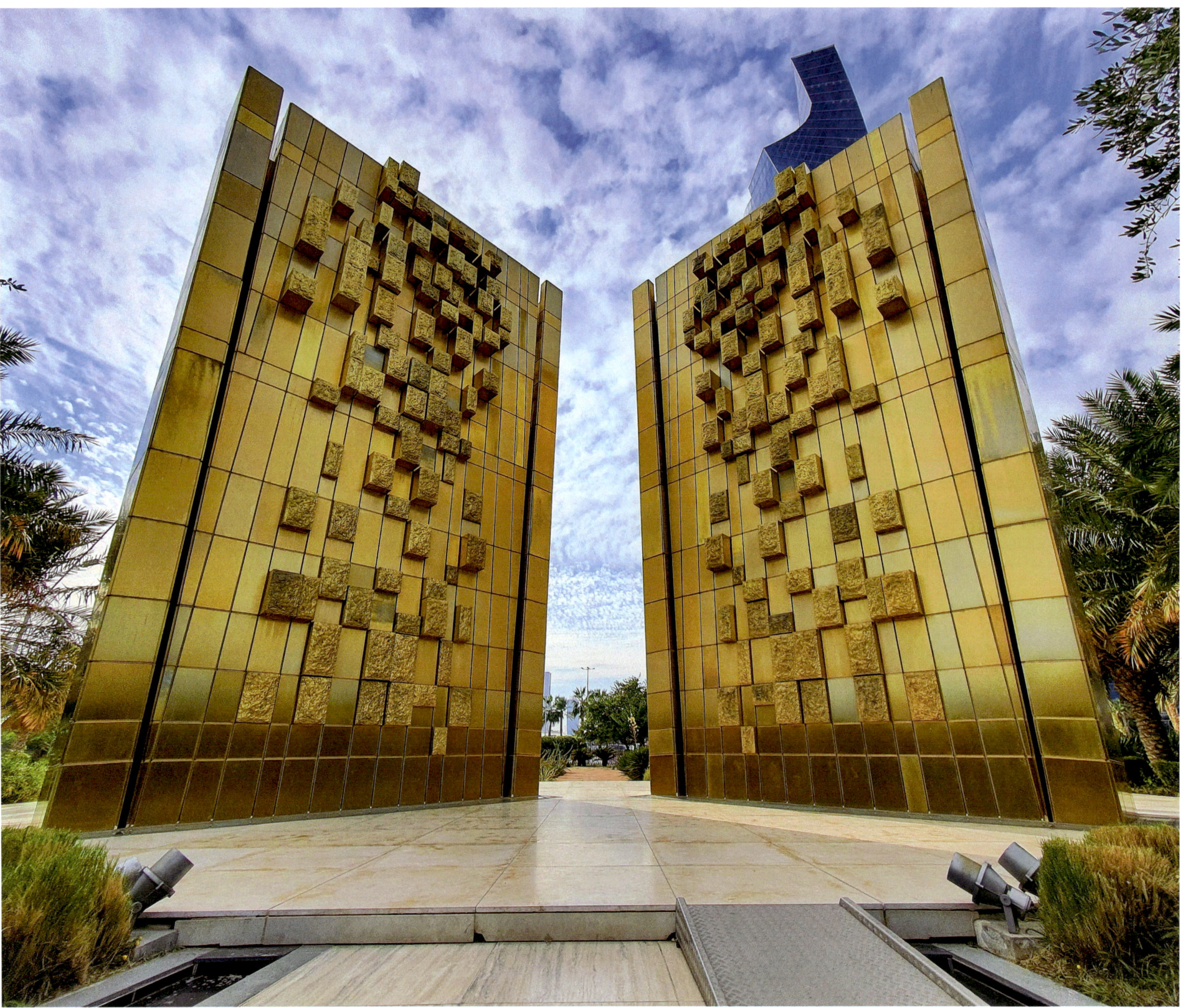

RIGHT:

Constitution Monument, Al Shaheed Park

Built in 2012 to celebrate the 50th anniversary of the Kuwaiti Constitution, this monument, featuring portals that reflect the past (the Old Age) and look to a prosperous future (the New Age), symbolizes the nation's journey towards democracy.

OPPOSITE:

Dhows, Kuwait City

These traditional sailing vessels, common throughout the region, define Kuwaiti identity long before the discovery of oil. Historically the economy and society were deeply intertwined with the sea, and dhows were essential for vital activities, from trade to pearl diving as well as fishing and transporting fresh water.

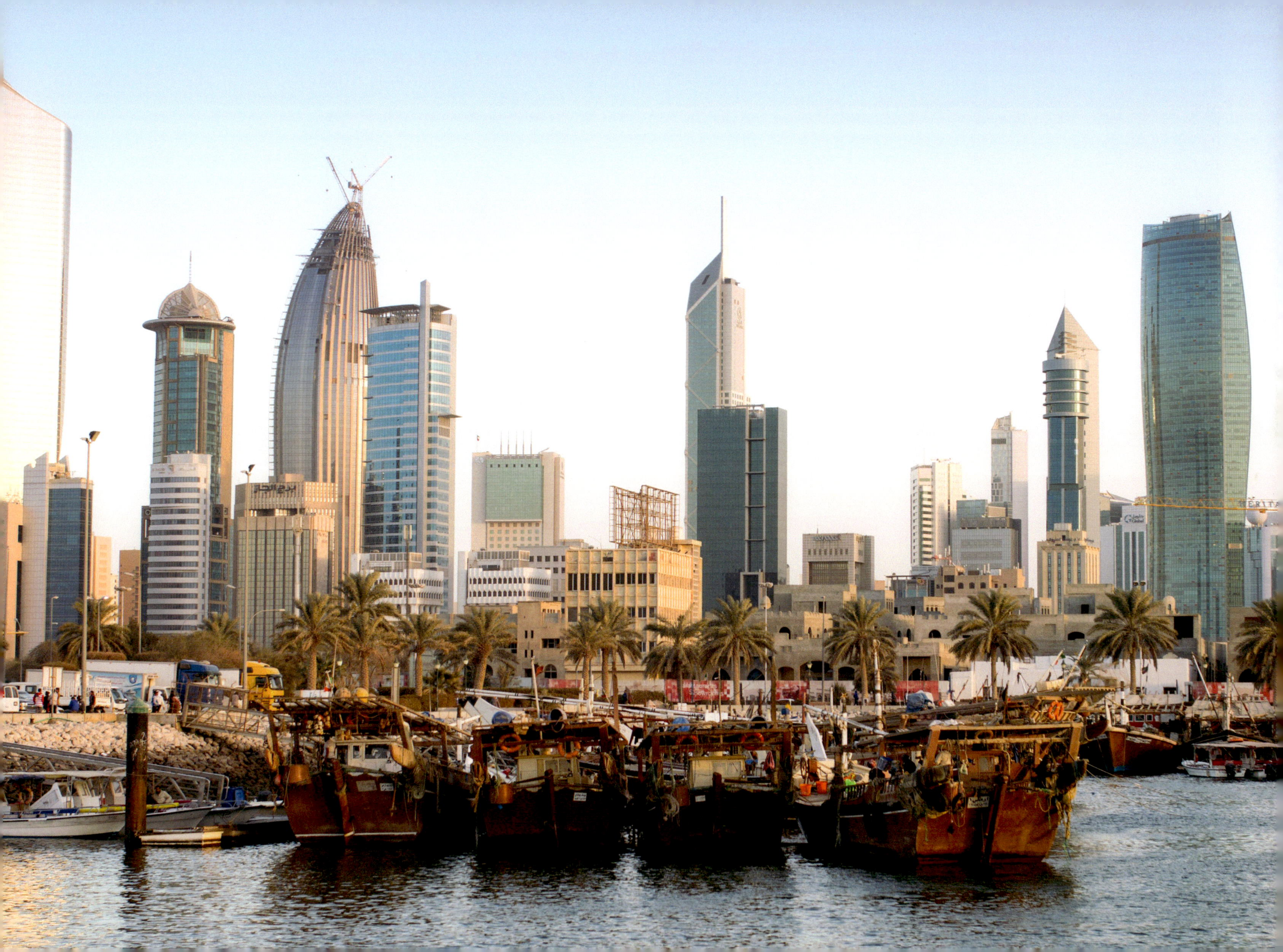

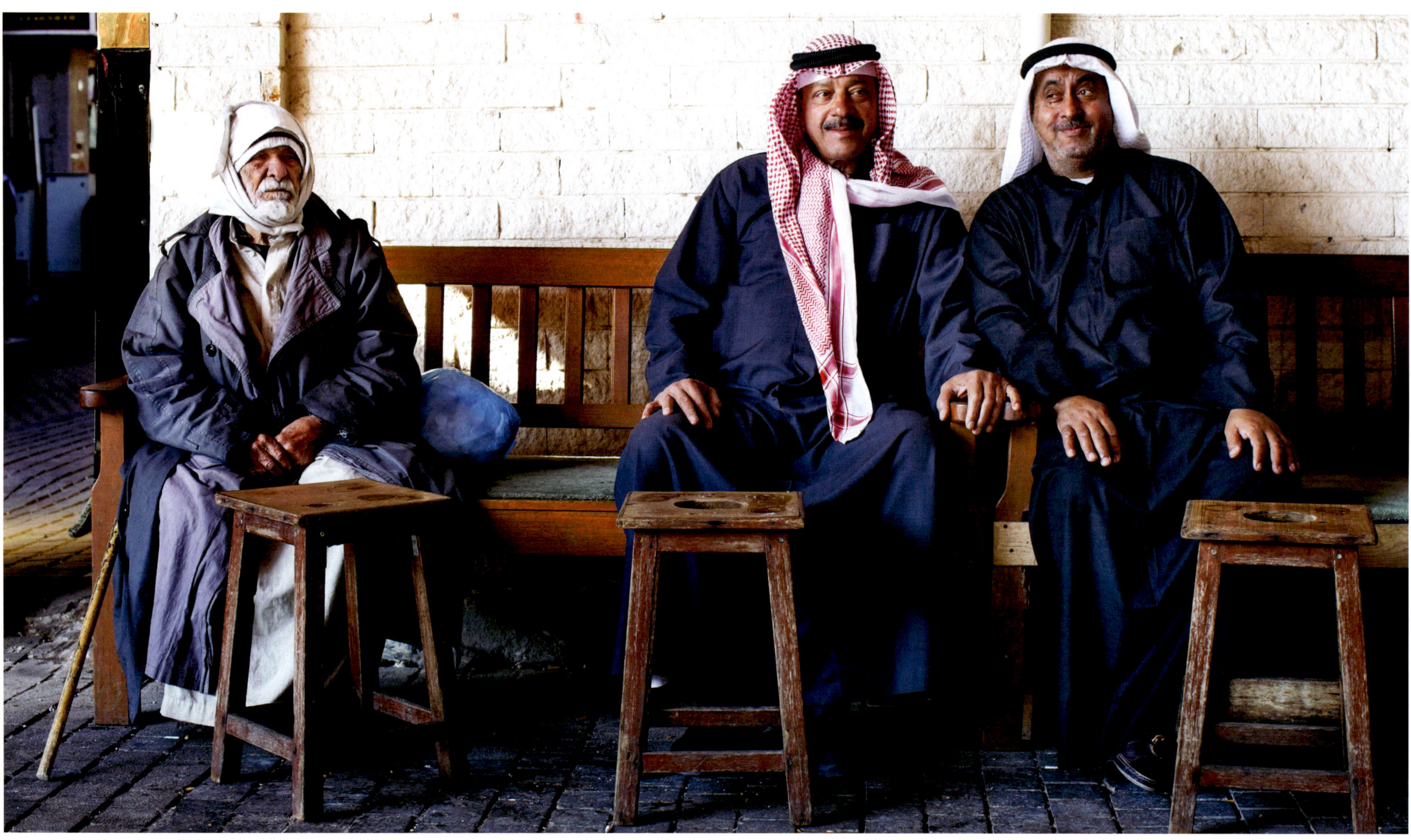

Souk Al-Mubarakiya, Kuwait City
In the Arabian Gulf, coffee is more than just a drink: it's the centre of daily life. Traditional, strong coffee is often infused with cardamom and is a Kuwaiti staple. Locals gather in cafes to sip coffee and socialize. Slow-paced conversation is a key part of the souq experience.

The Avenues mall, Kuwait
This monumental shopping, dining, and entertainment destination is one of the largest in the region. The Grand Avenue and Prestige area are home to high-end luxury brands and gourmet restaurants, where the most opulent gifts can be bought at a price. The mall is divided into several themed districts, each offering a distinct experience. Grand Avenue is a stunning, tree-lined boulevard with a transparent roof that mimics a European street. The Souq is a modern interpretation of a traditional Kuwaiti market, complete with winding alleyways and shops selling local goods. Other districts, like SoKu, are inspired by bohemian neighbourhoods and cater to a younger, trendier crowd.

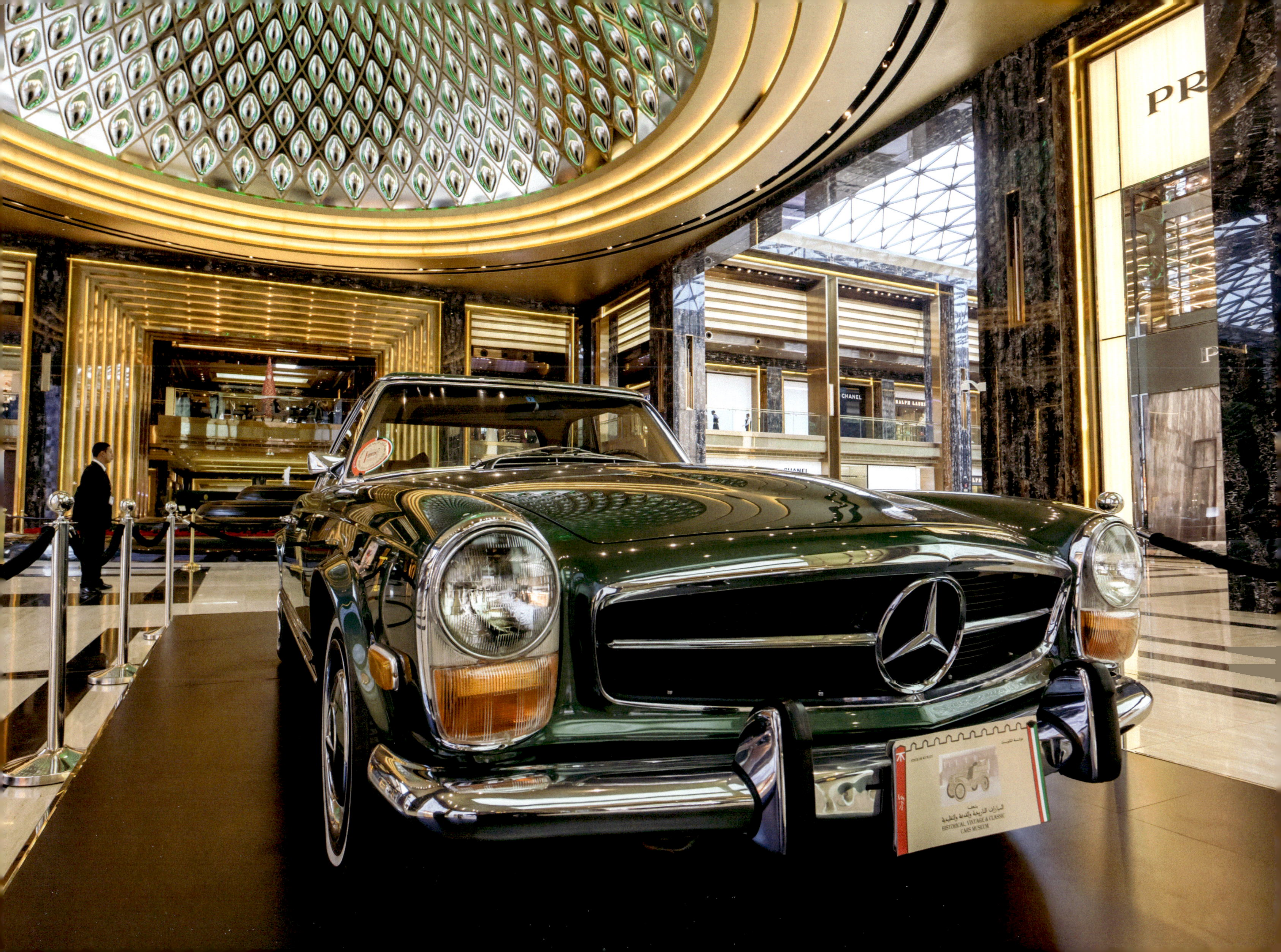

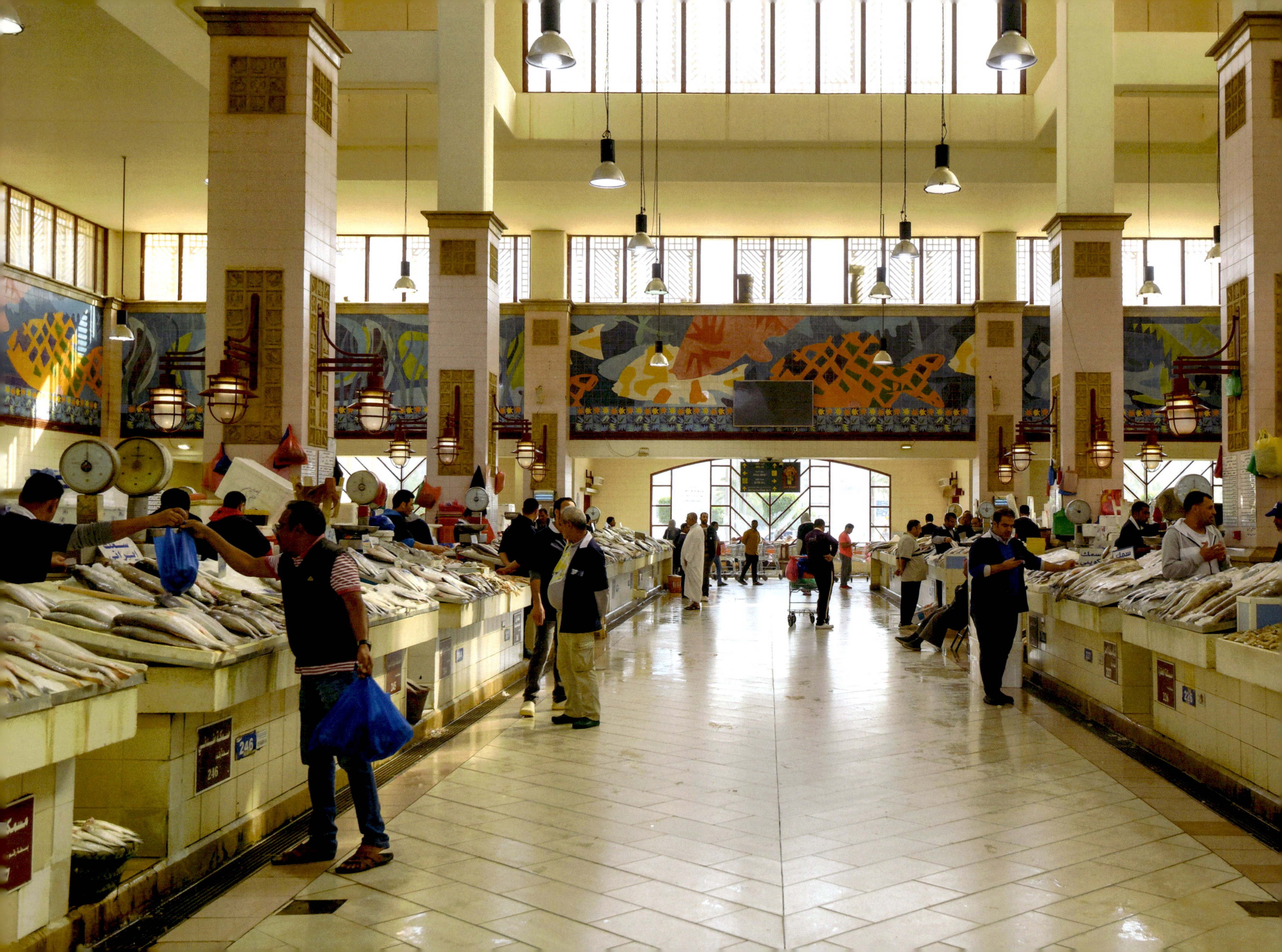

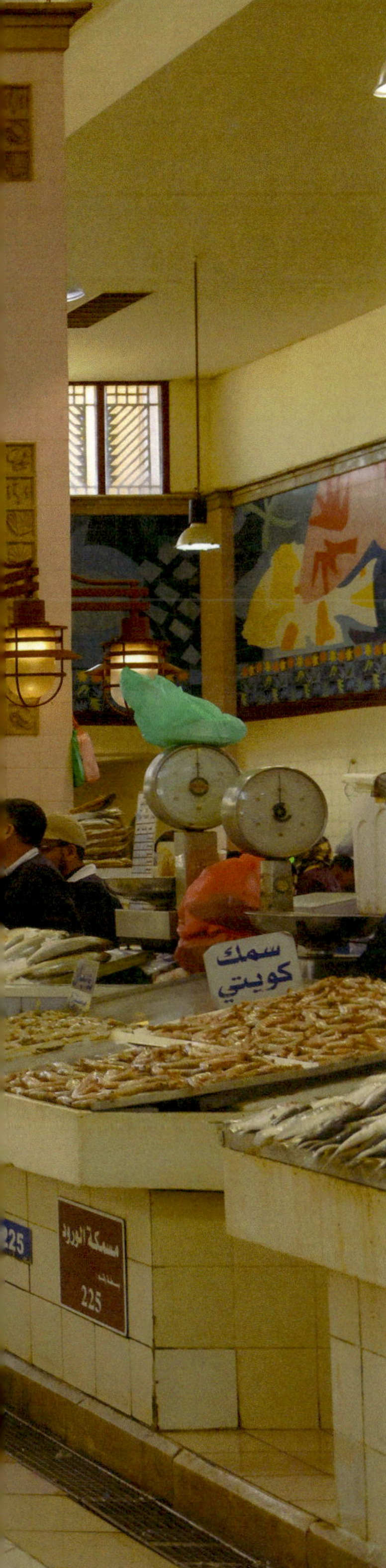

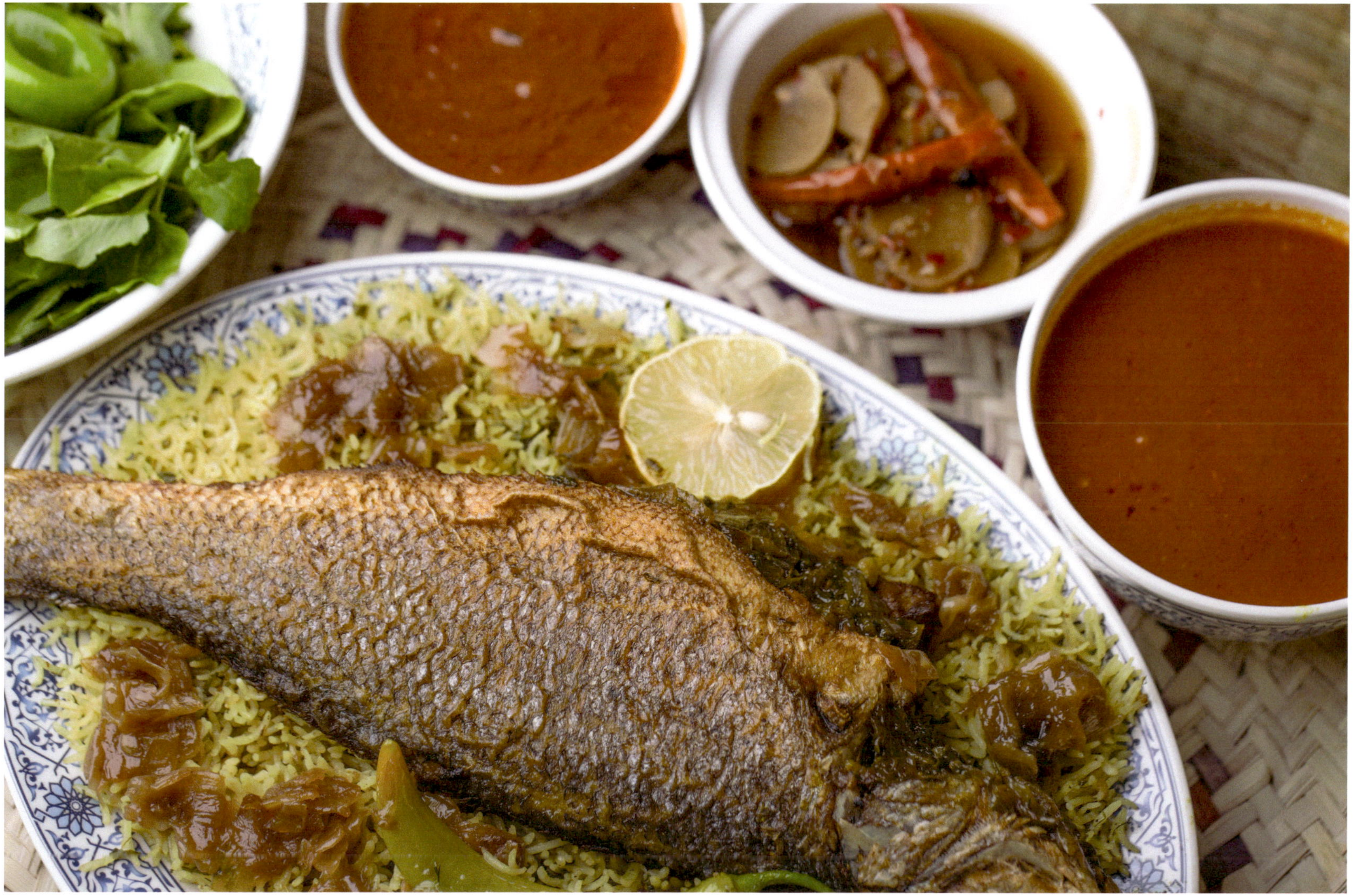

LEFT:
Fish Market, Kuwait City

The most famous fish market of Kuwait is also one of its oldest. The Central Fish Market sits on the Gulf Road waterfront and is busy every morning with shoppers and traders examining that day's fresh catch. Here the range of marine food will challenge even the best informed fish lover to name them or know a recipe to suit. Shoppers can also enjoy fresh cooked seafood.

ABOVE:
Mutabbaq Samak – an Arabian delight

This classic Arabian cuisine is considered a national dish of Kuwait, using spicy fried fish, such as silver pomfret, placed on a bed of rice cooked in fish stock with caramelized onions. Sometimes raisins are added, or cardamom.

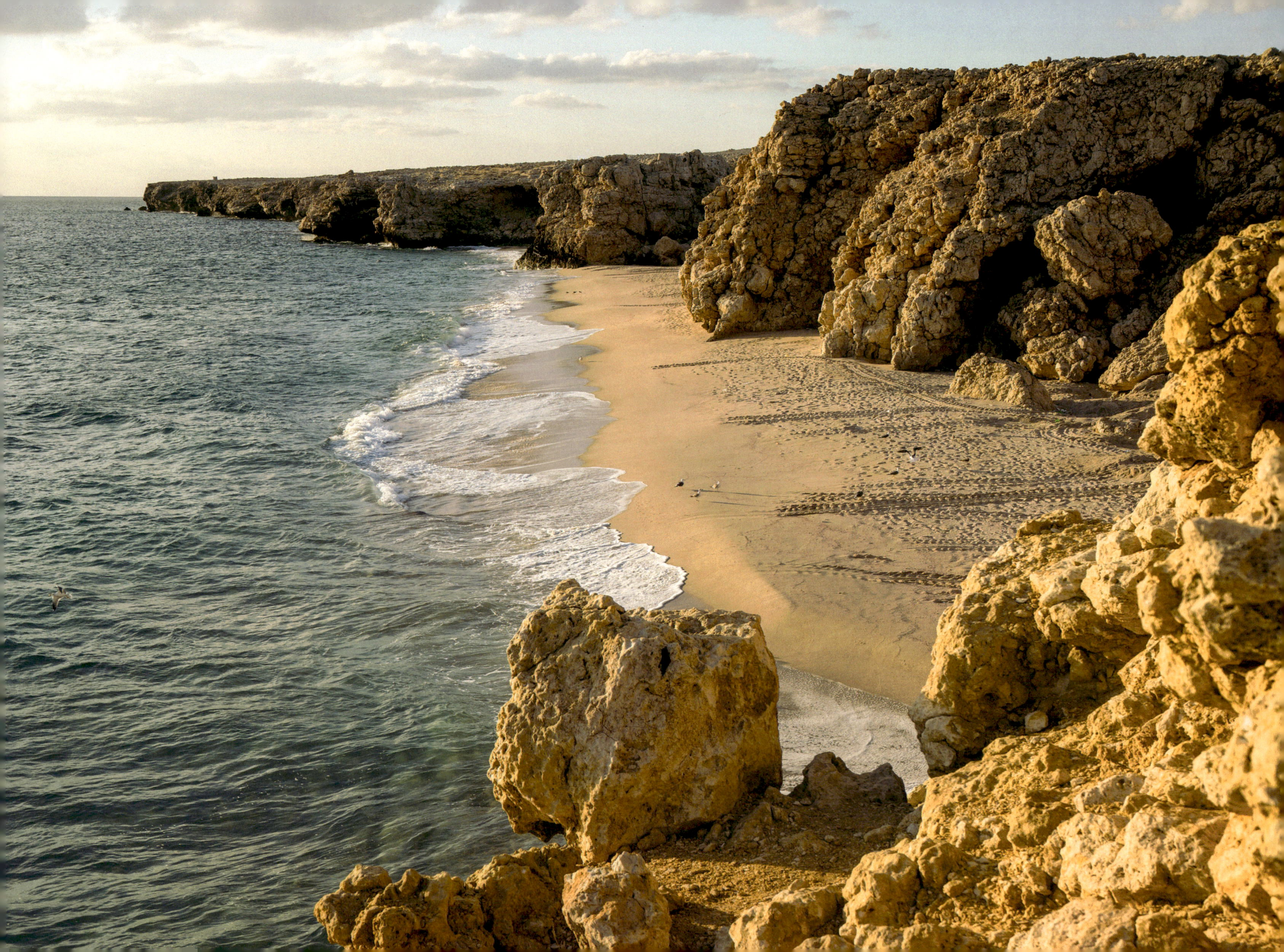

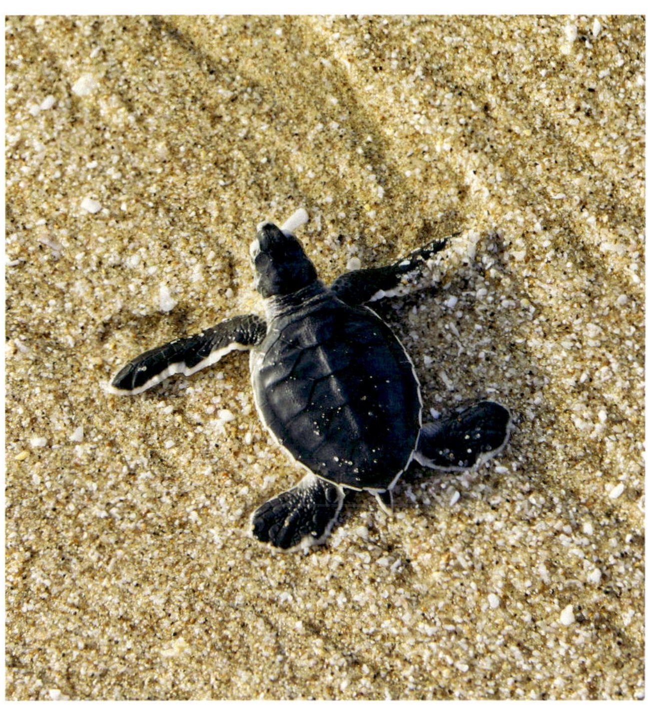

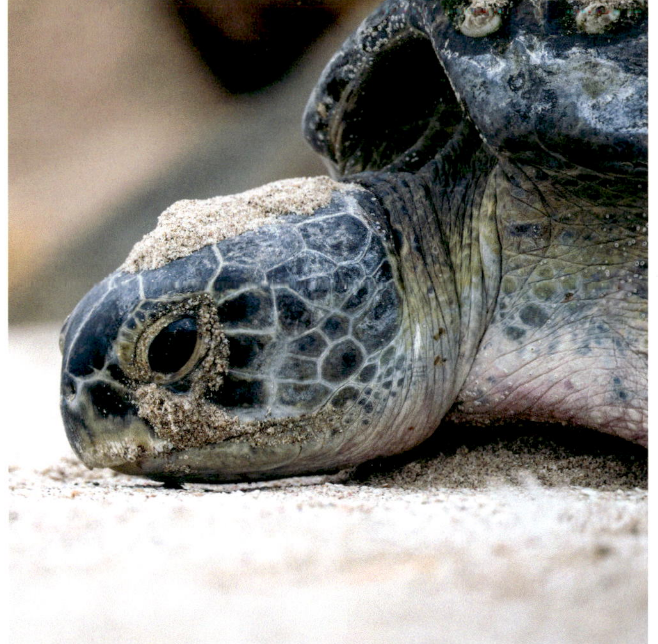

Ras Al Jinz turtle reserve
This beach in Oman is a vitally important nesting site for the endangered green sea turtle. It is possible to take guided evening and dawn tours to witness female turtles laying their eggs and tiny hatchlings taking their first steps of a perilous journey to the sea.

Turtle hatching, Raz Al Jinz
After approximately 55 days of incubation, these tiny hatchlings, just 5cm (2in) long and weighing 25g (0.8oz), emerge from their nests. Often they are guided by the moonlight reflecting off the ocean, as they dash to the warm waters of the Arabian Gulf. This is an awe-inspiring natural spectacle.

Traditional door and interior, Bahla Fort
The interior of this massive mud-brick fortification, built by the Banu Nebhan tribe between the 12th and 15th centuries, is a maze of rooms, corridors, and stairwells. Visitors can explore various sections of the interior rooms and the surrounding oasis. It is one of four such fortresses which were built at the foot of the Jebel Akhdar Highlands.

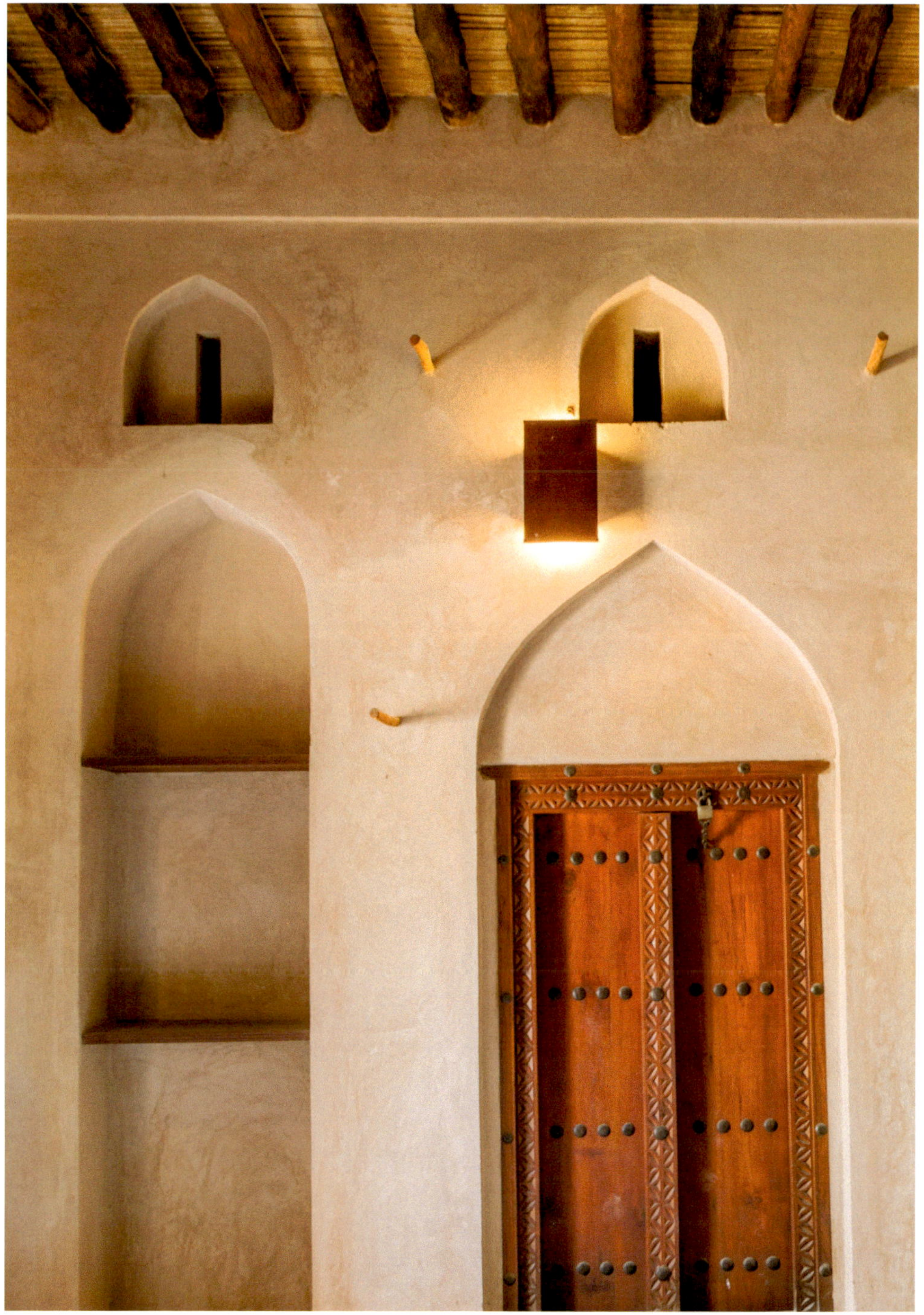

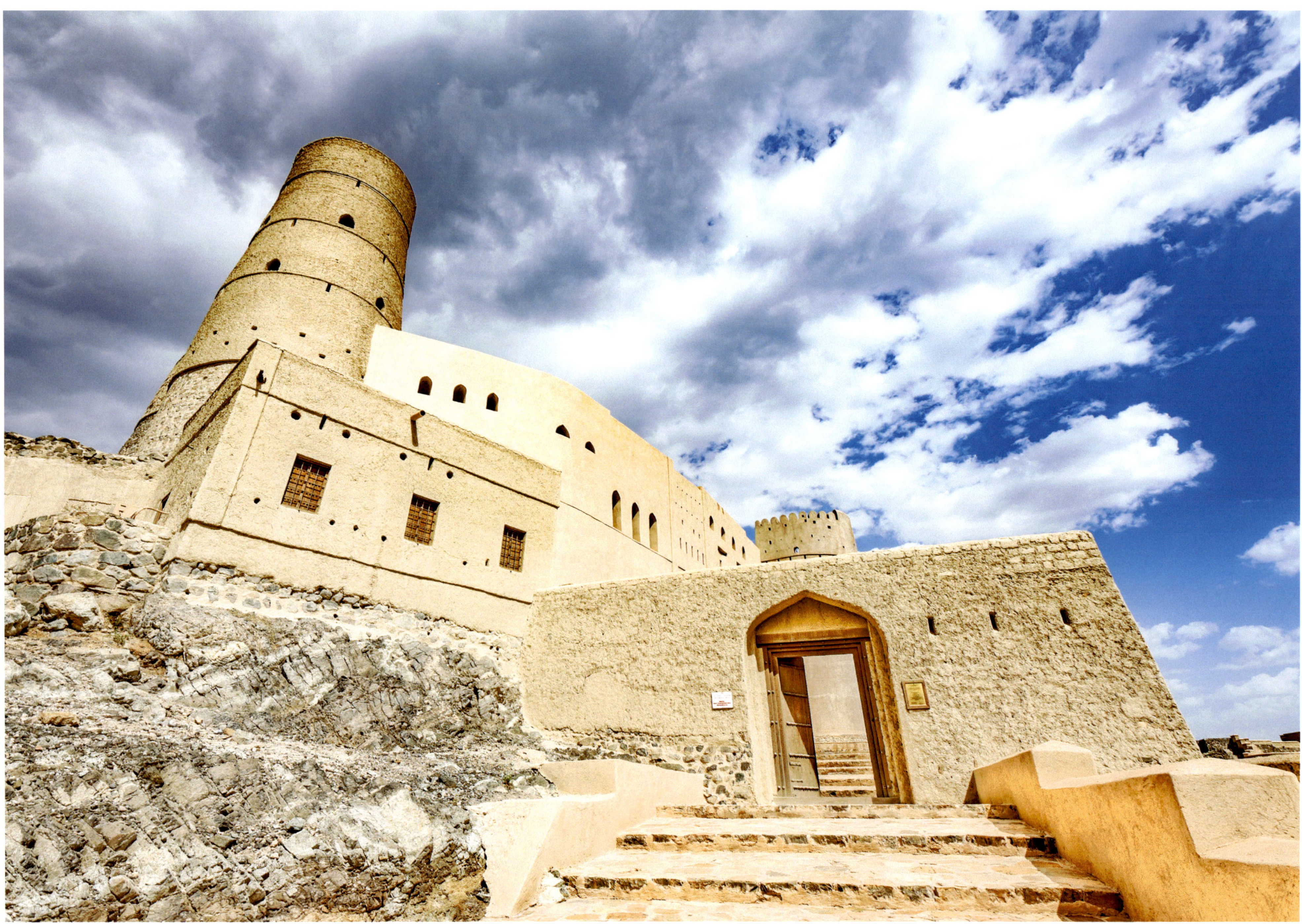

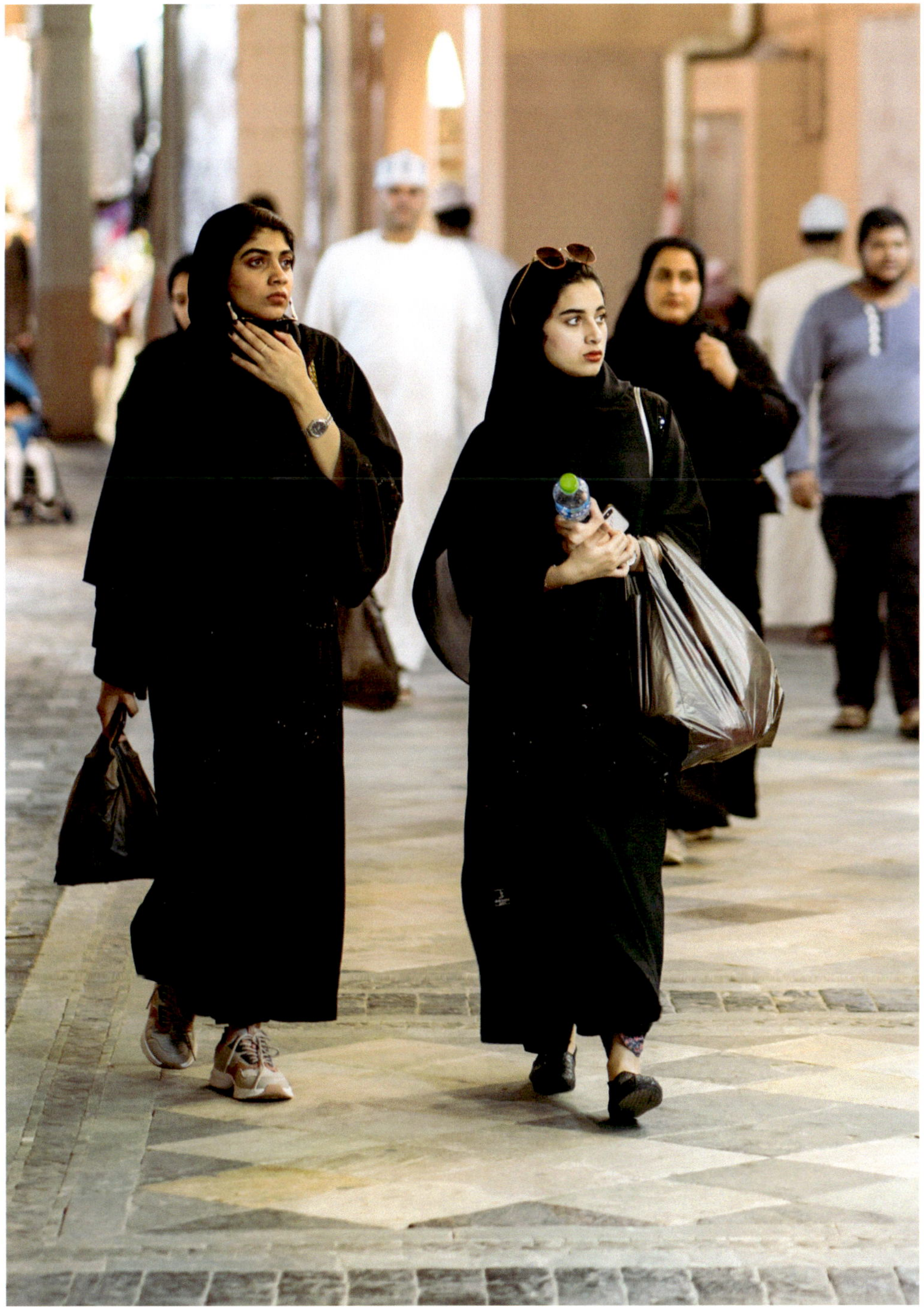

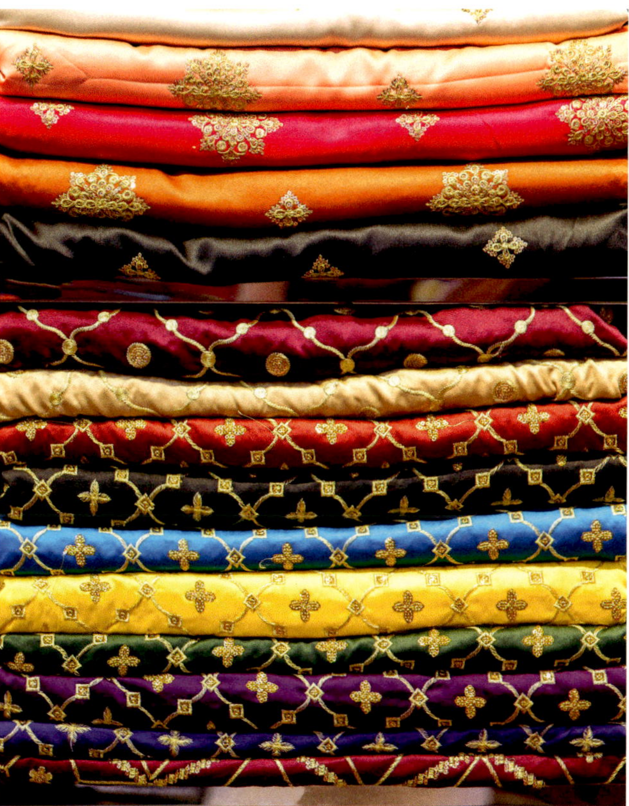

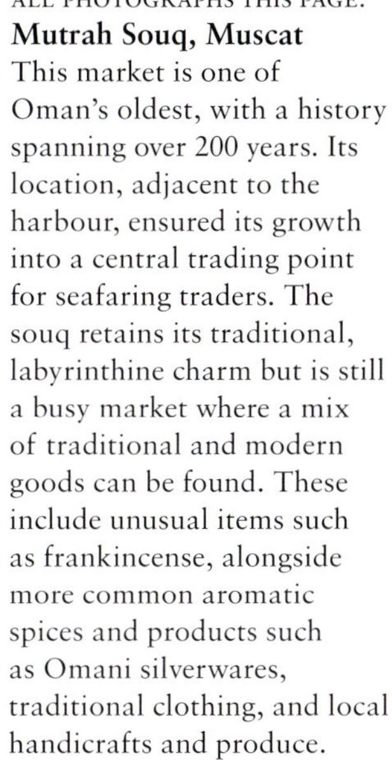

Mutrah Souq, Muscat
This market is one of Oman's oldest, with a history spanning over 200 years. Its location, adjacent to the harbour, ensured its growth into a central trading point for seafaring traders. The souq retains its traditional, labyrinthine charm but is still a busy market where a mix of traditional and modern goods can be found. These include unusual items such as frankincense, alongside more common aromatic spices and products such as Omani silverwares, traditional clothing, and local handicrafts and produce.

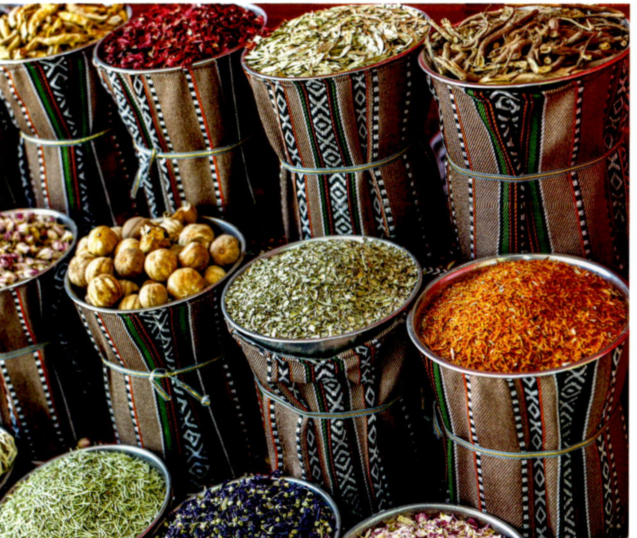

Bahla Fort
Known for its impressive scale, extensive walls, and oasis setting, this fort is also famously associated with many local legends. Bahla has been called the City of Jinn (supernatural beings in Arab folklore), causing some Omanis to avoid the place. The fort itself offers a glimpse into traditional Omani life and history. Inside there are rooms for multiple uses, such as a prayer room, a room where dates were processed into syrup, and old water wells.

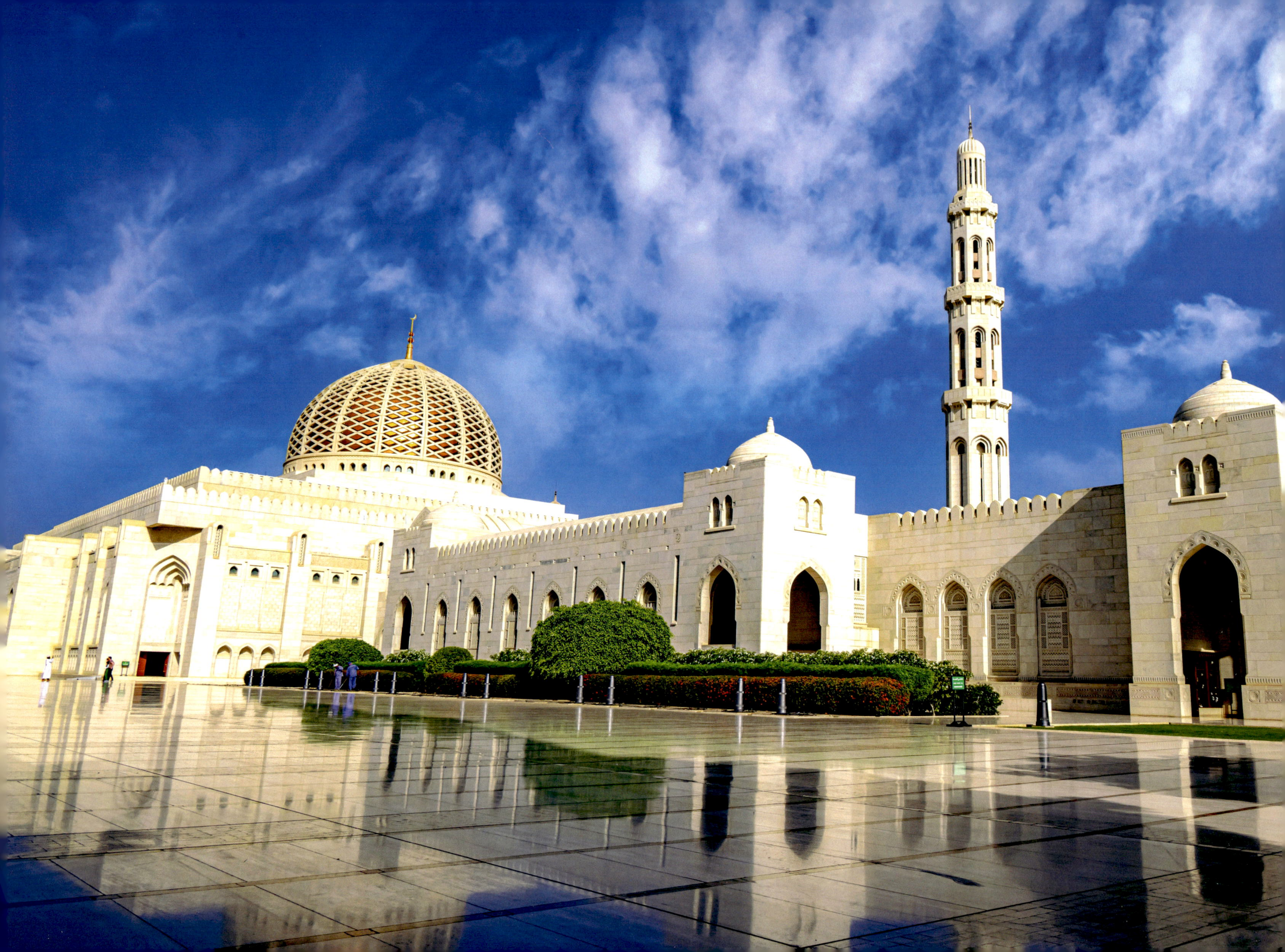

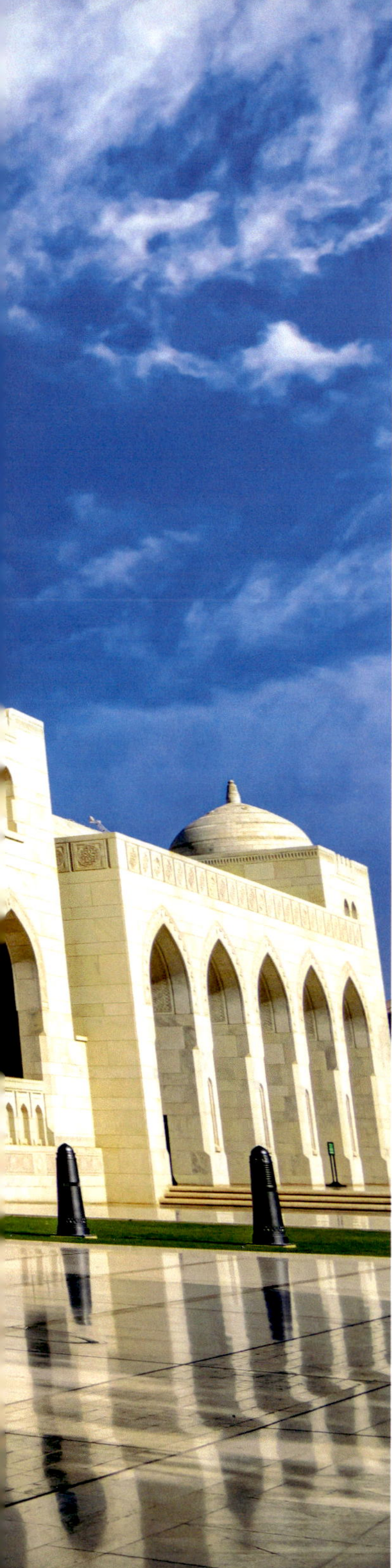

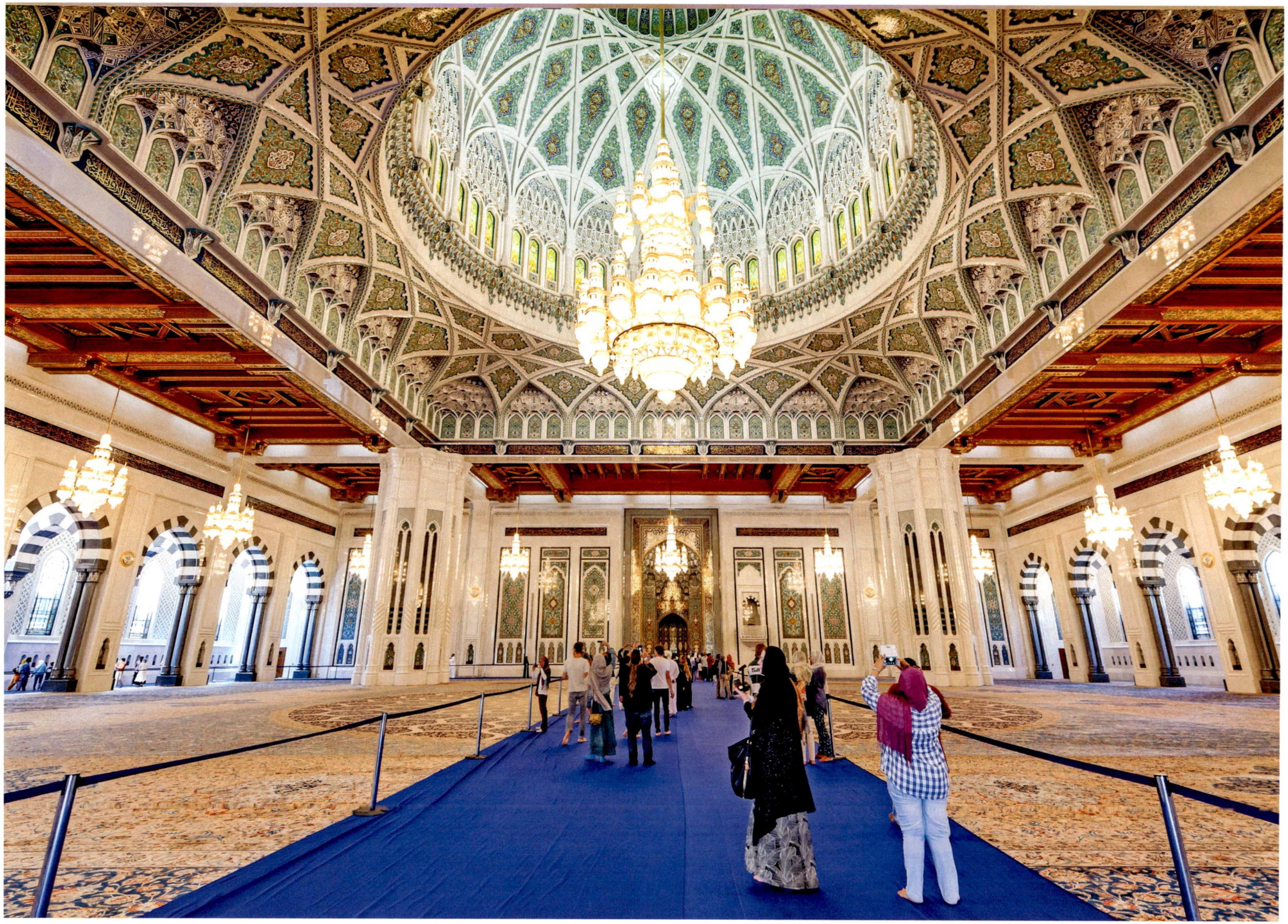

Sultan Qaboos Grand Mosque, Muscat

This marvel of Islamic architecture was inaugurated in 2001. It was built as a gift to the nation of Oman by Sultan Qaboos bin Said Al Said. It is one of the world's most beautiful and extravagant modern mosques. The central prayer hall is famed for its massive hand-woven Persian carpet, for many years the world's largest, and a spectacular Swarovski crystal chandelier. The mosque has five minarets, which symbolize the five pillars of Islam. The mosque, which welcomes visitors of all faiths, blends Omani, Islamic, and Middle Eastern styles.

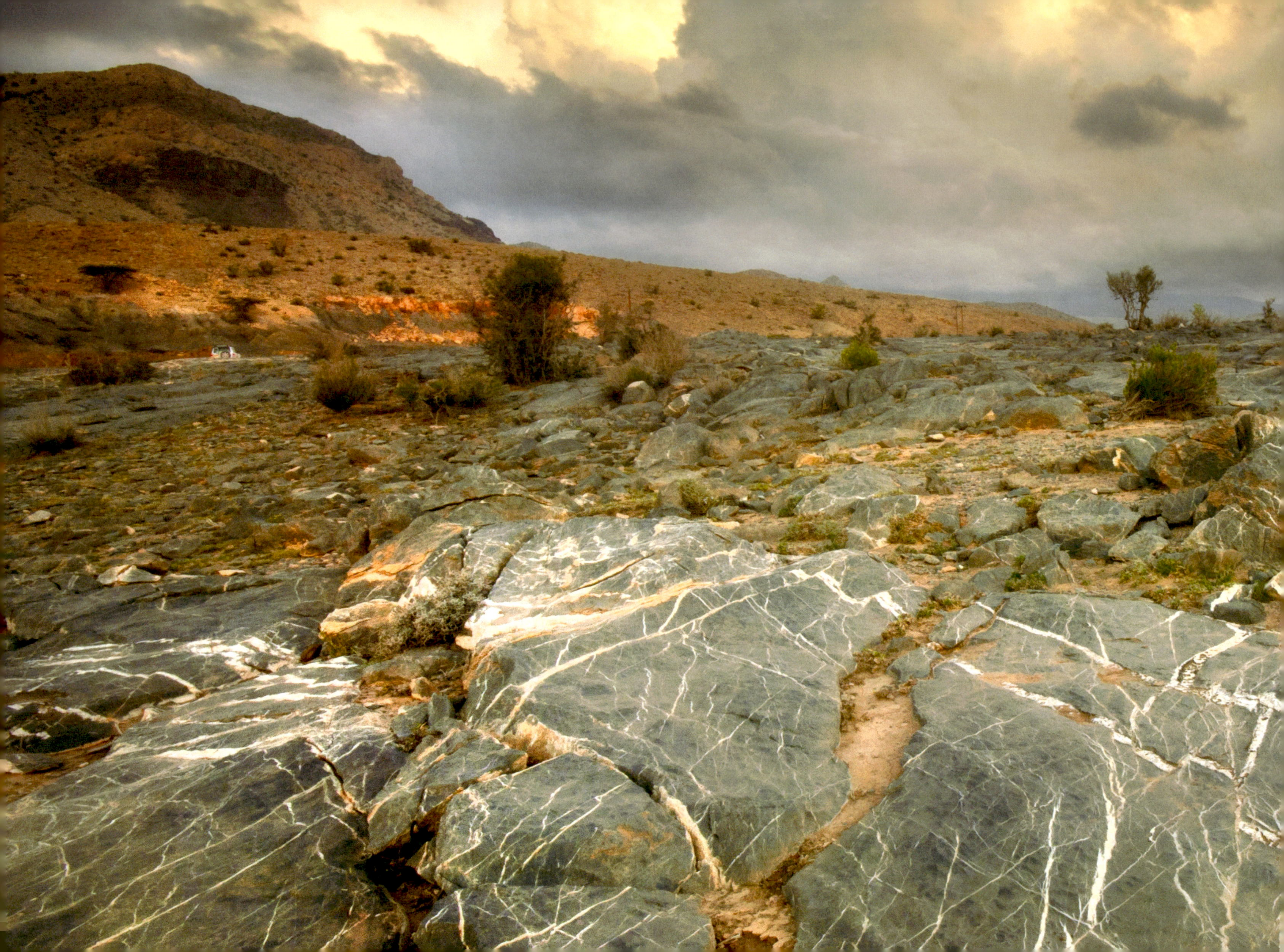

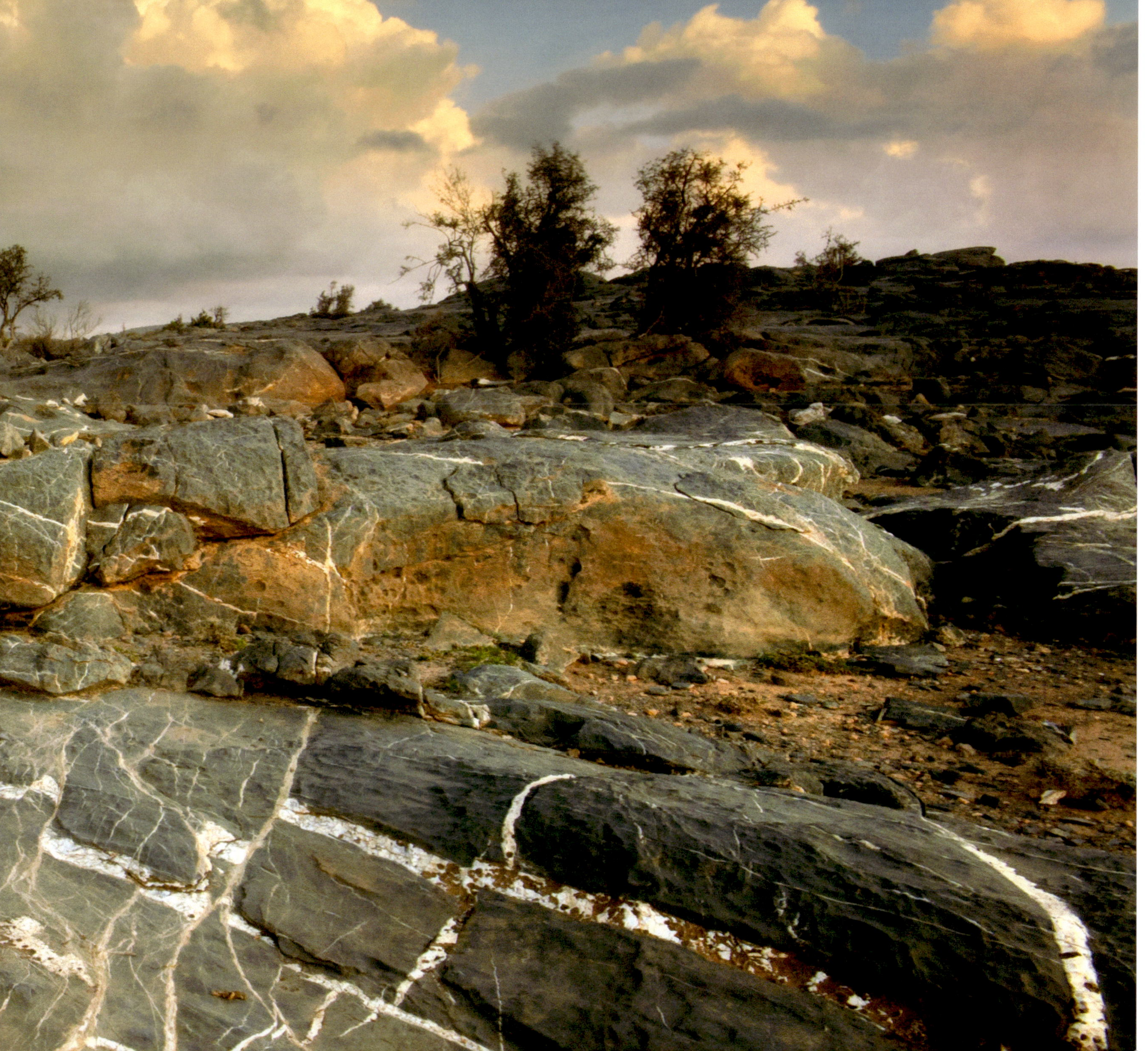

Jebel Shams Mountain, Al Hayar Mountain Range
This majestic peak is Oman's highest point, at just over 3000m (9840ft). It lies within the Al Hajar mountain range. Known as 'Mountain of the Sun', it is the first place to catch the spectacular sunrise, provided you rise at around 5 a.m. to take a hike known as the Balcony Walk to the top. This Jebel Shams Mountain area offers many hiking trails, cooler temperatures, and breathtaking scenery.

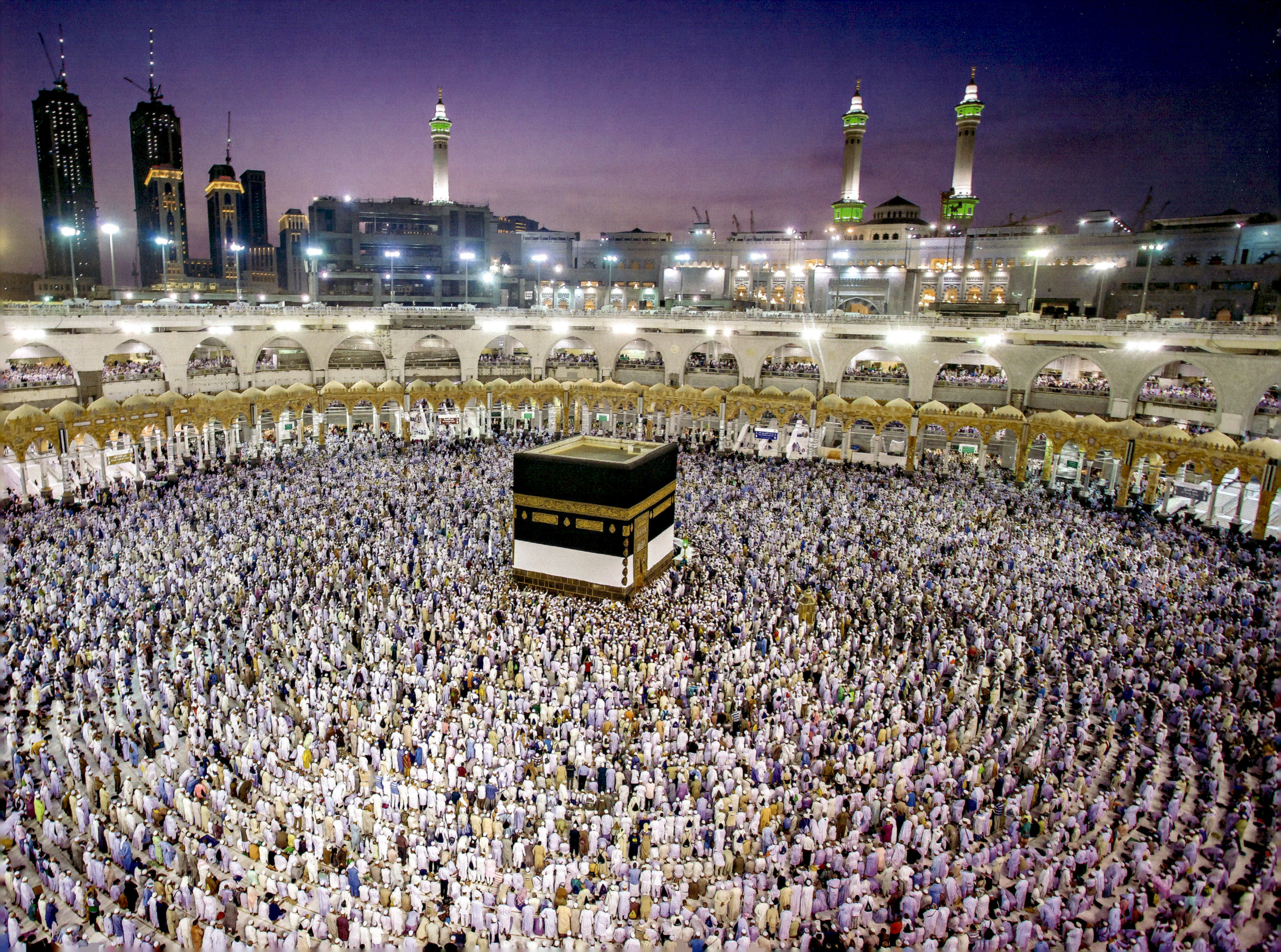

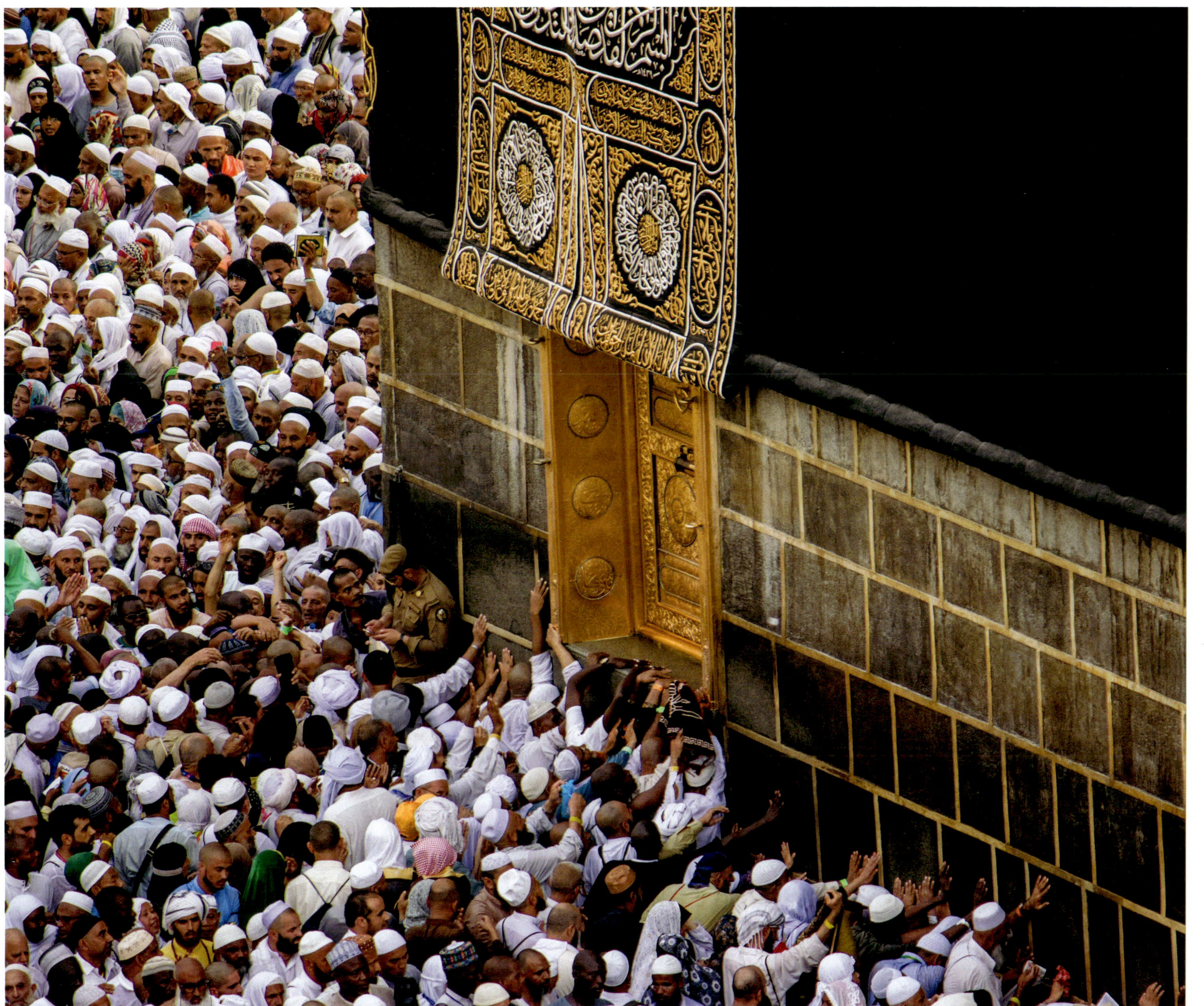

Masjid al-Haram, Mecca
Known in English as the
Great Mosque, this site
is the most sacred place
in Islam, surrounding
the Kaaba. According to
Islamic tradition, the Kaaba
was originally built by the
Prophet Ibrahim (Abraham)
and his son Ismail as the
first house of worship. The
Grand Mosque itself has a
long history of change, with
its first major construction
dating back to the Caliph
Umar ibn al-Khattab in 638
CE. The structure continually
grows as the number of
annual pilgrims grows.

LEFT:

**The Kaaba, Masjid
al-Haram, Mecca**
This cubical structure lies
at the heart of the Muslim
world. Islamic tradition holds
that it was first built by the
Prophet Ibrahim (Abraham)
and his son Ismail as a house
of worship dedicated to one
God. It contains the Black
Stone, a meteorite placed
there by Ibrahim and Ismail.
The Kaaba's importance lies
in its role as the qibla, the
direction Muslims worldwide
face during their five daily
prayers, symbolizing their
global unity. During the Hajj
pilgrimage, which is one
of the five pillars of Islam,
Muslims circle the Kaaba
seven times, a ritual known
as Tawaf.

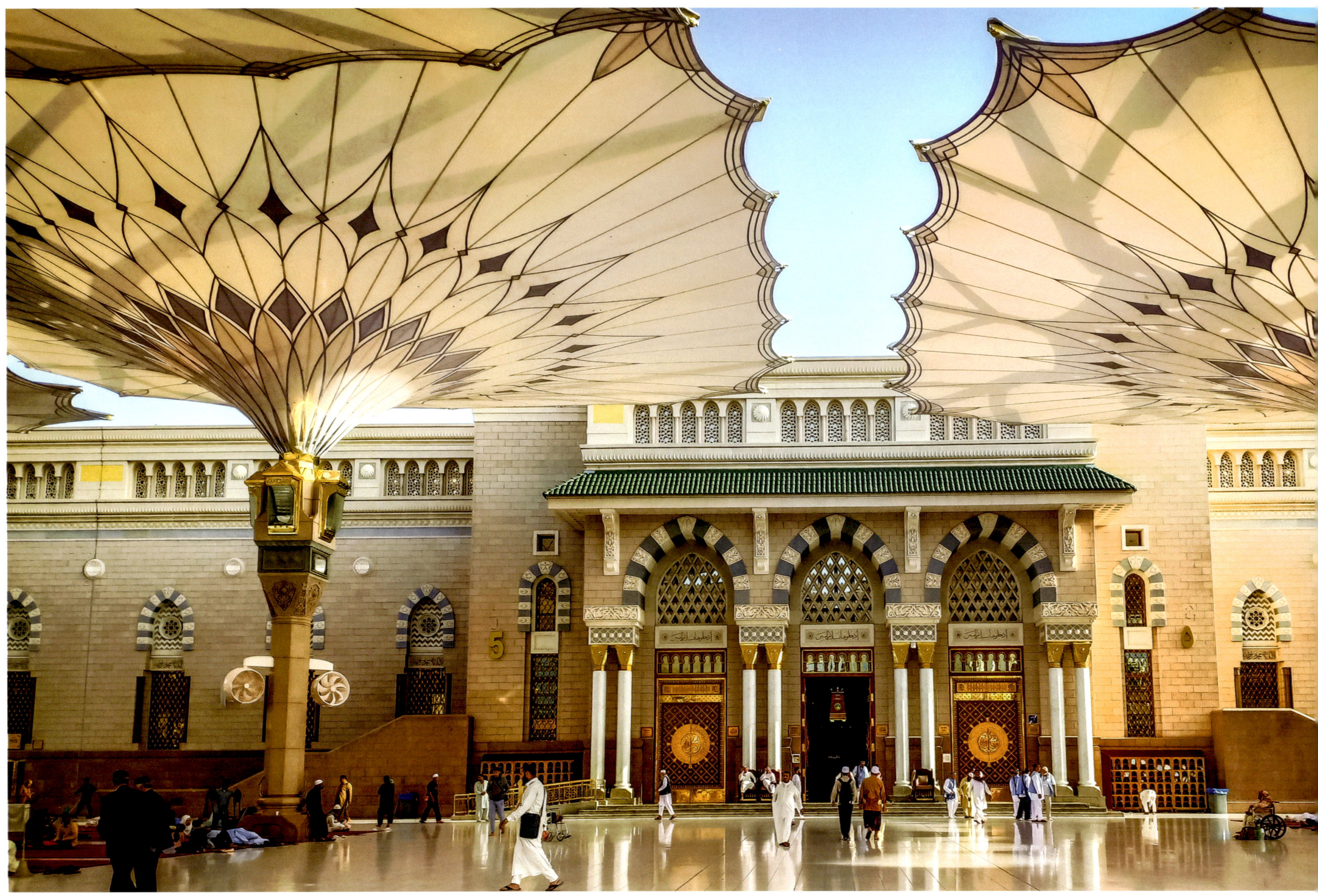

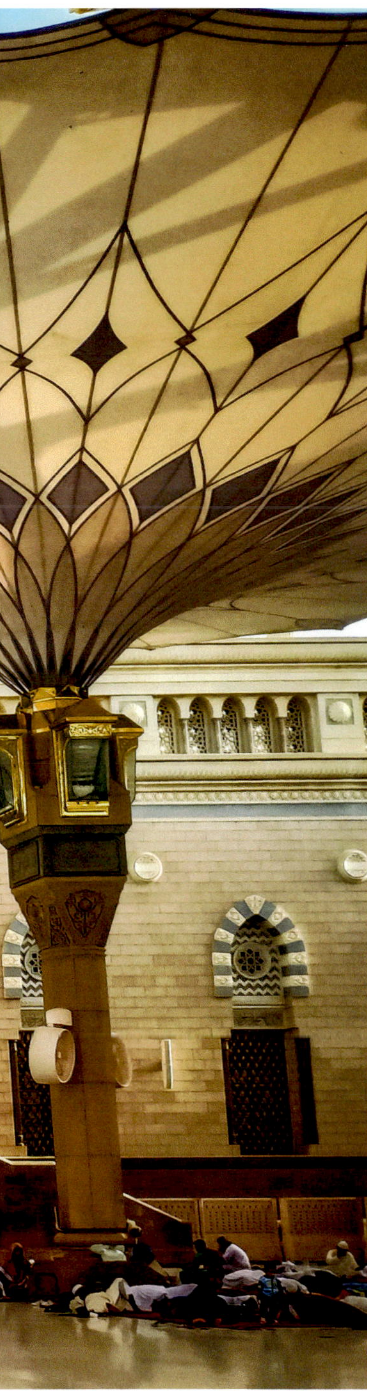

Masjid al-Nabawi, Medina

Known as the Prophet's Mosque, this is the second holiest site in Islam. It was built by Prophet Muhammad himself and is of immense importance as it is his final resting place. He is buried here in the Sacred Chamber along with his companions Abu Bakr and Umar. This chamber was originally the home of Aisha, the Prophet's wife. One prayer at Masjid al-Nabawi is considered more rewarding than thousands elsewhere.

BELOW:

Madain Saleh, Hegra

Also known as Hegra, this remarkable archaeological site is the second-largest city of the ancient Nabataean kingdom after Petra in Jordan. The area features over 100 monumental rock-cut tombs with well-preserved, intricately decorated facades. These tombs were a vital stop on the ancient incense trade route travelled by this nomadic Arab group who inhabited the deserts from the Euphrates to the Red Sea.

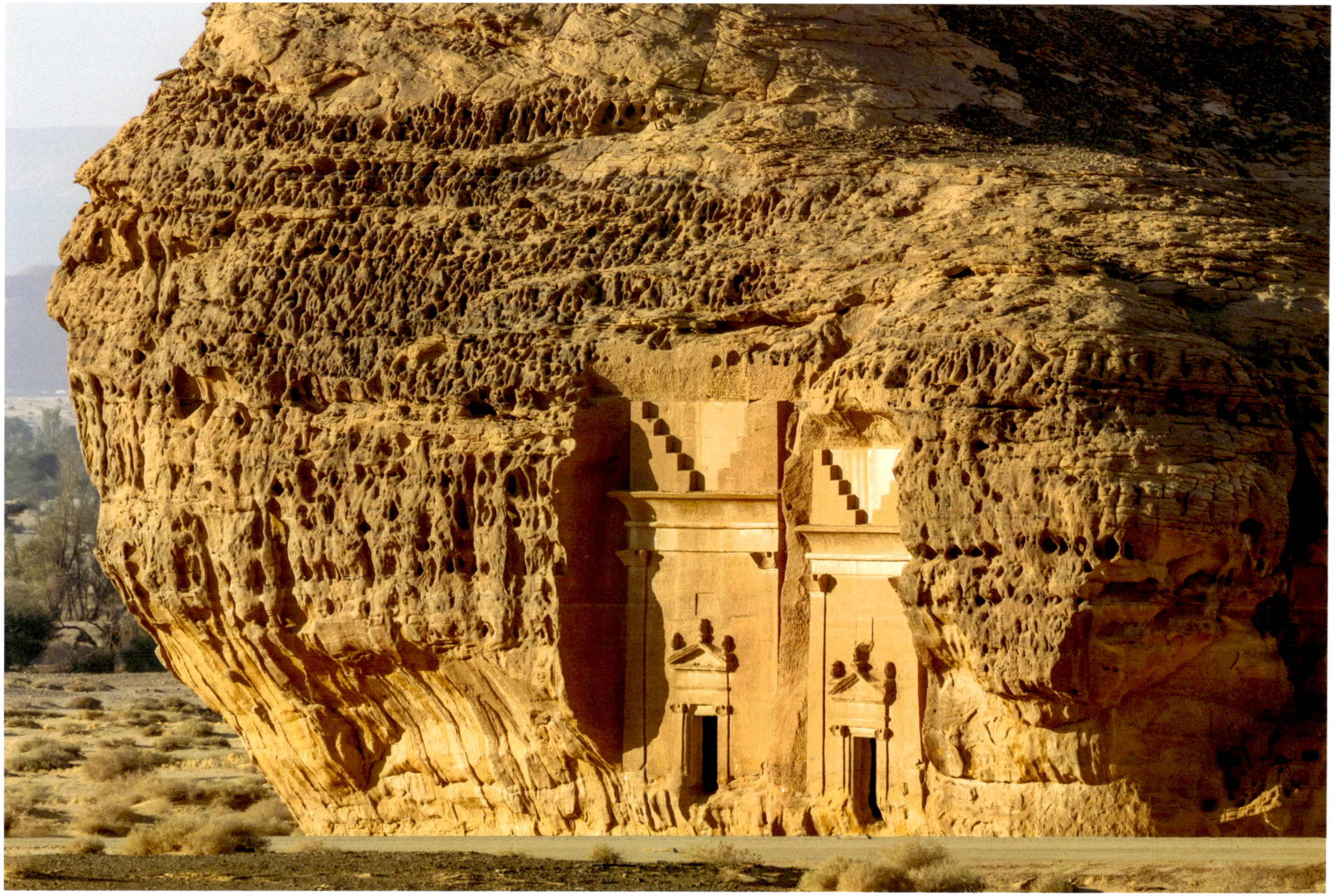

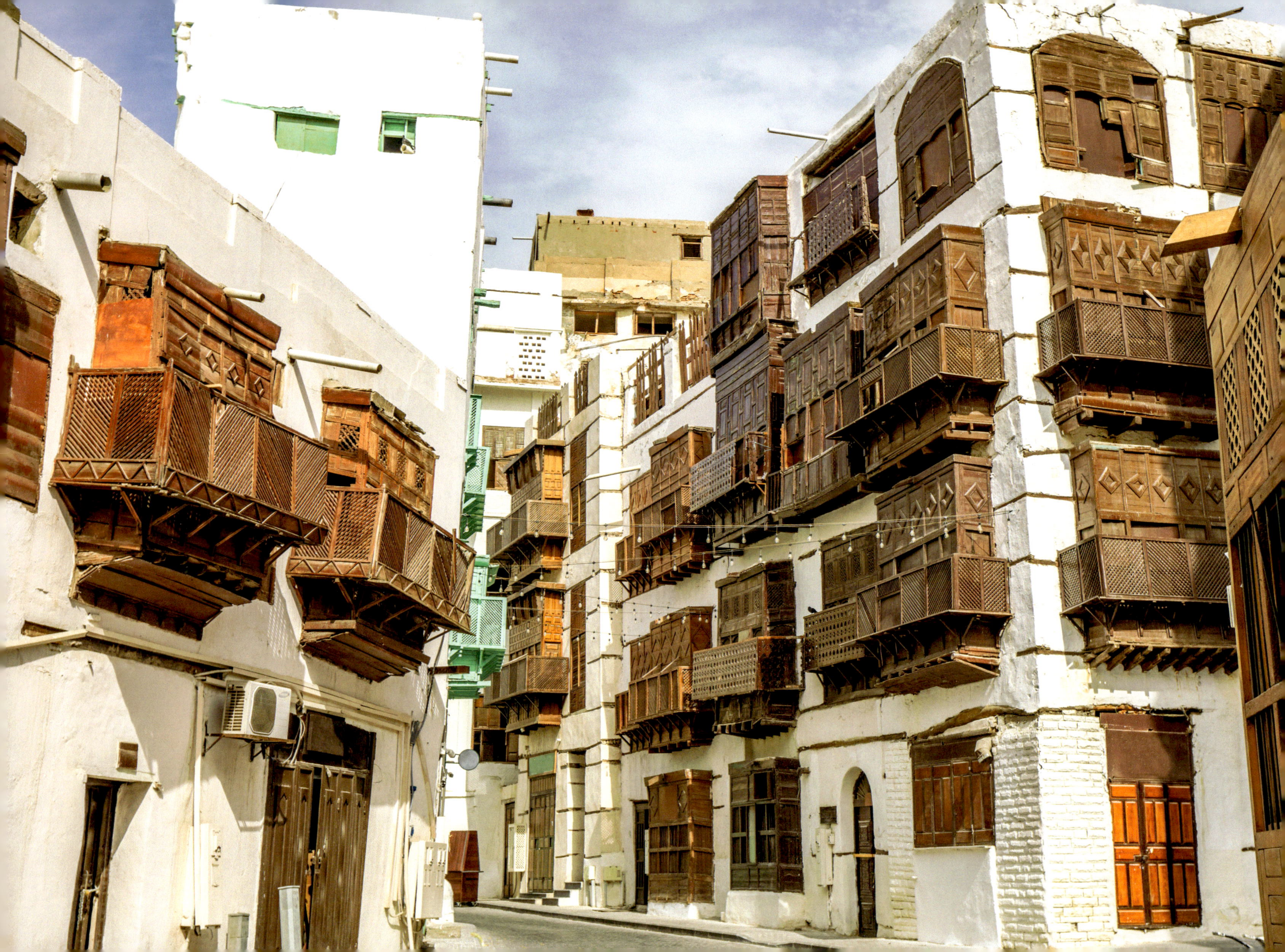

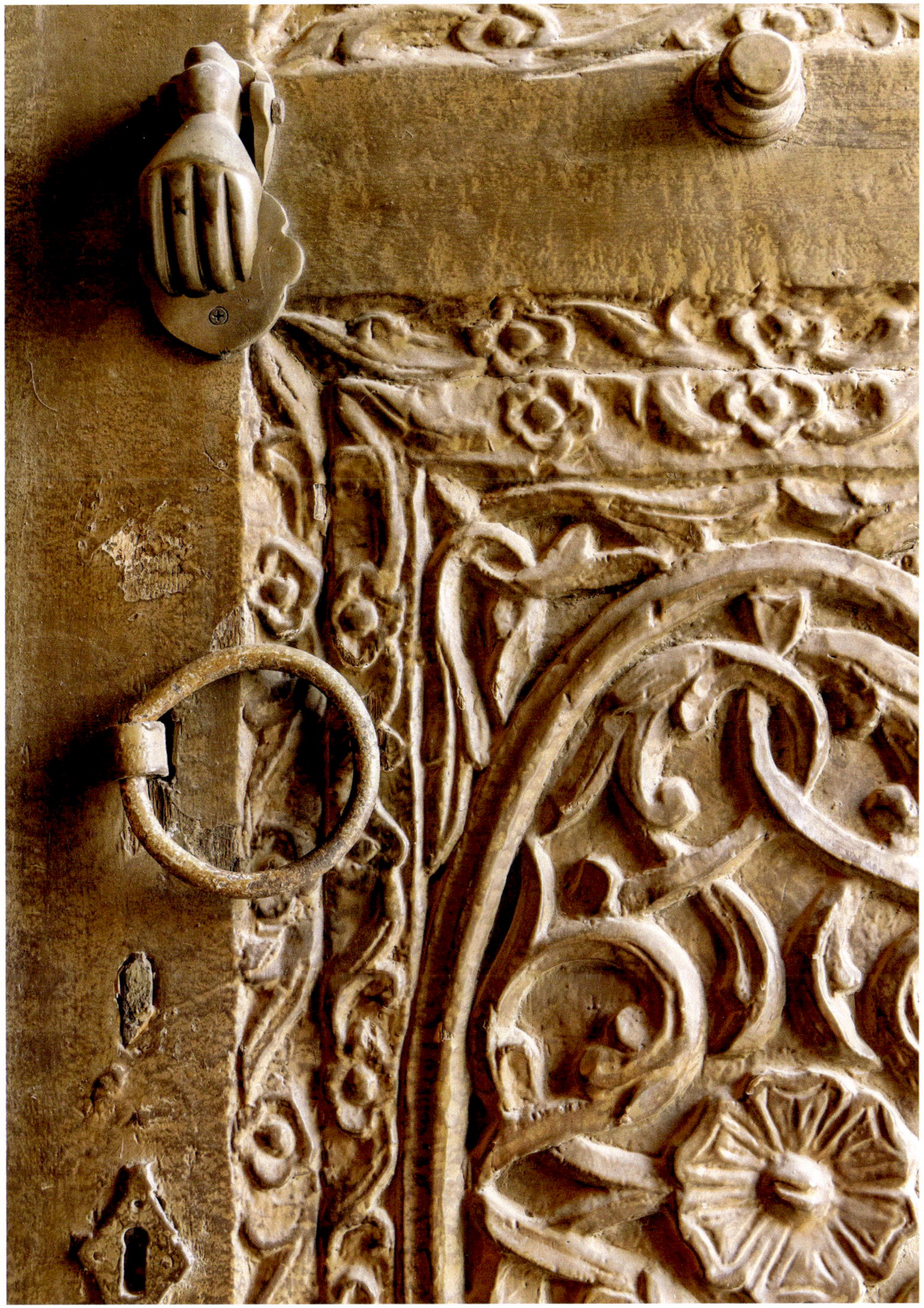

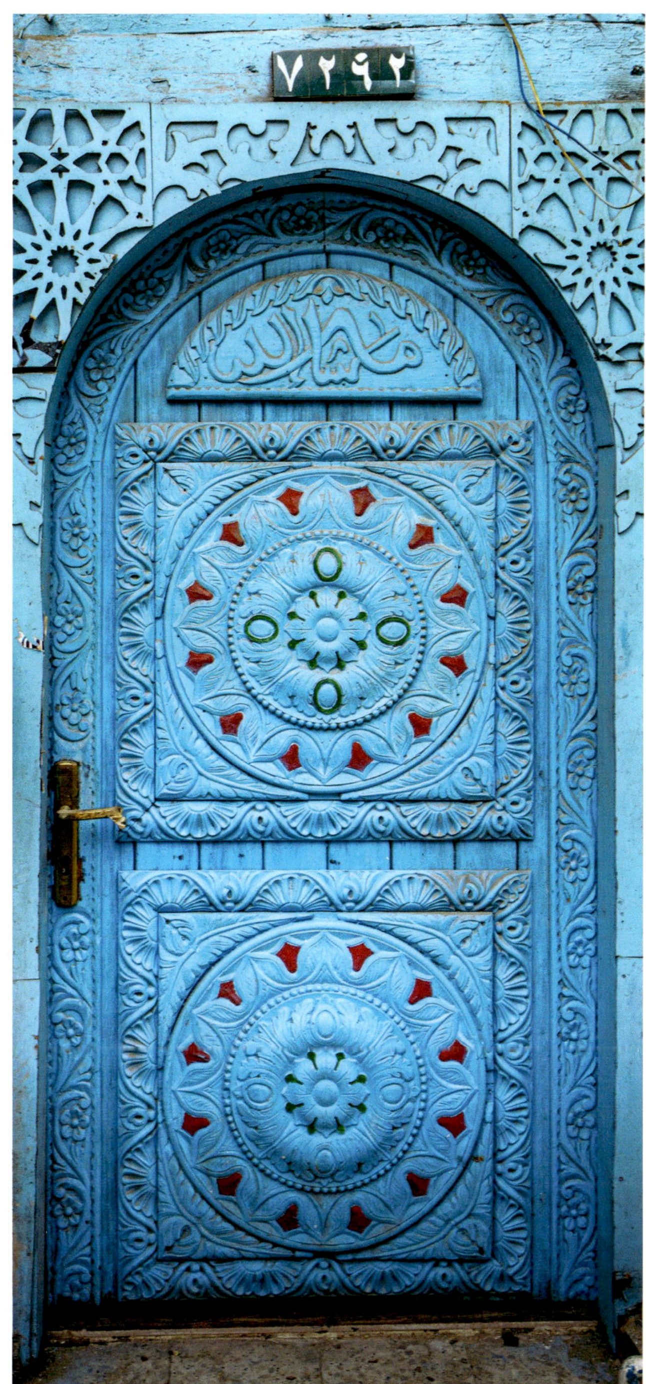

ALL PHOTOGRAPHS:

Al-Balad district, Jeddah
Jeddah's historic district is renowned for its unique Hijazi architecture, particularly the tall coral-stone houses adorned with intricate, projecting wooden balconies known in Arabic as rawasheen. This district is a labyrinth of narrow alleys and centuries-old buildings, providing the visitor with a chance to travel back in time to old Arabia. Al-Balad was established in the 7th century as a port for pilgrims to Mecca, arriving from Africa, India, and beyond. The area features many vintage doors of exceptional craftsmanship; these are often painted in vibrant shades of blue, green, or red, along with intricate carvings and decorative metalwork.

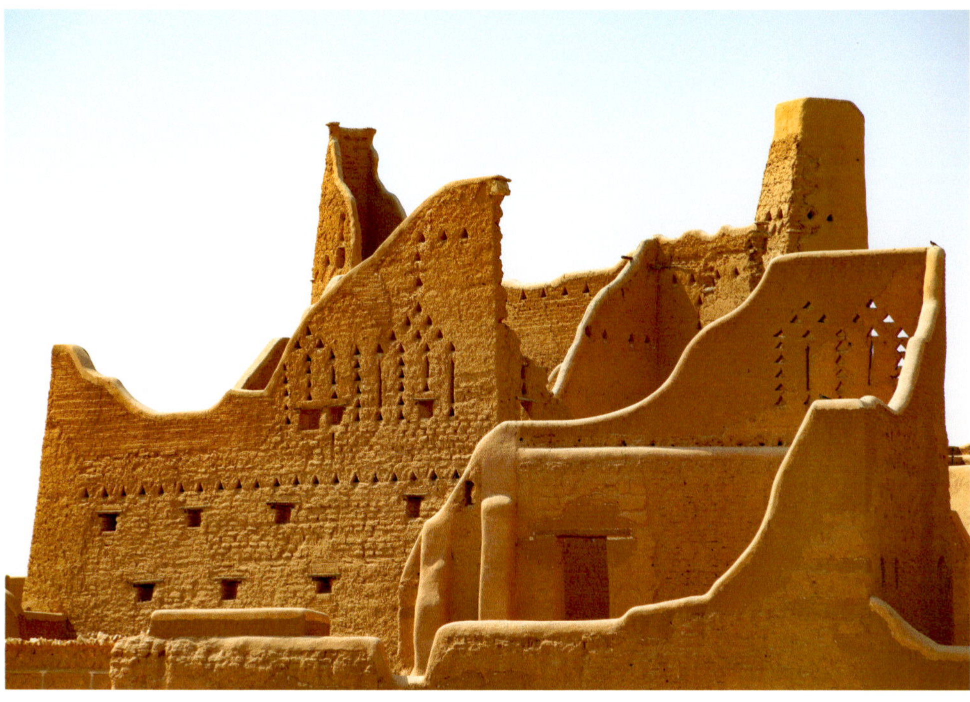

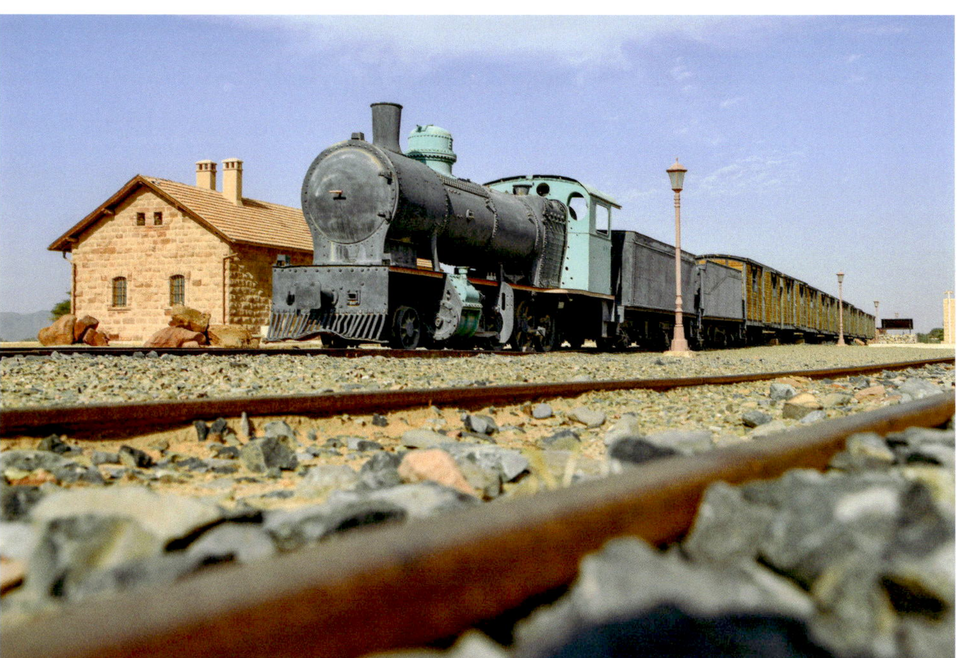

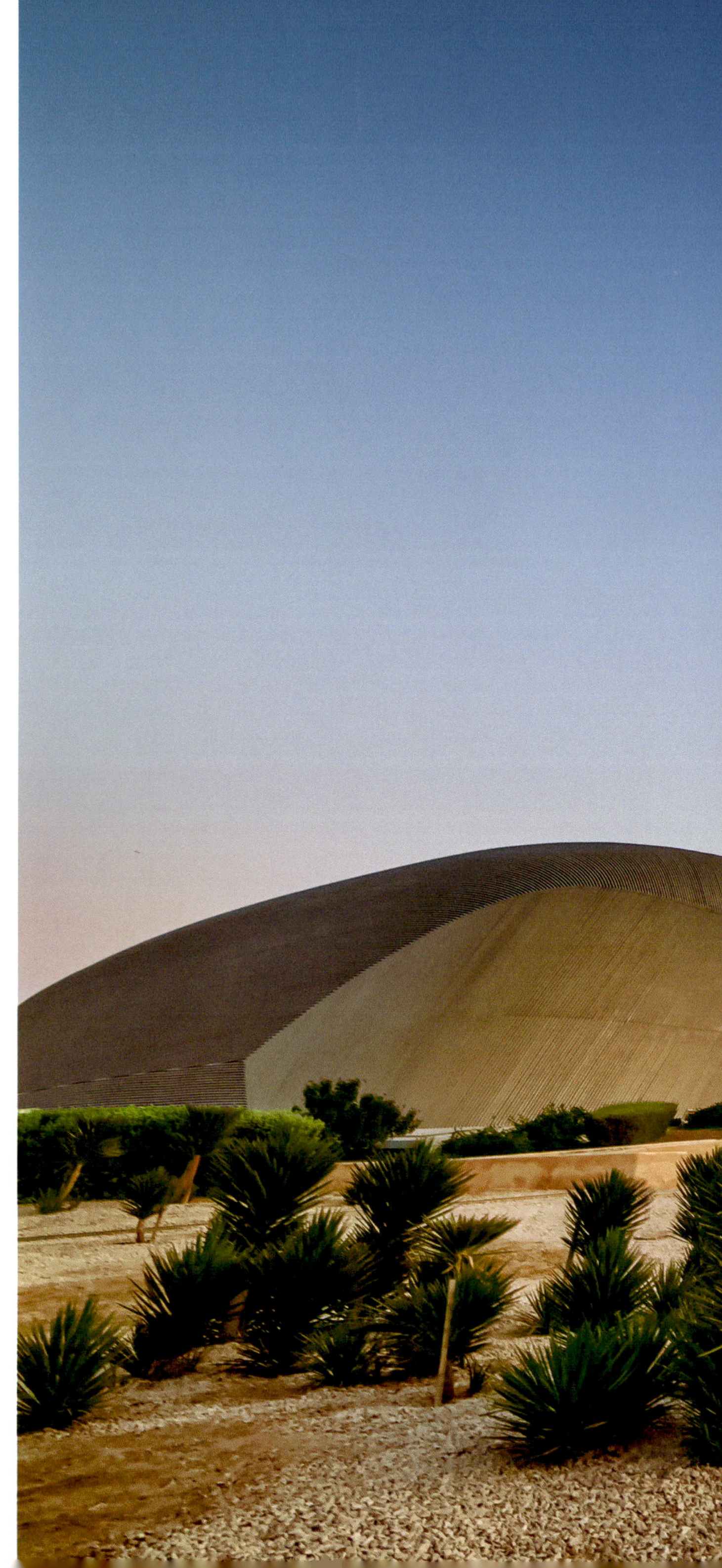

Salwa Palace, Diriyah
This UNESCO World Heritage site, near Riyadh, and capital of the first Saudi State, was established by Muhammad bin Saud in 1727 AD. As such it lays claim to being the historic heart of Saudi Arabia. This site now features cafes and craft shops for the visitors who can marvel at an impressive collection of Najdi mud-brick architecture, including palaces, mosques, and fortified walls.

Hejaz Railway Museum, Medina
This ambitious project, started by the Ottoman Empire and completed in 1908, was a system to connect Damascus with the holy city of Medina. It was built to both facilitate the pilgrimage to Mecca and to extend Ottoman control over the Arabian Peninsula.

King Abdulaziz Centre for World Culture, Dhahran
More commonly known as Ithra, this major cultural and creative hub aims to enrich Saudi society by providing access to knowledge, shared creativity, and cross-cultural engagement. It features a museum, library, cinema, theatre, and exhibition halls set within its distinctive architectural design.

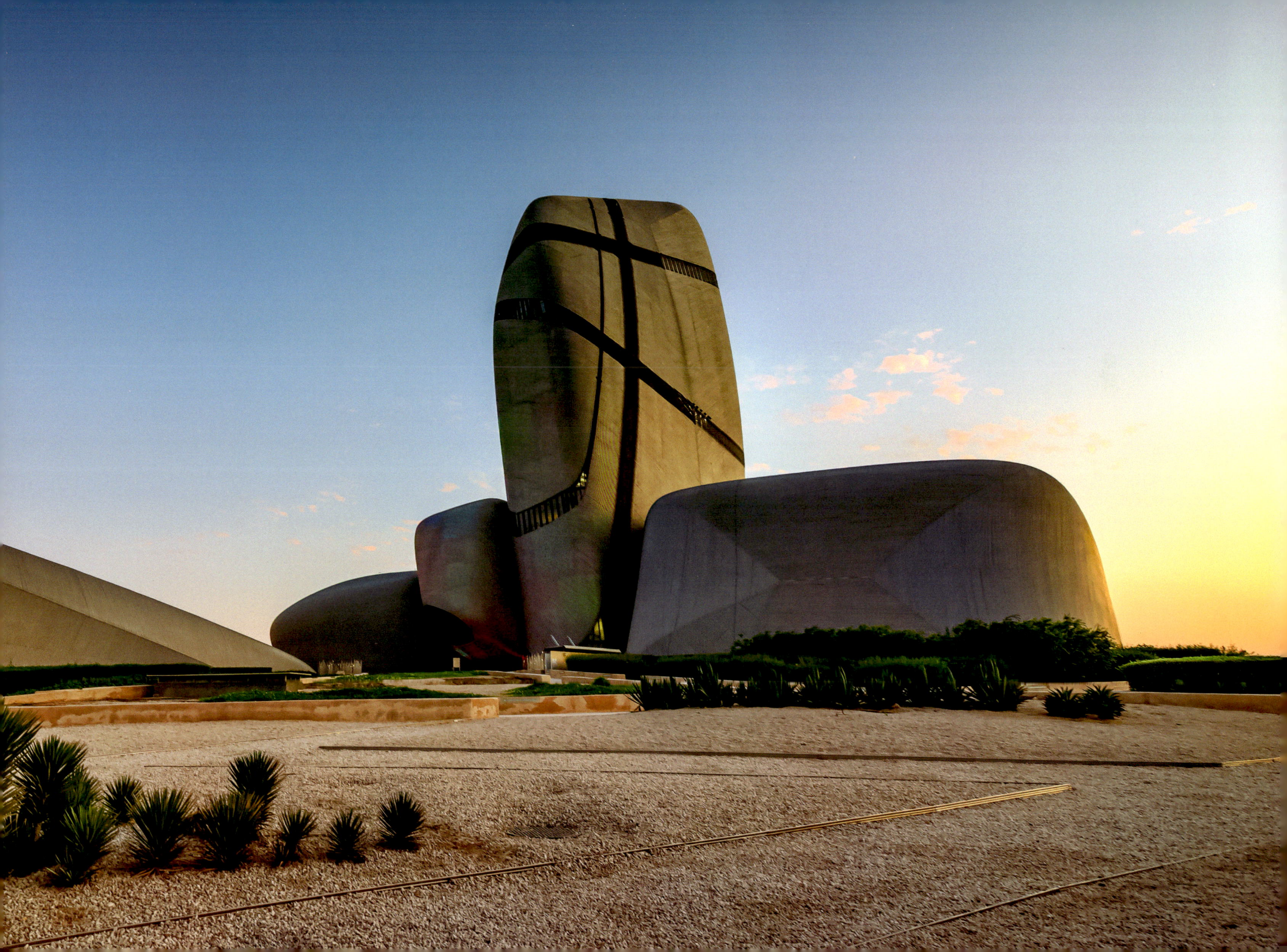

Taif Rose Festival, Makkah province

A rose festival in the heat of Saudi Arabia? Yes, this annual spring celebration of the city's famous Damask roses is held in the Al-Rudaf Park. Taif is a city set at an altitude of almost 2000m and enjoys cool spring weather. The festival showcases vast fields of multi-coloured blooms and a grand parade as the highlight. Visitors can also learn about the traditional methods of producing rose oil and rose water.

Camels, Rub' al Khali (Empty Quarter)

These tough, nomadic dromedaries have adapted to survive the world's largest sand desert, a vast area known as Rub' al Khali. These famed 'ships of the desert' are still crucial today as providers to the Bedouin people's lifestyle. Camels provide milk, meat, and transport, taking their riders across vast, waterless dunes. With their large, padded feet they can endure extreme temperatures, making them ideal for transport all year round.

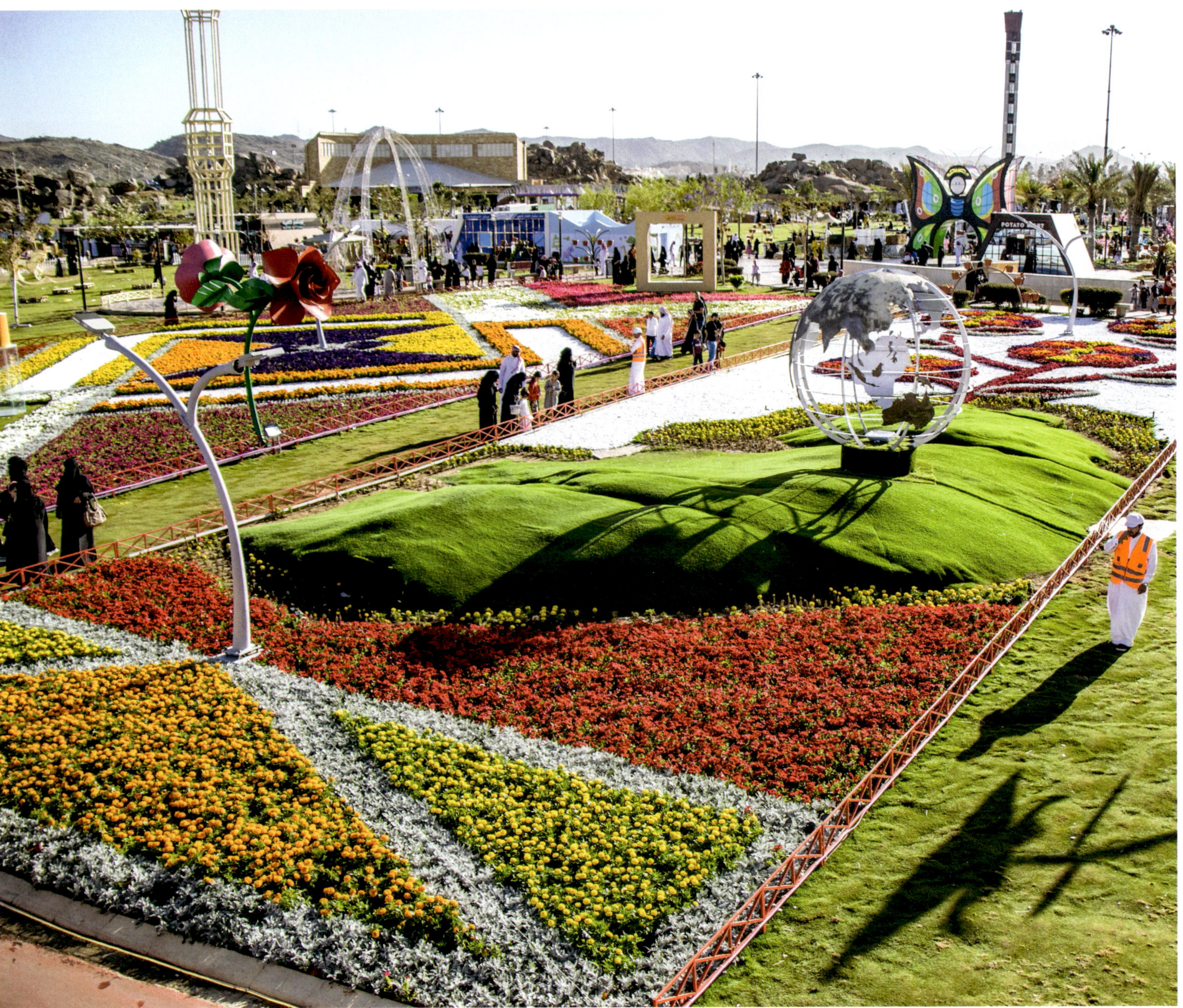

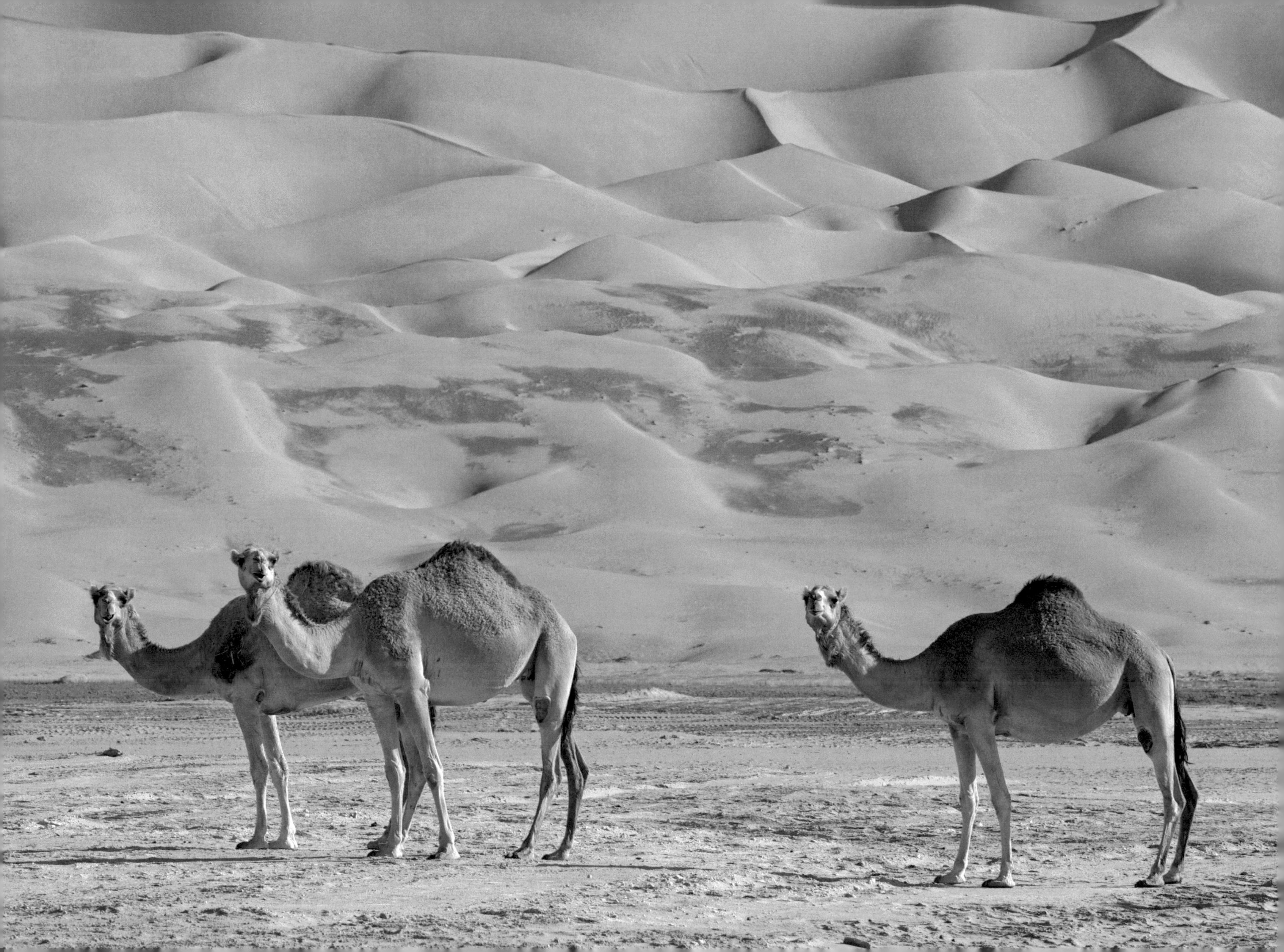

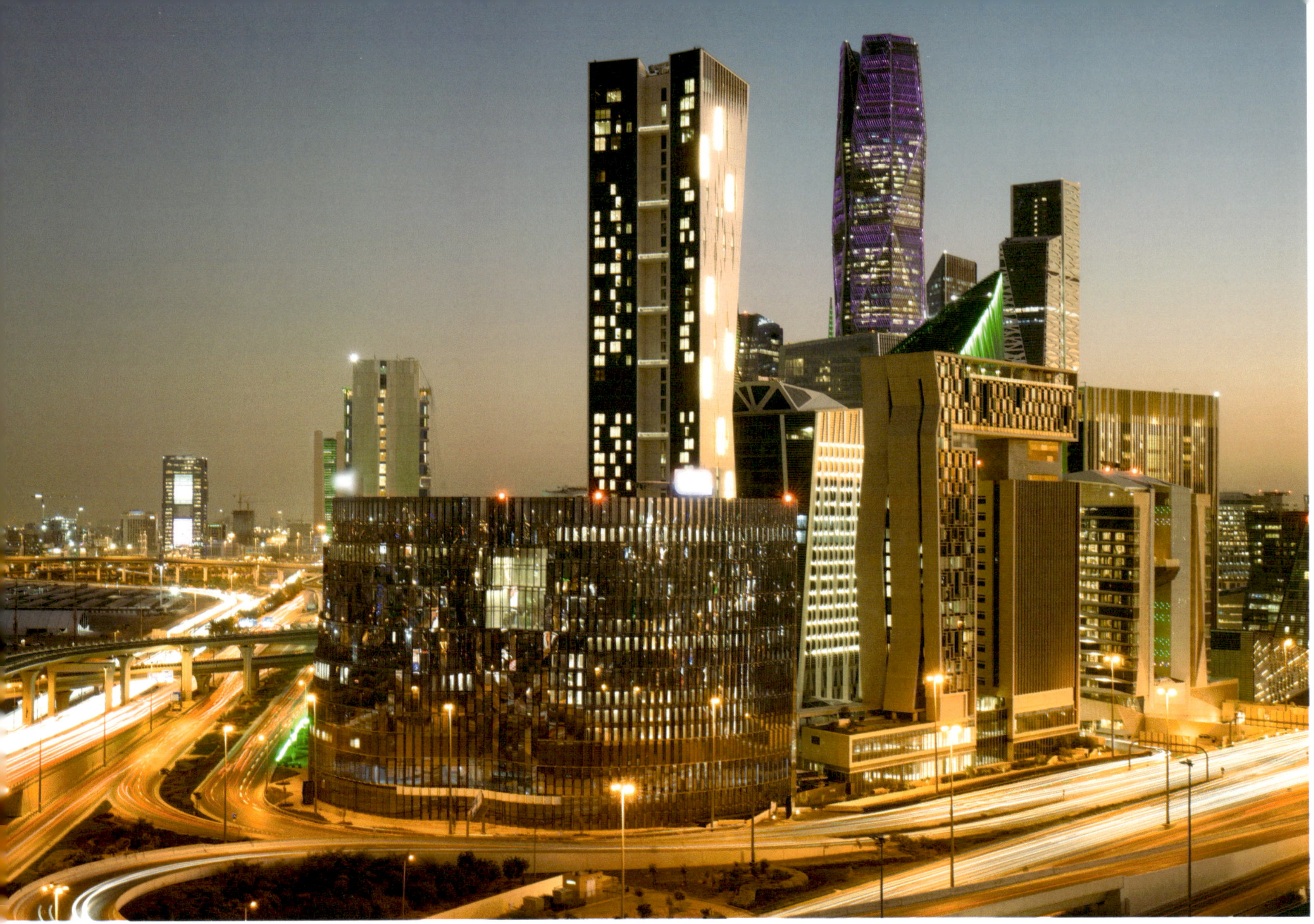

Nighttime skyline, Riyadh
This is the vibrant, rapidly modernizing capital of Saudi Arabia, and the largest city on the Arabian Peninsula. Its ever-changing skyline is defined by futuristic skyscrapers which challenge world records in height and architectural experimentation. This constant move forward is driven by Saudi Arabia's Vision 2030, and an expanding population looking to diversify to new lifestyles and digital technologies. Riyadh is a major, and growing, financial hub that is undergoing massive urban development, including a new metro system, and the largest entertainment centre in the Middle East, called Qiddiya, which is being built at a cost of $40 billion.

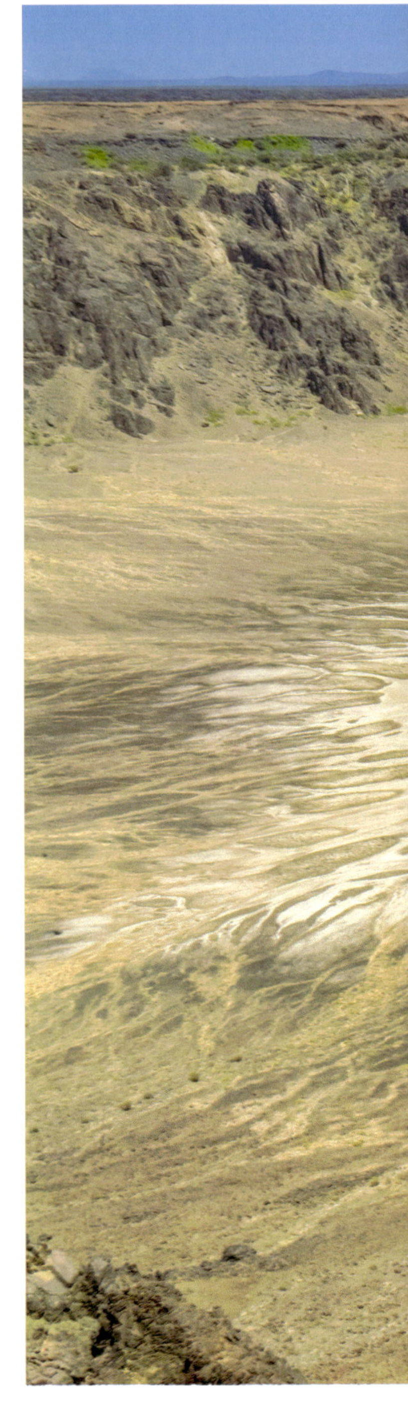

Wabah Crater
This vast area is the largest and deepest volcanic crater in the Kingdom of Saudi Arabia, with a diameter of 3000 metres (9840ft). It lies east of Jeddah, surrounded by the Al Luhayan, Umm Rilan, and Zabna mountains, all of which form a scenic view and offer hiking trails through the natural wonders of the region. The crater itself is 380 metres (1240ft) deep and attracts geologists from all nations.

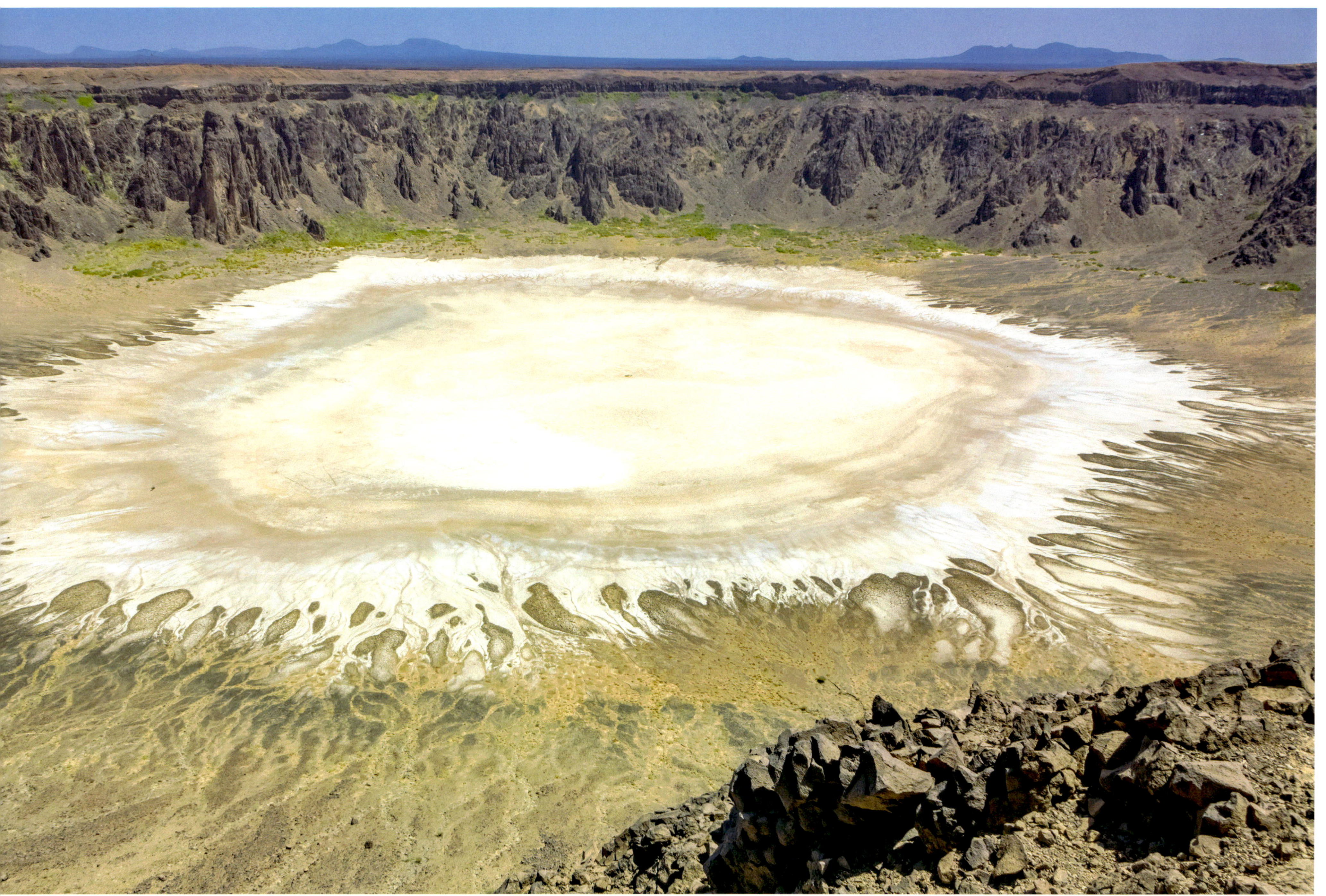

Burj Khalifa, Dubai

Inaugurated in 2010, this skyscraper was the world's tallest building. It was named in honour of Sheikh Khalifa bin Zayed Al Nahyan, the ruler of Abu Dhabi. Today it remains a stunning centrepiece of Dubai as it diversifies its economy and creates a truly global destination for business and pleasure.

The tower offers a variety of experiences. Visitors can ascend to the observation decks (pictured below), 'At the Top' on the 124th and 125th floors, or the even higher 'At the Top SKY' on the 148th floor, for the best panoramic views of the city and the Gulf.

The tower also offers fine dining at restaurants like At.mosphere and The Lounge. Surrounding the tower are lakes offering a spectacular fountain show each evening.

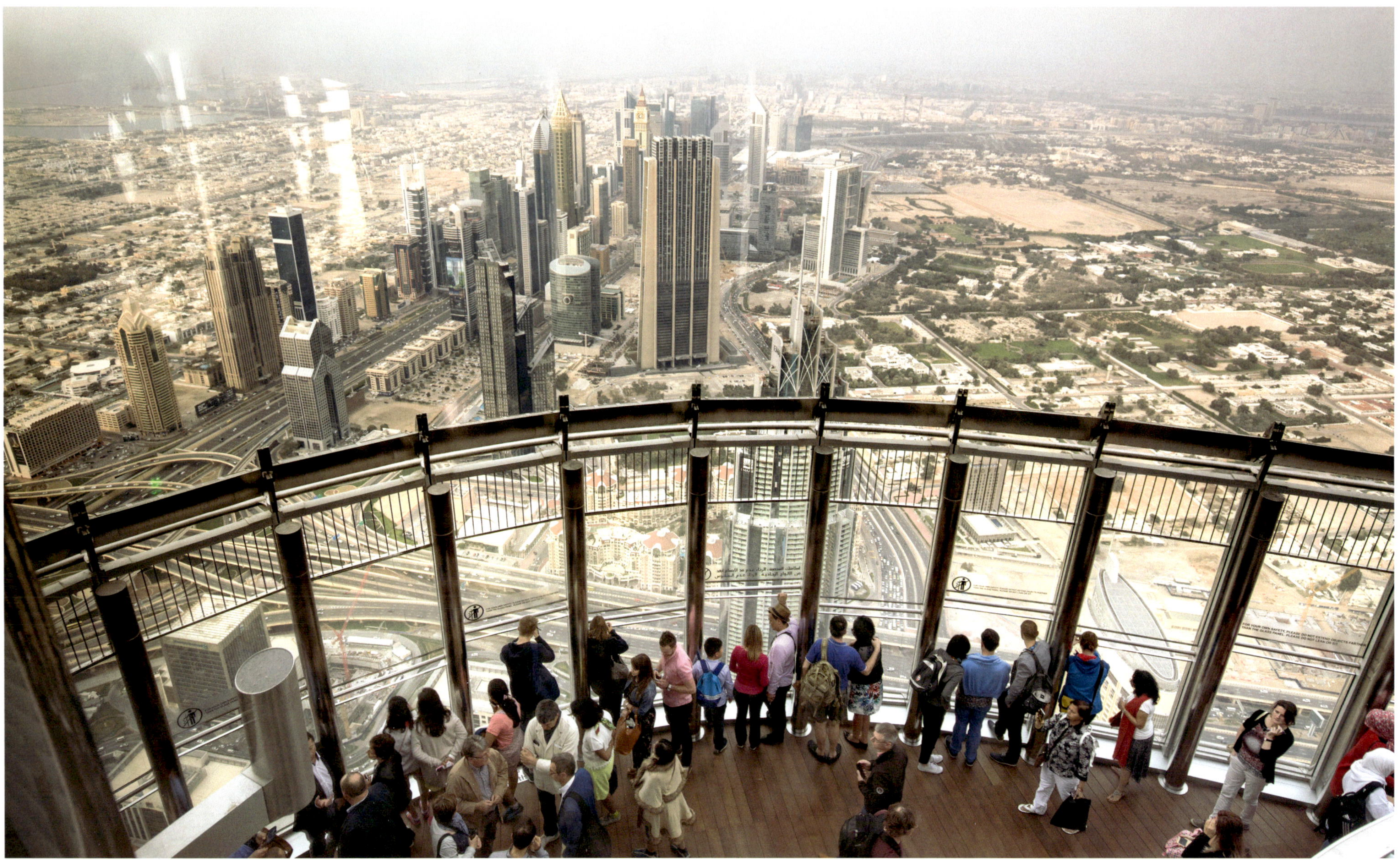

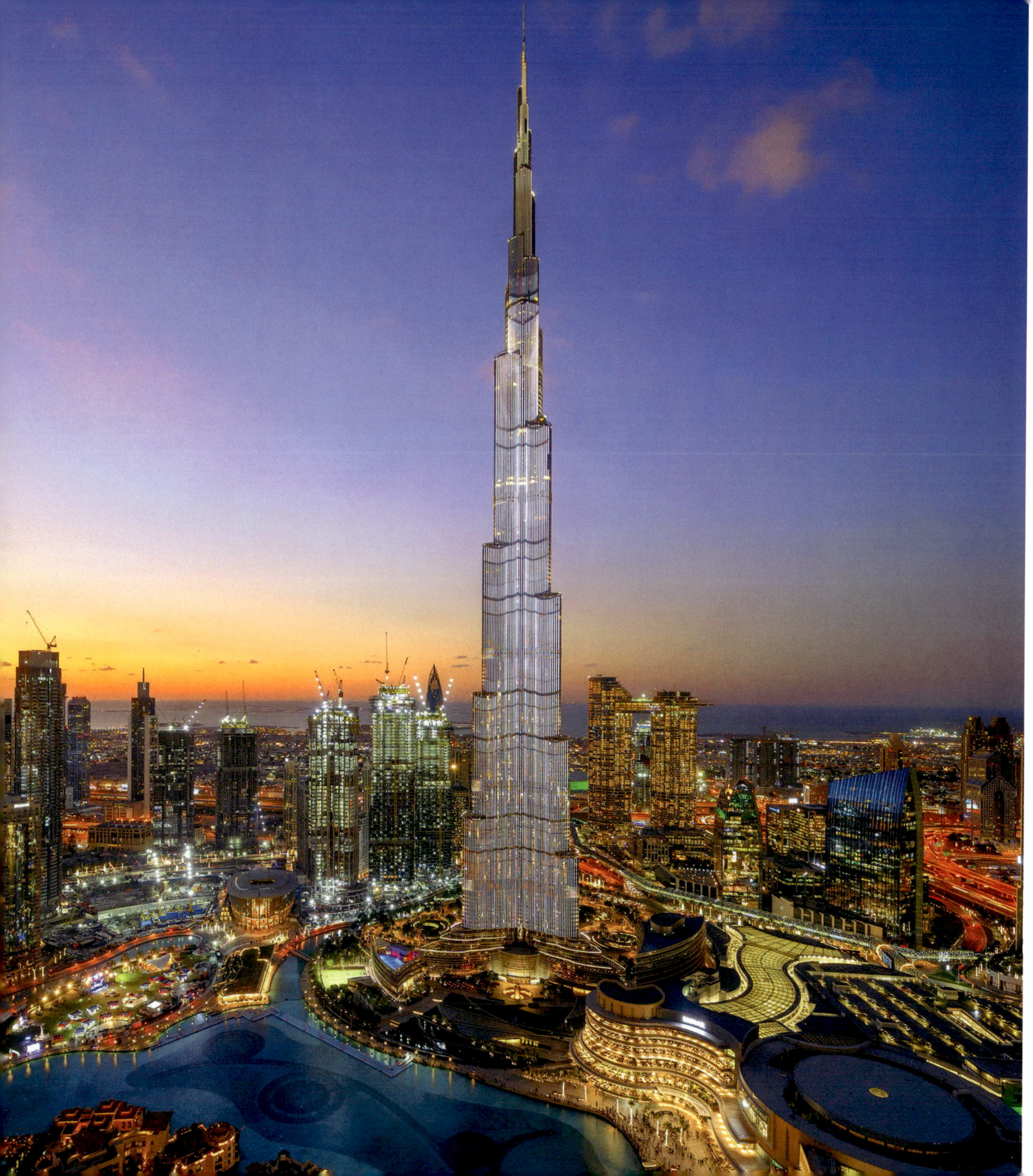

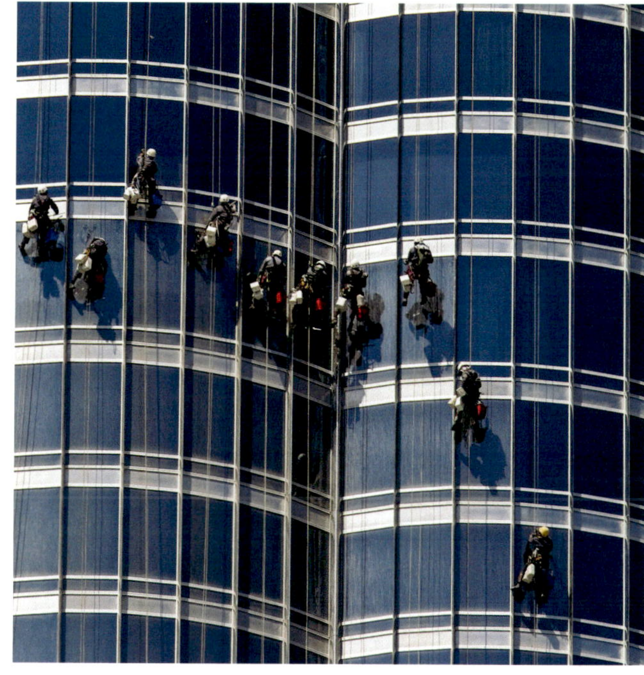

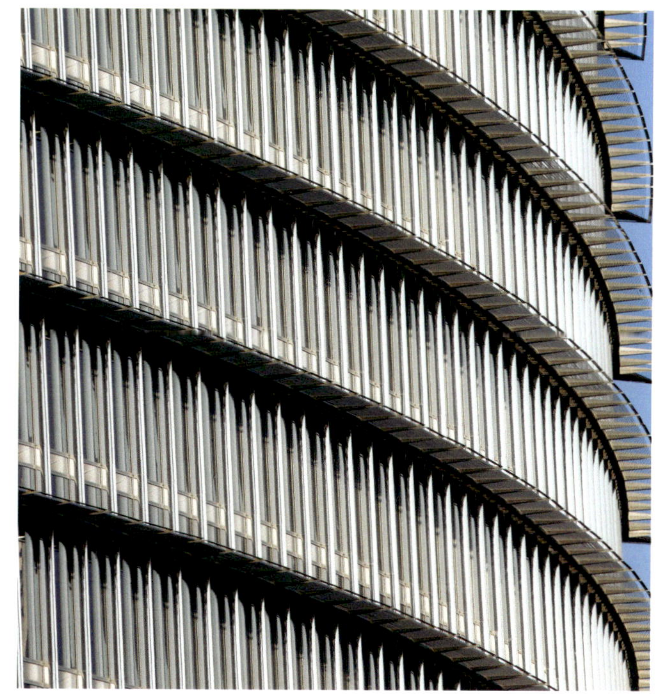

Museum of the Future, Dubai

Often called a 'living museum', this spectacular architectural landmark is a global hub for innovation. While showcasing the past, its important purpose is to actively explore future trends in science, technology, and humanity. Its awe-inspiring toroidal shape, adorned with Arabic calligraphy, represents humanity's journey toward an unknown future. The museum features futuristic, immersive, interactive exhibits aimed at educating people of all ages.

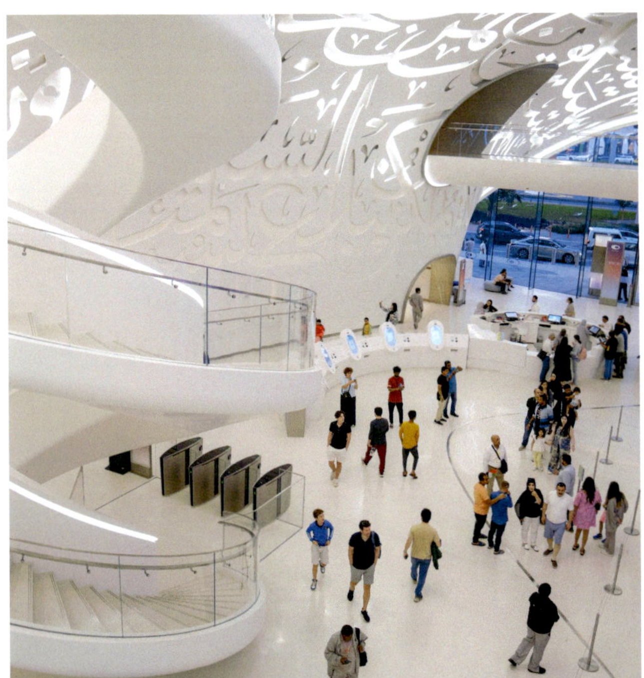

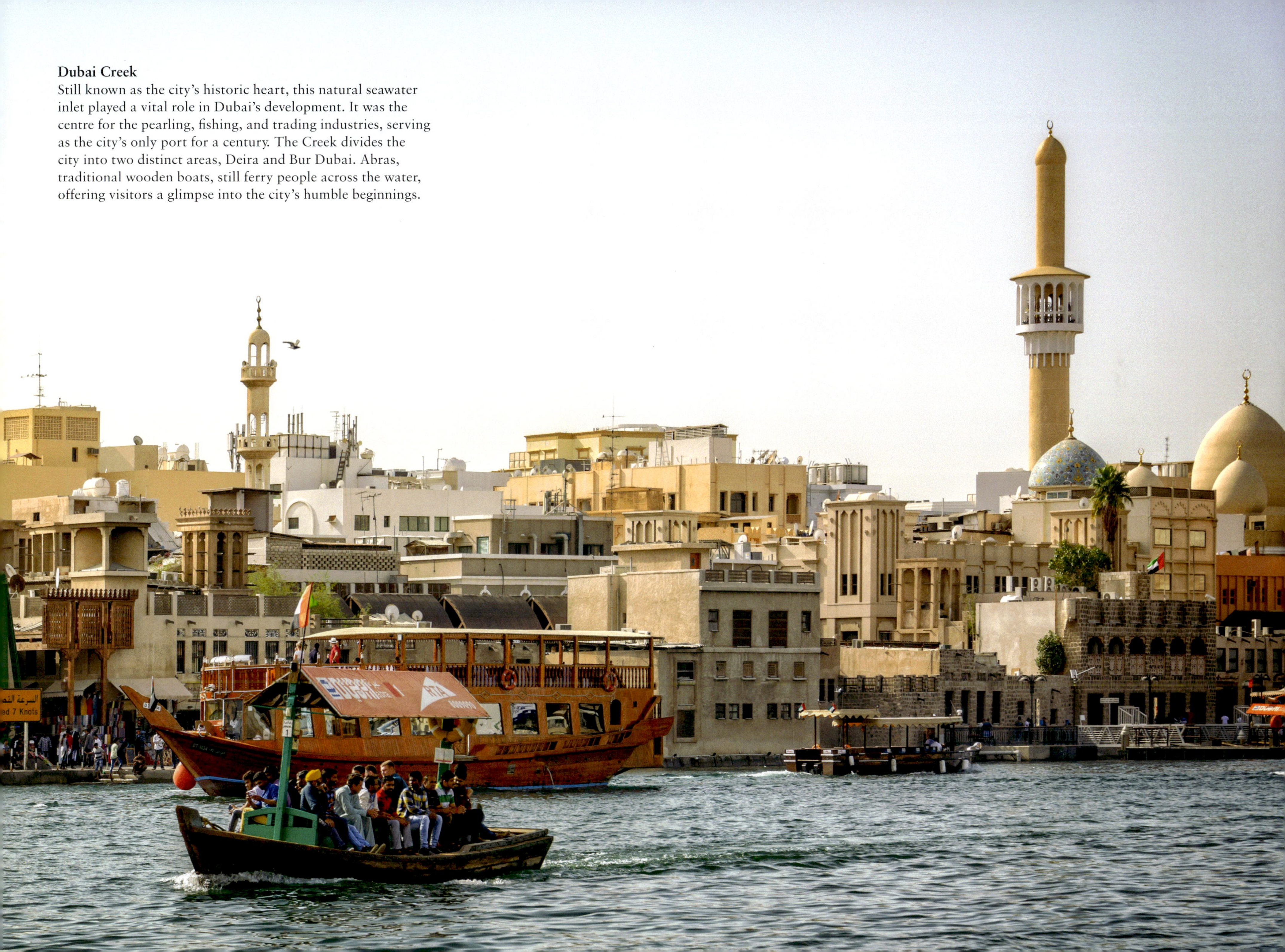

Dubai Creek
Still known as the city's historic heart, this natural seawater inlet played a vital role in Dubai's development. It was the centre for the pearling, fishing, and trading industries, serving as the city's only port for a century. The Creek divides the city into two distinct areas, Deira and Bur Dubai. Abras, traditional wooden boats, still ferry people across the water, offering visitors a glimpse into the city's humble beginnings.

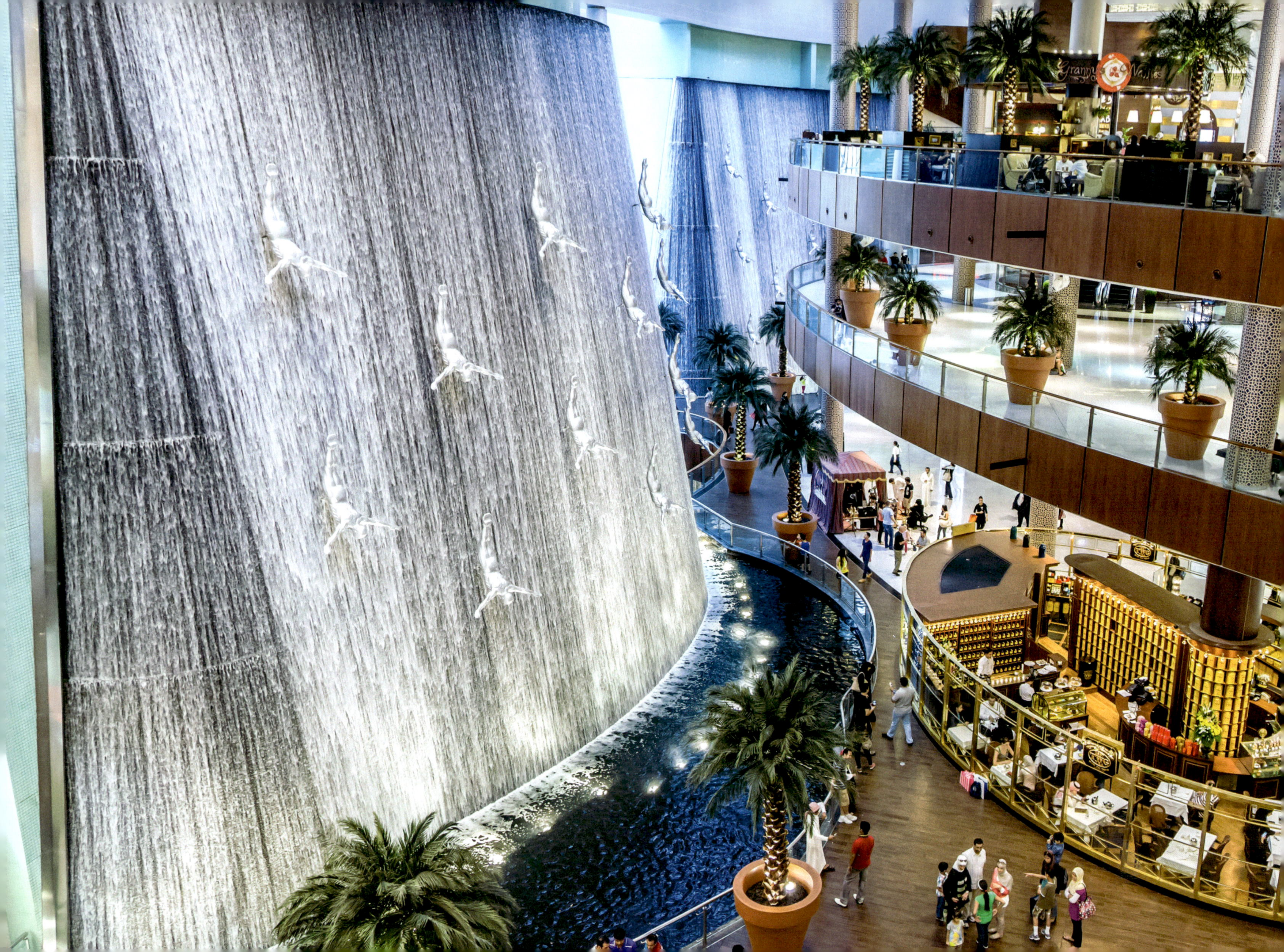

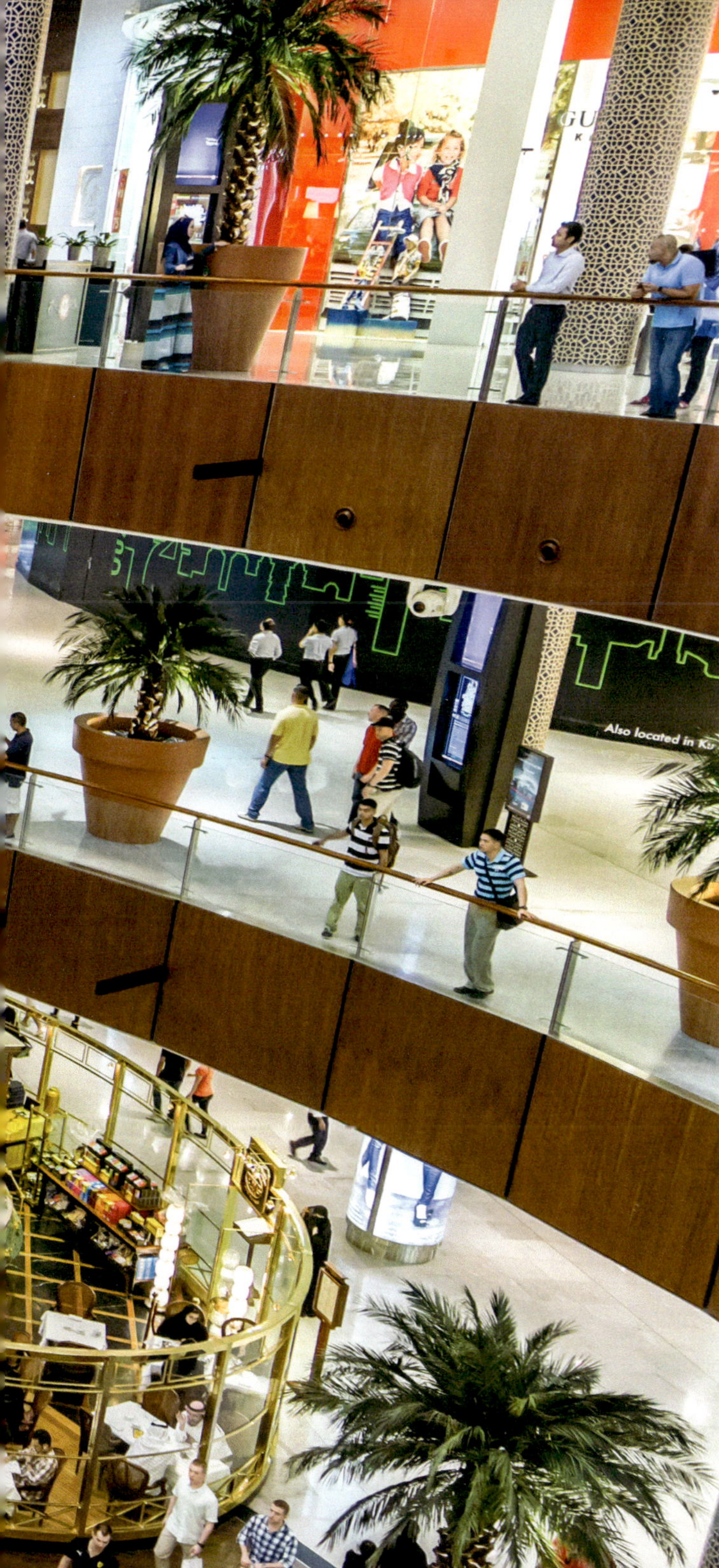

ALL PHOTOGRAPHS:
Dubai Mall, Dubai
Dubai is a world-renowned shopping destination and Dubai Mall lies at its heart. Opened in 2008 as part of the Downtown Dubai development, the mall is not just a shopping centre. Dubai Mall is also a massive entertainment hub featuring a variety of attractions, including the Dubai Aquarium & Underwater Zoo, an Olympic-sized ice rink, an indoor theme park, and a huge cinema complex. The mall's size and diverse offerings, including a huge variety of food options, while sitting alongside the Burj Khalifa tower, make it a whole day's fun.

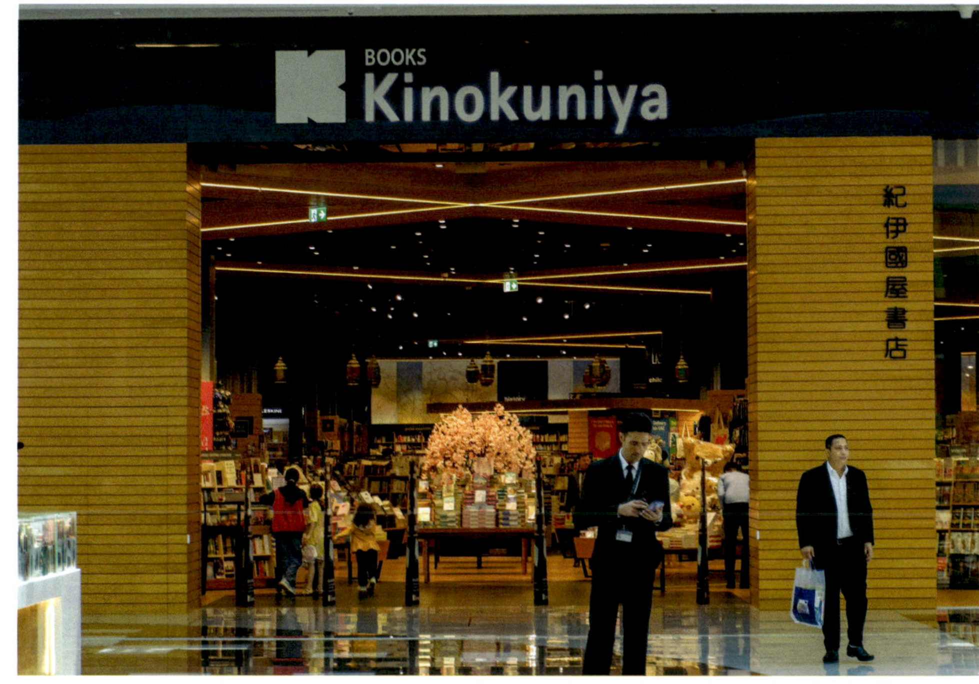

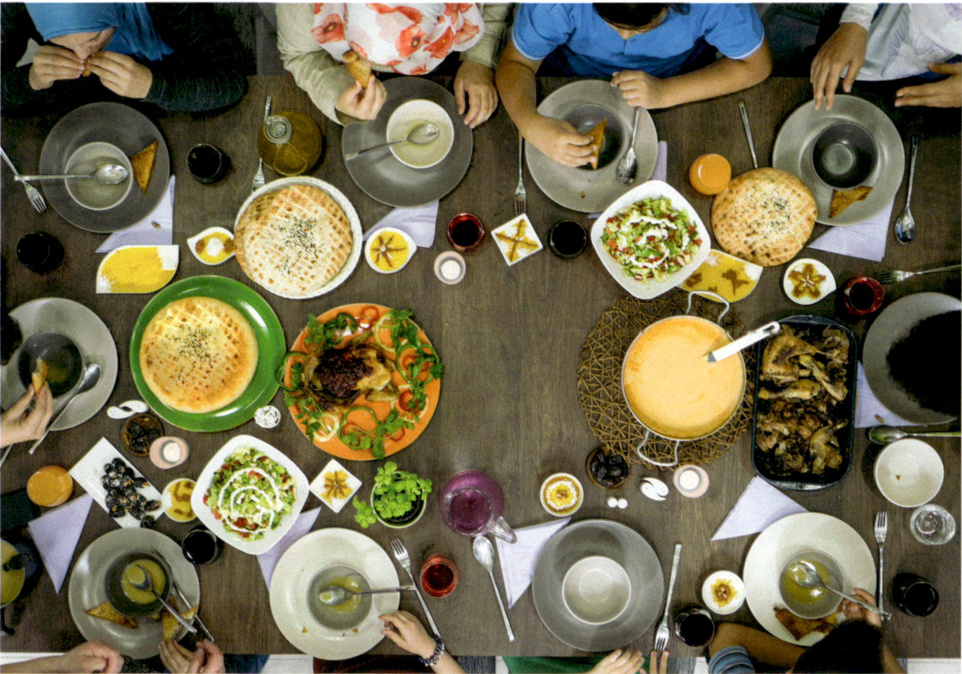

Lost Chambers Aquarium, Dubai

Situated at Atlantis, The Palm, this captivating aquatic experience is inspired by the mythical lost city of Atlantis. It houses over 65,000 marine animals, including sharks, rays, and tropical fish. The aquarium's design recreates the ancient ruins and tunnels of the sunken city, creating an immersive, maze-like environment. Visitors can explore 21 different exhibits, including the vast Ambassador Lagoon, which is home to hundreds of species. Visitors can also enjoy diving or snorkelling under supervision.

Palm Jumeirah, Dubai

This giant feat of visionary engineering was conceived in 2001, intended to expand Dubai's coastline and boost both the economy and Dubai tourism. The man-made archipelago, shaped like a palm tree, was built using millions of tons of sand and rock. When completed it was so large it became visible even from space. Today, it's a symbol of luxury, home to high-end resorts, private villas, and its own, multicultural community. It now attracts the richest tourists and residents enjoy a unique blend of lavish living and iconic attractions.

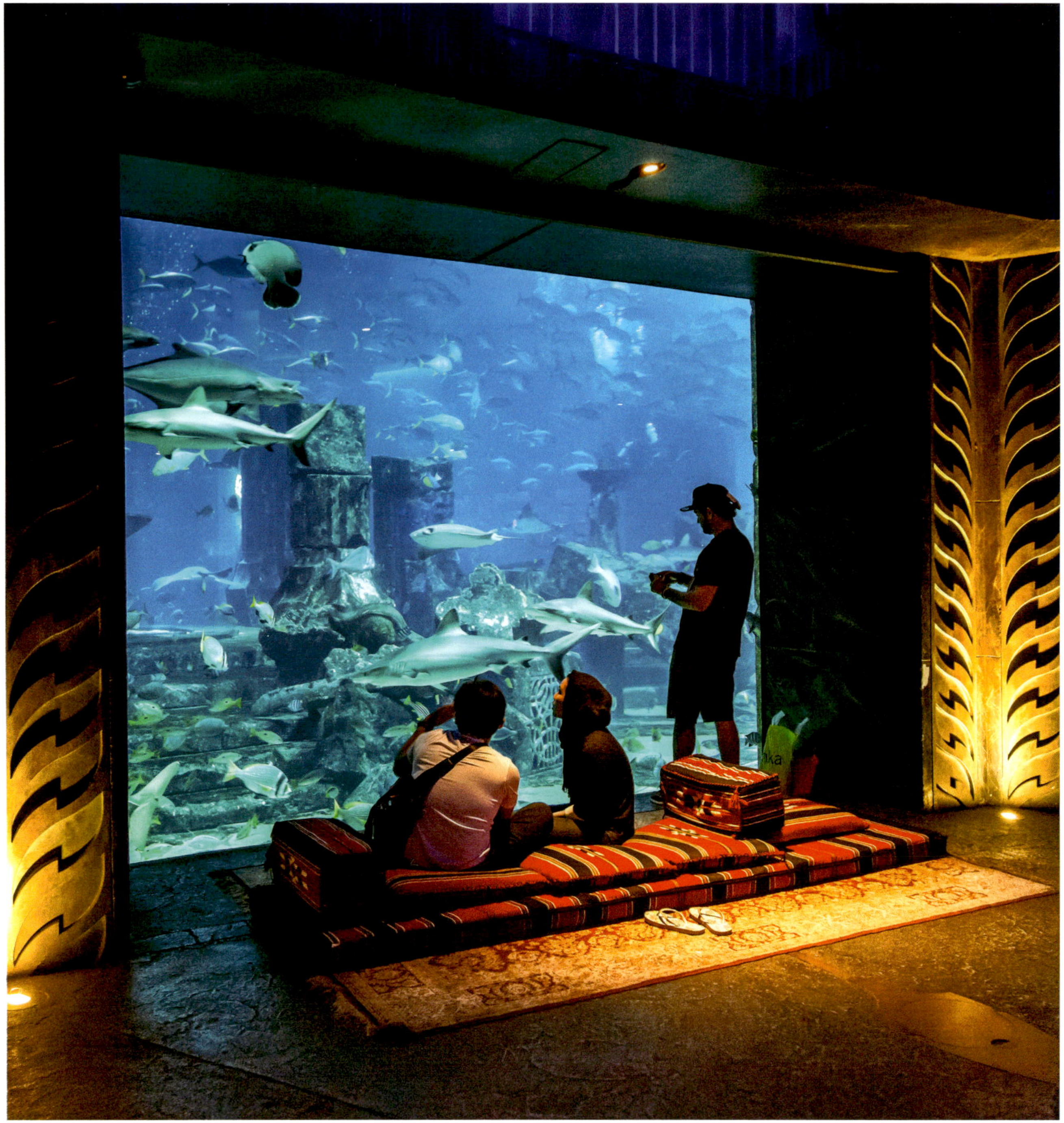

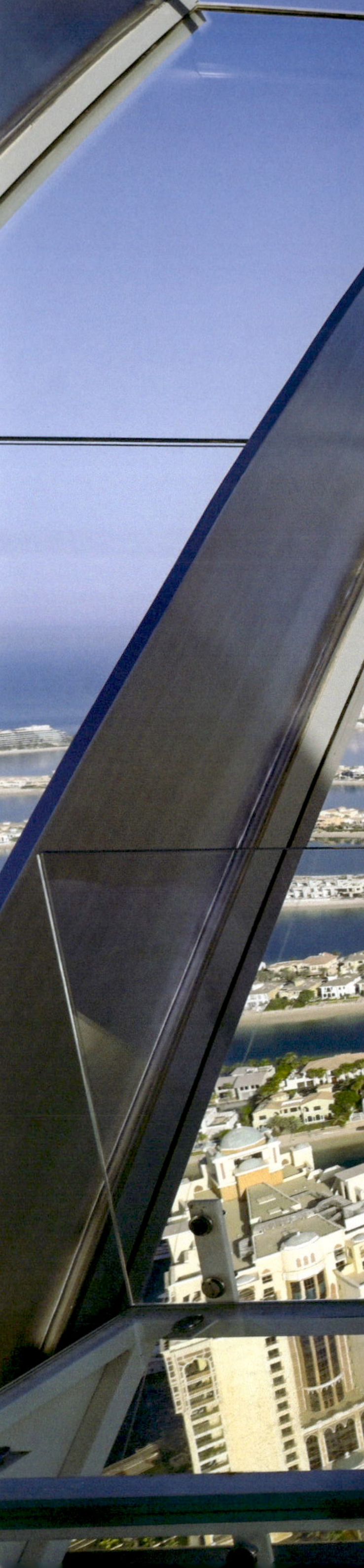

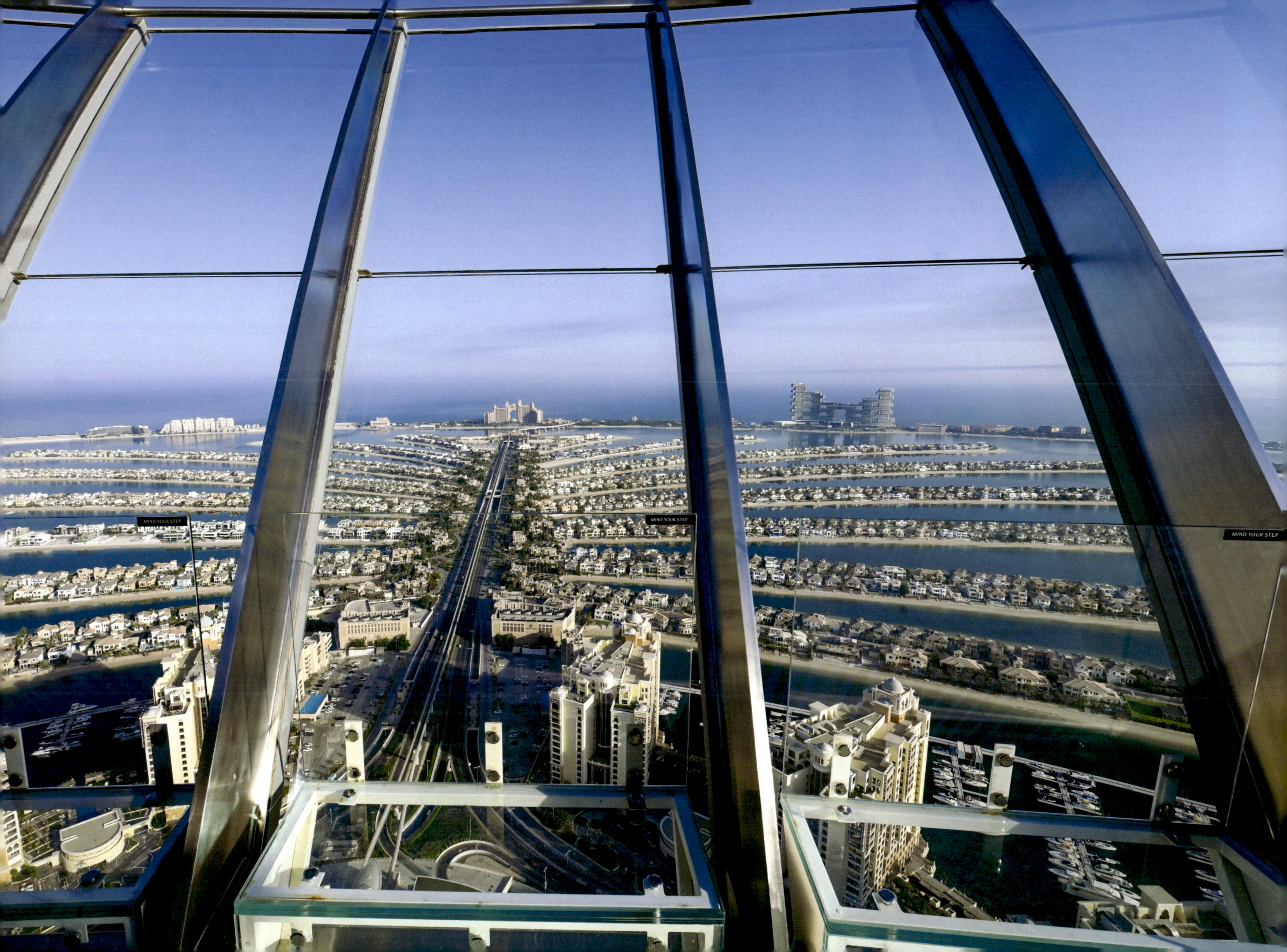

MIND YOUR STEP
MIND YOUR STEP
MIND YOUR STEP

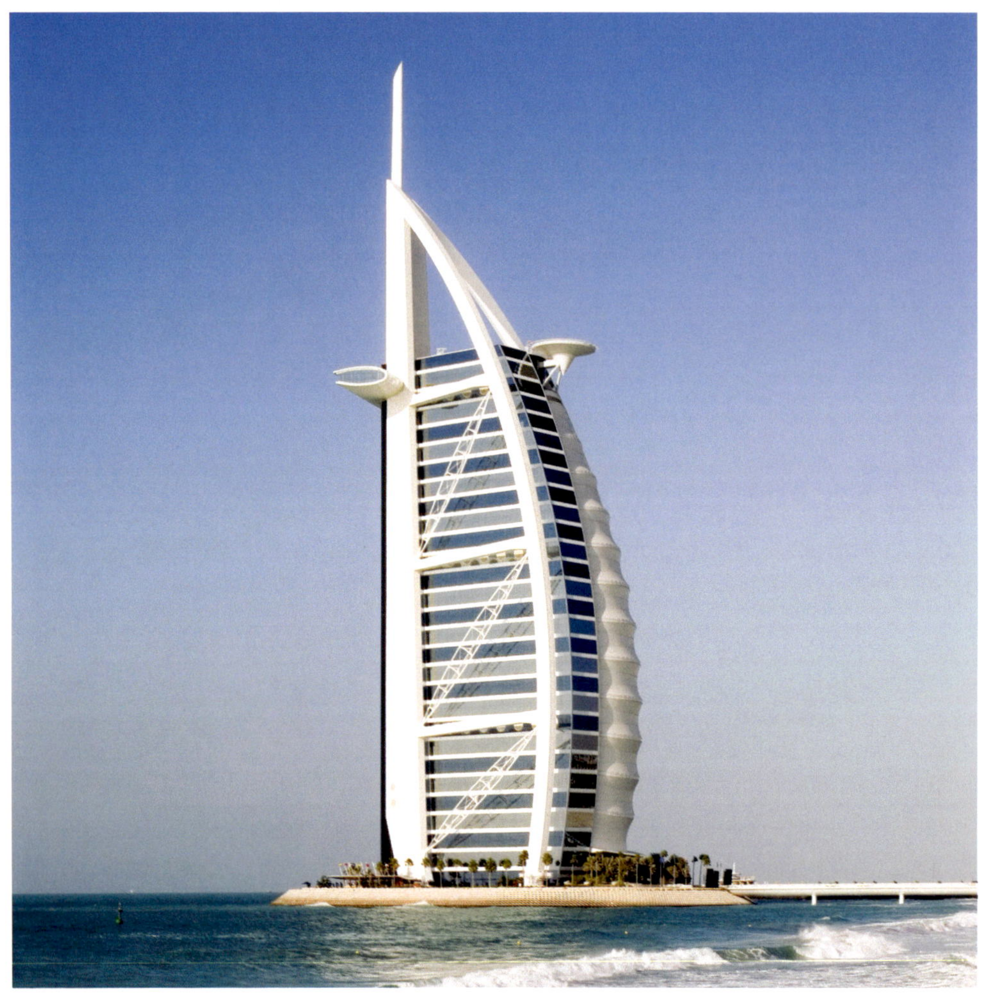

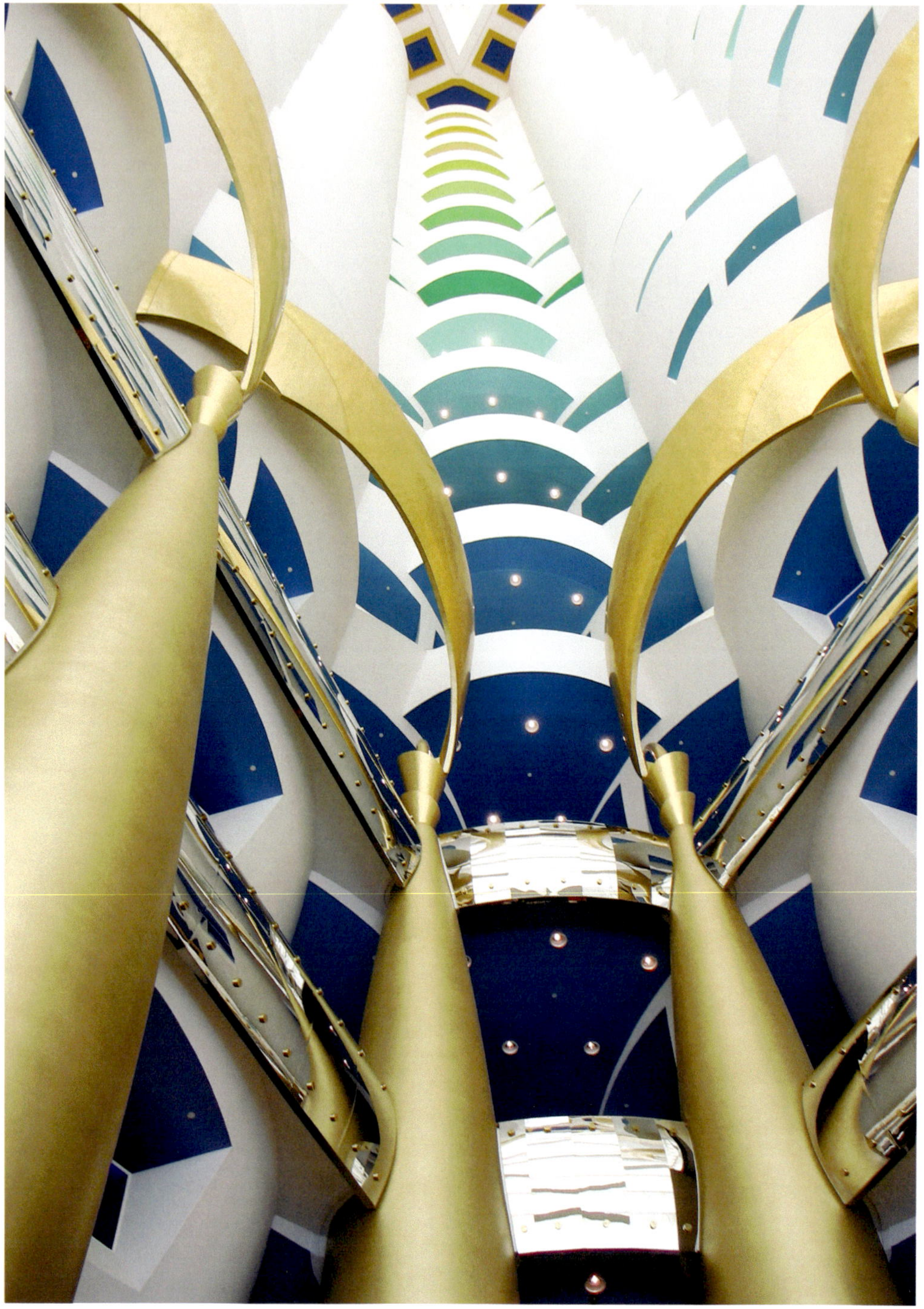

Burj Al Arab, Dubai

The Burj Al Arab is a luxury hotel in Dubai, UAE. It's famous for its unique sail-shaped design, which stands on an artificial island. It was designed by architect Tom Wright and opened in 1999. Often called the world's first 'seven star' hotel, it symbolizes Dubai's ambition and modern luxury.

Watersports, Dubai

With a pristine coastline and access to warm Arabian Gulf waters, Dubai is a premier destination for water sports enthusiasts. The city offers a wide range of activities, from high-octane adventures to more relaxed pursuits. You can enjoy jet skiing with stunning views of the Burj Al Arab, feel the rush of flyboarding, or get a unique, aerial perspective of the area while parasailing. For the less demanding tourist, paddleboarding and kayaking are more family-friendly options.

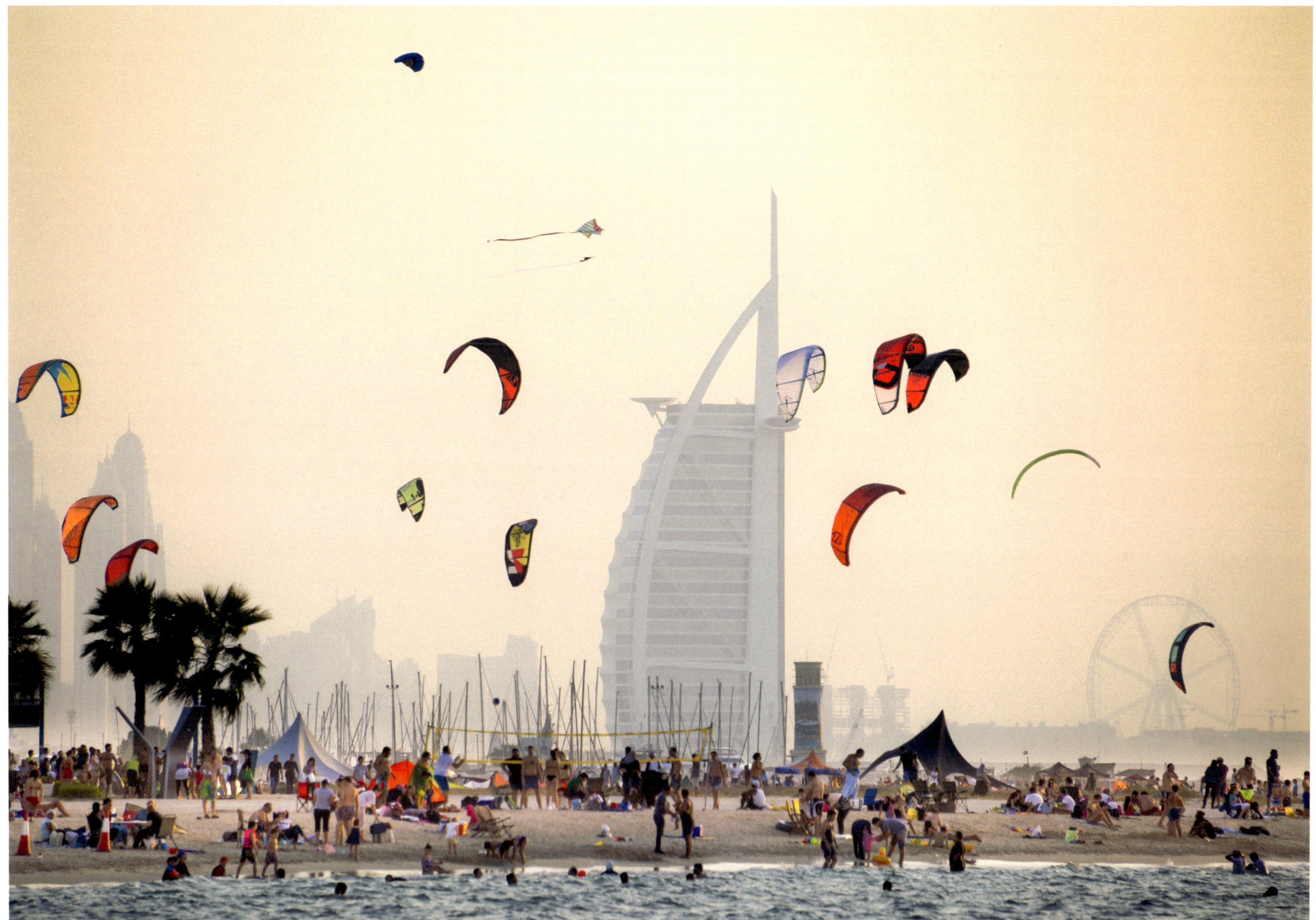

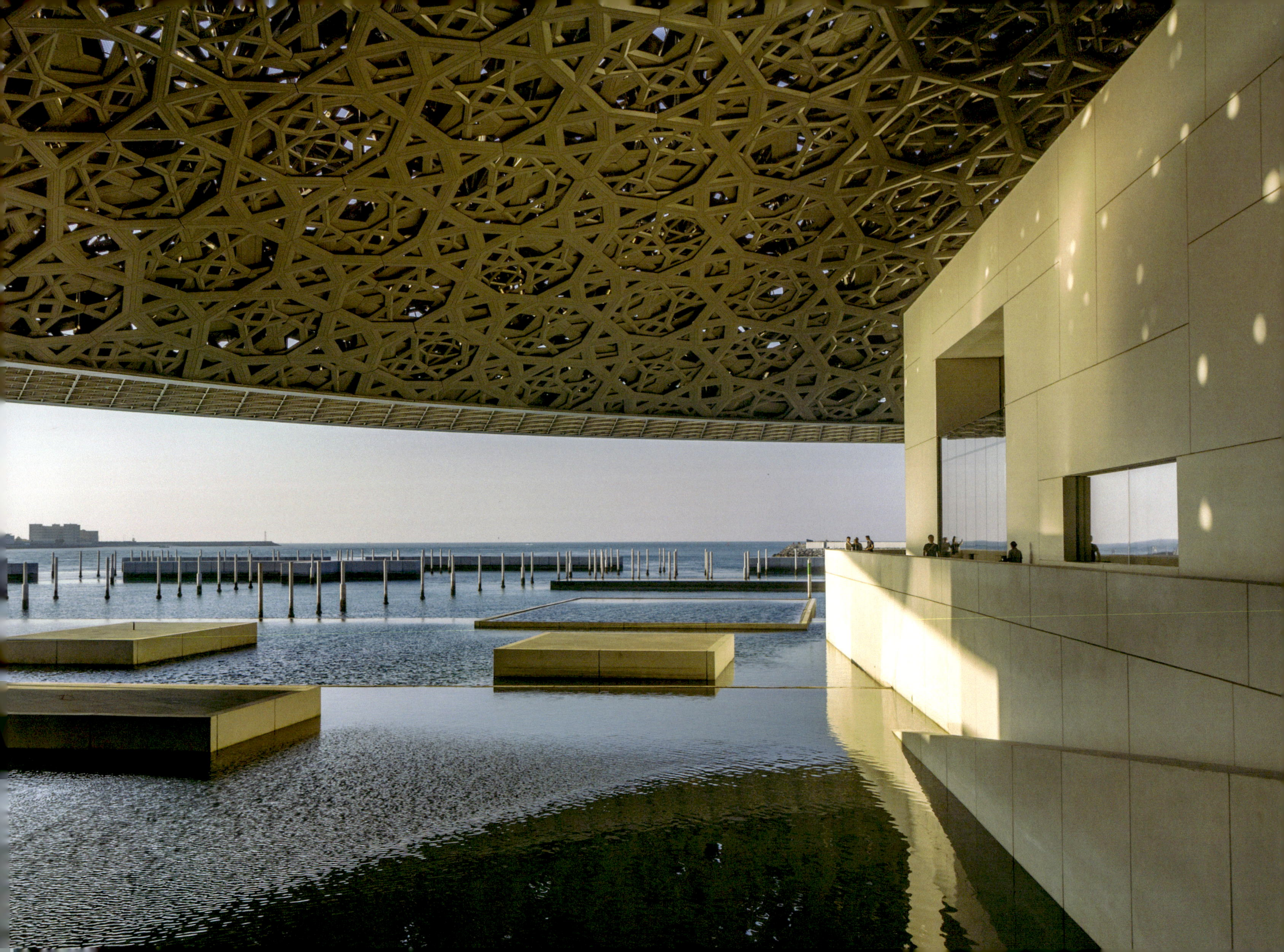

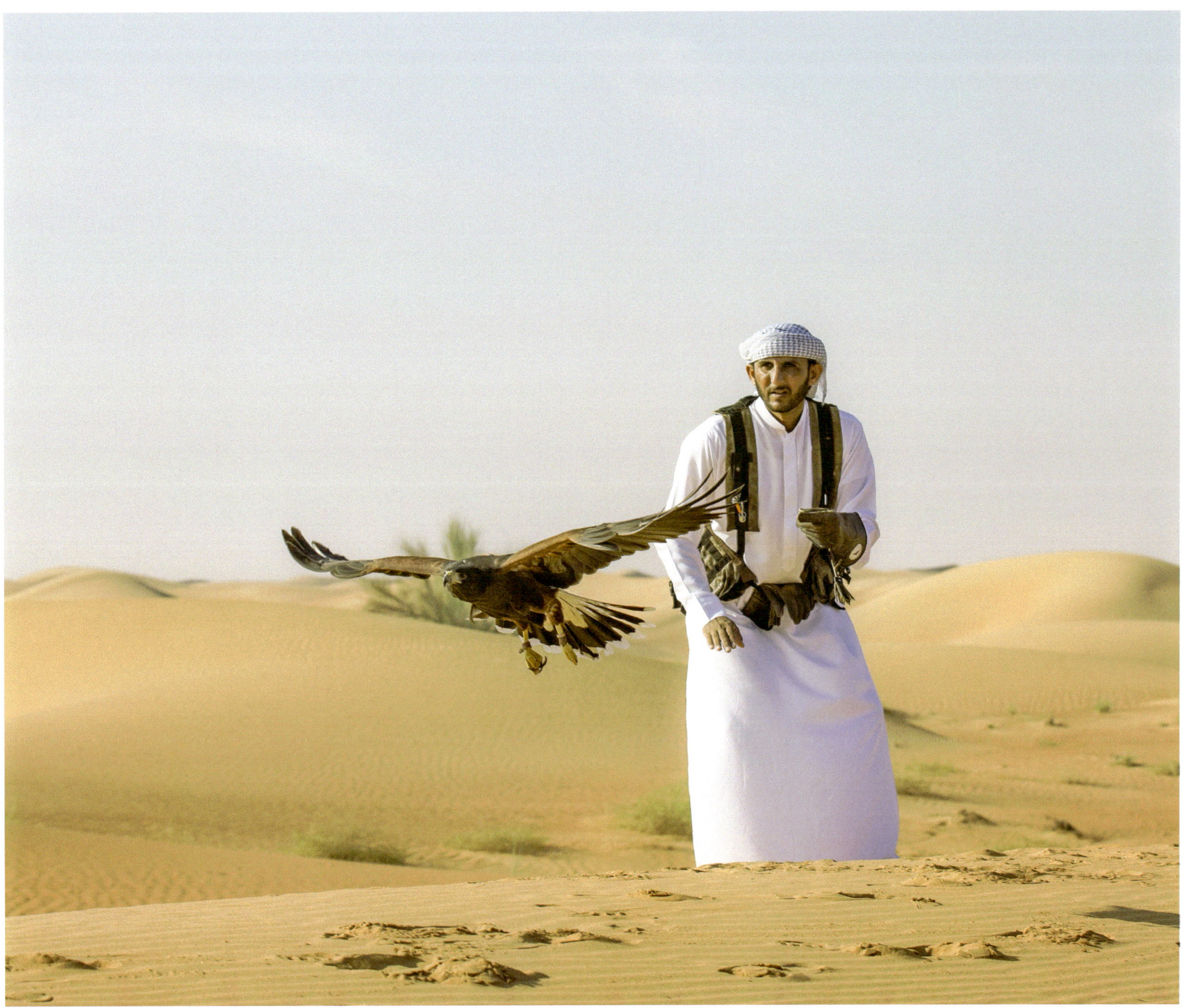

OPPOSITE:
Louvre Abu Dhabi
This universal, award-winning museum is a result of a partnership between the UAE and France. Designed by the architect Jean Nouvel, the Louvre is situated on Saadiyat Island. Distinctive for the massive, intricate dome that filters sunlight to create a 'rain of light', the museum goer experiences the feeling of being inside an oasis. The museum's collection is universal in content, explaining history, showcasing art and artefacts from diverse cultures, and highlighting shared human stories.

LEFT:
Falconry
Using falcons to hunt has been an integral part of Emirati culture for thousands of years, more recently transitioning from a vital survival skill to a cherished heritage sport. Historically, Bedouin tribes relied on falcons to catch food, with the relationship between the falconer and bird built on trust and respect. Today, falconry is a celebrated pastime and a symbol of national identity. While hunting is now regulated, the tradition continues through prestigious competitions, educational centres, and conservation programmes.

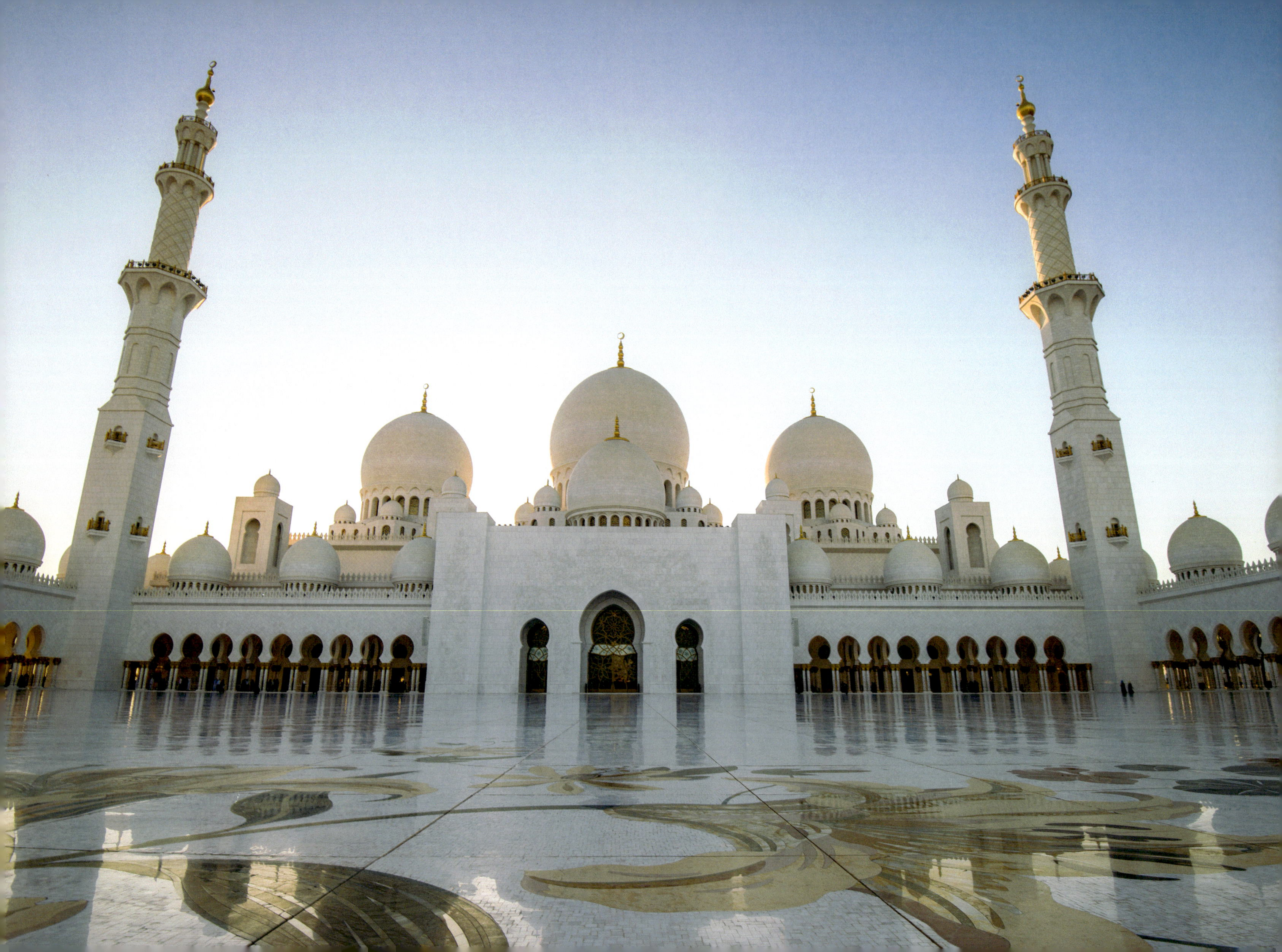

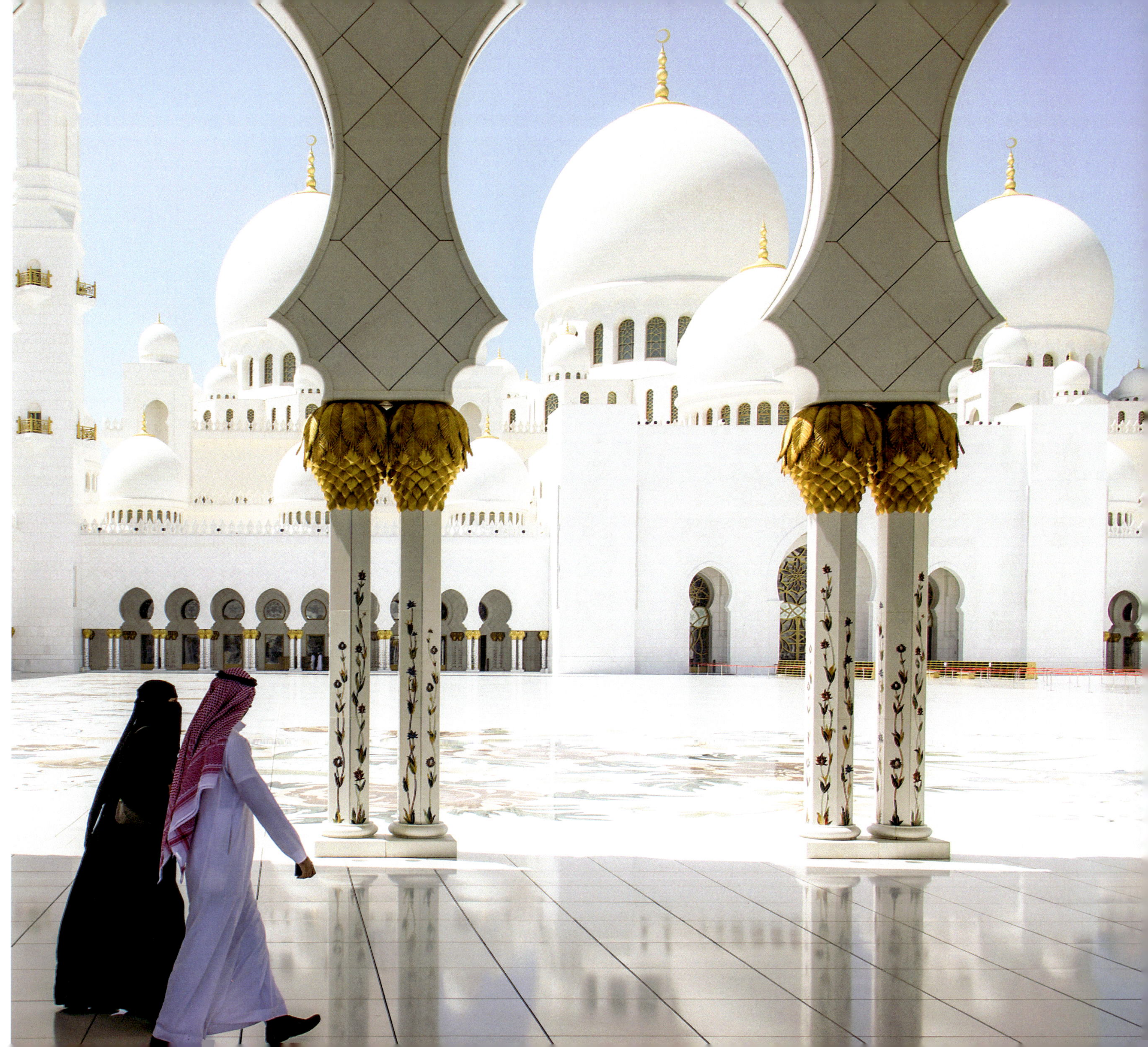

Sheikh Zayed Grand Mosque, Abu Dhabi

This astonishing architectural wonder is a testament to Islamic art. With 82 domes, more than 1000 columns, and containing the world's largest hand-knotted carpet, the mosque can accommodate up to 40,000 worshippers. The glittering design is a sumptuous blend of Mamluk, Ottoman, and Fatimid styles, adorned with gold, semi-precious stones, and multiple reflective pools. It was founded by Sheikh Zayed bin Sultan Al Nahyan, and was created as a beacon of peace and tolerance. Visitors of all faiths are welcome.

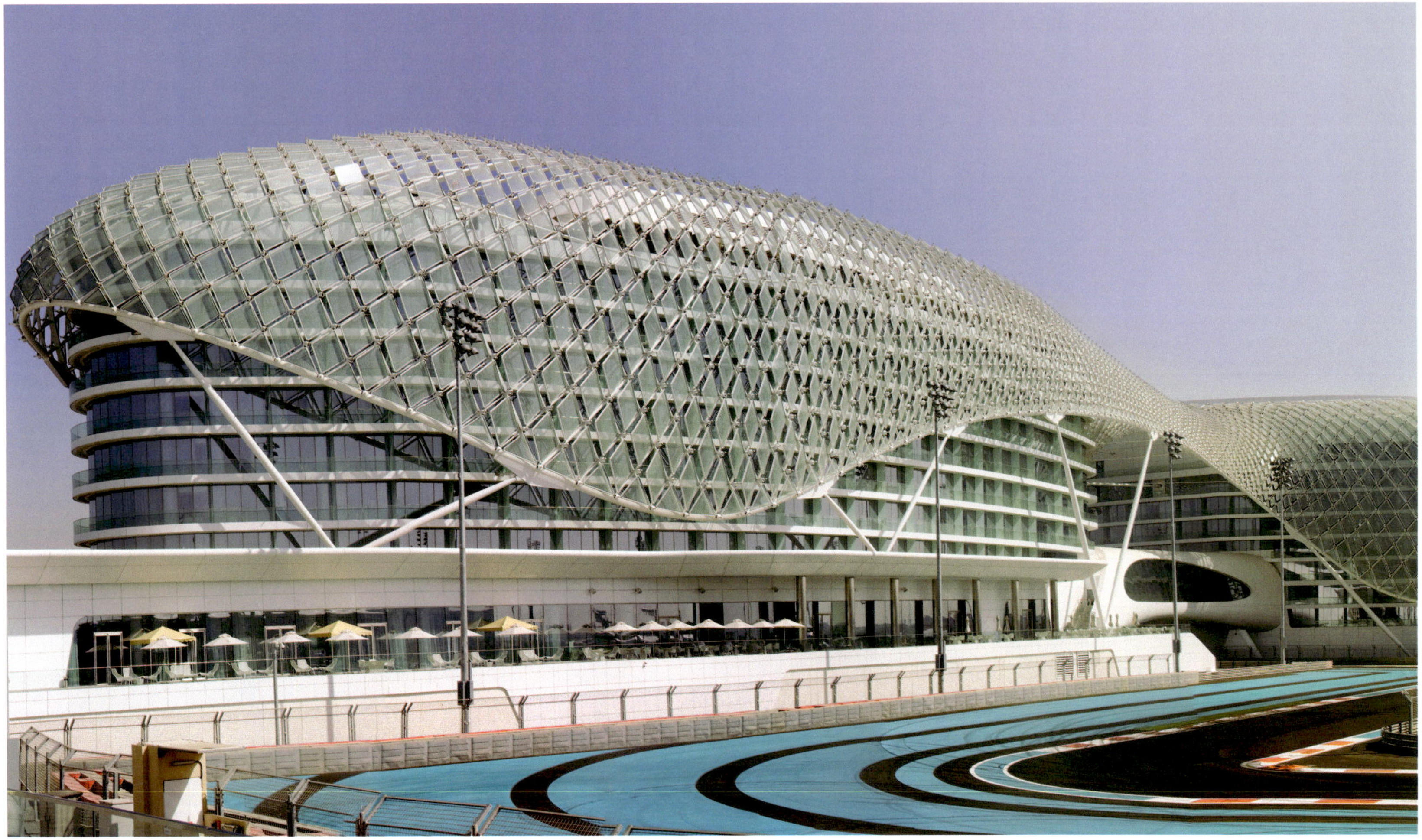

Yas Marina Circuit, Abu Dhabi

The Formula One racetrack in Abu Dhabi is the Yas Marina Circuit. Opened in 2009 on Yas Island, it is famous for its stunning twilight races and for hosting the final F1 race each season. Its state-of-the-art lighting system allows events to transition from day to night. It is situated close to Yas Island Ferrari World Theme Park.

Al Seef Heritage Souq, Dubai

This charming waterfront promenade blends traditional Arabian buildings with modern facilities. Shoppers can wander through winding alleys and explore the shops and stalls selling traditional handicrafts, textiles, spices, and Dubai souvenirs. The souq is an immersive experience, with the scent of spices and perfumes filling the air. It's an ideal spot to complete a visit to this Emirate.

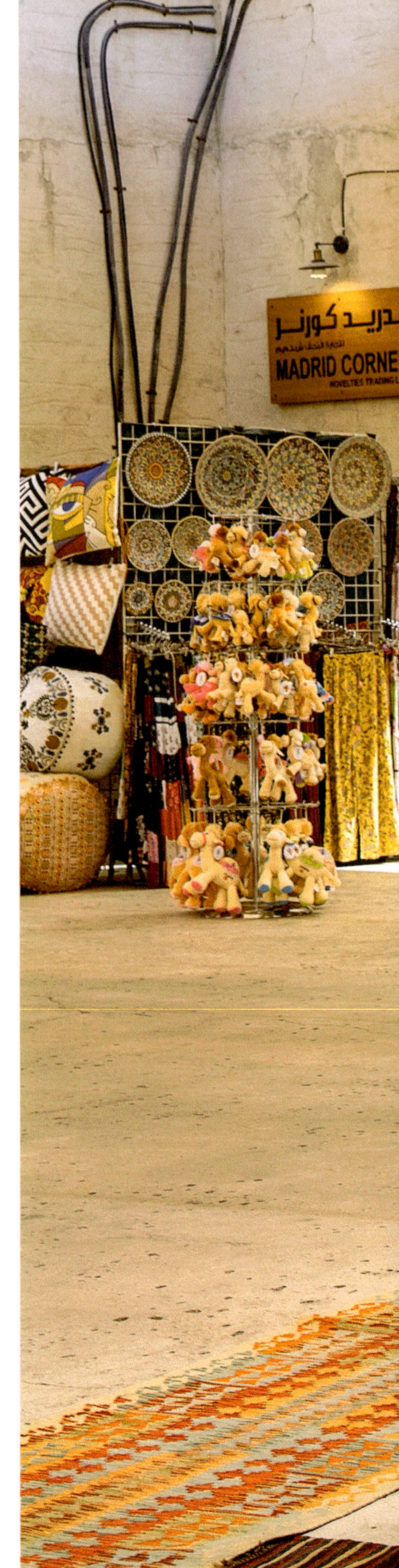

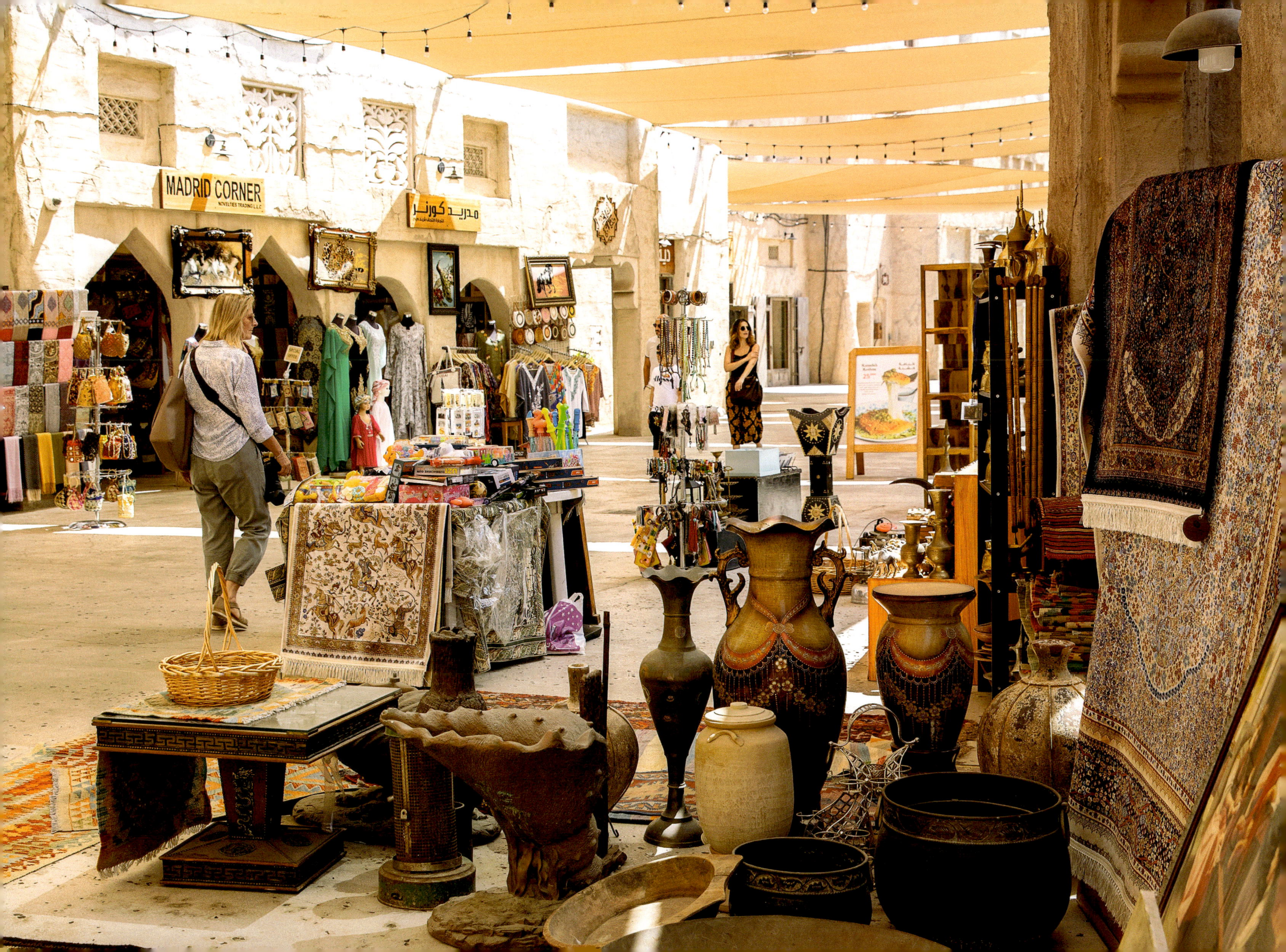

MADRID CORNER
NOVELTIES TRADING L.L.C
مدريد كورنر

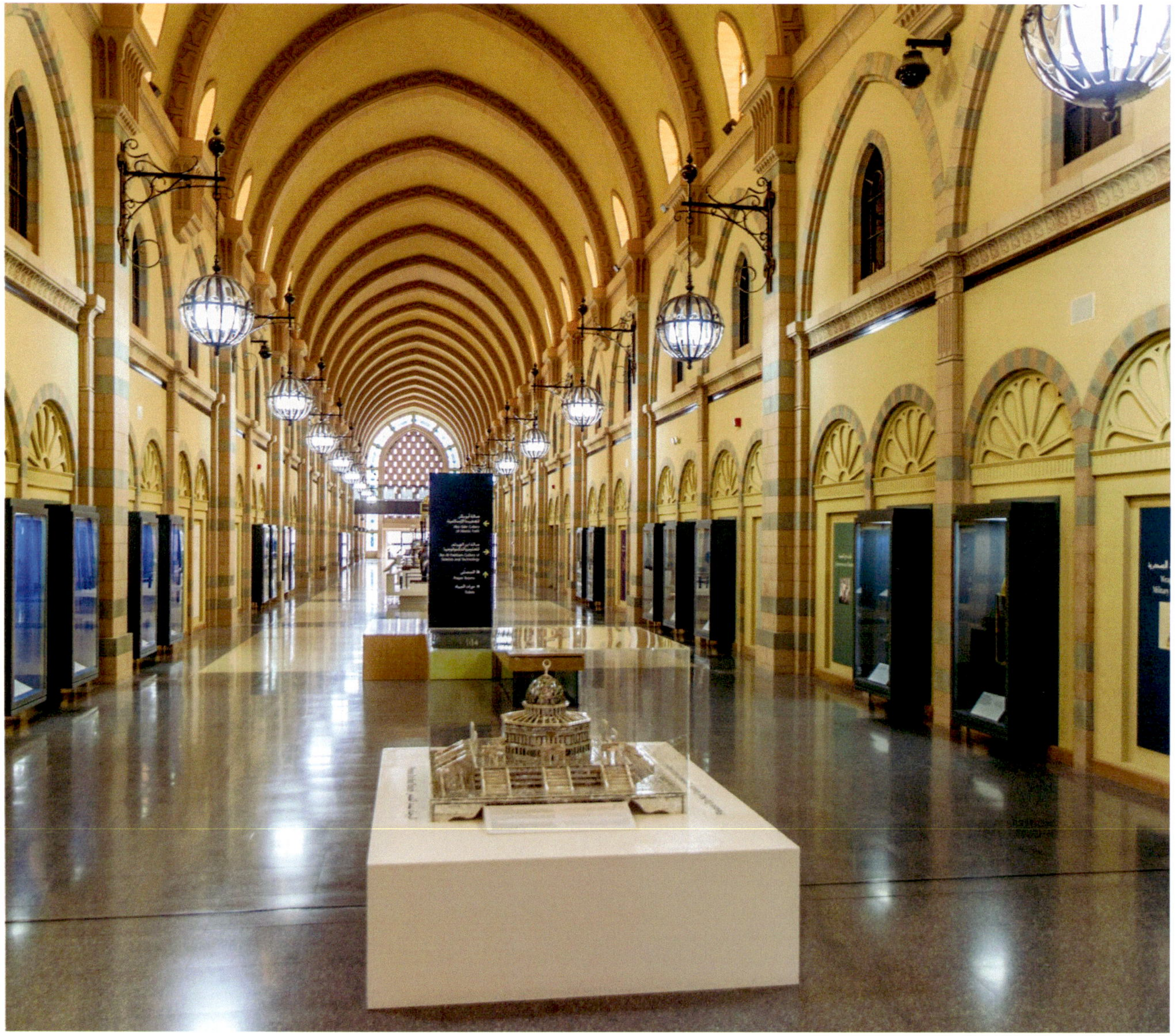

Sharjah Museum of Islamic Civilization, Sharjah
Located on the Al Majarrah Waterfront, this splendid cultural
landmark opened in 2008, after successfully converting a local
souq. It houses over 5000 fascinating artefacts from across
the Islamic world in the museum's seven galleries. Each area
explores a different aspect of Islamic civilization, such as faith,
scientific discoveries, and art. The highlight, however, is the
museum's central dome, which features an intricate mosaic
of the night sky, and celebrates the contributions of Islamic
scholars to astronomy.

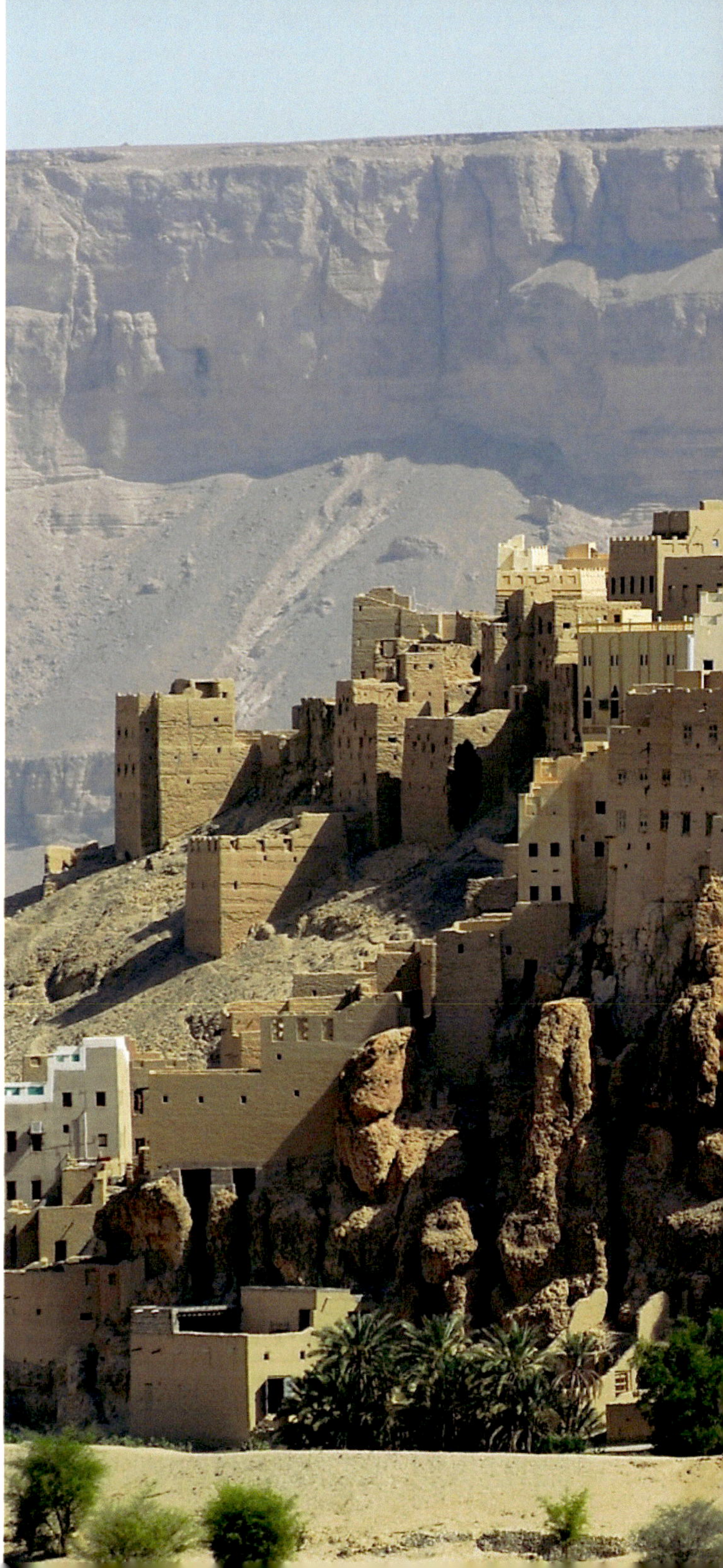

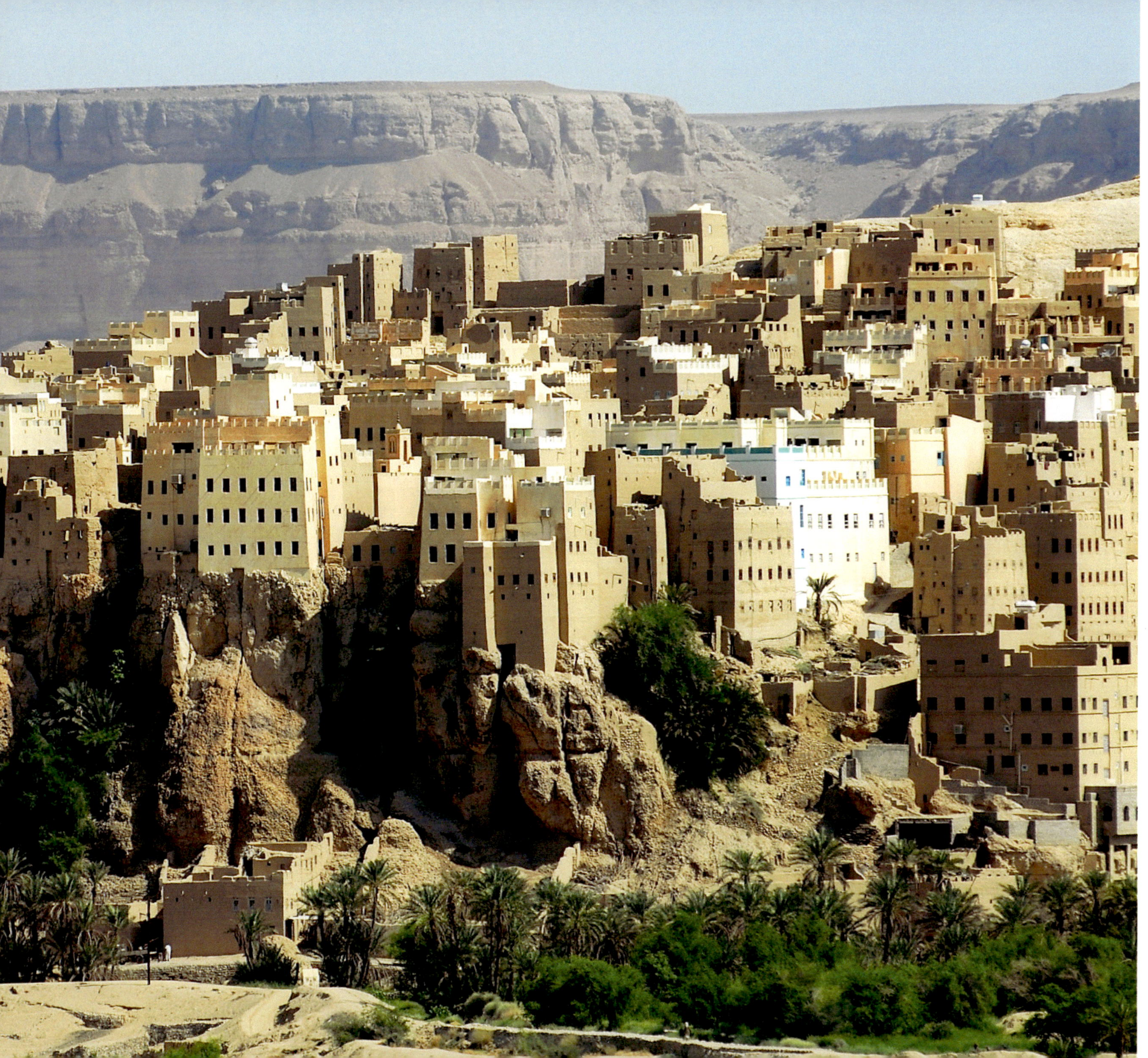

Seiyun, Hadramawt
This historical region is situated in eastern Yemen. Well known for its remarkable architecture and its rich history as a major trade and scholarly centre, the region is home to the iconic cities of Shibam, Tarim and Seiyun.

These places are famous for their mud-brick tower houses; indeed, Shibam is often called the 'Manhattan of the Desert' with some buildings reaching up to 11 stories high. The region's ancient trading story included the transporting of frankincense and myrrh, and its people, known as Hadhramis, have travelled widely, establishing new communities across the Arabian Peninsula and into Southeast Asia.

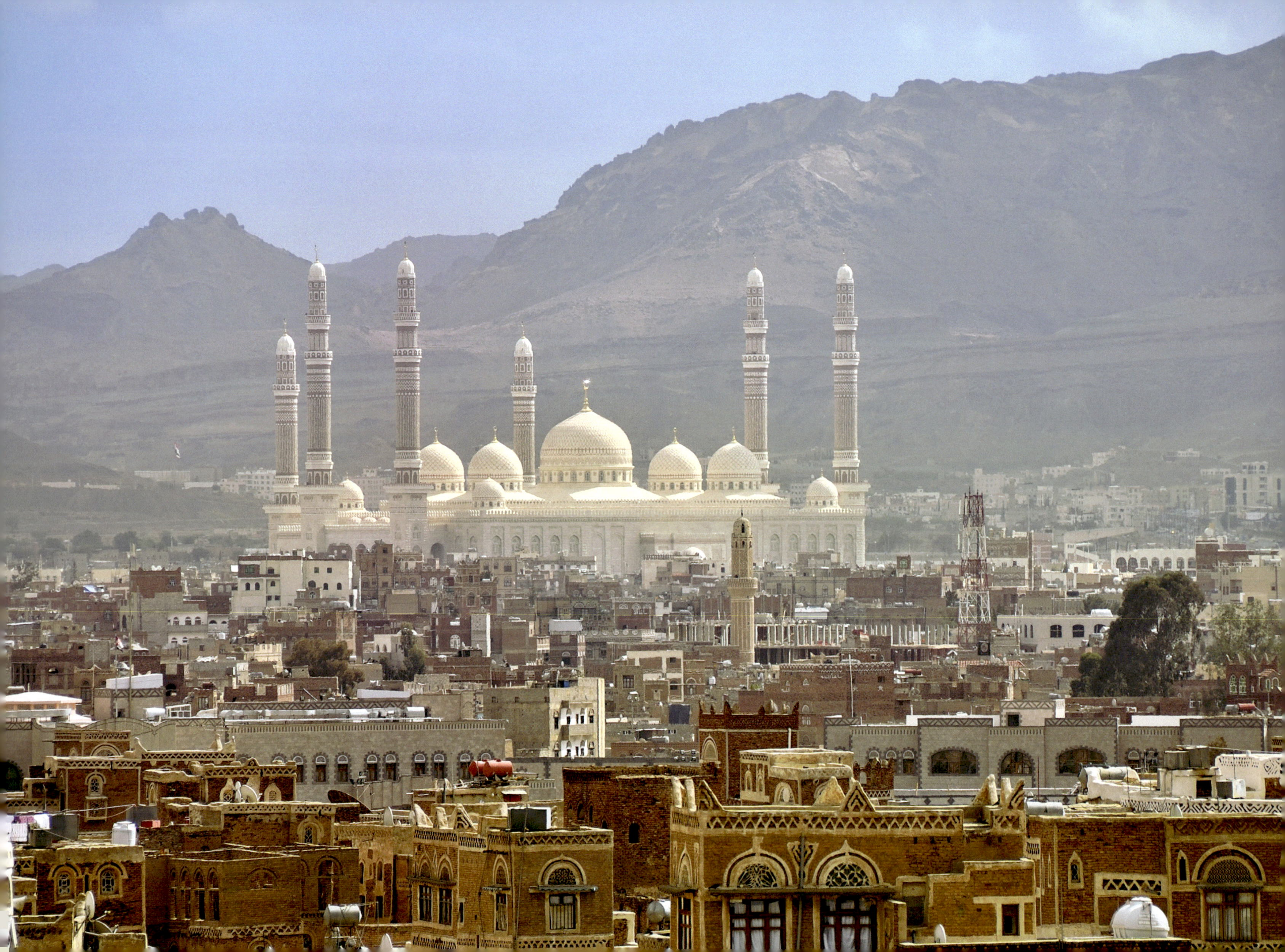

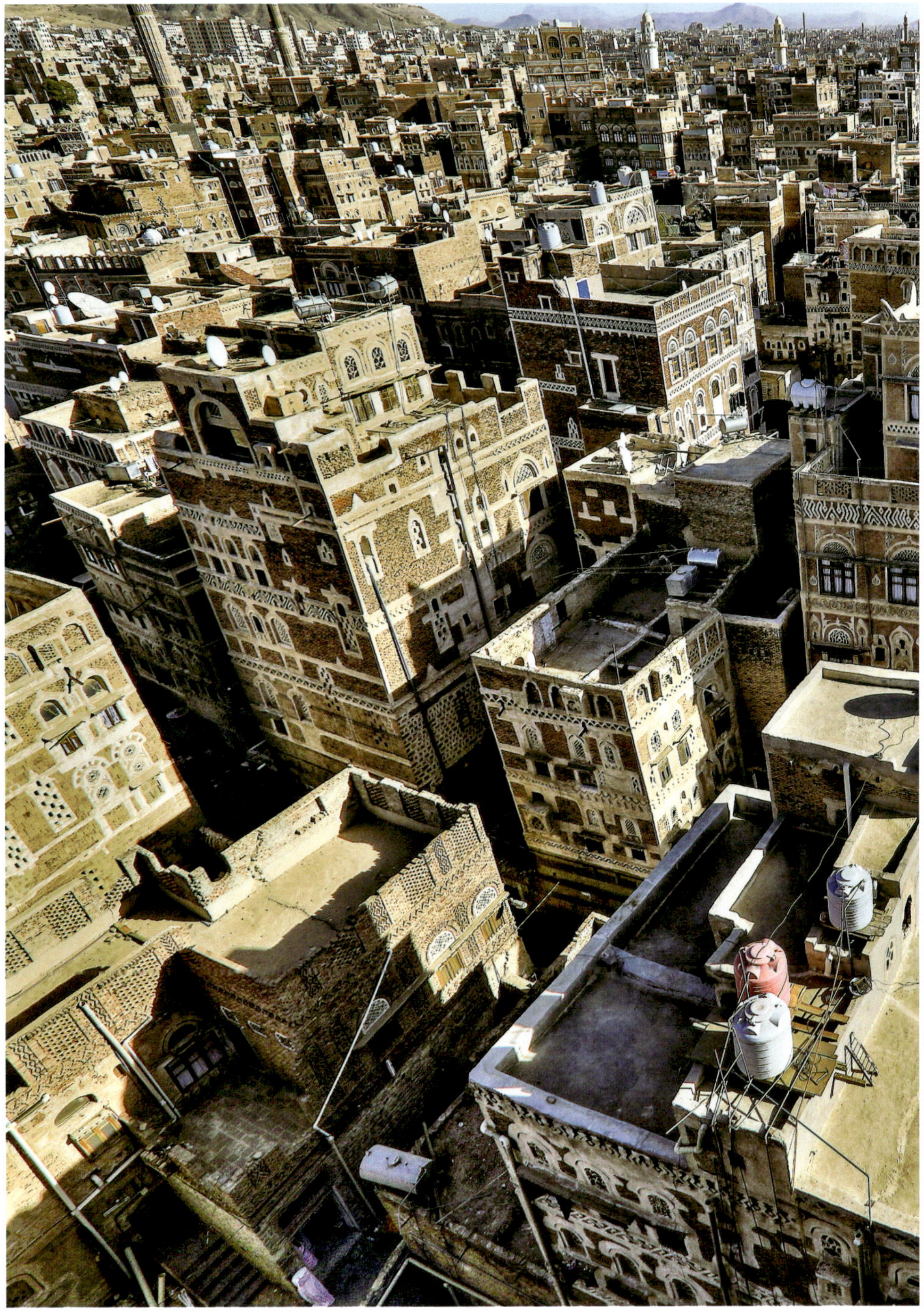

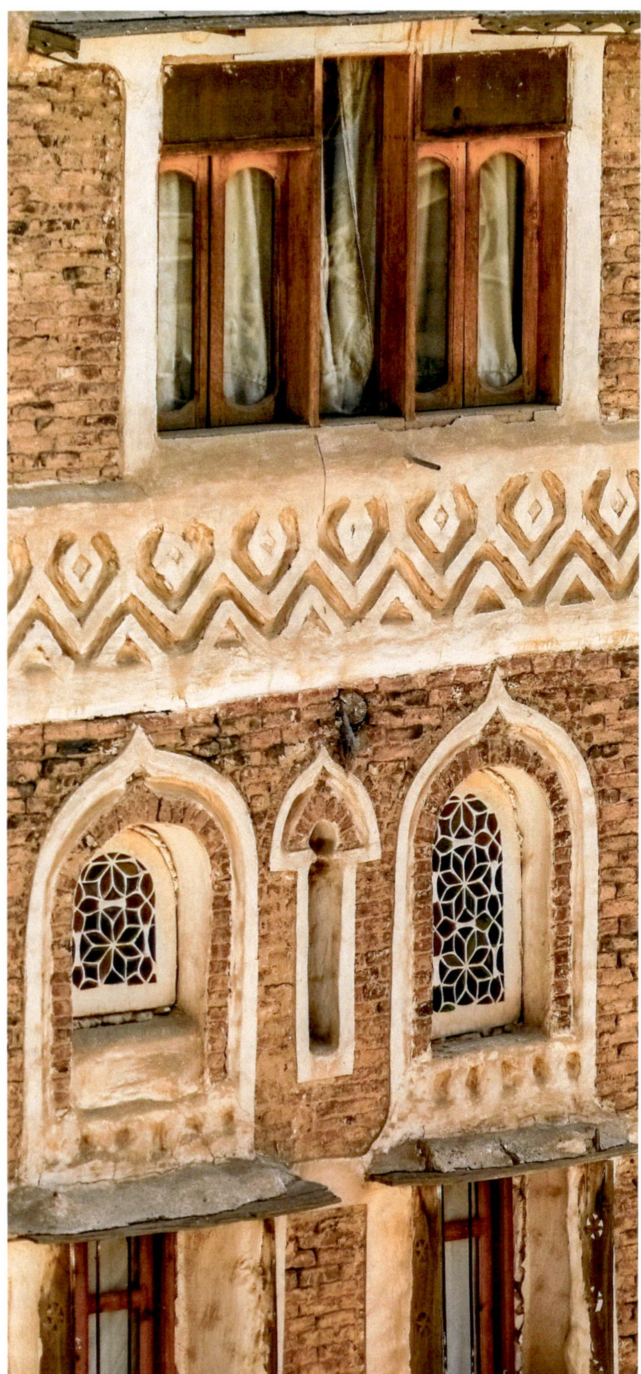

Sana'a

Sana'a is one of the world's oldest continuously inhabited cities and is a UNESCO World Heritage site best known for its unique multi-storey mud-brick tower houses and ancient souks. Sana'a was a major Islamic centre as far back as the Seventh and Eighth centuries.

The city's multi-storey buildings are better known as Tower Houses, and were constructed using a special blend of rammed earth and fired brick. They can be several stories high and often feature elaborate geometric patterns made from white gypsum and intricately carved wood. This unique architectural style has been used for centuries, creating a memorable urban landscape that is instantly recognisable as Yemeni.

More modern is Al-Saleh Mosque in Sana'a (pictured opposite), a new architectural masterpiece and Yemen's largest mosque. It was completed in 2008.

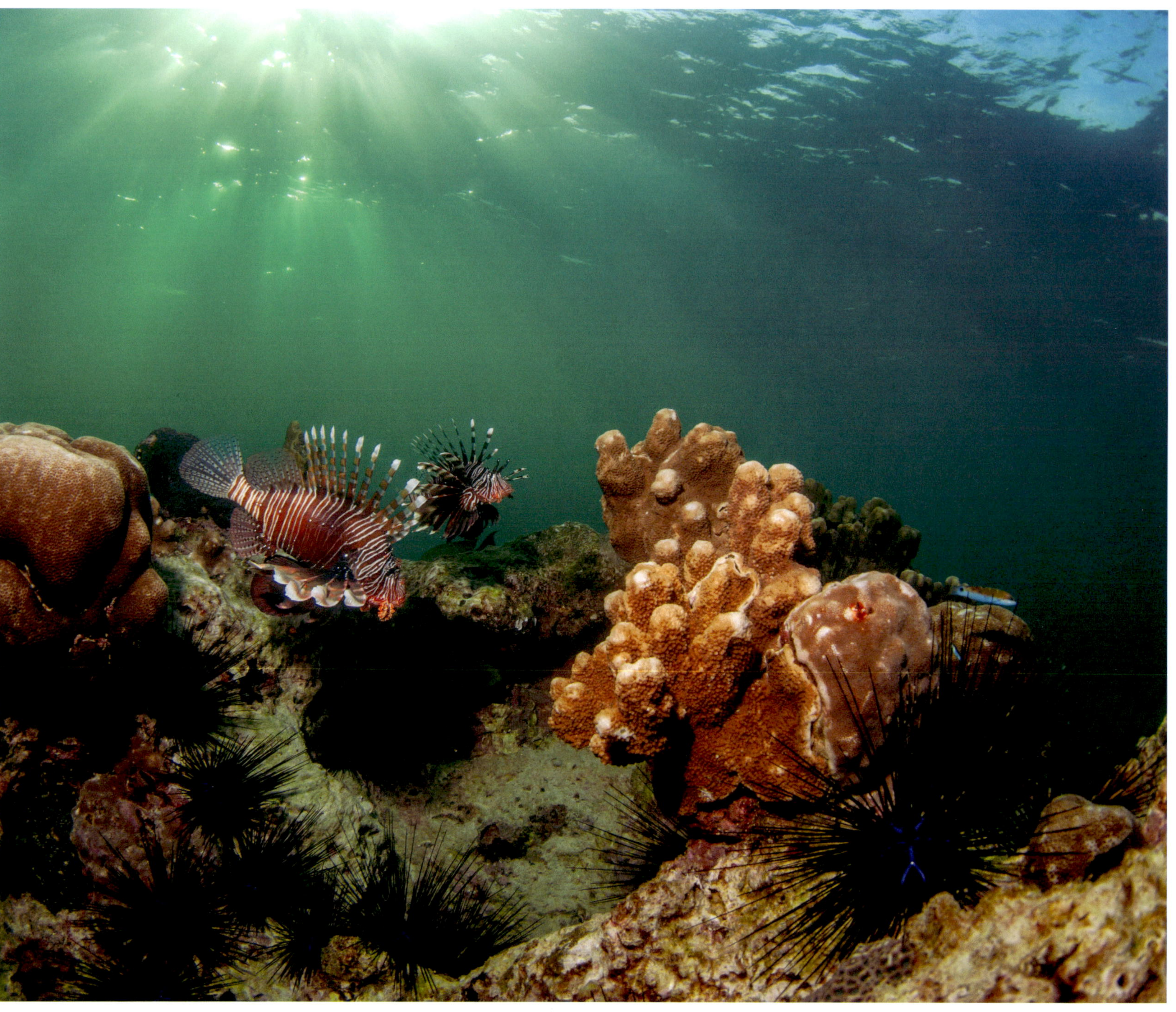

Socotra archipelago
Often called the 'Galápagos of the Indian Ocean', Socotra is in the Arabian Sea. This beautiful, isolated, biodiversity hotspot has an unusually high number of endemic species. Over a third of its plant life and 90% of its reptiles are found nowhere else on Earth. The coral reefs of Socotra are a special treasure, renowned for their incredible biodiversity. The waters surrounding the island contain a high diversity of species, with over 253 species of reef-building corals. Socotra's unique geographic location, at the crossroads of several marine zones, creates a hotspot for unique, hybrid fish species. The folklore of the Socotra islands is as unique as its endemic flora and fauna. Among the most prevalent beliefs are the stories of the Jinn, supernatural beings in pre-Islamic Arabian and Islamic traditions. On Socotra, these spirits are said to inhabit the island's remote and cavernous interior, including its deep caves and mountains.

OPPOSITE:
Bottle tree, Socotra island
This remarkable succulent is native to Socotra. It has a distinctive swollen trunk that stores water, a vital adaptation for surviving the island's arid climate.

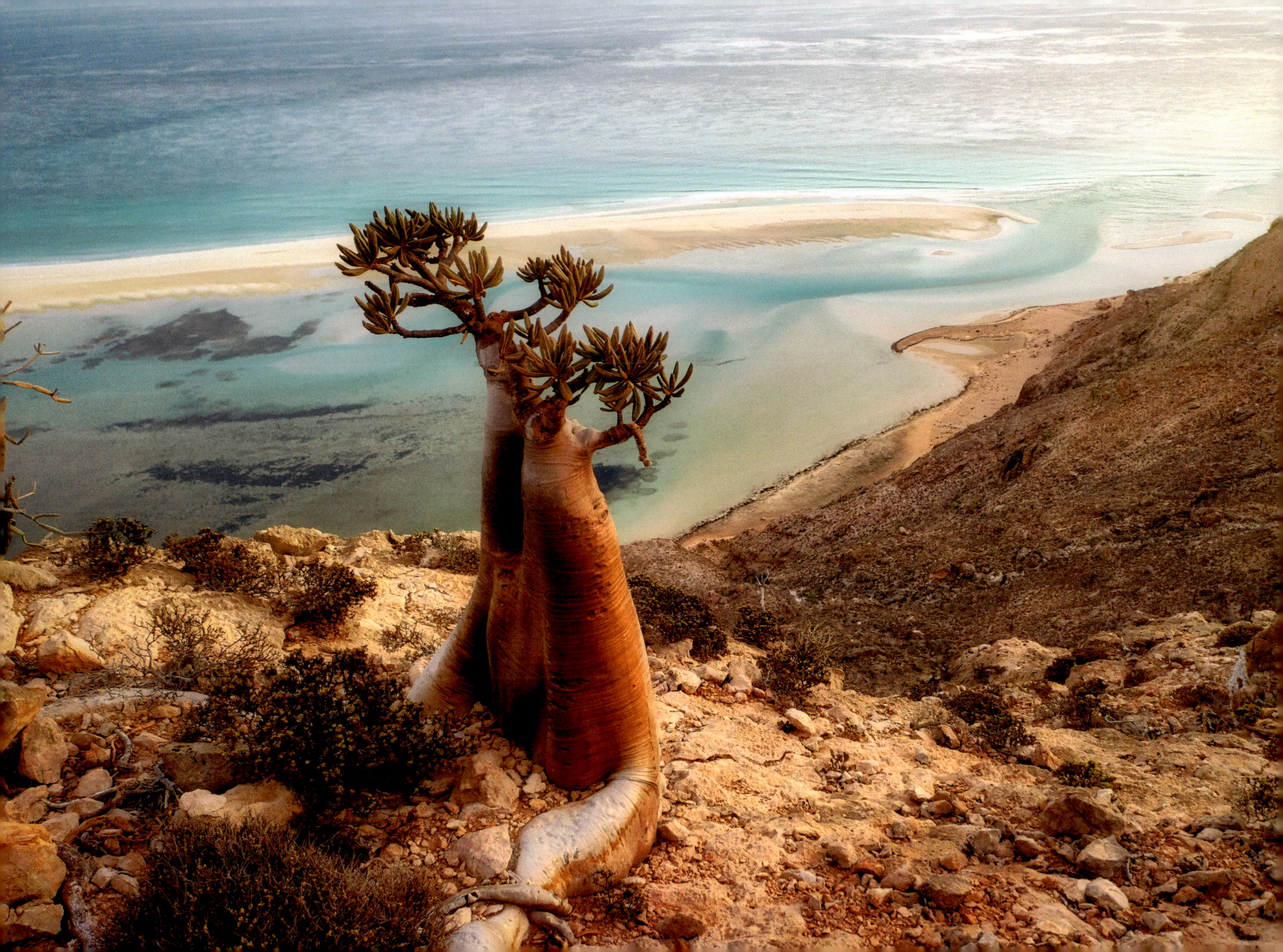

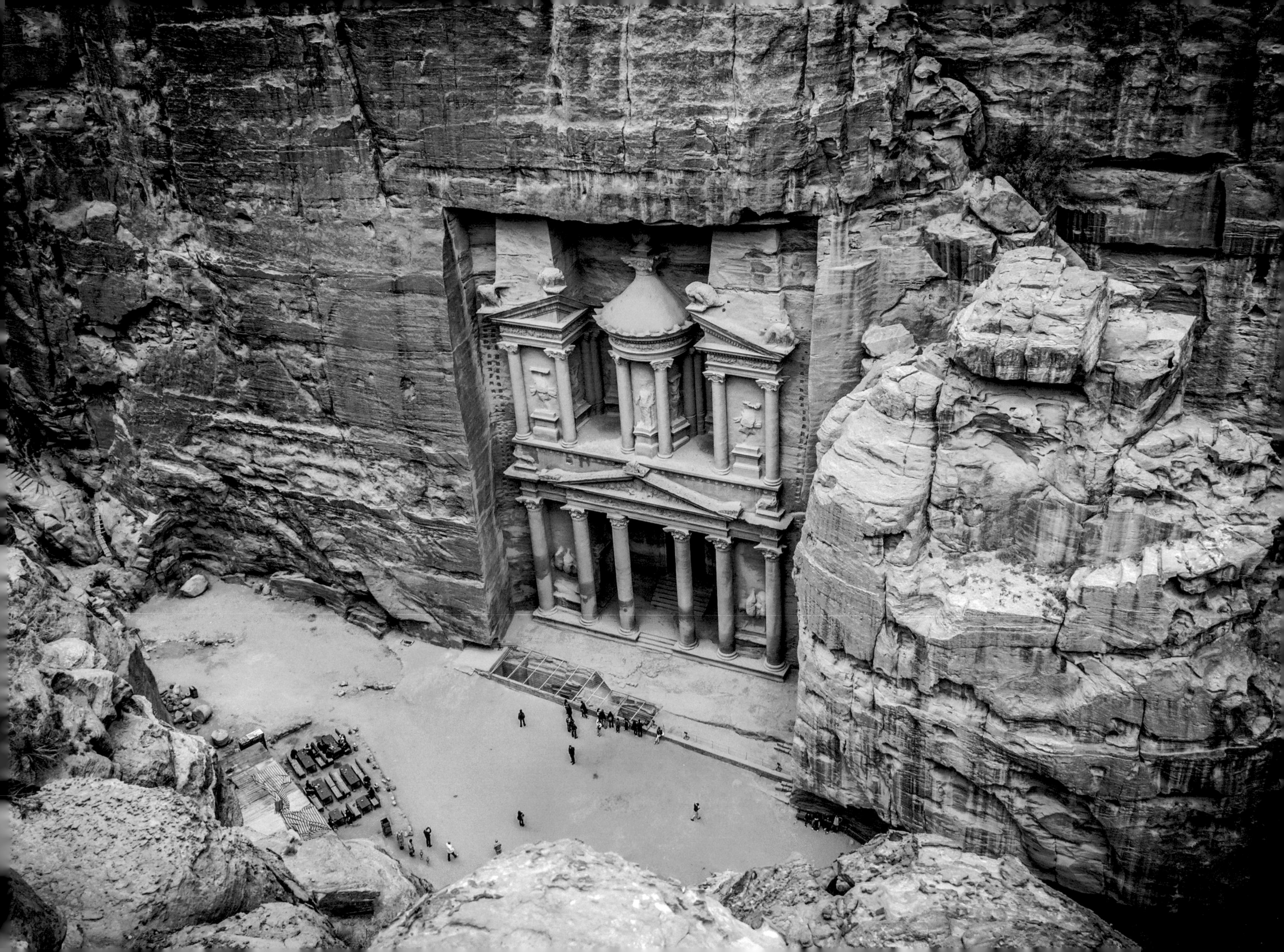

The Levant

Welcome to a region where history is etched into every sun-baked stone, whispered on the desert breeze and savoured in every delicious bite of local cuisine. In this chapter we embark on a time travellers' journey through the Near East, a special region bursting with ancient wonders, vibrant cultures and heart-warming hospitality. Imagine standing where civilizations began, where empires rose and fell, where the Crusaders roamed a thousand years ago, leaving behind a legacy that touches every modern visitor. Who can walk through the hallowed streets of Jerusalem, a city sacred to billions, without sensing the layers of spiritual history that lie beneath your feet? Or picture yourself crossing Wadi Rum, the so-called 'Valley of the Moon' desert landscape that shared its shifting sands with the legendary Lawrence of Arabia. By the enchanting Mediterranean coast you can discover the timeless Roman temples of Baalbek, their grandeur a testament to imperial power, or wander through the charming streets of Byblos, one of the oldest continuously inhabited cities in the world.

But the Levant is so much more than its incredible historical sites. It is a kaleidoscope of peoples and cultures, a melting pot of traditions that have coexisted, intertwined and flourished for centuries. This vibrant tapestry of Arab, Christian and Jewish communities, often living side-by-side, and each contributing to the rich cultural mosaic, creates a dynamic and cosmopolitan atmosphere. Then, there is the food. Prepare your taste buds for an explosion of flavours. Indulge in creamy hummus, smoky baba ghanoush and freshly baked pita bread that will redefine your idea of comfort food. Savour succulent kebabs, fragrant falafel, and crisp tabbouleh that sings with the taste of fresh herbs. From the bustling souks of Amman and Damascus to the chic cafes of Beirut, every meal is an adventure, a celebration of local ingredients and ancient recipes.

Treasury, Petra, Ma'an
Petra is included in the list of New Seven Wonders of the World, being just over 2500 years old. This iconic site exudes majesty and power. Its distinctive rose-red rock-cut architecture, enclosing entire temples and tombs such as the renowned Treasury, are carved directly into sheer sandstone cliffs.

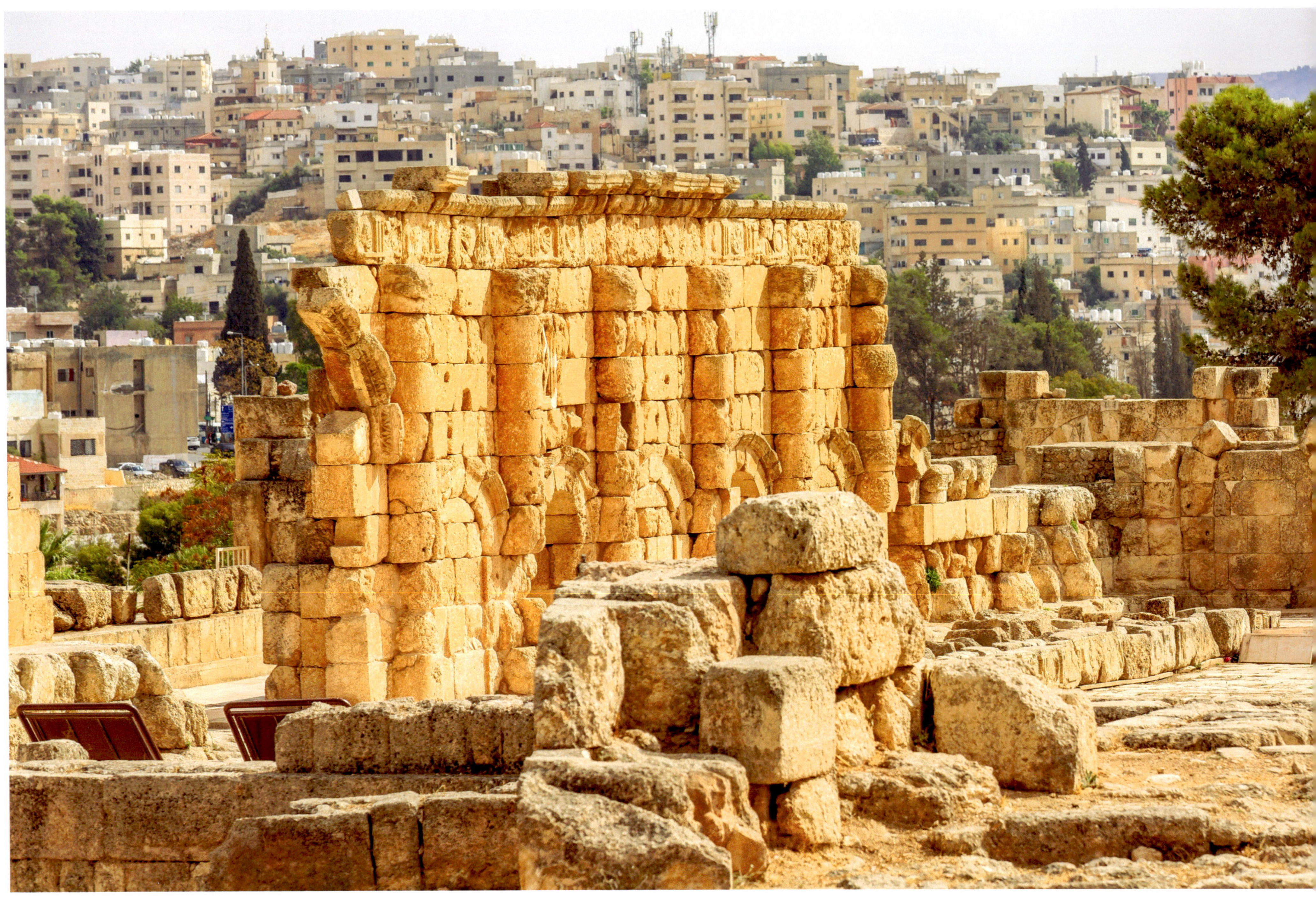

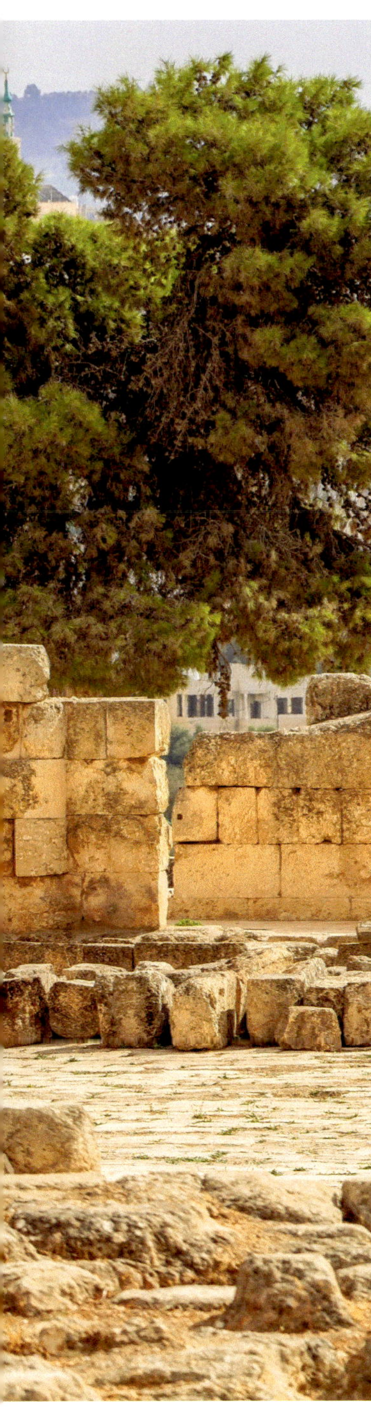

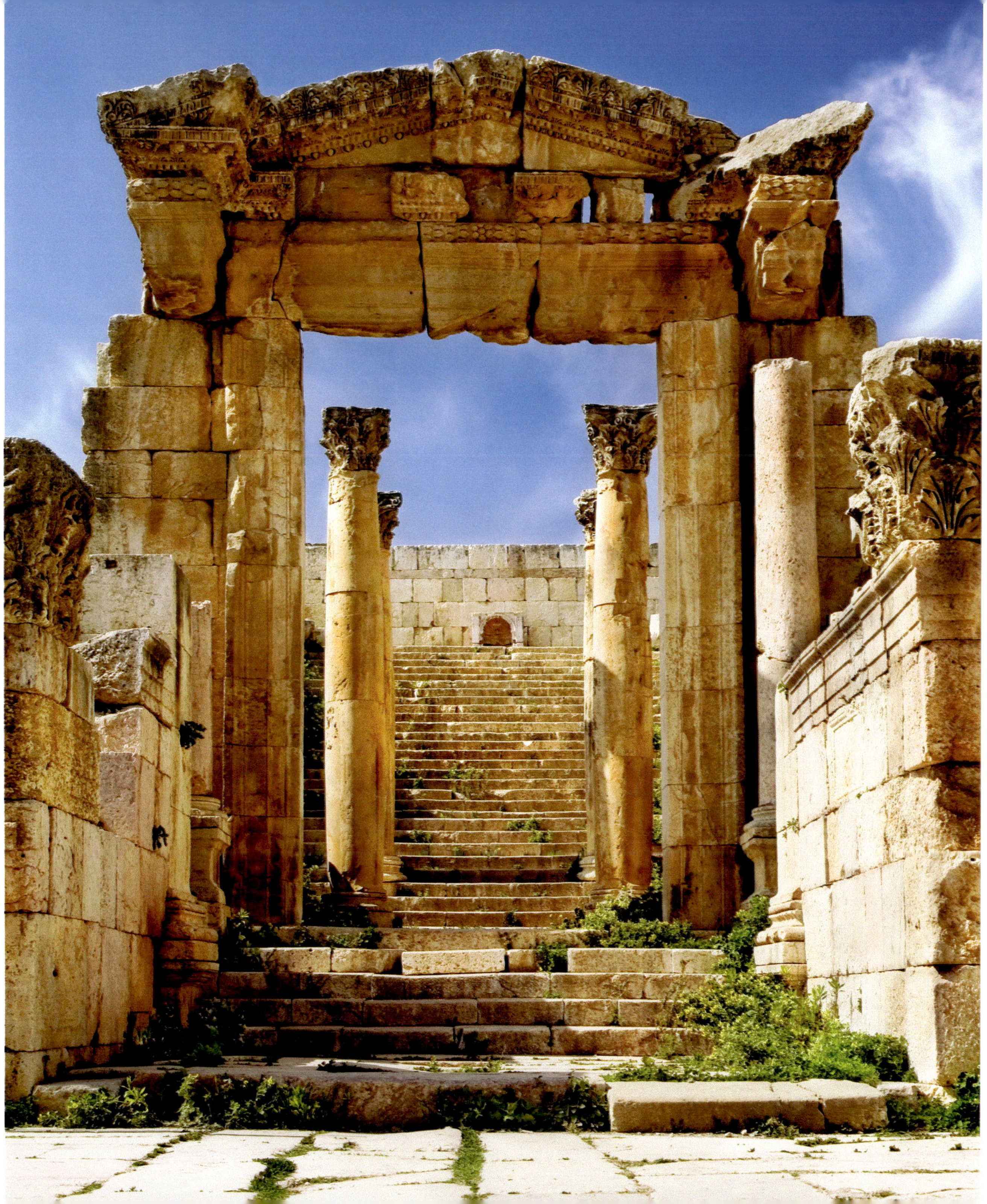

Jerash, Amman
These Roman ruins are among the best preserved in the world. Jerash is fascinating as the city was an ancient centre of trade and culture, and its ruins reflect a unique fusion of Roman and Middle Eastern traditions. The city was buried for centuries under sand, later revealing remarkably intact structures. Visitors can see paved, colonnaded streets with visible chariot ruts, and visit grand temples dedicated to gods like Zeus and Artemis.

**North Theatre, Jerash,
Amman**
The ruins at Jerash also
include two massive theatres
which are used today for
the annual Jerash Festival.
Built in AD 165 and
enlarged in 235, the smaller
North Theatre was most
likely used for government
meetings rather than artistic
performances. Many of
the seats in the theatre are
inscribed with the names of
delegates who voted in the
city council.

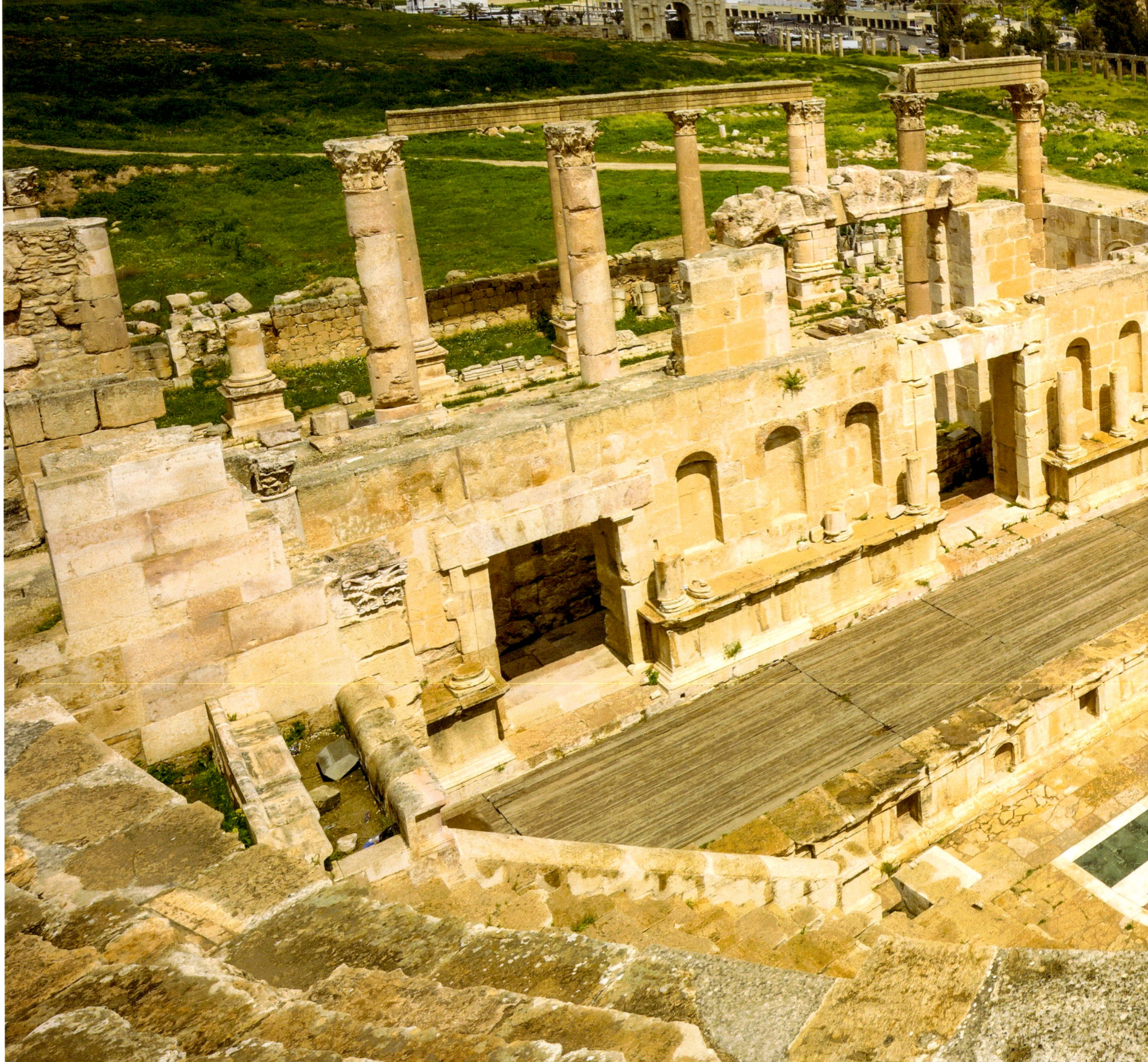

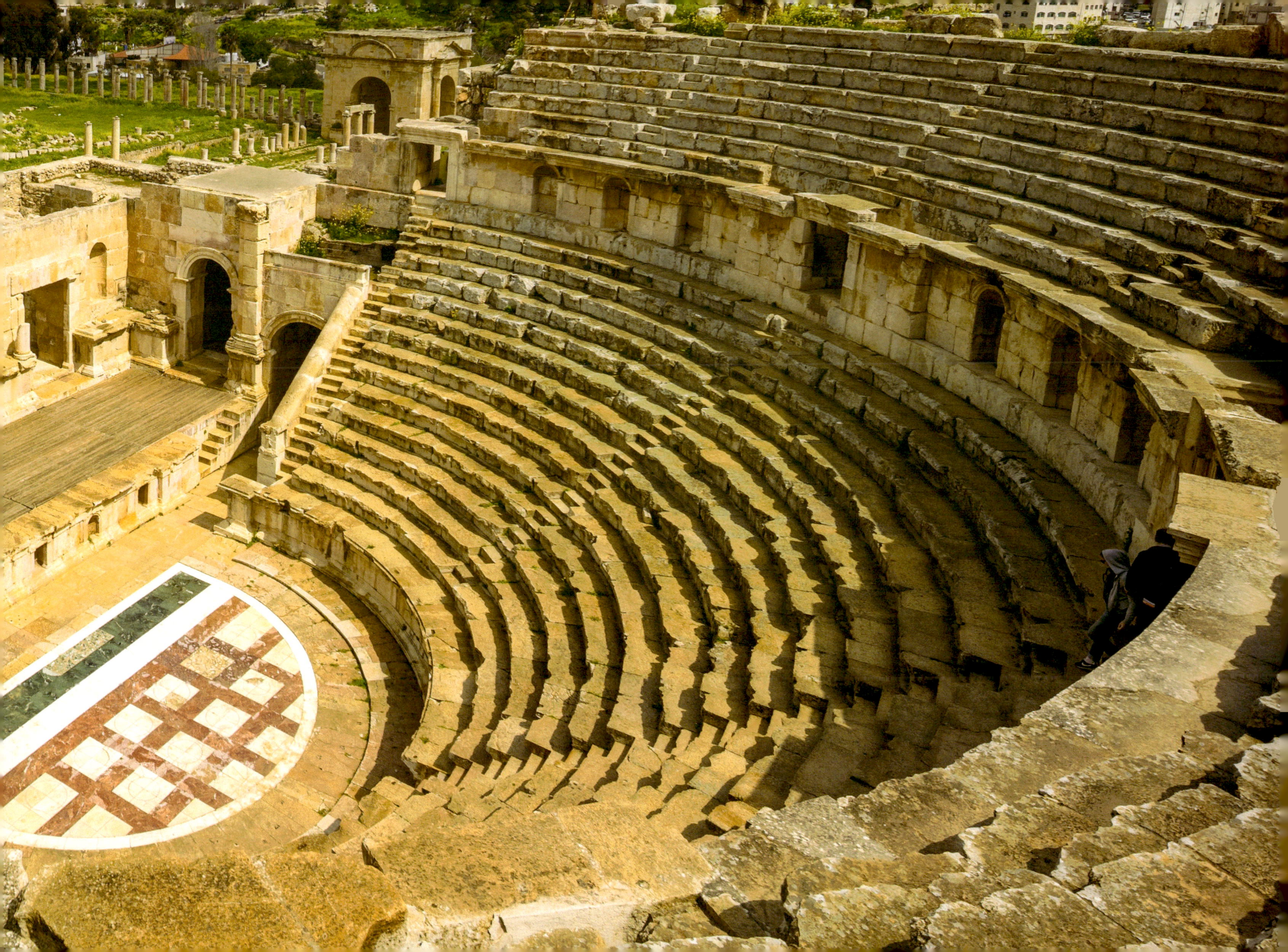

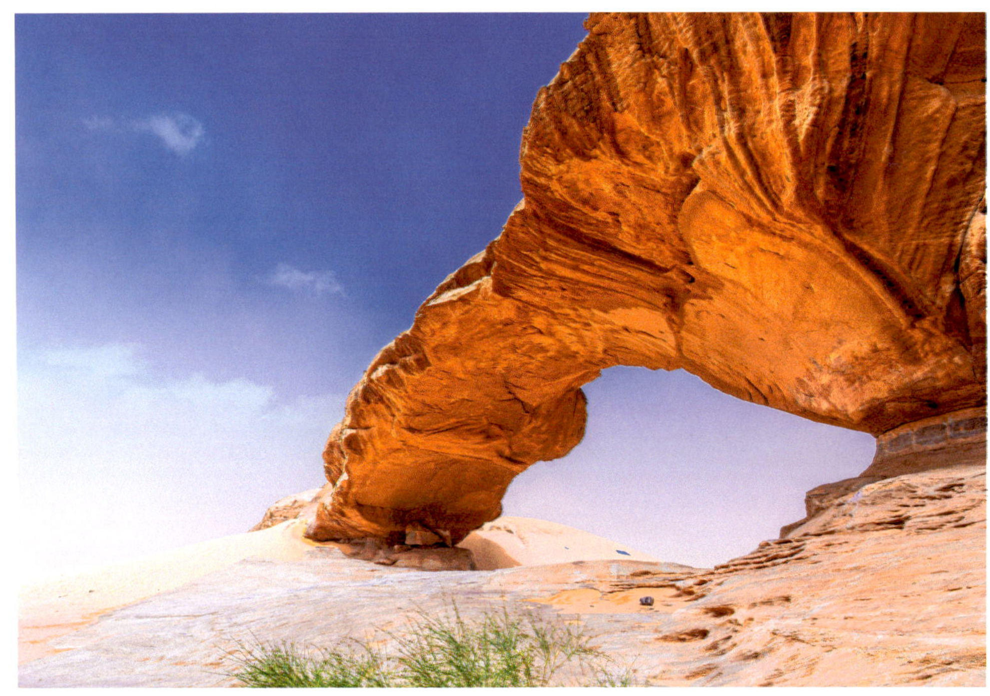

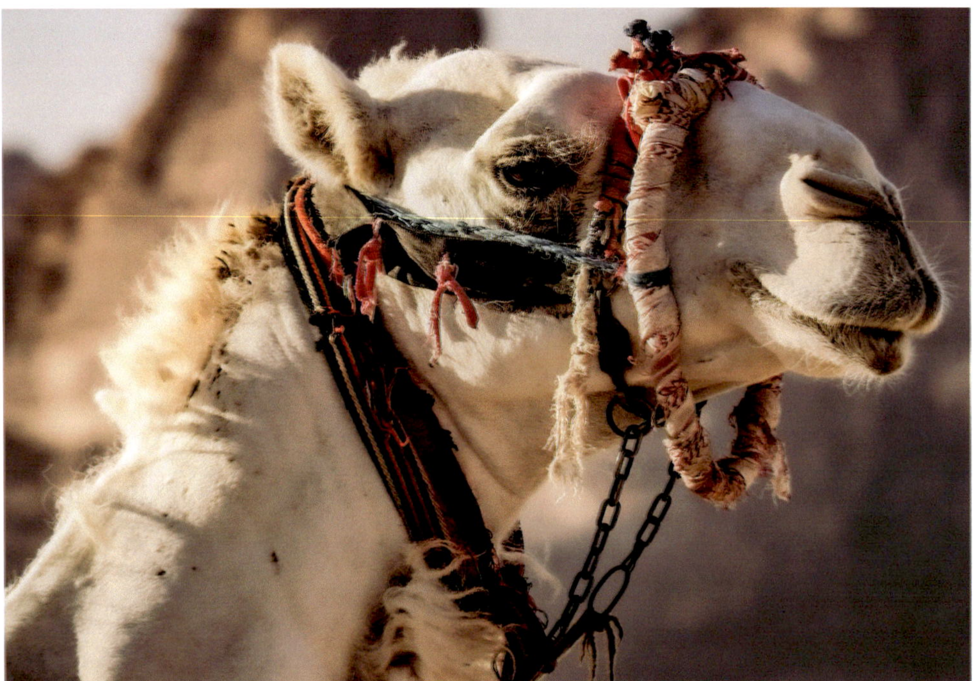

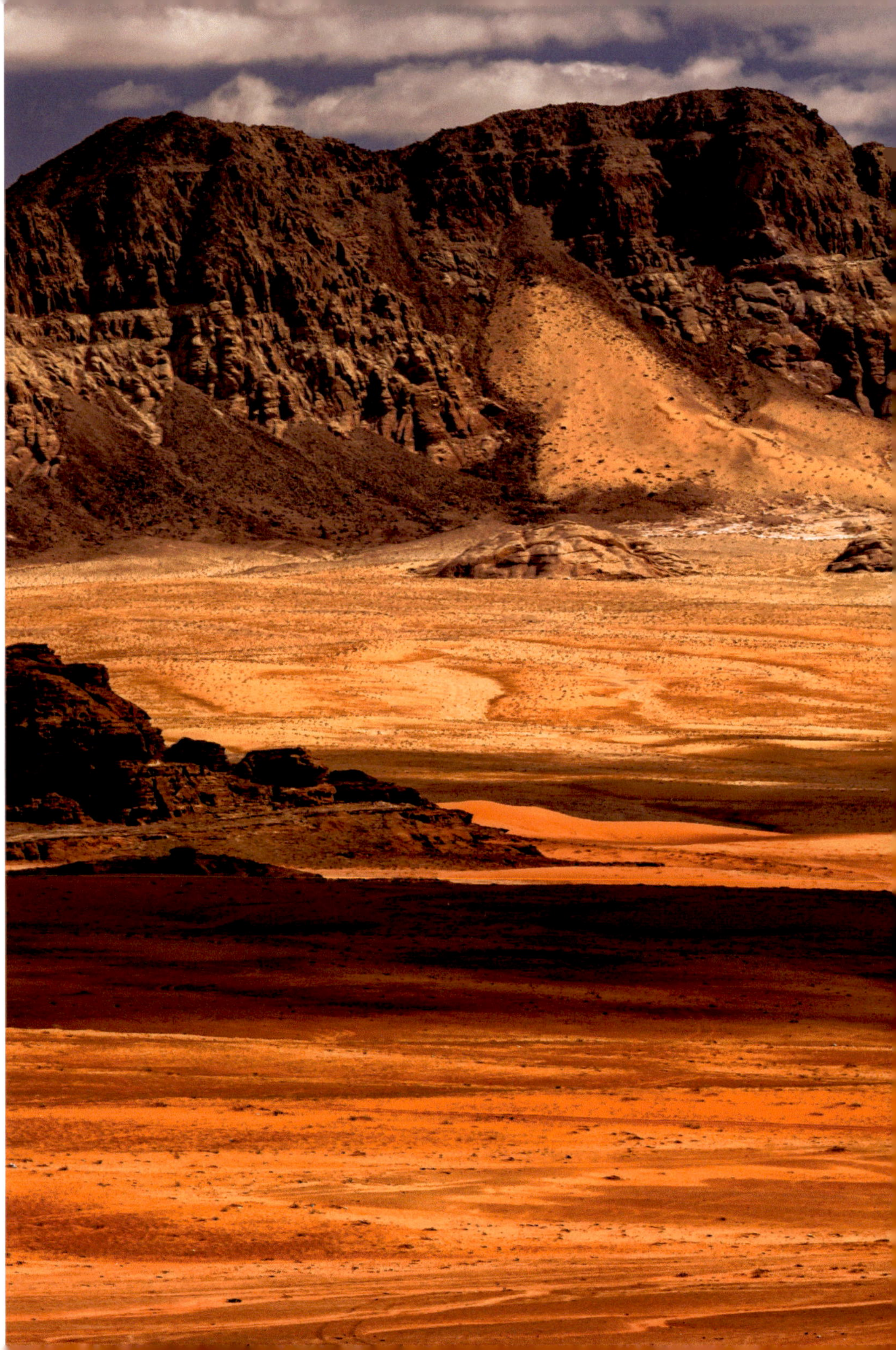

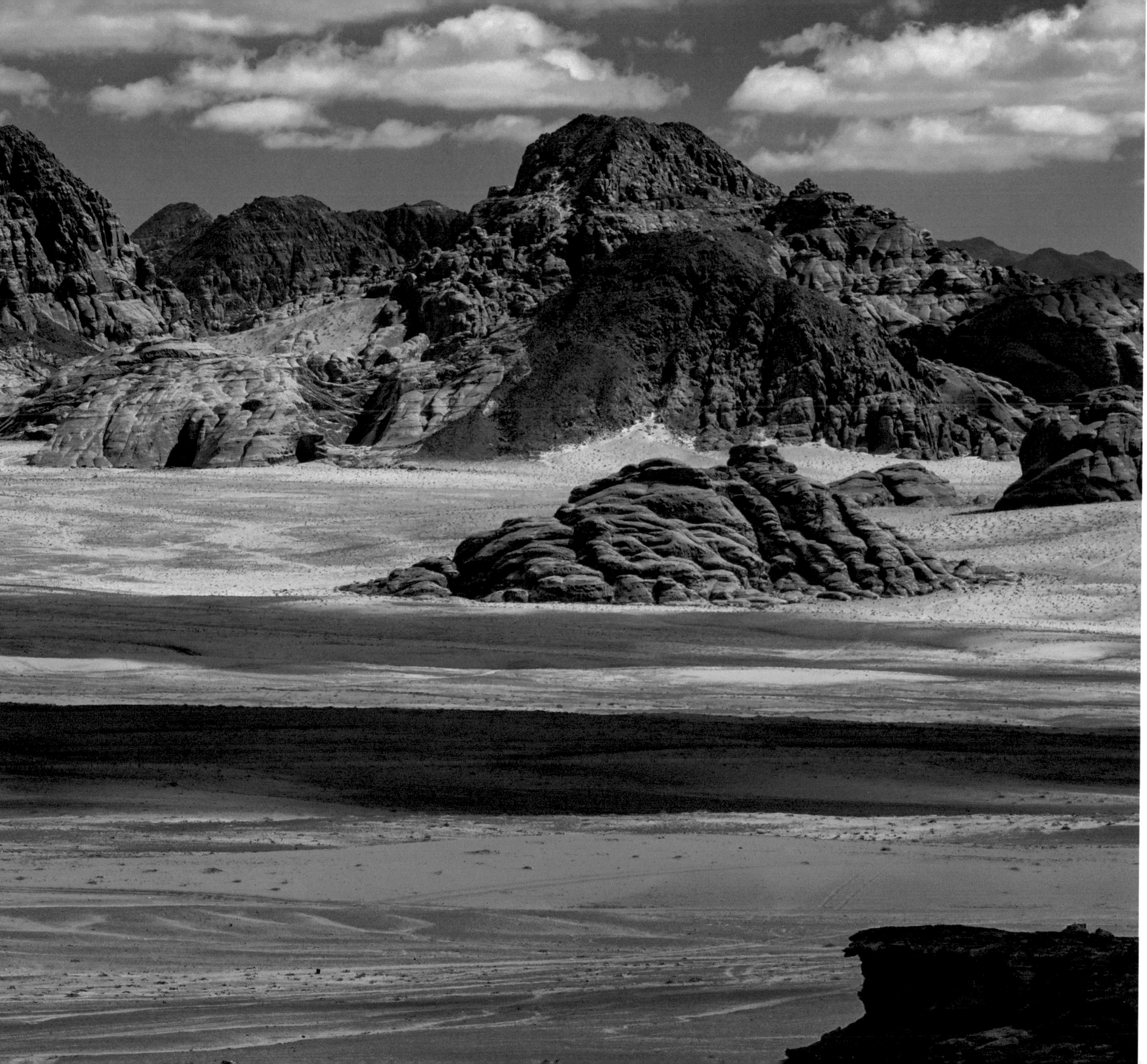

Wadi Rum

This breathtaking desert landscape of red sand dunes and awe-inspiring granite mountains is often named 'Valley of the Moon'. The other-worldly Mars-like appearance has led to the area being a popular filming location. The desert has served as a movie backdrop many times, most famously as the setting for much of the 1962 epic *Lawrence of Arabia*. Wadi Rum was also used to depict Mars in films like *The Martian* and as the desert planet of Arrakis in the recent *Dune* films. The area also holds significant historical value with rock inscriptions and petroglyphs testifying to 12,000 years of human activity.

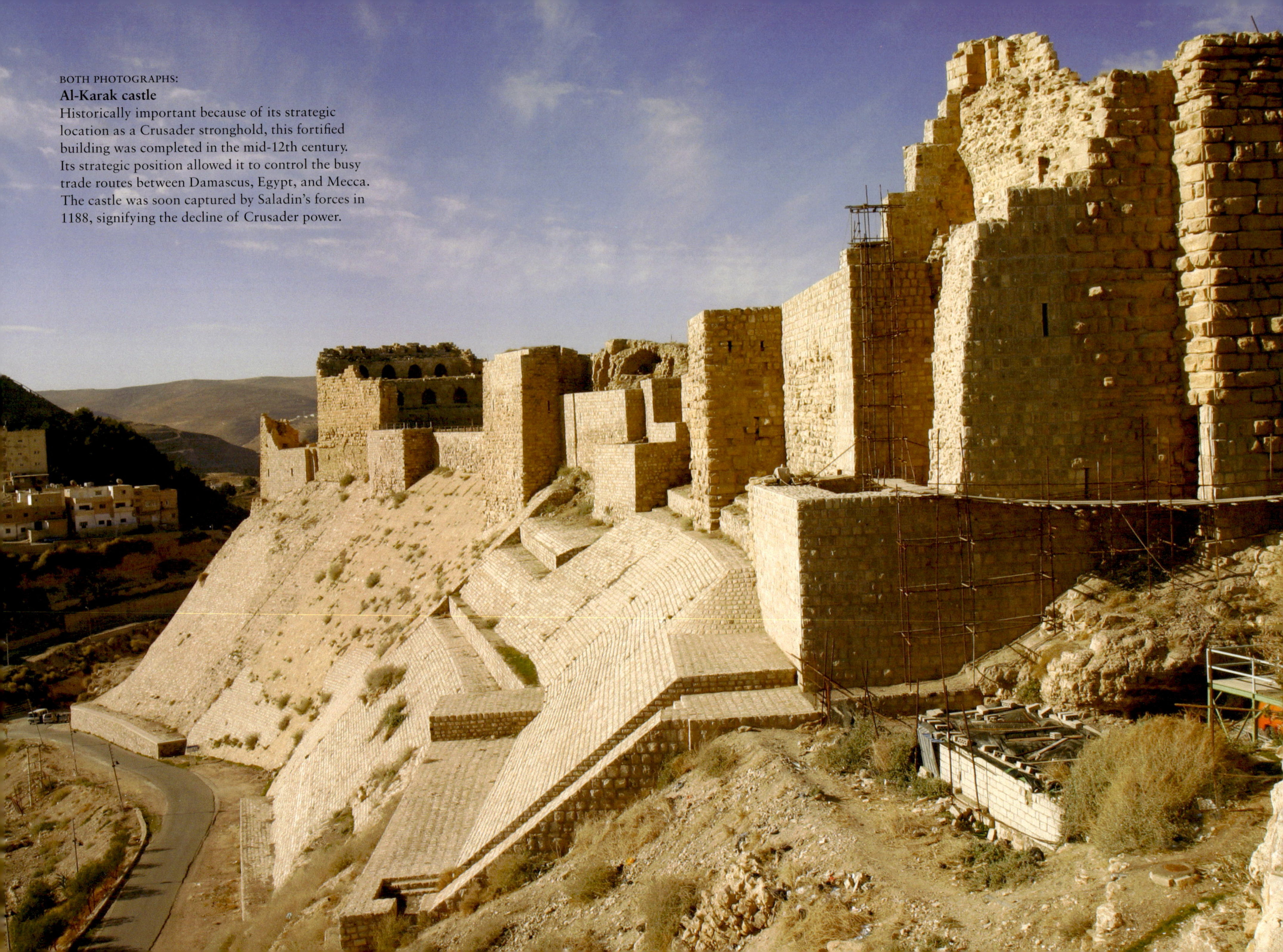

Al-Karak castle
Historically important because of its strategic location as a Crusader stronghold, this fortified building was completed in the mid-12th century. Its strategic position allowed it to control the busy trade routes between Damascus, Egypt, and Mecca. The castle was soon captured by Saladin's forces in 1188, signifying the decline of Crusader power.

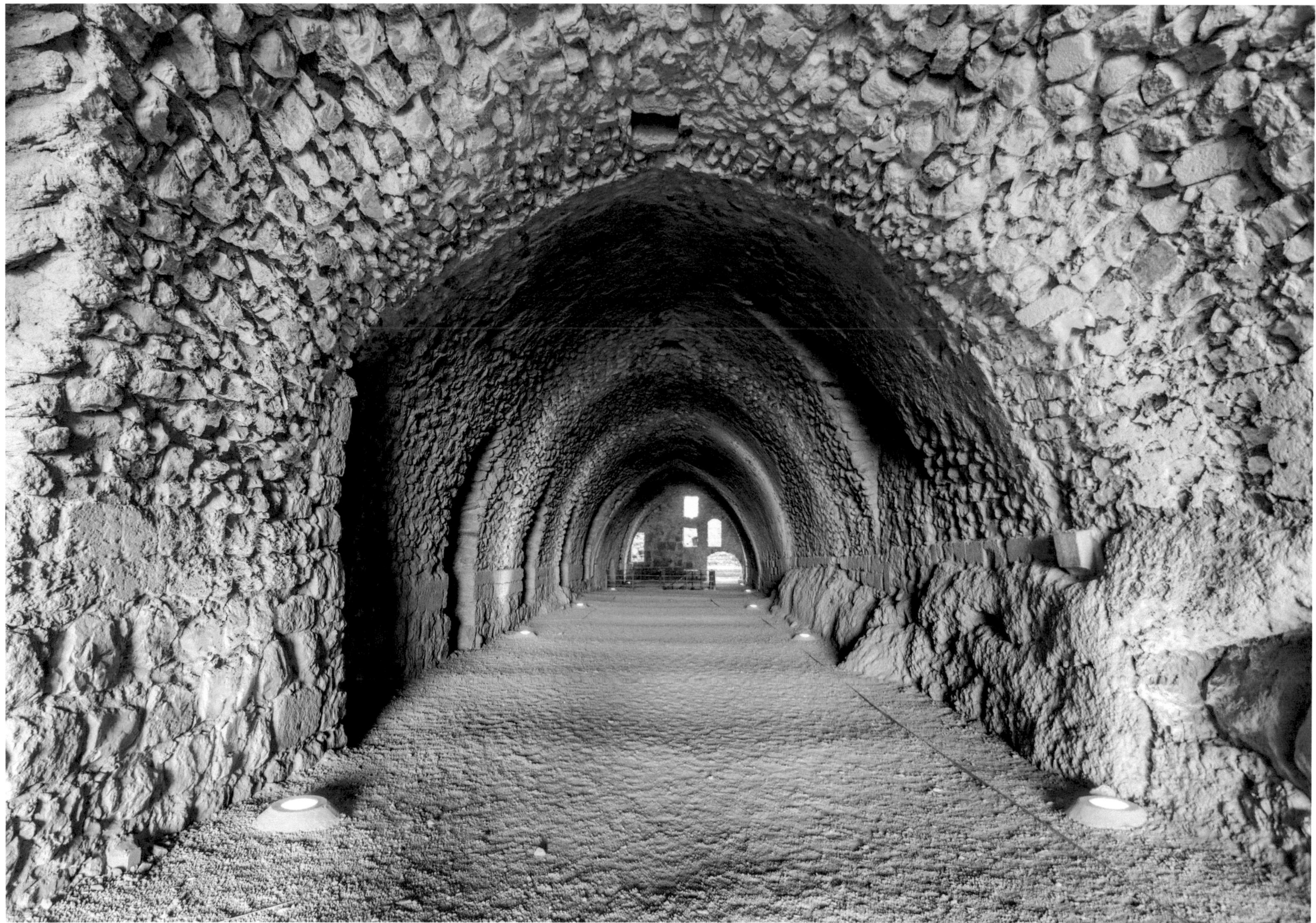

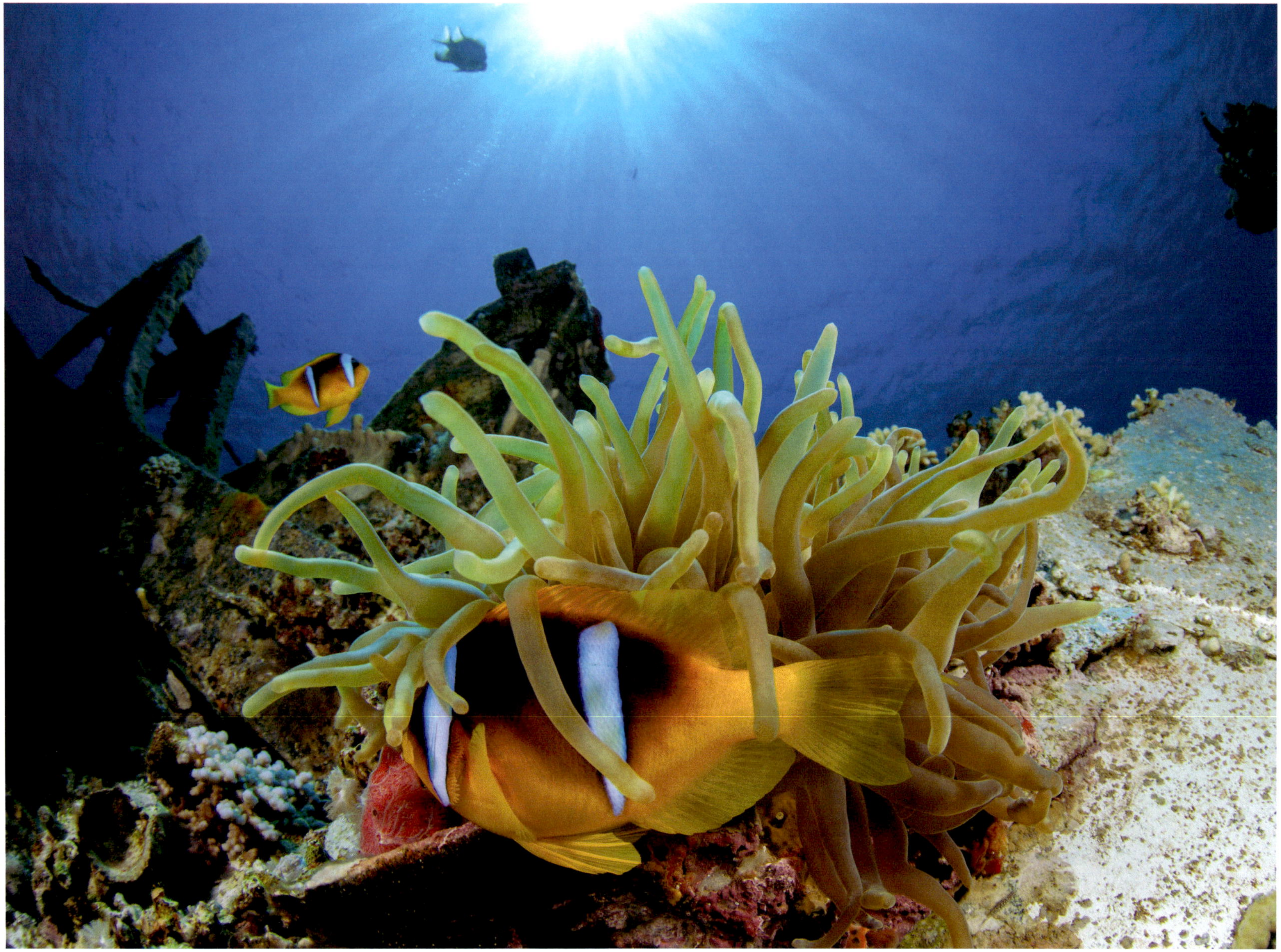

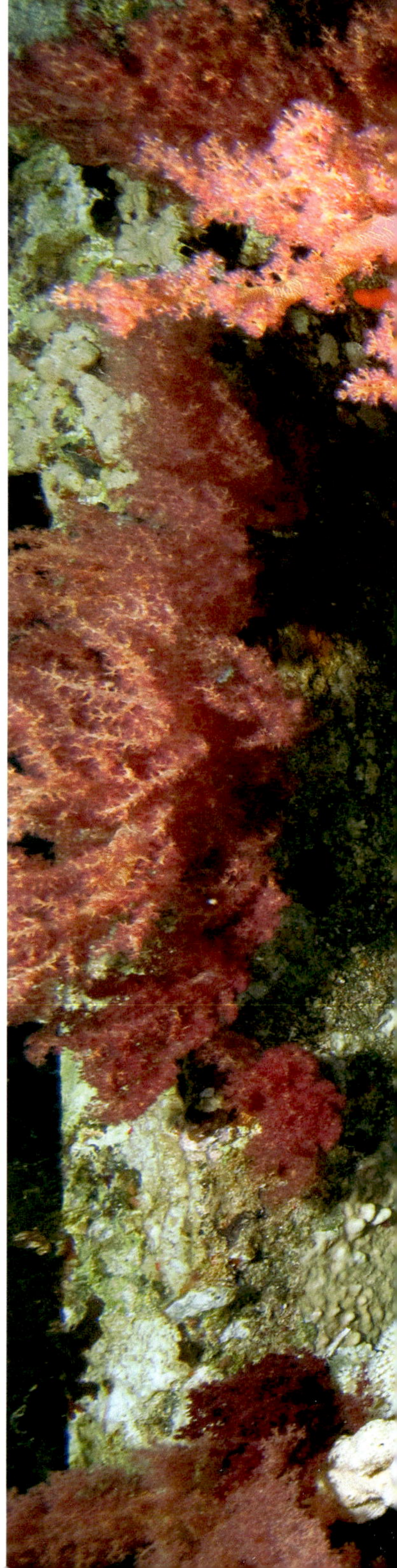

Gulf of Aqaba, Red Sea

The narrow gorge that ends at Aqaba provides calm, clear waters and a pristine marine environment. The Aqaba Marine Park is home to over 500 species of coral and more than 1200 species of fish. A myriad of reef fish such as lionfish, pufferfish and clownfish, as well as larger marine life such as sea turtles and rays, await divers here. Artificial reefs, including deliberately sunk wrecks, help protect the waters and increase fish numbers.

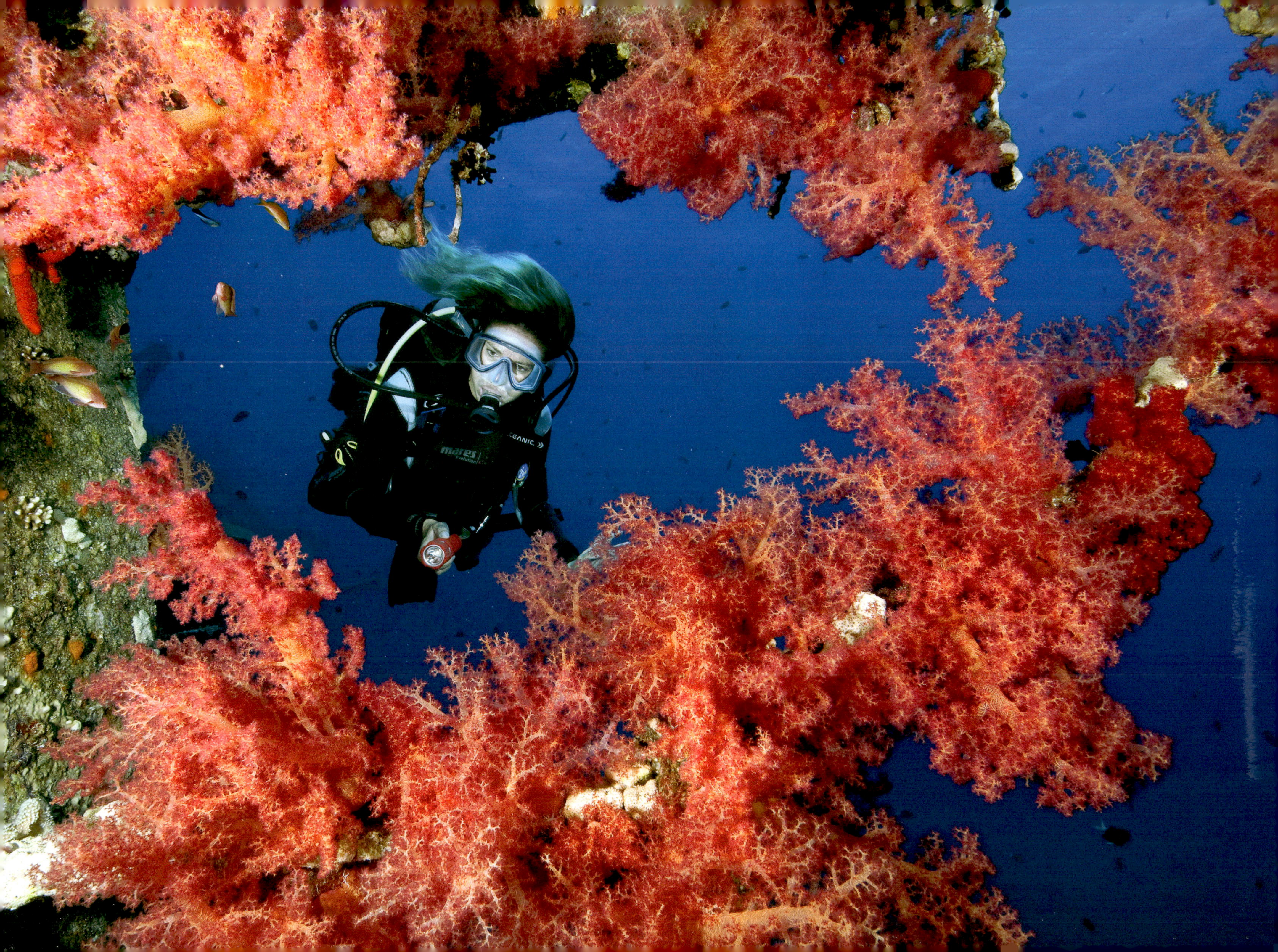

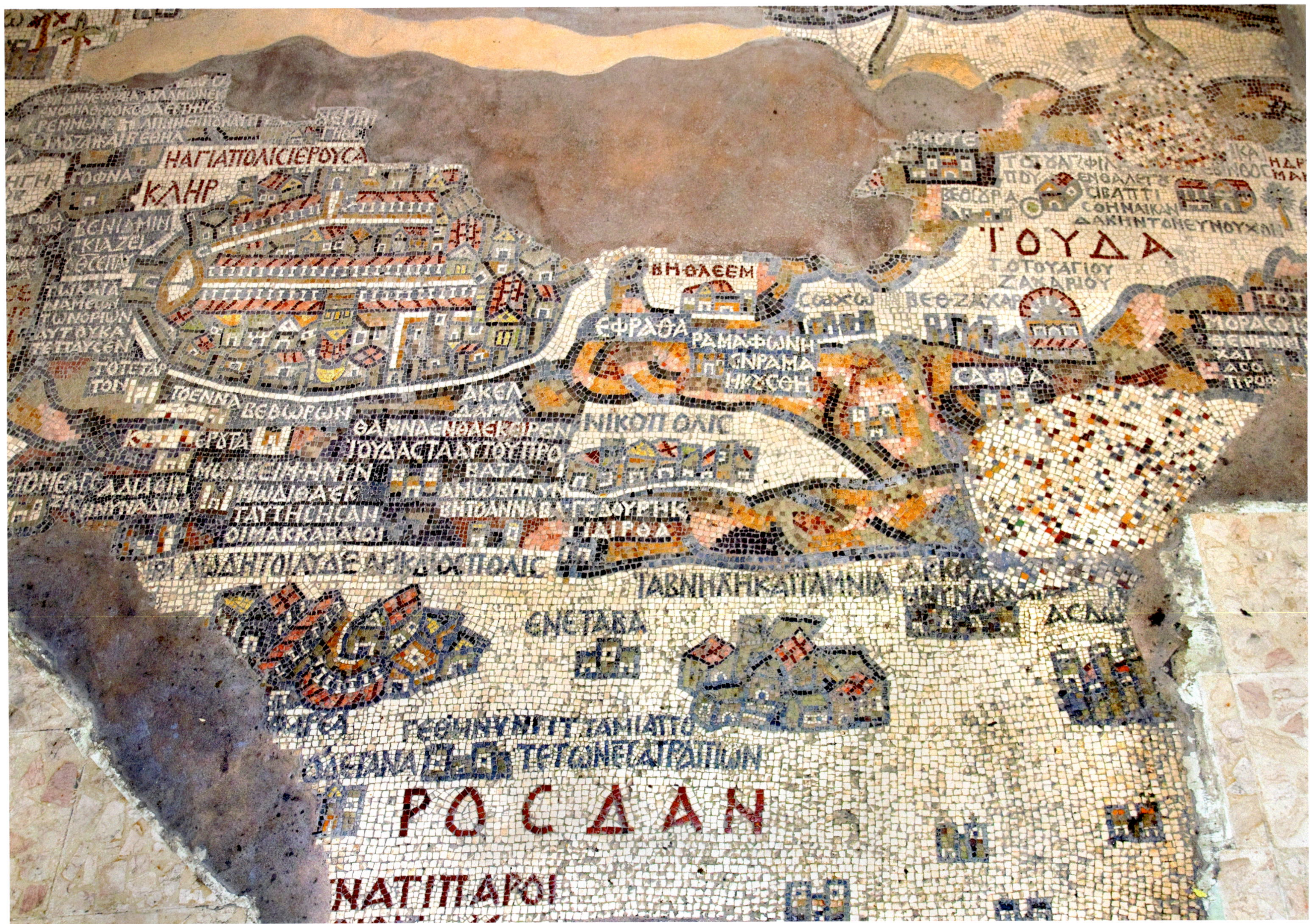
Η ΑΓΙΑ ΠΟΛΙC ΙΕΡΟΥCΑ
ΚΛΗΡ
ΤΟΥΔΑ
ΒΗΘΛΕΕΜ
ΕΦΡΑΘΑ
ΡΑΜΑ ΦΩΝΗ ΕΝ ΡΑΜΑ ΗΚΟΥCΘΗ
CΟΧΩ
ΒΕΘΖΑΧΑΡ
CΑΦΙΡΑ
ΝΙΚΟΠΟΛΙC
ΑΚΕΛΔΑΜΑ
ΟΝΕΤΑΒΑ
ΠΡΟCΔΑΝ

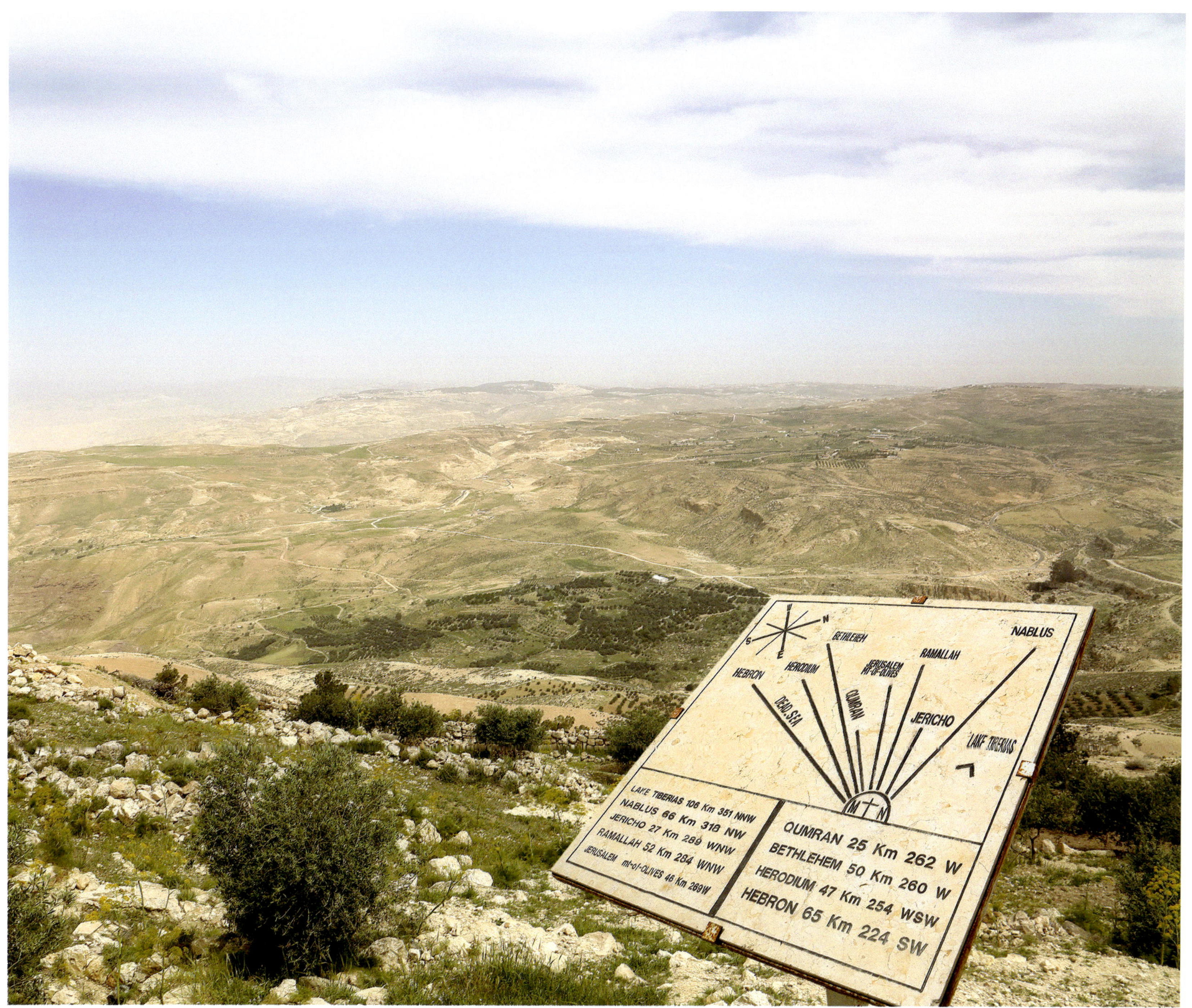

LEFT:

Mount Nebo

Mount Nebo offers a panoramic view of the surrounding region. Looking west, you can see the Jordan River Valley, the Dead Sea and the West Bank. On a clear day, the city of Jericho is visible, and sometimes even the rooftops of Jerusalem. The nearby city of Madaba, famous for its mosaics, is about 10 kilometres (6 miles) away.

OPPOSITE:

Madaba map, Madaba

This 6th-century Byzantine mosaic floor, the oldest surviving cartographic depiction of the Holy Land, can be seen in the Church of Saint George in Jordan. Its significance lies in its incredible detail of the Byzantine-era landscape, including a detailed plan of Jerusalem, making it a crucial historical and archaeological source for the study of biblical sites and the geography of the region.

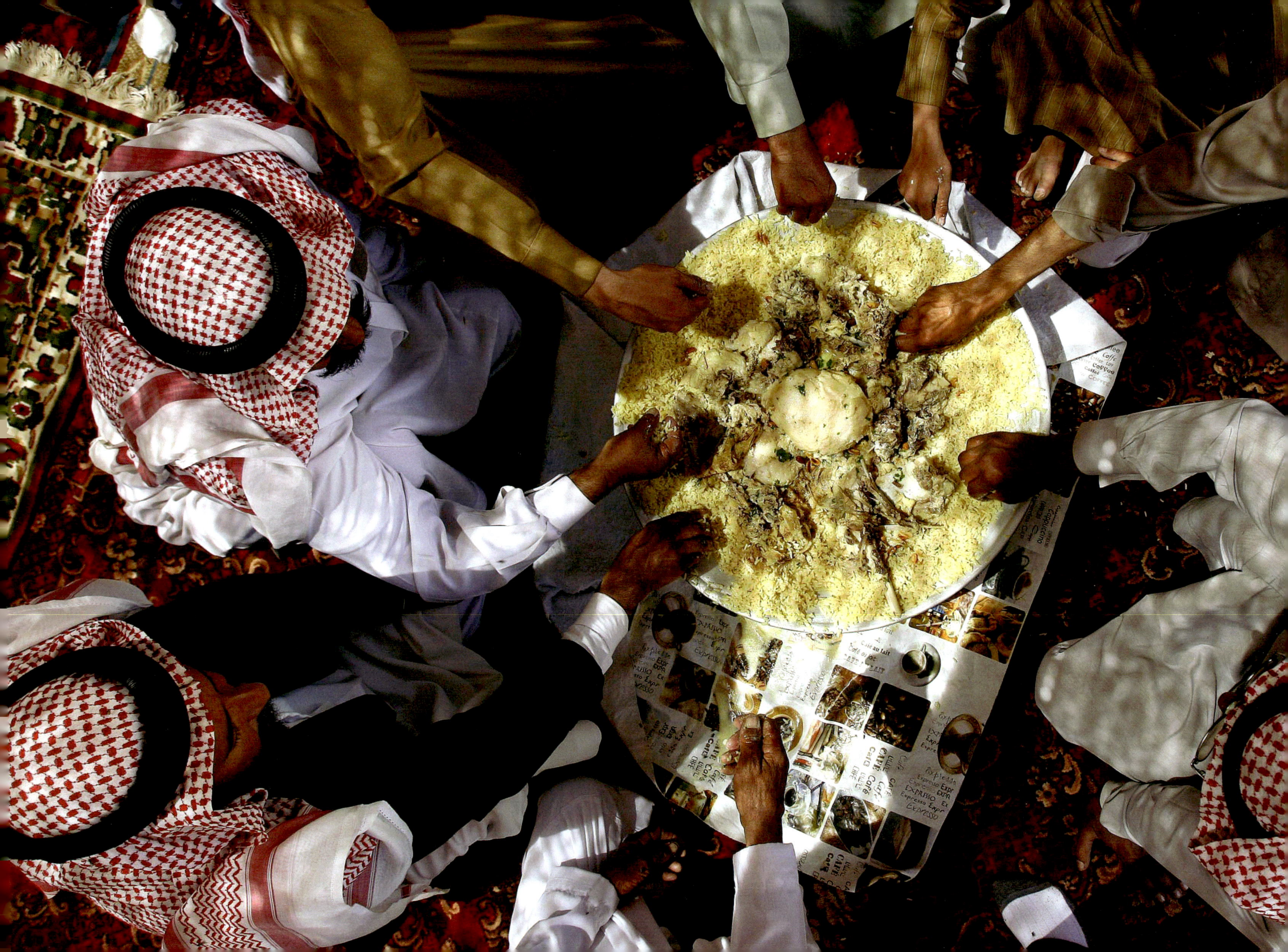

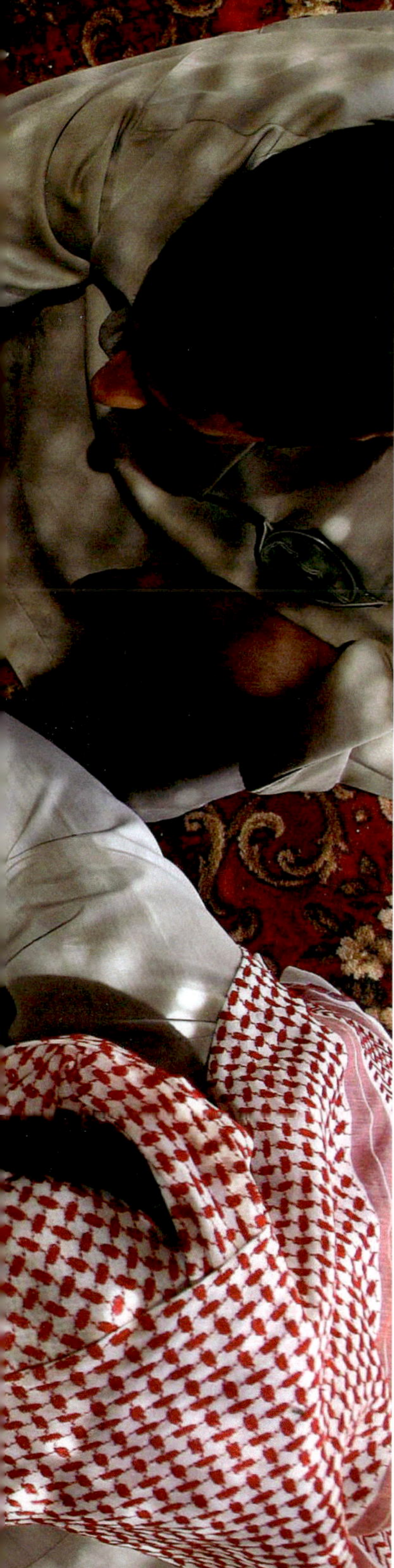

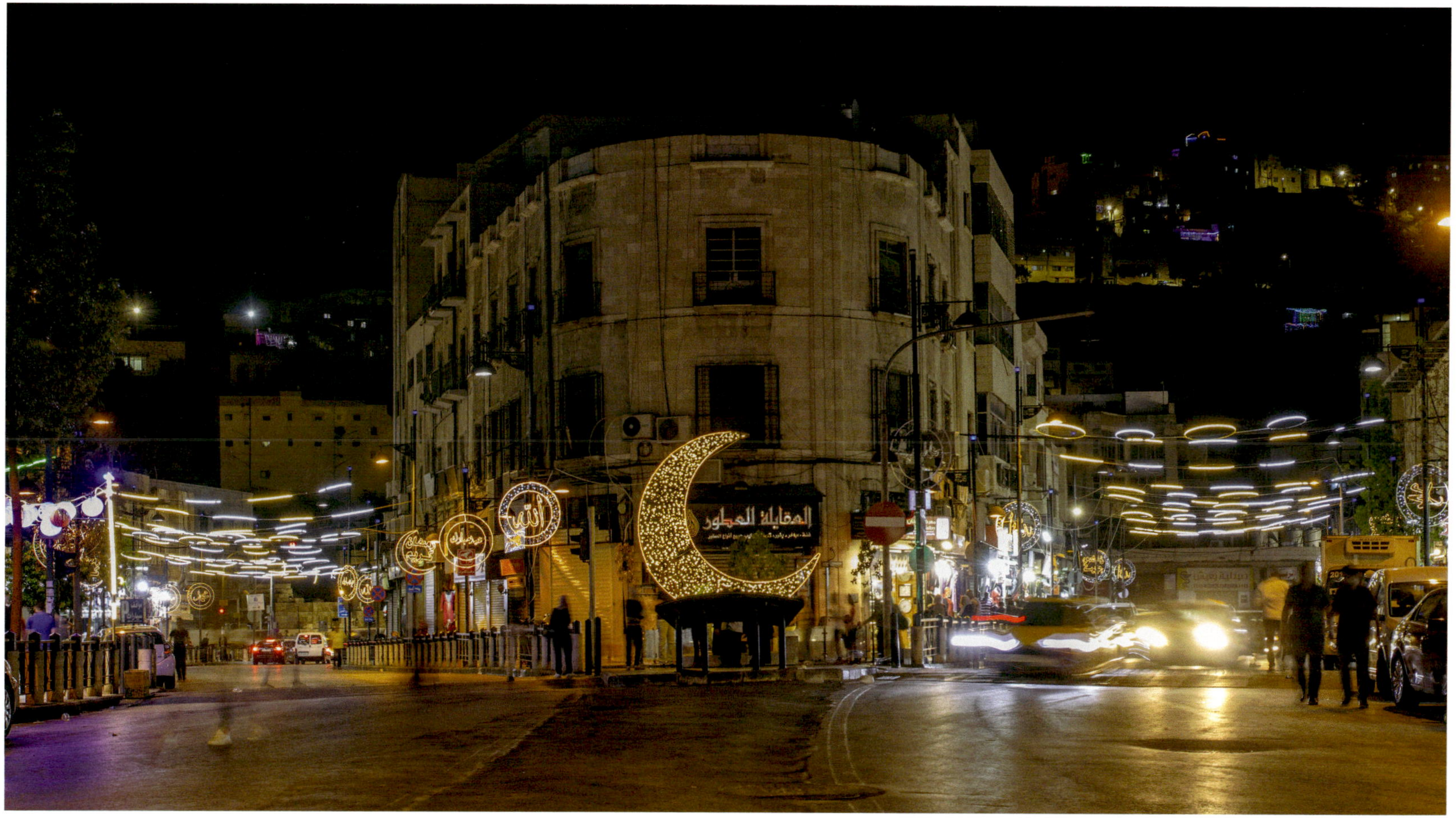

ALL PHOTOGRAPHS:

Ramadan, Amman

LEFT:

A Bedouin family is seen eating the traditional meal of mansaf (meat, rice, and yogurt) inside their tent in the Al-Jafr area, south of Amman, Jordan, where large populations of Bedouins live (pictured left). During Ramadan, the Jordanian capital of Amman is brightly decorated to celebrate the festival (above).

RIGHT:

Mansaf

Mansaf is the most famous Arab food for the Jordanian people. it consists of cooked lamb, rice and a tangy, fermented dried yogurt sauce (*jameed*) served on a bed of flatbread.

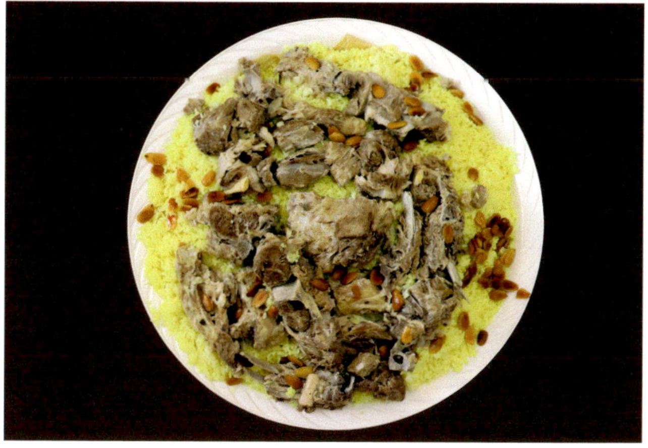

Cafe life, Amman

Jordan's recent food and cafe scene is a vibrant combination of traditional cuisine and new international trends. While classic Jordanian dishes like mansaf (lamb with yogurt sauce) and street food staples like falafel and shawarma feature large, a new, booming cafe culture has emerged. Hungry souls can enjoy traditional spots serving Arabic coffee and shisha or trendy, modern spaces with speciality coffee, Western menus, and a lively social atmosphere. These often stay open late into the warm Middle Eastern nights.

Steps of Al-Balad, Amman

A famed part of Amman's bustling downtown, these steps are not a single, central staircase. This network of steep, winding stairways covers the town's surrounding hills and is a vital part of the city's character. These pretty walkways connect the vibrant markets and Roman ruins of the valley floor to the residential neighbourhoods on the slopes.

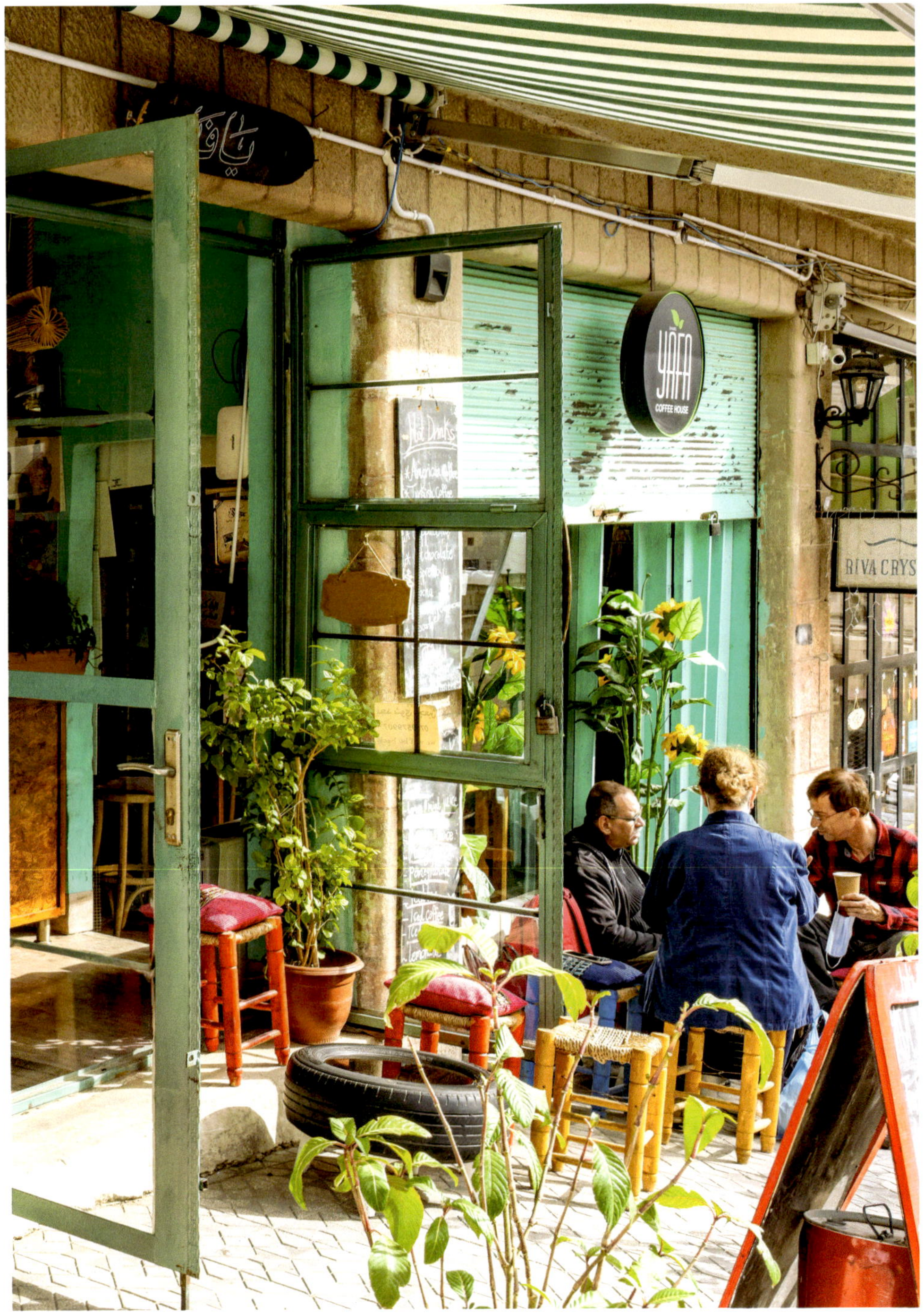

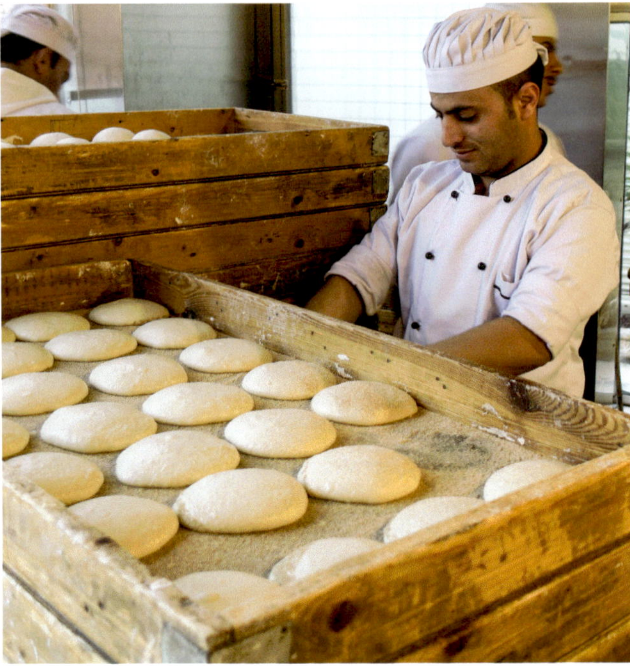

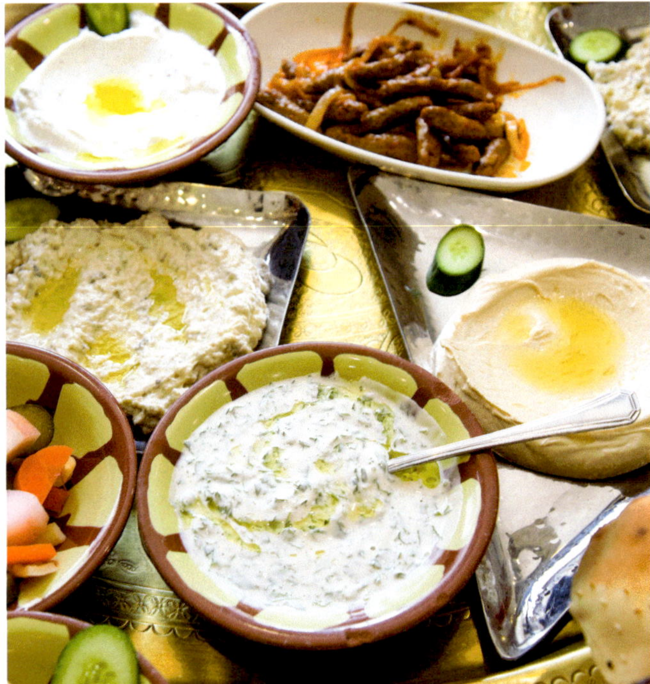

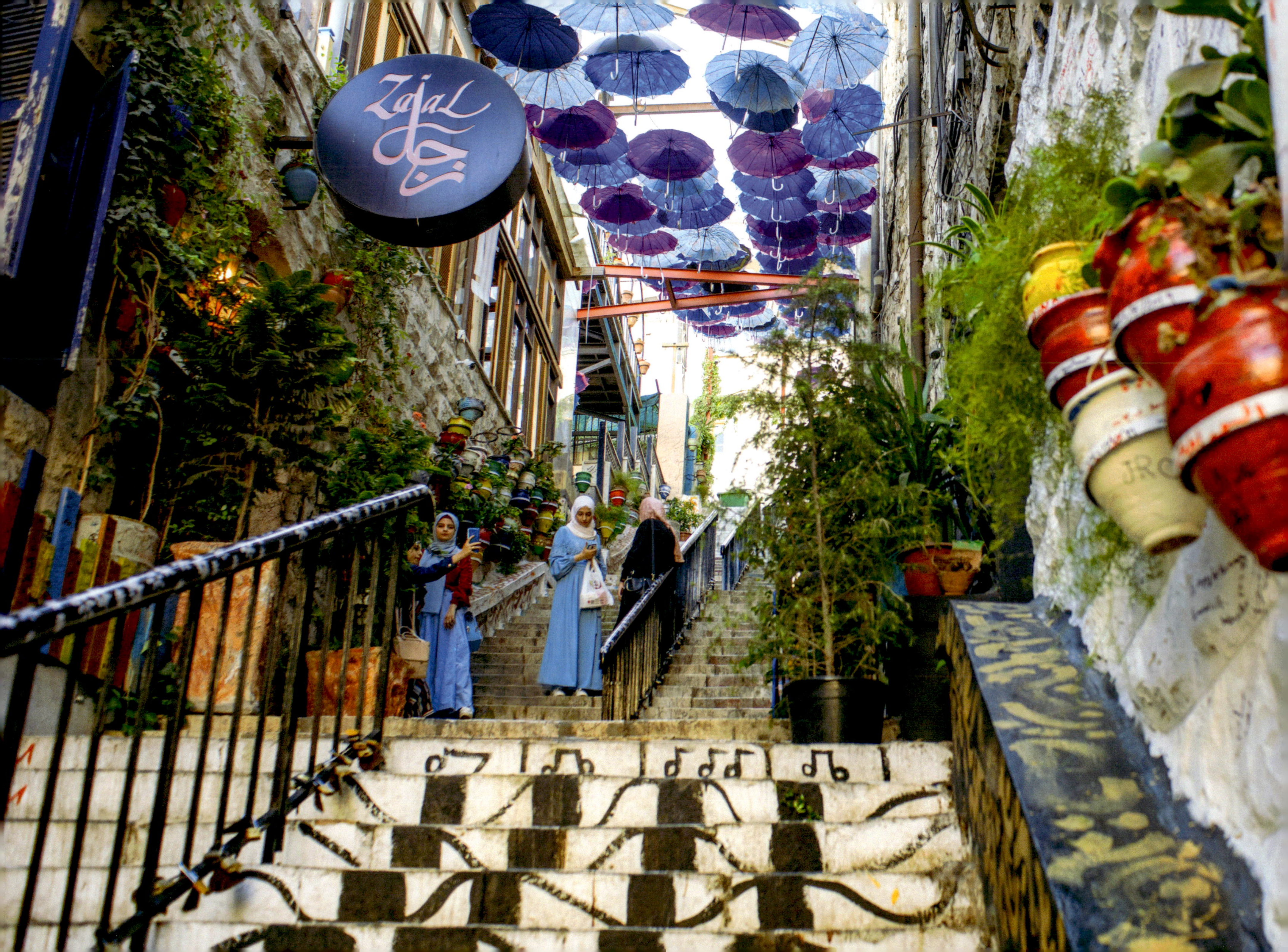

Zajal

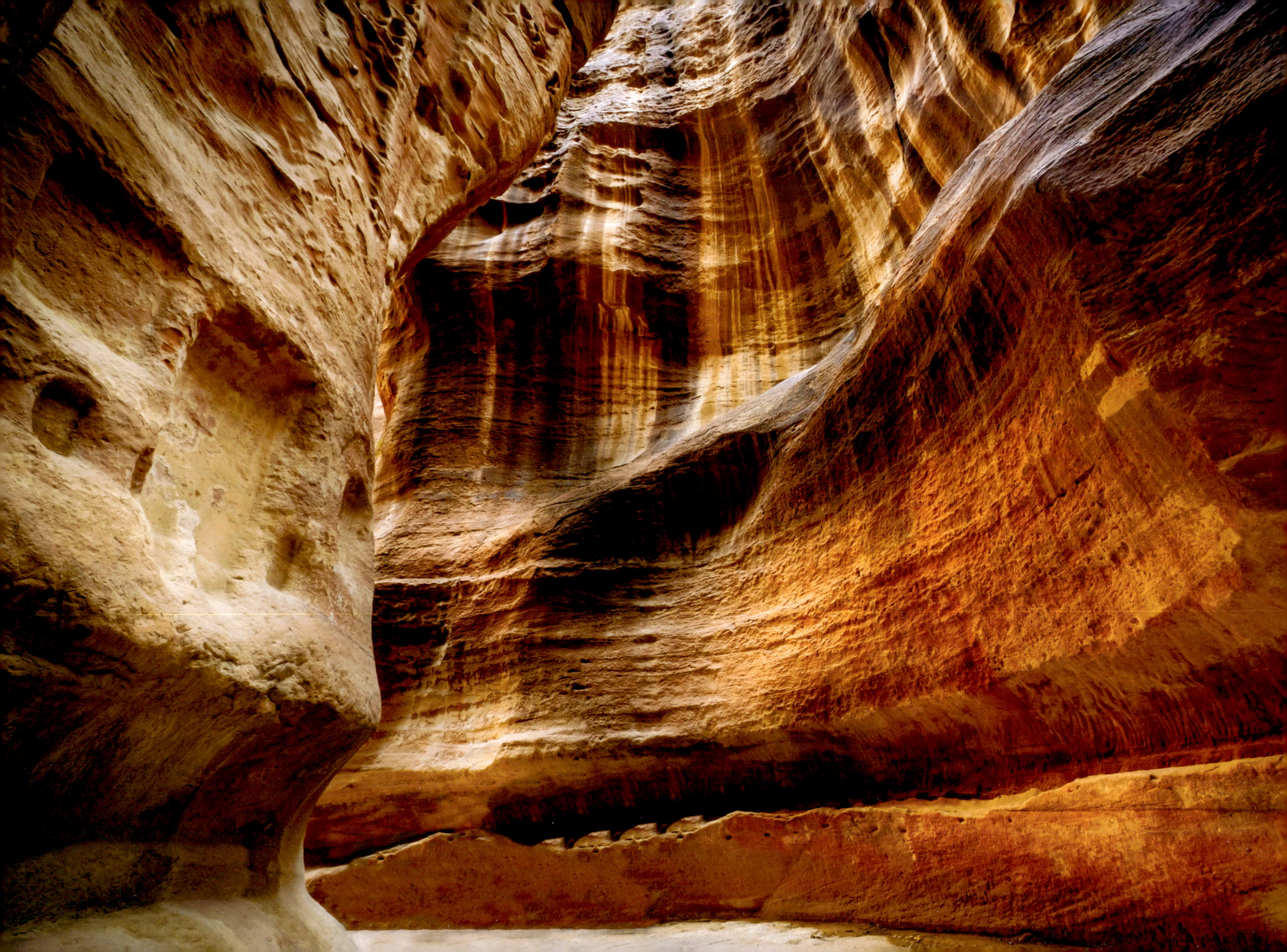

Petra, Ma'an

Petra is special. This unique place and its interiors have gifted many myths and legends over their 3000 years of existence. Perhaps the most famous tale about Petra's interior is a legend related to its most familiar spot, the Treasury (pictured right). A tale told by local Bedouins claims that a pharaoh's treasure was hidden in the massive urn visitors now see carved at the top of its façade. In the past, belief in this fable was so strong that Bedouins would fire rifles at the urn in an attempt to break it open, leaving bullet holes that are still visible today. However, the urn is actually solid sandstone, and the Treasury was built as a royal tomb by the Nabateans, an ancient Arab people, likely for King Aretas IV, and created a thriving city.

The vivid colours of Petra's canyon walls (pictured left) are sandstone formations that date to the Cambrian period. The rock's iconic red-to-orange range of bands vary due to different concentrations of iron and manganese oxides within them. This process, and the erosion which shaped the area, stem from groundwaters deposited over millions of years.

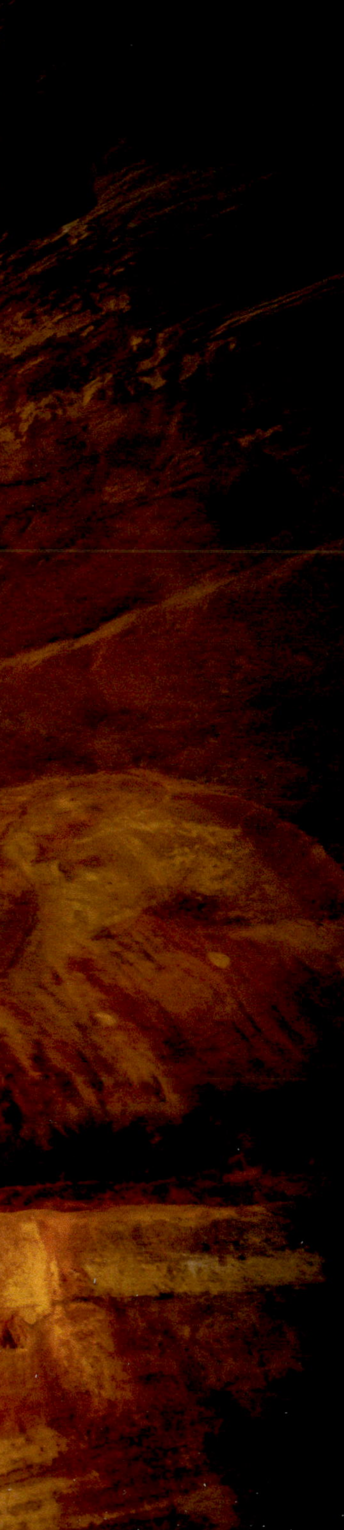

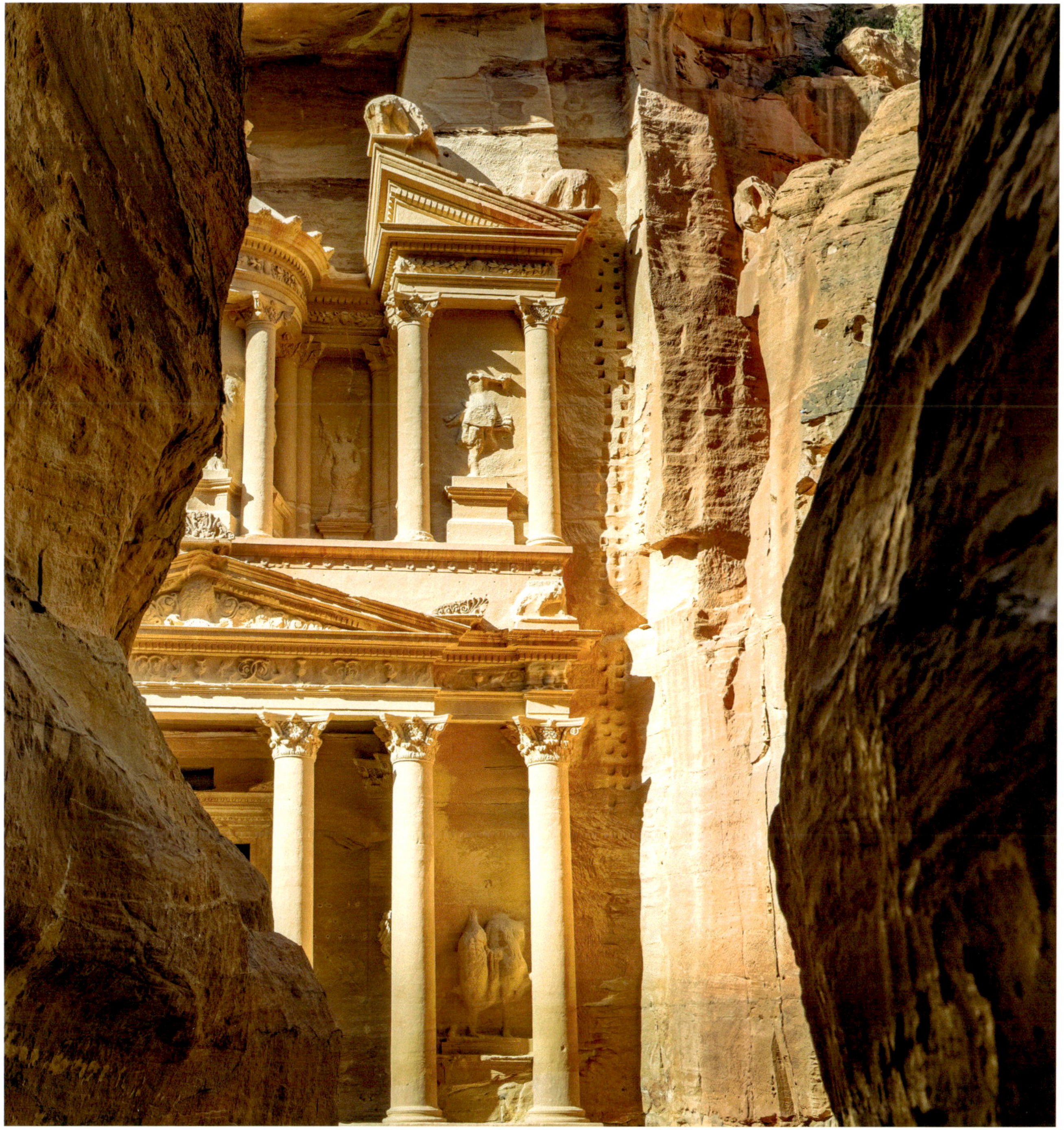

189

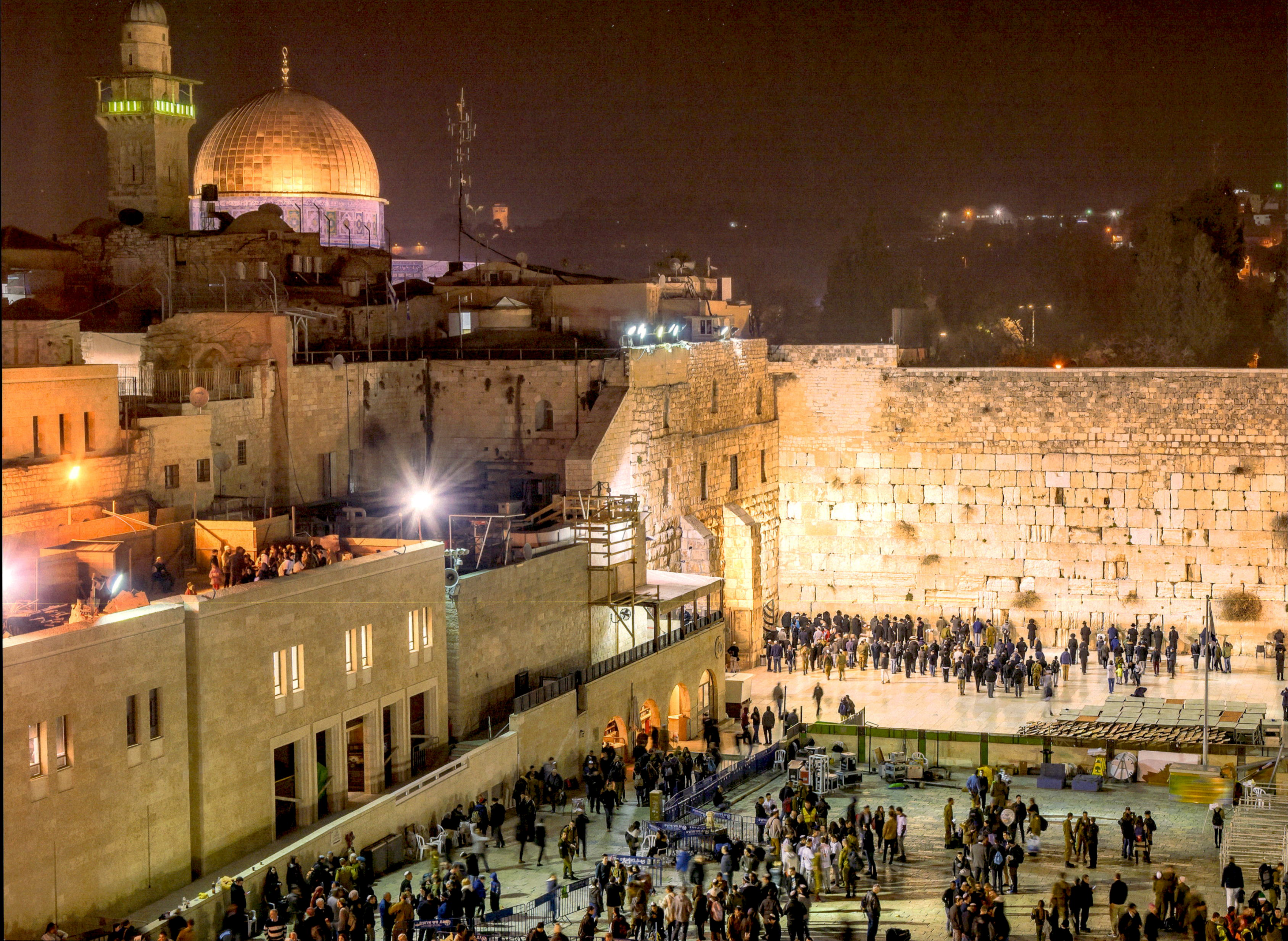

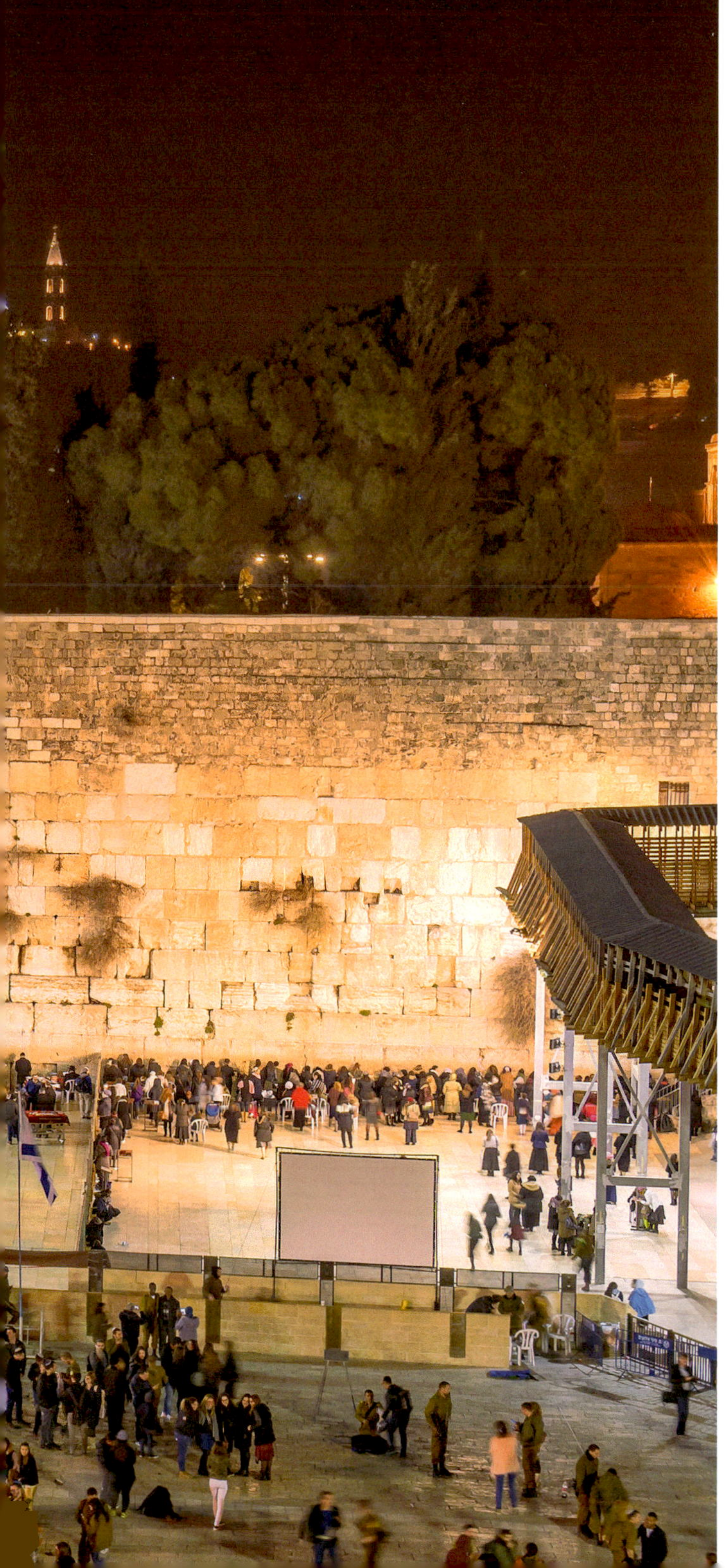

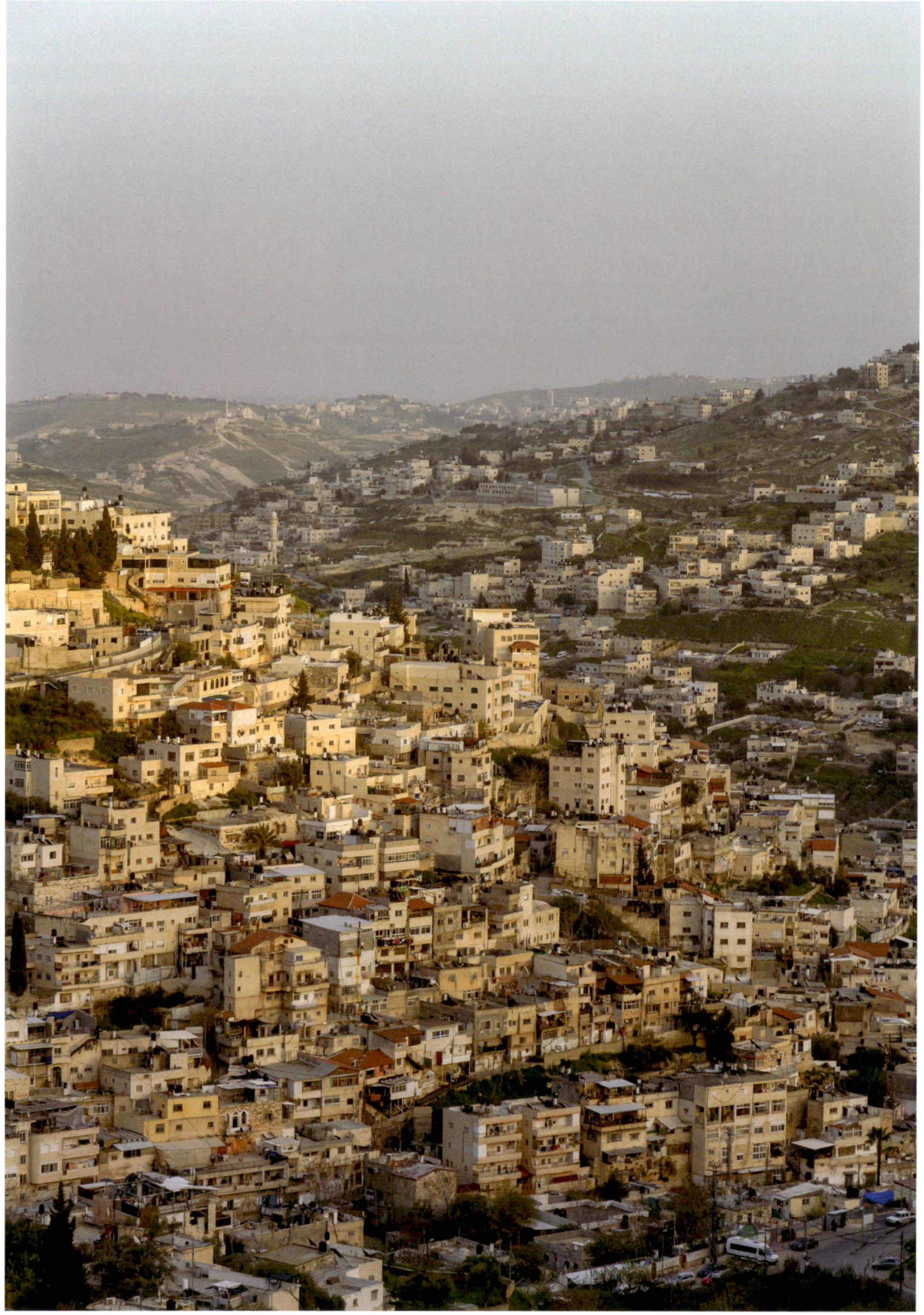

**Western Wall,
Jerusalem Old City**
The Wailing Wall, or Western
Wall, is a remnant of the
Second Temple complex and
the holiest site where Jews
can pray. It is a symbol of
endurance and the perpetual
yearning for the Temple's
restoration. Open all day and
night, people of all faiths visit
to pray, mourn and celebrate
in front of it. A famous
common practice is placing
written prayers into the
spaces in the wall, believing
that to be the closest point
to heaven.

**Residential district,
Jerusalem**
Jerusalem's residential areas
are built on terraced hillsides,
a necessity due to the city's
topography. This creates
distinct neighbourhoods
with breathtaking views,
often featuring stone houses
and winding streets that
follow the contours of the
landscape.

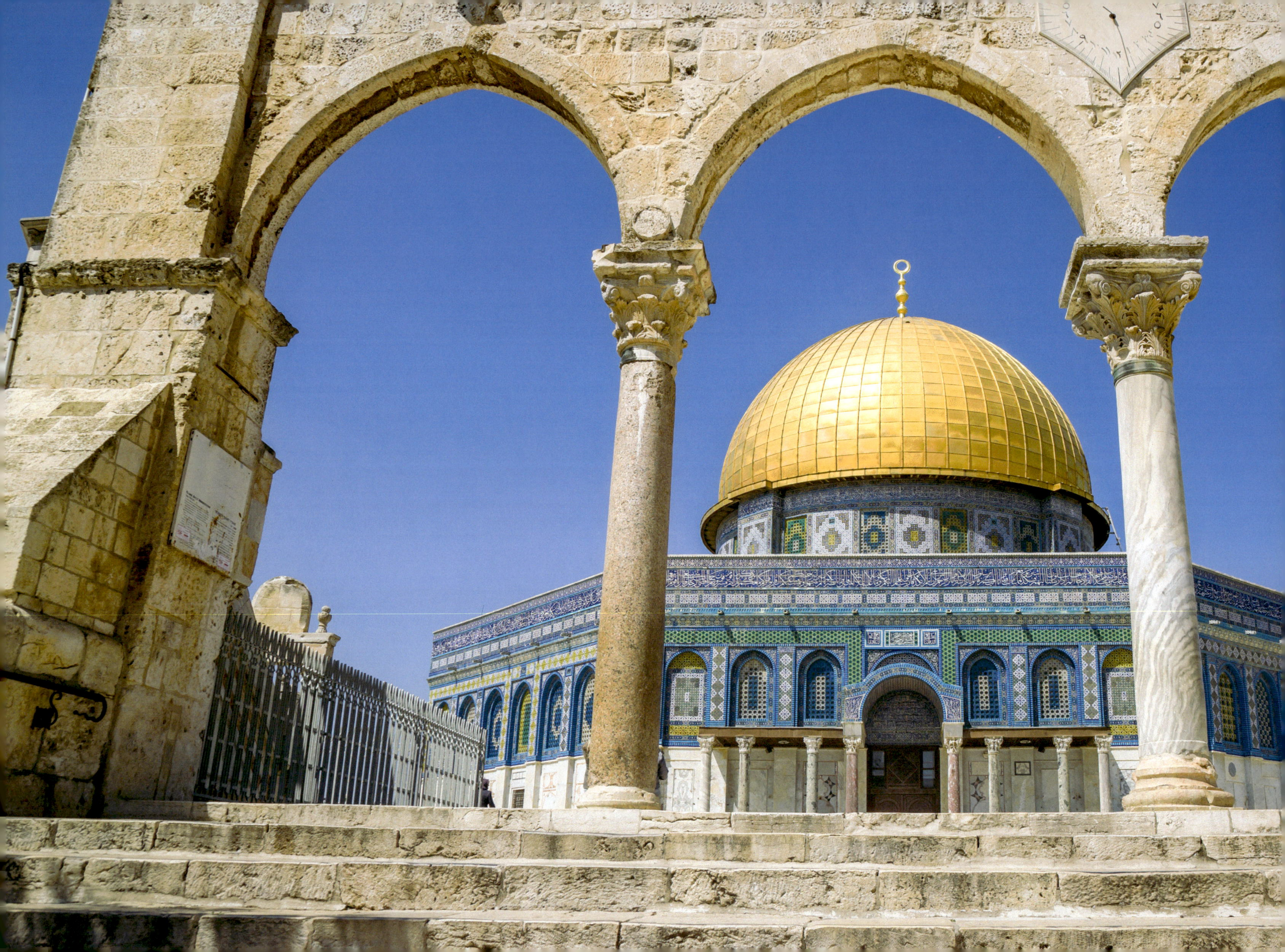

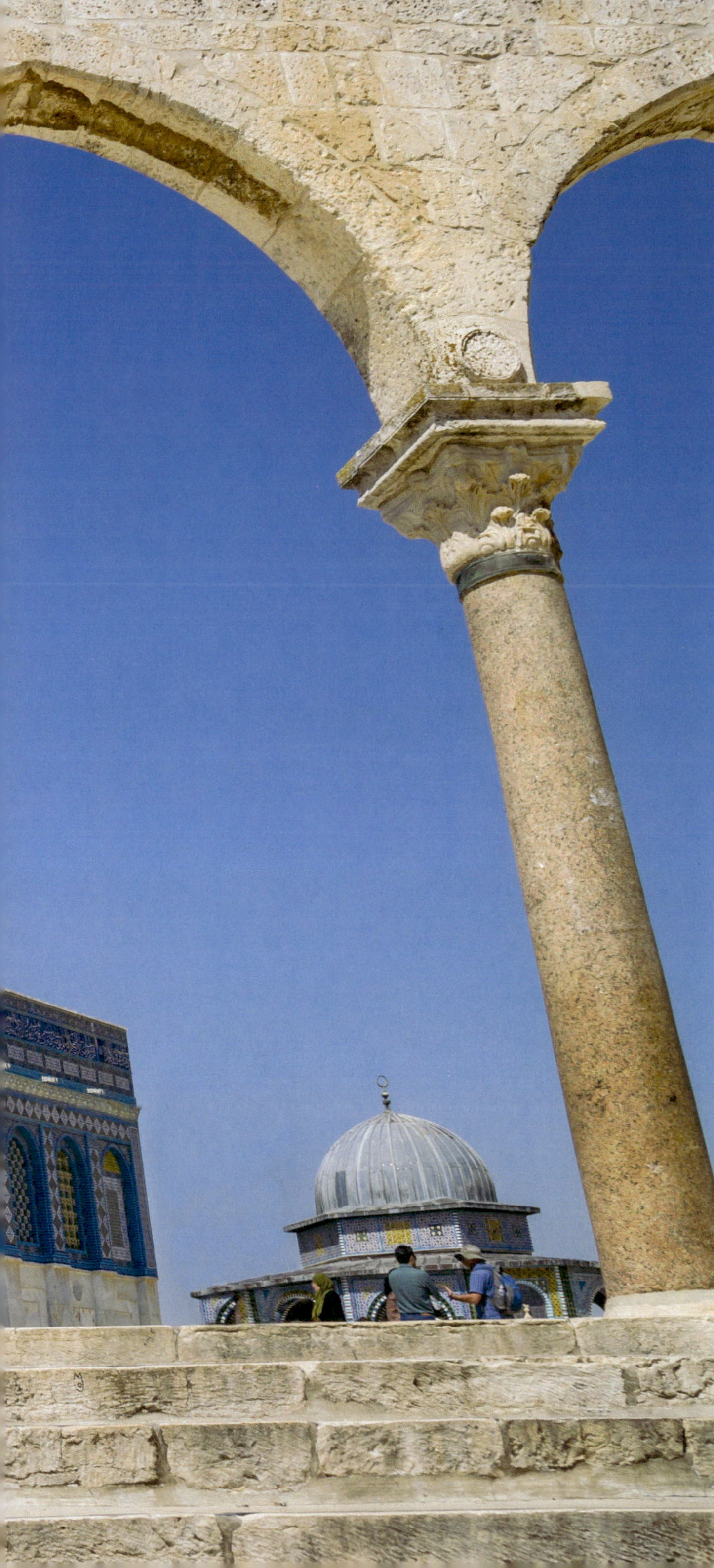

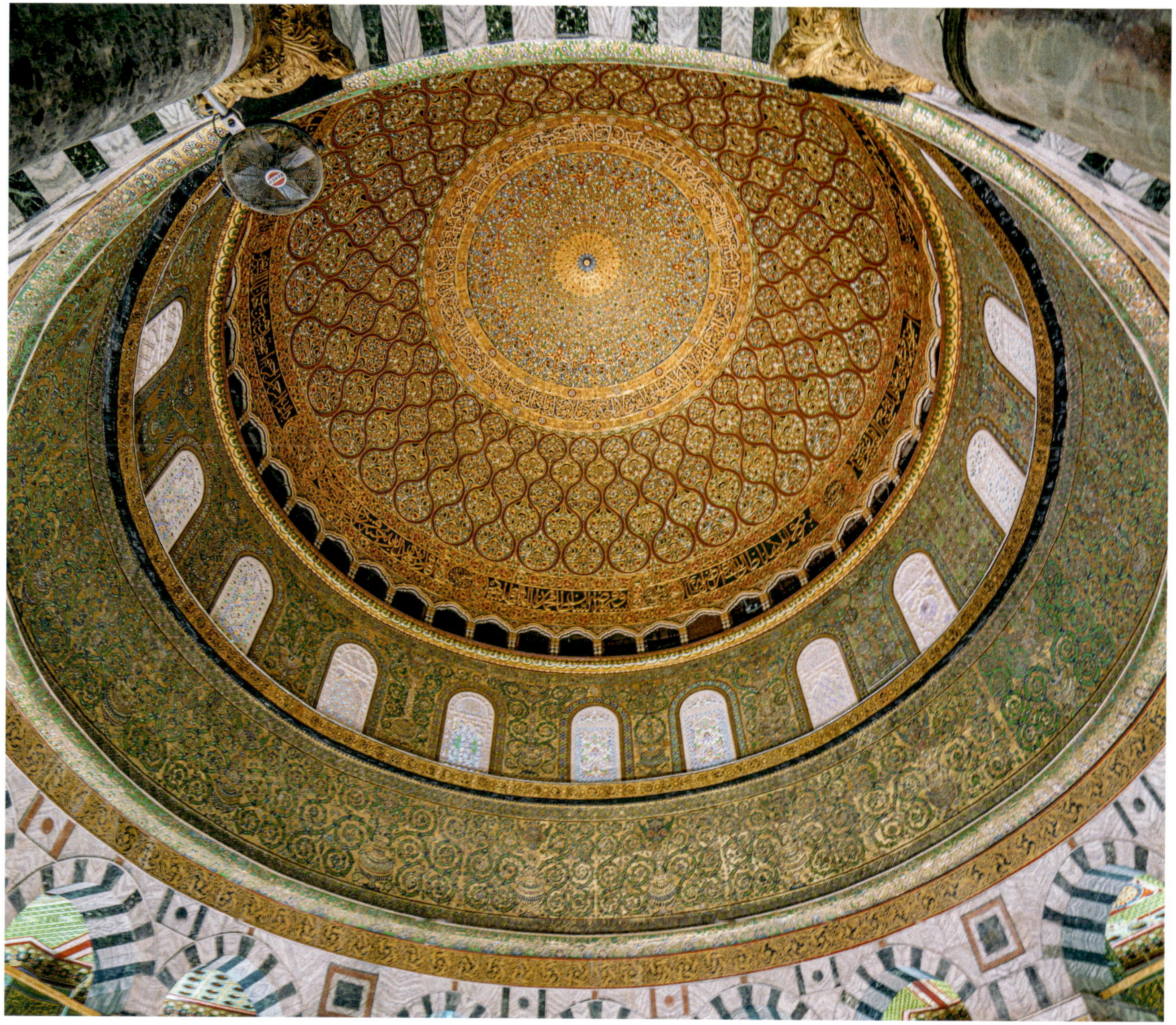

Dome of the Rock, Jerusalem

This world-famous building is one of the oldest and most significant Islamic structures and is located on the Temple Mount in Jerusalem. It was built between 688 and 692 CE by the Umayyad caliph Abd al-Malik. It is believed, though debated, that the caliph intended to commemorate the Prophet Muhammad's miraculous Night Journey and Ascension to Heaven, an event of immense importance in Islam. When constructed its architectural style and rich mosaics drew their inspiration from nearby Byzantine churches and palaces such as the Church of the Kathisma. The site is also sacred to Jews as the place where the Temple of Solomon once stood and where Abraham nearly sacrificed his son.

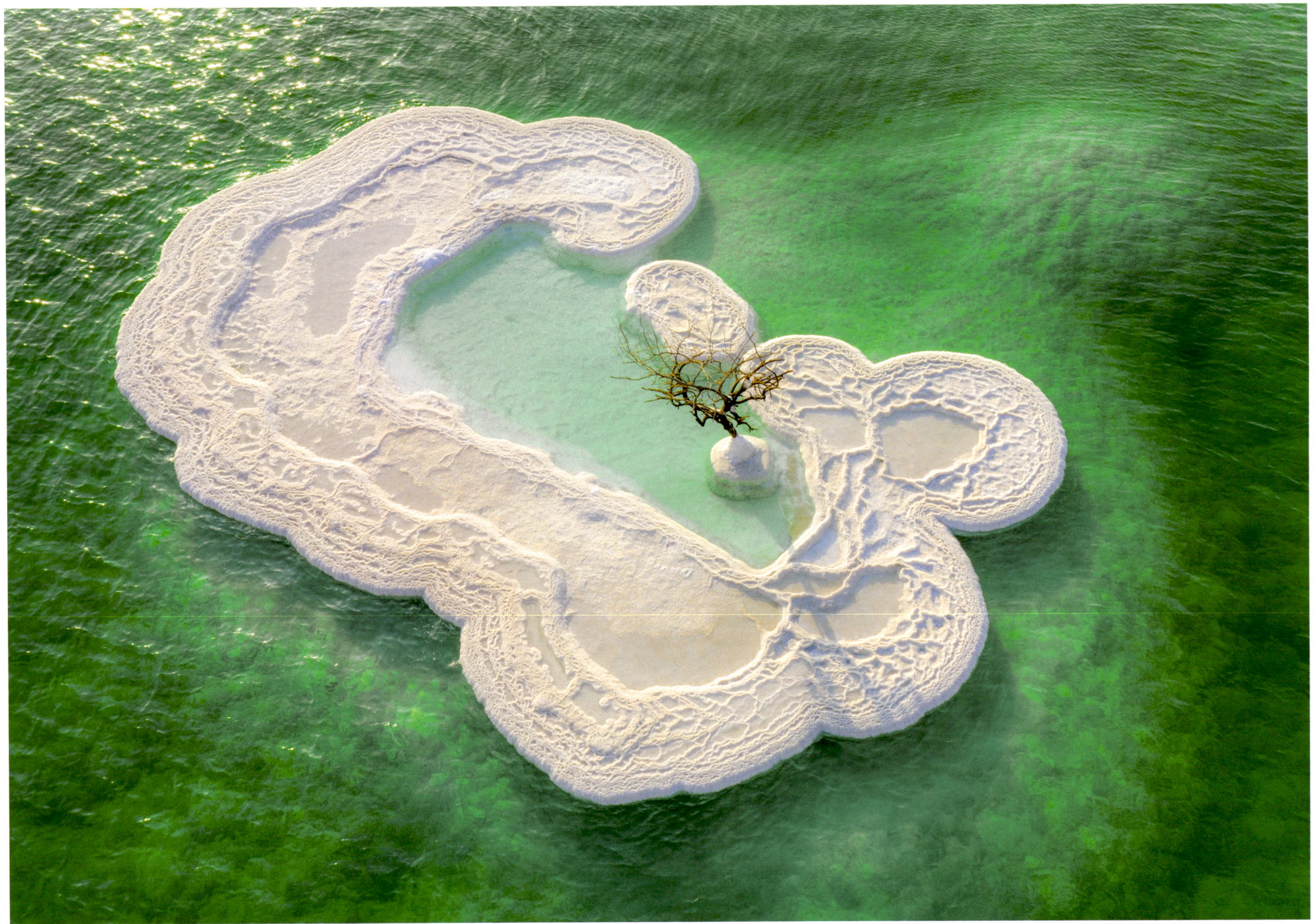

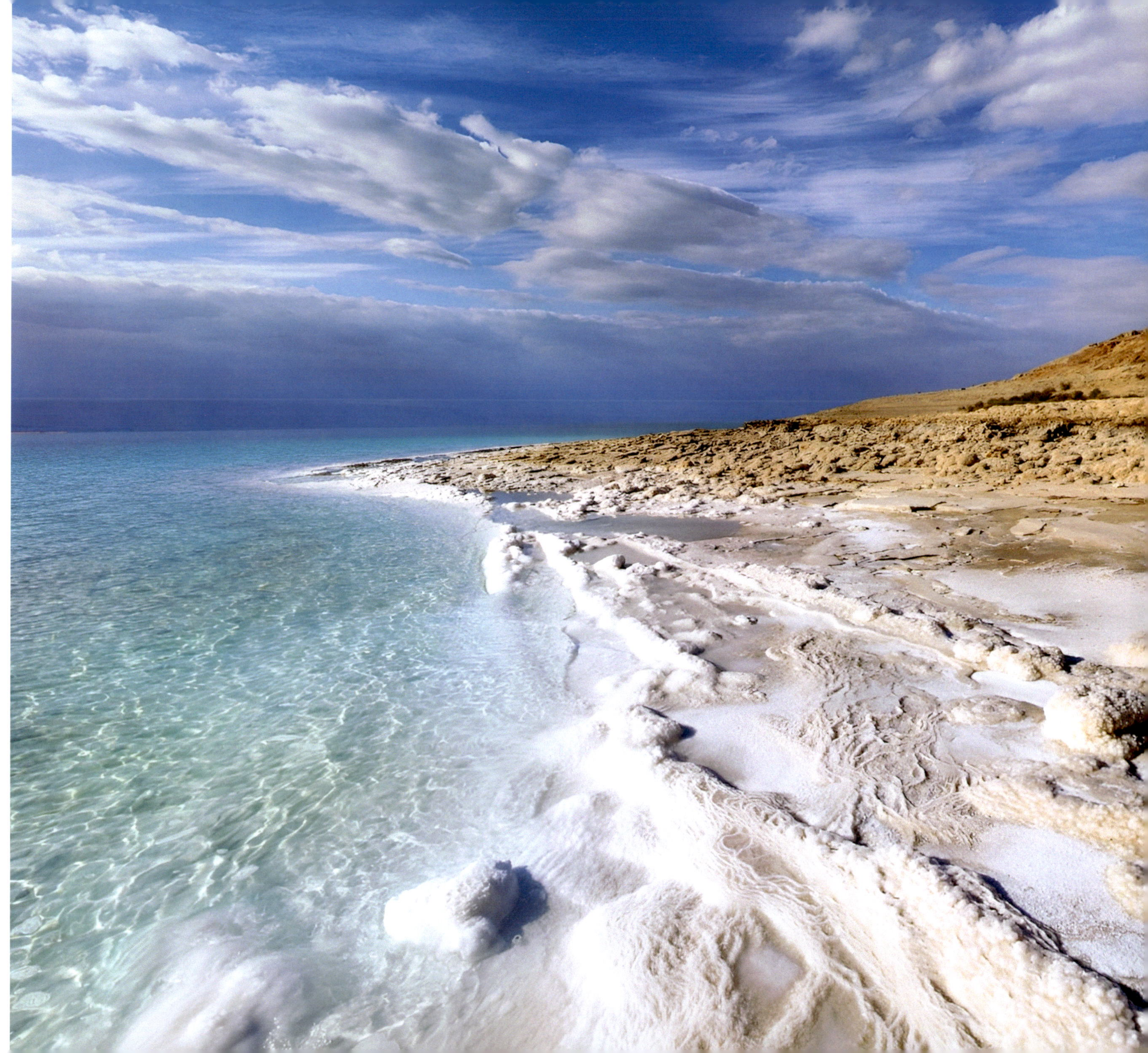

BOTH PHOTOGRAPHS:
The Dead Sea
This hypersaline lake originated in the Jordan Rift Valley, caused by a rift between tectonic plates. As the land sank, water from the Jordan River filled the basin, but with no outlet, evaporation left behind a high concentration of salt and minerals. Today, its unique properties are used by visitors from across the region and beyond. The extreme buoyancy allows people to float effortlessly, and the mineral-rich mud and water are used in therapeutic treatments for skin conditions, attracting visitors from around the world. This phenomenon is the lowest land-based earthly elevation and the waters are almost 10 times more saline than the world's oceans.

Street food, Jerusalem

This busy 24-hour city
delivers a vibrant mix of
flavours associated with
Middle Eastern cuisine. Old
Jerusalem's culinary scene
is deeply traditional, with
countless small family-run
eateries. Staples include
falafel and shawarma served
in fresh pita, often with
hummus, tahini, and various
salads. Another must-try is
the local ka'ak (Jerusalem
bagel), a long, oval-shaped
bread topped with sesame
seeds and often eaten with
za'atar, and don't miss the
famous mutabak (a cheese-
filled pastry) at Zalatimo
Sweets.

Falafel

The precise origins of falafel
are a subject of fun, lively
debate, though most food
historians agree it likely
originated in Egypt and that
the dish was invented by the
Coptic Christians as a meat
substitute during Lent, a
period of fasting. However,
in Jerusalem that will be
disputed as the vendors claim
this delicious street treat as
their own.

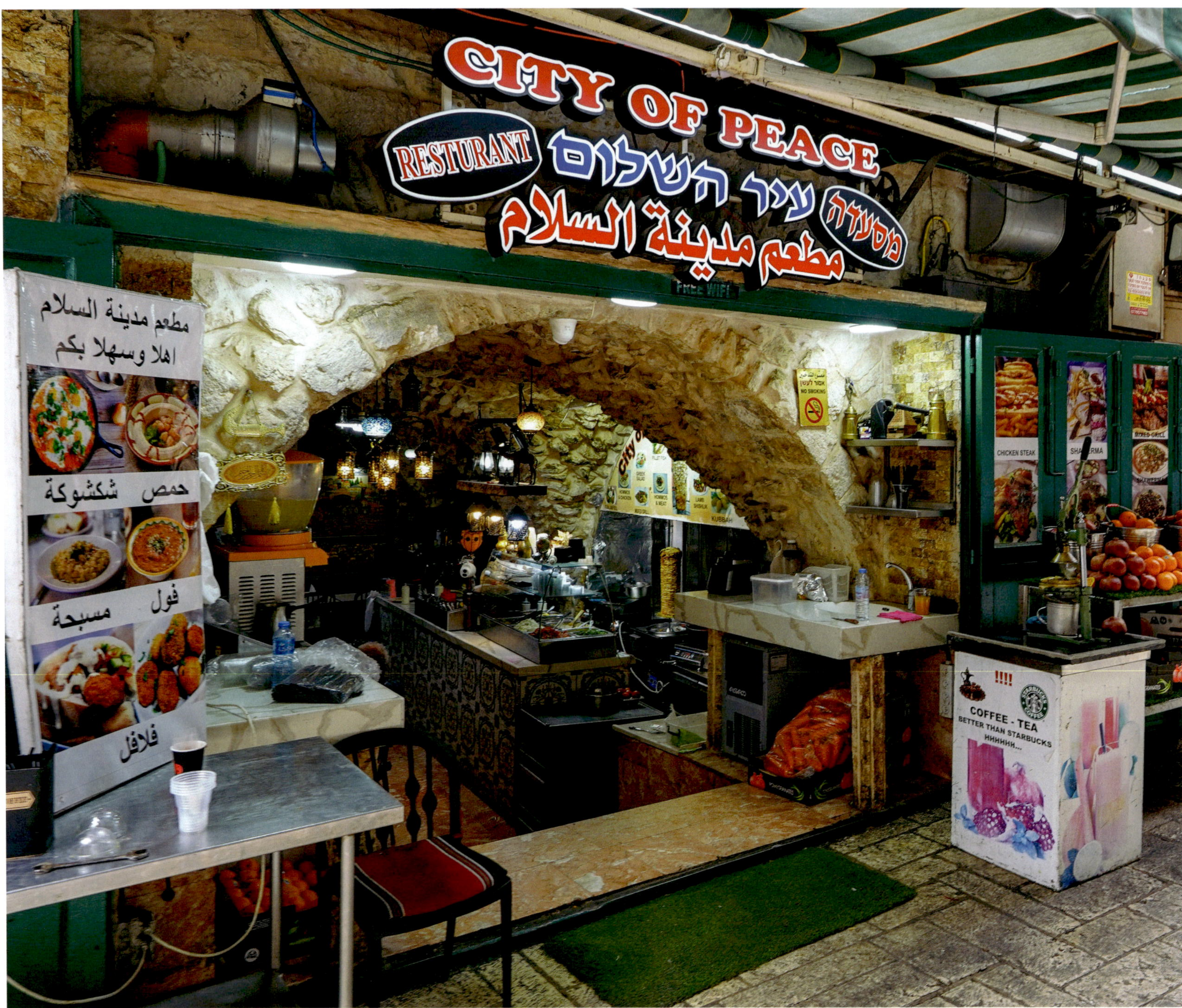

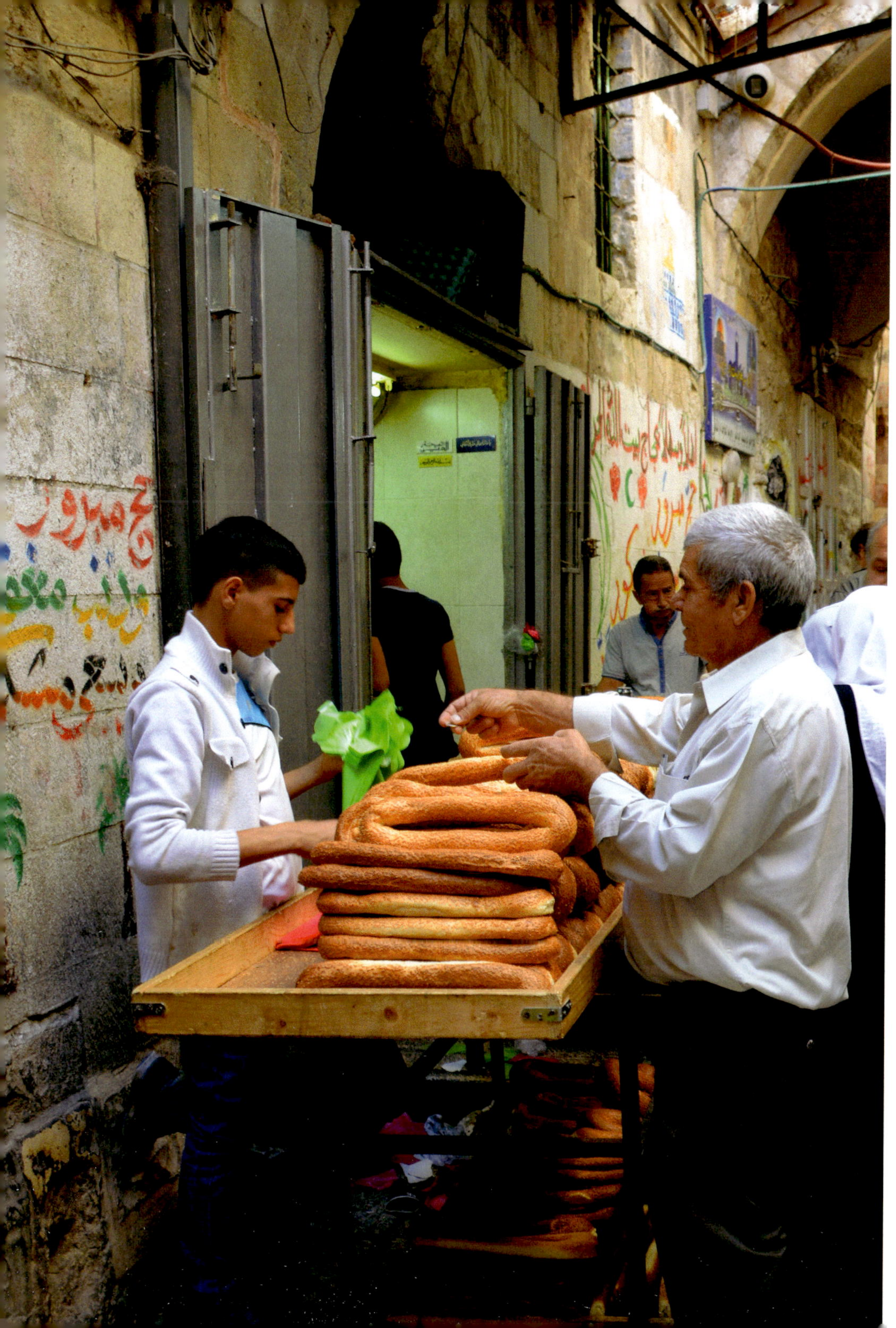

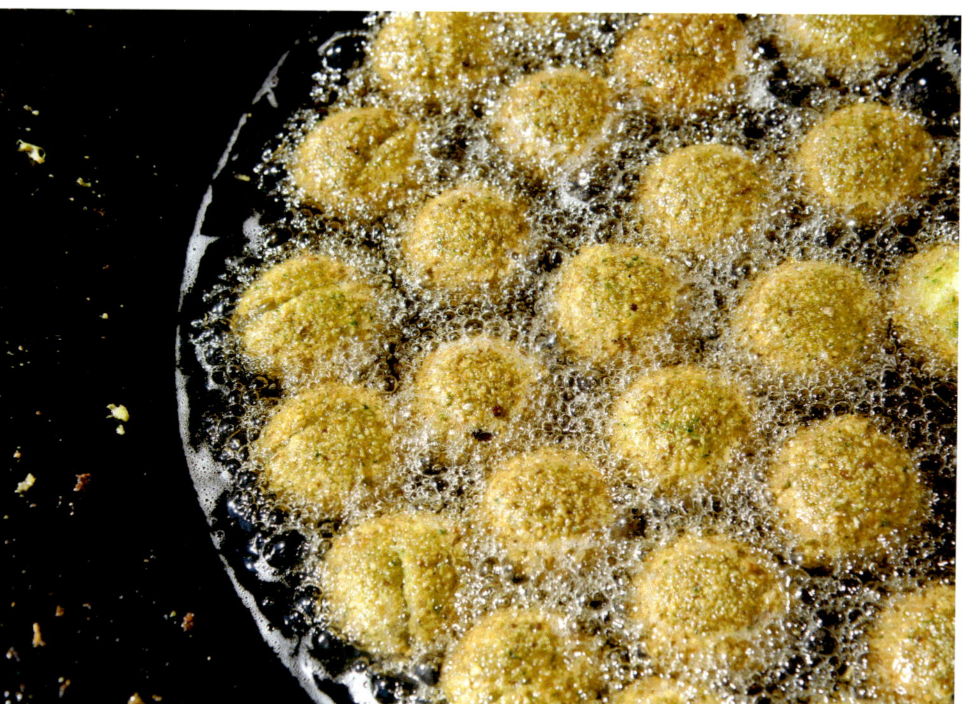

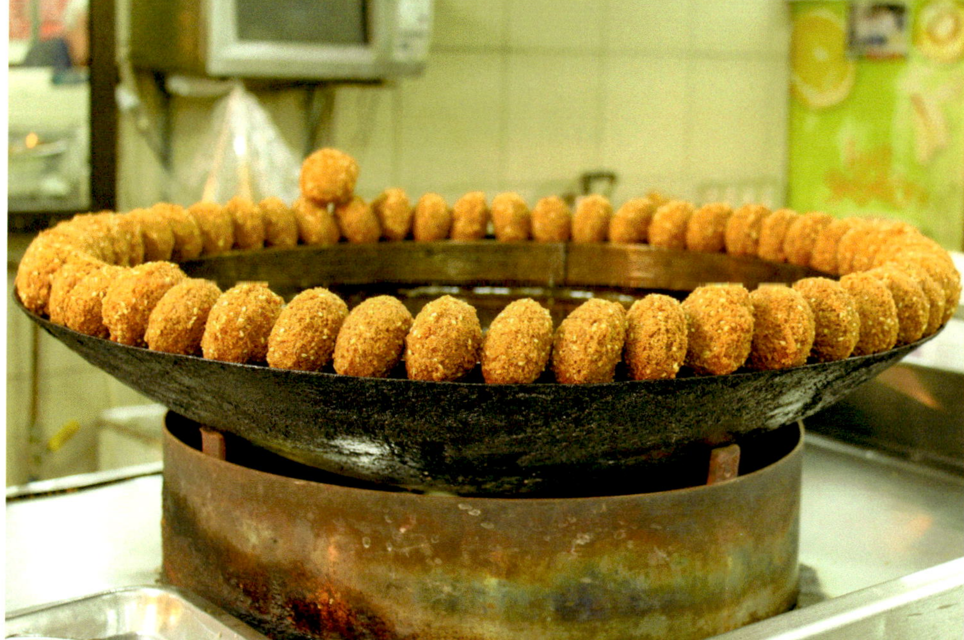

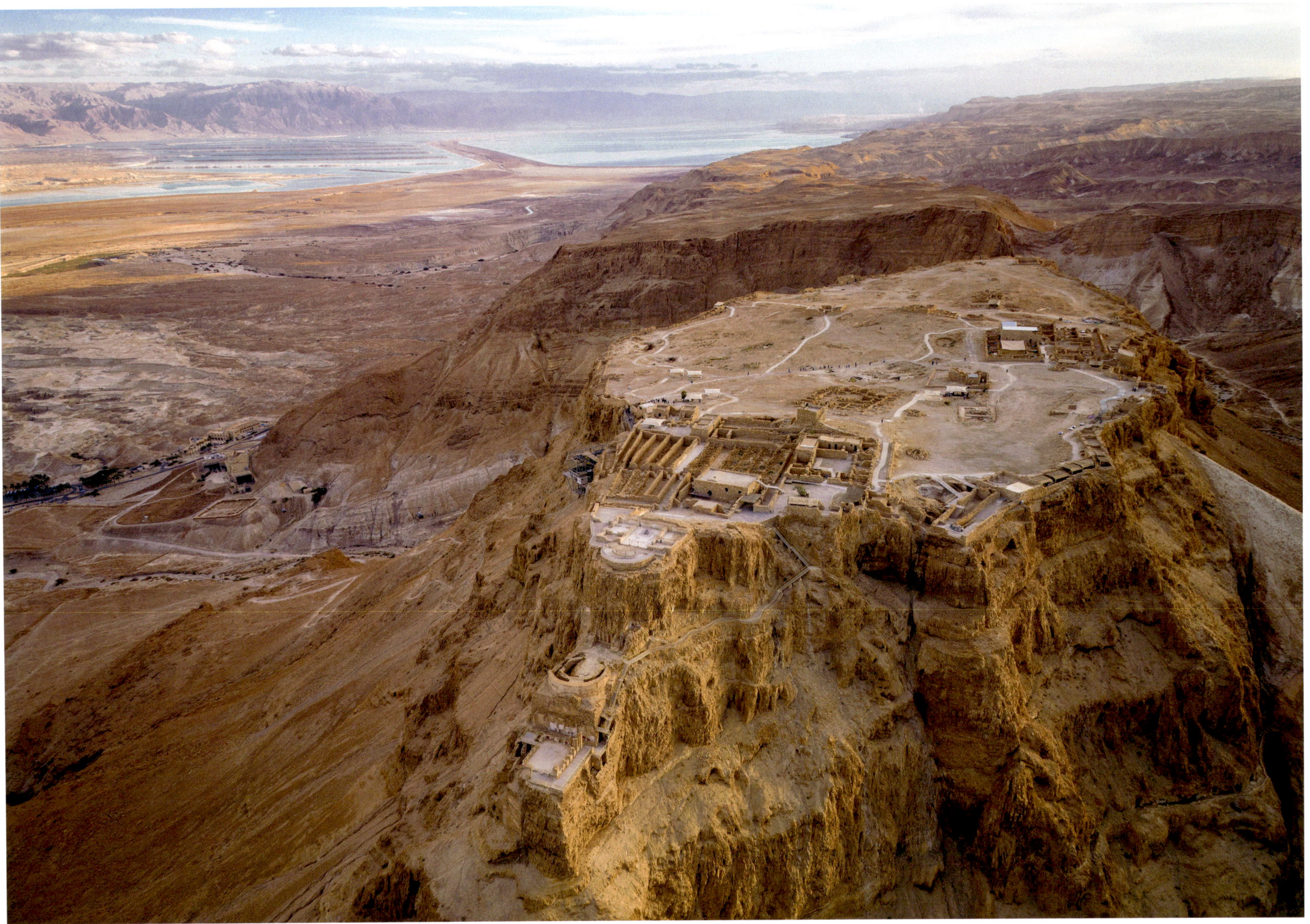

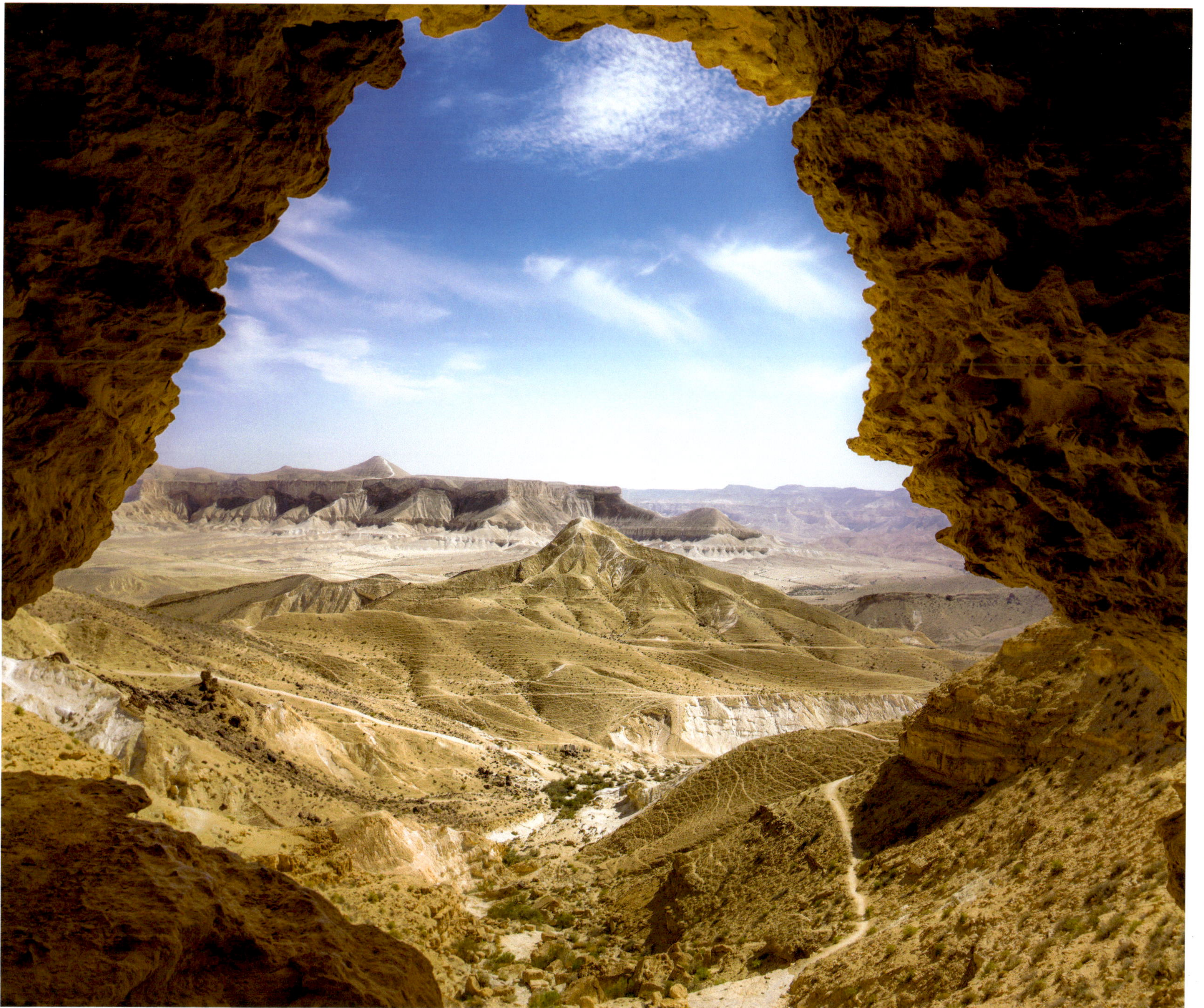

**Masada Fortress,
Judean National Park**
This site offers a powerful tourist experience at which Masada's tragic history is brought to life through the well-preserved ruins and informative displays. It was here, following the fall of Jerusalem in 70 CE, that a group of Jewish rebels called the Sicarii made their last stand at the Masada fortress. The Romans laid siege, but rather than surrender, the 960 inhabitants committed mass suicide, choosing death over slavery. Today, visitors arrive at the modern visitor centre where they can either take a cable car or hike the famous 'Snake Path' to the top where they'll find King Herod's palace, a synagogue, and Roman siege ramps, with endless views of the Dead Sea and Judean Desert.

Negev Desert
This huge area offers a mix of geological wonders, such as Makhtesh Ramon, the world's largest erosion crater, offering a breathtaking spectacle of colours and formations. Cultural experiences include visiting the Negev Wine Route, where vineyards thrive while still using ancient Nabataean irrigation techniques. More action-filled activities include sandboarding the massive sand dunes or taking a night-time drive to stargaze from this isolated, quiet landscape.

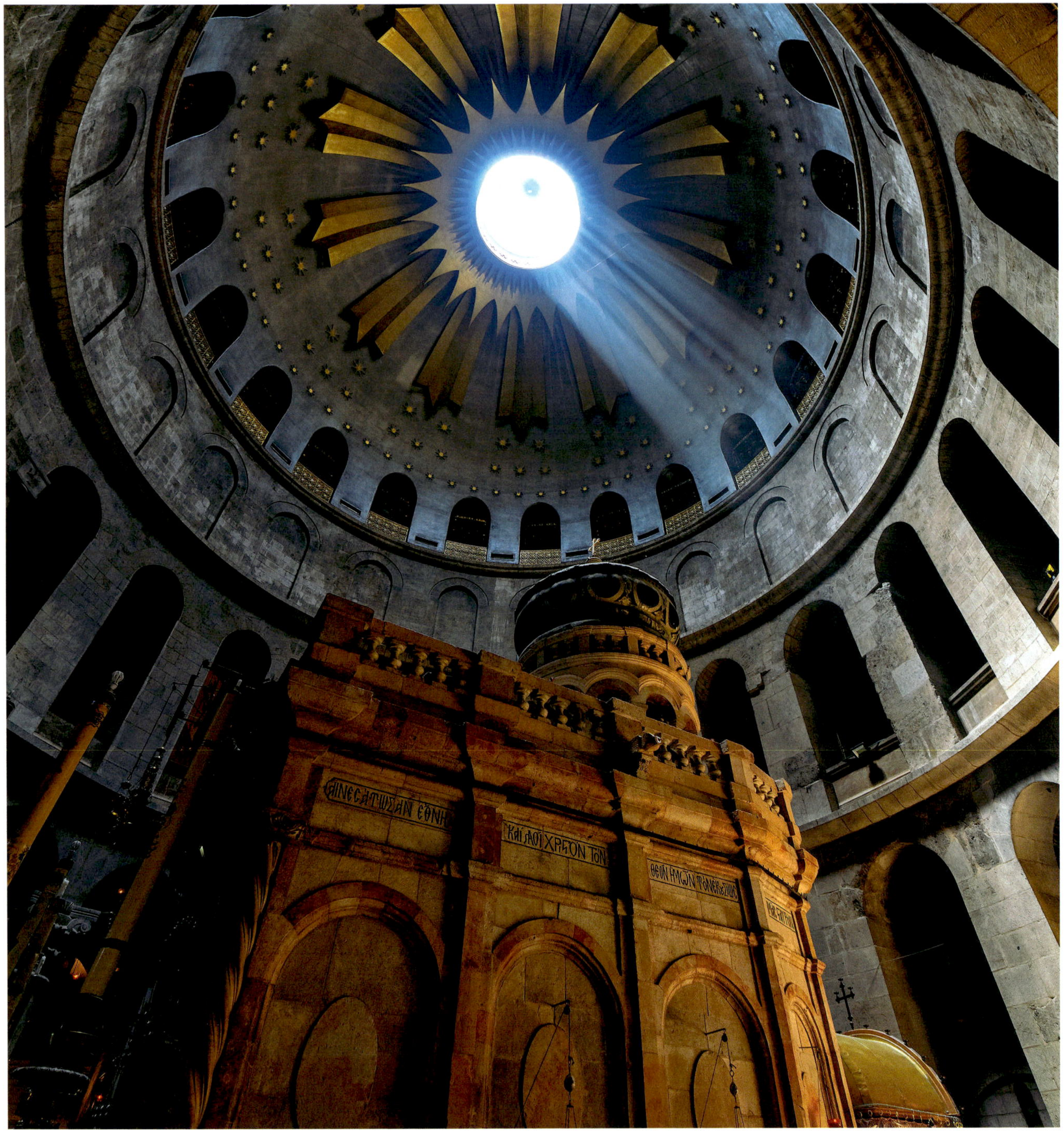

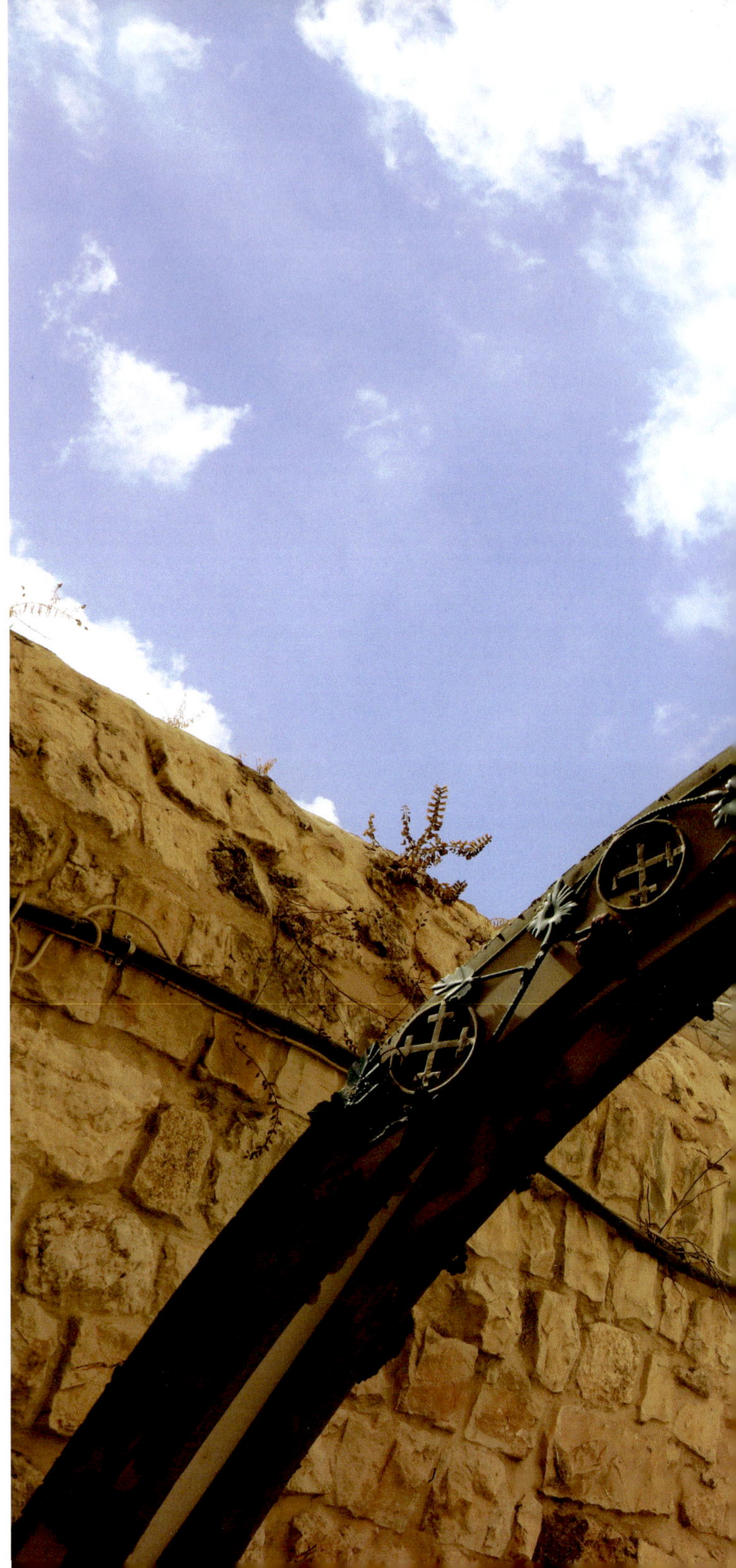

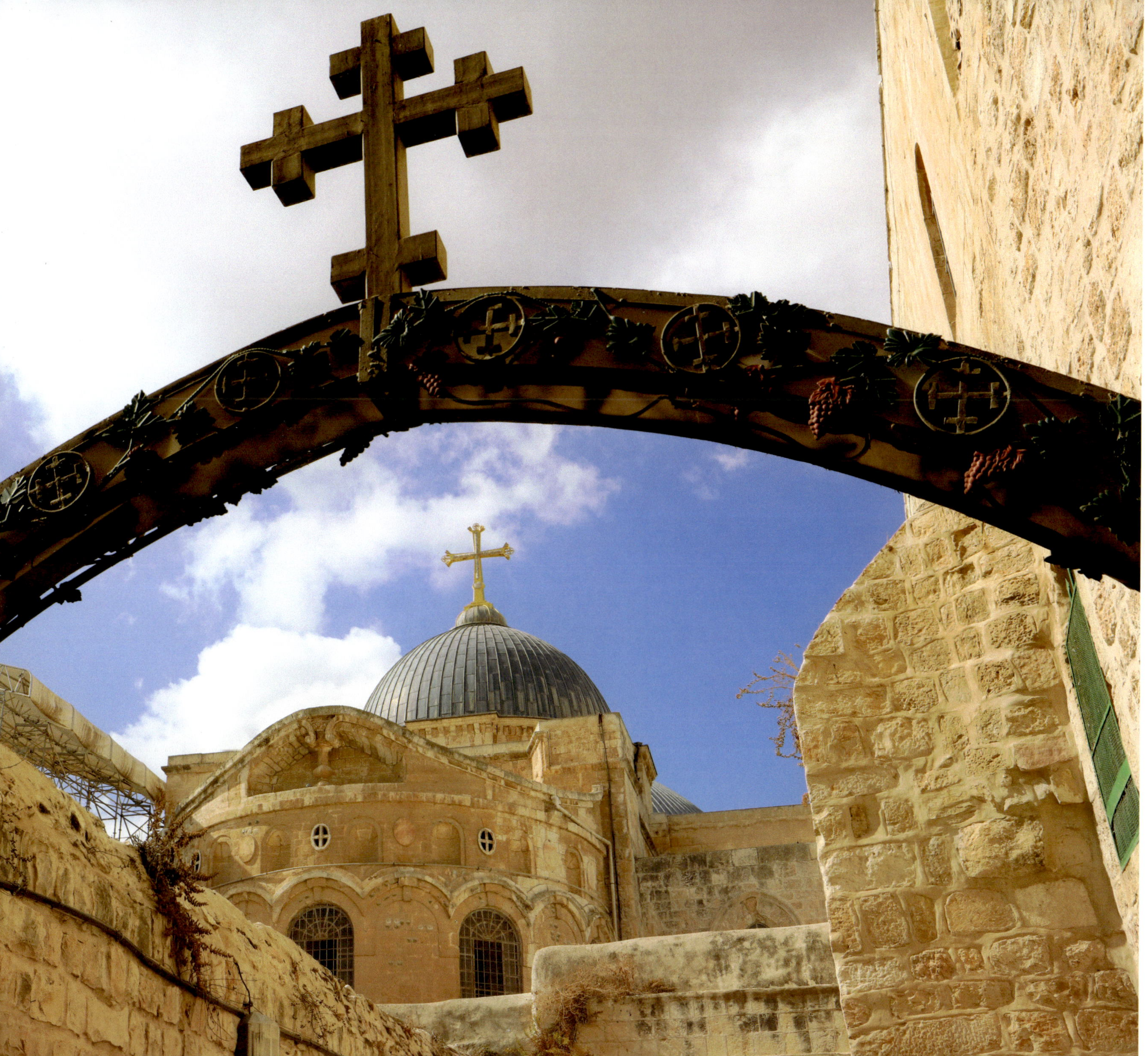

Church of the Holy Sepulchre, Jerusalem
This focal point of Christian pilgrimage is built on the sites where Jesus is believed to have been crucified (Golgotha) and where his tomb, or sepulchre, was located. The original church was built by Emperor Constantine I in the 4th century. The interior is a complex space, housing the two most sacred sites: the Rock of Calvary, where Jesus was crucified, and the Edicule, a chapel built over his tomb.

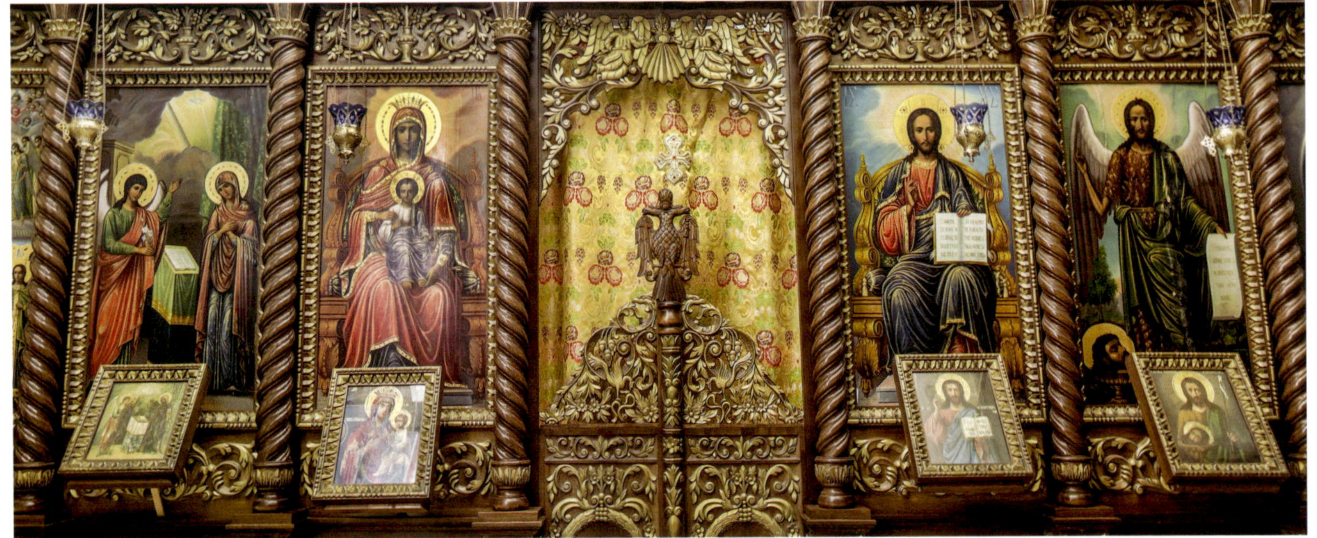

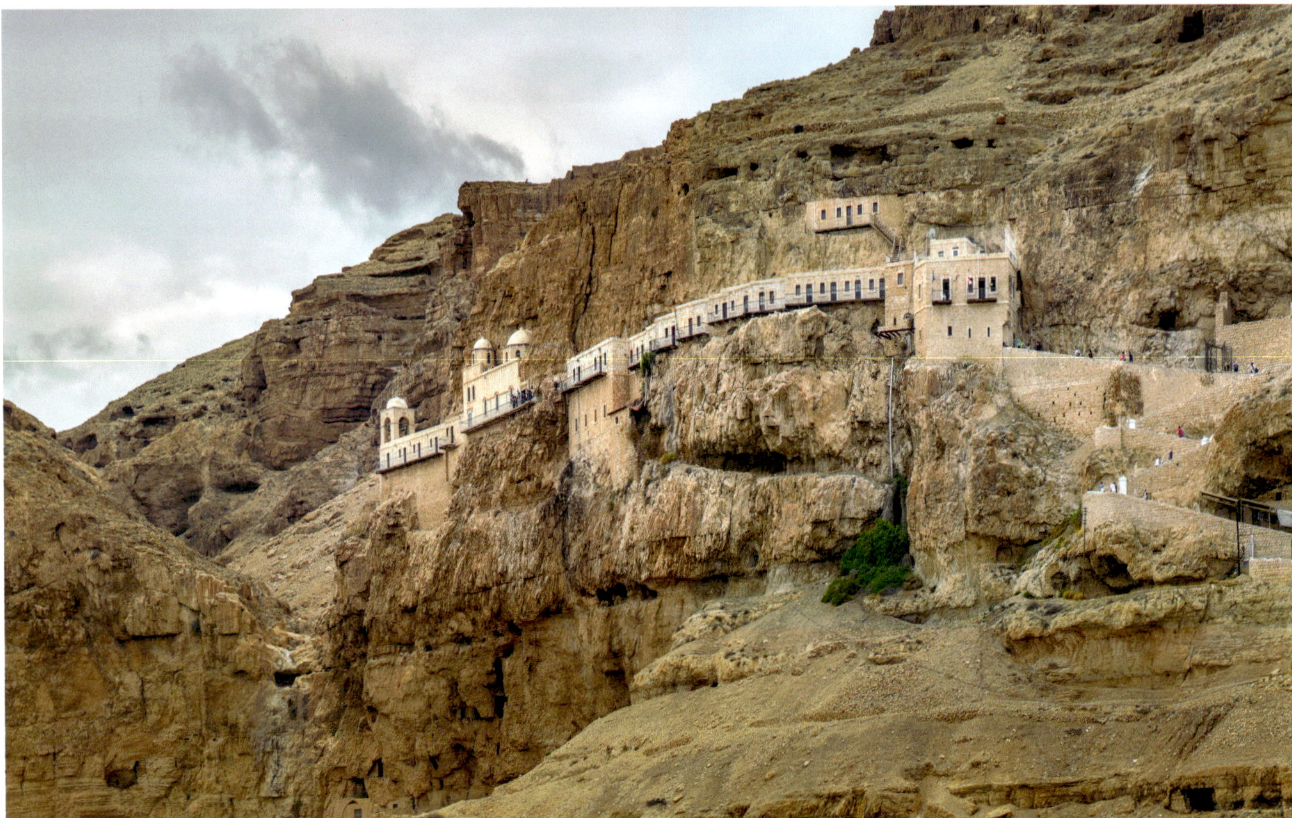

LEFT (BOTH PHOTOGRAPHS):

Monastery of the Temptation, Jericho

Built by the Greek Orthodox Church, this remarkable structure clings dramatically to the cliff face of the Mount of Temptation, which overlooks Jericho. Some of the monastery is carved directly into the rock and other elements are dangerously suspended. The monastery attracts pilgrims, and is adorned with many icons and religious art. The stone sitting inside a cave chapel is traditionally believed to be where Jesus sat during his fast.

RIGHT:

The Baha'i Gardens, Haifa

A different type of destination, these gardens are a stunning example of Persian horticultural design. Here the visitor finds terraces that are meticulously manicured and filled with symmetrical flowerbeds, sculpted hedges, and cascading water features. At the centre of the gardens stands the gold-domed Shrine of the Báb. These gardens attract international pilgrims as the designs symbolize the Baha'i faith's principles of harmony, unity, and human connection to a divine, universal order.

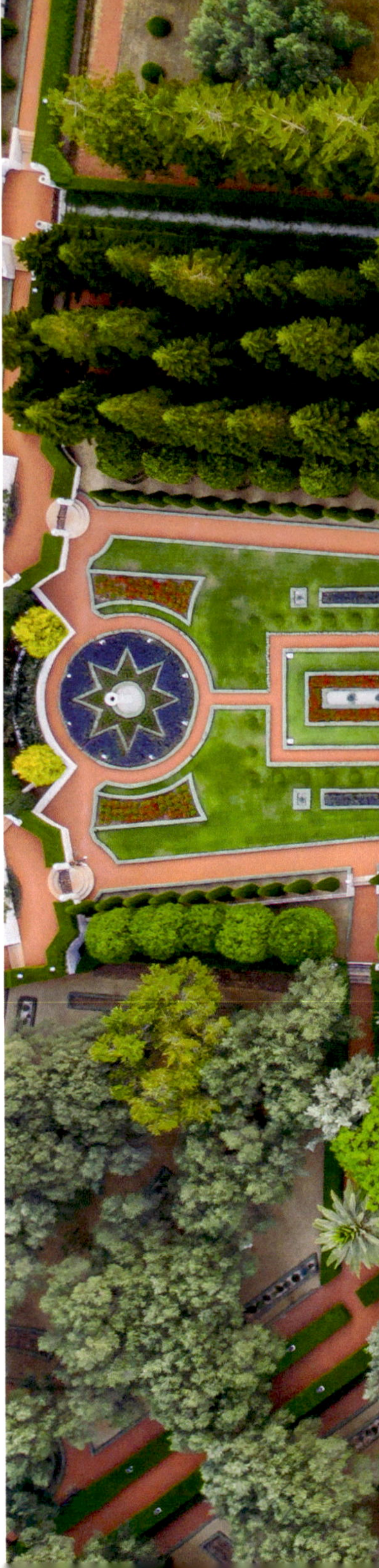

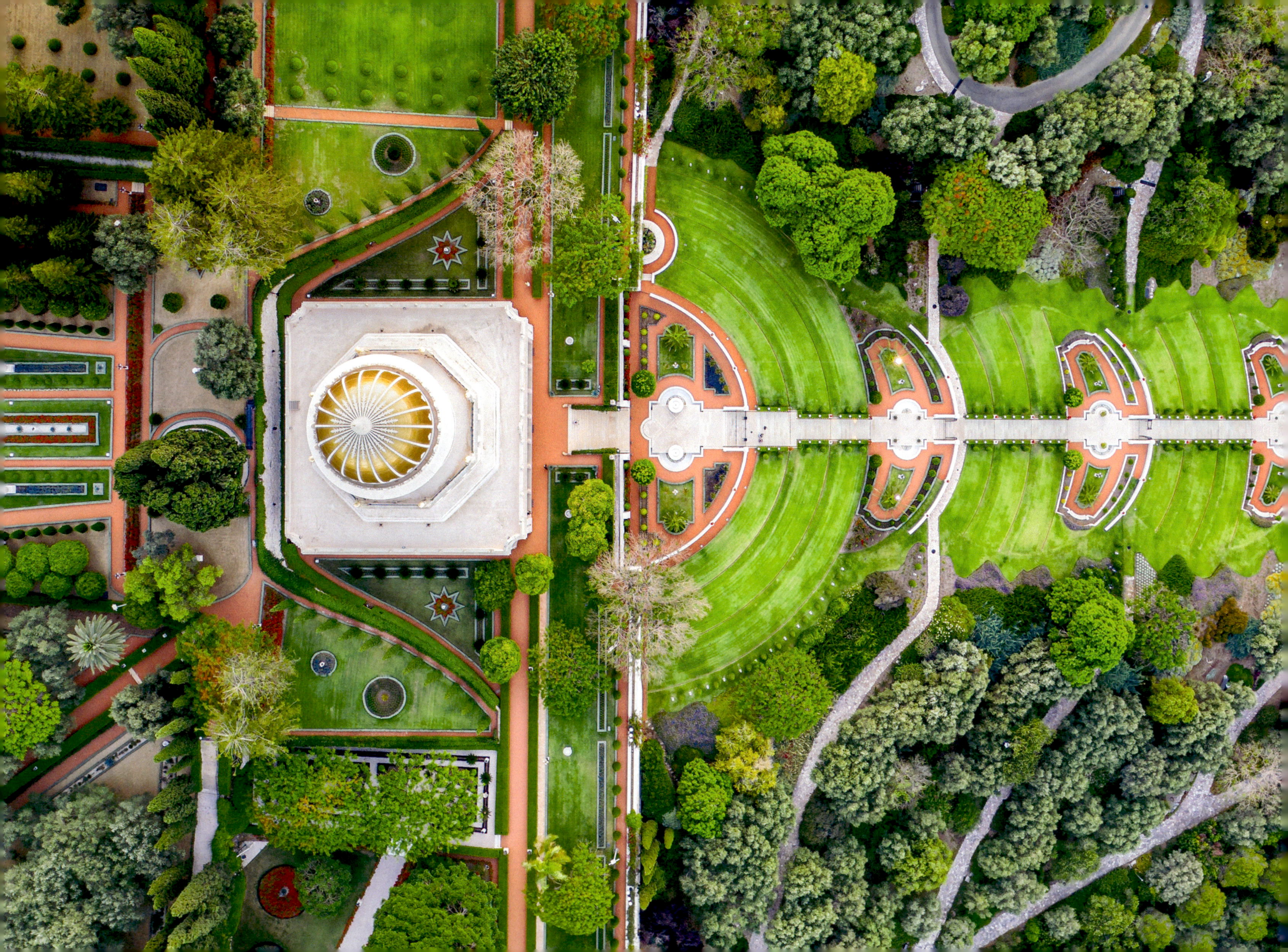

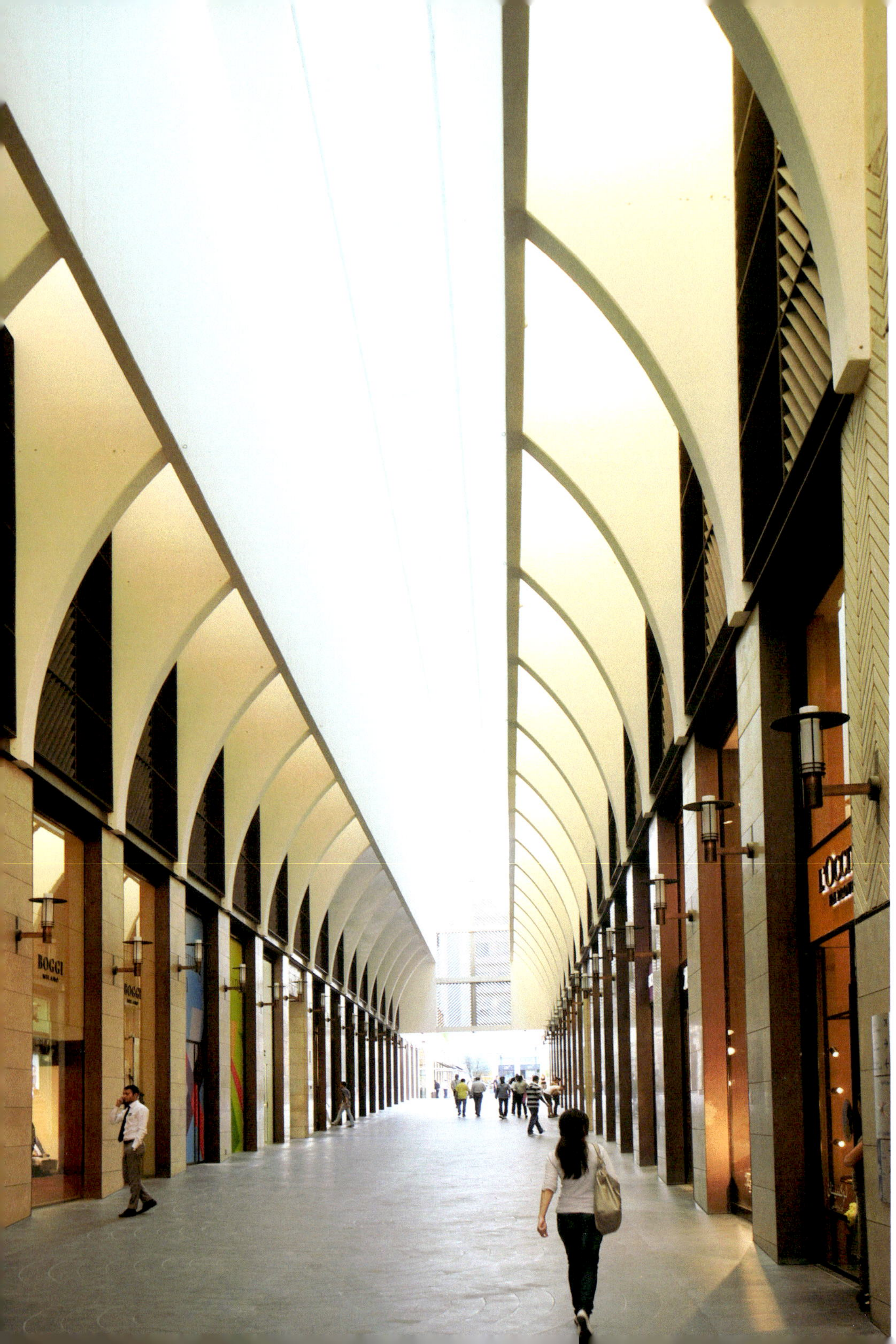

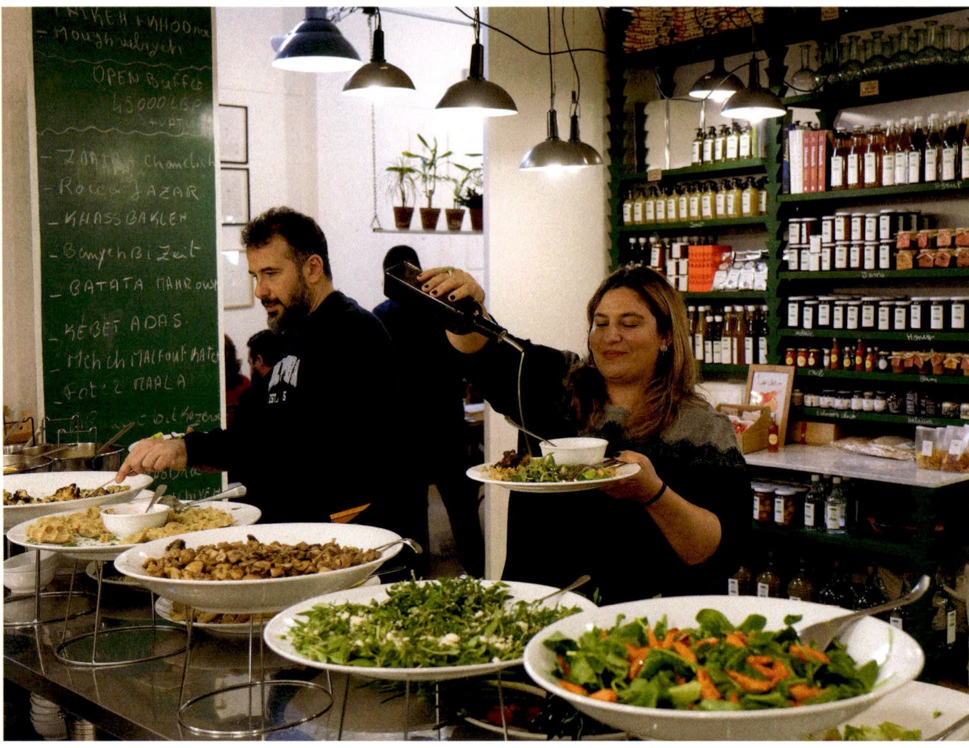

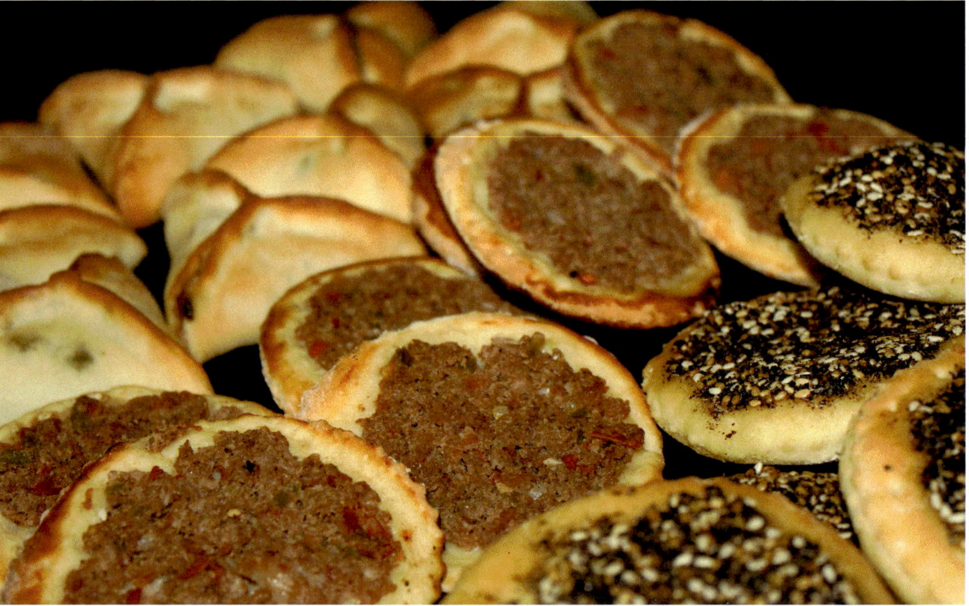

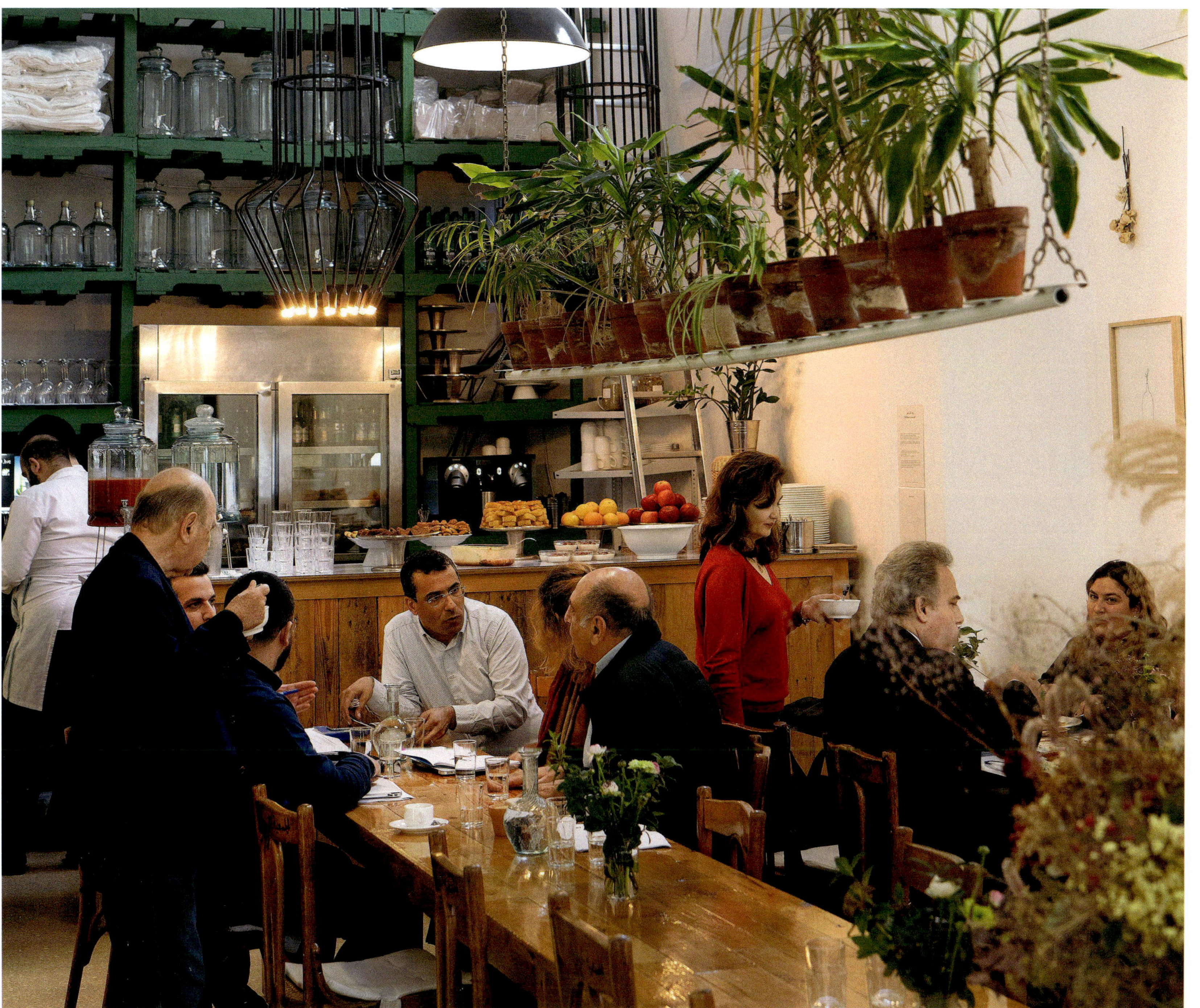

Tawlet community restaurant, Beirut

Tawlet, which translates as 'table,' is a famous spot in Beirut. It operates as a culinary showcase, inviting home cooks from different Lebanese villages to share their authentic regional recipes with a wider range of gourmet diners. The concept is to preserve and celebrate Lebanese culinary heritage, providing a fresh, seasonal and socially conscious dining experience in a welcoming communal setting.

OPPOSITE RIGHT BOTTOM:

Lebanese baked goods

The whole region is famed for its bakeries, creating delicious foods that are both sweet and savoury. The small flatbreads such as *za'atar* or *manakish* are delicious.

OPPOSITE LEFT:

Shopping mall, Beirut

Beirut is home to several prominent shopping malls as well as more localised souqs. Lebanese shoppers are drawn to these malls not just for the diverse range of international and local brands, but for the latest fashion offerings. Lebanese people have a historically strong passion for everything stylish, making shopping a joyful experience.

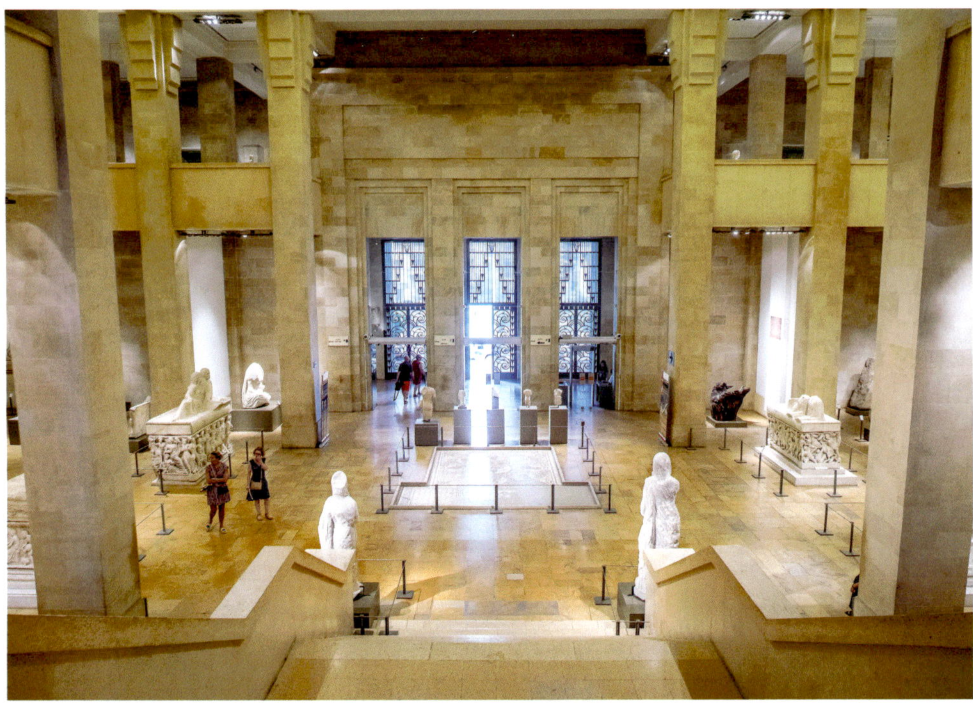

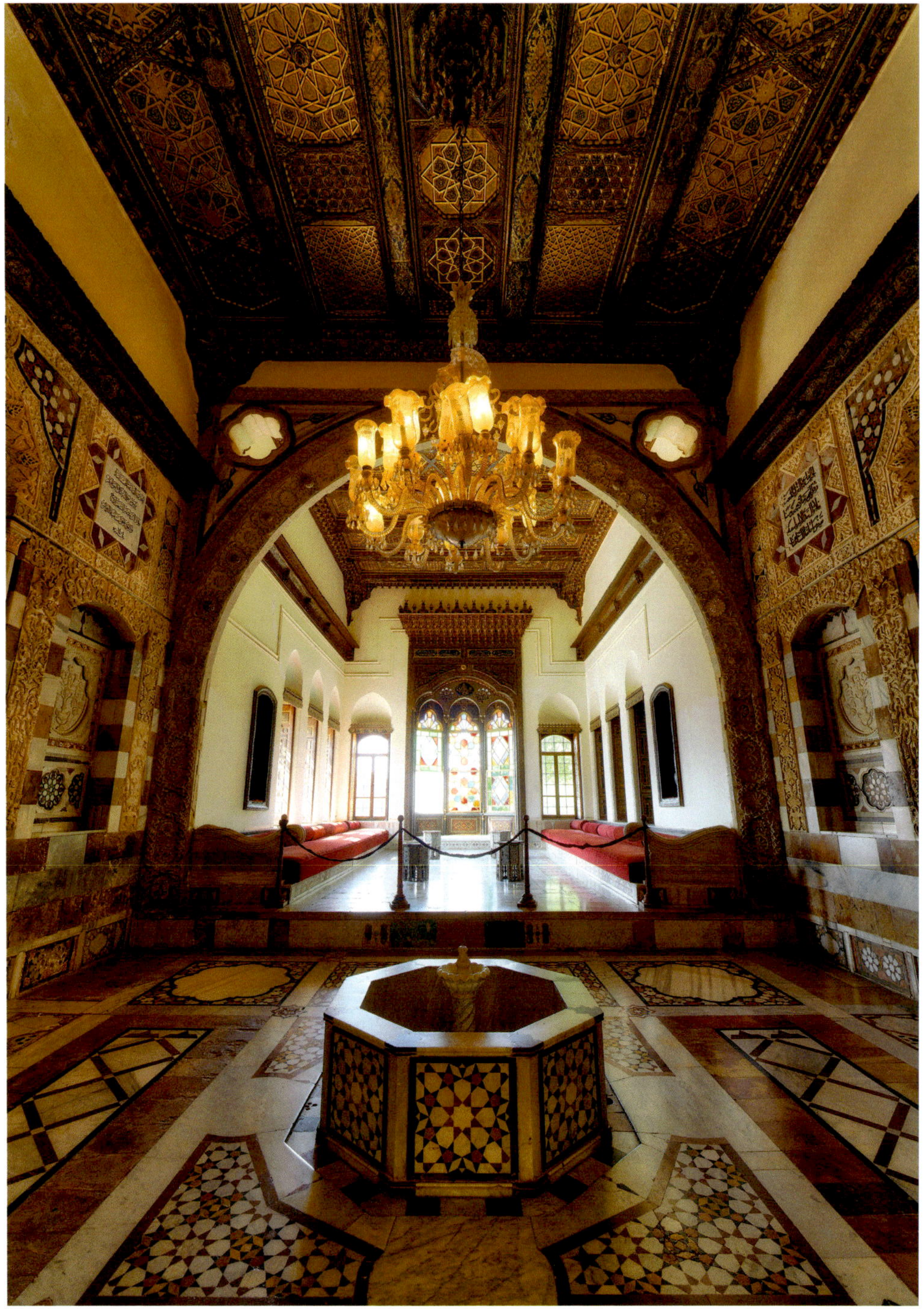

National Museum of Beirut
This testament to resilience, displaying collections successfully protected during the civil war, is located on the former Green Line. The museum is organized chronologically over three floors, with large, monumental artefacts like sarcophagi on the ground floor, and smaller objects arranged thematically in showcases on the upper floor, allowing visitors to follow a clear timeline of Lebanon's history, from prehistory to the medieval period. Among its highlights are gilded bronze Phoenician figurines from Byblos.

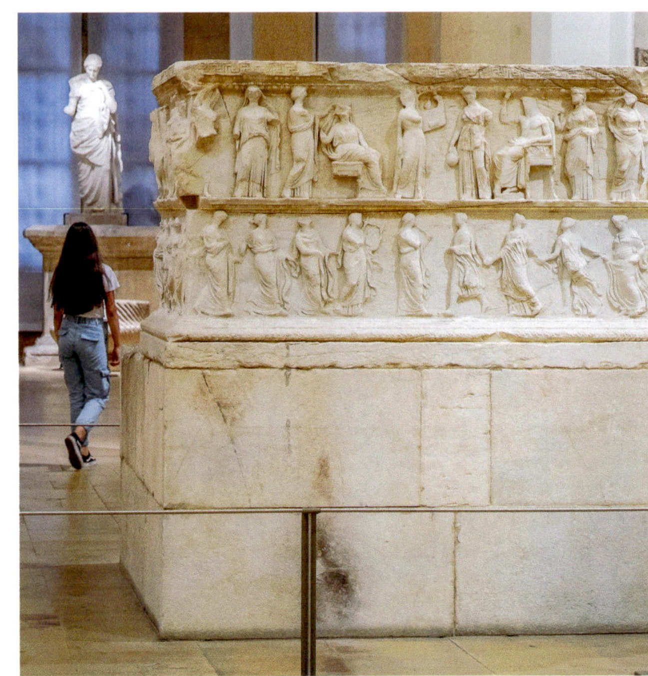

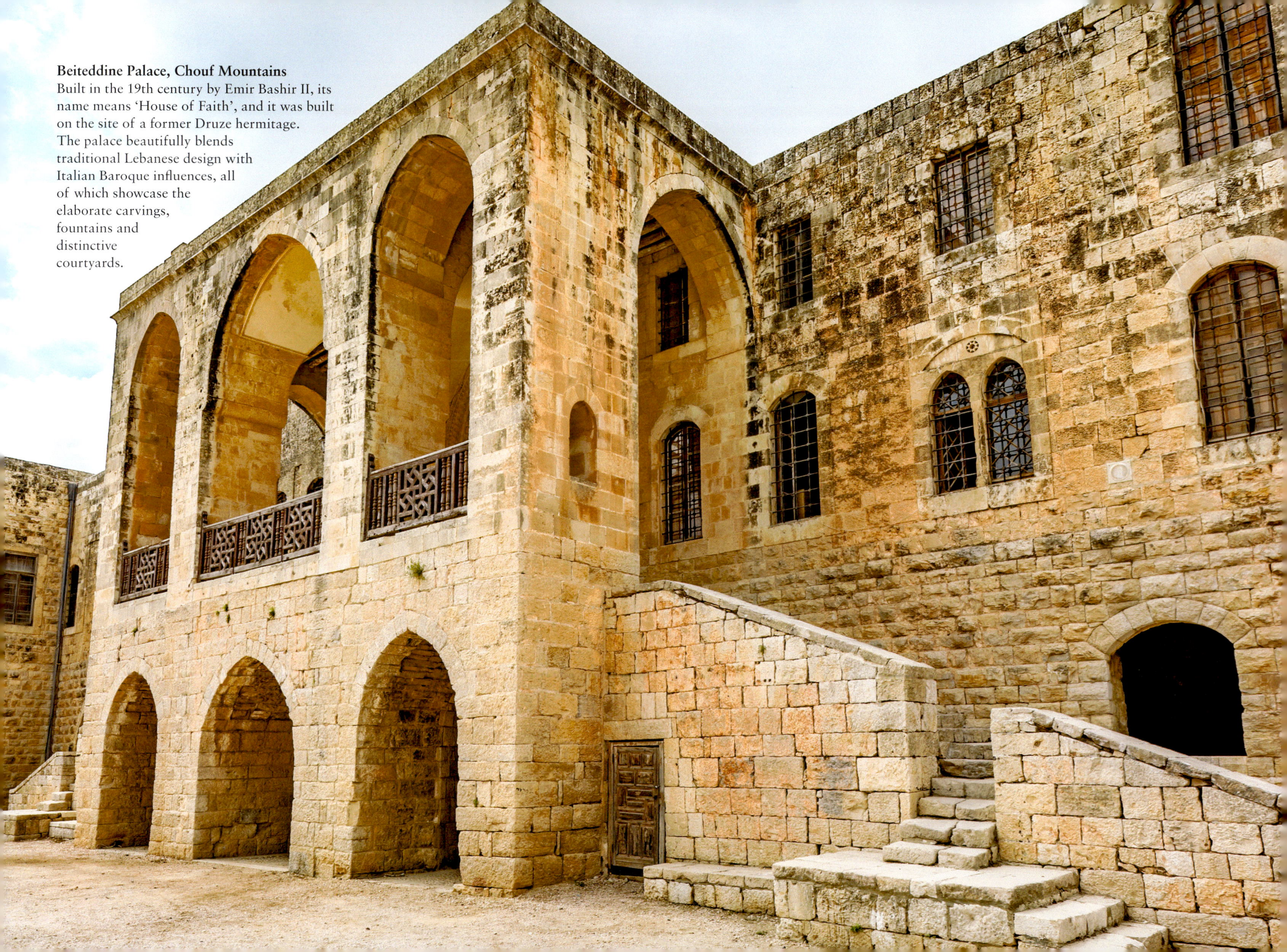

Beiteddine Palace, Chouf Mountains
Built in the 19th century by Emir Bashir II, its
name means 'House of Faith', and it was built
on the site of a former Druze hermitage.
The palace beautifully blends
traditional Lebanese design with
Italian Baroque influences, all
of which showcase the
elaborate carvings,
fountains and
distinctive
courtyards.

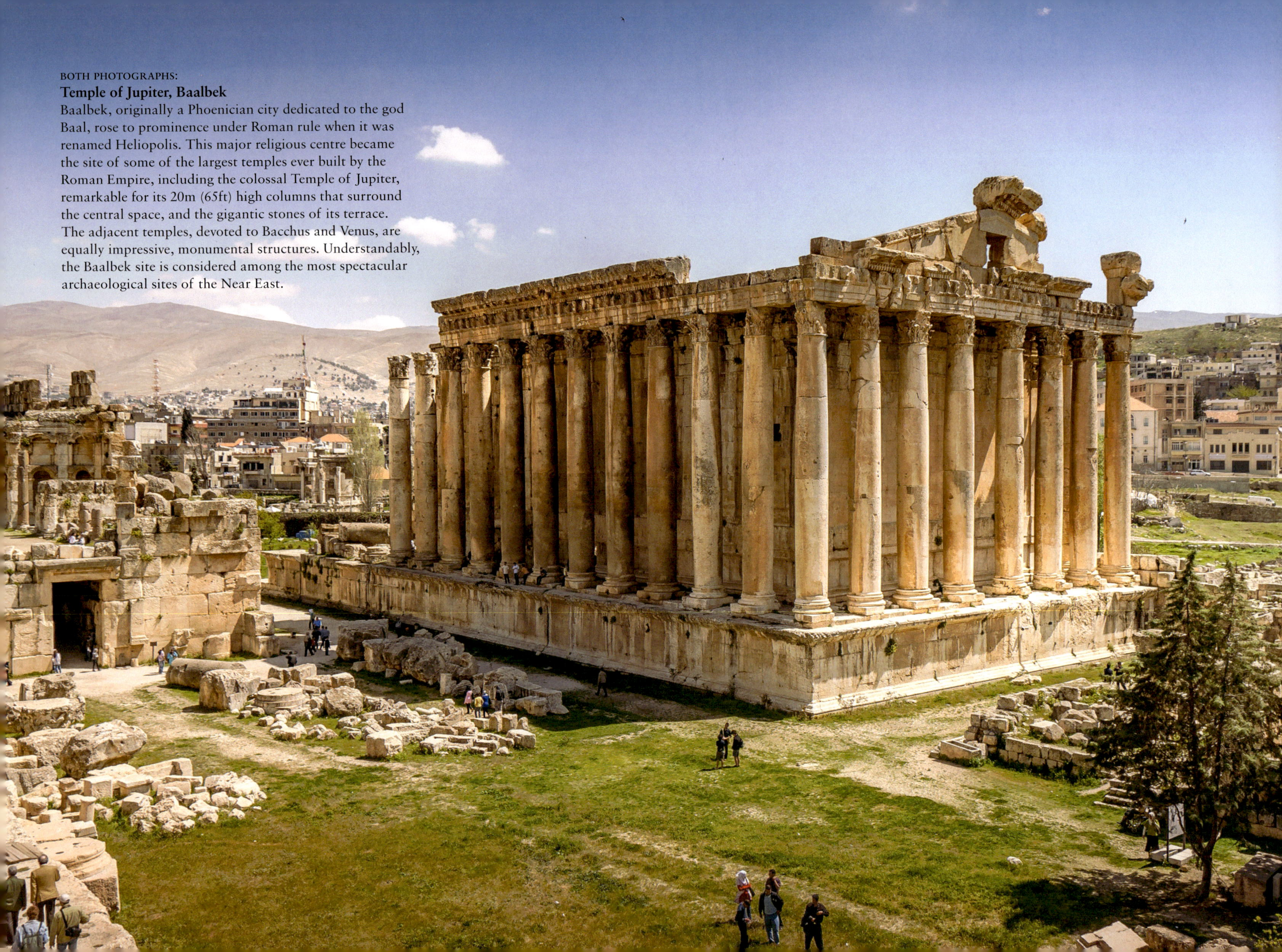

Temple of Jupiter, Baalbek

Baalbek, originally a Phoenician city dedicated to the god Baal, rose to prominence under Roman rule when it was renamed Heliopolis. This major religious centre became the site of some of the largest temples ever built by the Roman Empire, including the colossal Temple of Jupiter, remarkable for its 20m (65ft) high columns that surround the central space, and the gigantic stones of its terrace. The adjacent temples, devoted to Bacchus and Venus, are equally impressive, monumental structures. Understandably, the Baalbek site is considered among the most spectacular archaeological sites of the Near East.

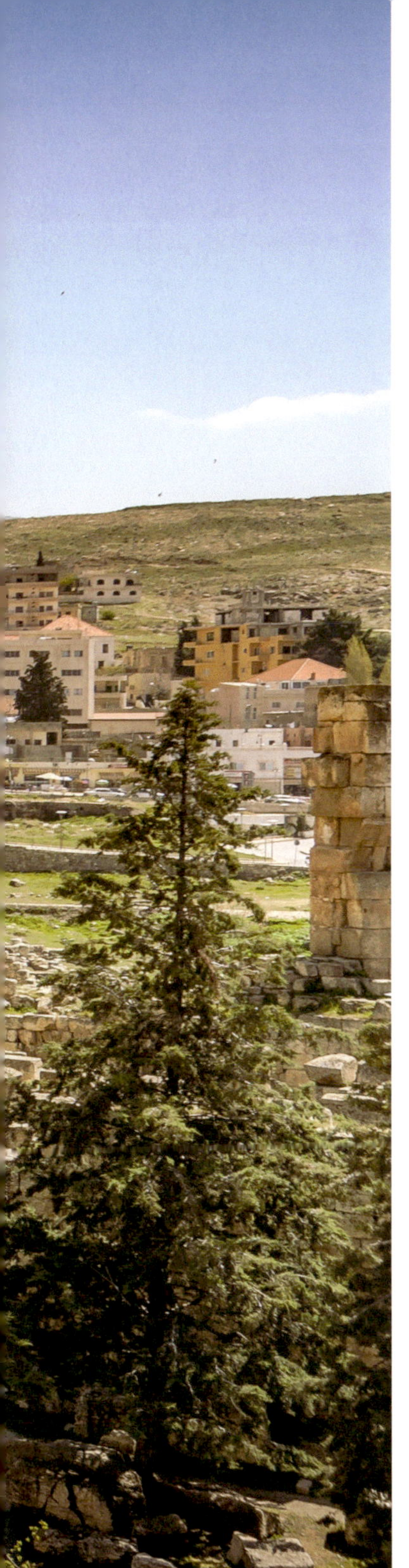

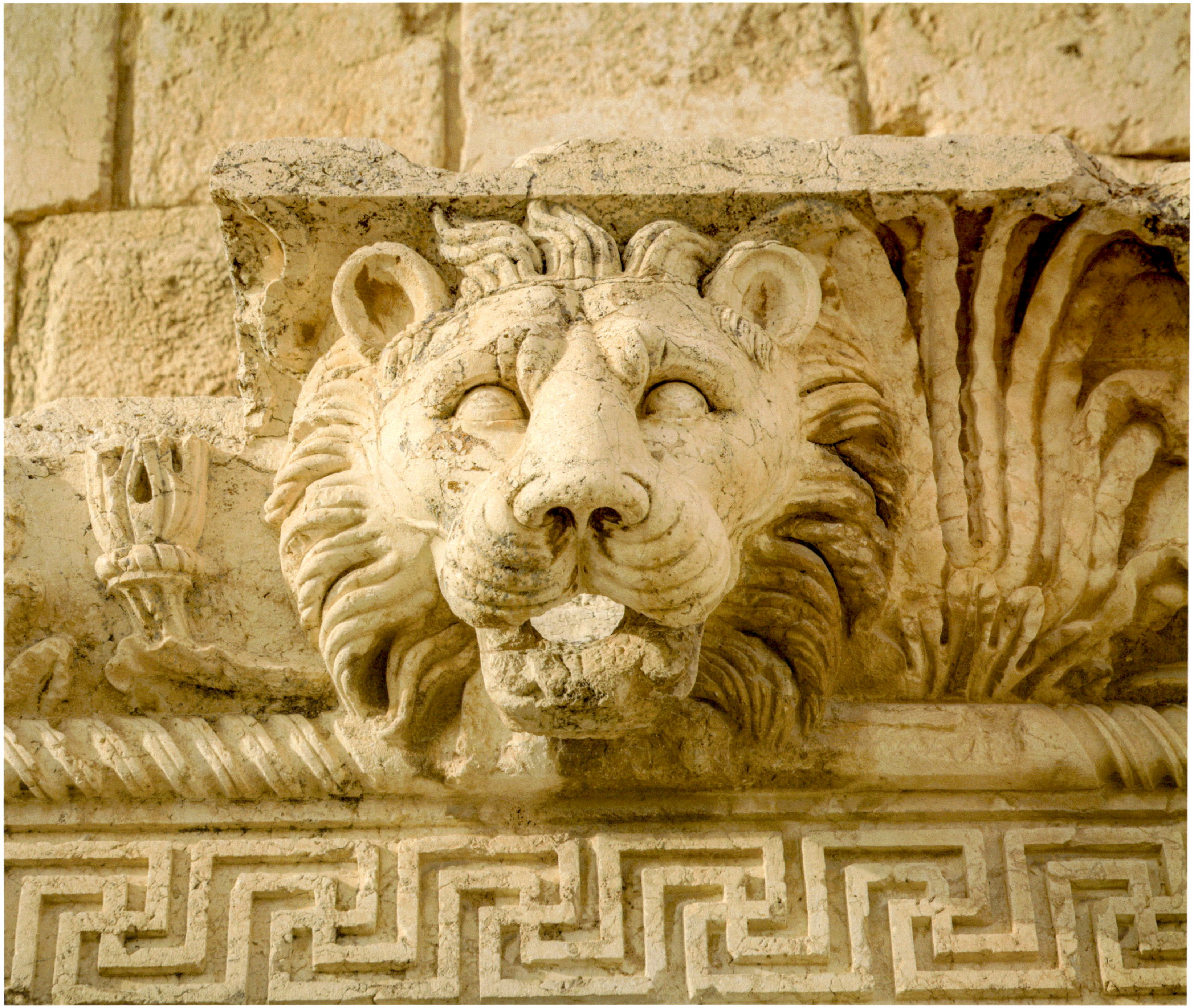

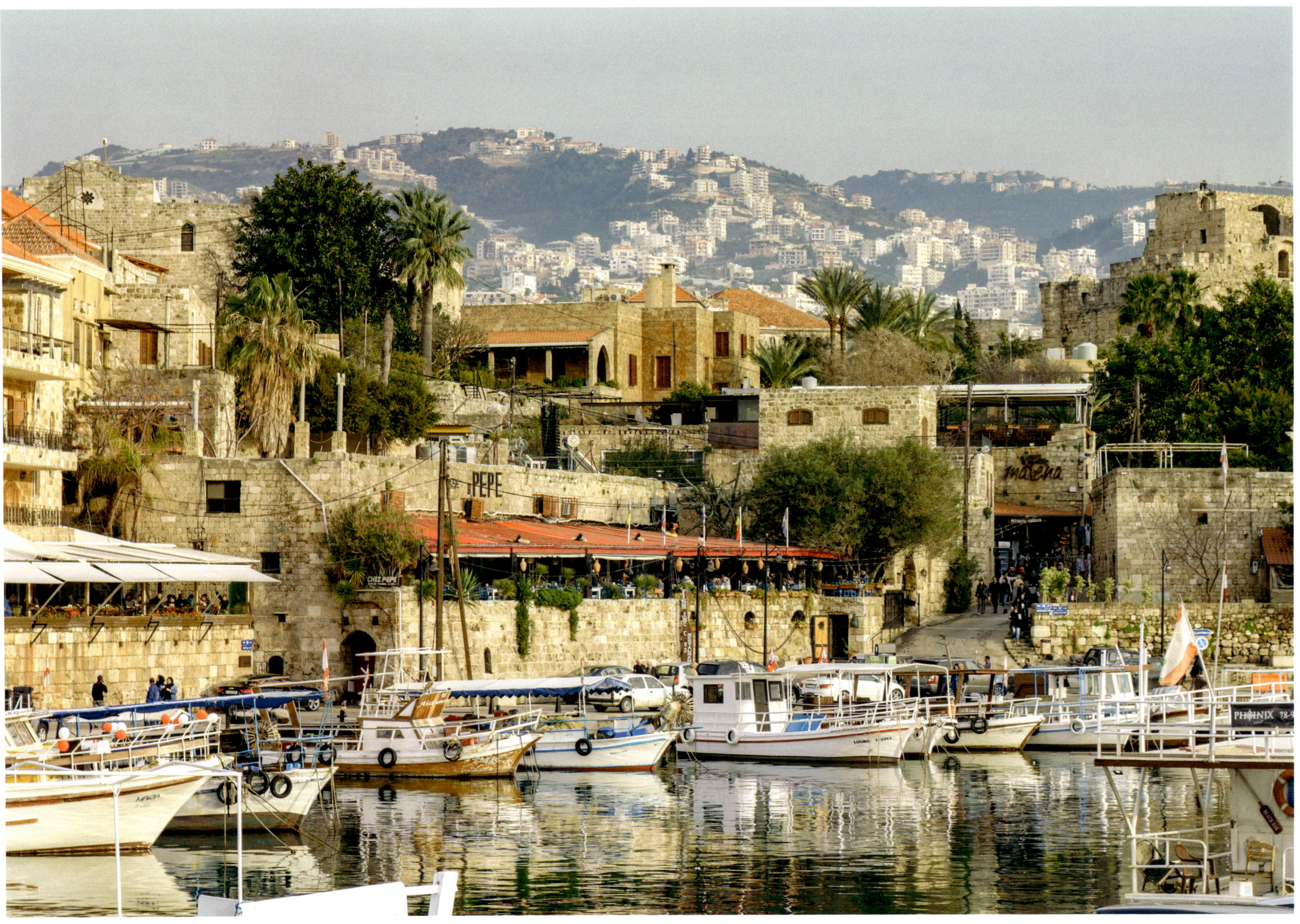

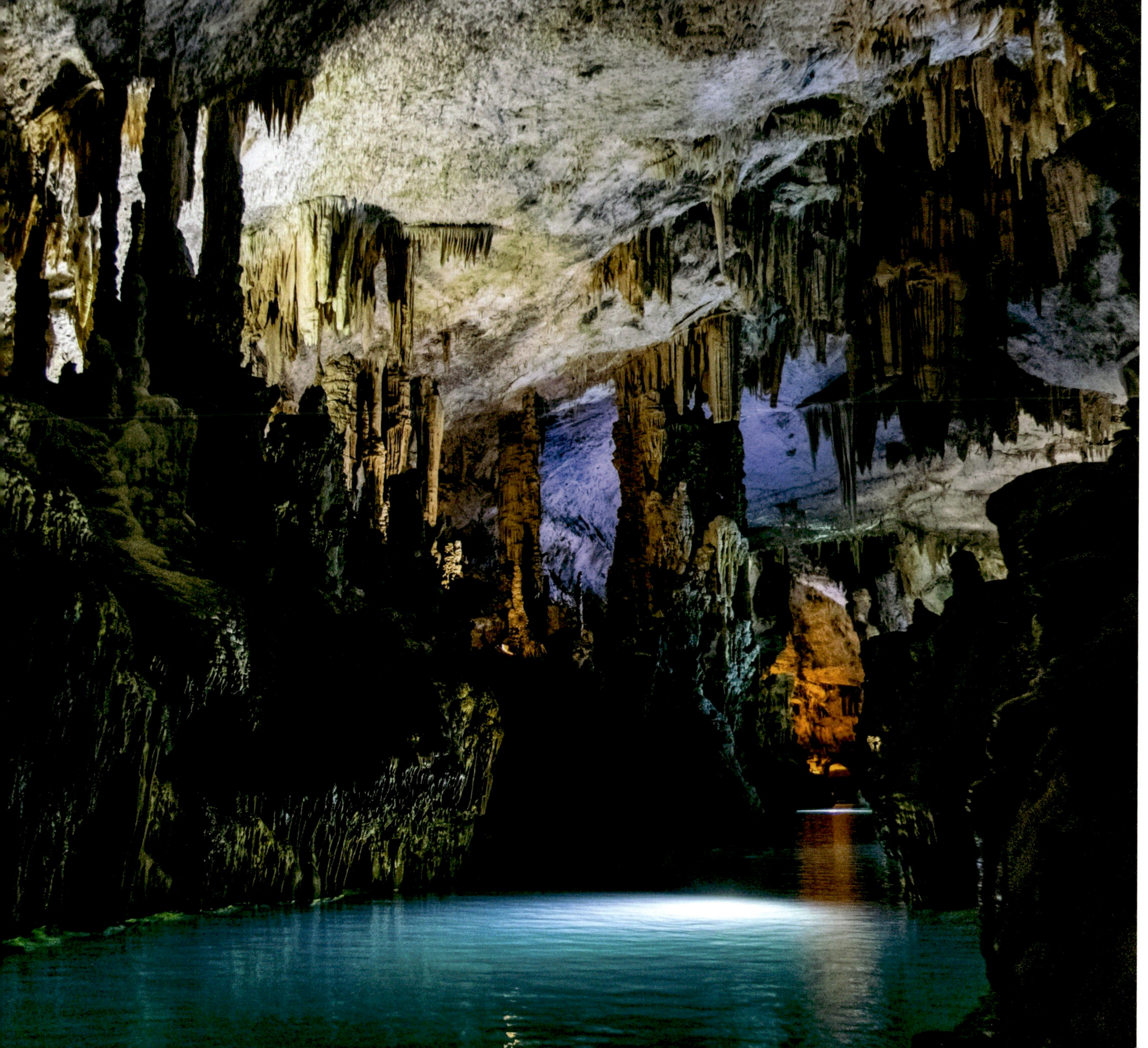

Jeita Grotto, near Beirut
This two-level system of stunning limestone caves is an unusual visitor experience. The almost 9km (5.6 miles) of caves are on two levels. The lower cave contains a tranquil, beautifully lit underground river explored by boat. The upper cave is a spectacular walk through spaces filled with incredible stalactites and stalagmites (including one of the world's largest), accessed by foot via specially built walkways.

OPPOSITE:

Byblos harbour
One of the world's oldest continuously used ports, Byblos is a special blend of Phoenician, Roman, and Crusader history. Today, this historical backdrop is filled with the vibrant energy of local fishermen, charming seaside restaurants serving fresh seafood, and a relaxed atmosphere where ancient ruins meet the gentle bobbing of small fishing boats and yachts. Byblos is a place where you can sense the past, enjoy Lebanese hospitality, and enjoy local cuisine and a fine view.

211

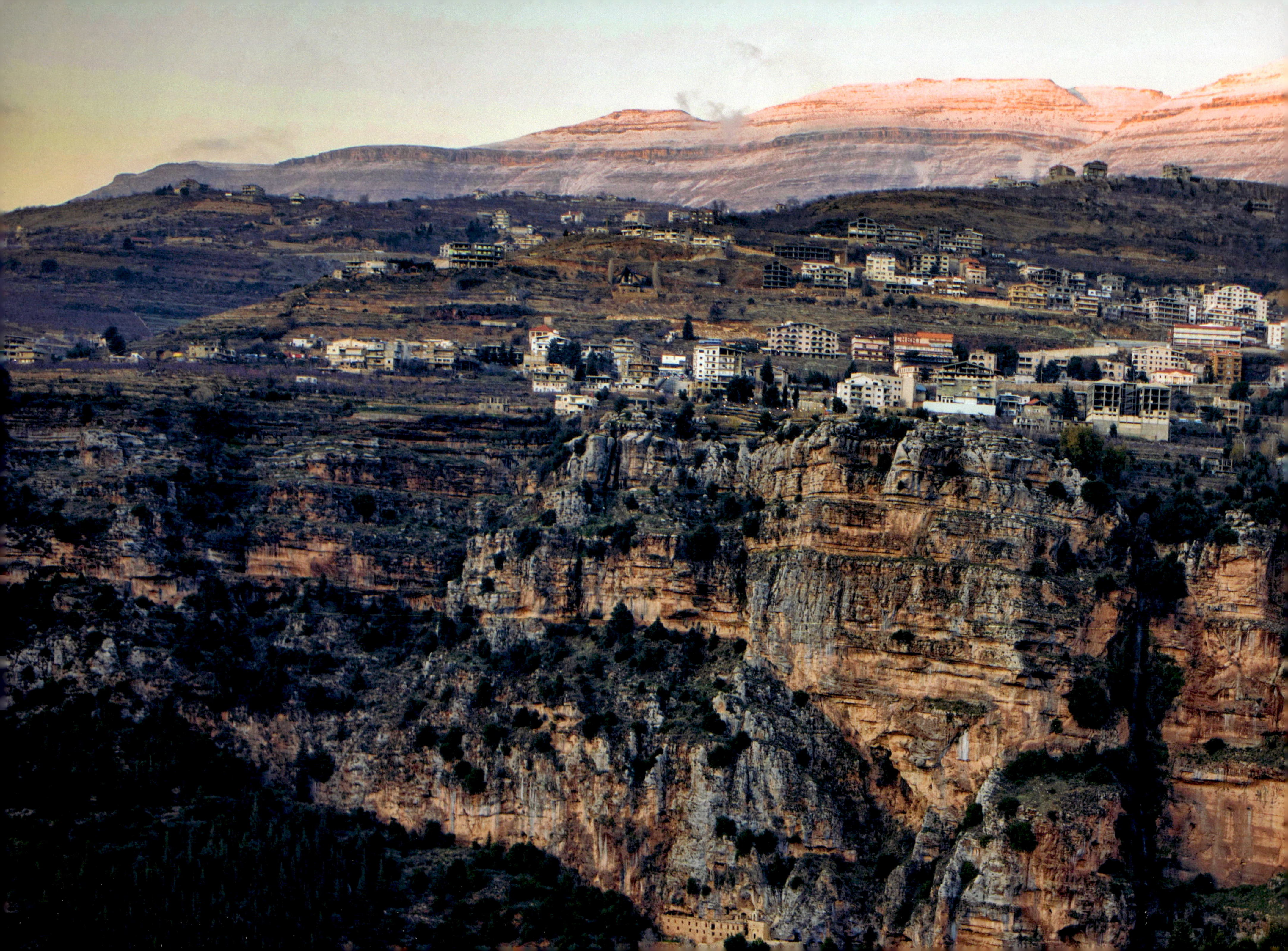

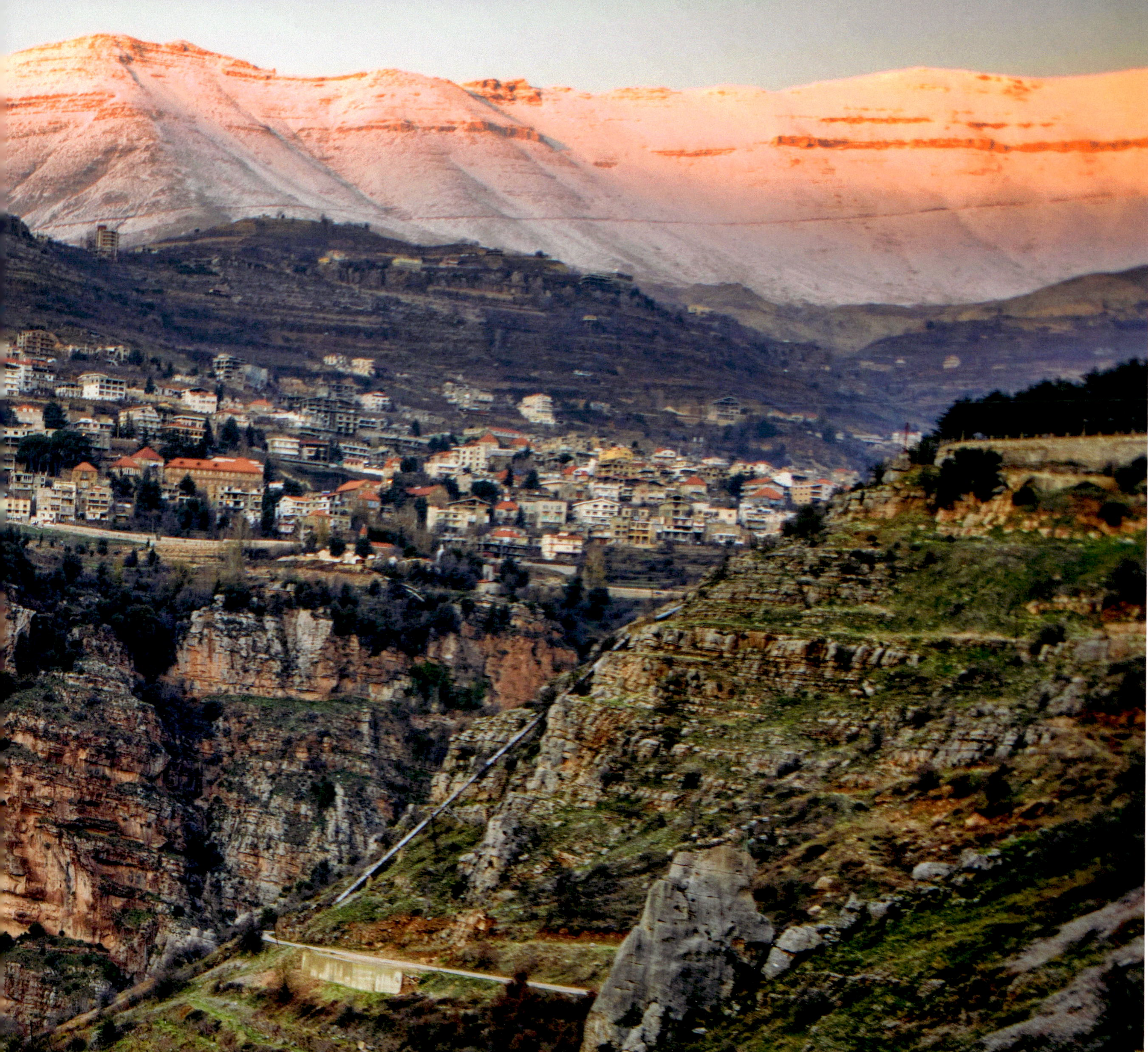

Bsharri, Qadisha Valley
This Lebanese mountain town is famous for being the birthplace of the great poet and artist Gibran Khalil Gibran, and provides a gateway to the Cedars of God forest. The Qadisha Valley is an area of spiritual and natural significance. Carved by the river, its rugged cliffs and deep gorges have provided a refuge for Christian monastic communities, particularly the Maronites, for centuries. The valley is dotted with monasteries and hermitages, often carved directly into the rock face, as examples of ancient ascetic life.

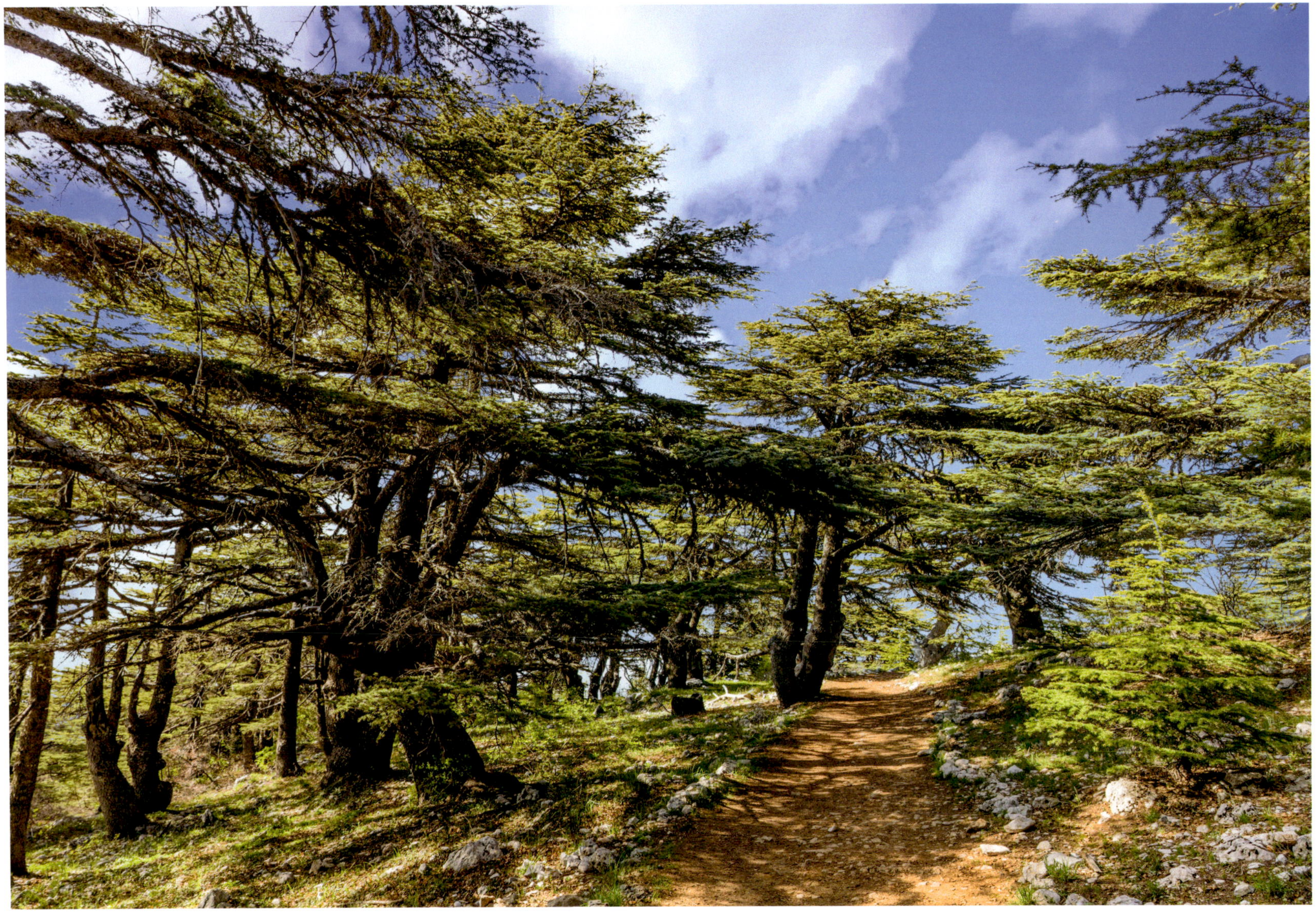

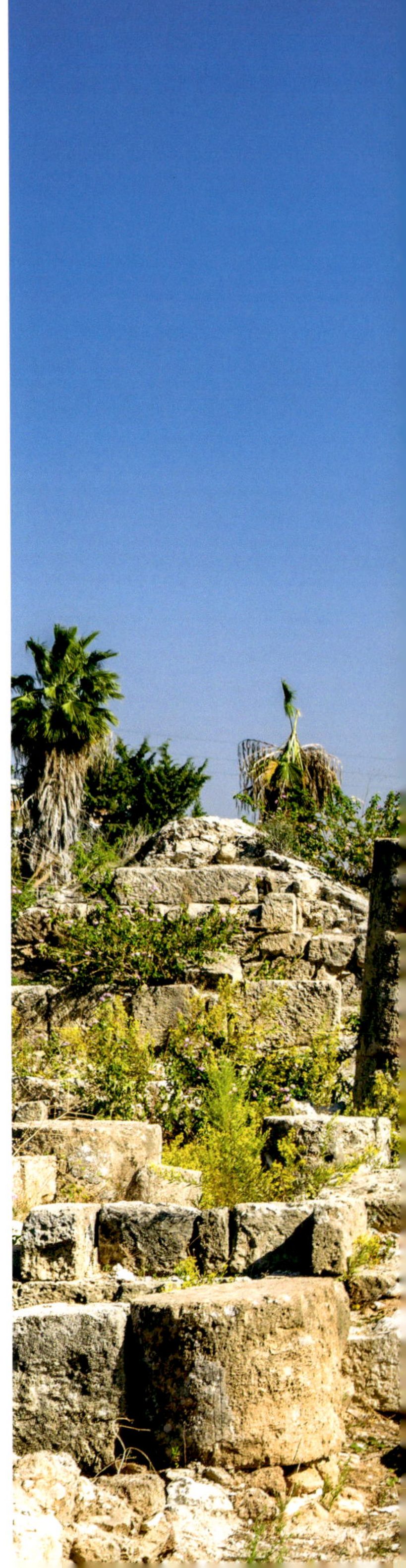

ABOVE:

Cedars of Lebanon, Shouf Biosphere Reserve
These trees are powerful national symbols and provide the central image of the Lebanese flag. As the last remnants of the vast forests that once covered Mount Lebanon, cedars have been prized since antiquity for their durable and fragrant wood. Cedars appear in the Bible and the Epic of Gilgamesh, and the trees were used to build King Solomon's Temple.

RIGHT:

Roman ruins, Tyre
This major Roman metropolis has a rich past, having been absorbed into the Roman Republic in 64 BC. Under Roman rule, Tyre flourished as a major commercial hub and grew to feature a spectacular Triumphal Arch, an expansive necropolis with hundreds of sarcophagi, and one of the largest and best-preserved Roman hippodromes in the world.

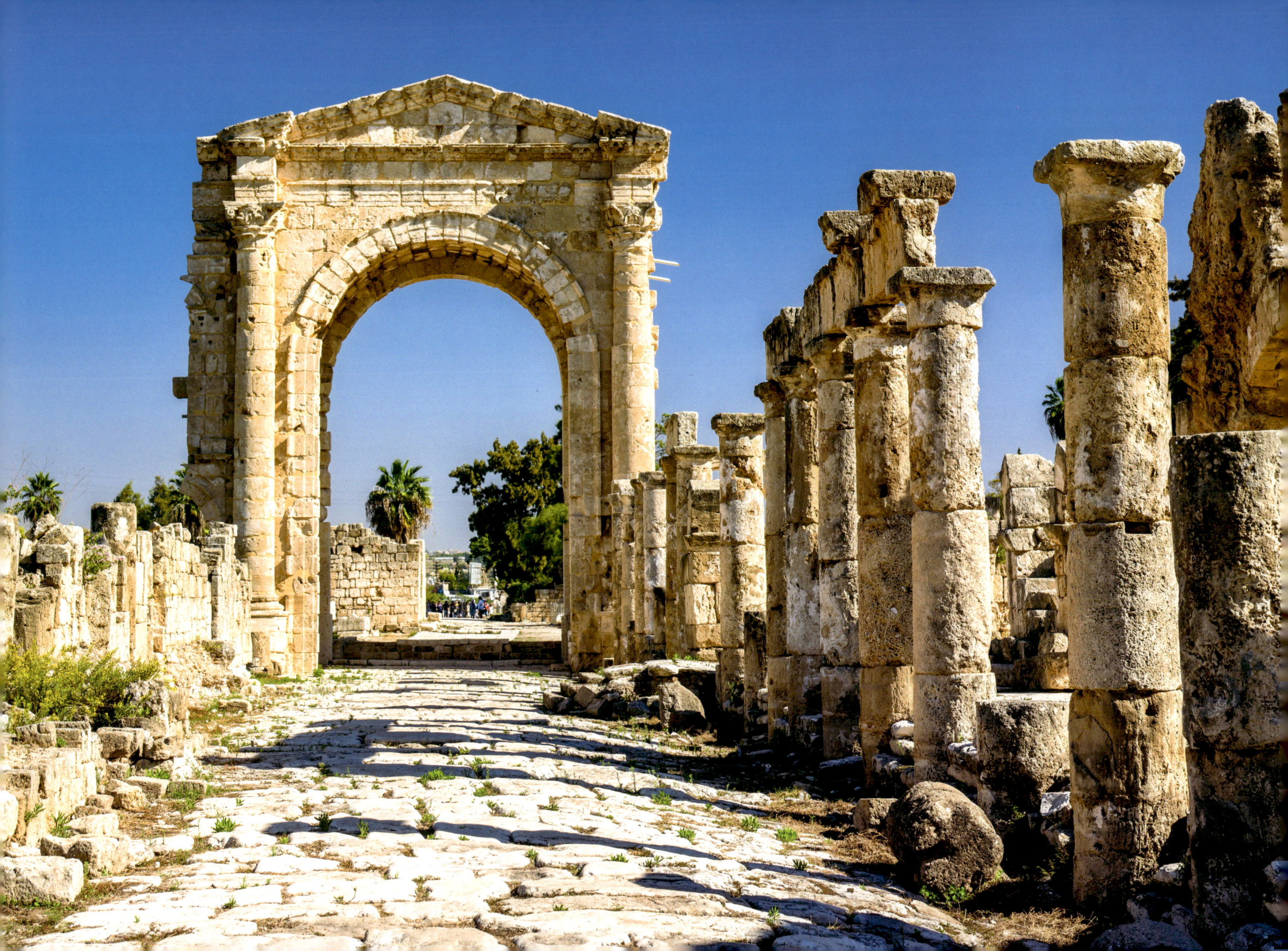

Old harbour, Kyrenia
This lovely spot was a
crucial port for centuries.
Dating back to at least the
10th century BC, it was
fortified by the Byzantines
and then expanded by
the Venetians. Today, the
harbour plays a more
serene role as a picturesque
tourist destination. The old
warehouses are now charming
restaurants, bars, and shops.
The jolly harbour is filled
with fishing boats, yachts,
and relaxed Cypriots and
visitors alike.

Rock of Aphrodite, Paphos
This famed spot is believed
in Greek mythology to be the
birthplace of the goddess of
love and beauty, Aphrodite.
According to legend, the
goddess emerged from the sea
foam here and was carried on
a seashell to the shore. The
site, with its dramatic rocks
and foamy waves, has become
a romantic symbol, with
local myths suggesting that
swimming around the rock
three times will bring eternal
youth and good fortune.

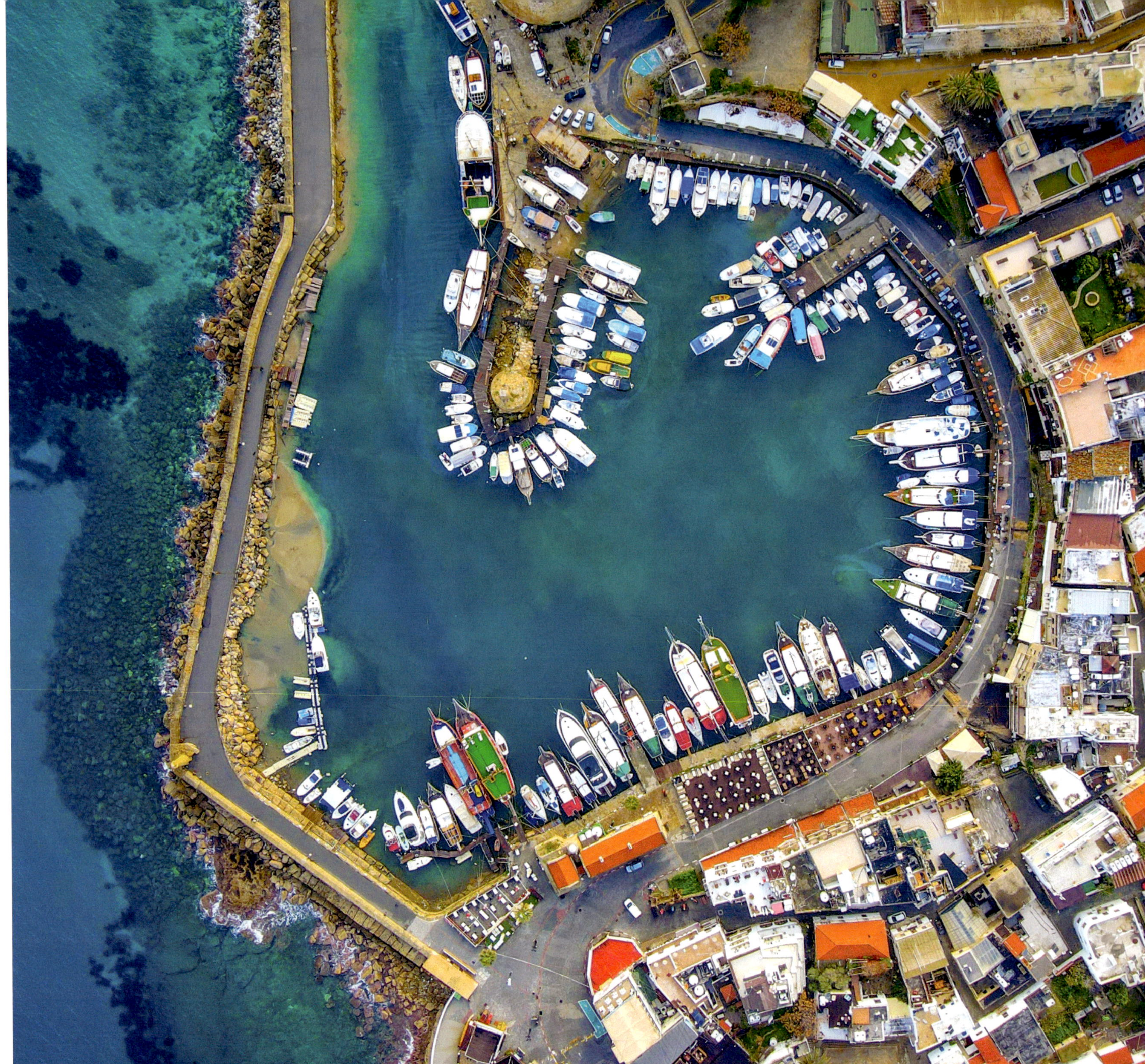

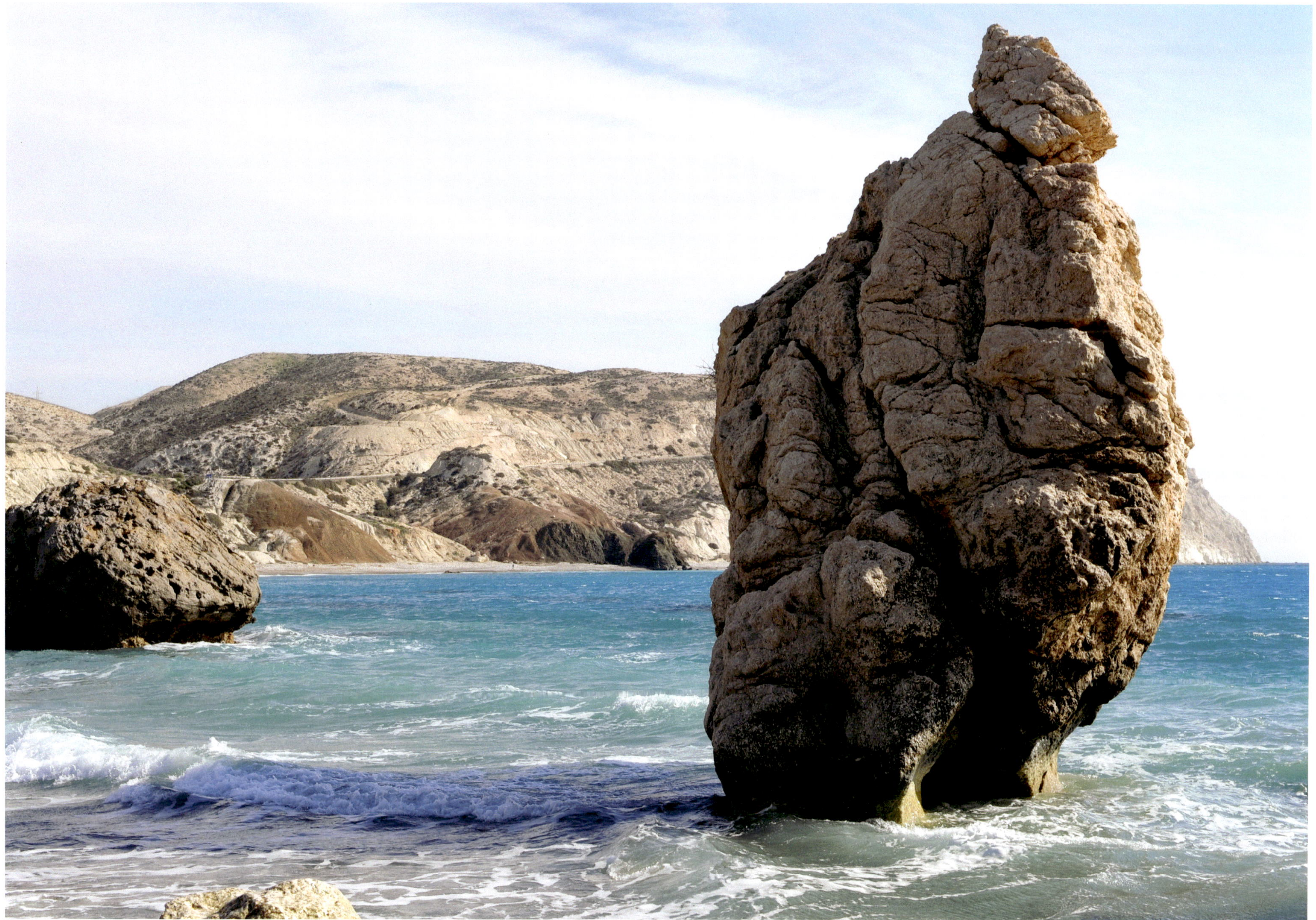

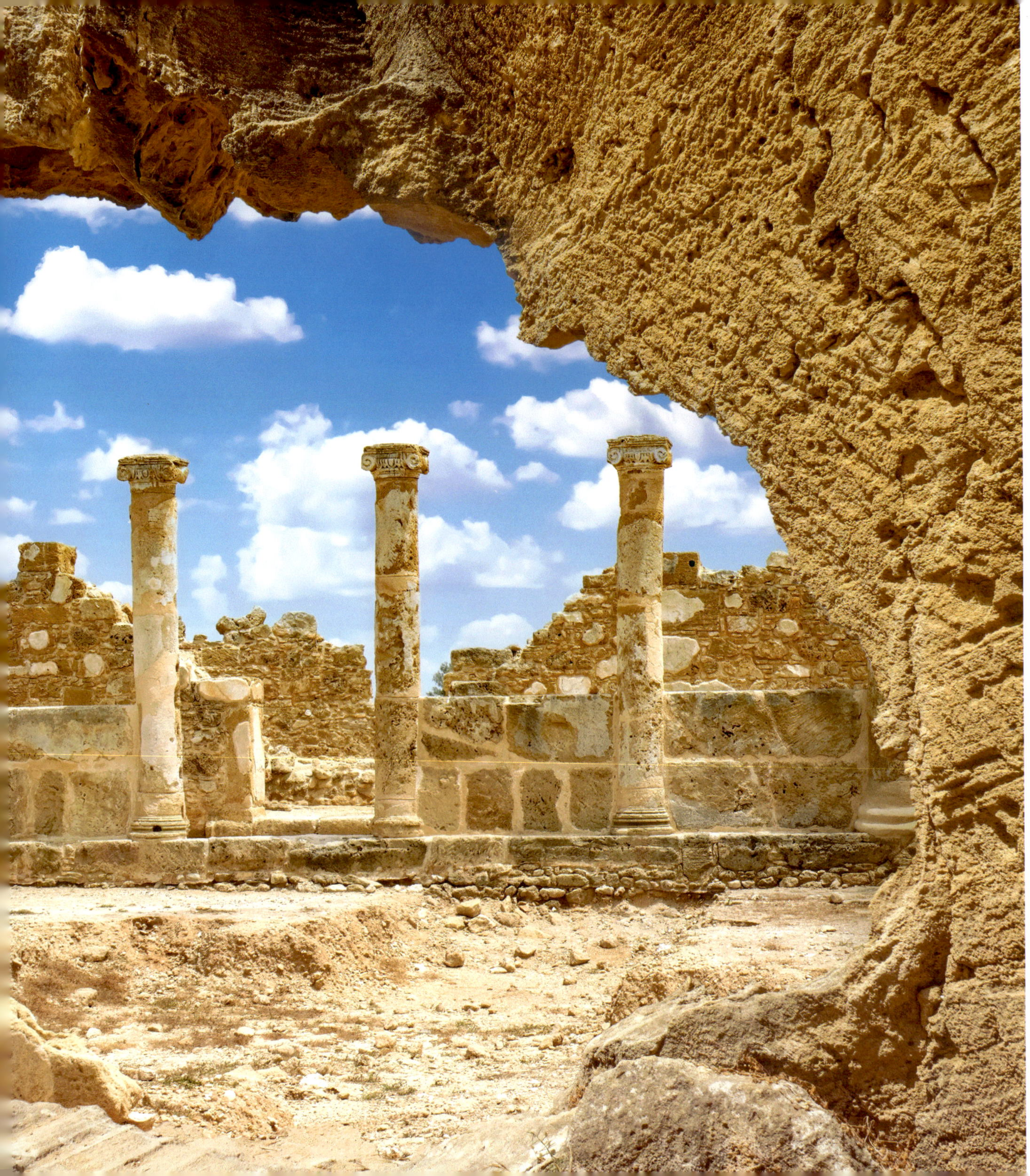

Paphos Archaeological Park
With a story traced to the Neolithic period, Paphos is most famously linked today with the Greek myth of Aphrodite. Legend states she was born from the sea foam near the city and this myth made Paphos, in ancient times, a major pilgrimage destination. Under the Romans, when it became the capital of Cyprus, the Roman proconsul Sergius Paulus arrived, marking a pivotal moment in the spread of Christianity on the island.

Paphos Archaeological Park is the site of Roman remains, including several villas, such as the House of Theseus (pictured left). The floors of these homes host a remarkable collection of intricate floor mosaics found by a local farmer in 1962. They are some of the finest examples of Roman mosaic art in the Mediterranean. Depicting elaborate scenes from Greek mythology, including the Houses of Dionysos (pictured right), Theseus and Aion, they provide a unique window into the daily life, beliefs and artistic sophistication of Roman-era Cyprus, during the 2nd to 5th centuries AD.

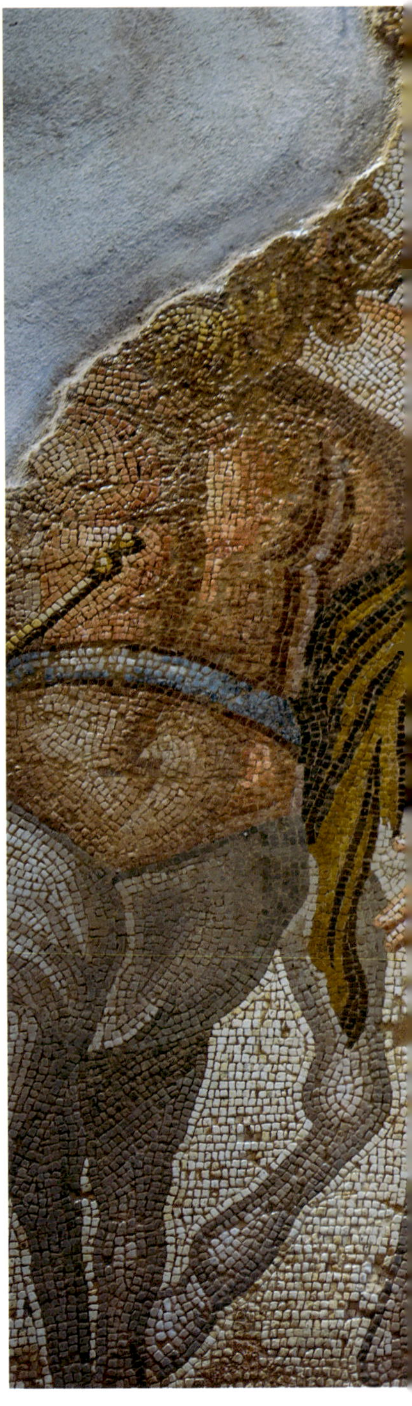

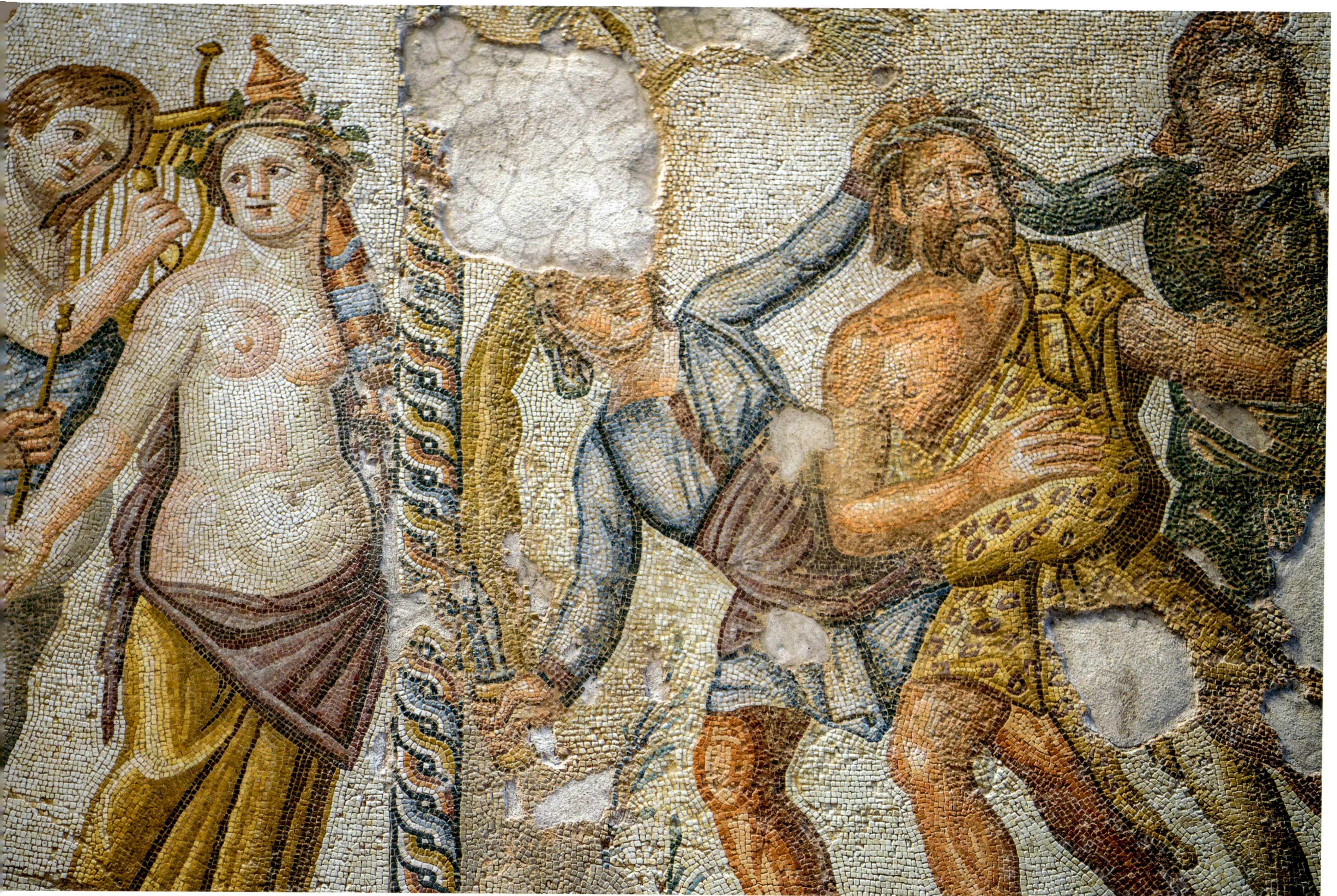

Cypriot Moufflon sheep
Known as 'Agrino', this wild sheep species is uniquely Cypriot, serving as a powerful national symbol. Shy and agile, these animals live mostly in the rugged Paphos Forest, representing a remarkable conservation success story.

Halloumi cheese-making, Letymbou
This staple of Cypriot cuisine holds a Protected Designation of Origin (PDO) status, meaning only cheese produced locally can be legally called halloumi. Traditionally made from a mixture of goat's and sheep's milk, it is most famous for its high melting point, which allows it to be grilled or fried to a golden-brown crisp without losing its shape. In local cuisine, it's also folded and preserved in a salty brine with mint leaves.

Troodos Mountains
These mountains are located roughly in the centre of Cyprus and are well known for two special things. They enjoy a unique geology, including a rare layer that allows sight of the ancient oceanic crust, and they have rich historical and cultural significance as a religious refuge.

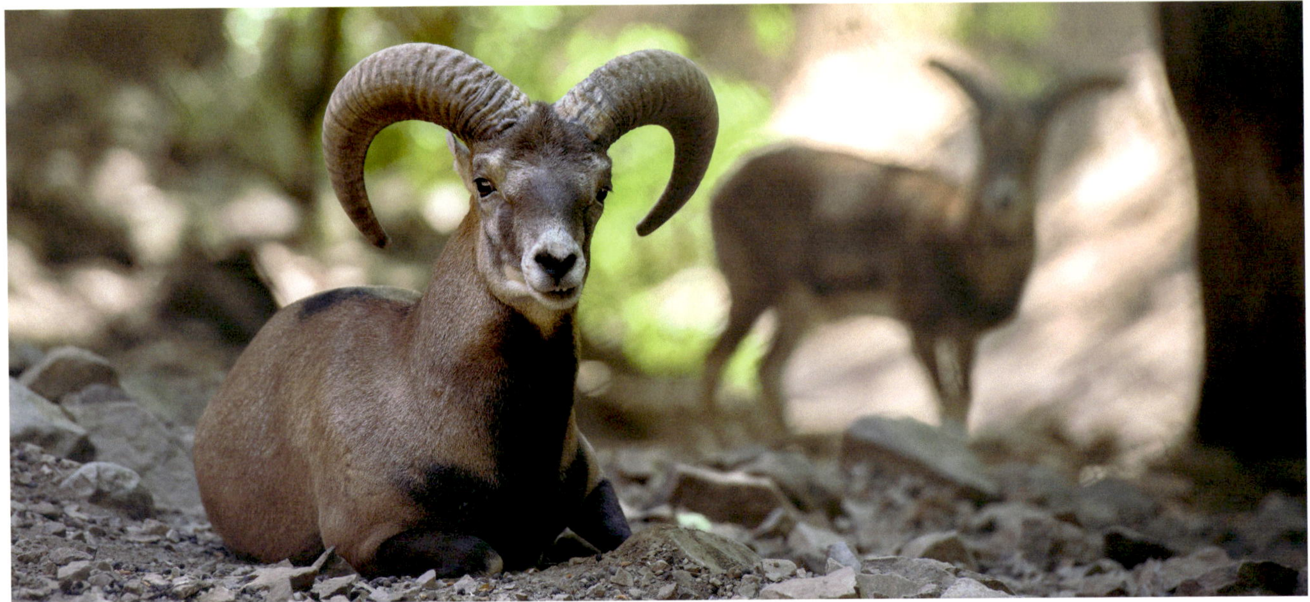

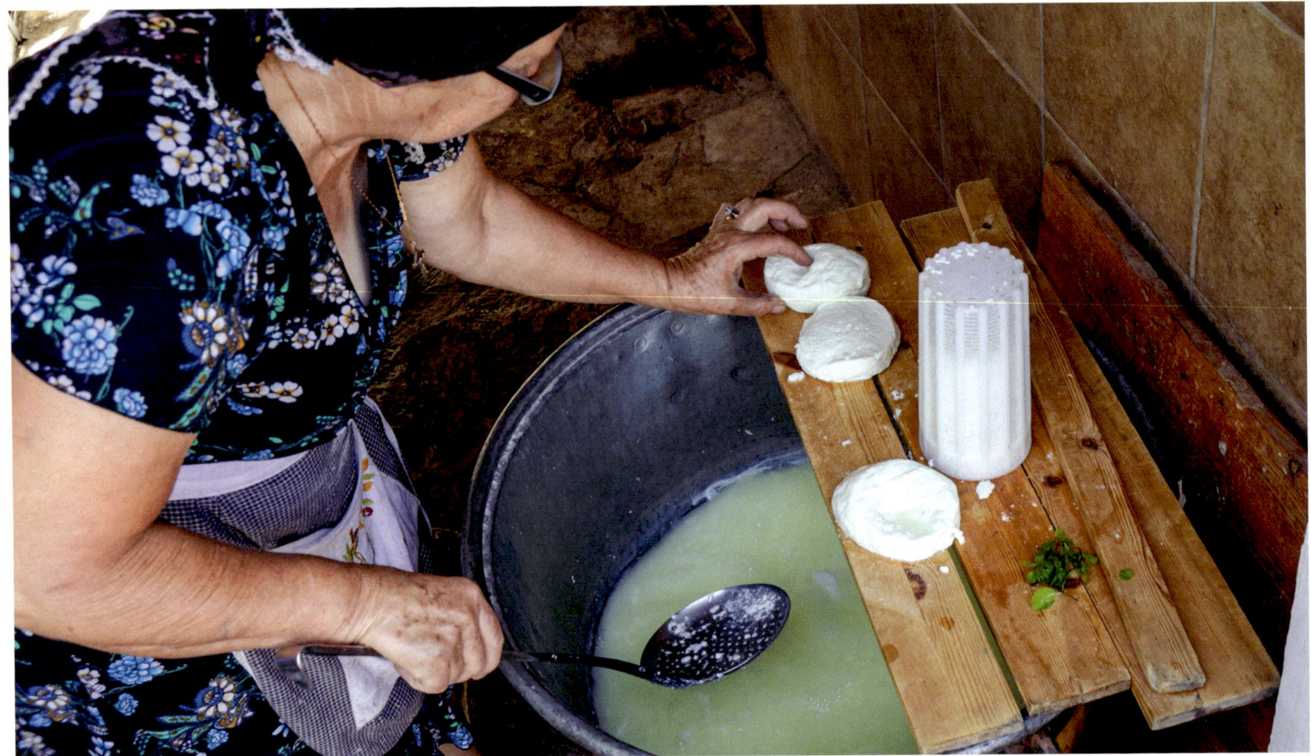

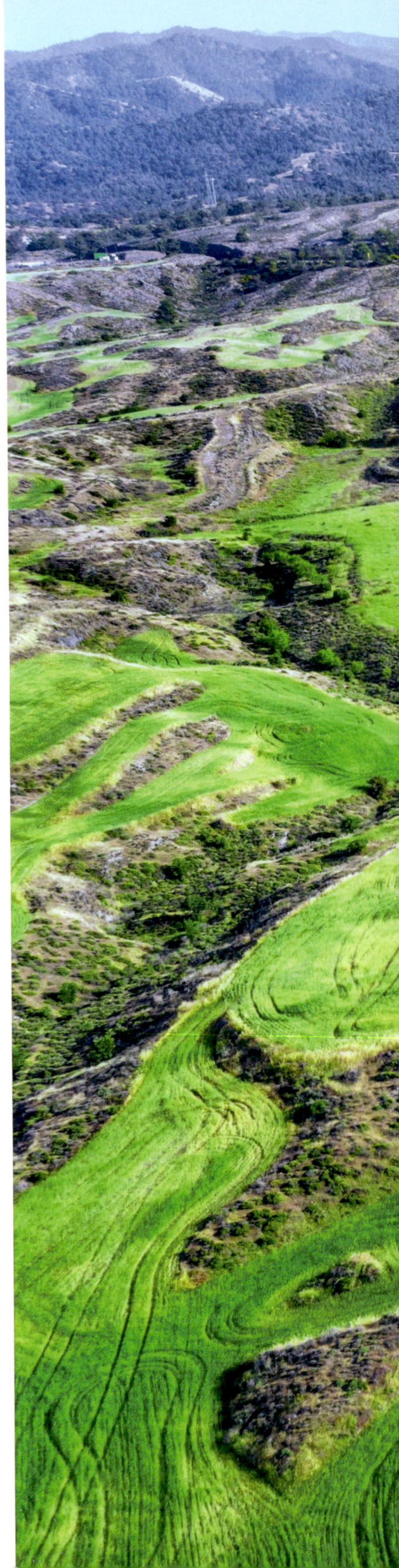

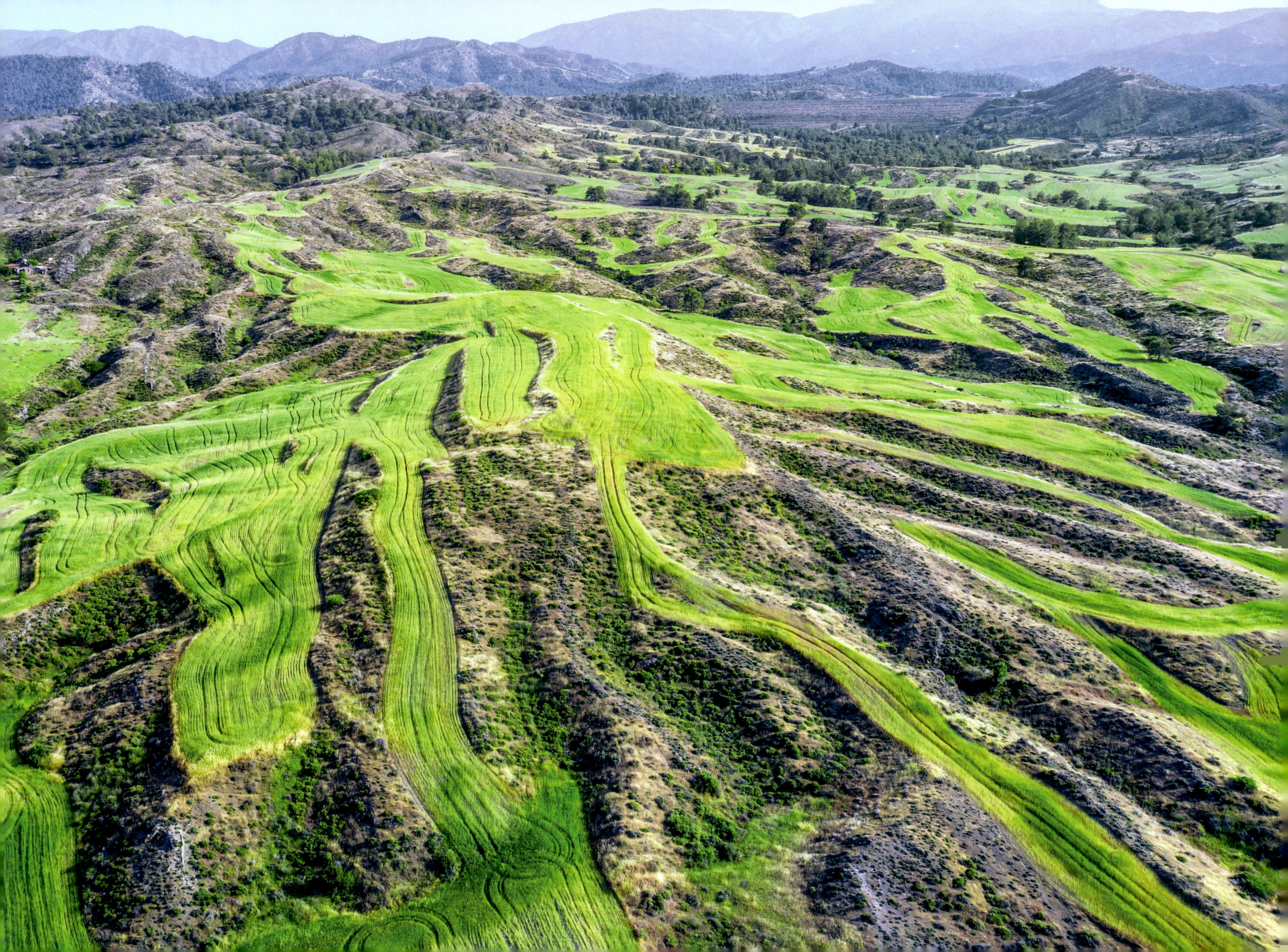

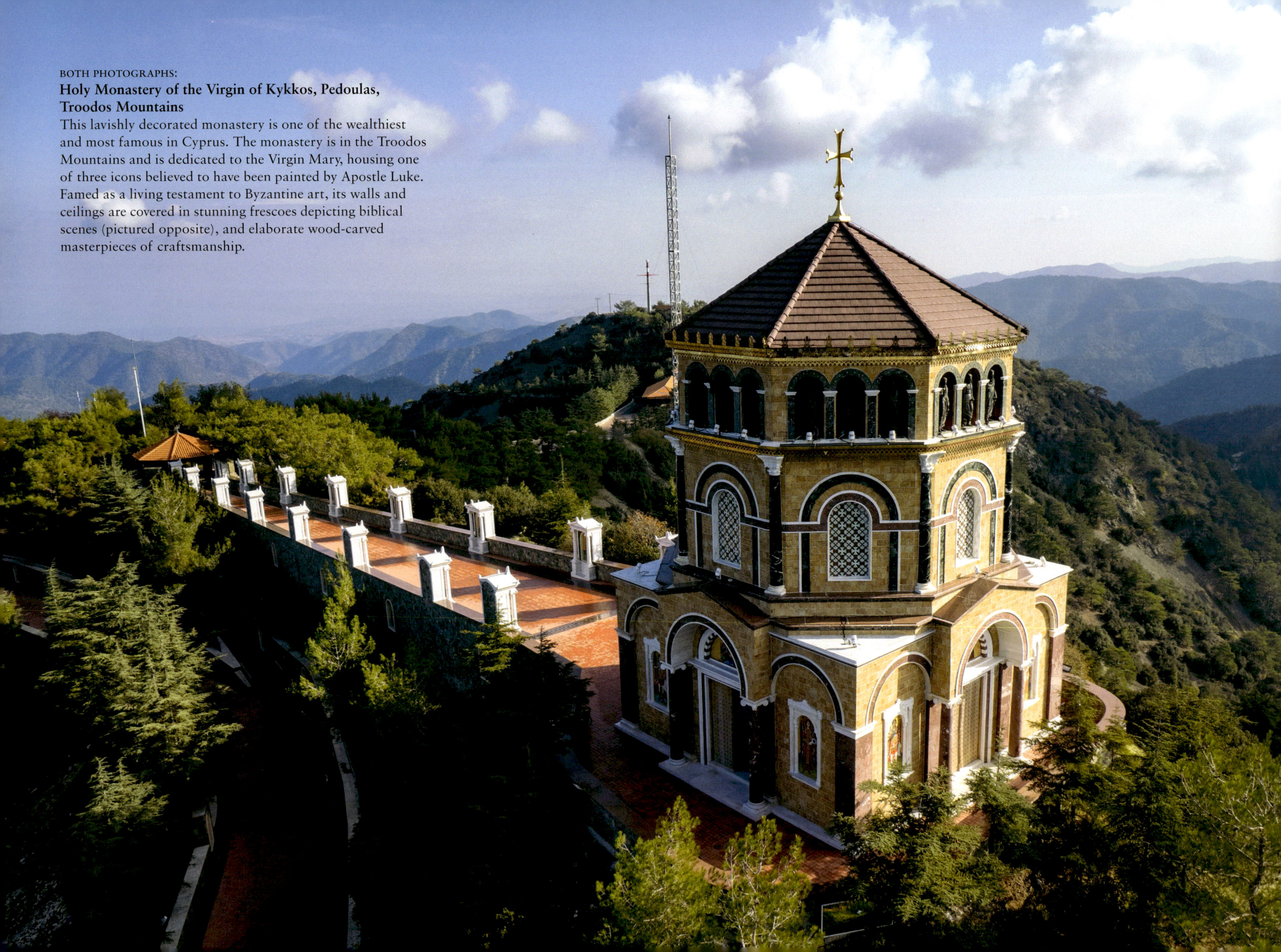
BOTH PHOTOGRAPHS:
Holy Monastery of the Virgin of Kykkos, Pedoulas,
Troodos Mountains
This lavishly decorated monastery is one of the wealthiest
and most famous in Cyprus. The monastery is in the Troodos
Mountains and is dedicated to the Virgin Mary, housing one
of three icons believed to have been painted by Apostle Luke.
Famed as a living testament to Byzantine art, its walls and
ceilings are covered in stunning frescoes depicting biblical
scenes (pictured opposite), and elaborate wood-carved
masterpieces of craftsmanship.

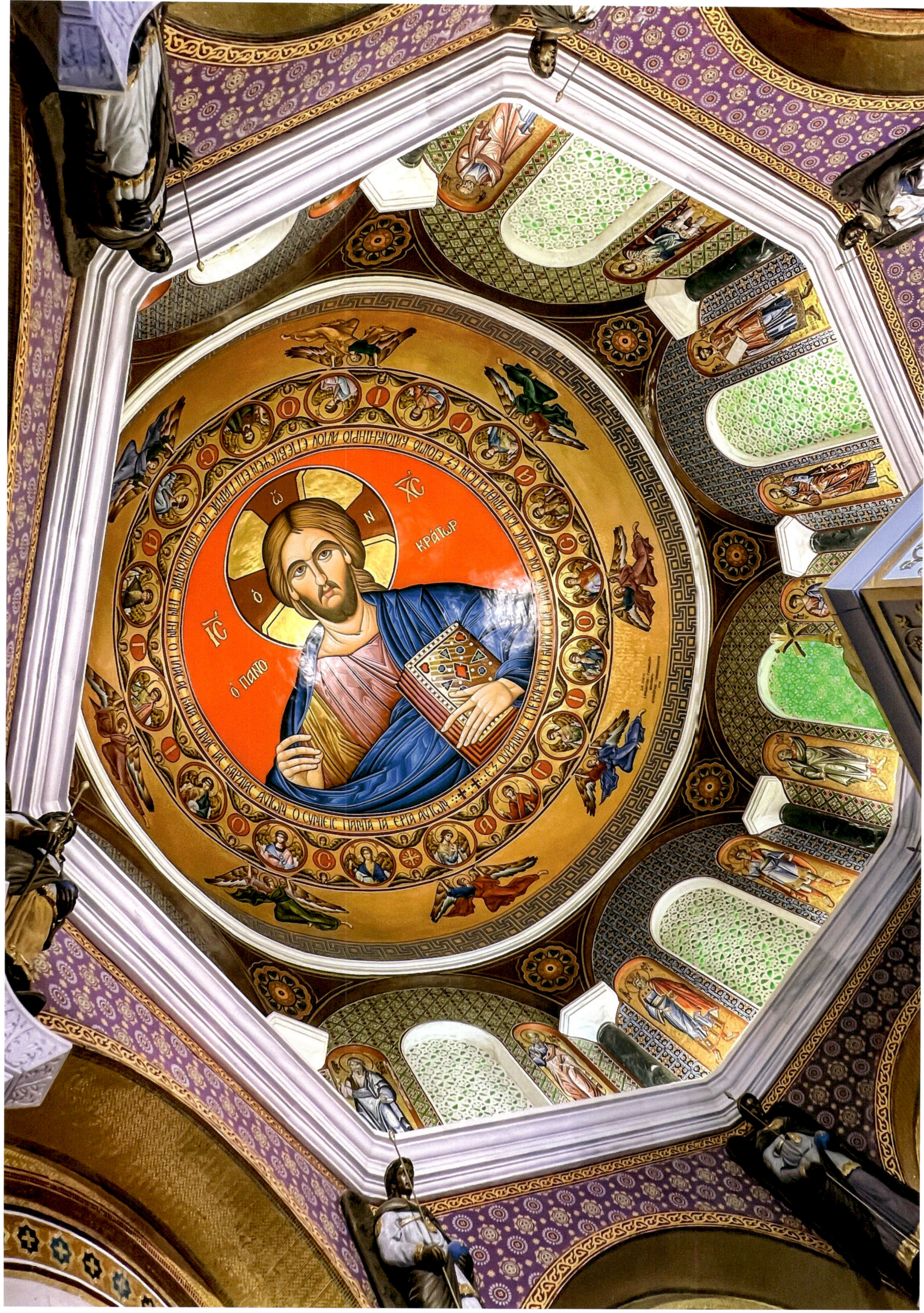

Picture Credits